PERSONAL FINANCE

SEVENTH EDITION

Robert S. Rosefsky

John Wiley & Sons, Inc.
New York   Chichester   Weinheim   Brisbane   Singapore   Toronto

ACQUISITIONS EDITOR	Marissa Ryan
MARKETING MANAGER	Rebecca Hope
PRODUCTION EDITOR	Edward Winkleman
DESIGNER	Laura Boucher
PHOTO EDITORS	Hilary Newman and Lisa Gee
ILLUSTRATION EDITOR	Anna Melhorn

Cover and chapter openings photo: Adam Cohen/Photonica

This book was set in Palatino by Digitype and printed and bound by R. R. Donnelley Crawfordsville. The cover was printed by Lehigh Press.

This book is printed on acid-free paper. ∞

Library of Congress Cataloging-in-Publication Data
Rosefsky, Robert S.
    Personal finance / Robert S. Rosefsky.—7th ed.
        p.   cm.
    Includes bibliographical references and index.
    ISBN 0-471-23822-8(alk. paper)
    1. Finance, Personal.   I. Title.
    HG179.R67   1998
    332.024—dc21   98-5649
                                                          CIP

Printed in the United States of America

10 9 8 7 6 5 4 3 2

To my wife and beloved companion, Linda Sue, and to our children: Debbie and Mark, and their Max and Samantha, Michelle and Paul, Adam and Linda, Joshua and Lindsay. And to the little ones on the way. Greater blessings or riches no person could ever have. And yes, I count them regularly.

About the Author

Dr. Robert Rosefsky's credentials—as author, educator, and professional financial consultant—uniquely suit him for the task of creating the definitive text on personal financial matters.

After receiving his B.A. degree from Yale University and his Juris Doctor degree from Syracuse University College of Law, Dr. Rosefsky practiced law and served as vice president and director of a commercial bank for several years, in which capacity he dealt with the public as a professional "problem solver," primarily in financial matters. He then directed his efforts toward the mass media, hoping to educate a broader audience in a field that had been long ignored: personal financial planning.

Dr. Rosefsky has written ten books on various financial subjects, and his advice has been widely syndicated through newspapers, radio, and television. Most recently he has served as Money Advisor for ABC's radio and television affiliates in Los Angeles.

His experience as an educator is both innovative and extensive. In affiliation with the Consortium for Community College Television, he has created, and presents, two college credit television courses: "Personal Finance" and "You and the Law." The "Personal Finance" telecourse has won an Emmy Award as best instructional series. Tens of thousands of students from all parts of the nation have received credits at their local colleges for completing these courses.

Dr. Rosefsky has taught Business and Economic Reporting at the university of Southern California School of Journalism, as well as financial planning programs for the UCLA Extension Program, for the University of Southern California College of Continuing Education, and for Coastline Community College.

Preface

You can run, but you can't hide.

The world is full of people who want to help you handle your money. For better or for worse. Such as,

Hello my friend, I'm J. Fairly Nicely of Intergalactic Capital Management and I'd like to tell you how to get RICH! If you will just let me be your Retirement Adviser/ 401(k) Guru/IRA Specialist/Insurance Counselor/Stock Portfolio Manager/Real Estate Tutor/Automotive Maven/Banking Guide/Financial Planner/Overall Money Management Mentor, I can solve all of life's problems for you.

Sound familiar? If it doesn't, it soon will.

The J. Fairly Nicely's will come at you over the phone, through the mail, across the Internet, and from every form of advertising now or ever to be invented. They will be convincing. Alluring. Intriguing. Hard to understand, yet hard to resist.

Many will have excellent ideas and well-proven techniques that can indeed help you with your financial concerns.

Some will be crackpots, scam artists, and poorly trained or overly greedy salespersons who want to make a fast buck from you.

So how do you cope? How do you sort it all out?

First you learn. You learn the basic concepts of managing your money. You learn how to identify and prioritize your personal goals and then construct plans that will help you reach those goals. You learn how to crunch the numbers that will help you make the right financial decisions. You learn the jargon of J. Fairly Nicely so that you can decipher the sales pitches and proposals that J. will heap on you. You learn what you can do on your own—thank you very much—and on what you will need professional help. And when you've learned all of that, you will be able to confidently choose which J. Fairly Nicely can be of help to you, and which of them you can dismiss.

That's what this book and this course are all about. To give you knowledge. To give you confidence. To give you the ability to control your own financial destiny.

We have all the tools you'll need:

- In addition to your instructor's caring guidance and this book, there is a Study Guide filled with exercises to help you sharpen your skills, plus carefully selected video supplements to expose you to an array of outside experts.

- There is the Internet, which has become one of the most dynamic and productive ways of acquiring financial information. We have invested heavily—in time, money, and expertise—to develop Internet activities that will enhance your learning. From the springboard of our Website—**http://www.wiley.com/college/rosefsky**—you will be able to access the following:

1. Exercises that will teach you how to use the Internet as a research and problem-solving tool for most of the subjects in the book. These were developed by Walt Woerheide of The Rochester Institute of Technology, with guidance from the Wiley staff and myself. Topics that have Internet exercises will be indicated by a WWW icon like the one you see in the margin.

2. Personal Finance Updates will be posted on the web site regularly to keep you on top of any developing trends that can impact on your financial well-being. There is also a tie-in with *The Wall St. Journal* that will help you understand the economics of everyday life.

3. The Decision Maker software will help you crunch the numbers needed to make wise judgments in common areas of financial concern. The software can be downloaded from the site.

Within the book itself you'll find some new elements that have been added since the last edition. The first part of the book has been restructured to put greater emphasis on the importance of planning and prioritizing. It's entitled "Family Economics," and it will help you understand and deal with the relationship between the economy and your career, your spending habits, and your goals.

Each chapter has a new feature, "For Better or For Worse," which will help you anticipate outside influences that can affect your financial well-being. The more you can anticipate the unexpected, the better you'll be able to dodge the bullets or take advantage of the good breaks.

And finally, there is, in every sentence in every chapter, my best effort to make these subjects easy to understand, all the better to help you achieve what you want for yourself. It's all there for the taking. Use it wisely, today for learning, and in the future as a continuing reference source. Good fortune to you.

Robert S. Rosefsky, J. D.

Words in the text that are underlined in color are more fully defined in the Glossary at the end of the text. The Internet icon refers you to our Website, from which you can choose the resources that you need. This site can be located at **http://www.wiley.com/college/rosefsky**

Contents

PART FOUR   MAKING YOUR MONEY GROW

PART FIVE   PROTECTING WHAT YOU WORK FOR

avoid taking home unsold watermelons, and you could end up a big loser. If the harvest is just right but the weather is cold, people might not be interested in buying the melons at all, and again you end up a loser. In the first case, the supply exceeded the usual demand. In the second case, the supply was customary, but the demand was low. On the other hand, if your harvest is just right and the demand is high because the weather is hot and dry, you could reap a tremendous profit.

- **Luck**   This is, to be sure, a very unscientific aspect of economics. But it is present in every one of the other influences. Whether good or bad, it's unpredictable. The ability to take advantage of good luck and avoid the ravages of bad luck can make a distinct difference between success and failure in an economic endeavor.

In many cases these influences overlap, intertwine, and influence each other. But whether taken individually, in combination, or as an aggregate, they do shape and give direction to the human forces that constitute an economic population.

Effects and Results

The forces go to work and are influenced one way or another by the various factors just mentioned. Here's a brief rundown of some of the potential effects we'll explore in the course of this chapter:

Exercise 1.1

- Inflation or deflation (rising or falling prices and wages)
- Employment or unemployment (good jobs or lack thereof)
- Growth of an economy or recession
- Survival of an economic entity or termination of the entity
- An attractive investment climate or an unattractive one
- Surpluses or deficits (having money in the bank or being excessively in debt)

Many of these effects and results can become influences in their own right. The football team suffers a loss, and the score against them is so lopsided that the players are humiliated. This effect—humiliation—lowers their morale to such a point that they lose their next game, which they had been heavily favored to win. The effect has become a cause in its own right. Or a company develops a highly touted product, only to have the public ignore it because of a poor advertising campaign. Not only does the company thus lose money, but also some of the top managers quit over the marketing program, and the company suffers even further as a result. The effect—poor sales—has become an influence in its own right on the future of the company.

FISH, BERRIES, AND LOGS: WHERE IT ALL BEGAN

To get a better idea of how these forces and influences interact, let's examine the history of three fictional primitive tribes: The Fish People, the Berry People, and the Log People. Any similarities between the economic concerns of these ancient folk and those of your own family, your employer, or your nation are not coincidental.

The Fish People lived at the water's edge, and they harvested a bounty from the sea. Their work was not physically demanding, but it required patience, cunning, and long hours. As long as they were willing to work, there were fish to be caught. An endless supply of fish seemed assured, and their leader, Mug, told them that they could become rich through hard work and through the expansion of their fishing grounds. The fish they didn't need for their own purposes they would trade with the Berry People for berries and with the Log People for logs. Men, women, and children all worked. They saw no limit to the amount of fish they could catch and thereby no limit to the amount of berries and logs they could acquire from their neighbors. Their energies and their expectations were high. They desired to expand and to become ever wealthier.

A few miles inland, on a plateau blessed by constant sunshine lived the Berry People. The plateau was covered with thousands of wild berry bushes of all kinds—black, huckle, rasp, straw, and goose. These delicious berries were always in demand by the Log People and the Fish People. Nature blessed the Berry People: The berries grew in abundance with little need for care. The only work that the Berry People had to do was to pick their crop. What they didn't keep for themselves they packaged to deliver to the neighboring tribes in return for their products. With the sun, the rain, and the soil doing most of their work for them, the Berry People tended to be lazy and greedy. Their leader, Wump, assured them that everything was going their way and they should take advantage of it and live the good life. Wump saw no need to plan for the future. The future, it appeared, would take care of itself.

Beyond the plateau the land rose into wooded hills. This was the domain of the Log People. They had devised tools to cut down the plentiful trees that surrounded them, and they traded the logs to their neighbors for fish and berries. The neighbors found the logs necessary for building fires, creating shelters, and fashioning additional tools for their own uses. Work for the Log People was physically demanding. Cutting down the trees and chopping them into pieces with their primitive tools was bone-wearying. It had become custom among the Log People for only the men to work at cutting the trees since their physical prowess was greater than that of the women. The women tended to the home and to the needs of their men, who returned exhausted from their work at day's end. The Log People were content with their modest lot and aspired to neither wealth nor power. Their leader, Theodore, had told them, "This is the way it has always been with us, and this is the way it probably always will be."

The three tribes had agreed that for trading purposes one fish equal in length to Mug's forearm would be equal to one basket of berries the size of Wump's head, which in turn would be equal to one log the length of Theodore's leg. Thus, if the Fish People wanted to acquire 10 logs, they would have to deliver 10 appropriately sized fish to the Log People. And so on.

The three tribes lived in harmony, trading among themselves as their needs and desires dictated. The following, in no particular order of importance, are some of the occurrences that shaped the lives of these tribes. As you read, bear in mind the economic influences that were outlined earlier.

The Empty Forest

For as long as the Log People could remember, the big trees had always been there. Many years before, when all the tribes were much smaller, all their needs had been filled by chopping down just two or three trees a year. But in recent years all the tribes had expanded considerably and were demanding much more wood than they had formerly needed. The Berry People were building more elaborate log huts, the Fish People needed logs to make rafts, and all three tribes were making more furniture, tools, fences, and fires for heat and cooking.

Whereas the big trees used to be just a few minutes' walk from the Log People's village, the choppers now had to walk much farther to get to the available trees.

Theodore had done too little calculating, and he had done it too late. Never before faced with the problem of not having trees close at hand, the thought of planting new trees had never dawned on him. And when he finally did realize that new plantings were needed, he was dismayed to discover that it took many years for the seedlings to grow into mature trees. Meanwhile, it was now taking the choppers three hours to get to the mature trees and six hours to drag the logs back to the village. The time needed to create a single log had multiplied many times, and thus it was costing the Log People dearly to acquire one fish or one basket of berries. Humankind was suffering its first energy crisis.

Though blessed with a natural resource that could be renewed, the Log People had failed to renew it, and they were suffering accordingly. Furthermore, by failing to anticipate the ever-increasing cost of acquiring the natural resource, their problems were compounded. Eventually Theodore would invent the wheel, which would make possible the creation of a wagon. This would sharply cut down the time and energy needed to get the logs. But in the meantime, waiting for their new plantings to mature, the Log People settled into an era of economic distress.

All Dried Up

As long as the Berry People could remember, there had always been enough rain. How shocking it was then when one year it did not rain. The drought was devastating. Many of the berry bushes produced no fruit at all; some bushes withered and died; and the berries that did grow were puny and tasteless. The Log People and the Fish People would no longer accept one basket of berries in equal trade for a fish or a log because the berries were of such poor quality. They insisted on two baskets for one fish or one log, and the Berry People found themselves with no choice. Until they could remedy the problems caused by the drought, they would have to do with fewer fish and fewer logs. The unpredictable forces of nature had seriously undercut the life of the Berry People, and Wump, their leader, vowed to do something about it.

Wump searched the surrounding countryside and discovered a solution to their problem: an underground spring. He told his people that their only salvation would be to carry buckets to the spring and bring water back for the bushes. But the Berry People had grown so lazy throughout the fat years that they were unwilling to work hard carrying water to save themselves. Many of them refused to accept Wump's warnings about the ultimate consequences of their failure to work hard, believing that the rains would come the next day, or the next, or the next. But the rains didn't come, and the Berry People were on the edge of extinction.

Fearing the worst, Wump retired to his private quarters to concentrate on how to save his people. It came to him in a flash! The head of the underground spring was at a point of land higher than the Berry People's plateau. Why not, Wump reasoned, fashion a trench leading from the spring to the plateau. "We could then direct the water to flow through the trench and onto our parched berry bushes."

He announced his plan to the people, telling them that it would take a lot of hard work to dig the trench, but that once it was completed, abundant water would flow to their bushes. Faced with the ultimate crisis, the Berry People did the necessary work. Within a few weeks, the trench had been dug and the water began to flow. Soon the bushes would be blooming again, and they'd be back to one basket of berries for each fish or each log. Prosperity was just around the corner.

Wump had researched the problem and had developed a means of coping with it. Wump's technology—the first irrigation canal—had overcome the adverse forces of nature as well as the weak spirit of his people. Wump also knew that they should never again take for granted that the rains would fall. Planning for the future was something that *had* to be done, for, Wump admitted to himself in his private moments, it *was* possible for the spring to dry up someday.

The Disappearing Fish

The fish always swam close to the shore settlement of the Fish People—until one strange day when the fish disappeared. Disbelief quickly spread throughout the village. In panic, they ran up and down the shore and put rafts out to sea. Far from their village the fish still swam, but why did they no longer swim near the village, where it was so convenient to catch them? Mug stood knee-deep in the water in front of the village and tried to reason the answer. It came through his nose. There was a strange and offensive odor to the water. Mug sniffed until the odor could be identified. It was the odor of human waste.

Mug realized immediately why the fish had disappeared. For as long as he could remember, the Fish People had disposed of their waste in the water near the village, relying on the tides to carry it out to sea. But over the years the pollution had become so dense that the tides could no longer wash the water clean. Simply enough, the fish were repelled by the polluted water and sought other grounds.

Mug told the village council that unless drastic action was taken immediately, their hopes and dreams would quickly fade. It would be necessary, he suggested, for the waste to be carried to some distant inland point and buried. He realized that this would drain the work power of the people, but only by doing so would the water eventually cleanse itself and allow the fish to return. The Fish People were motivated to realize their expectations. So they commenced an energetic program of waste disposal.

In just a few months the water had cleansed itself and the fish had returned. Even though it was more costly to the Fish People to remove the waste from the village, they were willing to do the necessary work.

They had realized that their well-being could be harmed by polluting their environment, and they were willing to pay the price to correct the problem. Had the price been much higher, Mug worried, the people might have objected to paying it and the village could have been split into factions moving up and down the coast, thus destroying the entity of the Fish People.

The First Price Wars

It had taken many years for the Log People to recover from their first energy crisis. To ensure that it would not happen again, they worked hard to plant as many trees as they could as close to their village as space allowed. But during the time it took for these new plantings to become mature trees, the Fish People and the Berry People had taken their own steps to avoid being caught in a shortage of logs from the Log People. The Fish People had started to collect driftwood and found that it was suitable for repairing their huts. The Berry People found that dead bushes made excellent fuel for their fires—better, in fact, than the Log People's logs. The Fish People and the Berry People began an active trade between each other in driftwood and dead berry bushes. That was the situation when the Log People's new trees came to maturity. Not only did they have more logs available than the other tribes needed, but there was now an added factor: competition. Berry bushes burned better and driftwood was more decorative. The supply of logs was too great and the demand too little. The Log People were again facing poverty. They literally had logs to burn.

Faced with stiff competition from their neighbors and being on the losing side of the law of supply and demand, the Log People had no choice but to cut the price of their logs if they were to survive. Instead of trading one log for one fish or one basket of berries, they traded two logs. In effect, the cost to the Log People had doubled. With the supply of logs so high the Log People saw no end to their dilemma. This dilemma—otherwise referred to as "too much money chasing too few goods"—has come to be known as the basic cause of a phenomenon called inflation. Another historical first for the Log People!

The Value of Good, Hard Work

The horror of the drought stayed in the minds of the Berry People for many years. Adding to this his constant fear that the underground spring could someday dry up, Wump succeeded in creating a force of energetic workers out of what had been lazy playboys and playgirls.

Wump organized the workers into efficient squadrons. One tended the underground spring and continually looked for new sources of water. Another tended to the irrigation canal to make sure it had no leaks. Another dug catch-basins to store excess water, and yet another tended to the pruning and fertilizing of the berry bushes. The Berry People knew that their crop would grow only on that particular plateau. They had no desire to plant in other areas, but they realized that by improving the yield on the plateau bushes, they could become wealthier.

Wump urged the workers to exert themselves, and he congratulated them for jobs well done. The workers appreciated Wump's concern for their welfare, and they cooperated with his plans to the best of their ability.

The fruits of their labors were soon evident: some of the bushes grew twice as many good berries as they had in the past; still others grew fewer berries, but they were much larger, much sweeter, and much more desirable. Because of this cooperation between Wump, the manager, and the workers, the Berry People had become more efficient. They were turning out more goods and better goods for a given amount of labor. Building on his earlier technological advance (the irrigation canal), Wump had succeeded in increasing the productivity of the population.

Smoking a Fish

After the Fish People implemented their waste disposal program, they found more fish than ever in the waters off their village. Now they faced a curious dilemma: they could catch more fish than they could trade to the other tribes. Still motivated by their desire for wealth and expansion, they deliberated on what to do with this excess of natural resource. The problem was that there was no way to keep a fish after it had been caught. It simply rotted and had to be thrown away.

If only there were some way that fish could be kept for an indefinite period. The village council met in Mug's hut to deliberate. They threw some fish on the fire for that evening's meal and commenced their discussions. Someone suggested inventing a freezer, but Mug noted that they did not yet have a place to plug it into. Other ideas flowed freely, with discussion and debate ensuing. The proceedings became so intense that the council forgot about the fish that were on the dying fire. Many hours later, still not having reached a conclusion, hunger got the best of them. They were dismayed to find that the fish had been too thoroughly cooked. The juices were dried out and the meat smelled of wood smoke.

Thus, they all went to bed without any supper that evening. But, on a hunch, Mug did not throw away the overcooked fish. He put them into a box to see what might happen to them.

Three days later, Mug sniffed at the overcooked fish. To his amazement, they did not smell rotten. He picked off a piece of flesh and tasted it. It was dry and smoky tasting, but curiously appealing. Mug said nothing of his discovery and three days later tried it again. It still tasted good. Then Mug announced the great breakthrough to the Fish People.

Purely by accident, technology had created a new product: smoked fish. Experiments began with different kinds of fish and woods to find the combination that would extend the life of smoked fish for the longest time. In the ensuing weeks the techniques were refined and perfected.

The Log People and the Berry People were at first skeptical of this new edible item, but on tasting it they found it satisfying. The popularity of the smoked fish spread rapidly among the tribes. In addition to providing a new taste sensation, it also solved two other important problems. One was that the people could never travel more than one day from their village, because they couldn't carry a supply of fish that would last that long. If they could carry a supply of fish that would last many days, they could explore realms far beyond their villages and expand their universe accordingly.

The other problem was that there were occasional shortfalls in the amount of fish needed to satisfy their daily appetites. By laying in a supply of smoked fish, they could get through those brief shortages comfortably. Needless to say, all these factors meant more sales for the Fish People. Here, technology (albeit accidental), as applied to the natural resources of the Fish People, allowed them to gain some control over the law of supply and demand. No matter how high or unexpected the demand, they could meet it with either fresh or smoked fish. And if demand should drop, they could either smoke the fish or leave it in the water until needed. And by ensuring themselves of a market for one form of fish or another during all seasons, the Fish People were able to keep their village budget on an even keel.

Bad News, Good News

Meanwhile, back in the Log People's village, Theodore and his advisors were trying to figure out a way to avoid the problem of an oversupply of logs. They reviewed what had caused the problem in the first place. Their major mistake was that they had relied on incomplete information in deciding how many new trees to plant. They couldn't remember precisely, but they thought they had either been told, or had let themselves believe, that there was a market for as many trees as they could produce. Thus, the over-planting. Now they realized how detrimental that information had been.

Theodore explained that they must seek correct information on which to base their planting decisions. "Let's determine just how many logs we can really sell at a fair price, and we'll plant accordingly." This was no easy task, for they all knew that it took many years between the planting and the cutting of the trees. Theodore assigned people to get the facts: How large will the populations of the tribes be when today's plantings mature? What kind of demand will they have for logs at that time? What kind of competition can be expected from driftwood and dead bushes? Are there other kinds of trees that can be planted that will be more salable? Can farming techniques be developed to make the trees grow taller and faster while still retaining the quality of the wood, if not improving it?

Theodore's people worked hard at their tasks and returned a year later with their recommendations. Theodore felt much more confident in guiding his people with this researched information than he had with the suppositions, guesses, and impulsive thinking that had guided them in the past. He took the conclusions to each of the clusters in the village who tended their own groves. He gave them lessons in how to plant, how much to plant, and how to tend the growing trees properly.

It took a full generation for all of this effort to pay off, but the rewards were worth the wait. The Log People had utilized education, market research, and the proper dissemination of information to stabilize and strengthen their economic well-being.

A Crushing Blow

Many years had passed since Wump had stirred the Berry People to new heights of productivity. Things were going perhaps a bit too well for the Berry People, and the old ways of laziness and greed had begun to recur.

Wump was much older now, and his influence was not as strong. His successor, Terwilliger, was intrigued by tales of the good old days when the Berry People had to do little work and were richly rewarded by nature.

In his zeal, Terwilliger cast about for ways that the Berry People could do less work and still earn more fish and logs. His idea was greeted with unanimous approval by his followers. They would double the size of the berry baskets. Despite the time involved in making the larger baskets, they were confident that the investment would be well worth it. By using the double-size baskets, they would save considerably on their packing costs and on overall handling. In short: less work, less expense, and more net income.

Terwilliger was delirious with the prospects, and his enthusiasm spread rapidly. So confident was everyone about Terwilliger's idea that nobody bothered to question it. Terwilliger sent messengers to the Log People and the Fish People to inform them of the forthcoming event: "New, bigger, better berry baskets for all!" He posted signs to extol the virtues of the new baskets and promised discounts for advance orders.

Mug and Theodore responded politely, saying that it sounded very interesting and that they'd certainly be willing to give the new baskets a try. Terwilliger interpreted their remarks as an enthusiastic endorsement of the new baskets. He was so sure that the demand would be great that he risked putting the entire crop on the market all at once.

The pickers picked their fingers to the bone to fulfill Terwilliger's orders. Thousands of double-size baskets were laid out on the delivery wagons. Terwilliger escorted the first wagon to the Fish People's village and presented the first basket to Mug. Mug was flattered by the gift and poured the double basket of berries into a large bowel for his family to taste. Then, to everyone's shock, they discovered that the berries on the bottom of the basket had been crushed by the weight of the berries on the top of the basket. Fully one-third of all the berries in the basket were damaged, and Mug responded angrily. "You told me I'd be getting two baskets' worth of berries in one, and in fact I only have a little more than one basket's worth of usable berries! You led me to believe that I was getting fair value for my two fish! I've been cheated!"

Stunned and embarrassed, Terwilliger apologized.He admitted that they had never tested to see whether the double-size baskets would create any crushing problems. They had just assumed that if a single-size basket did not result in crushing, neither would a double-size basket.

But it was too late for Terwilliger and the Berry People. Word of mouth spread quickly. Terwilliger had put the entire crop on the line and now found it difficult even to give it away. The bulk of the crop rotted in the double baskets, and the Berry People were flung instantly into poverty. Their underlying force—greed—had been thrown back in their faces by dreadful marketing procedures. Despite the quality of the product, the lack of research, poor packaging, and misleading advertising had resulted in a disaster for the people in the Berry village.

Help Wanted

One aspect of the smoked fish development brought unexpectedly good results: with several days' supply of fish, all the tribes were able to venture into previously unexplored areas. They found numerous other tribes specializing in their own products. To the north there were tribes that produced wheat, chickens, and apples. To the south there were tribes that produced barley, bananas, and a strange bubbling beverage that the natives called *beer*. None of these tribes had ever seen a fish—either fresh or smoked. The Fish People were eager to tap this vast new market. But they had some serious problems. All the available population was already working overtime to supply fish to the Berry and Log tribes. And the leader of the Fish People had long ago determine that only the Fish People should work the teeming waters by the village. How then could they catch more fish to sell to these outlying tribes?

First the leaders agreed that outsiders should be allowed to work in their village. Then they had to create a reason for outsiders to *want* to work in the fishing village. They decided to allow any outsiders a share of profits in addition to a basic wage for their labor. The women of the Log People found this an attractive proposition. By this time, cutting the logs and caring for the trees had become easier as a result of improved tools, and the women were freer to explore other opportunities for themselves. They welcomed the chance to receive payment for their work and were further satisfied that their village would benefit from the added wealth that they would bring home. Even some of the more energetic Berry People found the offer intriguing, and thus the first export business was created: selling to the outlying tribes.

Governmental policy, coupled with the creation of an incentive to invest (in this case time rather than money), was responsible for bringing a new era of prosperity to the three tribes.

Making Munny

The discovery of the outlying tribes and the opportunity to trade with them brought great changes to the Fish, Berry, and Log People. As the populations of the three tribes had grown, it was becoming ever more cumbersome to handle fish, berries, and logs each time a transaction occurred. The leaders agreed to create small tokens, made of stones, that would represent either a fish, a basket of berries, or a log. Thus, instead of trading the goods themselves, they could trade the tokens that represented the goods. Each token was referred to, in their primitive language, as a *Munny*. Now, if a Fish Person sold a large quantity of fish, he could take Munnies in exchange, rather than load himself up with berries and logs that he might not need at that time. Later, if that Fish Person wanted to acquire a basket of berries, he could trade a Munny for it rather than having to carry a fish clear across town.

Before long, the more enterprising members of the tribes began to accumulate large quantities of Munnies, and to protect themselves against thieves, they asked the leaders of the tribes to oversee the creation of a bank that would hold their Munnies for them.

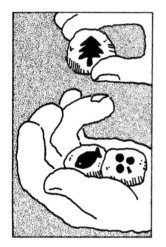

In addition to the Munny tokens, the three tribes had many other things in common. They were physically close to one another; they had many similar traditions and beliefs from centuries of living near, and trading with, one another; and they felt a need to help defend one another against any outside attacks. Eventually, they decided to formalize their common interests by creating a pact that would bind them together as an entity called the United Tribes. Meanwhile, and in similar fashion, the tribes in the north had joined together as the Wheat/Apples/Chicken Alliance. And the southerly producers of barley, bananas, and beer had joined together as the 3-B Federation. Each of these two other groups had created their own tokens representing their products, and the Alliance tokens, the 3-B tokens, and the Munny tokens were freely interchanged as the groups traded actively among one another. For many years all the peoples of these nations regarded one Alliance token as being equal to one Munny token, which was equal to one 3-B token. And for all those years the amount of trade among the nations was equal. Each bought and sold the same amount from one another, year in and year out.

The Building Binge (Fiscal Policy)

Then an unusual thing began to happen in the United Tribes. Their government decided to build a series of magnificent roads connecting the three villages. Many citizens objected, saying that the roads weren't needed and that no Munnies were available to pay for the building of the roads.

The United Tribes government responded, "We will surely need these roads in the future as our population grows. And having these roads will make us the envy of the Alliance and the 3-B Federation. Our national pride is at stake. And there's no problem about the Munnies—we'll borrow all we need from investors. If they lend us ten Munnies for one year we'll pay them back eleven Munnies at the end of the year. We'll get all the Munnies we'll need!"

Then the critics asked: "But where will you get the Munnies to pay back the investors?"

"No problem," said the government. "Since all of our citizens will benefit from these magnificent new roads, we'll have all of them pay us a certain number of Munnies every year. We'll call that a *tax,* and we'll use it to pay off the investors."

The road-building program got under way, and the government liked it so much that it then embarked on building parks and gardens and rest stops along the way. Some of the people in the government received favors from the builders. The more they built, the more Munnies they taxed the citizens. There seemed to be no end in sight to the government's spending. The more it spent, the deeper in debt it went, and the higher the taxes went for the citizens. Some citizens finally rebelled and said, "Stop! We're paying too many Munnies in taxes, and we're not getting benefits accordingly."

But some other citizens replied, "Keep spending. We make a very good living as road builders, and we want that to continue."

This incident describes what is known as fiscal policy, which has to do with how a government decides to spend money and how it will raise the money it spends—normally through taxation and borrowing. If a government's income and expenses are equal, it is said that the government, like a family or a business, has a balanced budget. If a government takes in more money than it spends, it has a surplus. If it spends more than it takes in, it has a deficit. The fiscal policy of a government can have many influences—for better or for worse—on the well-being of its people.

The Beer Bust (Monetary Policy)

Another unusual development in the United Tribes was the insatiable craving for beer, which was available only through the 3-B Federation. Despite warnings from the government, they consumed an ever-growing quantity.

The rulers of the 3-B Federation saw a unique opportunity: "Right now the United Tribes can get beer only from us. So let's raise the price as high as traffic will allow. Someday they'll figure out how to make their own beer, or they'll be able to get it from someone else, so we'll stash away a lot of what we earn today to protect us against that competition in the future."

The citizens of the United Tribes were shocked when the price of their beer doubled, from one Munny to two Munnies per flask. But the drinking continued without letup. Very soon the flow of Munnies from the United Tribes to the 3-B Federation became a flood. The United Tribes found themselves so short of Munnies that they could barely afford to buy berries and fish and logs, which they needed far more than beer.

"We will not be denied our beer!" shouted angry United Tribes protesters. "Carve more Munny tokens if you have to!"

"That would be wrong," replied the government. "Each Munny should be backed by something of value—either a log or a basket of berries or a fish, or by our credible promise that any of those items can be purchased in the future at a reasonable price."

The government's dilemma relates to monetary policy, which deals with how much money a government will allow to float through the economy. If there's not enough, the economy will shrink, and jobs and incomes will disappear accordingly. If there's too much, the value of the money becomes questionable, and sellers will raise prices to protect themselves against the possibly declining value of the money they receive.

Governments attempt to control economic health through monetary policy—in effect, controlling the amount of money available. There is no one formula that is guaranteed to work, but the wrong formula can be quite disruptive. In the United States major tensions have arisen over monetary policy with respect to buying oil, automobiles, and electronic goods from abroad. Our thirst for those items has been comparable to that of the United Tribes beer drinkers, and our money has flowed out accordingly.

The Banking Bombshell (Regulatory Policy)

The Building Binge and the Beer Bust caused serious problems for the United Tribes. One group, the bankers, came forward with a proposal to cure the ills. They said, "Our government is too strict with us. We take in depositors' Munnies, and the government guarantees that those Munnies will be safe in our hands. But in order to keep that guarantee intact, we are very limited as to how we can put that money to work. If the government will relax its regulations on us, and allow us to lend money more aggressively to builders and developers, we can help create jobs and incomes, and we can thus restore the health of our economy."

The government listened to these persuasions and was convinced of their value. Some people in government received favors from banks for helping to change the laws. Some people in banking received favors from builders and developers for helping to make loans to them. Some people who processed the loans received favors for saying that the properties being built were worth a lot more than they really were.

After a few years of this lending activity—during which, indeed, many construction and related jobs were created—the borrowers began to default on paying their loans. Many of them had built buildings that no one wanted to occupy. So the builders did not receive enough income from the buildings to allow them to pay their loans. But the people who had deposited their Munnies with the banks did not have to worry, for the government guaranteed that their Munnies were safe.

But if the banks had lost the Munnies on bad loans, where would the Munnies come from to pay off the depositors? From the taxpayers—and in huge amounts. Thus did the economic fortunes of the United Tribes suffer further from a failure of regulatory policy. This scenario was all too real in the United States during the late 1980s and early 1990s. It was referred to as the savings and loan bailout. Savings and loan companies (S&Ls) had been very strictly regulated: almost all of their lending was restricted to single-family homes. Then Congress gave in to demands from the savings and loan industry and allowed them very broad lending powers, while at the same time insuring the safety of depositors' money.

Hundreds of S&Ls went haywire, lending huge amounts of money on very high-risk projects. Unsavory promoters involved in these loans pocketed tens of millions of dollars in illicit fees. When the high-risk projects couldn't pay back their loans, the S&Ls collapsed. But the government—that is, the taxpayers—still had to pay off the depositors in the failed companies. Cost to U.S. taxpayers: hundreds of billions of dollars, and a severe drag on the economy for years.

This is but one example of flawed regulatory policy. The ripple effects can exert a harsh influence on the economic well-being of everyone directly or indirectly involved.

Tit for Tat (Trade Policy)

The Wheat/Apples/Chicken Alliance had been trading happily with the United Tribes for many years. Apples and berries went across their borders in great abundance. Two ripe apples for one basket of berries was the going rate of exchange. Many members of the United Tribes began to prefer the Alliance's apples to their own home-grown berries. So great was the appetite for apples that the jobs of many berry growers were in jeopardy.

"We must protect our workers' jobs," said the leaders of the United Tribes. "To do so, we must make apples more expensive: three apples for one basket of berries will be the price from now on. If the apple growers don't like that, then let them go sell their apples elsewhere."

This amounted to a tax on the import of apples. In trading terms, such a tax is called a tariff. When the apple growers heard about it they vowed to get even. "We can't stop another nation from putting a tariff on the apples they buy from us. But we can certainly retaliate. From now on we will allow a quota of only 1,000 baskets of berries into our country each week!"

Trade between the two groups quickly dwindled to a trickle, and both were hurt by the obstacles to free trade that each had imposed on the other. The trade policies of both groups had been counterproductive. Workers suffered instead of being helped. In addition to tariffs and quotas, a government's trade policy can include offering low-cost loans and tax incentives to producers of certain goods; these financial benefits can make the targeted products cheaper to foreign purchasers. But cries of "unfair" and "let's get even" are sure to follow.

Nations also may encourage or cease trading with other nations as a result of political, religious, or philosophical differences. Trading partners with the United States—the world's richest single market—cherish the designation of Most Favored Nation (M.F.N.) status, as that gives them the best terms for dealing with Uncle Sam.

Nations are continually negotiating with each other, and with blocs of nations, to seek fairness and advantage in their trading activities. Trade policies can thus affect the economic well-being of countless citizens.

Here Today, Gone Tomorrow (Industrial Policy)

The leaders of the United Tribes had an excellent idea: "Let us encourage the building of proper homes for our people. No more living in tents and caves. We shall have split-level condos and clustered housing on golf courses and spiffy single-family bungalows with jacuzzis and garage door openers." And so an industrial policy favoring home building was put into effect. Those who built homes received favorable tax treatment. Those who sold carpeting and appliances and furniture and paint and tile prospered handsomely. Investors in all of these companies reaped bonanzas. The leaders of the United Tribes awarded themselves generously for having satisfied so many people. Everyone connected with the home building industry boom was ecstatic!

But after a few years many people in the United Tribes became disgruntled. "Some people are getting rich at the expense of others. Home builders get fabulous tax breaks, but all the rest of us have to pay more taxes to pick up the slack. This is unfair. We should throw out our existing leaders and get new ones!"

So the leaders of the United Tribes replaced their industrial policy favoring home building with one favoring scientific research. This sent the home-building industry, and all its workers, suppliers, and investors, into a deep depression. But the research scientists loved it. Until the next industrial policy came along.

Although some might deny that the United States—epitome of the free market—espouses industrial policies, the fact is that we have had a succession of them for many decades. In the 1950s it was the building of the interstate freeway system. In the 1960s the space race began in earnest. Real estate development was favored in the 1970s and early 1980s, until the rug was pulled out from under it—with disastrous effects—by the 1986 Tax Reform Law. Sometimes industrial policy will disfavor a given segment of the economy, as tobacco makers and health-care deliverers found out in the 1990s. When the government bestows, or removes, its blessings by way of industrial policy, the results in jobs and incomes will be considerable. What effects have you felt, or might you feel from a change in industrial policy?

HERE AND NOW

The adventures and midadventures of these primitive peoples illustrate some of the most basic economic influences that we live with day to day. All these influences intertwine, overlap, and interact. Let's put these phenomena into a modern perspective.

Productivity

Productivity is a measure of efficiency: How much output can be generated by a given individual or group, considering the cost of raw materials, labor, capital, and overhead? Here are some examples of how conditions can affect productivity.

- You work in a factory that makes farnolas. At your average pace, you can turn out ten farnolas an hour. But your foreman is a mean person, and every time he makes the rounds, you get so aggravated that your efficiency drops, and for the next four hours you can turn out only nine farnolas an hour. The same goes for all your co-workers.

- The owner of the factory learns of the morale problem that's being caused by the foreman. The foreman is replaced with a much friendlier person, and you find yourself able to turn out eleven farnolas an hour. Your productivity has improved through a change in management, at no extra cost to the factory owner. This can mean greater profits for the owners of the company. And if you are paid on an incentive basis, it can also mean an increase in your pay.

- The owner of the factory installs an improved lighting system and better air conditioning. The added visibility and comfort factors for the workers enable them to become more efficient. The productivity of the factory has been increased as a result of capital investment.

Examine the various aspects of productivity in your home, your workplace, and your school. Where and how can matters be improved? Is the cost of making those improvements justifiable? Be your own efficiency expert. It could mean extra money in your pocket.

Government

The stories of the primitive tribes have already illustrated how government policies can affect the economic status of individuals and entire nations. Other activities of our government further illustrate these phenomena in very real terms.

For example, throughout the 1990s spending by our government resulted in annual federal budget deficits in excess of $200 and $300 *billion*. Where did the money that was spent come from? Most of it was borrowed and will eventually have to be repaid. Some of it was borrowed from U.S. individuals and institutions, but ever-increasing amounts of it were borrowed from foreigners. When a government owes money to its own citizens, it's relatively easy to establish a repayment schedule that everyone can agree to. But when a government owes money to foreign individuals and institutions, repayment plans are not as flexible.

The government spending did provide jobs and benefits for millions of Americans. But the repayment of the borrowed money that provided those jobs could mean higher future taxes.

How have specific government actions affected your individual economic well-being, for better or for worse? How can you anticipate future government actions that could affect you, and what defensive actions can you take to protect yourself?

International Matters

For the foreseeable future our involvement in the global marketplace will have the most indelible influence on our economic well-being. The previous discussion on trade policy illustrates some of the concerns, and the Consumer Alert section at the end of this chapter discusses other aspects. The best career and investment advantages will flow to those who are the most knowledgeable in international matters.

Technology

The irrigation canal the Berry People built and the fish-smoking technique that the Fish People developed were examples of technological development that improved conditions for the population. Advancing technology plays an extraordinary role in our economy. It relates directly to productivity in most cases, and lack of it can mean stagnation.

The most stunning example of technological advancement has been in the area of electronics. Improvements in computer chips have reduced the cost of doing calculations to a tiny fraction of what it was just a few years ago. Superconductors and fiber optics represent other areas of continuing technological advance. Major breakthroughs hold the promise of new materials that will permit electricity to flow with virtually no resistance. In time, this could result in computers that are vastly more efficient than the most powerful ones now in existence, medical diagnostic equipment that will make X-rays and scanning look primitive by comparison, electrical generating facilities that will be much more efficient than those we have today, and similar wonders that scientists once only dreamed about.

New developments in bio-technology and genetics hold the promise of better health and longer productive lives for all. What technological advances have affected you in your home and work life in recent years? Are they for better or for worse? How might advancing technology affect your job in the future?

Information

Information in the general sense is gathered from life experience, from education, and from what we learn through the media. To the extent that we take advantage of the information available to us, we can improve our lot considerably.

The creation and flow of information will have a major impact on the U.S. economy as the undeveloped nations of the world learn, grow, and become consumers of products that we will manufacture for sale to them. Roughly three-quarters of the earth's population is still considered undeveloped. In those nations, 60 to 90 percent of the people still work at agriculture to create enough food to feed the population. (In the United States, only about 2 percent of the population feeds the other 98 percent with a lot left over to be exported.) As the citizens of these undeveloped nations learn more about agriculture and health, they will become more self-sufficient and secure. As they learn basic trades and skills, they will become better able to support themselves and their families. As they continue to improve their lot—largely through education and training—they will have money to spend on such things as tools, medicines, books, and teachers. This, in turn, will beget more information, sharper skills, and more income. Sooner than later, these billions of people will be buying things that we've long since become accustomed to: running shoes and blue jeans, tape recorders and tennis rackets, furniture and television sets, movie tickets, and so on. For many years to come, these billions of people will look to the existing industrial nations to provide most of these goods—and our economies will boom. Eventually, those nations will be self-sufficient in most of those goods, and whole new patterns of international economy will emerge. But for the next twenty to fifty years, information will be the seeds planted abroad that will bear fruit back home.

STRATEGIES FOR SUCCESS

Keeping Up-to-Date Can Pay Off

It's difficult indeed to predict accurately the long-term fluctuations in our nation's economy. But, by keeping up-to-date on certain key statistics, you can gain a good sense of short-term trends, and you can plan your investments and other economic activities accordingly. Each month the government publishes the Index of Leading Economic Indicators. This tends to be the most reliable gauge of expected growth or shrinkage in the economy in the months ahead. Also, major borrowings by the U.S. Treasury tend to set trends for interest rates throughout the nation. The "Credit Markets" section of The Wall Street Journal carries news and analyses about these borrowings on a regular basis. Keep up with these matters, and see if your awareness doesn't help you manage your own personal finances.

Capital Investment

Even with all the skills, enthusiasm, and technology that an individual or business can muster, money is still needed to make things happen. Every large business—even a General Motors, an IBM, or an Exxon—started as a small business. And small businesses grow when they are able to attract money: capital investors. A company whose management, product, and profitability are attractive to investors will be able to raise more capital to improve and grow. Simply put, working for such a company can mean career advancement for you.

Not all capital investment comes from outsiders. Specific businesses must also have reason to believe that they can invest their own money internally and reap rewards accordingly. Here again we see the intertwining of various economic influences: the government can create incentives for a business to invest in its own future through tax credits and similar devices.

Forecasting

All economic entities must do some accurate forecasting if they are to survive. If the Log and Berry and Fish people had looked ahead, they might have avoided their troubles.

Likewise, in today's world we must be alert to future changes in the value of money, the cost of labor, the price of raw materials, the costs of shipping, building, communicating, traveling, litigating, medicating, everything else that goes into life and business.

Over the long run, with very few and short-lived exceptions, inflation will be a force to contend with. Costs rise. Workers expect pay raises. A drought in the Midwest makes the price of bread go up. A war between oil-producing nations makes the price of gasoline go up.

A government wants to ward off inflation, so it raises the cost of money by boosting the interest rates that banks have to pay when they borrow money from the government. "How can *that* work?" you ask. In recent years, governments have followed the theory that by boosting the cost of money, it will be more expensive to borrow. By making borrowing more expensive, you deter people and businesses from buying things. With the demand for things thus dampened, prices will stabilize. This has worked more often than not when properly implemented.

Since money is an ingredient of everything that is built, bought, stored, delivered and stashed away, sensing the future value of money becomes a basic part of economic management. The most common concern regarding the future value of money is: How much will the purchasing power of your work be eroded by inflation? In other words: If you have to work one hour today to earn enough to buy a six-pack, and the price of a six-pack increases by 10 percent a year, then next year you'll either have to work one hour and six minutes to buy a six-pack. Or you'll have to get a raise to offset the extra cost. If you don't do either, then your purchasing power will have been eroded by inflation: the future value of your money will be less—in terms of what it can buy—than it is today.

Long-term planning—retirement for individuals, new factories for businesses—must take this phenomenon into account. If, for example, you spend $100 a week on food, and inflation runs at an average of, say, 3 percent a year, then in thirty years the bill for the same food will be $190! (That's an increase of 3 percent each year for thirty years, or 90 percent. Compounding hasn't been considered to keep this concept simpler to understand.) If you plan to retire in thirty years, how much will you have to put away each year until then to be able to afford your current lifestyle?

The calculations can be tricky indeed, and they must take into account many unknowns. For example: your needs in thirty years may be less than they are now, such as needing only one car for a family instead of two. Your ability to put away money might get easier as your income increases—which it should. Say that you now need to save 8 percent of your annual income in order to reach your desired goals. If your income increases in the future, you may find that you'll only have to save, say, 5 percent of your annual income to reach your goals. And if inflation increases from its current level, the amount you can earn on your savings can also increase proportionately. Page 357 has further details on how to realistically evaluate this dilemma for your own personal purposes.

Marketing

Everybody is selling something. When you apply for a job, you are selling yourself. The "package" you present to the employer can determine whether you get the job. In addition to looking at your résumé and application, the employer observes how you dress, how you speak, and how you carry yourself. She takes account of your level of enthusiasm, your knowledge of the company and the industry, and your overall personality. In short, applying for a job is a marketing effort that you make on your own behalf. The better you market yourself, the better your chance for success.

Similarly, employers must make efforts to market their own products. Those efforts include knowing the marketplace, learning what the competition is doing and planning, designing a package that will appeal to the public, informing the public of the benefits of the product (advertising), and establishing a price structure for the product that the public will accept.

Nature and Natural Resources

Until we discover or invent some new kind of energy source to power our vehicles, our factories, and our homes, we will be living in the age of petroleum. Petroleum is a natural resource found in some of the most unreachable places on the planet: miles beneath the ocean, in the frozen wastelands of the polar icecaps, and in the middle of hostile deserts. Nature has given us the gift of petroleum as a fuel. But nature has also seen to it that access to this gift can be costly and challenging.

Just as the Log People found it necessary to go farther and farther afield to chop down their trees, we may soon find it necessary to go to ever-increasing expense to acquire our basic fuel commodities, as well as other important natural resources. Sometimes ingenuity will replace one natural resource with another resource that is more readily available. For example, nuclear power might someday replace petroleum as our primary source of energy. But what about clean water and clean air? As those natural resources—which we take for granted—become more scarce, what can replace them? The economic and social well-being of everyone on earth will be affected by our ultimate need to modify our habits or to replace some of these resources.

THE RESULTS

It has not been the intent here to give you textbook definitions of such things as inflation, recession, deficits, surpluses, and other economic phenomena. Rather, it is hoped that the foregoing discussion will help you understand the influences at work in the world, in our nation, and in your individual environment. At the end of each chapter in this book you'll find a section titled Ups & Downs: The Economics of Everyday Life. These sections will help you focus on the specific causes of economic activity as they affect your day-to-day personal financial affairs. Your better understanding of these forces and influences will enable you to become a better manager of your personal economy, and will help you to take advantage of opportunities that you might not have previously recognized.

PERSONAL ACTION WORKSHEET ——————————————————

How Do You React?

As this chapter has illustrated, a great many matters—both close at hand and remote—can affect your financial well-being. An awareness of these matters should alert you to defensive or corrective actions that you can take to protect yourself. Consider the following list of incidents that might have had a bearing on you in the past year. Think deeply about the not-so-obvious effects. What reactions did you have, or could you have had, either to fend off harmful effects or take advantage of good effects?

Incident	Effects on You, Direct or Indirect	Your Reactions, Actual or Possible
❏ Strikes (local, regional, or national)	_____	_____
❏ Weather conditions	_____	_____
❏ Business conditions for your employer	_____	_____
❏ Business conditions in your city, in the nation	_____	_____
❏ Your own health	_____	_____
❏ Health of your family	_____	_____
❏ Changes in tax laws	_____	_____
❏ Changes in working conditions	_____	_____
❏ International incidents	_____	_____
❏ Your acquiring more education	_____	_____

CONSUMER ALERT

The Global Marketplace

Exercise 1.2

You work at the XYZ Company—minding your own business, taking care of yourself as best you can, and saying, "I couldn't care less about international trade. It doesn't affect me now. And it won't affect me in the future. So why worry?"

Bad call.

Historic changes are taking place around the world, and new patterns of competition and opportunity in international trade will affect *virtually everyone*. Your company might find new markets in other countries; that could benefit your career. Or your company might be harmed by international competition; that could be bad for you. Your pension fund might be invested—for better or for worse—in companies involved in world trade; that could impact on your retirement income. There's really no place to hide. But an awareness of what's going on now, and what might happen in the future, can alert you to make the right moves.

These are the major trends that will be shaping world economic events in the years ahead.

North America   Trade pacts with Canada, Mexico, and the nations of the Caribbean can create a unified market of some 400 million people. Good news: easier trading with our neighbors, and more customers for U.S. made goods. Bad news: U.S. workers will have to compete with lower wage earners in those other nations.

Western Europe   A unified trading bloc in Western Europe can match North America in size and wealth. Money and labor and goods will move freely across borders, just as they now move across state borders in the United States. This will encourage giant multinational European companies, which will be stiff competition for Americans and Asians.

Eastern Europe   The former Soviet Union and its former allies are decades behind the West in basic infrastructure. They need incalculable billions of dollars to build new highways, factories, and power plants to get them into the twenty-first century on a par with the West. U.S. companies have a great opportunity to help Eastern Europe rebuild. In the long term, Eastern Europeans may become good customers for U.S. products and services. But competition for that trade with Western Europe and Asia will be ferocious.

Asia   Japan will be the hub of a giant industrial wheel encompassing more than 2 billion people from China to India and all points between. Low-cost labor coupled with huge amounts of money will result in an industrial juggernaut. But their infrastructural needs are equally gigantic, which the United States can help provide.

UPS & DOWNS   *The Economics of Everyday Life*

The Ingredients

The Ups & Downs sections in each chapter have been created to help you understand the ingredients in the economics of everyday life, to help you successfully ride the ups and downs of prices, interest rates, job opportunities, investments, tax laws, and even the whims of nature.

Following are the basic ingredients that go into the cost of almost everything. As they go up and down, so can your own financial well-being. Keep these basic ingredients in mind as you read the rest of this book, and particularly the Ups & Downs sections.

Capital   Every product or service you acquire has a capital ingredient: money, either cash-in-hand or borrowed. The farmer needs money to buy seed and fertilizer and equipment. The doctor needs money to pay for rent and staff and technology and continuing education. The bank needs money (from depositors and investors) to lend to borrowers.

Labor   The creation of every product or service involves some human efforts. Labor costs can vary widely, depending on the skills being used and the bargaining ability of the workers.

Social Costs   Capital and labor used to be considered the core elements of cost. But today much of the cost of any product or service also helps pay for—via taxes—social welfare programs, education, and a wide range of governmental activities.

Marketing   A lot of money goes into the design, packaging, and advertising of any product. You pay for it when you buy the product.

Governmental Regulations   Add up the costs of tax law compliance, payroll recordkeeping, pension plan administration, health and safety precautions, union relations, discrimination policing—it's a bundle.

"Postage and Handling"   A few decades ago the cost of delivering goods was relatively minimal. But now the costs and complexities are far more significant, involving fuel, equipment, insurance, and storage.

After-service   The age of consumerism has added its costs to an item after it has been purchased: namely, warranties, consumer hotlines, product recalls, defense of lawsuits, and supply of replacement parts.

These ingredients are examined more closely in later Ups & Downs sections.

?

WHAT IF . . . ?

How would you deal with these real-life possibilities?

As the world changes, any of the following could cause you to make adjustments in your own economic life. Consider each phenomenon, and evaluate how you might react. What adjustments might you make in your work, your budgeting, your style of living, your future plans?

1. The company that you (or your spouse) work(s) for announces that it's starting an export division. (Or your company provides goods or services to another company that is starting an export division.) There is every reason to believe that the venture will be a success. The initial target for foreign sales will be Central America. New opportunities at home and overseas will be available to those with skills in language, marketing, and customer service.

2. Your employer is being clobbered by foreign competition. Attempts to keep up are futile. It's only a matter of time—perhaps six months to a year—before the company folds.

3. The government announces a job retraining program offering instruction in high-tech applications, computer sciences and engineering. There's no cost, but you'll have to devote fifteen hours a week for a year to get the training, which holds promise but no guarantees of better jobs.

4. The government opens the door wide to new immigrants. Many foreigners, with skills like yours and willing to work for less money, are on their way here.

NUMBER CRUNCHERS

Do the calculations to make decisions in these real-life possibilities.

Exercise 1.3

1. Ask a bank what interest rate you'd have to pay today for a 36-month new-car loan of $10,000, and what the monthly payments would be. If you waited six months to buy the car (at the same price as today), and interest rates then had moved up by one percentage point, what would your monthly payments be then? What if rates had dropped by one point?

Exercise 1.4

2. What is the interest rate today and the monthly payments on a 30-year fixed-rate home loan of $120,000? What would your payments be if you took out the loan six months from now, after rates had moved up one percentage point? Down one point?

Exercise 1.5

3. Determine the current rate of inflation (the Consumer Price Index, or CPI). Using that as a rough gauge, what would happen to the price of a car, a home, or a year's worth of college tuition if the CPI was two percentage points higher each year for the next two years?

4. You invest $5,000 in a mutual fund that is pegged to move up and down in sync with the Dow Jones Industrial Average. What will your investment be worth if that average moves as follows over the next three years: (a) +5%, −8%, +12%? (b) −7%, +16%, −2%? (c) +12%, +9%, −8%. (Don't count taxes or dividends.)

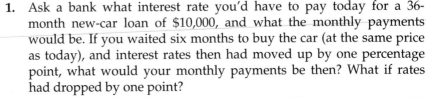

STRATEGIES FOR SUCCESS

Biblical Wisdom Helps You Manage Your Money

Remember the biblical story about the seven fat years followed by the seven lean years (Genesis 41)? Simply put, the message is: When times are good, put away something for the lean years. Any economy—your nation's or your family's—will go through times of relative prosperity alternating with relative austerity. When times are good, when income is high, it can be tempting to spend everything you're earning. But better to heed the ancient wisdom: Put some aside when the putting is good. You'll be happy you did when times aren't so rosy. A dollar put away during the fat years can grow to be $1.25 . . . $1.50 . . . or more to have on hand during the lean years.

FOR BETTER OR FOR WORSE

Things beyond our control often impact our personal and financial well-being, for better or for worse. Some are more predictable than others. How could you be affected if the following real-life phenomena happened? Could you have seen it coming? What steps could you have taken to minimize damage or maximize advantage? The better able you are to anticipate and recognize these forces, the better equipped you are to deal with them.

1. The Federal Reserve announces that interest rates will be increased by 0.5 percent, effective immediately.

2. Severe floods in the Midwest devastate the current grain crops. More than 30 percent of the expected harvest will be lost, and 20 percent of the next crop is threatened by expected weather conditions over the next six months.

3. Your state government announces that a maximum-security prison costing $80 million will be built ten miles from where you live.

Exercise 1.6

Working, Planning & Budgeting

Without work all life goes rotten. But when work is soulless, life stifles and dies.

Albert Camus

Shun idleness. It is a rust that attaches itself to the most brilliant metals.

Voltaire

You may call it *the rat race* or *the daily grind*. Someday you'll look back on it and wonder, "Where did all the time go?" This is the essence of family economics: (1) earning the money; (2) setting goals as to how you'll spend it, and (3) developing disciplined budget plans that will enable you to reach those goals. All of these matters are going on simultaneously, and they are subject to change at any given time. It's quite an exercise to coordinate them properly and to make wise adjustments when the need arises. This chapter will help you focus on all three of these "moving targets" so that you can plan, prioritize, and achieve what you want for yourself. Specific decision-making tools in this chapter include:

- How to accurately determine what a given job is worth: putting a dollar sign on the basic wage, the fringe benefits, and the longer term potential
- How to protect your legal and financial rights as an employee
- How to clarify your financial goals: setting them, putting the necessary priorities on them, and developing a workable plan to meet your goals
- How to use a financial statement as a planning and goal-meeting device

THE ROLE OF WORK IN YOUR LIFE

Work is perhaps the single most powerful force shaping your life. Your work creates the bulk of your income. It is that income, put to proper use, that allows you to be self-sufficient. It provides you with the necessities of life, as well as whatever luxuries may be within your reach. Income that isn't needed now can be invested for your future welfare.

Work can be a training ground. The job you do today gives you experience. That experience should enable you to accept future assignments that will be more challenging and rewarding and will promise greater benefits.

And work—for better or worse—can play an important role in many of the nonfinancial aspects of your life. The type of work you do can clearly shape a great deal of your social life, leading you into friendships and activities generated by the working environment.

As a well-planned working career progresses, it should create more leisure time, along with more dollars to spend in that leisure time. If you are to make the most of this powerful force that shapes so much of your life, it's necessary to look at work in a broad perspective. Your job is not simply a means of filling the hours from nine to five. You must look at not only what you might be doing today, tomorrow, or next week, but also where your aspirations and abilities can lead you. You must examine the ways you can maximize the rewards and pleasures available to you through work. Finally, you must consider how you can most efficiently use the fruits of your labor—your income—to satisfy current and future needs and desires.

FACTORS IN CHOOSING YOUR WORK

You have an extraordinary range of opportunity available to you in choosing your work. In every part of the country, there are community colleges and state universities, which offer relatively low-cost education that can lead to virtually any type of career. When the economy of our nation is dynamic and expanding, it offers new types of work opportunities and increasing chances for advancement within chosen fields of endeavor.

We are at the forefront of many new technologies, which will create challenging new opportunities in genetic engineering, laser technology, satellite communications, space exploration, weapons and defense systems, and much more. Even our leisure activities generate tens of billions of dollars a year in jobs for our citizens, ranging from neighborhood health clubs to professional sports teams to our worldwide exporting of movies and television programs.

Your ability to achieve your fullest work potential has few limitations. Achieving full potential is often interpreted as making a lot of money. That's not necessarily an accurate description of achieving full potential. Indeed, many people work so hard to make a lot of money that they never find themselves with the *time* to enjoy the *money* they've made. They may consider themselves failures.

There are important criteria other than money. Consider such rewards as a sense of self-satisfaction; the pride and pleasure you can feel from being creative, from being innovative, from being part of a winning team; a sense of personal growth that enhances your social, family, and community life. You can't spend these rewards, but they are invaluable.

You must determine your own balance of the rewarding aspects of work: money, leisure time, advancement, comaraderie, and pride in your achievements. That sense of balance is not easily achieved. Many people work years or decades before sensing that they have achieved it. Many people never find it, and many give up prematurely because they feel it's beyond their grasp. Others never strive to achieve it at all. There is no easy formula that can guide you toward the balance that is right for you. It's an ongoing quest, subject to change as your own needs and desires change. Your ability to achieve the right sense of balance will depend on your *desire* to do so and on a number of other factors, which we'll now examine.

Attitudes and Aspirations

Your choice of work, and your pursuit of success, will be shaped not only by your own attitudes and aspirations but also by those of others. Evaluate how each of the following influences might affect your work and career:

- Your ideas of what you want to achieve. For example: "I would like to have my own business."
- The degree to which you mold your own ideas of success based on other people. For example: "My friend Pat has everything going just right. If I could achieve what Pat has, I'd be very satisfied."
- The degree to which you are influenced by others. For example: A teacher may sense that you have certain aptitudes and, without your being aware of it, may motivate you to seek a career that you might not otherwise have considered. Or relatives may gently nudge, or emphatically push, you in one career direction or another, perhaps more for their own sense of self-satisfaction than for yours.
- The extent to which you are influenced by traditional social values. Will you be satisfied with the type of life that society has typically extolled: a good job, a nice family, living in a pleasant neighborhood, and becoming part of the community? Do you aspire to more than that? Or do you rebel against those values?
- The extent to which a change in your family circumstances can reshape your attitudes. For example: "I had great dreams for myself, but now I must make them secondary to the demands of my family."

Or, "I had great dreams for myself and, now, with the help and encouragement of my family, I can begin to achieve those goals."

- The extent to which you are supported by your employer. Can you profit from the support you receive from your employer? Can you overcome lack of support from your employer?

- The extent to which you view your current work as merely a job or as one step on the ladder of a long-range career. Are you just putting in your forty hours, or do you have ideas that will benefit the company and lead to your advancement?

How do you really feel about all these elements? Can you distinguish between the positive and negative influences as they affect your own attitude? Can you take advantage of the good influences? And can you walk away from the bad influences?

Education

Education is the major foundation on which a successful career is built. As Table 2–1 illustrates, on average, the more education people receive, the greater the income they'll receive.

If you project these figures out to a full working career, you can readily see that the college graduate in Table 2–1 will earn roughly double what the high school graduate earns. However, as attractive as the college graduate's lifetime earnings seem to be relative to the high school graduate's, the cost of obtaining that education creates a serious dilemma for many people. Table 2–2 illustrates the rising cost of obtaining a college education.

The debate over the value of *college* may never be resolved, but there can be very little argument that *education*—college, on-the-job training, or self-education—plays an integral role in career advancement and the achievement of one's fullest potential.

Bear in mind that educational facilities *alone* do not necessarily equip you for a more rewarding career. It's *what you do* with them that will make all the difference.

TABLE 2–1   **Income and Education**

Education of Householder	Average Annual Income, 1998 Dollars, Est.
Elementary school	$34,900
High school (4 years)	47,000
College (4 or more years)	91,500

Source: U.S. Census Bureau.

TABLE 2–2   **Rising College Costs**

If You Were to Start a Four-Year College Career in	Your Cost for the Four Years (room, board, tuition, books, transportation, and other expenses)* Would Be About:	
	Public (State) Colleges	**Private Colleges**
2000	$53,300	$112,500
2001	56,500	119,200
2002	59,900	126,400
2003	63,500	134,000
2004	67,300	142,000
.	.	.
.	.	.
.	.	.
2016	135,400	285,700

Exercise 2.1

*Costs are based on a 6 percent per year inflation factor.
Source: U.S. Department of Health and Human Services, 1996.

Aptitudes

In the career sense, aptitude generally means what you're best suited for. But what you're best suited for might not necessarily be the thing you enjoy most or from which you can generate the best level of income. For example, a young man worked in his father's clothing store during vacations. His father convinced him to take over the clothing store when he graduated. Because of the extensive on-the-job training, he had an *aptitude* for retailing; security and income seemed assured by following that course. But he never like retailing. Although the income and security were comfortable enough, he soon felt stifled, unproductive, discontented. By common methods of measurement, his aptitude was for retailing. But for him it was the wrong career.

What, then, is aptitude? It's a very precarious balance of many personal elements, some of which can be measured and some of which defy measurement. In the absence of a clear sense of direction, guidance counseling can be of some help in sorting out these various elements:

- What do you enjoy doing?
- What do you do well? (This is not the same as what you enjoy. Many of us do things well but don't necessarily enjoy doing them. And many of us enjoy doing certain things that, regrettably, we don't do that well. The difference should be noted.)
- What can you do to generate a desirable level of income and security?
- To what extent, if any, are you seeking to satisfy the expectations of others? Many people, such as the young retailer just noted, embark on careers because others expect it of them.

Personal Experience

Your personal experiences, both at work and in your private life, can affect your career choice and the success you may achieve. Any prior job can help you determine whether you like a particular type of work and whether you are good at it. Prior jobs can also lead to references that you can use later in seeking employment.

Other personal experiences—in or out of the workplace—can help you evaluate your comfort level in various situations:

- Do you enjoy being among other people, or are you more of a loner?
- Do you tend to be a leader or a follower?
- Are you content to be confined in a specific location for extended periods of time, or do you feel a strong need to move around in different locations?
- Is your span of concentration long or short on menial tasks? On more difficult tasks?
- Do you accept criticism constructively, or do you rebel against it?
- Are you a fast learner or a slow learner?
- Are you assertive or shy with other people?
- Are your ambitions greater or less than those of your peers?
- Can your energy be sustained for long periods of time, or does it come and go in spurts?
- Are you basically a patient or an impatient person?

Consider what kind of work opportunities and environments will most happily blend with your own traits to provide you with maximum satisfaction without forcing you into painful compromises.

The Changing Composition of the Work Force

Patterns of work life in the United States are changing. In the years to come, few individuals will be left untouched by the changes. To be aware of emerging trends that can affect your career is to be prepared to cope and to adjust. Let's briefly examine some of these trends.

The percentage of males participating in the work force is diminishing, while the percentage of females is sharply increasing.

Men are entering the work force later in life because of longer schooling, and they are leaving the work force sooner because of earlier retirement programs. Improvements in disability and health care benefits have also enabled men to leave the labor market when health problems have arisen.

A drastic drop in the birth rate has resulted in more women being able to work uninterrupted by childbearing. The availability of day-care facilities and tax benefits for child-care expenses have also aided many women wanting to enter the work force.

These factors, together with rapid gains by women in education and job opportunities, are resulting in dramatic shifts in the roles of men and women. Role separation is being replaced by role sharing for vast numbers of married couples. More than half of all married couples have two incomes, providing some protection to a married couple in the event of a layoff, compared to the once-typical family unit that depended predominantly on the man's income.

In the years ahead, the struggle will intensify between men and women for comparable jobs, comparably paid. What traditionally had been "male jobs" and "female jobs" are intermixing. With rare exceptions, sexual distinctions in the work force will all but disappear. How will these shifting demographic trends work to your advantage? To your disadvantage?

ECONOMIC TRENDS

The pendulum never stops swinging. As the primitive tribes in chapter 1 learned, many economic trends can create or threaten job opportunities. Awareness of these trends is essential if you want to take advantage of the good swings and avoid the troubles of the bad swings. Here is a summary of the most common trends; they can affect not only your career but your investment efforts as well.

- **Business Cycles**   On a national or regional level we refer to these cycles as *growth periods* and *recession periods*. One typical pattern: the economy is booming thanks to policies that make it easy to borrow money. Companies build new factories, buy new equipment, and hire new workers. When workers are in demand they can ask for, and get, higher wages. The higher wages translate into higher prices for the things that these workers make. The rising prices—inflation—hit a point where some people say, "I can't afford that." So they stop buying that thing, and the workers who make it are out of a job. Workers without jobs can't buy things either, so the layoffs spread. Pretty soon the economy's pendulum has swung from a growth period to a recession period. After a time, the laid off workers begin to find jobs again, and the pendulum starts to swing back the other way.

   The U.S. economy was booming in the 1980s, then went into recession in the early 1990s. By the late 1990s the pendulum had swung back the other way. Until? When the early 1990s recession hit, the buzzword for laying off workers was *downsizing*. Why was there so much downsizing? Because there was too much *upsizing* in the 1980s. Riding on boom times then, too many businesses thought that growth and prosperity would never end, so they took on more employees than the future would find prudent. Another way of looking at this phenomenon is to take into account the law of gravity: what goes up must come down. No one has yet been able to find a way around the law of gravity.

(It's amusing to note some of the econo-babble that companies use to make bad things seem not so bad. A sampling of other expressions used by major corporations to describe firing people: *Release of resources. Career-change opportunity. Rightsizing. Strengthening of global effectiveness. Normal payroll adjustment. Career transition program. Schedule adjustments.* Yeah, right.)

Business cycles also occur in industrial categories. The sudden popularity of sport utility vehicles was a boon to the automobile industry. The invention of the video cassette recorder was a boon to the movie industry and created the video sales/rental industry. The invention of the computer spawned countless new enterprises, from mouse pad makers to publishers who sell books explaining how to work the computers, and all points in between. Eventually, the causes of these phenomena fade, and the businesses and jobs fade as well. And the pendulum swings.

- **Geographical Shifts** When air-conditioning became cost-effective (after World War II) there was a huge shift of population from the chilly Northeast and Midwest to the sunny South and Southwest. Many cities throughout the Snowbelt began to shrivel as people left, resulting in more closings and lost jobs. When the Cold War ended around 1990, hundreds of thousands of jobs in the defense industry were wiped out. A huge percentage of those jobs were in the Sunbelt, and migrations began back to the Snowbelt. In the 1970s Americans were buying imported cars in record numbers, and auto workers in the Midwest began losing their jobs as a result. By the 1980s many of the foreign auto companies were building factories in the United States, so jobs started coming back to U.S. workers. In the mid-1990s the North American Free Trade Agreement joined the United States, Mexico, and Canada in a pact that would make it easier for those nations to trade with each other. Mexican wages were much lower than those in the United States and Canada, so a lot of U.S. jobs went south of the border. But then the Mexican economy began to improve, so Mexicans became customers for goods and services made in the United States and Canada. The pendulum swings. Can you cite any other examples, particularly that might pertain to you personally?

- **Political Changes** When the Democrats controlled Congress in the early 1990s they attempted a massive plan to revamp our health care industry (which represents about 14 percent of all the money spent each year in the United States). The health care industry shuddered with fear. In came the Republicans, and out went the health care overhaul. The health care industry breathed a sigh of relief, but in the meantime they had begun their own forms of consolidation to hopefully stave off governmental intervention. (See chapter 17 for more details.) Anyone remotely connected to the health care industry—including anyone needing medical care—was impacted by this political change.

Since 1969 the U.S. government has been unable to balance its budget. Spending outpaced income year after year. This was largely due to differing philosophies between the Republicans and the Democrats. The taxpayers made up the difference. In 1997 the two parties stopped their bickering long enough to pass spending and taxing laws that would supposedly balance the budget by 2002. We'll see, but while we wait some taxpayers get a break, and some who had been the beneficiaries of government spending will get broken. The pendulum swings.

Job Retraining

International competition, emerging technology, and changes in our government's industrial policies can also create or threaten job opportunities. The possible need to retrain yourself for a new type of work cannot be ignored. Various programs have emerged to assist workers in getting effective retraining. Keep yourself up to date on what's available. You never know when you might need it.

Financial Rewards

Of all the factors that might affect your choice of work, perhaps none is as persuasive as money. But, as the vignette at the start of chapter 1 indicated, that can be a mistake. As you may recall, the choice there was between higher income today but little advancement opportunity in the future, or less pay today with much more rewarding potential. You must, of course, evaluate actual potential with great care.

Beyond the base earnings you must carefully evaluate the full range of fringe benefits that may be available, and that can be worth thousands of dollars to you. Here are the major fringe benefits you should know about. The Personal Action Worksheet at the end of this chapter will help you evaluate and compare fringe-benefit packages at various places of employment.

Pension Plans

In a pension plan, the employer puts money aside every year for the benefit of eligible employees. In accordance with what is known as the *vesting plan*, you must work for the company for a given number of years before those benefits are locked up on your behalf. Normally, you don't receive the money in the pension plan until you retire. Pension plan benefits vary considerably from one company to another. (See chapter 18 for a more detailed discussion of pensions and vesting.)

Profit-Sharing Plans

These are similar to pension plans. A certain percentage of the company's annual profits are divided up among employees, and you're entitled to your share in accordance with the vesting plan. Commonly, your vested interest will not be paid out until you quit or retire. A particularly attractive aspect of pension and profit-sharing plans is that you don't have to pay income taxes on your employer's contributions during the years in which that money is credited to your pension or profit-sharing account. (See chapter 18 for more details.)

Investment Programs

A popular fringe benefit is known as the 401(k) plan. This is a form of investment program in which part of the employee's pay is placed in the plan, and that portion of pay escapes income taxes until the money is eventually withdrawn by the employee. The earnings of this plan are also tax-deferred. Employees generally have a choice of different types of investments, including a guaranteed income plan, similar to a savings program; a mutual-fund type of plan that invests in a variety of stocks; and a plan that invests in the stock of the company the employee works for. It's generally possible to mix and match among the different plans, and the mix can be changed at various intervals. It's also common for the company to chip in some money for each dollar the employee puts in. For example, for every dollar an employee puts in, the company might put in 25 cents. (See chapter 18 for more details.)

Health Insurance Plans

Health insurance plans are among the most common type of fringe benefits offered to employees. But not all employers offer this potentially valuable benefit. And plans that are offered can vary widely, from skimpy coverage to extensive coverage. As health care costs continue to rise, employees are being asked to bear part of the cost of the group insurance. See chapter 17 for more details.

Life Insurance

Life insurance is not as common a benefit as health insurance, but its inclusion in benefits packages is growing. As with group health insurance, the employer is able to purchase coverage for many employees at a lower cost than you could obtain on your own. Group life insurance may be a flat fixed sum or may vary in relation to your earnings at the company.

Educational Programs

Many employers will pay all, or a part of, the cost of courses that the firm recommends or that you wish to take in the furtherance of your career. That education is an asset you can take with you wherever you go.

"Family-Friendly" Benefits

Some fringe benefits might be more important in terms of family convenience than money. The number of holidays and vacation days—paid, unpaid, or any combination thereof—should be established. Sick leave is of major importance: How many days of paid sick leave—full or partial—would you be entitled to? When sick-pay benefits run out, is there a disability-income program that would kick in to pay all or part of your income?

Where and when you work is negotiable with some employers. Flextime, if offered, would allow you to vary the hours of your working day to coordinate with your family needs. Telecommuting—working at home and connecting with work through phone, fax and e-mail—is a benefit that many can enjoy; indeed, some employers are realizing that productivity increases with some workers when they telecommute.

Miscellaneous Benefits

The list of additional benefits grows each year as employers compete for good workers. Some of these may be negotiable—you don't ask, you don't get. Here is a rundown of some of the more popular benefits being offered:

- **Cafeteria plans**   This benefit lets workers choose between a number of various fringes, which might include insurance for life, health, and disability, investment plans, and vacation time. If you don't want one particular benefit you can dump it and get extra value on another benefit. These are also known as *flexible benefit plans*. If this is available, you must choose with great care and understand what options you have if you want to change the mix later on.

- **Flexible spending accounts**   With these you can set aside some of your earnings and avoid paying income taxes on that amount, provided you set the money aside to be used for certain qualified expenses such as dependent care or unreimbursed medical costs. Be careful: In order to preserve the tax-free status of those earnings, the money must be spent during the year on those qualified expenses. If it isn't, the money is forfeited. Learn what expenses qualify, and estimate very carefully what your actual expenses in those areas will be before you embark on the plan.

- **Education** This might include training that will aid you in improving your work skills, which, in turn, could lead to higher pay and job advancement. Free seminars on financial and retirement planning are also offered by some companies.
- **Stock options** This would give you the right to buy shares of stock in the company at a lower-than-market price. In some plans you obtain *warrants,* which give you similar rights. If you do partake of such a fringe benefit, investigate its limits: Do the options or warrants expire after a certain time? If you buy the shares through these plans, do you have to wait for any period before you can sell them?
- **Housing-related perks** Does the employer offer a relocation package that would pay all or part of your moving costs? Separate components of such a package can include paying for your closing costs on selling your former home and/or buying a new home; job hunting expenses for you or your spouse; and temporary living quarters while you wait for your permanent new home to be available. If your employer does not pay for any relocation costs, some of them might still be tax deductible to you. See the section on moving expenses in chapter 10.
- **Personal benefits** Day care, counseling programs, employees' cafeteria, recreational facilities, and on-site infirmaries are commonplace in larger companies.

Where the Jobs Are

Your job skills have to coordinate with other factors: that there is a need for those skills; that the need exists in a place you want to live; and that you're willing to move to a new place to match your skills with the need. If you

STRATEGIES FOR SUCCESS

How to Leave a Job the Smart Way

When you want to quit a job, emotions can overcome common sense. That's when costly mistakes happen. Before you hand in your resignation, find out *specifically* what will happen to your fringe benefits if you quit now, or if you wait until later. Will you lose vesting rights on your retirement plan? How much will it cost you to take over your health insurance protection so that you don't go uninsured until the coverage from a new job kicks in? The same with any other group plans—life insurance, dental insurance, and so on. Worried about being laid off? Don't quit in anticipation: If you do so, you could lose your right to future unemployment insurance benefits.

TABLE 2–3 **Fastest Growing Occupations, 1992–2005**

Occupation	Rate of Growth
Home health aides	+138%
Human services workers	+136%
Personal and home care aides	+130%
Computer engineers and scientists	+112%
Systems analysts	+110%
Physical and corrective therapy assistants	+92%
Physical therapists	+87%
Paralegals	+85%
Occupational therapy assistants and aides	+78%

Source: U.S. Bureau of Labor Statistics, 1996. Statistical Abstract of the U.S.

live in Omaha and are interested in marine biology, or if you crave a career in forestry and you live in Miami, you'd best start packing your bags. Every few years the U.S. Bureau of Labor Statistics ranks occupations expected to grow the fastest in the decade ahead. Table 2–3 shows the most recent results.

THE JOB QUEST

Exercise 2.2

Seeking a job—one that will lead to a career—is a matter of selling.

Any successful salesperson knows that advance preparation is essential if a sale is to be made. In the selling process that we call seeking employment, your *sales kit* consists of a number of different elements.

- **Your résumé** This is the history of your past experience in school and at work. It should succinctly inform your prospective employer of all the training you've had, as well as activities that would establish a broader profile of you as a person. The employer wants individuals who get along well with their fellow workers, who exhibit a constructive and productive attitude, and who are, in general, well-rounded members of the working team.
- **Your references** Written references include full-time work situations, part-time and charitable work and involvement with civic, religious, or social organizations. The references help to establish your reputation for trustworthiness, integrity, and industry. An accumulation of references from responsible individuals can enhance your opportunities for current employment and future advancement.

- **Your presentation**   This is perhaps the most critical aspect of your *sales pitch:* What can you do for the employer that other applicants for the job might not be able to do? Applicants normally have an opportunity to make their presentation during the job interview.

Self-Employment: A Working Alternative

You can perform many types of work—particularly in consulting and creative fields—as an independent contractor or as a sole proprietor instead of as an employee. As a self-employed person you have to pay your own Social Security taxes (self-employment tax), and you'll have to provide your own health and unemployment protection. You might be entitled to some attractive tax deductions, and you can establish a retirement plan that can offer benefits not available to regular employees. Before embarking on this path, you should get advice from an accountant. (See chapter 21 for a full discussion on self-employment.)

CHANGING CAREERS

Nearly one-third of all U.S. workers change careers in any given five-year period—*careers,* not just jobs. A job change implies going from one employer to another, but doing the same work. A career change is much more drastic: altering virtually the total structure of one's work, whether with the same employer or with a new one or on one's own.

Although there are no valid statistics concerning the success quotient in career changes (did the change bring the money, happiness, challenge,

STRATEGIES FOR SUCCESS

Prepare Yourself Well for Job Interviews

The better prepared you are for a job interview, the better your chances of getting the position you want. Attend to all the details of good grooming. Learn as much as you can about the company: Talk to current employees for down-to-earth information. For major companies, check *Standard & Poor's* listing at your local library. Also, inquire at your local newspaper for recent items about the company. Be prepared to tell your interviewer how you think you can help the company, and supply convincing reasons why you want to work there. Don't nag about what kind of pay, hours, and benefits you'll have. Don't smoke or chew gum, and try not to fidget. Rehearse interviews with a close friend to help you get over the nervousness.

contentment you were seeking?), changing careers can be an infectious phenomenon. Self-employment is a particularly powerful lure.

Children are asked from their earliest days, "What do you want to be when you grow up?" They are seldom asked, "*How many* different things would you like to do when you grow up?" Many choose a career at an early age with the assumption that it will be their one and only career. Too little thought is ever given to the possibility that the chosen career may be limited in its overall satisfactions. Many people are poorly prepared for the day they find their first careers have reached a dead end. They have acquired neither the skills nor the outside interests nor the flexibility that could assist them in a career change. Many recognize the value in making a change but are reluctant to move for fear of giving up the security they have already achieved. They might thus resign themselves to continuing an unsatisfying career.

Many others, however, will have acquired other skills, other interests, and a sense of flexibility that can broaden their perspective and allow them to adapt easily to a new career situation.

You may never have any notion of changing your career until you encounter one of the factors that can motivate you to seek a change. Figure 2–1 illustrates the typical flow patterns of a career change. Look at the far left column, Motivating Factors. Any one of those factors, or others not included in this chart, may prompt you to begin exploration, which can include diagnosis and testing as well as counseling and referral. Many will

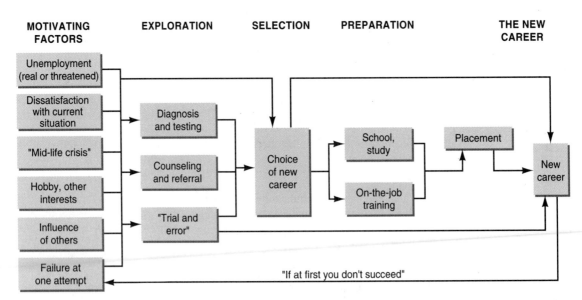

FIGURE 2–1   Typical flow patterns in a career change
Source: Adapted from a study by the Rand Corporation, "Mid-Life Career Redirections."

opt for the "trial-and-error" method of exploration, which can be costly, time-consuming, and frustrating.

Donald and Ellen

Let's briefly trace Donald and Ellen's career change patterns. Donald started as assistant manager in a shoe store. But when the owner's son expressed a desire to be the manager of Donald's store, Donald began to fear for his job. He had long enjoyed his hobby of assembling electronic kits, and he wondered if there might not be some better career opportunities for him in that field.

The motivating factors—suspected unemployment and an enjoyable hobby—led Donald to do some exploring. He had his aptitude in electronics tested and made careful inquiry in his community about job opportunities that would put his skills and interests to best use. After due exploration he made his selection. He would train himself to work on the development of video game cartridges. He took some appropriate courses in electronics at a local community college and did some apprentice work for a company that manufactured game cartridges. He was able to do this in the evening while maintaining his flow of income from the shoe store. In the months it took him to prepare for his new career, the game cartridge company hired Donald and he hit the ground running.

Ellen was not so successful. She had been happy as a musician, playing in a combo at local nightclubs. Her family was appalled. They nagged her about seeking a more respectable profession—working in a bank, selling insurance, becoming a stockbroker—a career *they* could be proud of.

The family's nagging was the main motivating force in Ellen's career change. She just wanted to get it over with and get them off her back. So she didn't bother with any diagnosis or counseling. She just looked through the want ads for the first opportunity in a white-collar position, and within a week she was in a training course for life insurance sales. Her first few weeks in the new career were disastrous. She neither liked the work, the people she dealt with, the hours, nor the need to sell life insurance. Ellen's failure at her first attempt finally motivated her to seek some professional counseling. The counselor told her that she'd do best as a musician and that her family would just have to learn to live with it. With new-found confidence in herself, Ellen went back to her old job with the combo and lived happily ever after.

YOUR WORK AND INCOME: PROTECTION AND REGULATION

Exercise 2.3

Your financial and legal rights as an employee are regulated and protected by a variety of federal and state laws. It's important that you be aware of how these laws can affect your work and income. Following is a brief summary of the most important such laws.

Your Paycheck

The Internal Revenue Service requires that your employer withhold some of your pay to be applied toward your income taxes, Social Security taxes, and other state and local income taxes. It's then the employer's responsibility to forward these amounts to the appropriate authorities.

The amount withheld should be as close as possible to your actual taxes for the year. More than 80 percent of all workers have more withheld than is necessary to pay their taxes. The result is that they get a refund for the amount that has been overpaid when they file their tax return the following year. The average refund check is about $1,400. These workers are, in effect paying about $117 a month into an account with the government on which they earn no interest at all.

W-4 Form

The amount withheld from your pay is based on the number of *allowances* you claim on the W-4 form you filed with your employer when you began work. The more allowances you claim on your W-4 form, the less will be withheld from your pay, and thus the higher your take-home amount. You can claim allowances for yourself and for members of your family. You can also claim additional special allowances if, for example, you itemize your income tax deductions and if you are entitled to certain income tax credits. A worksheet accompanying the W-4 form explains in detail how these special allowances work. You can easily amend your W-4 form as needed to reflect the proper number of allowances so that your take-home pay will be adjusted accordingly.

W-2 Form

By the end of January of each year, you should receive a set of W-2 forms from your employer. These forms reflect the total amount you were paid for the prior year and the total amounts that were withheld for taxes and for Social Security. The information on the W-2 form will assist you in completing your returns. The W-2 form enables the Internal Revenue Service to verify your total pay and the amount that was withheld.

1040 ES Form

If you receive income that is not subject to withholding you may have to pay an estimated tax quarterly during the year. The federal form 1040 ES contains a worksheet that will assist you in estimating your total tax obligation from income not subject to withholding. Income that is not subject to withholding can include such items as money received from independent contract work, tips, and investment income.

Workers' Compensation

If you suffer injuries in conjunction with your employment, you are entitled to certain benefits under the workers' compensation law of your state. You may be entitled to benefits even if the injury was your own fault. But if you injured yourself deliberately, or if you were drunk or under the influence of drugs, you may not be entitled to benefits.

Workers' compensation benefits can include both medical expenses and reimbursement for lost income.

In general, if you accept workers' compensation benefits from your employer, you might not be able to bring a lawsuit against him or her for loss or damages you may have suffered. If workers' compensation benefits and other medical insurance will not adequately compensate you, consult an attorney at the earliest possible time. Each state has workers' compensation review boards that will evaluate claims and pass judgments accordingly. Check with your employer to determine the extent of possible coverage.

Unemployment Insurance

If you are discharged from a job that is covered by unemployment insurance, you are entitled to a limited number of weekly checks to tide you over until you find employment elsewhere. If you are discharged for cause—such as for violation of your employer's rules—you might *not* be entitled to unemployment benefits. The unemployment insurance program is administered separately by each state. Unemployment insurance funds are generally paid in by employers, with some additional subsidy from the federal government.

If you are discharged, you should immediately file a claim with your state unemployment office. You will have to appear in person each week to claim your check. You must be willing to accept any suitable full-time job that becomes available. If the employment office offers you such a job and you refuse it, you could lose your unemployment benefits.

If you are discharged from a full-time job, you can take on a part-time job and still receive *partial* unemployment benefits. If, after discharge, you receive workers' compensation income, severance pay, or a pension from the former employer, you may be ineligible for unemployment insurance benefits. If your claim for benefits is turned down, you are entitled to file an appeal with the unemployment insurance office.

If you leave a job voluntarily, you will not likely be eligible for any unemployment benefits. The following dilemma can occur: Michelle worked at a job that was covered by unemployment insurance. She feared that her job was in jeopardy. She quit in order to have time to seek a more secure job. One week later she learned that she would have been discharged because of a mass layoff. It took her two months to find another job. During that time she did not receive any unemployment benefits because she had quit voluntarily. Had she remained on the job for one more week and been discharged, she could have been entitled to unemployment insurance for almost two months.

Many workers wrongly view unemployment insurance as a form of welfare. It is not: It is insurance. If you had a fire in your home, you certainly wouldn't refuse the payments from the insurance company. Unemployment insurance is the same type of thing: The benefits should not be turned down because of pride or lack of knowledge of the situation.

Employee Retirement Income Security Act (ERISA)

This complex law established a variety of protections for your rights under any pension or profit-sharing plan an employer might offer. One of the most important requirements of ERISA is that all employees covered by such plans be provided with a description of their benefits at least once a year. A great deal of your financial welfare—particularly for the future—may depend on your pension or profit-sharing plan. The description you receive should be read carefully, and if any part of it is not clear, seek clarification from your personnel office.

The Individual Retirement Account (IRA) was also created as part of ERISA. See Chapter 18 for further details on ERISA and IRA.

Your Right to Work and Discrimination

A number of federal and state laws protect workers from discriminatory workplace practices. If you are denied a job or fired from a job in violation of these laws, you can pursue your rights through the appropriate state or federal agencies.

Here's a rundown of these major federal laws. Most states have adopted parallel laws and have established agencies to administer them. If you have specific questions or problems, contact the nearest office of the U.S. Department of Labor or your state Department of Labor for assistance.

The Federal Fair Labor Standards Act

The Federal Fair Labor Standards Act protects minors from being employed in "oppressive" jobs. These can include jobs that are hazardous or detrimental to the health and well-being of minors. In most states, minors under age 14 are not allowed to take jobs, and work permits are required until they reach a prescribed age. These laws also limit the number of hours and times of day during which minors can work.

The Age Discrimination in Employment Act (1967)

The Age Discrimination in Employment Act applies to workers between the ages of 40 and 65. It is a violation of the law for covered employers to refuse to hire or wrongfully discharge individuals in that age bracket because of age alone.

The Fair Employment Practices Law

The Fair Employment Practices Law, also known as the Civil Rights Act of 1964, provides perhaps the broadest antidiscriminatory measures. Under this statute, "It is unlawful for an employer to fail or refuse to hire or to discharge any individual, or otherwise to discriminate against any individual, with respect to compensation, terms, conditions or privileges of employment because of such individual's race, color, religion, sex or national origin." Sections of the law apply such prohibitions to employment agencies and labor unions as well as to employers. A 1990 federal law extended these protections to disabled persons.

There are some exceptions under this law. For example, a Japanese restaurant has the right to hire a Japanese chef without fear of violating the law. An employer cannot be required to hire a worker of one sex when a job reasonably requires that a member of the other sex is more appropriate—such as a restroom attendant. Distinctions in pay and other employment matters can be allowed if the company has a good faith seniority or merit system or a system that distinguishes among employees who work in different locations.

The Equal Employment Opportunity Commission (EEOC) has power to begin actions in court to correct violations of the law. State agencies may also provide means of resolving a problem.

Wage and Hour Laws

The federal wage and hour laws apply to people whose work is in any way involved with interstate or foreign commerce. If your work doesn't fall into that category, you are probably protected under your state wage and hour law. These laws generally set a maximum number of hours you can be required to work each week and establish a minimum wage to which you are entitled. Check the current regulations associated with your job.

Plant Closings

A 1989 federal law requires that employees be given advance notice of plant closings or large-scale layoffs. This rule applies generally to companies with 100 or more employees.

Family Leave

A 1993 federal law, the Family and Medical Leave Act, gives employees the right to take twelve workweeks of leave during a twelve-month period to care for a newly born or adopted child, or to care for a spouse, child, parent, or oneself if that person has a serious health problem. The leave time is generally unpaid, but certain employment benefits are to continue during the leave time. The law pertains to employers with fifty or more workers; some states have overlapping laws. See your personnel office for more specific details.

Americans with Disabilities Law

The federal law bans employers from refusing employment to workers who might be mentally or physically disabled. Employers may not ask prospective workers about the existence, nature, or severity of a disability. However, employers do have the right to ask disabled persons—or any other prospective employees—about their abilities to perform specific tasks. The law also mandates that employers provide "reasonable accommodations" for the needs of disabled workers, including special equipment, working hours, and working conditions.

Employers with fifteen or more workers are required to comply with the law.

Health and Safety Regulations

State and local laws require building owners and employers to be responsible for safety conditions within work areas covered by the laws.

The federal Occupational Safety and Health Act (OSHA) sets standards to protect the health and safety of workers in their working environment. If an unsafe condition exists, an employee can complain to the Department of Labor, which can require the employer to correct the condition.

As a general rule, if you complain about an employer, under OSHA or the other federal employment laws, it is illegal for the employer to retaliate against you for having made a complaint.

Union Matters

Tens of millions of workers are members of labor unions. Labor unions negotiate wages and other benefits for members and can act on behalf of members if unfair employment practices occur.

The National Labor Relations Act of 1935 and the Labor-Management Relations Act of 1947 (also known as the Taft-Hartley Act) govern relations between management and labor with respect to unions. Under the National Labor Relations Act, *employers* are prohibited from:

- Unreasonably interfering with employees who are attempting to organize a union or bargain collectively
- Discriminate against workers by imposing hiring conditions that discourage union membership
- Interfering with a labor union in its formation or administration
- Refusing to bargain collectively with appropriately elected representatives of the employees
- Discrimination against any worker because he or she has complained against the employer under the law

The Labor-Management Relations Act generally prohibits *employees and unions* from:

- Forcing workers to join a union
- Refusing to bargain collectively with an employer once the employer has received proper certification of the union's status as the employee's bargaining agent
- Becoming involved in illegal work stoppages
- Requiring an employer to pay for work that was not performed
- Charging excessive initiation fees or union dues to employees belonging to the union

The federal National Labor Relations Board (NLRB) oversees laws relating to unions and management.

Garnishment

If you do not pay your legal debts, your creditors can sue you and obtain a judgment against you. That judgment may entitle them to garnishee your wages, which could require your employer to send a portion of your wages to the judgment creditors.

Under the Federal Consumer Credit Protection Act (1968), also known as the Truth in Lending Law, there are limits to how much of your pay can be garnisheed by a creditor. Most states have similar laws. Check to determine local regulations.

A garnishment can be extremely embarrassing to the employee. Federal Law prohibits an employer from discharging an employee just because his wages have been garnisheed. If, however, an employee's credit performance becomes so improper that the employer is overloaded with garnishment claims, the employer could make a good case for dismissing the employee.

Employment Policies and Contracts

The conditions of many workers' employment are covered by contracts between employer and employee or between employer and union. These contracts should spell out all pertinent matters relating to employment, including pay, raises, fringe benefits, vacation privileges, sick-pay provisions, and causes for rightful termination. If your employment is covered by a contract, you must acquaint yourself with all the provisions. When the contract expires, either you or your union representative will have to renegotiate it. Renegotiation should commence many months before the termination date.

Most workers are not covered by contracts but by the ongoing employment policies of the employer. Except where state or federal law prevails, many of these policies can be changed at the sole discretion of the employer. Such changes could occur with respect to fringe-benefit programs, sick-pay benefits, hours and place of employment, and pay-raise schedules. Protect yourself by obtaining current policies and advance notice of any intended changes in writing.

SUCCESS IS WHAT YOU MAKE IT

Your success in your work will depend on more than just fulfilling your basic duties as an employee. Your initiative, your creativity, and your willingness to cooperate can all help you move up the ladder toward higher pay, greater recognition, and career advancement. Your current job might not be what you have in mind for a lifetime career, but every good experience can build your knowledge, and every good performance can result in a positive reference that will help you achieve the ultimate potential you are seeking for yourself.

Viewed positively and patiently, your work can provide you with an ongoing sense of challenge and achievement. Viewed negatively and impatiently, your work and your personal life can end up in a rut. The choice is yours.

THE MASTER PLAN

You can go through life on a hand-to-mouth basis, living as best you can from day to day, spending when the mood strikes you and hunkering down when the money runs out. This is known as "having too much month at the end of the money." It's not fun. It's frustrating, often painful, and frightening when you don't know what next week or next month might bring. Of course, everyone's life has its fair share of uncertainties. But you don't want to live that way; you can have The *Master Plan*.

A Master Plan consists of a number of phases. First is the goal-setting: What do you want to achieve for yourself in the near term and the longer term? Second is the prioritizing: Which of your clearly defined goals deserve the most attention and earning power? Third is the risk management phase: How can you best protect your goal-path from the destructive risks that everyone faces? Fourth is the need to update: As your needs and desires change, as older goals get accomplished and newer ones appear, how do you adjust your overall financial patterns to remain in control of your own destiny?

Before we explore these matters in more detail, and consider tools you can use to build and maintain a master plan, here are some thoughts that will help you to tackle the challenge of creating The Master Plan.

Goal Setting

Exercise 2.4

First of all, understand that there is no single correct set of goals, budgets, or plans. Countless guidelines are suggested in consumer literature. There are statistics galore that will show you how much people spend and save. These can be helpful in giving you an overview, but when all is said and done, you must establish The Master Plan that suits *your own needs and desires*. Not your friends'. Not your parents'. Not your neighbors' or co-workers' or party-mates'. *Your own.*

The easy way might be to clip an article from a magazine that tells you how your household budget should work, and follow it to the letter. The hard way is to sit down with your family members, analyze what you want to achieve, crunch a lot of numbers, work out specific spending and saving patterns, and then embark on the rocky road. Have no doubts: the hard way is the better way.

Goals fall into many categories. The most obvious are the time-related goals: short term and longer term. Short-term goals mainly mean taking care of the here and now in comfortable fashion. Longer-term goals require a lot of advance planning: educating your children, going into business for yourself, retiring comfortably when you want to, and the like. We'll take a closer look at these issues later in this chapter.

One way to help you sort out the goals is to think of your money as Today Dollars and Tomorrow Dollars. Today Dollars are those you need for here and now. Tomorrow Dollars are those you put away today to be used in the future. Some Tomorrow Dollars have to be consciously put away: you have savings plans and investment programs that you contribute to regularly. Some Tomorrow Dollars will accumulate as a result of how you spend some of your Today Dollars. For example, some of your current earnings from work may be set aside in a pension plan and for Social Security. And part of your payments on your home loan go toward reducing how much you owe. Some of your life insurance payments may be building up a cash reserve that you can later tap into. In all of these cases, your Today Dollars are being turned into Tomorrow Dollars automatically. This book is designed to help you understand and keep track of it all.

Prioritizing

Some goals are more important than others. It's important to have the means to educate your children. It's not so important (for most people) to have a stash of money to take a gambling fling in Las Vegas every six months. Think in terms of *Must Goals* and *Maybe Goals*. Must Goals are those that you simply must accomplish: You must have a certain amount of money (or ability to borrow) at some fixed point in time. You don't want to have to say to your child, "Pat, I'm sorry we can't send you to college, but I spent and borrowed every penny on gambling flings in Las Vegas, and I lost it all."

Maybe Goals are those about which you can say, "Maybe, after we've embarked on a well-disciplined program to meet our Must Goals, we can start working toward some more fun goals. Failure to meet a Must Goal can be devastating: "I can't afford to retire," and so on. Failure to meet a Maybe Goal isn't that big a problem. "Okay, so we didn't go to Europe this year. Maybe, if we stick to our budget, we can do it next year, or the next." As you sort through your goals, use the Must and Maybe designations as your starting point in prioritizing.

Family Concerns

The changeover from single person to married person requires a complete new look at your goals, your priorities, your spending patterns, and your need to revise them all. The change from married person to parent takes you a giant step further in your need to re-examine everything.

Consider these important aspects of family financial planning. Some day you may have to deal with them all:

- **The costs in having children**   The thought of having to pay uninsured maternity expenses might be the single best form of birth control there is. Talk to your family doctor to learn what these expenses might be, and then examine your health insurance to learn the extent of your coverage for maternity.

- **Health care**   Family health care is quite a different matter from individual concerns. Will all family members be covered by an insurance plan? What deductibles and co-payments will apply? With children, a whole range of pediatric specialists can add to the mix of necessary care providers. How does your health plan cover this?

- **Educational costs**   The cost of higher education has grown faster than the normal rate of inflation (see Table 2–2). If you're going to have college-bound children, the time to start planning for their education is now, even if they are not born yet. Tax law changes in 1997 give some attractive tax breaks for the college-bound. See chapter 20.

- **Children's spending money**   Even this issue must be faced. Will they get allowances? How much? Who will determine the size of the allowances: you or peer group pressure? ("Gee, Mom, Fran gets twice that amount. Why can't I have that much?") Will they have to work (home chores and/or real jobs) to be entitled to a given allowance? The amount of an allowance, and the conditions under which a child gets it, can considerably affect a child's ability to establish a sense of self-sufficiency and self-worth.

- **Housing**   The roof over your head may need some enlarging as the family grows. To what extent might your family's well-being be affected by the size and facilities of your home? Considering gender and age of children, such matters as bedroom and bathroom sharing can impact on the family's comfort patterns. Buying a new home, or modifying an existing one, can be costly. You must evaluate the cost–benefit ratio and plan accordingly.

- **Role modeling**   As your children observe and are affected by your spending patterns, so will they adopt similar patterns, for better or for worse. If you know you spend too much money willy-nilly, and you know you're not being wise, it won't do much good to hope that your kids are smarter. They do as you do, not as you say.

"The good life" is something that we not only strive for; an avalanche of advertising tells us what we need in order to be happy. Common sense should prevent anyone from falling prey to this lure, but it doesn't always do the trick. Having The Master Plan and sticking to it is your best defense against the lures of instant gratification. Just as a guide to how your fellow Americans are chasing the good life, Table 2–4 illustrates some shifts in recent spending habits.

TABLE 2–4   Shifts in Spending Habits

We're Buying More Of	1989	1996 (increase as % of total consumer spending)	We're Buying Less Of	1989	1996 (decrease as % of total consumer spending)
TVs, VCRs	1.09%	2.74%	Food in restaurants	5.59%	5.42%
Computers	0.11	1.30	Doctors' service	3.73	3.61
Brokerage services	0.56	1.02	New cars	2.51	1.57
Toys	0.78	0.94	Furniture	1.04	0.94
Airline tickets	0.58	0.61	Tobacco	1.29	0.91

Source: U.S. Department of Commerce, Bureau of Economic Analysis, 1997.

The percentages in Table 2–4 may seem small, but remember that they represent percentages of *trillions* of dollars' worth of consumer spending.

Risk Management

Life, in a broad sense, is a series of risks. Success in life is navigating those risks safely. No one is immune to unforeseen catastrophes, such as illness, property destruction, premature death of family breadwinners, and loss of work. The Master Plan can succeed only if you establish sound risk-management techniques, the primary one of which is insurance: life, health, disability, property, public liability. These tools are discussed at length in the appropriate chapters of this book. The secondary form of risk management is self-insurance: "I can't afford, or don't want to spend, money for insurance policies, so I'll take my chances all the way." That's the easy way out. As with basic planning, discussed earlier, have no illusions: the hard way is the better way.

The Need to Update

As we mature, old goals are accomplished or abandoned, and new ones arise, perhaps unexpectedly. These shifts require a revision of our Master Plan. Moreover, as we achieve old goals and strive toward new ones, we may have to make certain tradeoffs—adjustments in priority to allow us to accomplish something that may not have been there yesterday.

In short, a workable Master Plan is only as valid as its revisions. In addition to developing the disciplines of saving wisely and spending prudently, we must develop the habit of periodically reviewing and revising the overall plan so that it will clearly satisfy the sought-after lifestyle. For the family, it may be a yearly meeting at which everyone sits down to evaluate and plan for the future. For the individual, it may be an annual meeting with a banker, accountant, lawyer, or other advisor to do the same. An important part of such a review is to go step by step through each item and ask ourselves: "Am I doing it right? Am I getting bogged down in unproductive spending habits? Will I arrive at my appointed destination on time with the right amount of dollars?"

A GOAL WORKSHEET: HERE AND NOW

Table 2–5 is a worksheet. It lists all the common expenses we have to meet and contains spaces for the amounts you are now spending (or setting aside), as well as projected amounts you will be spending one and two

TABLE 2–5   Goal Worksheet — Current and Ongoing Expenses

	Current Estimated Monthly Expenses	Estimated Monthly Expenses One Year from Now	Estimated Monthly Expenses Two Years from Now
Food and beverage			
Shelter			
Clothing and linens			
Protection against risk (insurance)			
Entertainment			
Education			
Health care costs			
Transportation			
Little rainy day fund			
Cost of credit			
Travel and recreation			
Personal business			
Children's allowances			
Miscellaneous personal expenses			
Luxuries			
Charity and religious expenses			
Income taxes			

Exercise 2.5

years from now. Filling out the worksheet serves several purposes: it will provide a clearer picture of your current financial situation; it will aid you in anticipating future goals as your needs change; and it can help you determine what expenses might be modified to supply more spendable dollars in another area.

Each of the items in the worksheet is discussed here in more detail.

As you calculate each expense, include any debt repayment that may be part of the total expense. In other words, any payments on an automobile loan would apply toward your overall transportation expense. Also, separate from debt payments that portion attributable to interest, and include those interest items under the category "cost of credit." It's important to get a clear-cut picture of what all your credit is actually costing you, and it may come as quite a surprise.

Table 2–6 sets forth average budgets for families of varying levels of income. Consider them only as broad guidelines, not as recommendations.

TABLE 2–6 Annual Budget for Four-Person Families

Item	Lower Budget (under $15,000), Percentage of Total	Intermediate Budget ($15,000–$30,000), Percentage of Total	Higher Budget (over $30,000), Percentage of Total
Food	31.2	24.7	21.1
Housing	19.0	22.2	22.9
Transportation	7.4	8.8	8.0
Clothing	6.9	6.9	6.1
Personal care	2.6	2.2	2.1
Medical care	9.7	6.1	4.3
Miscellaneous	4.2	4.8	5.7
Other items	4.1	4.3	4.9
Personal income taxes	8.0	14.7	20.6
Social Security and disability	6.3	6.3	5.1

Totals may not add up to 100% because of rounding.
Source: U.S. Department of Labor, latest data available.

Food and Beverage

This includes food and beverages consumed at home and at restaurants, alcoholic beverages, lunch money, snack money, and tips.

Shelter

Calculate each of the following components separately:

Basic Expense: Rent or Mortgage Payment

If you are an owner, remember that a portion of your mortgage payment applies to the reduction of your debt. This portion, referred to as principal, can be recovered when you sell or refinance the property. But because that future time is unknown, the total mortgage payment should be considered as a current expense.

Property Taxes

Owners are billed each year for property taxes. The bill may include separate allocations to the city, the county, the school district, and any other jurisdictions with the right to tax local properties.

Property Insurance

Property insurance for both owners and renters includes coverage for fire and other damage to your dwelling and its contents, public liability and medical payments coverage for costs incurred by people who may be injured on your premises, plus specially scheduled protection for loss or theft of valuable property.

Utilities and Communications

In an energy-conscious world, the cost of utilities (electricity, heat, water) cannot be taken for granted. Consider how those costs can be reduced by various energy-saving techniques. Ample literature is available from utility companies, home improvement dealers, and at your local library or bookstore.

The cost of communicating has multiplied in recent years. Once upon a time there were only telephones. Today cellular phones, fax machines, e-mails, pagers, and computers all talk to each other. In addition to the cost of the equipment, there are monthly service and usage charges to pay—to the telephone companies and the Internet providers. Just figuring out which local and long-distance telephone service is the most cost-effective takes some educated number-crunching. It's easy to spend more than $100 a month, just for the connections, let alone the usage charges. Calculate with care to determine if you're getting value for the money you're spending in this area; if not, you should have no problem getting along with less.

Maintenance and Repairs

A program of preventive maintenance can be decidely less costly than after-the-fact repair.

Renovation and Improvements

Whether you renovate your dwelling cosmetically (painting, landscaping, etc.) or functionally (adding new equipment, rooms, etc.), you must take into account how much of the expenses can be recaptured when the house is sold. Improvements that are too personal may not appeal to a buyer. Improvements that are too costly—that would cause the house to be priced much higher than other homes in the neighborhood—stand a poor chance of repaying the cost. See chapter 10 for more details on selling your home.

Appliances and Reserves for Replacements

Items in your home, such as the water heater, dishwasher, refrigerator, furnace, and other appliances, can be costly to replace. Rather than waiting for these items to die and then scrambling to find the money to replace them, put aside a few dollars each month now so that you'll have a replacement fund to buy new items later.

Clothing and Linens

Clothing expenses are based on two main factors: need and style. Too many budgets are thrown into disarray because of excessive purchases of clothing and accessories. And although sheets, towels, and blankets may be relatively minor budget items, shopping with an eye to durability and washability can keep replacements to a minimum.

Protection Against Risk

This is the insurance package that protects you against illness, accident, disability, claims by others for damages you may have caused them, and the premature death of the breadwinners. The workings of the insurance plans (health, life, disability, and auto) are discussed in later chapters, but the costs, taking deductibles into account, should be included here.

Entertainment

Much of the money spent on entertainment tends to be spent impulsively. This is natural; when we get the urge to escape, we don't always stop to examine how the expenses might affect our normal budgetary program. The frequent result: a severe budget "leak."

Take the time to make a detailed listing of all entertainment expenses so that you can determine where excesses might occur.

Education

This should include tuition for college, private school, religious education, and adult education, and all textbooks and related reading materials and supplies. Include also tutors and expenses for school clubs, uniforms, and equipment.

Health Care Costs

Over and above any premiums you may pay for health insurance, include here any costs you incur that are not reimbursable by any insurance program. In addition to visits to doctors, include prescriptions, dental expenses, eyeglasses, hearing aids, therapeutic equipment, and the costs of any other special treatments or devices needed.

Transportation

This should include the cost of both privately owned vehicles and public transit—and don't overlook the cost of motorcycles and bicycles, their maintenance, repairs, and parts. (Chapter 5 discusses transportation costs in greater detail.)

Little Rainy Day Fund

Distinguish "little rainy day" funds in your immediate budget program from "big rainy day" funds for your long-range budget. The little rainy day fund is a handy source of money—perhaps kept in a savings account—that can be used to equalize some of the inevitable fluctuations that occur in a month-to-month spending program. It should be added to regularly and tapped as little as possible. The more it can grow, the better off your big rainy day fund will be.

Cost of Credit

Apart from interest on a home mortgage, which is included in the shelter category, list all costs you are incurring for all your other credit uses. This would include all interest *and late charges* on all charge accounts, credit cards, personal loans from any source, loans against life insurance policies, and overdraft checking accounts. Not enough attention is paid to this cost, which can add roughly 10 to 30 percent *a year,* plus any late charges, to the goods and services you're purchasing.

Travel and Recreation

This is separate from your normal transportation and entertainment expenses. It refers primarily to vacations, travel to visit family and attend out-of-town weddings, and other functions. Expenses include transportation, lodging, meals, entertainment, tips, shopping (souvenirs, etc.) car rental fees, baby-sitting fees, special clothing and equipment, and any costs involved in maintaining your dwelling while you are away.

Personal Business

Include all expenses you incur in keeping your financial matters under control: legal fees, accounting fees, income tax preparation charges, investment and advisory expenses, safety deposit box rentals, checking account costs, and the purchase of necessary equipment and supplies related to these matters (a computer, stationery, filing equipment, etc.).

Miscellaneous Personal Expenses

When budgets fail to balance it's usually because too many dollars have dribbled away in unnoticed fashion. Big items—utility costs, rent, mortgage payments and the like—are easy to trace. But the variety of smaller "miscellaneous" expenses are too easily forgotten. This results in the *Miscellaneous Bulge,* and the *Dollar Diet* is the best remedy. The Dollar Diet costs nothing, and will help you solve the overspending problems. Here's how: In a separate notebook keep track of every nickel, dime, and dollar you spend for at least two months. You must write the item down before you spend the money. If you change your mind about buying the item, cross it off your list. At the end of the two months you'll not only be able to track your excess spending, you'll also have conditioned yourself to stop and question every expense before you make it. Here are the items to track:

tobacco	allowances	hygiene and toiletry
alcohol and tobacco	gum, candy, snacks	products
music (CDs, tapes)	gasoline and other car care	magazines, newspapers
beauty parlor/barber	videos, bought or rented	entertainment
minor clothing items	transit (buses, taxis, trains)	cosmetics
gifts, greeting cards	laundry, dry cleaning	dining and drinking out
school lunches		

Luxuries

This is an optional category for those who have a goal of acquiring certain luxuries as a part of their expense program. What are such luxuries? It all depends on the individual—obviously, what one might consider a luxury, another might view as an ordinary acquisition. Luxuries must be designated in terms of priority with regard to all your other expenses. What might you be willing to give up in order to acquire them?

Charity and Religious Expenses

This includes membership in religious organizations and contributions to them, as well as other charitable contributions, such as the United Way, Red Cross, medical-oriented charities (American Heart Association, American Cancer Society), and so on.

Income Taxes

List all amounts paid via withholding or otherwise for federal, state, local, and Social Security taxes.

SHAPING FUTURE GOALS

Table 2–7 lists people's most common major goals. These goals are not listed in any order of priority; that is for you to determine. Complete the columns accompanying the goals to get a better idea about what priorities you want to attach to them.

Sort out these goals using the *Must* Goals/*Maybe* Goals distinction that was discussed earlier. Some account must be given to inflation, but it is impossible to predict. Throughout most of the 1990s inflation was not of great concern, averaging about 2 percent to 3 percent a year. But there were periods during the 1970s and 1980s when inflation flared at double-digit rates, upwards of 10 percent to 12 percent a year! Our national policies have focused on avoiding dangerous inflation, but unpredictable economic forces can always bring it back.

TABLE 2–7   Major Future Goals

	How Much Will Be Needed?	When Will It Be Needed?	Amount per Year	Priority
Education	_____	_____	_____	_____
Housing (new shelter)	_____	_____	_____	_____
Retirement	_____	_____	_____	_____
Stake for your children	_____	_____	_____	_____
Stake for yourself	_____	_____	_____	_____
Care of elderly or disabled	_____	_____	_____	_____
One-shot expenses	_____	_____	_____	_____
Big rainy day fund	_____	_____	_____	_____

For purposes of this exercise you might want to do "best case" and "worst case" scenarios. As you project your future needs, build in a low inflation factor, say 2 percent a year, for the best case, and a high factor, say 8 percent, for the worst case. The Decision Maker software program that was designed as a companion to this book can help you with these calculations. The software is available on the Internet at http://www.wiley.com/college/rosefsky.

Also, in the study guide that accompanies the text there are chapter exercises titled, "What's It to You?" These are designed to help you prioritize concerns in the full spectrum of personal finance. The segment in chapter 2 will be of particular help.

Let's now take a closer look at each of the items in Table 2–6.

Education

This refers to higher education for children, and, in light of current trends, it can be a most challenging goal (see Table 2–2). College education traditionally must be funded at a fairly fixed point in time.

Preparations to meet this goal must begin as early as possible. These preparations can include a savings/investment program; awareness of loan, grant, and scholarship programs; and communications between parents and child regarding the child's own contribution to the financial needs, such as through work.

Housing (New Shelter)

Individuals and families owning a home have an advantage over those currently renting: they will be building equity that can be applied toward the purchase of a new house or some other goal. Current renters must accumulate a large enough down payment to enable them to obtain their first home. Later chapters on housing provide assistance in working out the arithmetic of buying versus renting and focus on how home ownership can be accomplished.

Retirement

With rare exceptions, this is the most predominant Must Goal for everyone. You don't have a chance to do it over if you reach a point when work ceases and there's not enough to live on. It's never too early to begin focusing on this important goal. (Chapter 18 contains more guidelines to help you achieve that focus.)

Stake for Your Children

Many parents want to provide their children with a stake to help them get started in life. The stake might be used to help them buy a home, to get them started in a career, or just to provide a cushion to assist them in coping with the world's vagaries. If this is one of your goals, you must give it priority in line with other goals.

Stake for Yourself

As discussed earlier, career changing is a prevalent phenomenon in our society. Many of these changes involve going into business for oneself, and often a substantial stake is needed. Put a priority on any such goal you may have, and keep it in mind each time you renew and revise this list. (See chapter 21 for a further discussion on self-employment.)

Care of Elderly or Disabled

This should be called a need rather than a goal, since we all hope that those near and dear to us will be able to maintain themselves throughout their lifetime. But it doesn't always work out that way. Parents and other close relatives might become dependent on us for a measure of support. If this is anticipated, it can be planned for and is easier to cope with.

One-shot Expenses

These might be must goals, or they could be maybe goals. They can include such items as a "once in a lifetime" trip, a large wedding for one's child, a major purchase of jewelry or luxury items, or a generous gift to a charity. These are voluntary goals, and their priority may be high or low. The higher the priority, the earlier the planning must be done.

Big Rainy Day Fund

We earlier mentioned the "little rainy day" fund. The big rainy day fund is directed more to major unanticipated expenses that anyone might confront—uninsured medical expenses; extended periods of layoff from work; emergency needs of other family members; uninsured losses; and so on. Generally, this item has a fairly high priority. Proper insurance can minimize much of the risk, and there's always the possibility that the fund will never be needed and can, at some point, be allocated to other goals.

THE SOURCES FROM WHICH FUTURE GOALS CAN BE ACHIEVED

In addition to keeping a careful watch on your goals and their shifting priorities, it's also important to be alert to the sources of money. They, too, are subject to change over the years, and it's important to be able to adjust goals and priorities in line with changes in the sources of income.

Income from Work

This is the primary source from which your current and continuing goals will be met. If you don't use all your current income in meeting your current goals, the excess can be put aside to meet future goals. Or it can be spent now on nonessentials. This extra money—what you earned minus what you spent—is called discretionary income. It's good to be in the position of having some. But the choice between spending it now or putting it away for the future can be quite perplexing.

Savings/Investments

Depending on the risks you take with your money, you may have a reliable or an unreliable source of dollars. Prudence can assure your future; speculation can demolish it. Be well aware of possible consequences before you make any decisions in this extremely important area.

Equities

Homeowners build a source of future funds as they reduce their mortgage debt and as the home (usually) increases in value. Owners of ordinary life insurance policies are also building a source of future funds. Both forms of equity—your share of ownership—can amount to substantial sums. If they are tapped too early, by refinancing your home or prematurely cashing in your life insurance policies, the ability to meet future goals may be seriously impaired. Know what these values are and what they can amount to in the future. Later chapters on housing and life insurance will assist you in determining those future values.

Borrowing

Borrowing is a convenient way of meeting goals. With regard to housing, transportation, and college tuition, borrowing allows you to accomplish what otherwise may take many years of accumulation. But beware: Borrowing means that you're accelerating the use of future income, with an added cost of roughly ten to thirty percent a year for interest. And since funds borrowed now must be repaid in the future, that repayment can impinge on your future cash flow. Prudent borrowing can enhance your current lifestyle; imprudent borrowing can devastate your future lifestyle.

Enforced Savings: Pensions, Social Security, Profit-sharing Plans

These represent current income shifted to future accessibility. To many people, these enforced savings represent all, or a substantial part of, the sources for meeting retirement goals. But a danger exists: Many people will find that their reliance on these sources has been *in error*—there isn't as much as was expected. Even though need for this money may be many years off, it's vital that a close estimate of what will be available is maintained on a continuing basis.

Inheritances, Gifts, and Other Windfalls

For most of us, this category may be a complete imponderable. But if you have any reasonable assurance that inheritances or gifts will be coming your way, it would be wise to try to determine the after-tax amount involved; this can have a considerable effect on your other ongoing financial plans.

THE FINANCIAL STATEMENT: A PLANNING TOOL

Can you imagine buying an automobile with no dashboard indicators on it? No speedometer, no gas gauge, no mileage indicator, and no oil, brake, or battery warning lights? And to top it off, the hood is sealed shut, requiring two days in the shop every time you want to check your oil, battery, and other innards. It might be okay for an occasional spin to the supermarket, but to take it out on the highway would be risky, to say the least.

In much the same sense, any individual, family, or business needs a proper set of *financial indicators,* as well as easy access to the inner workings, so that periodic tune-ups can be done quickly and simply.

A thoughtfully prepared and *regularly updated* financial statement is an invaluable package of gauges, meters, and warning lights. It can tell you how fast you're going, how your fuel is holding out, how much fuel you'll need in the future, and how smooth your ride is.

Financial statements provide a picture of the exact financial condition of the person or business involved. But financial statements reflect the condition *only on the given day.* The value of a single statement is limited. The true value comes in comparing it with past statements, so that strong and weak points can be spotted and evaluated.

The Elements of the Financial Statement

Exercise 2.6

The financial statement consists of three major elements: assets, liabilities, and net worth. Figure 2–2 illustrates these and other features of a typical financial statement in simplified form.

PERSONAL FINANCIAL STATEMENT

As of_____   (date)_____

Purpose of Loan:_____   Source of Repayment:_____

Personal Information: Name, current address, previous address, length of time at addresses, Social Security number, telephone (home and work), marital status, current employer, previous employer, length of time with employer

*Assets**		*Liabilities**	
Cash	_____	Loans payable to banks	_____
Securities (stocks, bonds, savings)	_____	Other debts (credit cards, charge	
Money owed to you (from friends,		accounts, finance companies, etc.)	_____
family, contracts, refunds)	_____	Taxes due (income, property, etc.)	_____
Life Insurance cash surrender value	_____		
Real estate (less loans against)	_____		
Personal property (autos, home			
furnishings, etc.)	_____		
Total Assets $_____		Total Liabilities $_____	

NET WORTH: Assets minus Liabilities $_____

Annual Income: Itemize salary or wages, rental income (net), business income (net), dividends, interest, other

Total Income $_____

Annual Expenses: Itemize loan payments (home, car, credit accounts), taxes, insurance, living expenses, other

Total Expenses $_____

NET CASH FLOW: Income minus Expenses $_____

FIGURE 2–2   Simplified Sample of Personal Financial Statement
*All assets and liabilities should be itemized as of *current value.* All insurance coverage (life, health, property, public liability) should also be detailed.

Assets

Assets are the sum total of everything you own, plus everything owed to you. The value of assets is figured as of the date of the statement. Because the value of many assets does change, it's essential to evaluate them anew each time a statement is prepared.

Included among your assets are your house, cars, personal property, bank accounts, cash value of life insurance, stocks, and other securities. Also included are money or property due you as a result of a pending inheritance, personal debts owed to you, property settlements, and so on.

Liabilities

Liabilities are debts—everything you owe. As with assets, these are figured as of the date of the statement, and values must be updated accordingly.

Included among liabilities will be the mortgage on your home, amounts owed on loans, contracts, and other personal debts. A detailed financial statement will break down liabilities into long term and short term. This can aid an analysis of your condition by distinguishing which debts will fall due within, say, one year and which will fall due at some more distant time.

Net Worth

Your net worth is the difference between assets and liabilities. You arrive at net worth by subtracting liabilities from assets. A storekeeper might see it this way: If he wanted to close up shop altogether, he would sell off all assets and use the money to pay off all liabilities. What's left would be his net worth.

Here's a simple example of how net worth is calculated on one particular item. Kim has a car valued at $10,000. However, she still owes the bank $2,000. Therefore, her net worth in this asset is $8,000. The asset (car) minus the liabilities (debt to bank) equals net worth, $8,000.

Other Aspects

Financial statements will also include a brief summary of your annual earnings and living expenses, as well as schedules of your life insurance holdings, your investments, and your property, both real and personal.

From time to time, you may be required to provide personal financial information to obtain credit. In such instances, you'll sign a statement that says that the information you have given is accurate; that you have given the information so that the other party can act in reliance on it; that you have not withheld any pertinent information; and that you agree to notify the other party of any adverse changes in your circumstances. In providing this information and then signing the statement, you are legally binding yourself to the accuracy of the information given. If you give false or incomplete information you may be putting yourself in jeopardy. An insurance policy can be voided, a loan can be declared in default, a debt can be refused discharge in bankruptcy proceedings. The way to avoid such concerns is to be certain that the information on any financial statement is *accurate.*

The Uses of the Financial Statement

As an Early Warning Signal

An ongoing program of updated financial statements can help you spot troubles before they get out of hand. A financial mess can be lurking beneath the surface for years before it begins to hurt. For example, you might be slipping into excessive debt. By tracing your debts over the years via your financial statements, the signals may become evident early enough to warn you to correct the situation. Or your nest egg might not be growing as rapidly as it should be, and this can be spotted by comparing a series of annual financial statements. It's all a matter of keeping track, and the financial statement program is a most important tool for this.

For Keeping the Reins on Your Credit

Good credit, wisely used, can be of immense value. Knowing well in advance your borrowing needs and your borrowing capabilities helps assure wise use of credit. Through your financial statements, you can maintain a close watch on your current debts, items that need replacement in the future, such as a car, and your anticipated future income (your ability to afford tomorrow's needs). You think that you'll need a new car two years from now. But considering what other things you might have to borrow for between now and then, how will that car loan fit into your overall plans at that time? The financial statement gives you the data that can help you cope with the future. See chapter 12 for more details.

In Helping to Protect You Against Loss

If you keep your financial statements up to date—at least yearly—you'll be forcing yourself to keep accurate current valuations on all your property. The value of any property is subject to change, and only by knowing true current values can you be sure of obtaining the necessary insurance to protect you against loss. See chapters 5 and 10 for more details.

In Maintaining a Sensible Life Insurance Program

Provision must be made to maintain comforts in the event of the premature death of a breadwinner. Life insurance is the most common means of ensuring this. A life insurance program should be planned in conjunction with the availability of other assets that can be cashed in to provide for needs. The financial statement is a reliable indicator of assets that can be converted into cash without undue sacrifice, should the necessity arise. This can help you tailor your life insurance program to your specific needs rather than guessing what that program should consist of. See chapter 17 for more details.

In Helping to Establish a Worry-Free Estate Plan

Your progressive financial statements provide the best possible at-a-glance gauge of what type of estate planning you need. Prudent estate planning requires a regular checkup of your net worth: which assets and liabilities are increasing and decreasing? At what rate? Until what time? Which assets have income potential, and to what extent? See chapter 19 for more details.

In Helping to Plan Your Long-Range Budget

The financial statement, regularly updated, is a simple device to keep your current and future goals in clear focus and to provide ongoing measurement of the sources from which those goals will be met.

As an Aid in Borrowing

On those occasions when a financial statement is required as a condition for getting a loan, you'll expedite matters considerably if you are prepared with a current statement, as well as statements from recent years. It will speed up application processing and serve as evidence of your financial good housekeeping.

SOME THOUGHTS ON SPENDING HABITS

One object of this chapter is to help you establish financial habits that will allow you to accomplish your goals. But all too often we are waylaid in the pursuit of those goals by commercials urging us to buy things that promise us happiness and satisfaction in almost every phase of life.

Spending habits born out of impulse, gullibility, or low sales resistance can be extremely counterproductive to one's financial welfare. We are all subject to impulsive spending, but we must control it.

Spending habits may have been unconsciously inherited from our parents, and we must evaluate their objective. Peer-group pressure—"keeping up with the Joneses"—can also influence spending habits, and succumbing to it can be costly and unsatisfying.

Spending habits are a powerful force in shaping your overall well-being. To the extent that spending habits control you, you'll have a much more difficult time achieving your own personal potential; when *you* control these habits, you will indeed be the master of your fate. Chapter 3 will help you develop wise spending habits.

 ## PERSONAL ACTION WORKSHEET

What Is Your Real Income?

Real income consists of both wages and fringe benefits. Wages are visible every time you get your paycheck, but fringe benefits are difficult to evaluate. Following is a list of common fringe benefits. Note the ones you now enjoy. If your employer didn't make them available to you, estimate how much it would cost you to obtain them on your own. Tally the total value of all your current fringe benefits. Compare the value of that package with what may be available from another employer you may be thinking of transferring to.

Benefit

Value, or Cost of Obtaining Benefit on Your Own (per Year)

- ❐ Health insurance $ _____
- ❐ Disability insurance _____
- ❐ Life insurance _____
- ❐ Pension contributions _____
- ❐ Profit-sharing contributions _____
- ❐ Investment-fund contributions _____
- ❐ Automobile _____
- ❐ Uniform allowance _____
- ❐ Educational programs, seminars _____
- ❐ Dental insurance _____
- ❐ Legal insurance _____
- ❐ Club membership _____
- ❐ Use of athletic, other facilities _____
- ❐ Retirement counseling _____
- ❐ Personal financial counseling _____
- ❐ Medical, psychological counseling _____
- ❐ Other _____ _____

_____ _____

Goals Should Satisfy Yourself, Not Others

Linda and Gary faced a dilemma common to many young married couples.

"We both have good jobs with a lot of potential, and we're confident that we can afford to buy a home in the near future. We've found a funky old cottage about twenty miles out of town right on the lake. It's run down and would need a lot of work, but the price is right, and we love the location. Even with improvements, it would still be funky, but it's 'our thing.'

"That's where the problem arises. Our folks, and a lot of our friends, have been hounding us to buy a place in a neighborhood that's the 'in' place for up-and-coming career couples.

"To us that's phony, but we can't deny that it does offer good contacts and whatever advantages may come from living in the 'right' neighborhood. It would cost a lot more than our funky bungalow, and we'd really be strapped to make the monthly payments. But, then, our friends and family say, 'You'll reap a bigger profit when you sell the "right" place, compared with what you might gain when you sell the bungalow.'

"When we boil it all down, it's the two of us against a lot of them. We know we're young and naïve. We respect the experience of others. But we feel guilty—if we buy the bungalow, we're being self-indulgent and foolish. If we buy into the 'right' area, we're being sensible and mature—supposedly. Just who are we supposed to be trying to please anyway?"

The ending, at least for Linda and Gary, was a happy one. They bought the bungalow and fixed it up, and eventually their friends and family admitted that they had done the right thing.

As Linda later put it: "The final decision came down to this: Do we strive toward goals that we ourselves have set, or do we live our lives as others want us to? Well-meaning though the others may have been, we have to express our own independence and live our own lives. Fortunately, we made the right choice. Other couples in the same boat might have done better to listen to the others. To each his (or her) own—as long as you know what your own is."

UPS & DOWNS *The Economics of Everyday Life*

Why Spending Habits Change

A lot of factors can influence how you spend your money. You're very conscious of some of them: You just got a raise, or you just got fired. There are also influences that sneak up on you, and some of them can be dangerous.

Inflated Expectations This is human nature at work in one of its most devilish ways. "I'm *positive* I'm going to get a raise . . . a bonus . . . a winning lottery ticket . . . a big profit on the stock I just bought . . . So why wait? I'm going to start spending that money NOW!" And worse: "I'm going to go into debt now and I'll repay it just as soon as the money flows in." The dangers are obvious. Keep alert to signals that your own expectations may be inflated.

Expectations of Inflation Yes, it sounds like the above, but it's quite different. From time to time the media will sound warnings that inflation is picking up—the cost of everything is rising. This often sends people on buying sprees: Buy now, before the prices go up. This buying activity prompts merchants to raise prices to take advantage of rising demand. And then you have a classic case of a self-fulfilling prophecy. The buying urge, in *expectation* of inflation, often causes people to buy things they don't need.

The Lure of Eee-zee Credit We're all bombarded with offerings of credit cards, home equity loans, and the like. All too often the lure is overpowering, and a spending spree ensues. Bear in mind: The fact that someone is willing to lend you money doesn't necessarily mean that you should borrow it or that you're in good shape to repay it.

Self-indulgence The cry of self-indulgence is "I MUST have that, and I MUST have it NOW!" Advertising, fads, trends, and just plain keeping up with the Joneses can open checkbooks by remote control. There's some self-indulgence in everyone. Beware.

Hunkering Down Spending cuts can be prompted by a concern over your employment prospects. This may prompt you to get back to basics and salt away what you can to see you through tough times. But determine the realities of the job market; don't rely on rumors or suppositions. Also, you might be hit by the reality of how much you have to start putting aside today to meet future goals. When you fully realize the importance of the following sentence, you're on your way to good financial health: "What I don't spend today I can put away and spend in the future."

? **WHAT IF . . . ?** ───────────────────────────────

Test yourself: How would you deal with these real-life possibilities?

1. Your parents will be retiring soon. You worry that they will not have enough income to live in the style to which they've been accustomed. How much, if at all, can you help them financially? What are you willing to give up for their sake? On the other hand, if you don't care to or can't help them right now, how will you react if they run into serious financial problems a few years from now?

2. Economic conditions are harsh, and your boss tells you that you're going to have to take a pay cut of 10 percent if you want to keep your job. Where will you cut your spending to offset this cut in income?

3. A major national company is opening a branch in your city and is hiring people with your skills. You'd like to apply there. Make up a shopping list of all the things you'd need to know about working for the company to enable you to make a wise decision.

4. There have been rumors that your company may be acquired by an-other—one with a reputation for running a "lean and mean" shop. You fear that your job is in jeopardy. What can you do, now and when the merger occurs, to protect yourself? If the worst case does occur, what sources of income can you tap—your savings, your former employer, and/or the government—to tide you over until you find a new job?

NUMBER CRUNCHERS ───────────────────────────────

Do the calculations to make decisions in these real-life possibilities.

1. Your place of work is a quick and easy bus ride from home. Dress is casual on the job, and there is a pleasant low-cost employees' cafeteria. You have a new job possibility that's in an upscale area ten miles from your home. There's no mass transit to that place, so you'd have to drive. The new job would require more fashionable clothing, and all of the lunch-hour restaurants are pricey: You'd have to pay two to three times as much for a lunch as you now pay in the employees' cafeteria. Considering the expenses involved in this new job (commuting, cloth-ing, lunches, etc.), how much of a pay increase would you have to get in order to earn the same take-home pay you're now earning?

2. You've become hooked on a new leisure pursuit—golf? scuba div-ing? photography? skiing? You really want to get involved, but it's going to cost a lot of money. You estimate it will take $1,000 to get set up. Then, at a low level of involvement, it will cost an average of $100 per month; at a high level, $200 per month. How much of your desire can you fit into your existing budget if you go for the low level of activity? The high level?

FOR BETTER OR FOR WORSE

Things beyond our control often impact our personal and financial well-being, for better or for worse. Some are more predictable than others. How would you be affected if the following real-life phenomena happened? Could you have seen it coming? What steps could you have taken to minimize damage or maximize advantage? The better able you are to anticipate and recognize these forces, the better equipped you are to deal with them.

1. The company you or your spouse works for declares bankruptcy.
2. You have a child who is a senior in high school. You've sacrificed so that you could save almost $30,000 to send your child Pat to college. Pat decides not to go to college and claims the decision is final and non-negotiable.
3. You're living on a very tight budget, with little or nothing going into savings. Your employer announces a 401(k) plan (see chapter 18 for details) that will contribute 50 cents to your account for every dollar you put in.

3

Sensible Shopping and Spending

"Money may be the husk of many things, but not the kernel. It brings you food, but not appetite; medicine, but not health; acquaintances, but not friends; servants, but not faithfulness; days of joy, but not peace or happiness."

Henrik Ibsen

You can be better off by $1,000 or more per year! That's how much a Smart Shopper can save in routine shopping for food, pharmaceuticals, and the like. And for big-ticket items—appliances, home furnishings, electronic goods, and vacation travel—you can reap big savings by following the guidelines in this chapter, which will tell you, among many other things:

- How to recognize built-in bad shopping habits and replace them with good money-saving habits

- How to cut 10 percent, 20 percent, and even more from much of your food and drugstore spending

- How to find affordable and enjoyable vacation travel

- How to shop for the best values in at-home leisure electronic equipment

- How to find no-cost or low-cost personal enrichment activities that can enhance your leisure time and your life

THE BAD HABITS

Every day we are bombarded with hundreds, if not thousands, of advertising messages: on television, radio, the internet and billboards; in newspapers and magazines; and in our mail. Advertising shows us the choices we have for products and services. But advertising must also be approached with caution: in addition to those instances when advertising is misleading (see chapter 4), advertising can create costly buying habits. It can motivate us to buy on impulse, spending dollars we might have put to better use. It can prompt us to buy a product that promises certain benefits when comparable products offer the same benefits at a lower cost.

Advertising isn't entirely to blame. No ad ever reached out and twisted anyone's arm to buy a particular product. We must accept the blame for our own impulsiveness and unwillingness to take a few extra moments to pick the product that can satisfy our needs at the best possible price.

If you have any doubts about the tendency toward poor shopping habits by the average American, conduct a simple experiment *after* you've read this chapter: Be a supermarket spy. Push a cart so as not to raise suspicion, and follow other shoppers up and down the aisles of the supermarket. Notice how they succumb to impulse, brand favoritism, and lack of adequate comparisons. After doing this you'll at least feel confident that *you* know how to save as much as 20 percent on the bulk of your shopping—and, for a family that spends an average of $100 a week on such items, or more than $5,000 a year, that's a savings of about $1,000 per year.

Let's now examine some of the specific Smart Shopper techniques, particularly those that can be employed at the supermarket, where the majority of our day-to-day shopping budget is spent. (All price comparisons referred to in the following material are based on regular prices, not on specials or discounts.)

THE GOOD HABITS: GROCERIES AND TOILETRIES

Unit Pricing

Suppose a 14-ounce bottle of Heinz ketchup is $1.39 and a 64-ounce bottle is $3.76. Which is the better buy? The smaller bottle is cheaper, of course, but it's not the better buy. On a *per ounce* basis, the bigger bottle is the better buy. In the small bottle the ketchup is 10¢ per ounce. In the big bottle the ketchup is 5.9¢ per ounce. The exact same product is 4.1¢ per ounce cheaper—almost 60 percent per ounce cheaper—when bought in the larger container.

TABLE 3–1   **Unit Pricing Comparisons**

Product	Size	Cost per Package	Cost per Ounce	Savings per Ounce with Larger Package
Taster's Choice Coffee	7 oz.	$7.89	$1.13	
	2 oz.	3.59	1.80	37%
Mott's Applesauce	48 oz.	2.67	5.6¢	
	23 oz.	1.58	6.9¢	12½%
Del Monte Corn	15¾ oz.	.69	4.4¢	
	8¾ oz.	.56	6.2¢	26%
Treetop Apple Juice	128 oz.	3.89	3.3¢	
	46 oz.	2.29	4.9¢	33%
Best Foods Mayonnaise	32 oz.	2.78	8.7¢	
	8 oz.	.89	11.1¢	22%
Del Monte Peach Halves	29 oz.	1.56	5.4¢	
	8¼ oz.	.79	9.6¢	44%

This is what's known as unit pricing: calculating the price of a product by the unit—ounce, pound, and so on—rather than by the container it comes in.

Consider Crest toothpaste: a 2.5-ounce tube at $2.29 comes to 91.6¢ per ounce. An 8.2-ounce tube at $2.99 comes to 36.5¢ per ounce—a difference of almost 55¢ per ounce, or a savings of 60 percent per ounce if you buy the big tube. See Table 3-1 for other examples.

Brand Label versus Generic Label

A box of 100 Lipton teabags: $3.65. A box of 100 store-brand teabags: $2.89—a savings of 76¢, or 21 percent. The difference in taste may be

insignificant, but even if there is a distinguishable difference in taste, is it worth the sacrifice for the 21 percent savings?

Brand-name products are those regional or national items whose names are known to us through advertising and general familiarity. Generic products, in the broad sense, are those that are privately labeled for specific stores or chains of stores. In many cases, the quality of generic products is equal to their brand-name counterparts. Indeed, many are made by the same manufacturers and to the same specifications. Some generic products may not have the same quality as their brand-name counterparts, but the difference may be so slight as to justify buying them for the savings that can be realized. At the very least, a trial of the generic products is certainly warranted. If you're dissatisfied, you can always go back to the brand label. But if you're satisfied with the generic label, you can reap substantial savings.

Pharmaceuticals and Prescriptions

Generic products also offer considerable savings in the drugstore. Table 3–2 compares some common items that can be purchased without a prescription. (The survey was conducted at a major chain outlet, and the pharmacist gave assurance that the generic products were comparable to the brand-name products.) Many prescription items are also available in generic form, and at considerable savings. If your doctor gives you a brand-name pre-

TABLE 3–2   **Brand Label versus Generic Label**

Product	Size of Package	Cost of Package	Savings
Advil 200 mg	100 ct.	$8.69	37%
Generic equivalent	100 ct.	5.49	
Q-Tip cotton swabs	500 ct	3.99	20%
Generic equivalent	500 ct.	3.19	
Pampers Baby Fresh wipes	96 ct.	3.79	26%
Generic equivalent	96 ct.	2.79	
Heinz vinegar	32 oz.	1.35	12%
Generic equivalent	32 oz.	1.19	
Carnation Coffee-mate	22 oz.	2.99	38%
Generic equivalent	22 oz.	1.85	
Neosporin	1 oz.	6.99	43%
Generic equivalent	1 oz.	3.99	
Johnson's baby powder	15 oz.	3.49	32%
Generic equivalent	15 oz.	2.39	

scription, ask whether there is a generic equivalent. You can also ask the pharmacist to call the doctor and request approval to substitute a generic prescription for a brand-name prescription.

Bulk Buying

Many stores will offer substantial discounts—10 to 20 percent—if you buy by the case. Indeed many cities have "warehouse"-type supermarkets that specialize in by-the-case merchandising at much lower prices than at regular markets. In addition to the discounts you can obtain, buying in bulk quantity protects you against inflationary price increases on those products.

Most common nonfood products have a virtually infinite shelf life—you can keep them in storage almost indefinitely without any deterioration in their quality.

Convenience Foods

A simple experiment: we cooked a six piece box of Aunt Jemima Frozen French Toast. Then, using ingredients from scratch that cost the same as the box of the frozen "convenience" food, we made a platter of fresh French toast. Almost the same exact time was involved. (It did take a few extra minutes to wash out the bowls that used the fresh ingredients.) Results: From scratch we got twelve slices of toast that looked, smelled, and tasted delicious. The Aunt Jemima toast had no aroma, and looked and tasted a bit like cardboard. The winner by a big margin: do-it-yourself. The loser, in value for money and taste: the convenience food.

Convenience foods might save a little time, but they rarely will save money. And what you get for your money with convenience foods is a

STRATEGIES FOR SUCCESS

Impulsive Shopping Can Cost You Plenty

One study revealed that shoppers will pay two to three times more for a given type of item if a credit card sign is visible near the cash register. ("Oh, what the heck, let's buy the better version—we can use our plastic!") And a psychologist reports that certain symbols and visual cues, such as "Discount" and "Last Day of Sale," can prompt impulsive and unnecessary spending. Stores know this, and they use every trick they have to move merchandise. Don't let your impulses get the best of your common sense, lest you spend more than you can reasonably afford.

compromise. Here are a few more examples. Fresh versus frozen strawberries: in the summertime an equal batch of each is about the same price. Is there even a close call in taste? In the winter imported fresh berries will cost more than the frozen. You be the judge.

Buttered frozen vegetables cost only a few pennies more than plain ones. Go for it? That little pat of butter works out to about $5 a pound for the butter. Ditto for pre-sugared cereals and the like. You're paying a bundle to have someone else spoon a bit of sugar for you. And the worst of all: paying upwards of $4 for a gallon of water at the market! Not you, you say? Don't bet on it. Read the Consumer Alert section at the end of the chapter.

Coupons and Specials

Cents-off coupons are offered by both manufacturers and stores. If you don't use coupons on products that you *regularly* buy, you're throwing money away. Smart Shoppers will take perhaps an hour per week to scour the ads looking for coupons offering discounts on all products they commonly buy. The savings can be many dollars per week—an hour well spent. In addition, savings can be multiplied at stores that double the value of many coupons. By combining coupons with sales prices on items you would buy anyway, you can really stretch your grocery dollars.

Miscellaneous Money Savers

Don't Shop While Hungry

If you shop while you're hungry, you're more likely to load up your basket with nonessentials, snack foods, impulse items, and so on.

Shop with a List

Carefully plan your needs in advance, and write them down on a list. Stick to the list if you want to keep your budget in line.

Avoid Snack Foods

Snack foods tend to be costly, and the nutritional value you get for your money is questionable. The following case history best illustrates this warning:

"I came home from work early one afternoon and found my children sitting around our kitchen table eating DingDongs. As I watched an entire box of DingDongs disappear, I realized that our household went through $10 worth of DingDongs and similar snack foods per week. That's more than $500 a year! I immediately ordered an end of all Ding-Dongs in our house. My children looked at me aghast. I didn't want to interfere with their after-school snacking, so I told them that rather than spend money on DingDongs, they could make cookies and cakes from scratch on their own. This delighted them, for three or four days. Then the task of cleaning up after themselves began to be too much for them. The baking tapered off and so did the snacking. Not only did our food budget go down noticeably, but I'm sure I detected a drop in our dental bills as well."

Bend a Little

In general, supermarkets stock their highest-profit-margin items at eye level. The better bargains for you—in terms of unit price and generic availability—tend to be on the lower shelves. A little bit of bending will save you a lot of money.

Look for Extra Bargains

Many markets will discount bread, pastries, and produce after they have been on display for a day or so. If the market doesn't advertise these items, ask your manager what is available. Many markets also have a "thrift" shelf, where slightly damaged nonfood items are placed. These can represent substantial savings.

Know Your Local Market

Habit often finds us shopping at the same market most of the time. It's also wise to get to know the other markets that are convenient to you. You might find that they offer a better price on most of the products you commonly buy. Also, get to know the individual managers at each of the markets. The managers are there to please the public, and the better they know you, the more likely they are to offer you that extra special little item: a better choice in the produce department or the meat department, a tip that a certain item you're buying will be going on sale the next day, an offer to sell you an overstocked item at a discount.

THE GOOD HABITS: CLOTHING AND ACCESSORIES

"That looks absolutely smashing on you. Wear it anywhere and you'll have them all drooling."

"Your taste is excellent. I can tell that you're a real fashion leader."

"That's what absolutely everybody is wearing today. If you want to be with it, you'll buy it now before we run out of stock."

"As long as you're buying the slacks, you ought to get some nice things to go with it. Here's a nice matching sweater."

Vanity, thy name is clothing shopper. Young or old, male or female, few of us are immune to the flattering persuasions of the clothing salesperson. But Smart Shoppers keep a firm grip on their common sense, never letting it succumb to moods, to ego, to fads, or to impulse. Smart Shoppers have carefully studied their practical needs for clothing and accessories and are willing to take the time to shop for those items that offer the best value (appearance considered) for the money.

Only you can decide how you want to look or how you should look. There's little argument that the well-dressed, well-groomed person can enjoy certain advantages over the poorly dressed or slovenly person. To that extent, appropriately attractive clothing and accessories can be considered an investment in one's social and business well-being.

On the other hand, excessive spending on clothing will not necessarily produce commensurate results. You must find the balance that's right for you. And that balance must include both the desired appearance *and* the cost of creating that appearance. The following material can help you with the budget-balancing tricks of affording the look you want.

Ego and Impulse

The salespeople's flattering remarks at the beginning of this section are samples of just a few of the tricks of the clothing trade. But long before we enter the clothing stores, our brains and our egos have been preconditioned. Few products are more lavishly and glamorously advertised than clothing. The advertising lets us believe that we can look like models in *Vogue* or *Gentleman's Quarterly,* and the salesperson confirms it.

Nothing can cripple a budget more devastatingly than vanity and impulse. You can't fit designer jeans on a nondesigner body. But we spend ourselves silly trying. True, a few salespeople will be honest enough to tell you that a particular outfit makes you look like a hippopotamus. But they are there to sell clothing, and they know well that nothing sells clothing more rapidly than flattery. Arm yourself accordingly: Don't act on impulse. And shop around before you make a decision.

Embellish the Simple

You can stretch your clothing dollars farther by sticking to basically simple outfits and embellishing them with attractive accessories. For example, a common men's outfit—navy blue blazer and gray slacks—can take on a variety of appearances, depending on the accessories, all of which give the basic unit a different look. Similar combinations are possible with basic women's outfits. A variety of simple accessories can offer much more diversity for the money than a variety of outfits can.

Miscellaneous Money Savers

A Sense of Timing

Use the calendar to your advantage. Buying clothing and accessories off season can represent substantial savings. You won't have as abundant a choice of fashions or styles, but you can pick up bargains that will be well worth your shopping trip.

For a better selection of merchandise, check out the seasonal sales at most large clothing and department stores. Major sales usually take place after Christmas and after Easter. Shop early for the best selection.

Consider Seconds

Seconds (or irregulars) are items of clothing with minor flaws in them. The price of a second can be well below the price of an otherwise identical item. And the flaw itself may be so minor that no one will really notice it. Factory outlets and discount stores are good sources of seconds.

Cleanability and Durability

How readily will a particular garment soil, and what will be required to clean it? Is it hand-washable or must it be dry-cleaned? The care labels on the garments indicate the recommended cleaning techniques. The durability and cleanability—or lack thereof—represent an important element in your overall clothing investment.

Beware of Counterfeits

People will pay a good deal extra for items that display the name or initials of a leading designer or manufacturer. Thus, manufacturers happily create counterfeit versions of designer items that might be woefully inferior to the genuine articles. So, beware: If you find yourself obsessed with an opportunity to buy a "genuine" Armani at a price that seems too good to be true, don't be disappointed if it falls into shreads after the first or second wearing. You're most likely to get stung buying such articles at swap meets, from street vendors, or from stores that seem to open one week and close the next.

Know Store Policies

If you buy a garment, will you be able to return it if it doesn't suit you? Will the store refund your cash, or will it simply allow you a credit against other purchases? Or will the store refuse to take it back altogether? If the store does allow return privileges, how long does that privilege last? Many items offered on sale are sold on an as-is basis, preventing you from getting any kind of refund or exchange privilege. Almost always, if you want to return any items, you must bring in your sales receipt in order to get credit or a refund.

Buying for Children

Young children outgrow most clothing before it has had a chance to wear out. Except for one or two dressy outfits, or items that might be handed down to younger children, it is false economy to buy top-of-the-line clothing for children. Look to factory outlets, discount stores, and special sales for the best bargains on children's clothing.

Rummaging

Have an annual rummage through your closets and dressers to get rid of unneeded clothing and other personal items. If you don't know a hand-me-down recipient, donate your used clothing to thrift shops. If you itemize your income tax deductions, you can claim a deduction for the donated clothing.

THE GOOD HABITS: MAJOR HOME FURNISHINGS

Your overall budget can be drastically affected by your need for major home furnishings: furniture, carpeting, and appliances. In weighing your housing/furnishings considerations, you must take into account the following:

- How long will you be living in the dwelling? If you're settling in for a long stay, a bigger investment in furnishings is more easily justified. If you'll be living there for only a year or so, it might not make sense to burden yourself with major expenses for furnishings. Determine whether your job, your marital status, or the growth of your family is likely to dictate a move in the near future.

- Are there youngsters (or pets) on the scene? Children (and dogs and cats) can wreak havoc on furnishings. A jelly spot on a sofa, a urine stain on a carpet, plus assorted other blemishes have to be expected when little ones are about. The family with young children and active pets must evaluate how the furnishings will withstand the onslaught. If you buy expensive furnishings while the children are very young, you may be faced with expensive cleaning and repair costs, or the furnishings could look a shambles by the time the children are grown and more responsible. It makes more sense to buy more modest furnishings while the children are young.

- Will your tastes change? Will your selections today still please you one year, five years, ten years from now?

  For example: Today you might be very excited about strong pastel colors in your upholstery and carpeting, accented by chrome and glass tables and accessories. It might indeed look beautiful. But say you weary of it within a few years. Or you move to a new location where the furniture absolutely clashes with your new surroundings. You may then look back on your original choice as money wasted, money that could tally many hundreds, if not thousands, of dollars.

  You might be better off choosing a more conservative design and color range for the major items and accenting those pieces with relatively inexpensive accessories, such as throw pillows, lamp shades, and area rugs. Those can be changed easily and inexpensively and can give your premises a very different look at a much lower cost than a whole truckload of new furnishings.

- What is the focal point of your social life? Will you be doing a lot of entertaining at home? Or do you prefer to go out a lot for your social life? It may not be possible to afford both fine home furnishings and a lavish outside entertainment budget. Many people don't realize this until after they've invested heavily in furnishings and then find themselves in a budgetary crisis. If you'll be spending a major portion of your social life at home, you can justify more expense for the furnishings. On the other hand, if you're not a homebody, you should structure your budget more to suit your "going out" needs and less to satisfy your at-home needs.

Furniture

- With wood furniture, how are the parts joined together? Is the piece all wood or does it utilize less expensive fiberboard in unseen places? Does it stand firm and solid? Do doors, drawers fit and operate properly? What is the quality of the hardware? What is the quality of the finish and any decorative elements? Bear in mind that for tables, a synthetic surface (such as Formica) can wear more durably than wood.

- With upholstered furniture, pay attention to the construction elements as with the wood furniture just noted. How is the fabric anchored to the piece? Do the patterns and colors match properly? How durable is the fabric? What are the sun- and soil-resistance factors of the fabric? What is the stuffing made of, and how long will it hold its shape? How does it sit? Test it for firmness, comfort, clothing against fabric. The more carefully you shop, the more readily you'll see that better quality costs more. Only you can decide whether the better quality is affordable and worth the price for you.

- If you're handy with a paintbrush, you might find that unfinished wood furniture offers you better value for your money. Secondhand furniture in good condition and "seconds" (new furniture with minor flaws) can also be feasible alternatives.

- What guarantees do you have if something goes wrong with furniture: a leg comes unglued, fabric detaches from the frame, cabinet doors fall off? Better furniture dealers will usually guarantee to fix or replace defects that are not due to normal wear and tear. Determine how long such a guarantee will last. "Cash and carry" stores may offer little or no guarantee. To erase any doubts, ask about the guarantee before you decide on your purchase, and then have it put in writing.

- Some furniture dealers will deliver and set up your furniture at no additional charge. Other dealers charge for delivery. Still other dealers, such as warehouse and factory outlets, may not offer delivery service at all. Depending on where you live and how easy the access is to the rooms in which the furniture will be placed, delivery and setup charges can add considerably to your cost. Shop these charges as carefully as you do the furnishings themselves. Naturally, if you have access to a truck and some strong helpers, you can save considerably by doing your own delivery and setup.

- Don't guess on color or size of furniture. If you guess wrong, you could end up with an expensive purchase that doesn't suit you. Take color samples of any carpet, wallpaper, paint, and/or drapes with you to furniture stores, or ask the furniture dealer to give you color swatches of the pieces to match against the existing room. Take careful measurements before you shop. Draw your room to scale on graph paper and test out different furniture arrangements. Most large stationery stores sell plastic cut-out templates showing various sizes and types of furniture. This can be a handy tool to help you determine what pieces of what size can go in any given room. If you are considering buying convertible sofas, reclining chairs or expanding tables make sure you measure properly for both the basic and expanded versions of each piece.

- Acting on impulse can be dangerous. Visit many stores, looking for those whose reputation and inventory suit your budget. Scour the ads for sales: home furnishings are very sale-prone, and the best buys are available to those who are patient and willing to hunt.

Bedding (Springs, Mattresses)

The consensus of consumer testers is that quality pays in bedding. A well-constructed box spring and mattress can last twenty years, perhaps even

Consider Renting Instead of Buying

In many circumstances, it may be wiser to rent rather than buy costly household items, particularly furniture. For example: if it's likely that you'll be doing a lot of moving within the next few years, moving your own furniture can become a costly proposition. Most cities have furniture rental businesses that can furnish an apartment or a house, top to bottom, in a few hours, in a wide variety of styles and colors. Also, look into rental plans that give you an option to purchase the items.

longer. An off-brand product may cost 20 to 30 percent less than a major brand, but it may last only half as long. Evaluate the choice accordingly. Dealers offer frequent sales on bedspring and mattress items that are similarly constructed but do not have matching covers. Since you see the mismatched covers only when you take off the sheets, there's no reason not to take advantage of these special buys.

Carpeting and Other Flooring

The possibilities—and the price ranges—are limitless. Area rugs, bare polished wood, linoleum, vinyl tile, brick, fake brick, stone, fake stone, ceramic tile, adobe tile, and carpeting ranging from synthetic grass to luxurious wood represent but a sampling of the types of flooring available.

Personal taste, budget, durability, and cleanability must all be taken into account when you choose flooring. Of particular concern in making a decision on flooring is the length of time you'll be in the home. Most flooring, once installed, can't be taken with you. The obvious exception is area rugs. Carpeting can be removed, but it's difficult to install it in a new dwelling. The cost of lifting, moving, recutting, and reinstalling old carpeting in a new dwelling can come close to the cost of brand-new carpeting.

All carpeting and other flooring materials should be shopped for as carefully as furniture. Note that medium shades tend to show soil and dirt least, that patterned and multicolored carpeting tends not to show wear patterns as readily as solid-color carpeting, and that different types of carpet fabric have distinctly different levels of soil resistance and cleanability. In addition to pricing the carpeting, determine the cost of padding and installation. And check the reputation of the dealer with the Better Business Bureau for reliability and willingness to adjust complaints.

Appliances

What you *need,* what you would *like,* and what you can *afford* are all up to you. Before you make buying decisions, bear in mind the following:

Installation

Will such appliances as dishwashers, disposals, and trash compactors fit into your existing space? Or will extensive work have to be done to accommodate them? If so, how much will that added work cost? Will any special installation be necessary for any given appliance? An electric clothes dryer may require special wiring. A gas clothes dryer will require a gas line. Both will require a venting outlet. Is your existing wiring suitable for air-conditioning? A refrigerator with a built-in ice cube maker will require a water line to the site. A gas water heater must be properly vented, as must a kitchen exhaust fan. Determine these special requirements and get cost estimates for them before you make your buying decision.

Service and Warranties

On major items (clothes washers and dryers, dishwashers, freezers, refrigerators, and room air conditioners), a one-year warranty for parts and labor is common. In addition, the sealed systems in such units might have warranties for as long as five years. Don't be content with the salesperson's promises: Examine the written warranty before you make a buying decision. Find out whether warranty service is performed by the dealer or must be obtained from another source. Determine the reliability of the service source. A check with the local Better Business Bureau is advisable.

With smaller units (television sets, food processors, CD players, and video recorders) much shorter warranties are common. With most television sets, the warranty for labor is ninety days, but some may be as long as one year. The warranty on the picture tube and other parts will commonly be one to two years. The source of service is again very important. Will the dealer or a nearby service center be able to correct problems under warranty? Or will servicing involve time, money, and inconvenience for you?

For example, a comparison of two similar brand-name food processors revealed the following: Although the warranties were identical, one brand had to be sent away for warranty servicing, whereas the other could be repaired locally. In the case of a breakdown in the first unit, the cost of packing and shipping it, plus the return postage required under the warranty, represented more than 10 percent of the original purchase price of the unit. The latter unit could be serviced simply by delivering it to the original dealer.

With most appliances you can obtain a service contract to take care of problems after the original warranty has expired. Refrigerators and freezers are constructed to last decades, and any major defects will usually show up during the initial warranty period. For such products, extended service contracts might not be worth the money. The cost of an extended service contract for an automatic clothes washer, dishwasher, or room air conditioner might be less than the cost of one service call. If you have a knack for maintaining appliances, you might find a service contract an unnecessary expense.

Periodic servicing of some major appliances is a must. Furnaces and central air-conditioning units should be checked and lubricated periodically, filters should be changed, and the entire systems should be checked for leaks. An annual check-up prior to the heating and cooling seasons, respectively, can be far less expensive than repairing a major breakdown.

Paying for It

If you haven't yet established credit or if you've had credit problems, you'll probably be attracted to stores that offer "easy credit terms, no down payments—past credit history no problem." What appears in the advertising to be "easy credit" may indeed be costly. If a merchant or a lender is taking a risk with you, you will be charged accordingly.

Home furnishings represent major budget items, and credit is commonly used to obtain them. Follow the guidelines set forth in chapter 12. Consider what financing terms a dealer offers and compare those terms with banks in your area. For buyers with no credit or with credit problems, it might be far cheaper to obtain a cosigner for credit purchases rather than get involved with high-interest-rate lenders that ply their wares at the "easy credit" emporiums.

Information Sources

Exercise 3.1

Consumer Reports magazine, available at your local library, is the best single source for learning about and comparing home furnishing items. To locate information on the product you plan to buy, check the index in the back of the latest issue. *Consumer Reports Buying Guide* indexes all subjects covered for the previous year. Kiplinger's *Personal Finance* magazine can be another helpful source.

With most appliances you can obtain specification sheets from the manufacturer or dealer. These give you abundant information about each product; you should read and compare different brands before you make your decision. The more time you take to compare, study, and shop, the better equipped you'll be to make the right buying decision.

RECREATION

How much of your disposable income should you devote to recreation and leisure? That's a very personal decision that each individual and family must make for themselves. Some people will go overboard on their leisure expenses, leaving them in a budgetary bind. Some people will consciously choose to curtail other types of expenses—living in a more modest dwelling, driving a more modest car—in order to enjoy their leisure freely. Others will forgo leisure activities so that they can live in a more elaborate dwelling and drive a more elaborate car. These are personal choices. If you're overspending on leisure, however, you can either make adjustments or suffer the consequences. The same holds true if you are not partaking of any meaningful leisure activities. The rest of this chapter will help you think about the balance you'd like to achieve, and it might motivate you to take action. We will explore two broad areas of leisure and the important financial considerations relating to them. Those areas are vacation and travel, and recreation at home.

VACATION AND TRAVEL

Exercise 3.2

From the weekend camping trip to the elaborate cruise or European junket, you want to be certain that everything goes right. It's a shame to waste money, but it's even more disappointing to have wasted time. You can always go out and make more money, but you can never go out and make more time. Careful planning is therefore essential.

Using a Travel Agent

The proper professional to assist you with your vacation and travel plans is a travel agent. Well-trained and experienced travel agents have many tools to help you get the most out of your vacation dollars. Among these tools are:

Exercise 3.3

- The *Official Airline Guide (OAG),* which gives complete information on virtually every commercial flight in the United States, as well as many international flights
- Directories of hotels, resorts, car rental agencies, and cruises, providing detailed information on costs, facilities, reservation requirements, and often the quality of the various services and facilities
- Publications by airlines, resorts, states, nations, and tour-packaging companies, providing an excellent means for familiarizing yourself with various opportunities, price ranges, available dates, and other useful information
- Personal experience, since agents travel extensively to examine locations of concern to their clientele
- Computer on-line services that can instantly show the agent the availability and times of flights, data on hotel rooms, rental car prices, and even weather reports in most cities of destination

A travel agent can give you advice and guidelines on choosing a vacation that will satisfy your interests and budget. Furthermore, the agent can make all necessary reservations for travel and accommodations. The more advance time you give the agent to work on your plans, the wider choice you'll have of flights, hotel rooms, rental cars, and the like. Visiting a travel agent at the last minute will probably prove frustrating, but even in such cases the agent can probably do more for you than you could on your own.

Travel agents earn their money in commissions they receive from airlines, hotels, cruise companies, and tour operators that they book for you. Agents normally charge their clients only for out-of-pocket expenses made on the clients' behalf, such as long-distance telephone calls. Some travel agents impose service charges for issuing and amending some airline tickets. Inquire in advance how much, if anything, a given agent would charge for given services.

In some cases, a travel agent can save you money by knowing of a group tour whose itinerary matches the travel you are planning. Making arrangements for you to take part in the group tour could cut your costs considerably. If agents don't volunteer such information, ask them if they know of any such possibilities.

Choosing a travel agent is like choosing any other kind of professional advisor. Personal recommendations are always worth seeking out. Also, the neatness and efficiency of the travel agent's office can often be a giveaway to the quality and efficiency of service, or lack of it. The agent should be a member of the American Society of Travel Agents (ASTA) and should have credentials from the International Air Transport Association (IATA).

The Internet also offers a wide array of travel information and booking capabilities, but with the Internet you don't get the benefit of a travel agent's personal experience and knowledge of various destinations, carriers, hotels and so on. Further, with the Internet, you might have to give your credit card number to a stranger at the other end of the Web. Do so at your own risk. (Why do you think they call it a Web?)

A Wealth of Information

In addition to the printed material a travel agent can offer you, there is an abundance of literature on travel that you should take advantage of at the earliest possible planning stages. Whether you're traveling on your own or with a group, the more you can learn about your destination, the more choice you'll have as to what you'll want to see and do. Visit your local bookstore and library and choose from among the following worthwhile publications.

Exercise 3.4

- The choice of good travel guidebooks grows every year. The Fodor and Dorling-Kindersley guides are directed toward the more affluent traveler. The Birnbaum guides seem more appropriate to the younger (thirties and forties) traveler who does not have to pinch pennies. The *Let's Go* and *Under $25 a Day* series will appeal to all those who must mind their travel budgets carefully.

- The Mobil *Travel Guides* cover the United States and are very detailed with respect to hotels, motels, and sightseeing facilities.
- Michelin guides provide excellent information on many major European cities and countries.
- Travel magazines abound. Also, you can write to the Chamber of Commerce of the cities you plan to visit and ask them for any tourist information they have available.

Air Fares

The pricing of airline tickets is an incredible jumble. If you want to fly from point A to point B, the price of your ticket will depend on how far in advance you make your reservations, the day of the week you're traveling, how long you're staying at your destination, and the class of service you choose. And, depending on the type of plan you choose, you might or might not receive a refund of all or part of your ticket if you have to change your travel plans. The best guide through this maze is a travel agent, who has access to all these fare structures. Each airline will quote you only its prices for a given trip. The travel agent can quickly determine all possible choices between points A and B. Table 3–3 illustrates the spectrum of fares

TABLE 3–3 Airline Fare Comparison

These fares were quoted on one specific date for flights on the same future date. All fares are round trip.	
Phoenix/Los Angeles	
Lowest	
Special excursion, must stay over a Saturday night, must book seven days in advance, no refunds	$68
Middle range	
No restrictions, but limited seats per flight; coach	$174
Highest	
First class, no restrictions	$390
Los Angeles/New York	
Lowest	
Special excursion, same restrictions as above	$462
Middle range	
Seven-day advance booking, 50% penalty for cancellation	$518
Highest	
Coach, no restrictions	$1,340
First class, no restrictions	$1,980

available between Los Angeles and Phoenix as a short-flight example and between Los Angeles and New York as a cross-country flight example.

Frequent Flyer Plans

Most major airlines offer frequent flyer plans, which enable travelers to accumulate points for distance traveled on a given airline. Once you've accumulated the necessary points, you are entitled either to free travel on the airline or upgrades. Many airlines also cooperate with hotels and car rental agencies, which in turn provide lodging and car rentals at discounts. The more you use the designated companies, the more points you'll accumulate. Be sure you know what restrictions the plan has. How long do you have to use the points you've accumulated? Are there exclusions as to days you cannot travel with your bonus points?

Most frequent flyer awards cannot be sold or given away to anyone else, but there may be exceptions; check with your airline for specifics.

Almost all airlines now have credit cards tied in with their frequent flyer plans, which allow you to earn miles by charging on the card. This is in addition to earning miles by using car rental, hotel, and other services tied in with the airline's frequent flyer program. If you're a frequent credit card user, this can be an excellent way to accumulate more miles toward your free travel. But please follow the advice in chapter 12 on credit and borrowing, and pay your credit card bills in full every month. That way you don't have to pay any interest on the credit card. If you find yourself paying interest on charges you incurred to earn miles, you're offsetting the value of the miles by what you're spending in interest.

Airlines impose blackout restrictions, which are days you can't use your frequent flyer miles to travel. Most of these days are around holiday seasons. Furthermore, airlines strictly ration the number of frequent flyer reward seats on all flights, which can make it very difficult for you to get flights on the days you want, unless you book many months in advance. For example, travel between Europe and the United States during the summer months is so heavy that frequent flyer awards have to be booked late in the previous year if you want to have a decent choice of flights from which to choose.

Some frequent flyer plans—British Airways is one example—offer a number of hotels that will give you rooms in exchange for frequent flyer mileage. This can be a good way to get around the heavily booked seasons. If you can't use your mileage to get a free flight, pay for the flight and use your mileage to get a free hotel room instead. That way you get extra mileage for the flight, and you can have a better choice of times to travel.

Frequent flyer mileage expires after a fixed time. Use 'em or lose 'em. Each airline will announce its own expiration schedule. If you're faced with losing points here's a tactic that can gain you an extra year. Before the points expire, get your award ticket, even if it doesn't have a specific flight on it. Once you have the award ticket, you have an extra year to use it.

Wholesalers (Consolidators)

You can achieve substantial savings on international travel by using wholesalers, who make available sharp price reductions. They advertise in the Sunday travel sections of major newspapers, particularly *The Los Angeles Times*, *The New York Times*, and the *Chicago Tribune*. If you can't find those papers at your local newsstand, check at your local library.

Wholesalers commit themselves to a number of discounted seats on given transoceanic flights, and they pass part of the savings on to their customers. Many also offer discounts on hotels in destination cities. Before you book with these companies, check how long they have been in business and the manner in which they conduct their business. These discounted tickets are usually nonrefundable if you alter or cancel your travel plans. Wholesalers, as a rule, offer a wide selection of regularly scheduled flights to different destinations on different airlines.

Seasonal Bargains

One good way to stretch your travel dollar is to take advantage of the seasonal bargains in many major resort areas. You might not have the best weather, but the low prices might more than make up for the climate. Off-season hotel prices in many tourist areas can be as little as one-half to one-third of the high-season price. Samples include resorts in Las Vegas, Arizona, and Florida, where summertime prices are a fraction of wintertime rates. Similarly, England and Europe can be much cheaper in the winter than during the hot and crowded summer months. If the weather is of secondary concern to you and you primarily want to see the sights and partake of the tourist opportunities, ask your travel agent for the off-season fare alternatives available. You can see more of the world for less money than you might think.

Near-home Vacations

If air, bus, or train fares threaten to use up too much of your vacation budget, consider the travel opportunities within an easy day's drive of your own home. How many New Yorkers have never been to Boston or Washington, or vice versa? How many San Franciscans have never been to Los Angeles, and vice versa? And so it goes throughout the nation. Close-to-home opportunities for fun, adventure, and enrichment are abundant, no matter where you live. Not to take advantage of these opportunities is to deny yourself recreation.

Good weekend getaway values can be found in hotels that cater to business travelers during the week. Packages can include sharply discounted room prices, meals, cocktails, and bargain tickets to local attractions.

Package Tours and Resorts

If you're not inclined to hassle over travel details, thousands of package tours are available to you. These offer an almost all-inclusive price for your vacation, which includes travel, accommodations, sightseeing, a guide where appropriate, and some meals and extras. Package tours are available through resorts, airlines, travel tour companies, and major travel agencies. Package tours can often save you money. It's wise to compare what the same travel would cost if you bought each component (air, hotel, rental car, etc.) separately. Experienced travelers probably prefer to create their own packages. The novice might appreciate the convenience and possible cost savings of the package.

If you are considering a package tour, study the brochure that details what you get for your money. Pay attention to the following:

- Most packages are advertised as costing from a certain amount of dollars. That little word *from* is vitally important. It describes the *lowest* possible price for the package. If you want a better choice of rooms, dates, or amenities the price can escalate rapidly.

- Many of the advertised "extras" do not represent a true travel bargain, though on the surface they seem appealing. A "free welcoming cocktail" or a "free bottle of champagne" in your room may sound alluring, but it's worth only a few dollars at most. The more important things to evaluate, in terms of cost, are the basic room accommodations and meals, if any.

- If meals are included as a part of the package, find out what kind of menu and what kind of choices will be available to you. The basic package price might include minimal food service, with anything extra at an added cost. You can avoid disappointment by finding this out in advance.

- If recreational facilities, such as tennis or golf, are included in the package, determine if those facilities are available any time you want them, or only at certain times, which might be inconvenient.

- If the package includes transportation, when will the flights leave? Night flights can knock your body clock awry and render you incapable of enjoying yourself at your destination.

- How much free time will you have, particularly on a multicity guided tour? There are horror stories of tour groups being herded around like sheep. After a few days of that, you might not know whether you're in Athens, Greece, or Athens, Georgia. To protect yourself, make sure you examine the day-to-day itinerary, which should be included in the travel brochure. Too little free time can leave you exhausted; too much free time can mean that you'll be out spending money on your own, and that can leave you broke. Look for the happy balance with your travel agent as your guide.

Do-It-Yourself Tours and Vacations

More-experienced travelers often prefer to make their own arrangements. This means more time spent in the planning stages but more free time during the trip rather than following the tour guide's timetable. Careful research is the key to a successful do-it-yourself trip.

For intercity travel, particularly on a foreign trip, rail, bus, and air travel passes may be available. These passes can represent a considerable saving over individual bookings from city to city. Some of these passes for European travel must be purchased in the United States.

When booking do-it-yourself travel, it's essential that you get all your reservations confirmed in writing from the hotels, car rental agencies, and any other facilities you'll be using. Make certain that those confirmations spell out exactly what you're getting for your money: the type and price of the room, the arrival and departure dates, and the type and price of the car you are reserving. Take these written confirmations with you. If you pay any deposit in advance, be certain to get a receipt for that deposit; and make sure when you make final payment for your stay that you are given the proper credit for that deposit.

Cruises

Cruises have often been thought of as an indulgence only for the wealthy. But when you consider that for one all-inclusive price you receive your room, meals, entertainment, all facilities of the ship, and transportation from port to port, the price of a cruise might not be much different than a stay of comparable length at a resort or a budgetwise trip abroad.

Cruises, like tour packages, are advertised on a *from* basis. The price in the advertising is for the lowest-priced stateroom on the ship. It will probably be on the lowest deck, inside (as opposed to an outside room with a porthole), and at the far end of the ship (either fore or aft) where the motion of the boat will be more noticeable than in the center. But aside from the stateroom, all passengers have equal use of all facilities on the ship at all times. The food is the same, the entertainment is the same, the access to all facilities is the same. If a minimum stateroom isn't available, the price of better staterooms escalates rapidly. Since life on a cruise ship is spent predominantly in the public rooms, and on shore, and the stateroom is used for little else than sleeping and changing clothes, the booking of a minimum stateroom should not prove a hardship to most travelers.

The all-inclusive price means just that: elaborate meals, snacks, and midnight buffet; nightly professional entertainment and dancing to live bands; daily movies; plus lectures and lessons on a wide variety of subjects. Not included are alcoholic beverages, laundry, tips, and on-shore expenses.

With respect to on-shore expenses, travelers should avoid buying things (jewelry, perfume, watches, and the like) they can obtain at home for a similar price. When shopping in foreign ports, it's always important to ask: "If I'm not satisfied with this when I get it home, how can I get the matter corrected?" It's one thing to visit a local jewelry store where you bought a watch that stopped working. It can be quite something else to try to get a watch fixed if you bought it in a tiny shop in some exotic Caribbean island.

Your travel agent can provide you with schedules of all ships leaving from accessible ports. Many cruises also offer substantial air fare discounts to get you from your hometown to the port city. The travel agent can provide you with deck plans of ships. Study the deck plans carefully. Notice where the minimum-rate rooms are and where higher rate rooms are. Choose a stateroom that will give you adequate comfort, cost considered.

Most cruise lines offer discounts if you book or pay for your passage in advance. If you're sure you're going to take a specific cruise, it can make good sense to take advantage of these discounts. Not only can you reduce your ticket price by hundreds of dollars, but also the savings you realize are not taxable.

Another way to cut the cost of a cruise—if you have a flexible schedule—is to take advantage of late booking discounts offered by most lines. If a ship sails with empty rooms, the revenue those rooms could have generated is lost forever. So cruise lines will often offer steep discounts on unsold rooms shortly (perhaps a few weeks) before sailing to generate what revenue they can before it's lost. Check with your travel agent for details.

Trip Insurance

Whether you're going on a cruise, a package trip, or a do-it-yourself trip, you can buy insurance that will provide a refund if you or a member of your family becomes ill and is thus unable to travel. Such insurance may also provide that if a close member of your family who was not taking the trip becomes ill or dies you can get a refund. Ask your travel agent for details on this trip insurance.

STRATEGIES FOR SUCCESS

Condo Rentals Can Mean Big Vacation Savings

Staying in a motel or a resort can be expensive. And the bigger your family and the longer you stay, the more expensive it gets. In most resort areas, it's possible to rent condominiums for a lot less than you'd pay for a hotel room. (Owners who use the condo for their own vacations during part of the year put them up for rent when they're not using them.) Condos usually come fully equipped (kitchen, linens, towels, etc.) and many have nice amenities, such as tennis courts, swimming pool, and the like. If you don't need the services of a hotel (room service, telephone operator, etc.), a condo can give you a lot more vacation for a lot less money. Check with the Chamber of Commerce or Visitors Bureau in the city you plan to visit for references on condo rentals.

Travel Scams

The travel industry is not without its fair share of con artists. The problem has become more severe in recent years, as telephone solicitations have blanketed the country offering all sorts of supposed free travel to innocent and gullible victims (See chapter 4.)

Home-exchange Programs

If you're the trusting type, a home-exchange program can offer you the best of both worlds: the chance to live in a distant city at very little expense. The idea behind a home exchange is that you swap residences with a family in another city—either in the United States or abroad. In addition to eliminating hotel bills, you also have kitchen facilities at your disposal so that you can save considerably on food costs. You might even swap the use of each other's automobile.

Ask your travel agent for the names and addresses of various home-exchange programs. Sponsors of these programs charge a modest fee for providing you with a subscription to a swapping listing. When you've found a good match you should correspond in detail with them to make certain that you both know enough about the home and facilities to satisfy each other. To the extent possible, get personal references on the other individuals so that you can feel a sense of trust, since they will be living in your home. But the fact that you are living in each other's homes does help keep the level of trust high. You needn't own a house to get involved in an exchange; apartments and condominiums can be just as acceptable as a single-family home.

Pocket Money

Traveler's checks are the best way to carry money with you on vacation. Personal checks are rarely accepted, but most tourist areas do accept common credit cards. Cash is convenient, but if lost, it's gone forever. If traveler's checks are lost, the issuing company can arrange for an immediate refund.

Traveler's checks are available at most major banks and through some travel agencies. They are issued by such companies as American Express, Bank of America, Citicorp, Visa, and Mastercard. The cost of traveler's checks is about $1 per $100 worth of checks. Many banks make traveler's checks available to their customers at no charge.

Foreign Money

If you are traveling to another country, you'll have to convert at least some dollars into the currency of that country. You'll probably be able to charge hotel bills and restaurant bills on most major credit cards, but you'll need local currency for such things as taxis, minor purchases, and tips. Unless you've established a bank account in the foreign country, it will be extremely difficult for you to cash a personal check. Traveler's checks, again, are the best way to carry money. Cash your traveler's checks at local banks. You'll obtain a much better rate of exchange than you will at hotels, shops, or restaurants.

ATM machines in major tourist cities allow you to withdraw the local currency from your checking account at home. You can also use your credit cards to borrow local currency. Mind the cost of doing the latter.

Precautions Before You Leave Home

Secure your peace of mind by taking a few simple precautions. If you don't have a trustworthy person to stay at your home while you're away, make certain that all valuables are out of harm's way. Either put them in a safety deposit box at your bank or leave them with someone you trust. Be certain to stop all mail and newspaper deliveries by contacting the Post Office and newspaper circulation office. For less than ten dollars you can buy timers that turn your lights on and off at various times of the day and night to make it appear that someone is at home. Ask neighbors to keep an eye out for any strange persons around your home. If you leave your car in the driveway, it will accumulate dust and tip off a would-be burglar that the home is empty. Leave a car key with a neighbor or friend and ask him or her to move the car around every few days and to keep it dusted off. Check with your property insurance agent to determine what coverage, if any, you have for valuables you plan to take with you. What additional coverage might be advisable? Alert your local police that you will be away; very often they will keep an extra eye on the property for you. Consider hiring a private patrol service to provide surveillance on your home while you're away. Check with your telephone company to see whether they have a call-forwarding service that will inform callers how you can be reached if you do, in fact, wish to be reached.

Make arrangements for all payments falling due during your absence. If that's not feasible, explain to your creditors that you will be gone for a while and ask them if they can waive any late charges or make other accommodations. If you neglect to take care of such matters, you risk having late payments show on various accounts, which could be detrimental to your credit rating. If you have investments with a stockbroker, determine what action, if any, you might want the broker to take in your absence. If that's not practical, leave word with the broker as to how you can be reached if the need arises. If you have any savings certificates or other securities maturing during the time you'll be absent, make arrangements with the bank or broker accordingly. The better you take care of such details before you leave, the better time you'll be able to have.

Know Your Rights

If you are traveling on a common carrier—particularly an airplane—make certain you know in advance what your rights are in the event you get bumped from your flight or your luggage is lost or damaged. Bumping means that there's no room for you on the plane. The Federal Aviation Administration (FAA) requires that airlines make payments to passengers who are bumped. There are limitations on how much an airline is responsible for in the event of lost or damaged luggage. Never pack valuables or needed prescriptions in luggage that is to be checked. Rather than risk the anguish of even a temporary loss, carry those items with you on the plane.

Buying Big-ticket Vacation Items

It's a curious facet of human nature: Most people are not in their "right minds" when they are planning a vacation or are actually on the vacation. During the planning stages, there's an aura of excited anticipation. That's when one might say, with a burst of wild enthusiasm, "Let's go for broke and *buy* that boat we've always wanted!" Or, while on the vacation itself, a similar loss of reality can occur, in response to which one might say, "It's foolish to spend money *renting* a place here—let's *buy* a place!"

Then, in the rosy glow of a vacation mentality, you find that you've plunked down a few thousand dollars and signed a whopping contract for the balance of payments on the new motor home, boat, or vacation home.

Before you write that check or sign that contract, consider the following:

- On a minimal purchase of any of those items—say $20,000—the interest alone that you will pay on your debt will be in the neighborhood of $2,000 to $3,000 per year. That amount, in itself, can pay for one or more very nice vacations every year. Is it worth it?

- For the first year or so you'll get great enjoyment out of your purchase. But human nature being what it is, we tend to want to change the scene for our vacations every few years. Three years from now, will you still want to go boating in your boat, or spend your vacation in a place that by now may have become boring to you? Your thoughts at the time you made the purchase may have been, "We'll love it forever!" But, a few years later, you may wish you'd never taken the plunge. The time to think of that is *before* you take the plunge.

If you're contemplating a big-ticket vacation expenditure, the best precaution is to proceed on a test basis. Rent for a year or two, and see if it's really your style. The rental will probably cost you less than the interest alone on a purchase, and if you don't like it, you can walk away. Contrary to what many salespersons may tell you, it's *not* always that easy to unload an unwanted camper, boat, or home in a distant resort area.

Time Sharing: Easy Solution?

Time sharing is a recent phenomenon. Simply stated, time sharing means that you buy the right to use a specific facility for one or two weeks during the year. Part of the time-sharing concept is that you can exchange your location for one of many others each year. If you weary of your condo in Waikiki after a few years, you can swap it for a villa in Switzerland or a resort in Miami or a castle in Spain.

Exercise 3.5

It all sounds very attractive, and some people have found great satisfaction in it. But the time-sharing phenomenon is also rife with misrepresentation and fraud. Many people have purchased time-sharing interests in resorts that were never built. Many find that the facilities are inferior to the way the salesperson represented them. Others discover that the so-called guaranteed cost is not guaranteed at all—that increasing assessments boost the cost much higher than was anticipated. And, to make matters worse, many find that the exchange privileges are not as represented.

Time-sharing sales pitches are very high-pressure. The most prudent approach to a time-share sales offering is to visit the place in person to be certain that it is as represented to you. Study your contract carefully to determine what your exchange privileges, if any, might be and what added costs you might have to incur in the future. All due caution is advised before you sign any contract.

RECREATION AT HOME

Major vacation travel may occur only once every few years, and only a few weekends may be devoted to camping, traveling, or sightseeing. But every day there are hours of leisure time to fill at home or in your community. Following are some considerations—financial and otherwise—on some of those ways of filling your leisure time at home.

Electronics

The electronics boom offers increasing sophistication at decreasing costs. As a new century dawns, virtually every home in the United States will have one or more of the following: cable television offering dozens of channels; dish antennas capable of receiving scores, if not hundreds, of television channels from satellites; video player/recorders; wide-screen television sets—five feet or more across; and computers capable of interacting with television for educational, work, and game-playing purposes.

And sooner than later there will be video/computerized facilities that will print newspapers and magazines on recyclable plastic right in our living rooms and that will permit us access to virtually everything that's ever been filmed or printed via giant computers reached through satellite connections.

In short, we're in an electronics revolution, and the emergence of new techniques and equipment will shape our leisure lives to a great extent.

With so many marvels due in the future, it is frustrating to deliberate today what investments should be made in electronic leisure equipment. "Should I buy something today only to have it become obsolete next month because of a more advanced model?" The point is well taken. But whatever you do invest in today, you can still enjoy for many years while planning the next investment in more advanced equipment. Let's examine some of the specific items that tempt you currently.

Video Cassette Recorders

Video cassette recorders can be used to record anything that is broadcast through your television set—including incoming cable and pay TV signals.

When VCRs were first introduced in the early 1970s, they were priced at about $2,000, and they had very little flexibility. Currently, you can obtain top-quality equipment for well under $500, and the machines are equipped with internal computers that allow you to set them to turn on, record, and turn off many days in advance. Other common features include fast-forward, slow-motion, and freeze-frame capabilities.

Prerecorded tapes, including movies, sporting events, and instructional material, can be purchased or rented. Rental rates for cassette tapes can be as low as a dollar. Compare that with the cost of taking the family to a movie theater. Blank recording tapes with a capacity of upwards of six hours can be purchased for well under $5.

In shopping for a VCR, bear in mind the following criteria: Will you benefit from the costly optional extras included in many sets, or will you be better off with a lower cost, no-frills set? What type of warranty comes with the set? If service is needed, can it be done locally, or must the set be sent away to a service bureau? Competition is very keen with these products, so it will pay to shop around and seek discounts at local dealers.

In addition to stores that sell and rent prerecorded material, many public libraries are now offering prerecorded cassettes to their local communities.

Video Cameras

One of the most popular items in the home electronics market is the video camera, which has replaced the old-fashioned home movie film camera. There is a wide selection of cameras priced under $500, and models with new features are always being introduced. This year's best deal might be obsolete before you get it home. But if you let yourself worry about that, you'll never enjoy using it. So, after doing the necessary homework, make your best purchase, and don't look back to see what you might have bought had you only waited another month or two.

Personal Computers

Technology is advancing so rapidly with these devices that it's difficult to predict what will be available to the public next month, let alone next year. The basic component is the home computer, which can be attached to a printer and/or to your telephone. The cost of these units ranges from a few hundred dollars to thousands of dollars, depending on their capabilities.

Popular uses of the home computer include accessing the internet, financial planning, word processing, instructional programming, and a wide variety of games. Many more sophisticated uses are available to the small businessperson and the professional person, including billing, inventory control, and a host of other bookkeeping and calculating functions

Shopping for a home computer, programs, and games will take a lot of careful homework. How much use will you make of the equipment? Can you justify the cost of doing your projected work on the computer, or can you get it done more inexpensively using more traditional methods? Rapid change is expected in the home computer market, so you must decide whether you will be buying something that will too quickly become obsolete or that will serve justifiable purposes for at least three to five years. And as with the video player/recorders, you must determine the extent of warranty as well as the availability and cost of service. Finally, beware of what has befallen many home computer buyers: After the novelty wears off, it is relegated to the expensive toy status, gathering dust in a forgotten corner.

The Internet

An interesting historical note: The previous edition of this textbook, published in 1996, made scant notice of the Internet. It was in its infancy, and who could have known what it might have grown into. Today the Internet is still little more than a baby, but it has become a rapid growth phenomenon of science-fiction caliber. Its ultimate future shape is still years away from clear definition.

Surfers beware: to the gullible, the Internet can be a dangerously costly place. For much of what is on the Internet there is no gatekeeper, no editor, no arbiter of taste or truth who controls what can be put there. Unlike a magazine, a book, a newspaper or a broadcast, no one with any authority has necessarily approved what is distributed. This opens the doors wide for fraudsters, tipsters, and just plain sloppy writers whose purported facts might be nothing more than rumors, disguised sales pitches, or just plain falsities. Further, anything that is put on the Internet can be altered by hackers, and this can go unnoticed by the original authors. Hackers have broken into the CIA and State Department computers. Very little is beyond their reach.

Scam artists go to great lengths on the Internet to get your credit card number or personal identification numbers for your ATM cards. Advice from a CompuServe customer service rep, who deals with such problems on a daily, if not hourly, basis: "Don't give your credit card number to *anyone* on the Internet. If the deal is valid, you can do it by mail." Someday there will be totally secure ways of doing electronic commerce via the Internet. Until then, follow the CompuServe advice. Shop on the Internet if you will, but pay for what you buy through the mail. (That way you also have added protection: If you're caught in a scam, the mail fraud laws may protect you. There is as yet no comparable protection on the Internet.)

Fax Machines

Fax machines are becoming as common as the toaster in the typical American home. The ultimate homeowner's version (already available in costly business models) will be the combined fax/answering machine/telephone/copier/scanner/computer. And it will be about the same size as your toaster.

Large-screen Television and Home Theater Equipment

Large-screen television sets range between $1,000 and $4,000, but technological advancement is expected to bring the price down over the coming years. Eventually, by utilizing fiber optics, large-screen television sets may be hung on a wall like a picture. In the meantime, the existing large-screen sets are strictly a luxury purchase. They definitely can enhance the pleasure you get from watching television; if you can justify the added cost of that extra pleasure, you may want to begin shopping around for a large-screen TV.

In development is a new concept of television, known as High Definition Television (HDTV). It promises movie-screen clarity on the home TV set, as well as a vast array of industrial and scientific uses. It may be well into the twenty-first century before HDTV becomes an *affordable* reality. When it does, it could replace existing TV sets and transmission modes.

Personal Enrichment

A great deal of your leisure time can be put to rewarding and productive use without your having to spend a lot of money. Look into the activities that may be available at your local library, college, church or synagogue, or community center, often at no charge. You're likely to find an interesting assortment of concerts, art exhibits, theatrical presentations, and lectures.

Carefully examine the continuing education catalogs of your local community college or university. You'll find a variety of courses and seminars that can amuse, entertain, and stimulate as well as educate. These programs are generally offered on weekends and evenings so that you can take advantage of them without interfering with your work.

Volunteer work—through religious and civic organizations—can be a very rewarding use of your leisure time. Volunteers are eagerly sought, and by helping others, you can help yourself.

Sports, Hobbies, and Out-on-the-Town

Athletic activities, whether individual, such as jogging, or organized in teams, such as softball, are among the most popular modes of spending leisure time.

Health Spas and Athletic Clubs (Tennis, Golf, Racquetball, Etc.)

Membership in such facilities can be very expensive, and you must determine whether the cost will be justifiable. You may be subjected to a rigorous sales pitch to convince you that you'll spend every nonworking hour on the premises becoming a better person. You will be expected to sign a contract committing you to monthly payments for your membership. If possible, take a trial membership to see whether this particular facility is really right for you. Will you use it as much as the salesperson tells you? And will the benefits to you be as delightful as the sales brochure suggests? Determine how long the facility has been in business, and talk with current members to ascertain their level of satisfaction. Be aware that many such facilities run into financial problems. This can result in a sharp increase in cost to members or, in the worst (and not that uncommon) case, the facility simply closes down and disappears along with your money.

Individual Sports and Hobbies

Many of these activities—such as skiing, sailing, scuba diving, photography—can involve considerable investment on your part. If you are already committed to such activities, you know what it is costing you. If you are contemplating embarking on any such activities, calculate in advance the cost of getting set up. Then, as with the health spas and athletic clubs, give it a trial run first to see if it's really right for you.

Professional Sports

If you're a "sports nut" and you live in a major league city (for baseball, football, hockey, basketball, soccer), you know how expensive it can be to satisfy your cravings. If you're a frequent spectator at any of these sports, consider sharing season tickets with other fans. The total cost over the full season might be considerably less for the same number of admissions as if you were buying tickets for each event. Also, inquire at the ticket offices to determine when discounts and group plans may be available. Your employer or union may also offer discount packages to sporting events.

A Night on the Town

Dining out and attending movies or concerts are regular items on many people's leisure-time schedule. Since we often do such things on impulse and since the activity finds many of us under the influence of alcohol, it's all too easy to ignore what the activity is costing. When you say, "Sure, let's have another bottle of wine" enough times in a month, you could unwittingly be impairing your ability to buy necessities the following month. And since a very high percentage of dining-out activity is paid for by credit card instead of hard cash, it's easy to succumb to the temptation to spend more than what is reasonable. Furthermore, if the credit card bill isn't paid in full by the end of the month, you'll start building up interest costs, which can end up increasing the price of that meal or that bottle of wine by 20, 50, or even 100 percent if you wait long enough to pay the bill.

In many cities you can purchase discount books that offer savings at restaurants, movies, sporting events, and tourist attractions. These books are often available through charitable organizations, so your fee goes to a good cause and you get benefits as well. You can also take advantage of the discount coupons for restaurants that appear in local newspapers and mailings.

Out-on-the-town expenses should be budgeted in advance and, whenever possible, paid for in cash or by check. Nobody is telling you not to have a good time. You just must be careful of having too good a time now at the expense of not being able to have a good time later.

The Ultimate Leisure

The poet William Wordsworth wrote these lines:

> The world is too much with us.
> Late and soon, getting and spending,
> We lay waste our powers.
> Little we see in nature that is ours.
> We have given our hearts away, a sordid boon.

Wordsworth, a nature lover himself, was bemoaning the fact that we get so caught up in the day-to-day business of life that we neglect the beauties and pleasures that nature offers us. We have, as he says, given our hearts away—sold out to the daily tumult of our regular work routine. Although that may have its own rewards, we may be missing out on more valuable things. A modern (and anonymous) philosopher put it more succinctly on a popular poster: "Don't run so fast that you can't smell the flowers."

PERSONAL ACTION WORKSHEET

Vacation Planner

No worksheet can help you determine how much pleasure you'll have on a vacation. But this planner can aid you in calculating and comparing the costs of various leisure holidays, Estimate each item carefully. A travel agent can be of great help, at no additional cost to you. Bon voyage!

Travel Expense Item	Estimated Cost		
	Vacation #1	Vacation #2	Vacation #3
Getting there			
❏ Airplane	_____	_____	_____
❏ Bus	_____	_____	_____
❏ Train	_____	_____	_____
❏ Car	_____	_____	_____
❏ Meals, lodging en route	_____	_____	_____
Getting about			
❏ Rental car	_____	_____	_____
❏ Buses, tours, excursions	_____	_____	_____
Room and board			
❏ Hotel, motel (are any meals included?)	_____	_____	_____
❏ Meals (not included in hotel price)	_____	_____	_____
❏ Snacks, drinks	_____	_____	_____
Activities			
❏ Equipment use and rental (boats, skis, lifts, horses, etc.)	_____	_____	_____
❏ Amusements (movies, amusement parks, concerts, plays, etc.)	_____	_____	_____
Miscellaneous	_____	_____	_____
Total estimated expense	_____	_____	_____
Cash available to pay for vacation	_____	_____	_____
Amount to be financed (loans, credit cards, etc.)	_____	_____	_____
Interest cost on amount financed (assuming you pay it off in 12 monthly installments)	_____	_____	_____

CONSUMER ALERT

Beating the High Price of Water

Would you pay $4.00 for a gallon of ordinary water?

Of course not, you say, but you may already have done so many times.

Example: The supermarket offers a six-pack of canned iced tea for $2.29. Six cans of 12 ounces each total 72 ounces. At $2.29, that's 3.18¢ per ounce. There are 128 ounces in a gallon, so at 3.18¢ per ounce you are paying $4.07 per gallon for canned iced tea. But all you are really getting is ordinary water, with a few cents worth of tea flavoring, added to it.

Likewise with juice products. How many quarts of Hawaiian Punch can you make from a can of the concentrated product? Compare the cost of doing so with buying regular canned Hawaiian Punch. What other products offer you the same choice? If you've been buying the canned instead of the concentrate, how much extra have you been paying to buy water and haul it home from the market?

Paying $4.00 per gallon for ordinary water is, obviously, absurd. It's bad enough to pay $1.30 or so for a gallon of gasoline—but at least that product is capable of propelling a 4,000-pound vehicle 20 to 30 miles at speeds in excess of 50 miles per hour. What will the water do by comparison?

You can't say that nobody is foolish enough to spend $4.00 for a gallon of water. The product wouldn't be on the shelves if nobody bought it.

Calculate how much money you might have paid in the last year to buy water at the supermarket. From now on, be a Smart Shopper. Buy the concentrates and use your own tap water. Think of what can be saved, in both money and energy.

UPS & DOWNS   *The Economics of Everyday Life*

Why Food Prices Fluctuate

Nature is the culprit with respect to produce, meats, fish, and dairy products. Seasons change regularly: you can buy strawberries in the summer for under a dollar a box, but the price zooms in winter when they are flown in from New Zealand. Floods, droughts, freezes, and hot spells also wreak havoc with prices.

Many other elements enter into the cost of food, some of which have nothing to do with the food itself.

New products   Each year about 12,000 new products are created for U.S. supermarkets. And about 80 percent of those new products fail. The makers pass some of the cost of these failed products onto the public by increasing the price of successful products.

Slotting allowances   Food manufacturers are in fierce competition to get the best display space in the best markets. Busy stores charge "slotting allowances" for the shelf space they offer to manufacturers. These extra fees can add to the cost of the product.

Failure fees   A retailer doesn't want to give up valuable shelf space to an unproven new product. Where competition is most intense, retailers ask for *failure fees*. If choice space is given to a manufacturer for a new product, and the new product fails to reach a given sales volume, the manufacturer will have to pay a penalty to the store.

Coupons and rebates   Each year the United States is flooded with some 270 *billion* cents-off coupons. We redeem about 7 billion of them, representing a "savings" to the redeemers of $3.1 billion. Add the cost of processing, printing, and distributing. There's no such thing as a free lunch. Someone is absorbing all that expense.

Technology   Scientific advances have been very much to the consumer's advantage. Genetic engineering provides bigger yields. New packaging allows for longer shelf life. At the checkout counter, the laser machine that reads the bar codes helps the market control costs, thus keeping prices down.

Human nature   As an experiment a supermarket set up two crates of identical bananas side by side, one unlabeled, the other with a popular brand label. The branded bananas were priced much higher than the unlabeled ones, but shoppers were loyal: They paid the higher price for the branded bananas, while the unlabeled ones went begging. This speaks for itself.

? WHAT IF . . . ? —————————————————————————

How would you deal with these real-life possibilities?

1. You're buying a new TV for $400, with a one-year warranty. The store offers an extended warranty for three years, at an extra cost of $150. You're no good at fixing electronic gizmos. Would you buy the warranty? If so, why? If not, why not?

2. Both your washing machine and dryer are on their last legs. Buying new machines will cost about $800, and you're strapped for cash, so you'd have to finance them. There's a nice laundromat nearby. What will you do to solve your dilemma?

3. Economic conditions are harsh, and you have to take a pay cut of 10 percent. How much can you reduce your food budget to offset that pay cut, without sacrificing good nutrition? What would you give up? What would you substitute? Now, look at the rosy side as well—a 10 percent pay raise. How much of that would go into your food budget? For what specifically?

NUMBER CRUNCHERS —————————————————————————

Do the calculations to make decisions in these real-life possibilities.

1. You're moving into a new dwelling and you have no furniture. Develop a list of all the furniture you'll need to live comfortably. Go shopping. How much would it cost you to buy everything for cash? How much would it cost you to finance everything, given varying amounts of down payment? (See the loan calculation tables in chapter 10) Visit a furniture rental store: How much would it cost you to rent everything?

2. Make a list of the ten items you purchase most frequently at the food market. Every week for one month compare the prices on those items at your own market and two other markets. Take all factors into account: coupons, special discounts, cost of getting to and from market, other conveniences. Where do you get the best deal, all things considered?

3. Ask your pharmacist to help you on this one: What are the ten most frequently prescribed drugs, and how much do they cost in typical dosages? Compare these costs with the costs of identical generic products. If you regularly use any prescription item, is there a generic equal, and how much does it cost?

4. Examine ads for book, record, or video clubs, particularly those that offer "12 for only $.99 each, as long as you agree to buy 6 more at our regular price . . . ," or comparable deals. Calculate how much you'd actually end up spending including shipping costs. Compare that with buying the same items at local stores or borrowing them from your local library. Which is the best deal?

FOR BETTER OR FOR WORSE

Things beyond our control often impact our personal and financial well-being, for better or for worse. Some are more predictable than others. How would you be affected if the following real-life phenomena happened? Could you have seen it coming? What steps could you have taken to minimize damage or maximize advantage? The better able you are to anticipate and recognize these forces, the better equipped you are to deal with them.

1. You've long been saving up for a once-in-a-lifetime three-week trip abroad, and now you've finally booked it and paid for it. One of your parents gets seriously ill just weeks before you're scheduled to go.

2. A new manager takes over at the supermarket you regularly use. He's an ogre. The staff morale goes from chipper to mean, and the condition of the market goes from sparkling to dingy. But their prices become more attractive. The next nearest market is three miles farther away from you.

3. A local furniture store has a going-out-of-business sale, and you charge $3,000 on your credit card buying goods that normally would have cost twice that. But the store goes out of business—totally—before they deliver your furniture.

4

Frauds and Swindles
and How to Avoid Them

There's a sucker born every minute.
P. T. Barnum

The statement is as true today as it was in Barnum's time. Despite all the consumer education material available today, an abundance of shady, misleading, and illegal business still goes on in every community every day. There are schemes that can relieve the unwary and the greedy of a few dollars or of many thousands of dollars. And more often than not, the swindlers get away with their schemes and skip from one city to the next, laughing at their victims all the way. Chances are good that someday you may be a victim of consumer fraud. But you'll have a strong defense against that possibility if you heed the techniques in this chapter:

- Spotting and avoiding the deals that sound too good to be true; that promise something for nothing; that promise instant wealth, health, or success

- Knowing whom to inform if you discover a fraudulent scheme in the works

- Knowing where you can get help if you find yourself the victim of a swindle

BARNUM WAS RIGHT

No one is immune to the wiles of the con artist or the shady business operator. Young and old, rich and poor, succumb to some scam at one time or another. Because most business activities are indeed legitimate, we tend to trust people. We believe what we're told. We believe what we read in advertisements. And despite the ever constant rule of *caveat emptor—buyer beware*—we are not wary enough. If we are led to believe that we are getting something that sounds too good to be true, or something for nothing, we tend to believe it. And we part with our money without even asking questions. Sometimes it's nothing more than our own greed that does us in. Sometimes we are simply gullible—believing preposterous statements. And sometimes a salesperson wins our confidence so totally that we act as if we're hypnotized when we write out our checks.

Consumer fraud will never go away. According to a presidential crime commission study, more than 90 percent of the victims of consumer fraud never do anything about it. The majority of the victims are not even *aware* that they've been defrauded until it's far too late to do anything about it. Those who are aware of having been defrauded are reluctant to report it to the police, either out of embarrassment or out of belief that the police won't do anything about it. Thus, with few exceptions, promoters and swindlers run free throughout our society, taking advantage of our weaknesses, our greed, our gullibility, and our basically trusting natures.

Exercise 4.1

This chapter will explore some of the more common types of consumer fraud. Every type of fraud has endless variations, so don't for a moment think that the schemes described here are the only ones. You must be aware of certain *basic patterns* that can alert you to possible fraud. These basic patterns appear in the following situations:

- You're led to believe that you're getting something for nothing or are offered a deal that sounds too good to be true. There is no such thing as something for nothing, and any deal that sounds too good to be true is usually neither good nor true.

- Someone tries to sell you something with such vigor that you find yourself on the verge of spending money for something you might otherwise have ignored. In such cases, you should immediately ask yourself, "If this thing is so good, then why is he willing to sell it to me? Could it be that he'll get more benefit by selling it to me than I can by buying it from him?"

- A salesperson or an ad offers you something that is not available through normal channels. This may be a miracle cure, a chance to get rich quick, or a chance to become famous. These offerings will do nothing but deplete your bank account.

Although most advertising media (newspapers, magazines, radio, television) attempt to police the advertising they present to the public, there are definitely flaws in the system. Some policing efforts are not adequate, and misleading advertising can slip past the censor's scrutiny. Moreover, misleading advertising that appears in an otherwise legitimate medium takes on an aura of legitimacy. "It must be so if it appeared in the daily paper. If it weren't legitimate, the newspaper wouldn't run it." Being constantly alert is no guarantee that you'll never get stung. But *lack* of constant alertness will almost guarantee that you *will* get stung.

One final warning before we embark on tales of the wild and woolly world of consumer fraud. Nothing could please Snake Oil Sam more than a brand new medium where he can offer his scams and ripoffs with virtually total impunity.

That medium is the Internet. For all the good things available on the Internet, we're just beginning to see the tip of the tip of what is going to be the biggest iceberg in history: consumer abuses beyond measurement.

Sam makes billions of dollars every year through the legitimate advertising media—print, broadcasting, mail, and so on. But at least with those media there is some policing; some ads do get censored or are refused. Those that do reach the public are susceptible to prosecution if they turn out to be scams. The advertisers can be found. State and federal agencies can step in. And if the mail is used as part of a scam, federal mail fraud laws can be used to nab the culprits. Still, Sam gets away with an incredible haul.

Now imagine the Internet, where nothing has to be edited by any responsible authority. And if something is responsibly edited, hackers can break into the system and change it, and you'll never know the difference. On the Internet virtually anything can and does get published. There are no regulators or official censors. The advertisers can hide themselves in cyberspace, far from the reach of any law enforcement. Snake Oil Sam is in absolute Cyber-Heaven!

All of the swindles outlined in this chapter can be initiated on the Internet and through e-mail with lightning-like suddenness. Snake Oil Sam lurks in chat rooms waiting for the gullible and the greedy. The investment arena is particularly dangerous on the Internet. If a salesperson from a legitimate firm sells you a deal over the phone, through the mail, or in person, you have at least some hope of getting some help from the firm, from the National Association of Security Dealers, from the Securities and Exchange Commission or from your state's Department of Securities. Dealing with an unknown entity on the Internet leaves you with absolutely no recourse. You'll be out there flapping your wings in cyberspace, and Snake Oil Sam will laugh all the way to the bank. (He knows better than to entrust his money to strangers on the Internet.) Surf accordingly.

BAIT AND SWITCH

This is probably the oldest game of all. The bait is an attractive enticement to lure you into a store in a buying frame of mind. The switch occurs when you are in the store and the salesperson diverts you from the bait item to another item that offers him a higher profit. The switch can happen in many ways.

For instance, you're watching late-night television, and here comes good old Gideon Gotcha "out here in automobile land ready to sell you folks some beautiful cars of all makes and models. Here's a 1998 Cadillac with only 1,600 miles on it, in perfect condition, with brand-new radial-ply-biased-steel-double-whitewall-hand-autographed tires, and a built-in Hammond organ in the back seat! And how much would you expect to pay for this beautiful car? About $25,000? Maybe at some other place, but not at Gideon Gotcha's! Would you believe only $8,995!"

You rush down to Gideon Gotcha's where you find that the lot is closed for the night. You camp on the doorstep and when Gideon comes in to open up, you hand him an envelope full of cash and tell him you want the $8,995 Cadillac you saw on television just a few hours ago.

"Oh, I'm really sorry," says Gideon, "but we sold it during the night. I got a call at my house from a customer who sent a courier at 4 A.M. with the cash. But now that you're here, maybe I can interest you in a brand-new Caddie whose classic beauty will withstand the years better than the Mona Lisa. And since you came down so early in the morning, I could make a special deal for you. . . ."

Or you see an ad in the newspaper offering an entire side of beef for only 79¢ a pound. A fantastic deal! You rush to the place, and the butcher is happy to show you the side of beef that was advertised.

"Of course," he points out, "It's got some funny green spots here and there, but maybe we can cut them out. Anyway, if you boil the meat for fifteen or twenty minutes, it should kill any contamination that may have gone deeper. Now, if you don't like that particular side, we've got some regular sides over here in the cooler for $3.99 a pound."

Bait and switch tactics are outlawed by the Federal Trade Commission, as well as by many state and local laws. Nonetheless, they still occur in abundance. Your best protection against getting involved is your own careful scrutiny of the advertising, your willingness to shop around for similar products, and your ability to resist the temptation in the first place.

A distinction should be made between bait and switch and "loss leaders." A loss leader is a product offered by a merchant at a lower-than-normal price to entice you into the store where, it's hoped, you'll buy other merchandise as well as the loss leader. Supermarkets and discount stores use loss leaders all the time, and there's nothing wrong with this practice if you are getting the goods as represented and not a cheap replacement.

Where loss-leader advertising is employed, legitimate merchants will note in their advertising any catches in their offering, such as a limited supply, or will make clear that the offer is good only at certain stores or at certain hours. The Federal Trade Commission says that if a loss leader or other kind of promotional product is offered, the merchant is expected to have a sufficient amount on hand to meet what he reasonably expects to be the demand. Many merchants, realizing the value of pleasing their customers, will offer rainchecks if they run out of the supply of a loss leader.

If you detect a bait and switch operation in action in your community, alert the newspaper (or radio or TV station) where the advertising was placed. You may also want to notify the local Better Business Bureau and the police department. Very likely, nothing much will be done to the merchant who employed these tactics, but he'll be warned, and he might even promise not to do it again. Until next time.

MAIL-ORDER MADNESS

In terms of both dollar volume and number of incidents, the U.S. Postal Service is probably the single biggest carrier of fraudulent activity. Although many billions of dollars' worth of perfectly satisfactory goods are sold through the mail each year, the level of abuse also runs very high. Mail-order swindlers owe their success not just to the greed and gullibility of victims but also to the fact that the fraud inspection division of the U.S. Postal Service is woefully understaffed. A false or misleading advertisement can cover the country for many months before postal inspectors are able to gather enough evidence to put a stop to it. In the meantime, the promoters will have made their fortune and disappeared, only to reappear shortly thereafter using a different name and selling a slightly different product. And the chase begins again, with the promoters usually the winners.

Mail order starts with an advertisement printed in a newspaper or magazine, broadcast on radio or television, sent through the mail or beamed on the Internet. You are dealing with people you don't know. If something goes wrong, you might not be able to get it corrected. If you're dealing with *legitimate* mail-order purveyors, most problems should be fairly easily corrected. But if you find yourself in the hands of a mail-order swindler, it is safe to assume that there's virtually no chance of your ever getting satisfaction or your money back.

Following is a brief sampling of mail-order swindles, based on actual experience: To determine how cleverly the promoters toy with the minds and bank accounts of potential victims, I became an intentional victim of a number of offerings. The results should speak for themselves.

Vanity Rackets

The price of an ego trip can be high indeed. Vanity rackets prey on the desire of so many people to be recognized. Ads offer to publish your book, your song, your poem, or even your baby's picture in a directory that is to be sent to television producers.

Anyone who has ever tried to have a song or a book published through normal channels knows how frustrating it can be: Rejection slips pour in, and it seems as though there's no way to achieve success. How wondrous it is, then, when you see an ad by a publisher soliciting your work. "Authors wanted." "Songwriters wanted."

In the legitimate publishing world, most books and songs are created by established artists—usually with the help of agents—under contract to the publisher. In the vanity publishing world, publishers print virtually anything, provided you pay them enough money. The veiled promises of fame and fortune will never materialize. You will have paid a high price to have your ego massaged.

Do vanity publishers really seek quality? Or will they publish anything that comes in attached to a big enough check? Seeking an answer to this question, I wrote an intentionally atrocious song and sent it off to three different vanity music publishers. If they were looking for any kind of quality, they would have rejected my lyrics instantly. Here are the words to my song:

Ethel Is My Only Love
(sing slowly)

Oh oh oh oh Ethel
Ethel Ethel will you be my blessing
Cuz when I look at you and sigh,
It makes me feel high. Oh me oh my.
It seems like only yesterday that we were in high school together.
I can't believe how old we are now, forever.
Oh oh oh oh Ethel
I feel just lousy without you
You are my only love—not Rita anymore.
Seriously, I mean it.
Oh oh Ethel. Yeah, yeah, yeah.

This drivel was accepted, not once, not twice, but all three times by the vanity publishers. Here is a sampling of some of the literature they sent me:

Dear Mr. Rosefsky:
We have good news for you! Your song has been rated #5 on our top 30 evaluation chart. We sincerely believe that your song poem, with the proper servicing, has the potential for a hit song. We have already contacted nearby publishers, and the response to it was positive. Publishers' acceptance seems assured. If you have as much faith in your song as we have, you will want to take advantage of our offer.

Each of the acceptances requested that I send in $80 to $90 for "servicing" of the song. The next step would be to pay them $200 to $300 for complete scoring or orchestration. Following that, the sky was the limit. I could pay for as many records to be pressed as I wished to, and they would distribute them and I would receive royalties. Legitimate music publishers assured me that a product from a vanity publisher stood no chance of being played on a radio station or distributed to music stores.

Tabloid newspapers and the Internet are the primary sources of potentially fraudulent advertising. I found an ad offering $300 for my baby's picture. If the baby picture was "acceptable," it would be published in a magazine that was distributed to movie and television producers looking for child talent. I sent in a picture of my 30-year-old cousin, Herbie, who at the time weighed in excess of 200 pounds. The photo was taken in the midst of an attack of indigestion. The magazine "accepted"the picture for publication, provided I send them $12.95. Responsible people in the motion picture and television industries assured me that they had never heard of the magazine, nor would they ever hire talent through such a publication. Yet it's likely that many thousands of checks for $12.95 each were sent by parents eager to have their children achieve fame and fortune.

Would-be inventors are also easy prey for swindlers who promise to patent and market products in exchange for big up-front fees.

Get-rich-quick Schemes

How far wrong can you go? You send away $30 for a book that promises to make you rich overnight. and if you don't like it, they promise to send you your money back. Such ads abound because it's difficult to prove them illegal. You will indeed receive a book. Judging from all those I've seen, it will be a cheaply produced paperback that will teach you how to become rich: Write a similar book on your own, take out ads in magazines, and let people send *you* money. You'll also get your name on dozens of other mailing lists, one of which is likely to hit you for big money in the future.

Other get-rich-quick schemes are nothing more than blatant chain letters instructing you to sent $30 to a name at the top of an enclosed list. You're then to duplicate this letter five times and put your name at the bottom of the list. Within weeks you are promised thousands of people all over the country will be sending you $30. Chain letters are illegal. Not only do such schemes never produce money for you, but they could involve you in a federal lawsuit.

Work-at-home Schemes

These promise ways to supplement your income by working at home. They appeal to people who can least afford to lose money—the elderly, the invalid, the poor.

- **Addressing envelopes.** You send $20 to the promoter and receive instructions on how to approach local businesses to sell them your services as an envelope addresser. But you are competing with professional mailing houses that can turn out thousands of envelopes in the time it would take you to do a few dozen.
- **Handicraft kits.** For your $20, you'll receive a kit of materials with instructions on how to turn them into baby booties, key chains, and the like. The promise is that the company will buy it back from you in finished form at a profit to you. You make the product and send it back to the company, only to be told that it's not up to their standards. They're very sorry, they'll say, but perhaps you'd like to try again by ordering another kit.

The postal fraud authorities and the Council of Better Business Bureaus agree: They have never seen a work-at-home scheme that worked, except for the promoters.

Quackery

Lose weight . . . cure baldness . . . look younger . . . live longer . . . improve your sex life. Shades of Snake Oil Sam, who sold caramel-flavored alcohol to the gullible from his traveling sideshow wagon.

Example: The ad told me that I could grow taller. Cost: $15 with a money-back guarantee if I wasn't satisfied. I received a single sheet of paper with a program of exercises titled "Erecto-Dynamics." I was to do these calisthenics for at least twenty minutes every day for a full year. But most important to the growing taller program was that I should stand up straighter. As for the money-back guarantee, it was contingent on my having my height verified by a doctor before the start of the year's program and at the end. The expense of having a doctor verify my height would be more than the money I'd get back from the promoter.

Quackery is of particular concern to the postal fraud authorities, for not only can you lose money but your health can be endangered if you fail to seek proper medical attention, relying instead on the pufferies of Snake Oil Sam. If your condition can't be helped by a professional, you certainly won't be helped by these mail-order offerings.

One aspect of the quackery phenomenon seems to grow without any end in sight, and it must be raking in billions of dollars from the gullible and the lonely: so-called psychics who clutter up the television airwaves and other media. Do Number Cruncher exercise 2 at the end of this chapter if you have any doubts about the money being generated by this nonsense. And bear in mind: There's no such thing as a "free" psychic.

As with so many other fads and scams, they will run their course and disappear. But the people behind the scenes—the ones who create and administer new scams—will not disappear. They'll be out there drumming up new ways to separate you from your money as long as there's a you and as long as there's money.

FRAUDS ON THE STREET

When you respond to an advertisement, you have time to consider your response. But when you're confronted by a stranger on the street, the surprise element can be enough to embroil you in a money-losing proposition.

The Pigeon Drop

This classic old scheme, the pigeon drop, has dozens of variations. In a typical operation, a person is approached by a stranger who chats with the victim for a few minutes to win her friendship and confidence. Then the stranger announces that he has just found a wallet that contains a lot of money but no identification.

The stranger offers to split the find with the newfound friend, the victim. At this point, the victim, taken in by the con man's friendship and generosity, is willing to do almost anything the con man advises. The con man then quickly suggests that before they split the loot, they should double-check the legality with a lawyer and that the victim, in order to show good faith, should put up an equal amount of cash and let the lawyer hold it while a decision is made as to who is entitled to the money.

It seems crazy that the victims would put up the cash, but they do time and time again—and often thousands of dollars are involved. As soon as the victim delivers the cash, the whole package is left with the con man's "lawyer," who promptly disappears. The victim's money? Gone in a flash. Elderly people are traditional marks for this scam. They tend to be more easily won over by the confidence game, and they're less likely to give chase. But no one is excluded from the potential of the pigeon drop.

Phony Goods

This type of swindle occurs mostly during the Christmas season, but it can pop up at any time, in any place. The scheme is decisive in its swiftness and simplicity. You're approached by a stranger offering to sell you anything from watches to jewelry to perfume to a color TV set "still in the carton." The price is too good to be true. It won't be until you get the item home that you find that the watch has no innards, the perfume is kerosene, the jewelry is cut glass, and the color TV set still in the carton is nothing more than a wooden box. Similar shenanigans can take place at flea markets and swap meets.

If you do fall prey to such a scheme, you can be certain that you will not be able to get your money back. If you are able to find the seller, he'll deny ever having seen you, and it's unlikely that the police will bother to assist you in what they would consider a relatively petty matter.

FRAUDS IN THE HOME

You don't always have to go out to encounter con artists. Sometimes they'll come to you, knocking on your door, calling, or sending e-mail. As with street schemes, the element of surprise works in favor of con artists. They are prepared to sell to you, and you're totally unprepared for a sales pitch. You have no way of finding the swindler if things go wrong.

"900" Scams

There are, it seems, 900 ways you can get taken if you are careless in making "900" calls on your telephone. The sales pitches are intriguing: You can talk to psychics, acquire credit cards, pour your heart out to the opposite sex, be lured into dangerous investment schemes, and much more. And the costs of doing so will be on your next month's telephone bill. Many people make the mistake of thinking that the deals must be legitimate because the telephone company is involved. Wrong! Abuses with "900" numbers, ranging from excessive charges to outright swindle, have been rampant. If you get trapped once, the telephone company might waive the charges for your first misadventure. But that's it. Beware also of seemingly toll-free numbers such as "800" and "888" which rack up the charges on your credit card. Know before you dial that those expenses can mount up and that if you fail to pay you can lose your telephone, your credit card, and your good credit standing.

Cellular Phones

How's this for a growth business? In 1991, when cellular phones were still in the novelty stage, Snake Oil Sam racked up $100 million in fraudulent activities with the phones. By 1995 his take had grown to $600 million, according to the Cellular Telecommunications Industry Association. How did/ does he do it? Easier than you may think. He can sit by the side of the road and scan any phone in use. With the data he retrieves he can program a clone phone with your number. He sells that cloned phone to an eager buyer, who proceeds to use your number to make and receive calls, tallying up hundreds of dollars in costs in just a few hours.

How can that hurt you? If your phone is cloned and you don't check your monthly bill (or your employees' bills) you could be paying for some-one else's calls. If you do discover improper use, your carrier might remove the invalid charges from your bill the first time. But $600 million of fraudu-lent calls were not reported to carriers' attention in 1995, the last year for which such statistics were available.

Fraud prevention programs are available on most cellular systems at lit-tle or no cost to you the user. But you have to use it regularly. You never can tell when that person by the side of the road has a scanner aimed at you.

Courier Services

Whether the scam involves investments, "free" vacations, or any other of-fering in which money has to be delivered to the con artists, victims are quickly won over when they are told, "We can send a Federal Express (or UPS) courier right over to pick up your check." The use of these well-known services adds legitimacy to the pitch and convinces many victims who might otherwise have avoided the scam. So when you hear that a courier service will fetch your check, don't let that sway your opinion of the offer's credibility.

Scholarship Scams

College students (perhaps such as yourself) face heavy costs for their schooling. The money pressure makes them easy targets for Snake Oil Sam. In recent years over 300,000 students and their families have been victim-ized by upwards of 200 scholarship scam artists. Their pitch is devilishly simple. Victims are told that they have qualified for a scholarship that can help them meet school expenses. All they need to do is send in, say, $279 or so for processing fees. Bye-bye money.

So many swindles are based on the eagerness of people to get their hands on needed money, and they're willing to pay good money in advance for the hope of getting the money they seek. Be well aware that legitimate scholarship donors do not ask for money up front. If you become aware of such a pitch, contact the Federal Trade Commission. They're on the lookout for these criminals.

HOME IMPROVEMENTS

Our homes are our castles. They're also among the favorite targets for swindlers. The stakes are large in home improvement frauds and the legal consequences can be devastating. Note the similar patterns that emerge in the following three case histories—stories that might almost be amusing if, in fact, they were not true.

The Squirrels

An elderly widow lived alone in a house surrounded by overhanging oak trees. Although she was financially secure, the loneliness of her days left her an easy mark for any unscrupulous person who could win her confidence.

The home improvement salesman was well trained to win her confidence. She soon told him of a grave concern of hers: she had antique furniture stored in her attic, and she was worried that squirrels that lived in the oak trees would gain access to her attic and gnaw the furniture into ruins. The salesman had a ready solution: he would install "squirrel deflectors" on her roof. These aluminum panels would reflect sunlight; when the squirrels tried to jump from the trees to the roof, they would be blinded by the reflected light and would fall to the ground.

The elderly widow couldn't sign the contract fast enough, and the deflectors were installed. The price: $1,500. The installation was defective; serious damage was done to the roof, and a legitimate roofer had to repair the damage at considerable cost.

The Furnace

An innocent homeowner was approached by a succession of rip-off artists as follows:

Day One: A young lad offers to clean out the homeowner's furnace for a very minimal sum of money. The homeowner agrees, the work is done, and the lad is paid.

Day Two: A "work inspector" asks the homeowner if he can see the furnace. He is supposedly checking up on the work that his furnace-cleaning crew has been doing in the neighborhood.

Day Three: A man representing himself as a "furnace inspector" asks to see the furnace. He tells the homeowner that the furnace has serious cracks in it and that he must "condemn" the furnace.

Day Four: The man from Day Two returns, telling the homeowner that he is sorry to hear that his furnace has been condemned. But he has a wonderful deal on the new furnace that can be installed immediately.

The homeowner buys the whole scam. He signs a contract for the new furnace. The contract is immediately sold to a finance company. The installers leave the old furnace in the homeowner's yard, and the homeowner has it checked by another furnace company. It is then that he learns that there is nothing at all wrong with the original furnace, but by that time he has no energy to fight the matter any further.

The Model Home

The salesman told the gullible young couple that their house had been chosen as part of an advertising program. They would receive "free" aluminum siding on the house. All they had to do was tell their friends and neighbors who had done this magnificent work. Thereby, the home improvement company would receive many referrals and everybody would be happy. The young couple couldn't sign the contract fast enough.

The work was done and, a month later, to the couple's amazement, they received a bill from a finance company for the first installment on a very expensive contract. Then—too late—they read the contract in detail. It stated that they had to pay for the installation, but that they would receive a discount for every referral that resulted in another installation. If they made enough referrals that resulted in enough contracts, then presumably their own job would have cost them nothing.

Is this a fraud or not? The contract was explicit, but the young couple failed to read it or understand it. Then the siding began to peel, and their "model home" began to look a shambles. They called the improvement company to repair the shoddy work, but the company's phone had been disconnected. The finance company that had purchased their contract was demanding payment. The couple had to hire a lawyer at a considerable cost to void the contract, and had to repair the house at their own expense.

Warning Signals

In addition to the "too good to be true" and "something for nothing" appeals of the home improvement pitch, there are some other aspects of the sales presentation that should cause you to be wary.

The "Perfect" Guarantee

The materials and installation may be accompanied by an "unconditional lifetime money-back" guarantee. The guarantee is only as good as its written statements and only as good as the ability of the guarantor to perform. A guarantee should be spelled out in explicit detail, and you should understand exactly what is and is not guaranteed. A guarantee is meaningless if you can't locate the guarantor.

Listen for the "Uh-oh" Music

Filmmakers use this gimmick to increase the audience's sense of anticipation: Just before the monster leaps out of the closet, or just before the bad guys ambush the good guys, you'll hear "uh-oh" music—music that signals that something bad, or frightening, is about to happen. Most of us, if we're reasonably cautious, have a sixth sense that plays "uh-oh" music in our minds before we find ourselves on the brink of being swindled. The melody may differ from time to time, but the lyrics are generally: "This sounds like something too good to be true," or "How far wrong can I go?" "Listen for the "uh-oh" music. It's telling you to beware. And most of the time it's exactly right.

Big Savings

You might be told that the work will save you hundreds of dollars over what it would cost through other contractors. You can never know this for sure unless you have properly drawn plans and specifications and obtained bids from reputable local contractors. Until you have done that, the salesperson's words are nothing more than puffery.

"Will Last Forever"

The salesman might say that materials, such as aluminum siding, are "maintenance-free forever." No substance yet discovered by science and affordable to the average homeowner is maintenance-free forever.

"Sign Up Now or Never"

Salespeople will be very anxious to get you to sign a contract right away. They know that if you don't, and if you have time to think about the deal, they may lose you. This is where the pressure begins. They may try to convince you that getting other prices will be a waste of your time; that their price is certainly the lowest; and that their low price won't be available later. This "now or never" kind of pressure can be convincing. Note well: When you're dealing with legitimate contractors, any contract can wait for a day or so. If you feel that by not signing right away you're losing out on something special, you had best begin preparing yourself for the worst.

Credentials

A reputable home improvement contractor's past history will speak for itself. You can visit his place of business, and you can talk to customers who have used his services. The shady promoter will make a big fuss about his credentials. He may have become a member of the Chamber of Commerce and he may have established a bank account and lines of credit with local suppliers. But all these credentials don't mean that you're getting good value for your money. It can be difficult to spot the credential-laden con artist. It's necessary to look behind the credentials and try to spot the warning signals.

Brand Names

Home improvement swindlers use the names of national firms to convince customers that they themselves are legitimate. The impression given is that the promoters are in direct alliance with the manufacturers and that such national firms certainly wouldn't condone anything but the highest quality workmanship with regard to their products. Thus the salesperson must be of the highest caliber.

Anyone can buy most of these name-brand products. Many homeowners have been bilked, believing that the contractor will use such brand-name products, only to find that inferior materials were used.

How to Avoid Home Improvement Rackets

Unless you are absolutely certain of a contractor's integrity, follow these steps to avoid being swindled on a home improvement project:

1. Do not sign any home improvement contracts unless you have firm, clear, detailed plans and specifications.
2. Do not sign any contracts until you have comparable bids from other licensed contractors based on those plans and specifications.
3. Do not sign any contracts until you have had the documents checked by an attorney.
4. Do not sign any home improvement contracts until you have discussed with your banker the overall financing of the project.
5. Be aware of state and federal laws that give you the right to rescind (cancel) a contract, particularly if it involves your giving a mortgage on your property to the other party. See the truth-in-lending law in chapter 13.

If you want the job done right and you want to get the most for your money, there are no shortcuts around these steps. It is a lot of work, but when you are spending thousands of dollars and risking damage to your house if you hire unqualified people, it is worth the effort.

INVESTMENT SCHEMES

"Here's the deal, with a rock-solid guarantee: You give me your money—$1,000, $5,000, $10,000, whatever—and if at any time you're unsatisfied with what I'm doing with it, just let me know and I'll immediately return the unused portion thereof."

Who would fall for an offer like that? You'd be surprised. When it comes to the area of investments—making your money grow—greed and gullibility reach their peak, and the opportunities for fraudulent activities are infinite. The fast-buck artists promise instant fortunes and huge tax savings in stocks, commodities, gold, silver, gemstones, land, and virtually anything else that might capture a victim's attention. You might be solicited through the mail, through advertising, or through the Internet but one of the most common media used by investment promoters is the telephone.

The Boiler Room

In a boiler room operation, fast-talking, hard-driving salespersons telephone would-be victims across the country, offering their latest miracle for getting wealthy. How do they get your name? Probably from mailing lists: If you subscribe to any financial periodicals or if you have bought any money-related books through the mail or the internet, your name will be on those lists, sold by the list owner.

Following is a sample—with little exaggeration—of what you're likely to hear if you receive a telephone call from a boiler room operation:

"Good morning, Mr. Rosefsky, this is J. Fairly Nicely of Mammoth Investments on Wall Street. I'd like to tell you how you can double your money within six months. Would you be interested in hearing that? . . . Mammoth has been authorized to sell stock in Amalgamated International—you've heard of them, of course—they've just discovered one of the world's largest linoleum deposits, and mining of the linoleum is expected to start next week. I'm authorized to offer you 500 shares at $10 per share, but the offer is good only for the next hour. Now get this: We know for a fact that the big brokerage firm Merrill-Lynch-Shearson-Webber is going to the market with a public offering price of $20 per share. You'll double your money, but you've got to buy *now*. Could you hold on just a moment, my other phone is ringing . . . (You now hear him supposedly talking on another phone.) . . . Yes, Mr. Gates, we still have some shares left in the linoleum venture. How many would you like? . . . Yes, Mr. Gates . . . 10,000 shares at $10 apiece . . . you've got it. Now Mr. Rosefsky, as I was saying, I just sold 10,000 shares, so I can offer you only 300, but if you really want the 500, maybe I can arrange it. . . . You seem hesitant; is there any reason why you wouldn't want to double your money?"

Yes, people do run to their checkbooks and send money to J. Fairly Nicely and his ilk without hesitation or fear. And that's probably the last they'll ever see of their money. But that's not the last they'll hear of J. Fairly Nicely, for he'll sell their name to other boiler room operations and, some other day, in some other way, they'll be offered a partnership in a veal farm, a future interest in a grove of velcro trees, or syndication rights on a herd of prize-winning naugahydes.

The pitchman's spiel is so frenetic that it doesn't give the victims time to think about anything other than doubling their money. If the would-be victims did stop to think, the first thought might be: "If this deal is so good, how come you're selling it to me? Why don't you just keep it all yourself?" If that question is asked, the answer will be: "I've hocked my house, my wife, my kids, and my gold fillings to raise every penny I could to buy into this. I can't buy it all, but I'm buying all I can." He may even sound all choked up at this point.

Your best defense against the wiles of the boiler room operator is to take advantage of a technical device built into your telephone. It's called the hang-up button. It works like a charm.

Ponzis and Pyramids

Charles Ponzi was a hustler who plied his skills in Boston during the 1920s. He so popularized an ancient scheme that it has carried his name ever since—the Ponzi scheme. It was simple and straightforward, and it attracted victims like a magnet. It worked like this:

Ponzi told victims, "You give me $100 today, and in 30 days I'll give you back $120." Thirty days later he did just that. His initial investment of $20 paid off, since now his believers would do exactly what he said. "Want to try again for another 30 days?" The first wave of investors took the plunge again. Ponzi had no trouble soliciting a second wave, and he used their money to pay off the first wave. Then he would solicit a third wave, and use their money to pay off the second wave, and so on.

In a Ponzi scheme new investors are constantly solicited and their money is used to pay off older investors. Keeping the investors happy keeps the money pouring in, but at some point the promoter will skip.

Closely related to the Ponzi scheme is the pyramid scheme, which is the basis for chain letters and multilevel distributorships. The promoters who start these schemes can make money, but at the risk of jail sentences, for the schemes can be illegal. Here's how the concept works: You have to pay money to someone to get in on the action. You are then entitled to seek money from others below you in the pyramid. As new players pay you, they, in turn, solicit others. This might involve a simple exchange of money. Or it might involve a business venture in which participants receive territories or licensing rights.

Participants succeed depending on how well they enlist subparticipants. If you carry the concept to its logical conclusion, you can quickly see how foolish it is. For example: You buy into a scheme that requires you to enlist ten other people. Each of those ten other people must then enlist ten additional people, and so it goes. If you carry this out to the tenth level down, 10 billion people must be involved in the pyramid for everyone to be satisfied. That's double the population of the entire earth.

Pyramid schemes collapse because they run out of people who are willing to participate, and the victims find that their names never move high enough on the list to recoup their investment.

Who Can You Trust?

Across the nation, talk radio has become a vehicle for all sorts of brainwashing activities, political, psychological and, in frightening dimensions, financial. People hear advice given on the radio, and for some unfathomable reason they take it as gospel. I have personal experience in this field. For ten years I hosted a financial call-in show in Los Angeles, and it never ceased to amaze me how much personal information people would give to me—a stranger—on the air while tens of thousands of other strangers listened in, and how avidly they followed my advice. My wife is a psychotherapist, and she is equally amazed at how the instant-shrink given out over the airwaves is gobbled up by the public, and how dangerous that can be: What's good for Pat from Peoria in two minutes of chat can be catastrophic for others who follow the same advice.

One popular radio talk show host whose program was carried daily for fifteen years in almost 200 stations recently pleaded guilty to nine felony charges, including fraud and conspiracy, for misleading his listeners to the tune of more than $21 million. Among his dirty deeds on the air: Unbeknownst to his listeners, he was paid to tout investments that he knew were worthless. He claimed that he had investigated various ventures when in fact he had not. He became involved with telephone pitchmen to further urge his listeners to part with their money in various schemes. He urged listeners to invest in certain precious metals by claiming falsely that he had put his own money into those metals. And before all of these felony counts, he had pleaded guilty to perjury and tax evasion charges. This was not a nice person, but he had the attention and respect of millions of listeners, and countless others who got hot tips from those listeners.

Who can you trust? Never, never make an investment that you learned about through the media—print, broadcast, Internet, mail, e-mail, or whatever-else-is-yet-to-be-invented—without doing your own independent investigation and then getting at least two other opinions from reputable people in that business.

LEISURE AND LUXURIES

Land Frauds

Will Rogers once said, "Land is the best investment there is cuz they ain't going to print no more of it." Tens of thousands of people have taken that remark seriously and have lost uncounted hundreds of millions of dollars on land swindles. They may not have realized that Will Rogers was a comedian, and this statement was one of his biggest jokes.

Land fraud schemes flourished in the 1970s and then slowed down as the impact of a newly created federal agency—the Office of Interstate Land Sales Regulation—began to be felt. Unscrupulous salespeople sold unwitting victims worthless swampland in Florida and barren desert in Arizona under the guise of "future retirement communities," "vacation rancheros," and just plain double-your-money-in-a-hurry investment opportunities.

Time Sharing

The swindlers didn't stop just because of the creation of a new federal agency. Many of the land salespeople switched to a new concept that emerged in the 1970s and 1980s called "time sharing." Time sharing is legitimate. However, abuses have been considerable. In a typical time-sharing situation, you buy the right to use a vacation facility for one or two weeks per year. The sales pitches are very high-pressure affairs.

Abuses occur when the facilities are not built in accordance with the original promises, when the facilities are never built at all, when the facilities are so poorly managed that you can't enjoy them, and when you learn that six other families have been sold the same space for the same time that you thought you had exclusive use of it. Promoters lure buyers to the sales meetings by promising what seem to be expensive gifts, such as television sets, automobiles, and free travel opportunities. Often, however, after you've sat through a two-hour presentation, you find that the gift is a cheap, perhaps worthless, electronic gadget. (Chapter 3 contains more information on time sharing.)

Vacation Ripoffs

It's hard to say no to an offer of a "free" vacation in some exotic place: plane fare, hotel room, rent-a-car, meals all included, plus $1,000 cash to spend as you wish! All you have to do is pay a $250 registration fee up front. That secures your airline ticket and hotel room, and it's fully refundable when you check in. What have you go to lose? $250 is what you've got to lose if you fall for this scam—and more, if you give the caller your credit card number. Your common sense may tell you to stay away from such a deal, but when they offer to send a Federal Express courier around to pick up your check, that may just convince you to take the plunge. After all, if Federal Express is involved . . . ?

All That Glitters . . .

Gold, silver, and precious gems have been the subject of fraudulent schemes that show no sign of abating. Examples include:

- **Counterfeit coins** Countless counterfeit gold coins have been circulated across the nation. Speculators have snapped them up without making any attempt to verify their legitimacy. When those speculators dig out the phony coins to sell, they're in for severe disappointment if buyers recognize that the coins are phony.
- **Gold-painted lead** Tens of millions of dollars were lost by eager gold investors who dealt with companies that promised future deliveries of gold bullion. The investors had to pay up front, but the future deliveries never took place. In many cases investors learned that the bars of supposed gold sitting in the promoters' vaults were nothing more than lead covered with gold paint.
- **Junk gems** Tons of worthless stones were passed off to gullible buyers as valuable rubies, sapphires, emeralds, and diamonds. Intriguing ads made it appear that phenomenal bargains could be had in these stones. To make matters worse, once the junk gem buyers had completed their mail order transactions, their names were sold to other sucker lists. The more sucker lists your name appears on, the sooner you'll fall for another scheme.

SNAKE OIL SAM'S MISCELLANEA

Advance Fee Loan Schemes

Snake Oil Sam is adept at filling his pockets through a pitch known as the advance fee loan scheme. Those who need money and who are having difficulty borrowing it from their bank are easy prey for this rip-off. The scheme promises that you'll receive the loan you need if you pay a sizable amount of money up front. Once the up-front money is paid, the swindler disappears with your money.

Credit Repair Clinics

Credit repair clinics appeal to people who have more debt than they can handle or bad credit histories. Unscrupulous credit repair clinics promise to relieve you of your debt problems, for a large sum of money, of course. As you can guess at this point, the up-front money you pay disappears without your getting any benefit from it.

Home Equity Loan Swindles

If borrowers give lenders mortgages on their homes in order to borrow money, the interest paid on these loans can be tax deductible. Such transactions are known as home equity loans. (See chapter 12 for more details.) Borrowers who don't think they can meet the lending criteria of banks may be lured into paying unconscionable fees and interest in order to obtain such loans from private, nonbank lenders. And if repayment is not made properly, unscrupulous lenders will be swift in starting foreclosure proceedings, which could cost the borrowers dearly.

Health Insurance Scams

Employers are frightened by increasing health care costs, yet they don't want to give up their plans for fear of losing valued employees. Enter the con artist selling phony health insurance plans that feature low costs and generous benefits. The employer pays the initial premiums, which quickly disappear into Snake Oil Sam's vast bank account. Doctors and hospitals end up holding the bag, having provided services in the honest belief they'd get paid. And employees end up uninsured, and perhaps uninsurable.

The Double Whammy

Pity the poor victims of the double whammy. They've already lost money in one swindle. Now they've been approached by the "Federal Consumer Protection Service" (or some other such phony but governmental sounding agency), which offers to recover the money they lost in the first swindle. That's right, they have to pay a hefty fee up front to get this service. If you don't know the outcome by now, please send me your name and address; I have a treasure map you might want to buy.

STRATEGIES FOR SUCCESS

Protect Yourself with Second and Third Opinions

If someone is trying to sell you something, no matter how convincing the sales pitch may sound, you must remember that the seller stands to benefit from making the sale. Maybe the seller will benefit more than you, the buyer. This can be especially so if what's being pitched is a fly-by-night investment scheme. Before you part with your money, or before you sign a contract, get a second opinion on the matter from someone who is not selling anything and who has no ax to grind. Protect yourself further by getting a third opinion. The more money at stake, the more this strategy will protect you.

WHAT TO DO ABOUT IT

Exercise 4.2

The sad fact is that if you do become a victim of a fraudulent scheme, there's little chance you'll get your money back unless you're willing to spend a lot of time and a lot more money on legal fees. And even if you are willing to spend money on legal fees, you can't sue someone you can't find: the con artist knows how to disappear quickly and totally.

Even though the chances of getting your money back may be slim, you still should take action if you believe you've been defrauded. If nothing else, your action may help put a stop to the fraud, thus benefiting your fellow citizens. And if they do the same, their actions will benefit you. Here are the main places to file complaints:

Federal Trade Commission

The Federal Trade Commission (FTC) is an agency that deals with deceptive business practices. FTC officials emphasize, however, that they do not represent individual consumers.

The FTC does not have the staff or the funds to investigate every complaint that comes to its attention. When there are enough complaints against a company, the investigative staff will look into it. If the FTC has reason to believe that a deceptive practice has occurred, the agency calls this to the attention of the alleged offender and attempts to work out a "consent order." A consent order is a document in which the alleged offender promises not to do what he has been accused of doing but does not admit that he was guilty of doing it. If he does violate the consent order, serious punishment can follow.

From the time that consumer complaints start trickling in until the time a consent order is obtained, many months can elapse. If an out-and-out fraudulent activity has been underway, the perpetrator may long since have vanished by the time the consent order is issued.

The FTC can function only if it gets input from the public. Although the victim of fraud may derive little direct benefit from reporting the case to the FTC, doing so does help the agency in its attempts to bring such practices to an end.

The Postal Service

Contact the Mail Fraud Division of the U.S. Postal Service if you suspect that the U.S. mails have been used to perpetrate a fraud. As with the FTC, the postal service cannot track down every complaint. The more complaints there are on a given matter, the better chance the Postal Service has of obtaining a satisfactory conclusion.

State and Local Governmental Agencies

All fifty states have some form of consumer protection office. Frequently, it's associated with the attorney general's office. Many large cities also have consumer protection agencies. As with the aforementioned federal agencies, lack of money deters these agencies from direct aid to the victim of a fraud, but they should be contacted anyway, immediately, and with all pertinent details. If there is any hope at all of apprehending the promoters, your local police or sheriff's office should also be contacted.

Your Local Newspapers and Broadcast Services

Newspapers, radio stations, and television channels throughout the nation have increasingly reported on consumer fraud. These reports are provided at considerable expense by the media as a public service. Very often they're able to resolve matters right on the spot.

Better Business Bureaus

Better Business Bureaus can be helpful before the fact. A call to your local BBB prior to a transaction might disclose whether the firm you're dealing with has a record of complaints with the bureau. BBB personnel might give you general guidelines as to types of suspect business endeavors. The BBB might also provide arbitration services to help you iron out a dispute you have with a local business. If you're dealing with a business located in another city, you should contact the Better Business Bureau in that city to determine whether the firm has a clean record. Understand that if a business has a clean record with the BBB, it does not necessarily mean that all is on the up and up. The clever con artists will know how to keep a BBB record clear and will also time activities cleverly enough so that he or she can be out of town before the complaints begin hitting the BBB office.

Financial Institutions

Banks, savings and loan associations, credit unions, and consumer finance companies are all actively involved on a day-to-day basis with the flow of IOUs generated from all kinds of business activities. If a deceptive practice is under way, an alert to these institutions could bring an end to the activity. Such institutions might be buying fraudulently induced IOUs, before anyone is aware that a fraud is in the works. The sooner the institutions know of it, the sooner they can stop buying the IOUs, and that can be the death knell for the fraudulent endeavor.

Your financial institution can also help you if you consult it before you sign any contracts. An astute loan officer might spot trouble that you missed.

Small Claims Court

Your local small claims court can assist in settling a claim of fraudulent or improper business practices *if* you can locate the party who has wronged you. Small claims courts differ from place to place, but, in general, you do not need a lawyer to represent you. If the amount of money involved in a claim exceeds the court's limit, it will not hear your case. Contact your local court to determine their rules and procedures.

YOUR BEST DEFENSE

No one is immune to the wiles of Snake Oil Sam. Your common sense is your best defense against losing money. To successfully manage your finances, heed the following cautions:

1. Analyze your needs and desires before you make a commitment to buy anything.
2. Obtain a basic knowledge of the product you're seeking to buy.
3. Compare the product you're interested in with that offered by other manufacturers and retailers.
4. Study carefully the guarantee behind the product, as well as the reputation of the manufacturer and retailer.

5. Realistically analyze your financial ability to buy the item, and shop carefully for financing arrangements.

6. Take prompt and appropriate action in the event the product or service does not live up to your expectations or to the representations made by the seller.

 PERSONAL ACTION WORKSHEET

Fraud-avoidance Techniques

This is a two-part exercise. First, answer the following questions—*before* you enter into any dealing with persons whose reputations are uncertain or unknown. Since you have read this chapter and answered the questions honestly, your choice should be clear.

Second, write down for future reference the telephone numbers of the indicated consumer protection sources.

1. If I'm not satisfied with the product or service I get from this person, what assurance do I have that I'll be able to get my money back?

   _____

2. Does this deal sound too good to be true or as though I'm going to be getting something for nothing? _____

3. Am I being pressured to sign up right away, or to buy right away, lest I lose the chance forever? _____

4. If the secret method (or investment technique, etc.) is so good, why is the salesperson selling it to me? Could it be that he or she will make more money by selling it to me than I can make by buying it?

   _____

5. Have I checked with the appropriate consumer protection sources to learn what I can about this company? _____

6. Do I really need the product or service that's being sold? And can I get it through other sources without any worry about satisfaction?

   _____

Consumer Protection Source	Telephone Number
❏ Better Business Bureau	_____
❏ City, state consumer protection agency	_____
❏ Small claims court	_____
❏ Consumer journalists (radio, TV, newspaper)	_____
❏ Federal Trade Commission (nearest office)	_____

CONSUMER ALERT

Learning to Say No Can Save $$$

Many good products are sold door-to-door, but there are also many flim-flams conducted in that mode. Your best protection is to learn how to say no. An old friend, best known as Sybil the Intrepid, had a way of saying no with such style and flair that anyone can benefit from her tactics. Here is how Sybil the Intrepid once handled a door-to-door vacuum cleaner sales-person:

Sybil: Oh, I've heard about your product, and I understand it's simply mar-velous. I'd like you to give me a demonstration right now, but first I must see your identity card.

Salesperson (enthusiastically):   No problem. Here's my card from the com-pany.

Sybil: No, that's not what I meant. I mean your *identity* card.

Salesperson (now slightly flustered and confused):   Well, here's my driver's li-cense . . . my voter registration card . . . my library card . . .

Sybil (deceptively calm):   No, no . . . those aren't what I mean. I mean your *identity* card. Your card that verifies that you aren't a member of the Commu-nist party.

Salesperson (now almost apoplectic):   But I've never heard of such a thing. I don't have such a card.

Sybil (with a straight face that would make your hair curl):   There, there now . . . that's all right. You just come back anytime with your proper identity card and I'd love to have you demonstrate your vacuum cleaner. We just can't let Communists in the house. You understand, I'm sure. 'Bye now. (The door closes ever so gently.)

UPS & DOWNS *The Economics of Everyday Life*

Why Scams Come and Go

Home improvement scams predominate in the spring and summer months. Holiday shopping cons and counterfeit goods are most evident in November and December. But many other kinds of fraudulent activities ebb and flow with changes in economic trends.

High interest rates and other conditions that make borrowing difficult—such as lenders going through an overly cautious phase—stimulate the advance fee loan scheme and similar abuses. Lenders offering "eeezee credit" pop up out of nowhere. Some demand fees up front; some charge exorbitant interest; some demand more collateral than need be pledged; some do all of the above. Be prepared for tough dealings if you don't pay it back as agreed.

Low interest rates, and/or rising inflation will spawn a host of investment scams. This is what the victims hear: "Because of today's low interest rates, your hard-earned savings accounts aren't paying you what they should. . . . And/or, rising inflation is eating up too much of your investment earnings. . . . Follow me, and I will lead you to investments with higher earnings and/or less erosion by inflation. . . . Trust me, for I am only interested in your well-being." At the very least, following that siren lure will result in your money being exposed to higher risk. At the worst, the money could disappear. If you leave your money where it is, in a safe harbor, it might not earn as much as it could, but at least it will be there when you need it.

Fads and trends can include collectibles such as plates, dolls, figurines, sports cards, and memorabilia. The more knowledgeable get in early, knowing how to buy and sell wisely. The more naive and gullible get in late, when the good bargains have been had, and the shysters are creating items for sale that will prove worthless.

Legal loopholes and lax enforcement The greatest financial debacle in American history—the savings and loan crisis—was largely the result of fraudulent appraisals and fraudulent accounting. It came about because of government laxity in regulating lenders' activities, and then its failure to stop the guilty parties quickly enough. The victims—American taxpayers—will foot the bill for a generation or two.

? *WHAT IF . . . ?*

How would you deal with these real life possibilities?

1. You learn that a friend is involved in a scam—not as a victim, but as a perpetrator. This person is naíve and without malice, but he or she can get into serious trouble if the authorities catch up with the con artists. Your friend is making good money in the endeavor and is unaware of the danger. How can you help your friend without exposing him or her to legal problems?

2. A stranger telephones you and very cleverly gets you to divulge your telephone credit card number or your bank credit card number. A few weeks later it dawn on you that you have blundered in giving out your number. What can/should you do to protect yourself against having unauthorized charges rung up on your account?

3. Your mail contains a packet announcing that you might have won $10 million in a Grand National Sweepstakes. You're encouraged to subscribe to magazines, but you need not make a purchase to win the prizes. However, you do subscribe to a few magazines, hoping that that will improve your changes of winning. When you do this, you alter your normal name slightly (spell out your middle name, for example, or misspell your last name) so you can trace how many other sucker lists your name will be sold to over the next year or two. Keep track. How many?

NUMBER CRUNCHERS

Do the calculations to make decisions in these real-life possibilities.

1. You receive a chain/pyramid letter instructing you to send $10 to the name at the top of the list of five names, then send copies of this letter to the other names, removing the name on top and putting yours at the bottom. Soon, the letter promises, as your name reaches the top of the list, you'll receive $10 from each of five other people—a total of $50 for your $10 investment. As each level of mailing multiplies the number of names by five, calculate how many levels there would be before every person living in your city would be on one of the lists. (Remember, this activity is illegal. Don't really do it. Just do the calculations.)

2. Identify a few "900" telephone pitches. (They abound on late-night cable TV stations and in tabloid newspapers.) Assume that each number receives 1,000 calls every day from all around the nation and that each call lasts 10 minutes. Based on their quoted rates, calculate how much revenue each "900" advertiser generates every day, week, month, and year.

FOR BETTER OR FOR WORSE

Things beyond our control often impact our personal and financial well-being, for better or for worse. Some are more predictable than others. How would you be affected if the following real-life phenomena happened? Could you have seen it coming? What steps could you have taken to minimize damage or maximize advantage? The better able you are to anticipate and recognize these forces, the better equipped you are to deal with them.

1. Hoping to reap a bonanza of thousands of dollars, you've put $300 into what turns out to be a pyramid scheme. The promoters promise to give you your money back, but before they do the police arrest them and bust the whole scam.

2. Interest rates have gone up, and banks are cutting back on their lending. You need to borrow $5,000 urgently. A stranger calls and tells you where you can get the money you need if you're willing to pay a small fee up front.

3. A site on the Web offers a hard-to-resist tip on the stock market. A friend of yours tells you she made a bundle on it.

5

Transportation: Buying, Financing, and Insuring Your Cars

You show me someone who's drowning in debt, and I'll show you someone who bought too much car, and whose payments for it are like concrete shoes.

Robert Rosefsky

Urban sprawl is a very accurate way of describing today's typical U.S. city, whether large or small. We have a lot of space to use, and we've used it. In the process, we've put a lot of distance between our homes, our places of work, our shopping centers, and our recreational facilities. The cost of moving about is a serious matter and must be taken into account in anyone's financial planning. This chapter will help you solve the common problems you face in trying to keep your transportation expenses in line:

- How to make the best choice when you buy a car
- How to deal with car dealers
- What kind of financing arrangement is best for you
- How much car insurance you should have, and how much it will cost
- What your car warranty is worth
- Leasing as an alternative to buying a car

THE COST OF GETTING FROM POINT A TO POINT B

The average cost of owning, financing, operating, and insuring an automobile is about 35¢ for each mile driven. This means:

- If you drive a mile or two to pick up a loaf of bread at the supermarket, the cost of getting to the market and back can be higher than the cost of the bread itself.
- That inexpensive treat of not so many years ago—the weekend drive in the country—can now cost you $20, $30, $40.
- If you drive a twenty-mile round-trip commute to work, it's costing you $35 per *week* to get to your job and back.

In short, driving from point A to point B is an expensive proposition. And new technology (air bags, anti-lock brakes, etc.) and new gadgets (cruise control, tilt steering wheels, etc.) continue to add to the cost.

Decades of conditioning have patterned much of our lives around the car: getting to work, shopping, school, recreation all depend largely on the availability of a car. In many cities, mass transit provides a less costly (and often less convenient) alternative. For the most daring, motorcycles and mopeds provide less costly (and less safe) transportation. For the energetic, bicycling, walking, and jogging may be the best alternatives of all.

For most people, driving is a major budget item, and an increase or decrease in driving can have a definite bearing on the budget. If you are choosing a dwelling or seeking a job, the cost of commuting must definitely be calculated.

As noted previously, a twenty-mile daily round-trip commute can cost $35 a week—$150 per month. That $150 per month in commuting costs is what you'd pay on $18,000 worth of mortgage at a 10 percent fixed annual interest rate. In other words, if you didn't have to drive to and from work, that $150 per month in commuting costs could be used to pay off an $18,000 higher mortgage on your home.

Your overall ability to make ends meet and manage your money prudently requires that you keep a tight control on all your transportation costs.

Figuring the Cost per Mile

The 35¢ per-mile figure noted earlier is, of course, an approximation. It's based on a small-sized car being driven 15,000 miles per year and kept for four years. It takes into account the following:

- The depreciation (difference between the purchase price and what it might be worth when you later sell it or trade it in)
- Operating and maintenance costs (including tune-ups, oil, tires, lubrication, and average necessary repairs)

- Operating and maintenance costs (including tune-ups, oil, tires, lubrication, and average necessary repairs)
- Interest (presuming that the car is financed for an average of three years)
- Taxes and fees (including sales tax, property taxes, registration, titling fee, license costs, necessary inspections)
- Insurance (public liability, collision, comprehensive)
- Gasoline (the amount can vary considerably, depending on your driving habits and the maintenance of your automobile)

The following factors will affect the cost per mile of driving your car:

Equipment

Cost, weight, and usage of optional equipment can have a distinct bearing on your overall operating costs. Example: An air-conditioning unit is one of the more expensive optional extras that can be installed in a car. The cost can exceed $700. In addition, the cost of registration, insurance, and interest will increase accordingly. The use of the air conditioning can also decrease your gas mileage by as much as 12 percent (see Table 5–1).

Maintenance

Proper, regular tuneups can improve your gas mileage by almost 13 percent (see Table 5–1). Proper tire inflation and rotation can also improve gas mileage as well as the overall ridability of the car. And a periodic troubleshooting checkup by a reliable garage can help prevent costly problems before they occur.

TABLE 5–1   How Speed, Air Conditioning, and Tuneups Can Affect Gas Mileage

Miles per Gallon	Speed				
	30 mph	40 mph	50 mph	60 mph	70 mph
With air conditioner on	18.14	17.51	16.42	15.00	13.17
With air conditioner off	20.05	19.71	18.29	16.23	14.18
MPG increase with air conditioner off	10.5%	12.6%	11.4%	8.33%	7.7%
Before tuneup	19.3	18.89	17.29	15.67	13.32
After tuneup	21.33	21.33	18.94	17.40	15.36
MPG increase after tuneup	10.5%	12.9%	9.54%	11.04%	15.3%

Source: U.S Department of Transportation, 1994.

Insurance

The number of cars on your auto policy, the number of drivers, and the safety record of the drivers can have a major effect on your car insurance costs. The section on car insurance later in this chapter explores these matters in greater detail.

Driving Habits

Hot-rodding, drag racing, speeding, and jackrabbit starting can diminish your gas mileage and also create more wear and tear on the basic mechanical aspects of the car. It may seem like fun, but it's going to cost you.

Knowledge

Knowing how to buy right, finance right, and insure right can definitely save you money. the more you know about the care and maintenance of your car, and the more of it that you can do yourself, the more money you'll save. A car care book or a short course in basic car maintenance can be an investment that pays for itself many times over each year.

BUYING A CAR

With individual tastes, habits, needs, and budgets as different as they are, there is no firm rule of thumb that describes the "best" buy for anyone's dollars. And with an almost infinite variety of cars to choose from—differing in age, condition, size, equipment, and cost—even general guidelines are difficult to set forth. The following considerations, however, weighed carefully as you shop, can help you find the vehicle that's right for your needs and for your budget.

Needs versus Desires

Exercise 5.1

You must clearly distinguish between your automotive *needs* and your automotive *desires*. The difference between the two can cost you thousands of dollars, with little to show for that money but some chrome, vinyl, and extra things that can go wrong in the car. For generations, American car buyers have been conditioned to believe that the automobile is a reflection of an individual's power, prestige, sex appeal, and success. If you can afford to succumb to that kind of hypnosis, feel free. The other side of the coin—never advertised by automotive manufacturers—is that when people find themselves in a financial jam, very often it's because they're paying far more for their car than their budget realistically can allow. If you're willing to sacrifice in other areas (housing, clothing, food, future savings, recreation) for the sake of a more luxurious car, that's your choice. Just be aware of the potential consequences.

In examining your automotive needs, be honest with yourself and with your budget. Three factors can boost the price of an automobile, and you must be careful that the price of your automobile does not exceed your ability to pay. These three factors are size, *flair,* and optional extras.

Size

How big a car do you really need for the bulk of your driving purposes? Larger cars cost more than comparably equipped smaller cars and can consume considerably more fuel. Can you justify a larger car because of your use of it—such as extensive traveling for business purposes or frequent hauling or children or cargo? If you don't need a large vehicle much of the time, consider purchasing a smaller car and renting a large vehicle for those rare occasions when you might need one.

Flair

Flair refers to the sportiness, the "muscle," the luxurious aspects of driving that many people crave. Make no mistake—flair is very expensive, and it won't get you from point A to point B any more safely or quickly than a basic set of wheels will. Your choice. Your money.

Optional Extras

In fact, optional extras aren't really optional. They're already built into the car, and you can't have them taken out. Optional extras can add $3,000 and more to the basic cost of the car, and many of them may be of marginal value. Racing stripes, fancy wheel covers, vinyl roofs, luxurious upholstery,

and an assortment of electronic gadgets provide very little in the way of essential transportation. In many cases, they just provide something extra to break down and need repair, usually after the warranty has expired.

New versus Used

Exercise 5.2

A used car in good mechanical condition can provide you with decent transportation for many years and many tens of thousands of miles—at a much lower cost than a similar new model. Note the qualification "in good mechanical condition." A prerequisite to buying a used car is a thorough analysis by a responsible mechanic. The buyer of a used car has no way of knowing what accidents or operating problems the car had in the past. The seller may not divulge all that is known about the car's history. Indeed, if the car has had more than one prior owner, the current owner may not have any idea about the car's history. The cost of a thorough inspection can be a very inexpensive way of finding out whether you're getting a good or a bad deal, but the bad deal will end up costing you many times what the inspection will cost.

If you buy a used car from a private individual, you'll take it on an as-is basis, unless the seller agrees to some sort of private warranty, which should be in writing. See the discussion on warranties, later in this chapter, for details on used car warranties.

Shopping Criteria

Since this textbook is devoted to money handling and not car handling, we'll leave the details of road testing and comfort testing up to the individual reader. Here are some of the financial considerations to be borne in mind when shopping for a new car.

STRATEGIES FOR SUCCESS

Alternative Sources of Good Used-car Buys

Used-car dealers and private parties are the common places to buy used cars. The dealers can be expensive. The private parties might not reveal hidden defects. (Dealers might also hide hidden defects, but reputable ones frequently offer at least some minimum warranty, which can give you some protection.) You could do better on a used-car purchase at a car rental agency's disposal lot. Major agencies, such as Hertz and Avis, sell rental cars to the public after they've been driven for a certain distance and time. These cars may have been better maintained than privately owned cars, and they may have decent warranties. Check wholesalers, too: middlemen who take trade-ins from new-car dealers and sell them to used-car lots. Don't expect any warranties, but the price might be right.

Exercise 5.3

After you've decided what pleases you with respect to size, color, equipment, and handling, refer to the Personal Action Checklist at the end of this chapter for a guide to what you'll get for your money. In addition to the base price, list separately each optional extra and its cost. This will cause you to stop and think twice about the value of those extras and will also give you a better comparison of the total product you're getting for your money.

The dealer will quote you a price that's different from the sticker price, taking into account the value of any car you are trading in. Haggling over the price of a new car is still one of the great old American traditions. The dealers almost expect that you'll haggle, and, if you don't, you could be spending hundreds of dollars more than you have to.

Don't guess: Be precise with each dealer's offerings with respect to warranty, extended service contracts, insurance, and financing terms.

To the extent possible, check the dealer's reputation in the community for service and adjustment of complaints. With respect to service, determine whether he offers pick-up and drop-off when the car is taken in for work, and whether the dealer has loan cars available, and at what price, in case you have to leave your own car there for an extended period.

Games Dealers Play

The automobile business is extremely competitive. Competitiveness breeds anxiety, and that, in turn, may cause dealers to bend the ethics of good business practices in order to win a sale. Some of these practices are illustrated in the following tale. Try to spot the pitfalls as they occur.

You're planning to buy a car, and you've set your heart on a Rammer-Jammer XJKB. You've priced it at two dealerships, which are within a few dollars of each other, and about $4,000 in cash will be required over your old trade-in. You want to try one more dealership, which advertises heavily that they will "meet or beat any deal in town."

You and your spouse take a drive to that dealership one evening. A pleasant chap takes you for a test-drive of the model you've been admiring. You're very impressed with the seeming honesty of this nice fellow, and you're intrigued when he suggests that the trade-in value of your old car might be $1,000 more than what other dealers have quoted you! He explains that this dealer's inventory of used cars is very low and he's offering better deals on trade-ins to build up his inventory. What's more, he thinks the boss has been overcharging too many customers, and he doesn't like people to get a raw deal. Thus, he tells you, he's going to take it upon himself to see that you get the best possible deal available.

He takes you into his office to do some calculating. After a few moments, he looks up at you with a smile. "If I can get the boss to take $3,000 plus your trade-in, would you sign the contract tonight?"

STRATEGIES FOR SUCCESS

Get Price Quotes in Writing

If you're quoted a price on an automobile, have the salesperson put it in writing. Make sure it's adequately detailed, including any extras, financing terms, down payment, and so on that may be part of the deal. And be certain to have the salesperson indicate—again, in writing—how long this price quote will last. If you go out comparison shopping and return to the original dealer two hours later, you don't want to be told, "Sorry, that price quote was good for only 10 minutes." If they won't put the quote in writing, you have nothing to go on later. And, if they won't put it in writing, maybe it's because they don't want to have to honor it. What does that tell you?

Three thousand! You were almost willing to pay $4,000 for exactly the same car at a different showroom. Of course you'd be willing to take a deal for $3,000. The salesman spots your enthusiasm and proceeds.

"Look," he says, " the boss doesn't like me to approach him unless he's sure the customer will take the deal. Let me fill out the contract showing a $3,000 trade difference, and you give me a good faith check for $50. That way, he knows he's got a firm deal *if* he signs the contract. If he doesn't go for the deal, I'll give you back the contract and your check and you can rip them both up. What have you go to lose?"

You've got nothing to lose, or so you think. You're sitting there planning how you can spend the $1,000 you've just saved and itching to get behind the wheel of the new car that's just a signature away.

"Okay," you say, "fill out the contract and I'll sign it."

He leaves the room with the signed contract and the check, and you and your spouse sit and snicker over the tremendous deal you're getting. "I was ready to pay $4,000, and we're stealing it for $3,000," you say. (There's a little bit of larceny in all of us.)

You sit and wait for 10, then 20, minutes. Just as you're about out of patience, the man sticks his head in the door and says, "I think everything is okay. I'm going to take the car to the service department and get it ready so you can take it home tonight if you want."

Another man enters the room. He is the assistant boss. He tells you that he appreciates how anxious you are to get into that new car. But, sadly, there seems to have been a snag. The pleasant man that you were so fond of has been doing a lousy job for the dealer. As a matter of fact, the assistant boss continues, it seems as though he was off by $1,000 on your deal. He vastly overestimated the value of your trade-in. "We'd love to have you in this car because I know you want to be in it," the assistant boss says, "but we've just got to talk about a $4,000 trade difference, not $3,000." The bubble has burst.

"In the first place," the assistant boss goes on, "we didn't even give your trade car a test-drive. Let me have the keys to it so our service manager can check it out and give you a fair trade-in price." Bewildered, you hand over your keys, and he disappears with them.

You and your spouse debate the matter in the closing room and agree that if you can strike a deal between $3,500 and $4,000, you'd still go for it since it would be better than any of the other quotes you'd been given.

The assistant boss reappears with your contract and you tear it up. "Where's my $50 check?" you ask. "Don't worry," he says, "I'll get it for you in a few minutes. Now, about your deal," he begins. "We've given your trade-in a good look, and it needs a lot of work and new tires. A good deal for us would be $4,300 plus your trade-in, but, since you've been here so long and have been so patient, we can bend some and let you have the new Rammer-Jammer for $4,100."

The grind is beginning to wear you down. You're starting to wonder when you're going to get back your $50 check and the keys to your old car. You're tense now, but you feel that you can get the deal for $3,900, which is still $100 better than the next best deal. You discuss it with your spouse and decide that since you've been here this long, you might as well hang around a little longer and hope the deal can be wrapped up for $3,900.

A few minutes later, salesman number three comes in. This is the boss, and he's high pressure all the way. The hour is getting later, and you're getting more and more tired. The boss now is pushing hard to close you at $4,050, which, as he says, "I'm losing money on."

Then comes the clincher. You again demand your check and your keys, and he informs you that the cashier has left for the night and the check has been locked up. The used-car appraiser has also left for the night and, thinking that your old car had been accepted as a trade-in, he parked it in the lot and locked up the keys in his office. "Don't worry," says the boss, "we can give you a ride home tonight and pick you up in the morning to get your old car and the check. I assure you, there's absolutely no problem. Now, about this deal. . . "

The final thrust: "Look folks, I know how late it's getting, and I want to get out of here as badly as you do. Let me ask you this—if I give you the deal for $4,000, will you take it? Then we'll all go out and have a drink." Resignation has set in, and you agree to the deal. After all, it's still as good as the best deal you had any other place. Wearily, you reach for your pen.

Interwoven throughout this intrigue are four types of sales tactics (Did you recognize them?), which have brought a poor reputation to a small segment of the automobile sales industry. These are:

The Highball

The salesman quotes a much higher trade-in value on your old car than is reasonable, which causes the first strong opening pull on your purse strings. The opposite of the highball is the lowball, in which the salesman looks at the sticker price on the new car and suggests a too-good-to-be-true discount from that price. The tactic here is to lead you to believe that you're going to get a better deal than you thought possible, all the quicker to get you into the showroom where the heavy pressure can be applied.

The "T.O." or "Takeover" Operation

This is a ploy involving a succession of salespeople ranging from low pressure to high pressure. The first one's job is to soften you and win your confidence. Subsequent salespeople increase the pressure until the closer takes over. The process is designed to wear down your resistance gradually. The first salesman's job was accomplished when he got you to sit down in the closing office, not just in a mood to buy, but with a raging desire to buy, albeit at a price that would later turn out to be impossible. The success of the takeover operation depends on the next phenomenon.

The Bugged Closing Room

It doesn't occur to most people that a closing room might be bugged. This is a devious trick and is not employed by a legitimate dealer. By listening in on your conversations, salespeople know where your soft spots are and how far they can take you. If they determine that you have strong sales resistance, they can always fall back on the following.

The "Disappearing Check" Trick or the "Keys are Locked Up for the Night" Gambit

This is the last straw. By claiming to have "misplaced" something of value, such as a check or car keys, salespeople are, in effect, nailing you to the wall until your resistance breaks. The best way to avoid being trapped in this manner is not to write any checks and to stand by as they test your trade-in car so you can retain the keys until the deal is either made or not made.

If you fall prey to these tactics in your car shopping, you might sign a contract you otherwise wouldn't sign. Even though, in the above case, you thought you got the same deal you could have had elsewhere, that isn't necessarily so. Had you gone back to the other dealers for a follow-up bargaining session, you might have gotten a still better deal. Awareness of these tricks and a willingness to walk away from shady tactics are necessary weapons when shopping for a car. The dealer sells hundreds of cars each month. You buy only one every few years. He knows a lot more about the tricks of bargaining and striking a deal than you do. He's entitled to a fair profit, but that doesn't give him the right to take advantage of you—all of which leads back to the most important point: Know the person with whom you are dealing. There's no substitute for integrity.

Your Old Car: Selling It Yourself versus Trading It In

Exercise 5.4

It's difficult to determine whether you can do better by selling your own used car or by using it as a trade-in on a new purchase. First, check the used-car price directory and used-car lots to see what cars similar to yours are selling for (see Table 5–2). The directory is available at all dealerships and at most banks. Bear in mind that the prices on cars at lots are the asking prices, not necessarily the selling prices. If you can find a buyer who will pay your price, it may be wise to make a deal. But before do, you must go to various dealers to determine the different prices you'd be expected to pay with and without a trade-in.

If you can't find a buyer quickly, you might be in for more headaches than the project is worth. You'll have to advertise the car for sale, and you'll have to be available when interested buyers want to take it for a test-drive. Not only could that be inconvenient; you could feel uncomfortable having a stranger take your car for a good long test-spin.

The way in which sales taxes are calculated can make a big difference in whether you should sell your old car on your own or trade it in to a dealer. You must determine these matters for your locale. (1) If you sell to a private party, are local sales taxes payable? (2) If you trade the car to a dealer and buy a new one, is the sales tax figured on the total cost of the new car, or on the difference between the cost of the new car and the trade-in value of the old car? For example, say the price of a new car is $12,000, the trade-in value of your old car is $4,000, and the sales tax is 7 percent. If the sales tax is figured on the price of the new car, the tax will be $840. If it's figured on the difference ($8,000), the tax will be $560. Do your research accordingly.

How Much Haggling Room Do You Have?

There is no rule of thumb, but here are some broad guidelines. Your haggling room will depend on the value of your trade-in, whether you're fi-

TABLE 5–2   Abbreviated Listing from Typical Used-Car Price Directory as of Summer 1997

1995 Chevrolet Model	Trade-In	Market
Cavalier 6 cylinder 2-door convertible	$9,170	$11,185
Corsica 4 cylinder 4-DR sedan	6,000	7,225
Lumina V6 4-door sedan	8,565	10,320
Camaro V8 Z28 2-door convertible	11,815	14,065

Note: Optional extras, destination charges, preparation charges, taxes, and licensing fees not included. Average wholesale and retail prices are for clean, reconditioned cars ready for sale. See separate listings in directory for increase/decreases in price due to equipment, condition, and mileage.

nancing through the dealer (see the next section, "Financing"), and how anxious the dealer is to move his current inventory. Generally speaking, dealers work on a mark-up of about 20 percent. Thus, it might not be unreasonable to expect a discount of 5 to 10 percent off the sticker price. To get much more than 10 percent is going to take some hard bargaining, but if you don't ask for it, they're not going to volunteer it. *Consumer Reports* magazine publishes annual price listings of new model cars, which can serve as a more specific guideline to your bargaining powers. Consult these lists before you go shopping.

When Is the Best Time to Buy?

Late summer and early fall tend to be when dealers are clearing out their old inventory to make room for the new model cars shipped from the factories. There may be a smaller assortment of cars to choose from at this time of year, but there's a strong chance that you will get a better price than you might have earlier in the model year.

This is also a time when dealers tend to sell their demonstrator models—cars that have been driven by employees of the dealership. Demos can be very good bargains. They tend to be well equipped and well taken care of, and many dealerships offer them with full warranty, even though they have been driven for a few thousand miles or more.

FINANCING: DIRECT VERSUS THROUGH THE DEALER

Assuming you have the necessary trade-in or down payment and acceptable credit, most dealers can arrange financing for you right on the spot. You can also make your own financing arrangements through your bank (and in many instances, your car insurance company). Which is better?

It can be very convenient to have the dealer arrange for the financing. It saves you time, but it can cost you extra money. Determine the Annual Percentage Rate (APR) the dealer will charge you for the financing. (See chapter 12 for a more detailed discussion of interest rates and installment loans.)

Exercise 5.5

Compare the dealer's APR with that offered by other lenders. The APR is the apples versus apples way of comparing interest rates. Have any APR quote put in writing and signed by the salesperson. If the dealer is charging more for financing, then obviously it wouldn't pay to borrow through the dealership unless there are extenuating circumstances, such as a desire not to increase your borrowing any further at your regular bank.

Dealers can receive benefits from lenders worth hundreds of dollars, depending on the amount of financing involved. Thus, dealers are anxious to arrange financing for you. If you play the game advantageously, you'll let the dealer believe that you're going to do the financing through him before you make a commitment to purchase the car. This is liable to result in a lower price for the car, since the dealer will anticipate additional profit through the financing. He may, if he suspects your wise buymanship tactics, give you two prices for the car—one if you finance with them; one if you don't. Act accordingly.

Another important advantage in dealing with your own bank is that you are dealing with people who know you and who can help you, should problems arise. If the dealer arranges the financing for you, it may be with a bank or finance company you've never dealt with. In such a case, if you run into problems with lateness or other financial distress, the institution is liable to regard you as little more than a number in their computer, and any help may be hard to come by.

Interest Rate and Rebate Incentives

Exercise 5.6

Dealers often offer incentive plans involving either low interest rates for financing or cash rebates, which will reduce the price of the car. When such opportunities are available, it can be wise to examine their benefits. But the incentives do not necessarily get you the best all-around deal. The incentives might be available on only a limited number of models. And there may be little or no room for haggling over the price on such models. In short, you might end up spending more for a car then you otherwise would have in order to get the incentives.

Wherever you arrange your financing, it's essential that you do not allow the loan to last longer than you expect to own the car. If you expect to trade every three years, you shouldn't finance for more than three years. (See the section on "Credit Abuses" in chapter 12 on how this timing of your loans can be important to you.)

Leasing as an Alternative to Buying

Exercise 5.7

Leasing has become an extremely popular way to acquire a new car. As previously leased cars come back onto the market—when the leases expire and the roughly 75 percent of lessees choose to return the cars to the dealers rather than buy them—there is also a dynamic business in the leasing of used cars.

The main good and bad points of leasing new cars are well known:

- **Basic cost**   Leased cars generally involve a lower down payment and lower monthly payments than purchased cars. But the small print in the leasing ads and contracts can narrow the gap. Read it with care, and add up all the numbers. Note that leasing is subject to a more stringent credit review than normal financing.
- **Purchase option**   At the end of the lease, which may run from two to five years, you'll have an option to buy the car. In a "closed end" lease, which is the most common type, the purchase price will be spelled out in advance. In an "open end" lease the purchase price will

depend on market conditions. Make sure you have the option you want specified in writing. If you don't want to purchase the car you can just walk away from it, after paying any applicable costs noted in the next paragraph.

- **Unanticipated costs**   If you want to end a lease before the term is up you might have to pay a hefty early termination fee. Also, whenever you do turn the car in, you have to absorb the cost of any repairs needed—including dings, dents, scrapes, stains, scratches—which can add many hundreds of dollars to your expense. In addition, if you drive the car more miles than the lease allows (usually about 15,000 miles a year) you have to pay an excess mileage fee, which might be 10 to 15 cents a mile.

- **Tax considerations**   If you lease a car for personal use, the lease payments are not tax deductible. Neither is the interest on your car loan if the car is for personal use. (A possible exception: If you buy a car with the proceeds of a home equity loan the interest may be deductible. See chapter 12 for more details.) Cars used for business purposes may offer some deductibility for either lease or interest costs. See your tax advisor for the latest regulations.

One of the problems with leasing cars has been the complexities of the lease contracts and the way in which leasing is advertised. Too much misleading information and consumer abuse resulted in an outpouring of complaints from the public. To combat this problem, the Federal Trade Commission issued new regulations that went into effect in October 1997 designed to clarify the language in leasing contracts. All dealers' lease plans must conform to this simple one-page form. Items covered include the specific amounts of down payments and monthly payments, any other charges that are part of the deal, the value of any trade-in, and clear language warning of any early termination penalties that must be paid. The new form will not be required for leases totalling more than $25,000, so *buyer beware* is the order of the day for anyone signing up for the big-ticket items. Others should review this FTC-mandated contract carefully before it's signed.

WARRANTIES

Many manufacturers now offer *limited warranties* on new cars extending for as long as seven years. These limited warranties generally cover the basic drive train and transmission in the car. Many other items, such as power windows, windshield wipers, radio, and dashboard circuits, may still be restricted to a twelve months or 12,000-mile limitation, whichever comes first.

The matter is further confused by the availability of additional warranties that extend beyond the basic manufacturer's warranty. Some of these plans are offered by the manufacturers themselves, and others are offered by private insurance companies. These extra warranties can cost hundreds of dollars, depending on how many miles and/or how many months they run. Often, the price of these warranties can be negotiated along with the price of the automobile. If you are mechanically inclined or know a good, trustworthy mechanic, the extended warranties may be of less value to you. If you're a novice when it comes to dealing with a broken-down car, the warranty might give you peace of mind. The best bet of all: Take an automotive repair course at your local community college, or buy one of the many good guidebooks on automotive repair. This might not enable you to do your own repairs, but at least you'll be able to determine whether an item can be fixed at minimal cost or whether the $700 estimate the garage gives you is an honest one.

Used car warranties from dealers have traditionally been limited to thirty days, which offers little protection to buyers. Some have no warranties at all: you take the car as-is.

But many manufacturers now have extended warranties for used cars, particularly for the growing number of formerly leased cars that are being returned to dealerships. Before these expanded warranties are offered, the cars are refurbished as needed, and thusly certified by the dealer. The cost of the refurbishment and the cost of the warranty will be passed along to the buyer. Also, in some cases, buyers must pay a certain portion—a deductible per repair—as part of the deal. The warranties are further limited to cars of a certain age or maximum mileage. In other words, if a car's age or mileage exceeds the set limit, it will not be eligible for the expanded warranty.

Table 5–3 illustrates a sampling of expanded warranties that may be available on certified used cars. Note that the length of the expanded warranties differs considerably from maker to maker. What does this program offer? By paying for the refurbishment and the warranty on an older car, you could get a lot more vehicle for the same money as you'd pay for a new car, and with a reasonably good warranty standing behind it. For example, you might get an older certified Lexus or Infiniti for the same price you'd pay for a new Chevrolet. The choice might not be easy to make, but at least there is a choice.

TABLE 5–3   Used Car Warranties from Selected Manufacturers in Late 1997

Make	Maximum Age/Mileage	Expanded Warranty	Deductible
Ford	3 yrs./50,000 mi.	1 yr./12,000 mi.	$100
G.M.*	3 yrs./60,000 mi	1 yr./12,000 from purchase or 4 yrs/50,000 mi. total	-0-
Toyota**	4 yrs./55,000 mi.	6 yrs./100,000 mi.	$ 50
Honda	3 yrs./60,000 mi.	6 yrs./72,000 mi.	-0-
Volvo	5 yrs./75,000 mi.	1 yr./12,000 mi.	$ 50
Acura	4 yrs./50,000 mi.	5 yrs./62,000 mi.	-0-

*Includes Buick, Chevrolet, Geo, GMC, Oldsmobile, and Pontiac.
**Warranty is on power train only. Broader coverage available at extra cost.

AUTOMOBILE INSURANCE

Automobile insurance protects you against the hazards inherent in owning and using an automobile—damage to the machine itself, and damage it may cause others for which you may be responsible. Each state requires motorists to maintain a minimum level of financial responsibility against their being involved in an automobile accident. Most commonly, this minimum responsibility is met by obtaining an automobile insurance policy that includes the all-important public liability protection.

Types of Coverage

Exercise 5.8

The typical automobile insurance policy packages many different types of insurance together. These types of coverage are as follows.

Public Liability for Bodily Injury

This is the single most important financial aspect of your automotive insurance policy, and possibly of your entire personal insurance program. Should your car injure or kill other people, this coverage will defend you against claims and will pay, up to the limits of coverage, any claims for which you're found to be legally responsible. Coverage is generally in two phases, one for injury to a single individual involved in an accident and a second phase for all individuals involved. The limits of coverage are usually expressed as follows: $10,000/$20,000. This coverage would protect you for up to $10,000 worth of claim from any single individual and for up to $20,000 for all parties injured in the accident. The amount of protection you choose is up to you. You may have to comply with a minimum required by your state, which may be as low as $10,000/$20,000 (more commonly expressed as 10/20). Or, if you are prudent and aware of the potential circumstances, you might choose much higher limits, perhaps as high as $100,000/$300,000, or even higher if it's available. The difference in cost between the minimal coverage and the more extensive coverage is only a few dollars per month—an investment that many would have a hard time turning down.

Public Liability for Property Damage

If your automobile causes damage to the property of others, this coverage will defend you against claims and will pay claims for which you are found to be legally responsible. The limit of coverage is usually expressed as a number following the limits for bodily injury liability. For example, public liability limits of 25/50/10 would mean that your property damage liability limits are $10,000 (following the bodily injury limits of $25,000 and $50,000).

In this case, if you caused injury to the property of others, you would be protected for up to $10,000 of such damage.

Property damage liability covers damage to the property of *others*—not to your own property. It can include damage to the automobiles of others or damage to buildings. Property damage coverage will usually not be less than $5,000, and a ceiling of $50,000 should be adequate in most situations, unless you crash into a new Rolls-Royce or career through a commercial building.

Your public liability protection for bodily injury and property damage will cover you in your own car or if you're driving someone else's car, as well as covering other persons who drive your car with your permission. It also provides legal defense for claims made against you.

Medical Payments

If you, or members of your household or guests who are driving in your car, are injured while driving (or even struck while walking), the medical payments provision will reimburse all reasonable actual medical expenses arising out of the accident up to the limits of the policy. Generally, these payments will be made regardless of who was at fault. The minimum may be as low as $500, but much greater coverage than that can be obtained at a reasonable added annual cost. As with the public liability portions of the coverage, the prudent motorist does well to consider taking much higher than minimal limits on the medical payments provisions, for the added extra cost is small indeed compared with the immediate protection obtained.

Uninsured Motorists

Regrettably, not everyone who drives an automobile is properly insured. You might be caused serious harm by a motorist with little or no insurance protection. You could be out tens of thousands of dollars in medical expenses and lost income, and the party at fault may have little or no money with which to reimburse you for the damage. Although the courts may find the person legally responsible for making payments to you, you may never be able to recover. Uninsured motorist protection is designed to take care of this problem, providing you with reimbursement for your losses through your own insurance company.

Recent statistics from the National Association of Insurance Commissioners reveal that a shocking number of drivers are not insured. Table 5–4 illustrates the percentage of uninsured motorists in a sampling of states.

These figures may actually *understate* the number of uninsured drivers, since many drivers will obtain insurance in order to register their cars and then let the insurance lapse when payments are due on it. These lapsed policies may not show up in the count of "insured" drivers.

TABLE 5–4   **Uninsured Drivers in Selected States**

State	% of Drivers Uninsured
Alabama	24%
California	24%
Florida	31%
Illinois	19%
Maine	15%
Missouri	15%
Oklahoma	15%
Texas	18%

Unfortunately we don't have a choice as to who might cause us harm in an automobile. It could be an adequately insured individual, or it could be an uninsured individual, or a hit-and-run driver we will never see again. This form of protection is quite inexpensive, and the motorist is assuming an unnecessary risk by not having it.

Comprehensive Insurance

This is a broad form of protection for loss caused other than by collision. It includes loss due to theft and damage to your car due to fire, glass breakage, riots, windstorm, hail, and other causes. Limited protection on contents is also available. Deductibles are common in such policies. If the deductible is, for example, $50, the motorist will have to pay the first $50 worth of any such loss, and the insurance company will pay for damages over the deductible amount. Check your policy to determine whether you are protected against theft if you leave your car unattended and/or unlocked. Some policies will not protect the motorist under these circumstances.

Collision Insurance

This coverage protects you against damage done to your own car, should you be in a collision with another car or an object such as a telephone pole or a building. Collision insurance usually carries a deductible. If car A and car B collide and the accident was the fault of the driver of car A, his or her property liability insurance will pay for the damage to the owner of car B, and the collision insurance covering car A will pay for the damage to car A. Collision protection tends to be fairly expensive. If you're driving a car more than five or six years old, the cost of collision protection might be so high that it discourages you from maintaining collision insurance in view of the limited recovery you can expect on an older car. Weigh the cost and the protection accordingly.

How Much Will It Cost?

Exercise 5.9

The cost of automobile insurance can vary considerably depending on the age, safety record, and occupation of the owner, and the purposes for which the car is used. Younger drivers have to pay a higher rate for their automotive insurance, primarily because those drivers have a generally bad statistical record for accidents and claims. Some companies will offer discounts for drivers with safe records and for younger persons who have taken driver education courses. Other discounts may be available where more than one car is insured and where compact cars are involved. In shopping for the best automobile insurance all available discounts should be inquired about from each agent.

The amount of the deductibles have a bearing on the total premium cost. As with deductibles in other forms of personal insurance, you are assuming a higher risk in exchange for paying a lower premium. The premium saved is an actual saving, whereas the higher risk may never occur.

If You Are in an Accident

If you are in an automobile accident, you should obtain the following information from the other party: the driver's name and license number, the plate number of the automobile, and the insurance policy number covering the other driver. The other driver will expect the same information from you. Depending on the extent of personal injury or property damage, a police report may or may not be taken. Also determine whether your state requires a detailed report to be filed with the state department of motor vehicles. Notify your insurance company at the earliest possible time. Your own insurance company can arrange for you to have your car repaired; they will later recover the amount for the repairs from the other driver's insurance company if the other driver was at fault.

If you were at fault and the other driver is paid for a claim against your insurance policy, that might result in an increase in your insurance rates. You might prefer to pay for the other party's costs directly rather than incur higher insurance premiums for the next few years. Discuss this possibility with your insurance agent before you proceed either way.

If injuries or damages are extensive, there may be a lawsuit by one driver against the other. Some states have no-fault laws, which allow a determination as to who can receive what payments, regardless of who might have been at fault in the accident. In other states, it might take a jury trial to determine who was at fault and what damages should be paid to the injured party. It could take years before such claims are heard by a jury. In reality, most such claims are settled out of court by the parties within a few months after the accident.

Personal injury lawyers who represent injured parties usually take 30 to 40 percent of recoveries as their fee, plus out-of-pocket expenses. Such fees are based on the amount you receive over and above your own medical and repair expenses. In other words, if you retain a lawyer who is able to get you an award of $10,000 for your pain and suffering, you may end up netting $6,000. And it might take you many months before you can get that much. On the other hand, you might be able to negotiate on your own with the other insurance company for $3,000 to $5,000. That would be cash right on the spot, compared with an unknown amount that you might or might not receive many months later. In short, the personal injury lawyer can be helpful where circumstances indicate more severe injuries, lost work time, extensive suffering, and so on.

Automobile Clubs

Another form of worthwhile insurance can be obtained through automobile clubs. For a modest annual fee, these clubs provide towing insurance, which will get your car to a service station at no out-of-pocket cost to you should your car break down on the road. Auto club insurance can also provide you with bail in the event of arrest; travel services are an added plus included with the price of the annual premium.

CAR POOLING

It can definitely pay to become involved in a car pool. Whether you're car-pooling to work, to pick up and deliver children at school, or even to shop at a supermarket, there can be considerable saving in the cost of operating your automobile. Table 5–5, based on a U.S. Department of Transportation study, gives some examples of the annual savings that can be realized by continuous participation in a car pool.

TABLE 5–5   Annual Car-Pool Savings

Round-trip Commute (Miles)	Type of Car	Cost of Driving Alone	Cost of Shared-driving Car pool	
			2 Persons	4 Persons
20	Subcompact	$944	$517	$282
20	Standard	1,380	756	410
40	Subcompact	1,640	933	517
40	Standard	2,414	1,369	756
80	Subcompact	2,852	1,625	933
80	Standard	4,226	2,397	1,369

Projected savings, based on $.35 per mile cost, as described earlier. Savings reflect the fact that all the parties in the car pool own and maintain a car.

CAR RENTAL

Aside from the commonplace airport and hotel car rental agencies used with business travel and tourism, car renting is increasingly popular with residents of cities where the ownership and parking of automobiles is costly and inconvenient. There are a number of major national rental firms with computerized reservation services and garage facilities well located in most major cities. These include Hertz, Avis, National, Dollar, Budget, and Thrifty. There are hundreds of smaller firms that, because they don't have the high advertising and rental overheads, can offer lower prices on rentals.

Rental Terms

Whatever your rental needs, it definitely pays to shop around for the best deal. Many rental firms regularly offer discounts at special times of the week, month, or year. Discounts are also available through auto clubs and through a corporate account that your company may have with one of the major rental firms.

Rental plans vary considerably. Most popular are those that charge a fixed amount per day which includes unlimited mileage or you may pay a fixed amount per day plus an added amount per mile. In both cases, the customer pays for gasoline used. If you can determine the number of miles you expect to drive you can figure which of these two plans would be cheaper.

The major rental firms allow you to pick up a car in one city and leave it in another. Depending on the cities involved, there may be a drop-off charge. Determine in advance what drop-off charges will be connected with intercity usage.

Rental Car Insurance

Car rental firms also offer you two different types of protection: collision and medical. The typical car rental contract states that you are responsible for the first $1,000 or $2,000, or more, of any damage to the car as a result of a collision, such as your running the car into a tree. The rental company will offer what's known as a collision damage waiver (CDW) for roughly $8 to $12 per day. If you pay for this collision damage waiver, that clears you of the responsibility of paying that initial amount in case of a collision. However, for the CDW to be effective, you must be using the car in accordance with the strict terms of the rental agreement. If the collision occurs when an unauthorized driver is at the wheel or when the use of the car is unauthorized, you may lose the advantage of the collision damage waiver. Your own personal auto insurance policy may cover you for some of these expenses. Check with your auto insurance agent to be sure. In addition, some major credit card companies now cover these expenses if the rental is charged on their card.

Also, ask your agent the extent of your protection for medical expenses if you are injured while driving a rental car. If you are comfortable with the protection you already have, either on your auto policy or your own health insurance program, it may not be wise to spend the extra money for the car rental company's medical insurance protection.

PERSONAL ACTION WORKSHEET

Car Shopping Comparison

Use this checklist to help you compare offerings from various dealers. Remember, the price of the car itself is not the only factor that determines how good the deal is.

	Dealer A	Dealer B	Dealer C
❏ Base price of car	_____	_____	_____
❏ Cost of operational extras (list items separately) _____ _____ _____	_____	_____	_____
❏ Dealer prep, delivery charges	_____	_____	_____
❏ Total sticker price	_____	_____	_____
❏ Trade allowance on your old car	_____	_____	_____
❏ Trade difference: new car cost less trade-in	_____	_____	_____
❏ Sales tax and license cost	_____	_____	_____
❏ How long will this offer be good?	_____	_____	_____
❏ Financing: What APR is offered?	_____	_____	_____
❏ Insurance: If offered, terms and cost	_____	_____	_____
❏ Reputation for fair dealing	_____	_____	_____
❏ Reputation for service and adjustment of complaints	_____	_____	_____
❏ Convenience in getting to and from when service is needed	_____	_____	_____
❏ If buying a used car: physical condition mechanical condition extent of warranty	_____ _____ _____	_____ _____ _____	_____ _____ _____
❏ Treatment by sales person	_____	_____	_____

CONSUMER ALERT

Service Station Sharpies Commit Highway Robbery

Most service station operators are honorable and reliable businesspeople. Sad, then, that a few sharpies smudge the reputation of an otherwise honest industry.

Long-distance travelers are particularly vulnerable to these tactics—far from home, in strange territory, they stop for gas and find themselves facing such money-gouging abuses as

- **Tire "Honking"** While you're not looking, a swift kick at your tire with a boot that has a sharp nail point embedded in the toe gives you a sudden flat and a sales pitch to buy a costly new tire.
- **Slashing** A few quick slices with a well-hidden razor blade can destroy a fan belt or a radiator hose in an instant.
- **The White Smoke Trick** The attendant sprays a few drops of a chemical on your hot engine, and a cloud of white smoke erupts. It's actually harmless, but you're then susceptible to a pitch for costly engine repairs—which, of course, aren't needed in the first place.
- **Bubbling Battery** Drop a few grains of Alka-Seltzer, or the like, into a battery and watch it bubble over. The unwary will find themselves paying for a new battery before they have time to say "plop, plop, fizz, fizz."
- **Shocking Shocks** A few dribbles of oil under the shock absorbers is enough to convince many drivers that the absorbers need replacement. The same can hold true for the transmission and so on.

The common ploy following any of these tactics is a statement by the attendant that "you ought not drive more than a few hundred feet with your car in this condition. . . ."

The best protection against such events is to have your car properly serviced before you set off on a long trip; never leave the car while it's being serviced; keep your eye on the attendant at all times. If you really do suspect a problem, take it to another station for a second opinion, or to a dealer who sells your make of car.

UPS & DOWNS   *The Economics of Everyday Life*

Why Gasoline Prices Go Up and Down

Geopolitics   This includes wars and other disputes involving oil producing nations. When Iraq invaded Kuwait in 1990, oil prices soared. Refiners feared that a war would cut off a major supply of oil, and the law of supply and demand forced prices up. By the time Iraq was defeated, it was clear that supplies would be adequate, and thus the price came back down.

Monopoly   Most of the world's oil comes from the OPEC nations—the Organization of Petroleum Exporting Countries. When they agree on the quantity of oil they will produce and the price they will charge, that can have enormous impact on world oil prices.

Taxation   Federal and state taxes on gasoline have a direct effect on what you pay at the pump. California boosted state taxes a nickel per gallon to generate money for mass transit and environmental projects, and in 1993 new federal taxes added 4.3 cents per gallon.

The cost of money   Oil drillers, refiners, and distributors borrow money just like other businesses do. As interest rates move up and down, those borrowing costs are felt at the gas pump.

Competition   Oil companies and individual stations constantly battle to win your business. Price is their most common weapon.

Speculation   There are commodities exchanges where speculators can bet on the future price of oil. (See chapter 16). Heavy enough betting in one direction or the other can influence the price you pay.

? WHAT IF . . . ?

How would you deal with these real-life possibilities?

1. You're involved in an auto accident in which the other party is clearly at fault. Your total costs will be about $4,000, plus another $1,000 in lost income. The other person's insurance company offers you $6,000 to settle the matter right away, leaving you with $1,000 cash-in-hand to pay for possible future medical costs. A lawyer who specializes in such matters tells you she can probably get $15,000 from the insurance company, of which $5,000 will cover your costs and losses and $5,000 will go to the lawyer, leaving you with $5,000 cash-in-hand. You are cautioned that this may take many months, possibly a few years, and that the amount of money is not guaranteed but is highly assured. What would be your course of action? Why?

2. You lend your car to a friend for a few days. Later, you have second thoughts: What kind of insurance, if any, does your friend have that would protect you if she was in an accident and hurt someone else? How much protection does your own policy offer you in such a case? What can you do to adequately protect yourself?

NUMBER CRUNCHERS

Do the calculations to make decisions in these real-life possibilities.

1. Dealers are pushing hard to sell cars. They're offering incentives that include low interest rate financing, rebates on the purchase price, or discounts on "special options" packages. Get all these details from one or more dealers and crunch the numbers to determine which of the incentives will be the best for you. (Note that the low-interest financing may be limited to loans of certain length and that the "special options" packages might include items that you ordinarily wouldn't want or need.)

2. How would your overall budget be affected if you gave up your car? Calculate how much you'd save by doing so, and how much it would cost you to get around, including using mass transit, car pools, rental cars as needed, taxis as needed, and more efficient use of another car in your family. Don't forget to include the cash you could get by selling your car, and the down payment and interest you wouldn't have to spend by not buying another car.

3. How much can you lower your car insurance premiums by raising the deductibles? How much more risk will this create for you? Is it worth it? What about reducing your risk by decreasing the deductibles? Get actual figures from your agent; don't guess.

FOR BETTER OR FOR WORSE

Things beyond our control often impact our personal and financial well-being, for better or for worse. Some are more predictable than others. How could you be affected if the following real-life phenomena happened? Could you have seen it coming? What steps could you have taken to minimize damage or maximize advantage? The better able you are to anticipate and recognize these forces, the better equipped you are to deal with them.

1. As you are driving out of the city after work on Friday for a nice weekend getaway, you remember that you forgot to renew your auto insurance policy the day before, the last day of the grace period.

2. You were planning to buy a car when the new models come out in September. Planned price tag, about $20,000. An increase in local sales taxes of one percentage point is announced to take effect on August 1, long before the new models arrive, and when the selection of current models is fairly thin.

3. The deal you've been offered on a new car is mouth-watering. Then you hear rumors that the manufacturer plans to discontinue that line next year.

6

Buying a Home

"The eyes of other people are the eyes that ruin us. If all but myself were blind, I should want neither fine clothes, fine houses, nor fine furniture."

Benjamin Franklin

Where to live? House, apartment, condominium? Central city, suburb, or somewhere in between? How much of your available budget should be devoted to housing? Scrimp now for the sake of something better in the future? Or spend now and not worry about the future?

There are no easy answers to these questions. Individuals and families must decide what will best suit their specific needs and desires, taking into account applicable financial, geographical, architectural, and personal factors. This chapter will help you evaluate those important factors and will also help you resolve these other common problems:

- How to find a dwelling in the right price range
- How to make the best use of real estate agents
- How to handle the contracts and other documents involved in a housing transaction
- How to get ready for the closing when you buy a house or condominium
- How to know your legal rights as a home buyer

THE DILEMMA

Financial Factors

A house (or condominium) is the single largest purchase most people will ever make, and they generally have to live with it longer than most other purchases. A mortgage loan is the biggest debt most people will ever incur, and monthly payments (including utility costs and maintenance obligations) represent a major portion of most budgets.

If you have the down payment to allow you to purchase a home and if you can meet the monthly payments without crippling your budget, owning a home can offer very attractive financial benefits. Property taxes and interest paid on your mortgage are allowable income tax deductions (see chapter 20). The money saved on taxes can be applied toward your housing costs. Through these tax breaks, the government, in effect, subsidizes homeownership. (Tax aspects of homeownership are discussed in greater detail in chapters 9 and 22.)

Homeownership also offers the possibility of attractive profits. Home values have historically increased over the years and are likely to continue to do so, despite occasional regional downturns, as happened in the late 1980s and early 1990s. In general, considering the initial costs of acquiring a home, a profit is not likely if the home is owned for only one or two years. If ownership continues for three years or more, however, the likelihood (and amount) of potential profit increases. Not only are the profit potentials attractive, but also tax laws favor those who sell their homes at a profit. (Taxation on the sale of a home will be discussed in more detail in chapter 10.)

Geographical Factors

You cannot afford to overlook the cost involved in getting to and from work, shopping, schools, and other places, whether by private automobile or by mass transit.

Consider, for example, choosing between house A and house B, which are identical in all respects (including price) except one. House A is closer to work, schools, shopping, and entertainment facilities. You estimate that if you buy house A, your overall transportation costs will be, say, $100 per month less than if you bought house B. Furthermore, if you bought house B, you'd have to spend, on average, an extra twenty hours a month driving or on mass transit, as compared to house A. How will these factors affect your choice? See Figure 6–1, the Travel Time/Cost Worksheet.

You must also evaluate the condition of the neighborhood: whether stable, declining, or improving, not only can it affect your state of mind and comfort level but it can also be of great importance to the future resale

FIGURE 6–1   **Travel time/cost worksheet**

All other things being equal between house A and house B, the location of which house will involve more travel time and travel cost to get you and your family to common destinations? Use this worksheet to help calculate the differences. Calculate both minutes of driving time and miles driven per month.

Destination	Distance to and from (Minutes/Miles)	
	House A	House B
School(s)	_____ / _____	_____ / _____
Major shopping places	_____ / _____	_____ / _____
Church/synagogue	_____ / _____	_____ / _____
Major entertainment places	_____ / _____	_____ / _____
Work (husband)	_____ / _____	_____ / _____
Work (wife)	_____ / _____	_____ / _____
Carpooling	_____ / _____	_____ / _____
Other	_____ / _____	_____ / _____

Exercise 6.1

value of your house. Evaluate: Two houses are identical, except that one is less costly than the other. But the less costly one is in a declining neighborhood. Today it might seem to be the better buy, but what of the future?

Architectural Factors

When making a housing decision, consider the architectural aspects: design, layout, size, and physical condition. They all have a bearing on getting the best value for your money.

Design

The design that appeals to you is largely a matter of taste, but added or unusual features come at a price. To what extent can you justify what could be costly design elements? If you expect to do business entertaining in your home, the extra investment in appearance might pay off.

Layout and Size

Exercise 6.2

The arrangement and size of the rooms and the size of the house are practical considerations. The house should suit your household's needs as they exist today and as you expect them to be for many years to come. It's uncomfortable to live in tight quarters, and it can be very costly to expand later.

Physical Condition

Invest in a professional service that can inspect all the physical aspects of the house: roof, walls, foundation, heating system, plumbing, and so on. Any contract to purchase should be contingent on your approval of the building inspection.

Personal Factors

Sometimes we base major financial decisions not on what we prefer but on what we think others think best for us. (Reread the Consumer Alert section at the end of chapter 3.) That can be a sorry mistake. A house is the major element in your personal lifestyle. You have to live in it, deal with it, and enjoy it. To that end, consider the following:

Privacy

A house has a lot of privacy; condominiums and apartments have relatively less. On the other hand, if you prefer the closeness and camaraderie of others, you might find that in a condo or an apartment.

Leisure Activities

Assuming that a given house and a given condo are about equal in space, location, and quality, the house will cost more than the condo. If most of your leisure activities are home-based, it can make sense to spend the extra money and buy the house. On the other hand, if most of your leisure activities are outward-bound (skiing, fishing, hiking, and traveling), it might make more sense to buy the condo, so that you'll have more money available for those leisure activities.

Fix-it Chores

If you have a knack for patching, painting, fixing up, and taking care of things, you might feel more comfortable in your own home, whereas if you have ten thumbs, you're likely to feel put upon if faced with taking care of the myriad items that need attention in a home. An apartment or a condominium might be preferable, particularly if the landlord or condominium developer is responsible for most of the maintenance on the premises.

The Future

Spending less on housing now than you can afford will allow you to have still more money in the future. Evaluate this reality as it might apply to your situation.

The Personal Action Worksheet at the end of this chapter will help you evaluate all these factors.

TYPES OF HOUSING

Houses

Although it is possible to rent a house, outright ownership is the more common means of acquiring this type of dwelling. The typical purchase involves a cash down payment that may represent as little as 5 percent of the purchase price, up to the more common range of 20 to 30 percent. The balance of the purchase price is paid over an extended period of time, with payments projected for as long as 20 to 30 years. The buyer's promise to repay the remaining balance is secured by signing an IOU commonly preferred to as a mortgage. (In some states this is referred to as a *trust deed*.)

Table 6–1 illustrates common features in new houses, and cost factors, comparing recent numbers with those in earlier years.

TABLE 6–1   Bigger, Better, and Not a Lot More $$$$

What do typical home buyers get for their money? Following are important characteristics of new single family homes in 1975, 1985, and 1995. Figures are national averages. The last line, Income to Cost Ratio, indicates how much new homes cost relative to current earnings. As you can see, a new home now costs only slightly more, relative to income, than it did in 1975. And you get a lot more for your money.

	1975	1985	1995
Central air conditioning	46%	70%	80%
2½ baths or more	20	29	48
4 bedrooms or more	21	18	30
1 fireplace or more	52	59	63
2-car garage or larger	53	55	76
1,200 square feet or less	25	20	10
2,400 square feet or more	11	17	28
Average square feet	1,645	1,785	2,095
Median selling price	$39,300	$84,300	$135,000
Per capita personal income	$6,053	$14,170	$22,560
Income to Cost Ratio	15.4%	16.7%	16.7%

Sources: U.S. Bureau of Economic Analysis; Bureau of Census, 1997.

Condominiums and Cooperatives

Condominiums and cooperatives are somewhat similar, and so are often confused, but their differences should be clearly understood. Both refer to multiple housing complexes, and, in each case, an individual resident has a form of ownership. In a *cooperative,* each resident owns an undivided percentage of the total building. In a condominium, the resident owns his or her own specific dwelling unit.

Here's how they work. Picture an apartment house, five stories high, with four apartments on each floor. All the apartments are of equal size and value. On a cooperative basis, each of the twenty residents would own an undivided one-twentieth of the total building. In effect, it's like twenty partners owning the whole project, each having an equal vote. The cooperative owners enter into an agreement that sets forth what type of vote is necessary to take various actions. For example, it may require a simple majority vote—eleven out of the twenty—to commit the group to improvements or repairs of a certain value. It may take a three-quarters vote to commit all the members to major expenses. And it may take a unanimous vote to reach an agreement to sell the project. Each cooperative group determines its own rules and regulations.

All the members of the cooperative have individual lease agreements with the cooperative for the premises they occupy. A master agreement among all the cooperative members will also spell out such matters as the right to sublease one's apartment to nonmembers; the right to sell one's interest to outsiders; and the right to bequeath their interest in the cooperative to members or nonmembers of their family. Usually, any members of the cooperative who wish to dispose of their interest are first required to offer it back to the other members of the cooperative, perhaps at a preagreed price or based on a preagreed formula for setting a price.

The business affairs of the cooperative may be run by a volunteer member of the group or by a hired professional, depending on the size and complexity of the building management. Cooperative members are responsible for their share of property taxes, property insurance, utilities, and maintenance. If the cooperative has borrowed money—a mortgage—each member will have to sign the mortgage to ensure payment.

In a *condominium,* each of the twenty occupants owns a separate and distinct unit. As in a cooperative, all the individual owners enter into agreement with all the others regarding basic management of the property, maintenance of the common areas, and rights of the individual owners to sublease and sell to parties of their own choosing. Each owner is responsible for individual property taxes and property insurance and, as with a cooperative, is additionally responsible for taxes and insurance applying to the common areas of the building.

Condominiums and cooperatives can come into being in one of two ways: An existing building can be converted into condominium or coopera-

Co-op owner owns undivided 1/20 of whole building, with right to live in one specific unit.

tive ownership, or a new structure can be developed and sold to occupants on a condominium or cooperative basis.

In the former situation—conversion—the contractual consent of the occupants is required in advance. Occupants who don't want to go along with the conversion may find themselves having to move.

In the latter case—new construction—there can be many potential pitfalls before the building is completed and all the units are sold. During the construction period, there is dual ownership: the developer owns all the unsold units and buyers own their separate units. A developer who is not able to sell all the units may rent the unsold units to tenants. This can cause serious friction between the tenants and those who have already purchased their units.

Other problems that can occur in new developments include:

Condo owner owns one unit outright.

- Developers may reserve ownership of recreational facilities, charging occupants a fee for their use. If developers are not contractually limited as to the amount they can charge for recreational facilities, the fees can grow to unsatisfactory levels.

- Developers may scrimp on construction, knowing that once each unit is sold, it's up to the individual owner to take care of its maintenance. This can cause costly maintenance and renovation headaches for individual owners.

- Developers may run into financial problems before the projects have been completed. This can put owners who have already bought units into financial jeopardy. The financial condition of the developer should be carefully checked before a purchase contract is signed.

In a house, owners can do as they please as long as they don't break any laws or create nuisances for their neighbors. They can sell when they like, to whom they like, at the price the market will bear. But in condominiums and cooperatives, many of the rights of the owners are subject to their contract with the association, and also possibly with the original developer. Although many people regard condominiums and co-ops as the best of both worlds—offering the convenience of apartment living with the advantages of homeownership—such contractual agreements often prove that this is not the case.

Mobile Homes

A mobile home customarily involves a combination of ownership and rental. The unit itself is purchased from a dealer and is often financed on a long-term installment loan basis. The unit is then shipped to the owner's destination, usually at the owner's expense, where it is moored on its pad and hooked up to the available water, gas, and electricity. The owner pays a rental for the pad to the park management and is responsible for individual insurance and utility costs. In some instances mobile home purchasers may have the units installed on property that they already own, thus avoiding the rental fee.

Because mobile homes are not of the same permanent construction as regular houses, an owner should be alert to the possibility of depreciation in value compared with the customary increase in value that permanent homes enjoy. If you are shopping for a new mobile home, compare the prices of similar *used* mobile homes to get an idea of the likely future value of your current purchase. Before making a final decision, evaluate this depreciation carefully.

It's also important to consider the rental arrangements for the site on which a mobile home is placed. Commonly, such sites are rented on a month-to-month basis. If the owner of the park decides to sell the entire property, that could mean eviction on short notice for the site renters, requiring a costly move.

Multiple Units

Other forms of dwellings are represented by multiple-unit buildings and townhouses (or, as they're called in some parts of the country, rowhouses). A common form of multiple-unit housing is the *duplex*, in which two dwelling units occupy the same building, either side by side or one above the other. Similar structures may house three units (a *triplex*) or four units (a *fourplex*). Beyond four units, the buildings would normally be referred to as apartment houses. You might buy a duplex, triplex, or fourplex with the intention of living in one of the units and renting out the others. This can be attractive if the style of living suits you, for the rental income can offset your own dwelling costs and provide a tax shelter. (A detailed discussion of the tax-shelter benefits of rental real estate is provided in chapter 16.)

HOW TO BUY A DWELLING AT THE RIGHT PRICE

Exercise 6.3

Buying a dwelling—and whether it's a co-op, a condo, or a house, we'll use the all-encompassing term *house* for purposes of simplicity—may be the largest and most complicated transaction you'll ever enter into. It's worth doing it right, even if it means spending a lot of time and energy in the process.

The critical elements in buying a house are:

- Knowing your price range
- Using a real estate agent
- Timing
- Looking for the anxious seller
- Driving a hard bargain
- Knowing your needs
- Finding comparable values
- Evaluating the age of the dwelling

STRATEGIES FOR SUCCESS

Shop for Financing Before You Shop for a Home

If you're planning to buy a home, shop for the financing before you shop for the property itself. Most lenders can give you at least a tentative commitment as to how much of a loan you can get. Some lenders will even prequalify you for a loan, subject only to their appraisal of the property you select. Knowing in advance how much you can borrow allows you to zero in on the right price range from the start. More important: If you know in advance that you can get a loan, you are in a better bargaining position with sellers. You're talking from strength. The sellers know they won't have to wait to find out if you can get the financing you need.

- Understanding warranties
- Determing financing costs
- Estimating utility costs
- Estimating furnishing costs
- Determining property taxes
- Evaluating resale potential

Knowing Your Price Range

Exercise 6.4

Consider how large a down payment you can afford and what monthly payments you can handle. The higher your down payment, the lower your monthly payments, and vice versa. It is reasonable to assume that monthly housing costs for most families will exceed 40 percent of their after-tax income. For many families, two incomes are needed to buy a house. (For more details on financing, see chapter 7.)

Using a Real Estate Agent

Exercise 6.5

Many people think of using a real estate agent only when they sell a house. But there are many advantages to using a real estate agent when you are buying.

Most agents belong to an association of local real estate professionals called a multiple listing service. This service publishes a directory, usually weekly, of all houses in the area that are for sale through real estate agents. Listings contain extensive information on each house, including its physical features and costs. The listings provide considerably more information than you can glean from the classified ads. By using the listings, a real estate agent can help you locate the right house in the right neighborhood at a considerable saving to you of time and energy.

A good agent is a skilled negotiator and should be able to help you bargain for the best possible price. And good agents are in constant touch with the financial markets so that they can help you obtain financing. Furthermore, the services of a real estate agent cost the buyer nothing; the agent's commission is paid by the seller.

It's not easy to find a good real estate agent to represent you as a buyer. Many agents are leery, and perhaps rightfully so, of would-be buyers who are really just "lookers." They can't afford to spend much of their time unless they know that a would-be buyer is really serious. If an agent thinks a buyer is serious and will, in fact, work with the agent all the way, the agent is more likely to work hard on the buyer's behalf. A contract between the real estate agent and the buyer is not customary; the agent acts on good faith between the parties.

When you do find an agent who will work with you to find the right place, be sure that he or she is willing to show you properties that are listed by agencies other than the listing broker. You want to be sure that you are getting a good look at all available properties in the community.

Timing

Timing can be critical in the purchase of a house. To the extent possible, make certain that your financing arrangements for your new home coincide with the expected closing date. Also, arrange as far in advance as possible for your departure from your current dwelling. If you're living in an apartment, be certain to give proper and timely notice of your departure to your landlord. If you're living in another house or condo, do as much as you can to assure that your dwelling will be sold as closely as possible to the time you take possession of the new dwelling. If you fail to coordinate these transactions, you could become an *anxious seller* of the dwelling you now occupy. As the next paragraphs indicate, the plight of the anxious seller is not a happy one.

Looking for the Anxious Seller

The *anxious seller* is the person from whom you are most likely to get a good buy and, accordingly, is worth seeking out. A real estate agent can be of considerable help in locating anxious sellers. The listings referred to earlier often contain information that can help identify anxious sellers.

Here are the situations in which you will most typically find anxious sellers:

- The house has been on the market for a particularly long time. The seller realizes that each month that goes by is costing an extra month's worth of payments. The sooner the *anxious seller* can unload this house, the sooner the drain on his or her funds will cease.

- The house is vacant. The seller has moved into a new dwelling and is making payments on both. Nothing makes a seller more anxious to sell than making payments on two dwellings.
- There has been a major change in the family, such as divorce or death. In either instance, the owner is often more anxious than usual to wrap up the sale of the property, if only for relief from the legal complications that go with such situations.

Driving a Hard Bargain

It's traditional for a seller to ask one price and for the buyer to offer a lower price; buyer and seller will ultimately settle for something in between. Unless the demand for houses vastly exceeds the supply, this type of bargaining is almost taken for granted. It may seem distasteful to you to bargain over the price, but be forewarned that when *you* sell a house, buyers will haggle with *you* over the price. The real estate agents representing the buyer and the seller will generally convey the offers and counteroffers back and forth, so that you don't actually have to come face to face with the seller on this matter. This is all the more reason to consider a real estate agent when you buy: the agent is better able to handle this delicate phase of the purchase than you might be. Agents can show you the difference between asking prices and actual selling prices on recent sales in the area. This can help you determine your bargaining leeway.

STRATEGIES FOR SUCCESS

Exercise 6.6

Pros and Cons of Buying Foreclosures

No one likes to capitalize on someone else's misfortunes. But you might be able to buy a home that has been foreclosed for a much lower price than market value. Check with local lenders to find out what they have taken over in foreclosure. Better still: a friendly banker or real estate agent may know of properties about to go into foreclosure. You may be able to get first crack at it before the general public does. Beware, though, of the dangers in foreclosed property: the physical condition may be sorely neglected, and costly work may be needed. There may be other liens hiding. Don't buy without a thorough inspection, title search, and legal advice.

Knowing Your Needs

A good price on too small a house today may prove to be a regrettable decision if, in a few years, you have to enlarge the house or tolerate the inconvenience of inadequate space. Similarly, if a house later proves to be too large for your needs, you may look back at the original purchase as having been more costly than necessary. Although changes in household size aren't always predictable, the possibilities must be considered, particularly when you're putting out many thousands of dollars for a down payment and signing an IOU for a great deal more.

Finding Comparable Values

Once you've located an area in which you want to live and have taken into full account the costs of commuting to work and other facilities, you should determine if a specific house is priced comparably to others in the vicinity. Your real estate agent can help you by examining the records of recent sales in the area. All other things (size, quality, location) being equal, comparable houses should sell for comparable prices. You might be fortunate in finding a seller who is disposing of property on a distressed basis—that is, personal circumstances require a quick sale at less than might otherwise be obtained. Such circumstances could be a job transfer, a drastic change in family situation, or the need for cash. On the other hand, you might find someone who is asking the maximum he or she thinks the traffic will bear. Unless you do some checking, you might succumb to a high asking price when, in fact, you could have obtained a better buy if you had researched comparable sales in the neighborhood.

Evaluating the Age of the Dwelling

Be careful not to compare apples with oranges. This is particularly true concerning houses that are equal in size and quality but differ in age. The age of a house can have a distinct bearing on the value you get for your money. Aside from decor, you have to evaluate physical deterioration. In certain neighborhoods, the old saying, "They don't build them like they used to," may be perfectly true. Certain older homes have been built with better-quality materials and finer craftsmanship than more recent homes. However, an older house can mean expensive repairs. A detailed inspection by a qualified contractor will reveal the current condition and the need to spend money on such things as foundations, sidewalls, roof, heating system, plumbing, wiring, and appliances.

One advantage of older homes might be an assumable mortgage that carries a lower rate of interest. Another advantage can be that as you make payments on the older mortgage, you build up your equity at a faster rate.

TABLE 6–2   **Rate of Debt Reduction on Mortgage ($60,000 Mortgage, 30-Year Term, 9% Fixed Interest Rate)**

During	% of Debt Paid Off	Dollars Paid Off	Dollars Still Owed at End
1st 10 years	10.6%	$ 6,360	$53,640
2nd 10 years	25.9	15,540	38,100
3rd 10 years	63.5	38,100	–0–

Example: During the first 10 years of this loan, you will have paid off 10.6% of the debt, or $6,360. But during the second 10 years, you will have reduced the original debt by 25.9%, or $15,540. Thus, if you stepped into a seasoned mortgage as opposed to a brand-new mortgage and you stayed for 10 years, a much larger portion of the payments would come back to you when you sold.

The older a mortgage gets the greater portion of each monthly payment goes to principal. Table 6–2 illustrates an example. Offsetting this advantage, a larger down payment is probably needed with the older mortgage. Careful analysis is needed.

Understanding Warranties

Unless warranties are specifically spelled out in a contract and agreed to by the parties, they may not be enforceable. Customarily, brand-new homes are sold with a one-year warranty by the builder. Limited warranties on used homes can be purchased from companies that specialize in such matters. The buyer and seller must negotiate which of them will pay for such a plan, if it's to be included in the deal. New-home warranties generally cover the premises with respect to cracks, leaks, and breakdowns of mechanical equipment. In addition to such warranties, the buyer and seller might agree to other specific clauses. For example, if the roof leaks within the first twelve months, it will be repaired at the seller's expense. This agreement between the two parties, if properly drawn up and executed, binds the seller to make good on the promise if, in fact, the roof does leak. A seller might offer such warranties as an inducement to a buyer; or a buyer might request such warranties from the seller as part of the overall bargain. There is no legal requirement that a seller offer such warranties, and, lacking anything in writing, the buyer has little protection.

Another form of warranty is on specific mechanical equipment. For example, a water heater may be installed with a seven-year guarantee. During the seven-year period, the house changes hands. The remaining guarantee on the water heater could accrue to the benefit of the new buyer. The same might be true of any other mechanical equipment.

In the purchase of a new house, the buyer should determine what mechanical equipment warranties are included in the builder's overall warranty. For example, the warranty on a water heater may begin as of the date of installation. The unit may actually have been installed a year prior to the sale of the house to the ultimate buyer. Thus, one full year of the warranty may have already elapsed before the buyer even begins to use the appliance.

Any warranty—on a house, an appliance, or any other product or service—is only as good as its specific legal statements, and it's only as good as the ability of the warrantor to perform.

Determining Financing Costs

"How much down, and how much a month?" Those are the predominant questions asked when considering any kind of financing. It's not always as simple as that, however. You have to determine how much of a down payment you can make without interfering with your other predictable financial needs. Bear in mind that once money has been used for a down payment on a house, that money can't be retrieved unless you refinance or sell the house. Both transactions can be costly and time-consuming, if in fact they're feasible at all. Before you commit your down payment dollars, think about what else you might need that money for, such as emergency medical expenses or other personal matters.

The monthly payments must be in line with your overall budget. Examine the terms of the proposed mortgage to determine if the payments can change in future months or years. This can be the case if you have an adjustable rate mortgage or some other plan that allows the lender to alter the interest rate and thus the monthly payments. (These escalation possibilities are discussed in more detail in chapter 7.)

To your advantage will be the tax breaks given to homeowners: The interest you pay on your mortgage is tax-deductible (as are the property taxes you pay). This can result in a sharply lower income tax bill each year. You can realize those tax savings immediately, instead of having to wait until you get your tax refund, by amending your W-4 form at work to reflect your deductions and increasing your take-home pay accordingly. You can use that extra spendable money to meet your mortgage payments.

Estimating Utility Costs

If you're buying a used home, determine the utility costs the former owners incurred. Obviously, not all families will utilize the available energy in the same way, but that's at least a beginning guideline to help you determine the costs you'll be facing. If you're buying a new home, this task is more difficult. But if the same builder has erected comparable homes in the immediate vicinity, talk to the owners of those homes and inquire about their utility expenditures. A visit to the local utility companies might also be helpful in getting these preliminary estimates. Also, a physical examination of the insulation in the house can be important. If insulation is inadequate, you should evaluate the cost of bringing it up to standard compared with the cost of additional fuel you'll use if you don't correct it. Your local utility company can assist you in these considerations.

Estimating Furnishing Costs

Beyond the cost of the house itself, your mortgage payments, and utilities, you must also consider furnishing the house to suit your tastes. If the decor is not satisfactory, how much will it cost to repaint, repaper, and otherwise change it? Other items that can run into considerable expense include carpeting, draperies, and cabinetry. You'll also want to determine how much of your existing furniture can be used and how much additional furniture you may need to complete the interior satisfactorily. Evaluating these elements is part of your initial buying decision. Where will the money come from to provide the necessary furnishings and changes in decor? Do you have the cash? Will you finance these purchases over the customary three- to five-year term of a home-improvement loan? Can you add these purchases to the overall cost of your home and include them in the mortgage? Whichever step you take, how will it affect the balance of your regular budget?

Determining Property Taxes

You should research not just what property taxes are on the home you're planning to buy, but also what they might become. People in the local tax assessor's office can be of some help, as can members of the City Council and the local news media. If economic conditions indicate that property tax increases are likely, you should attempt to budget accordingly. Property taxes can be deductible on your federal income tax returns.

Evaluating Resale Potential

When buying a house, it might seem foolish to guess what you might be able to sell it for in five, ten, or fifteen years. Granted, there's no reliable way to predict what any property in any community might bring even a year or two after purchase; but it is foolish to ignore the question altogether. Some neighborhoods show signs of slow and gradual deterioration, whereas others seem to have a fairly certain future of increasing property values. There may be subtle changes underway in the neighborhood that can deflate the value of property. If you envision reselling the home within a relatively short period of time—say, four to seven years—your real estate agent can help you estimate the possibility of increase or decrease in value. If you'll be in the home longer than that, you'll do best to put your thoughts into the hunch category and hope for the best.

Once you've made all the necessary evaluations, you're ready to visit your attorney and discuss the terms of the sale.

MAKING THE PURCHASE

You've found a house that is desirable and affordable. You've made an offer and the seller has accepted. What happens next? Commonly, the seller's real estate agent prepares a brief memorandum of agreement setting forth the basic terms of the deal. Both parties sign this memorandum, and the buyer may be asked to pay some earnest money to bind the deal. The memorandum controls until a formal purchase contract is entered into.

The Purchase Contract

The purchase contract is a very important aspect of a real estate transaction. It sets forth the names of the parties involved, describes the property, dictates the terms and conditions of the sale, stipulates the kind of deed the seller will deliver to the buyer, and states where and when the closing is to take place. Generally, a purchase contract is prepared by the seller's representative, either a real estate agent or an attorney. Note well: If the other party's representative has prepared a contract for your signature, you must assume that the contract will favor the other party. Only by having your own representative review the document can you be assured of the fullest protection of your own interests.

The Parties to the Contract

The names and addresses of the parties are set forth in the contract. Customarily a married couple will acquire the house jointly. Laws differ from state to state as to the specific ways joint property can be held. Examples include: "Mr. and Mrs. X as joint tenants"; "Mr. and Mrs. X as tenants by the entirety"; "Mr. and Mrs. X as tenants in common." You must determine the different ramifications of each form in your state and have your title listed accordingly.

If there has been a change in the sellers' status since they purchased the property, such as through divorce or the death of one spouse, steps must be taken to assure that the proper current legal status of the sellers is incorporated in the contract. This is for the buyers' protection.

If the contract gives the buyers a "right of assignment," then the buyers can transfer their rights to buy the property to other persons. This can be beneficial to the buyers if, for example, an expected job transfer is cancelled, thus eliminating the need to buy the house. In general, where a right of assignment is given, the sellers reserve the reasonable right to approve the new buyers.

Description of the Property

The purchase contract should contain the full legal description of the property—not just the street address. The proper legal description should be either a surveyor's description or a subdivision description. The surveyor's description indicates the boundaries and their length, all relating to a particular starting point. The subdivision description may refer to a specific parcel within a larger subdivision, whose map has been filed under local legal requirements by the original developer of the property. Such a description might refer to a lot as "lot #17 of the XYZ subdivision, which is registered in the County Recorder's book of maps #576, at page 148."

Title

Your title to a piece of property represents the rights you have regarding that property. There may be certain restrictions as to how you can use any given piece of property; and your use of the property may be subject to the rights of other people. The purchase contract will commonly state that you are receiving "title free and clear of all liens and encumbrances, except as otherwise noted." What does this mean? It means that you are receiving the property without any restrictions and subject to no other rights of other people, unless such other restrictions or rights are specifically spelled out. If your contract says that you are receiving the right to use the property "free and clear," when in fact you are not, you may have the right to get out of the contract. Your lawyer or your title insurance company will search the appropriate records to determine whether any other such rights or restrictions do exist. If you take title to property having restrictions you could find it difficult to finance or sell the property. It could also mean lawsuits to resolve whether the rights and restrictions are valid.

"BLOTS" ON THE TITLE   Restrictions on your use of the property and rights that others may have to use your property are referred to as *blots* on the title. The most common form of blots are easements, liens, and restrictive covenants.

- **Easements**   Many years ago, the owner of a piece of property might have given a neighbor the right to lead cattle across the property to a watering hole. The neighbor may have paid for this right and, in return, received a document setting forth that right. Later, when the owner of the property sold to another buyer, the neighbor's right to cross the property was included as a part of the deal. Thus, the new buyer acquired the property subject to the neighbor's right to use it. Until the owners of the adjoining properties agree to terminate this right, it will continue through all subsequent transfers of the property.

This is a form of easement, and it exists today in many forms. It's not uncommon for a utility company to have easements across residential property for the purpose of installing utility lines and underground piping. These rights may have been reserved but not yet exercised by the utility company. That these rights have not yet been exercised does not mean that the easement has expired. Easements may have been created many years before, yet they will continue to run with the property until they are terminated by mutual agreement.

• **Liens** Laws on the subject of liens differ from state to state. A lien on the property comes into being when the owner of the property has a debt that has not been paid, and the creditor takes legal action to collect the debt. If the legal action is successful, the creditor may wind up with the right to force the owner to sell his or her property (real estate and personal) in order to satisfy the debt.

For example, John borrowed $10,000 from Mary and could not repay it when the debt became due. Mary began legal action, but John still refused to pay. Mary won a judgment against John that technically gave her the right to force a sale of John's house to satisfy the debt. Mary, in effect, had a lien on John's house. The lien was properly recorded according to state law. Anyone then buying John's house would own it subject to Mary's right to force a sale in order to satisfy John's debt to her.

Other liens can arise out of a property owner's failure to pay taxes, in which case the government will have a lien. Or, if a property owner has failed to pay contractors or workers who have performed work on the property, a so-called mechanic's lien can arise.

Note that a debt alone does not give rise to a lien. The creditor must pursue the legal requirements set forth in the state in order to "perfect" the lien. Not until the lien is legally perfected does the creditor have any claim on the property. Because many months often elapse between the signing of a purchase contract and the final closing of a real estate transaction, a lawsuit could occur in the meantime and result in a lien coming into being prior to the actual date of closing. Thus, it's common for a title search to occur both on the signing of the purchase contract and again just before the closing to make certain that no liens have arisen in the interim. A proper purchase contract should disclose the existence of any actual liens. If the contract does not disclose liens that do exist, the seller is promising to sell something that he or she cannot in fact deliver: a *free and clear* title. In such a case, the buyer should have the right to bow out of the contract, recoup any monies paid in, and possibly collect damages suffered as a result of entering into the contract.

- **Restrictive covenants**   Such covenants prevent you from doing certain things on your property. For example, a restrictive covenant might state that you may not build a house of less than a certain value. Such a covenant, or promise, may have originated with the subdivider of the property, who wanted to ensure that the subdivision was developed with homes of at least a minimum quality, thus protecting the financial interests of all those buying lots. Buyers want to know that their investment would not be diminished by the construction of buildings of lesser value.

Exercise 6.7

TITLE INSURANCE   Even though the proper record books have been searched and no blots against your title have appeared, that doesn't prevent someone from making a claim against your property. Such claim might be invalid, but it can be a costly nuisance for you to prove that it's invalid.

To prevent such problems and losses, homeowners acquire an insurance policy known as title insurance. This insurance policy protects both the homeowner and the mortgage lender against such claims. A title insurance policy does not establish the *value* of your property. It sets forth the maximum amount of monetary damages you can expect to recover if a claim is made against your title.

The Deed

The deed is the legal document by which the title to the property passes from the seller to the buyer. It's the actual symbol of ownership. The purchase contract should spell out when you will get it.

The contract should also stipulate that the deed will be transferred at the time of closing. If the contract does not call for the deed to be delivered at the closing, you should receive an explanation before consenting to sign the contract.

There are different kinds of deeds, and they convey different interests in a piece of property. The highest and most complete form of deed is called a *full warranty deed.* In such a deed, the seller warrants that he or she has clear title to the property (subject to any stated exceptions), is conveying the title to you, and will protect you against any outside claims made against the property.

The lowest form of deed is called a *quit claim deed.* By this document the seller conveys to you whatever interest the seller has in the property, with no further assurance as to title. By virtue of a quit claim deed, the seller is saying, in effect, "I hereby quit, or give over to you, the buyer, any claim I may have to this property." If, in fact, the seller has full and complete title to the property, this is what is conveyed to the buyer. If, in fact, a seller has no claim whatever to the property, that too is what is conveyed to the buyer. In other words, a seller could convey to a buyer via a quit claim deed "all of my right, title, and interest in the Grand Canyon." The seller has no interest whatsoever in the Grand Canyon, but it's still a valid deed. He or she is simply giving over any rights he or she may have, and it's up to the buyer to determine that those rights are worthless.

Once buyers take title to a property, they can convey only the title they have received. You can't convey more than you actually own. If you receive a quit claim deed to a piece of property and later want to sell it, you can't give anything more than a quit claim deed—unless it's been otherwise legally established that you do, in fact, have free and clear title.

The buyer should demand the highest form of deed the seller is capable of delivering. If your purchase contract calls for you to receive a certain type of deed and, at the closing, the seller does not deliver the type of deed promised, you technically might be able to void the deal or bargain for better terms.

In a type of property transaction known as a *land contract,* the right to use the property transfers to the buyer, but the buyer does not obtain a deed until certain contractual terms have been complied with. This might take many years. (This type of transaction is discussed in greater detail in chapter 7.)

Manner of Payment

The purchase contract sets forth the manner in which the buyer pays the seller for the property. (See chapter 7 for a more detailed discussion of where the buyer gets the money to pay the seller.)

Buyers planning to obtain their own financing for a purchase should make certain that a financing contingency clause is in the contract. This clause will state, in effect, that if the buyer is not able to obtain financing at an agreeable rate of interest by the date of the closing, the buyer can back out of the deal with little or no penalty.

Closing Date

The purchase contract should set forth the date and place of the closing. The closing is the official event at which the transfer of deeds, checks, and IOUs takes place. When a closing date is fixed, both parties must perform by that date or risk forfeiture. Of course, the parties can agree to amend the date of closing. This is done when financing arrangements have been delayed or where personal circumstances unavoidably alter the plans of either or both of the parties.

In some states, the signed contracts and other documents are held by a third party pending completion of all the buyer's and seller's obligations. This is known as *escrow* and is commonly performed by an attorney, an escrow company, or the escrow department of a bank. The party holding the papers in escrow (the escrow agent) will have been instructed by both buyer and seller not to release the papers for the closing until all the obligations of buyer and seller have been performed as agreed. In cases where an escrow agent is used, the *close of escrow* is the same as the closing date.

The parties will usually agree to have the closing date (close of escrow) from one to three months after the signing of the purchase contract, though any other agreement is possible if both parties are willing.

Seller's Obligations

As part of the negotiations, the seller may agree to perform certain services or work on the property. For example: The seller agrees to have the house painted for the buyer's benefit. If the seller fails to perform as agreed, what recourse does the buyer have? It all depends on how the seller's obligation was worded in the original purchase contract. If the buyer was careful enough, the seller's obligations would have been spelled out in detail, including the color and type of the paint to be used, the number of coats to be put on, and specific damages should the seller not perform in accordance with the contract.

Default and Recourse

What if either party fails to perform in accordance with the agreement? What are the rights of the other party? Much depends on the nature of the default and how serious it is in relation to the overall transaction.

For example, if the seller has agreed to paint the house at his or her own expense and has done so substantially but has omitted some minor touchup, this type of default would probably not destroy the entire transaction. In such a case, the parties could negotiate a quick and simple settlement. But more serious defaults—by either party—can create serious questions as to the rights of the parties. The broadest remedy to either party is to bring a lawsuit against the other for *specific performance.* A judgment of specific performance would require the defaulting party to perform in accordance with the specific terms of the original contract.

Perhaps a simpler way of resolving disputes and defaults is for the buyer and seller to agree to arbitration proceedings in the event that one of them does not perform as promised. Arbitration may provide a quicker and less expensive means of resolving disputes than lawsuits do.

The Closing

The closing may take place at the offices of the escrow company or the mortgage lender, at one of the attorney's offices, or at the offices where the recording of the documents will take place. The signed deed, in accordance with the purchase contract, will be delivered to the buyer, and the appropriate monies or IOUs delivered to the seller. Also, the appropriate "adjustments" will be made, and payment passed accordingly.

Adjustments and Closing Costs

The adjustments are a prorating of any expenses that will have been incurred on the property by the seller. For example, property taxes on the house total $800 per year, payable in installments on January 1 and July 1. The closing takes place on April 1. The seller will have paid a $400 property tax installment on January 1. This covers the first six months of the year. Thus, the buyer will have to reimburse the seller for $200 worth of property taxes, representing April 1 to July 1, during which the buyer will have occupancy of the property.

By the time of the closing, the buyer should have also made arrangements with an insurance agent to have the property insurance in effect in the buyer's name. The buyer should also arrange with the local utility companies—gas, electricity, water—to have the name on the meters changed, effective the date of closing. The buyer is responsible for these costs from the time of closing onward.

Other sums of money can change hands at the closing. The closing is the time for the seller to pay any real estate commissions to the agent. The lawyers and the title insurance company will also receive payments due them. Perhaps the single biggest closing cost will be the fees that the borrower has to pay to the lender who made home financing arrangements. Under a federal law, the Real Estate Settlement Procedures Act (RESPA), a lender is required to give advance notice to a borrower of the closing costs, or a reasonable estimate thereof. This law will be discussed in more detail in chapter 7.

Recording

Individual state laws govern the recording requirements for the appropriate documents. The recording of the mortgage agreement is the responsibility of the lender, and the recording of the deed is the responsibility of the buyer. Recording these documents as required by state law puts the world on notice that the lender has a mortgage lien on the property and that the owner has ownership of the property. The buyer's attorney or title insurance company should have searched the title to the property up to the time of closing. But if the search was concluded days, or even hours, prior to the closing, it is possible for a lien to have sneaked in against the property. Although this happens rarely, it can cause tremendous problems. Thus, the ultimate precaution is to have a search conducted at the time of closing to be certain that no liens have attached themselves to the property prior to the actual moment of transfer and then to record the documents immediately.

PERSONAL ACTION WORKSHEET —————————————————

Home-buyer's Guidelines

The following evaluations can be helpful in your quest to buy a home or condominium. Seek the aid of a real estate agent in doing this analysis.

Factors	Home #1	Home #2	Home #3
❏ Condition of neighborhood (present and future trend)	_____	_____	_____
❏ Approximate miles driven per month			
to work	_____	_____	_____
to schools	_____	_____	_____
to routine shopping	_____	_____	_____
to other	_____	_____	_____
❏ Transportation costs per month	_____	_____	_____
❏ Physical condition of building			
walls, foundation	_____	_____	_____
roof	_____	_____	_____
plumbing	_____	_____	_____
wiring	_____	_____	_____
heating, air conditioning	_____	_____	_____
landscaping	_____	_____	_____
appliances	_____	_____	_____
insulation	_____	_____	_____
❏ Estimated refurbishing costs	_____	_____	_____
❏ Asking price	_____	_____	_____
❏ Down payment	_____	_____	_____
❏ Terms offered by seller	_____	_____	_____
❏ Price seller will probably accept	_____	_____	_____
❏ Monthly mortgage payments	_____	_____	_____
❏ Property taxes and insurance	_____	_____	_____
❏ Estimated utility costs	_____	_____	_____
❏ General maintenance and upkeep	_____	_____	_____
❏ Closing costs	_____	_____	_____

CONSUMER ALERT

Check, and Double-check, Statements by Sellers

A home seller, or her real estate agent, might be tempted to stretch the truth when discussing certain features of a house or condo. If you're a buyer, the following precautions might be helpful in clarifying matters that would otherwise not be spelled out in the contract.

If the Seller, or the Seller's Real Estate Agent, Says:	You Should:
"Our utility bills are amazingly low— this home is really energy efficient."	Ask to see the last year's actual bills. If the seller doesn't have them, check with the utility companies. Understand, however, that different families will consume different amounts of energy.
"That water stain on the ceiling is from an old leak. We had it patched up watertight years ago."	Get a garden hose and, with the owner's permission, simulate a heavy rain on the roof. You'll find out soon enough whether the leak is still there.
"The basement is dry as a bone, winter and summer."	Check for watermarks around the basement wall. Better still, hire a contractor, who'll know better what to look for.
"Oh, we're just a quick 5/10/20 minutes from the school/ freeway/airport . . . etc."	If traveling time is important to you, drive these routes yourself, at various times of day, to find out what is involved.
"You'll just love the neighbors."	Go knock on the doors. Find out for yourself. They won't be there forever, but they can make a difference.

If both parties agree that the seller is to correct certain conditions, make certain that such corrections are clearly spelled out in the contract. Then, make certain that the corrections are completed before the deal is consummated.

UPS & DOWNS   *The Economics of Everyday Life*

Why Housing Costs Go Up and Down—Part I

Whether you're buying or selling a home, you can't ignore the ebbs and flows in housing prices. Hopefully, you'll buy low and sell high. Unfortunately, the ups and downs don't always coincide with your personal plans.

As the housing industry goes, so do many others. Makers of appliances, carpets, drapes, paint, wallpaper, furniture, gardening tools, furnaces, water heaters, and so on, all depend on a robust housing market for their own successes. So, a slow housing market hurts more than just the builders and building trades. Conversely, in a booming market the ripple effects are felt far and wide.

Many factors influence housing costs. Let's examine them here, and in the Ups & Downs section of chapter 10, which deals with the same concerns.

Timing   It can take years for a housing development to go from scratch to move-in date. A developer must acquire the land, obtain permits, and arrange for financing before construction begins. Once the developer projects the building of 5, or 50, or 500 homes in a targeted price range, it's very difficult to change course. But if a lot of conditions change in that time, it can make a shambles of sales and price projections. If he finds himself with too many homes for sale in a down market, he may have to drastically cut prices. If his completion date coincides with an up market, he may be able to command higher prices. These price fluctuations in new developments can spread to pricing on existing homes as well.

Jobs   Local employment is an extremely important influence on housing prices. In a growing area, where new jobs are being created, people's confidence in the future is strong and they are willing to make the financial commitment to buy a home. The law of supply and demand kicks in: More people wanting to buy will boost prices; more people wanting to sell will depress prices.

Interest rates   Home loans go hand-in-hand with home purchases. As interest rates come down, it becomes easier for people to buy homes: They can more easily qualify for a loan because their monthly payments will be lower. This can spark a rally in home buying, which will exert an upward pressure on prices. As interest rates move up, it's more difficult for buyers to qualify for the higher monthly payments. This can prompt home sellers to lower prices in order to attract the shrinking number of buyers. (See Ups & Downs, chapter 7, for a discussion on what causes the movement in long-term interest rates, and the Ups & Downs in chapter 10 for more on housing costs.)

? WHAT IF . . . ?

How would you deal with these real-life possibilities?

1. You've found the house of your dreams. The asking price is $150,000. Your "comfort zone"—the price range you can live with—is $120,000 to $130,000. You offer $125,000. The seller counteroffers $140,000. What are your options from this point?

2. You've found a house that's priced in the low end of your comfort zone. It's smaller than what you really want, but you can see ways to add on to it. The cost of the add-on, however, will boost the overall cost of the house above your current comfort zone level, and perhaps overprice it relative to other houses in the immediate neighborhood. All things considered, this house comes closest of all you've seen to meeting your criteria. How do you resolve the dilemma?

3. It's a buyer's market out there! Housing prices are low, and interest rates on home loans are as low as they're likely to be for years. You're anxious to buy, and you know you can qualify for a loan, but you're coming up short in the down payment department. What steps can you take to become a homeowner, before the market turns against you?

NUMBER CRUNCHERS

Do the calculations to make decisions in these real-life possibilities.

Exercise 6.8

1. Assume three housing prices: $120,000, $150,000, and $180,000. Further assume down payments of 5 percent, 15 percent, and 25 percent. With an interest rate of 10 percent and a mortgage term of 30 years, calculate the dollar amount of the down payment and the monthly payments required for each house at each down payment level. The mortgage tables in chapter 7 will enable you to crunch these numbers. The purpose of this exercise is to prompt you to become adept at working out these formulas; this skill will come in handy when you apply for a home loan.

2. You're considering buying a house that meets all your criteria except for one: the floor coverings. You'd want to replace 130 square yards of carpet and 300 square feet of vinyl tile. Get cost estimates, including installation, in various price ranges. What does this do to your budget?

3. Compare the cost of hiring a professional moving company to get you from your current abode to your new home, with the cost of a do-it-yourself move. Consider everything: packing, manpower, gasoline, wear and tear on yourself, the value of your time. What's the best deal, all things considered?

FOR BETTER OR FOR WORSE

Things beyond our control often impact our personal and financial well-being, for better or for worse. Some are more predictable than others. How would you be affected if the following real-life phenomena happened? Could you have seen it coming? What steps could you have taken to minimize damage or maximize advantage? The better able you are to anticipate and recognize these forces, the better equipped you are to deal with them.

1. You are negotiating to buy a new dwelling. The realtor tells you that some empty farmland a few blocks away may be rezoned from agricultural to industrial.

2. You've signed a contract to buy a new dwelling. The seller has moved out. Before the closing, and before you move in, a thunderstorm reveals some serious roof leaks that you hadn't been aware of.

3. You've just moved into your new home, and a neighbor informs you that she is converting her home into a halfway house for delinquent teenage girls.

Exercise 6.9

7

Financing a Home

It is impossible to win the great prizes of life without running risks. And the greatest of all prizes are those connected with the home . . . the intimate and homely things that count most.

Theodore Roosevelt

The great American dream has long been to own one's home. Is the dream beyond reach? Probably not. This chapter will acquaint you with methods of home financing and will equip you with the knowledge you'll need to pursue your own dreams of owning a home. Among the techniques you'll learn about are:

- How to evaluate different types of home financing plans
- Where you can shop for home financing
- Which home financing terms are negotiable
- How to structure a financing package that suits your housing budget

HOW HOME FINANCING WORKS

Not many years ago if you were shopping for a home loan you might have visited a dozen different lenders and found very little difference between their home financing plans. Most lenders would have quoted approximately the same interest rate, which would remain fixed for the entire term of the loan, usually thirty years.

But that's not so any longer. If you visited a dozen different lenders today, you'd find several dozen different plans based on fixed rates, adjustable rates, or some combination. Sorting them out can make your head spin.

A home loan is probably the largest IOU you will ever sign, and it will be with you for years, perhaps even decades. A difference of one-quarter of a percent in interest can mean a difference of thousands of dollars over an extended period of time. If you want to get the best arrangement for your money, it's essential to do the homework before you commit on any home loan.

Your First Step

If you're planning to finance a home purchase, you should, after reading this chapter, begin to shop for available financing plans *before* you start looking for houses. Talk to various lenders in your community and get an idea as to the kinds of financing that are available to you: how much down payment will be required, how much in monthly payments will be required, and what other terms and conditions the lender will impose. This exercise will give you general guidelines as to the type of housing you can afford and will make it easier for you to do your house shopping in the appropriate price range.

Furthermore, if you can get a tentative agreement from a lender as to a financing arrangement, you'll be more confident in your actual house hunting, knowing that you can probably conclude a deal that falls within your price range. Also, knowing in advance what kind of financing you can realistically obtain can enable you to bargain better with a seller. A seller who is convinced that you won't have to wait around for weeks to find out whether you can get the financing may be willing to drop the price in order to save that waiting time. You have a lot to gain and nothing to lose from such a tactic.

Say you're interested in buying a house that costs $150,000. You've saved up $20,000 of your own money, but that's all you have. How can you buy the house?

You can borrow the other $130,000. You can go to a bank or any other lender that offers home financing and make arrangements to borrow the needed amount. If your application is approved you will sign a document promising to repay the full amount to the lender over a period of time, plus an agreed-on amount of interest. This document is commonly called a <u>mortgage</u>. (In some states, the document is referred to as a trust deed. There are some minor technical differences between a mortgage and a trust deed, but the basic concept is the same.) This mortgage might be referred to as a *purchase money mortgage,* or a *first mortgage.* With a purchase money mortgage, as in this case, you borrow the money to purchase the property. The designation of the mortgage as *first* means that the lender stands first in line to take back your property in the event you default in your obligation to make the payments. Table 7–1 illustrates various relationships between income, down payment required, size of loan, and payments thereon.

Or there may already be a mortgage on the property that you might be able to <u>assume</u>. Say that there is a mortgage on the property for $130,000.

TABLE 7–1   **How Large a Home Loan Can You Get?**

Lender's limit, as a percentage of monthly income	If you have this much monthly income							
	$2,500	$3,000	$3,500	$4,000	$4,500	$5,000	$5,500	$6,000
	Here is what you can get, on a 30-year loan, at 9 percent fixed rate (upper figure is amount of loan, lower figure is monthly payment, in dollars).							
25 percent	77,600	93,800	108,700	124,200	139,800	155,700	170,800	186,300
	625	750	875	1,000	1,125	1,250	1,375	1,500
30 percent	93,800	111,800	130,400	149,100	167,700	186,300	205,000	223,600
	750	900	1,050	1,200	1,350	1,500	1,650	1,800
35 percent	108,700	130,400	152,200	174,000	195,700	217,400	239,100	260,900
	875	1,050	1,225	1,400	1,575	1,750	1,925	2,100

Example: If your monthly income is $3,500 and your lender will make a loan whereby your monthly payments will not be more than 30% of your monthly income, you could get a loan of $130,400, with monthly payments of $1,050. Income tax implications are not taken into account, but you should calculate your own.

You could become the owner of the property by paying the seller your $20,000 in cash and then stepping into the seller's shoes as the person responsible for making the payments on the existing mortgage. In effect, you assume the seller's debt. You take it over. What if the existing mortgage on the property is only $120,000? After paying the seller your $20,000 in cash, you'll still be shy of the total purchase price by $10,000. In such a case, the seller might be willing to take your IOU for the $10,000. Your IOU would be known as a *second mortgage*. The terms of payment would be whatever you and the seller agreed to, and the seller, holding your second mortgage, would stand second in line behind the holder of the first mortgage to get paid in the event that you defaulted on the debt.

A mortgage contains two very important legal considerations. First, you are legally committing yourself to make the payments to the lender as agreed. Second, you are giving the lender the right to take steps to take back the property from you if you fail to make the payments. In other words, you have given the lender a security interest in the property as collateral for the loan.

If a borrower fails to make payments as agreed, the lender can begin a legal action known as a *foreclosure proceeding*. Foreclosure proceedings differ somewhat from state to state, but basically they allow the lender to cause the property to be sold at public auction. The lender recovers whatever money is owed out of the proceeds of the auction sale. The first mortgage holder gets first crack at the auction proceeds. If there is any money left over after the first mortgage holder is paid off, that can go to a second mortgage holder, and so on. For example: William owes $60,000 on a first mortgage and $10,000 on a second mortgage. William defaults and the property is foreclosed. The property is sold at auction, and, after foreclosure expenses are taken out, $66,000 remains. The first mortgage lender recovers the entire $60,000 owed. The remainder, $6,000, goes to the second mortgage holder. This means, obviously, that the second mortgage holder has suffered a $4,000 loss on the transaction.

The basic costs of a mortgage are the same whether the mortgage has a fixed interest rate or a variable interest rate:

- The interest, which is the *rent* you pay for the use of the lender's money
- The acquisition fees
- The insurance costs

How Interest Is Figured

Fixed Rate Loans

In the standard fixed interest rate mortgage, your interest cost is calculated on the unpaid amount of the debt at each given monthly point. Here's an example:

On a $70,000 mortgage, set to run for thirty years at a 12 percent interest rate, the monthly payments for interest and principal would total $720. During the first month of the mortgage loan, the debt the borrower owes is the full $70,000. Since 12 percent of $70,000 is $8,400, that would be the total interest for the full year if the debt did not change.

But we're interested now only in the first month, which is the first one-twelfth of the year. One-twelfth of the full year's interest is $700. (One-twelfth of $8,400 equals $700.) Therefore, $700 is the amount of interest due for the first full month of the mortgage. Thus, in that first month, the total payment of $720 is broken down as follows: $700 for interest and the remaining $20 applied toward the debt.

Going into the second month, the debt due has been reduced by $20, from the original $70,000 to $69,980. During the second month of the mortgage, the interest is calculated on this new debt of $69,980. One-twelfth of 12 percent of that amount equals $699.80. That's the amount of interest due during the second month. In the second month, therefore, your total payment of $720 is broken down as follows: $699.80 for interest and $20.20 to reduce the debt.

The debt has now been reduced by an additional $20.20, leaving a full balance owing of $69,959.80 going into the third month. In the third month, the interest due is one-twelfth of 12 percent of $69,959.80, or $699.60. The payment for the third month is broken down as follows: $699.60 for interest and $20.40 to reduce the debt. A breakdown of the first three payments would thus be as follows:

Exercise 7.1

	Interest	Principal	Debt Remaining
First month	$700.00	$20.00	$69,980.00
Second month	699.80	20.20	69,959.80
Third month	699.60	20.40	69,939.40

That's the basic formula on which fixed mortgage interest is figured. As each month goes by and the amount of the debt shrinks, the amount of interest paid gets smaller and smaller. As the interest portion of your total monthly payment decreases, the principal portion increases. As you can see from this example, and from Table 7–5 (later in this chapter), the payments during the early years of a mortgage are mostly interest. It's not until many years into the mortgage that the interest and principal portions of each monthly payment equal each other. In the last few years of a mortgage, the principal portion is substantially greater than the interest portion.

Adjustable Rate Loans

An adjustable rate loan, most simply stated, means that your interest rate can be adjusted up or down over the months and years. By adjusting the interest rate, your monthly payments might also change. In the last twenty years, the standard interest rates for home loans have fluctuated wildly, ranging from under 7 percent to almost 20 percent. No one knows which way they will head in the future. But if you are concerned that interest rates might move higher than they are now, you might be uncomfortable with an adjustable rate loan.

In order to make an intelligent choice between a fixed rate loan and an adjustable rate loan, you have to understand the jargon of the adjustable loan and how it works. The following statements may not make any sense to you when you first read them, but they're not far from what you might be told when you apply for an adjustable rate loan:

"Your initial rate will be 8 percent. The base rate will be 9 percent, with semiannual adjustments. The index will be the floating Treasury Bill rate, which is now 6.8 percent, and there will be a margin of 3 points over that. You'll have an annual cap of 1 percentage point, a lifetime cap of 5 percentage points, and you can avoid negative amortization by making the full payment upon each adjustment."

Is that enough to make your head spin? Let's take it one small piece at a time.

- **Initial rate**   The initial interest rate might be attractively low, designed to lure you to a given lender. The initial rate will last only until the first interest adjustment occurs, which is usually after six months.

- **Base rate**   The base rate is the interest rate on which the lifetime cap is calculated. If you have a lifetime cap of 5 percent, that means that your interest rate over the life of the loan cannot be greater than 5 percentage points above the base rate. In the earlier example, the base rate is 9 percent and the lifetime cap is 5 percent. That means that your interest rate over the life of the loan cannot exceed 14 percent. Borrowers can be confused by thinking that the lifetime cap is calculated from the initial rate, which in this example is 8 percent. In that case, the maximum interest you could ever have to pay on the loan would be 13 percent. You must determine the exact terms and conditions of these items before you commit to the loan.

- **Index**   The index is an arbitrary number, beyond the control of the lender, which is used to determine interest adjustments. The common indices are the so-called *cost of funds* for certain savings institutions or an interest rate that the U.S. government pays when it borrows money. In the example above, the index is based on the interest rate the U.S. government pays on its very short-term borrowings (Treasury Bills). At the time you were quoted the terms of the loan, that index rate was 6.8 percent. All indices will move up and down as interest rate trends change.

- **Margin**   The index plus the margin equals the interest rate you'll be required to begin paying at the start of each adjustment period. For example, if, after the first six months of your loan, the index has increased from 6.8 to 7.2 percent, the interest rate you will have to pay on your loan from that time on will be 10.2 percent: the index of 7.2 percent plus the margin of 3 percentage points. Similarly, if the index rate goes down, so will the rate you pay.

- **Lifetime cap**   As explained earlier, this fixes the maximum interest rate you will pay during the life of the loan. The lifetime cap is added to the base rate to get the ultimate maximum. If you commit yourself to an adjustable rate loan that does not have a lifetime cap, and if there are no laws otherwise protecting you, then there will be no limit on how high your interest rates can go over the life of your loan. This situation is obviously not desirable.

- **Annual cap**   The annual cap puts a limit on how much your monthly payments can increase during the course of a year. (In some loans, this cap may be based on a shorter period of time, such as six months.) Let's look at a rather extreme example. Assume you have a loan of roughly $120,000 and your current interest rate is 10 percent. That would require monthly payments of approximately $1,050. Assume also that during a one-year period, interest rates soared to 13 percent. If you did not have an annual cap of 1 percent as stipulated in the example, your monthly payment at the 13 percent rate would jump to $1,330. But because you have the 1 percent annual cap, your monthly payment cannot exceed $1,140, which is the payment that would be required for an interest rate of 11 percent. This brings up one of the most troubling dilemmas in the entire adjustable rate loan arena: the possibility of *negative amortization*.

- **Negative amortization** Following along with the preceding example, the 1 percentage point annual cap on your loan meant that your monthly payment could not increase by more than $90 during the one-year period—it couldn't go beyond $1,140. But, in reality, interest rates increased from 10 to 13 percent. Without the cap you would have had to take on a monthly payment of $1,330, which is $190 more than the $1,140 limit. What happens to that $190? Does the lender just forget about it? In most instances, the lender does not forget about it. The annual cap simply put a limit on your monthly payments during that set period of time. It did not stipulate that you would never have to pay extra interest over and above the limits set by the annual cap. Here we have a case of negative amortization: Technically, you would owe an extra $190 in interest each month. But since the annual cap prevents you from having to pay it each month, that amount is added to your overall debt. In other words, your debt would be growing by $190 each month if you fell into a negative amortization situation. Needless to say, if negative amortization continues for an extended period of time, it can leave you with a much bigger debt that you originally started with. You can avoid the negative amortization trap by increasing your monthly payments to cover all interest that may be due, regardless of the annual cap.

It should be quite obvious by now that all these terms have to be clearly understood and explained to you before you make a commitment to an adjustable rate mortgage.

Fixed versus Adjustable

Choosing between a fixed rate loan and an adjustable rate loan is a perplexing choice. With the fixed rate loan, you know exactly where you stand today, and where you'll stand any number of years from today. The fixed rate loan is easy to understand, and it holds no surprises for you. The adjustable rate loan may look more attractive because it will generally have a lower starting interest rate. And, of course, there's always the hope that interest rates may go down. Indeed, in recent years, they have gone down. But then they have gone back up again. And then they come back down again. You'll never know where you are on the roller coaster until you get to the end of the ride and look back.

One of the simplest rules of thumb in making the choice is to determine, as best you can, how long you expect to be living in the dwelling with the mortgage. If the base rate on the adjustable loan is 2 to 3 percentage points lower than the fixed rate that might otherwise be available to you, and if you are reasonably certain that you will be in the house no longer than three to five years, then the adjustable rate loan will probably be better for you, assuming that you have reasonably good caps on the loan. On the other hand, if you expect to be in the house for five to seven years or longer, the fixed rate loan will probably be better for you. It won't necessarily be cheaper over the long run, but it will be more stable, and that stability is important in the overall management of your finances. Put another way, over the long pull, you may end up having paid somewhat more in interest, but you will have gained considerable peace of mind over that long term.

Another feature of the adjustable rate loan should be noted: Commonly, adjustable rate loans are assumable by a creditworthy buyer. In other words, having an assumable loan might make it easier for you to sell your home in the future, if the buyer wants to take on your existing assumable loan. But again, timing enters the picture. If you are not going to sell for, say, seven years, the value of the house may have increased enough so that the balance due on the assumable adjustable loan is relatively low. That would mean that the buyer at that time would have to come up with a much larger down payment in order to meet your price. Under such circumstances, the assumable loan might be less attractive to both buyer and seller. Furthermore, it could well be that at that time the buyer would prefer a fixed rate loan, in which case your assumable loan is of little or no value to either party.

Exercise 7.2

Many lenders offer added attractions to their adjustable rate plans, and new ones are occasionally introduced. There are special plans for first-time buyers. Some plans allow very low down payments, with outside parties (such as an employer) being permitted to contribute part of the down payment. Some plans start out as adjustable rate loans but carry an option to switch at some later time to a fixed rate loan. And some plans start off at a fixed rate but can be converted to an adjustable rate at some agreed upon future time. It can all become very confusing—yet another reason to start shopping for the financing before you shop for the house itself.

Acquisition Costs

Exercise 7.3

In addition to the interest you pay on your mortgage, you will probably also have to pay certain fees to lenders for putting the mortgage on their books. Lenders may expect you to reimburse them for the legal expenses involved in preparing the papers, for the credit bureau costs involved in checking your credit history, for expenses for appraisals on the property, and for the cost of the title search.

In addition to these fees, you may be asked to pay points to lenders. Points are a one-time added fee that lenders impose on you to improve the yield on their investments. Generally, a point equals 1 percent of the amount of the mortgage. Thus, two points on a $70,000 mortgage would total $1,400. All these added costs—the fees and the points, and the ways you have of paying them—should be explained to you at the time you make application for the mortgage.

Insurance Costs

A lender may require you to obtain insurance to protect its interest primarily and your own interest secondarily. Title insurance, as discussed in chapter 6, is almost universally expected by the lender, the cost of which will be borne by the borrower. The lender will also expect the borrower to carry adequate fire insurance on the premises, so that the lender will be protected in the event of such catastrophe. The lender might also urge the borrower to obtain life insurance, so that the mortgage can be paid off by the insurance in the event the borrower dies. And default insurance may be involved: this insurance guarantees that payments will be made for a set period of time in the event the borrower defaults. FHA and VA loans include this kind of protection for the lender. In addition, many private firms offer default insurance, which, if required by the lender, will be at the borrower's expense.

Exercise 7.4

If you are required to carry default insurance, it can add approximately a quarter percent to your interest costs. That can mount up into a sizable sum over the years. After you have proved your good payment record to the lender, the lender may be willing to release you from the default insurance requirement. This release would reduce your monthly payment by the amount that was allocated for the insurance. This should be negotiated at the outset. If you have the right to be taken off the default insurance program, it should be spelled out in your initial agreement. The lender might not be willing to give you this right, but if you don't ask for it, you certainly won't be able to get it later on.

Escrow, or Reserve, Accounts

In some mortgage arrangements, the borrower may be required to pay an added monthly sum, which will be used to pay property insurance premiums and property taxes as they fall due. This is commonly known as an escrow account or a reserve account. Example: Your property taxes are $900 per year and your property insurance is $300 per year—a total of $1,200 per year. With an escrow account, you will pay an additional $100 per month over and above the basic monthly payment. The lender will pay your property taxes and insurance premiums out of that fund as those bills come due. Some lenders may require an escrow account; some may offer it as an option. In some states, lenders pay interest on the funds they hold for your benefit. Budget-conscious homeowners often find that an escrow account can be a simple way of leveling out their total annual budget program. It can be easier and more convenient to pay out a fixed monthly amount rather than have to meet large insurance and property tax bills when they come due. The lender normally analyzes escrow accounts once a year to determine how much will be needed in the account for the following year. The lender will notify the borrower of any adjustments in the monthly payment.

Other Important Clauses

Mortgages can contain other important clauses that can affect your legal rights as well as your monthly payments.

Balloon Clauses

The balloon clause allows the lender to demand that the entire loan be paid off at a set time. If you're not aware that such a clause is in your mortgage, it could come as a shock if the lender exercised this privilege.

Due on Sale Clause

A due on sale clause states that if you sell the home, the existing loan must be paid off at the time of sale. A new buyer can negotiate with the lender to keep the loan in place, but at currently prevailing interest rates.

Assumption Clauses

An assumption clause means that the owner of a house can sell the house to another party and the new buyer can assume the existing debt. The new buyer, in other words, steps into the shoes of the former owner and becomes liable for the balance on the debt, as well as all other terms and conditions of the mortgage. Assumption privileges are subject to the lender's right of approval. The lender might, for example, refuse to allow a person with a bad credit history to assume an existing mortgage. If you are buying a house that has an assumable mortgage, you should determine in advance whether or not you will be permitted to assume the mortgage. If you are entering into a new mortgage, the existence or absence of an assumption clause can affect your ability to sell the house later.

Prepayment Clauses

You might come into a sum of money and wish to make advance payments on your mortgage, either wholly or partially. Do you have the right to do so and, if so, will it cost you anything? Some mortgages contain prepayment privilege clauses that allow you to make such advance payments on your debt without suffering any penalty. On the other hand, some mortgages have prepayment penalty clauses stating that you must pay a penalty if you do prepay.

SHOPPING FOR FINANCING: WHERE TO GO, WHAT TO LOOK FOR

If you buy a house with an existing mortgage that you plan to assume, you'll be locked into the terms of that mortgage. But you can still discuss revision of any of the terms with the lender. It might be worth your while to do so to help tailor a different payment program that would better suit your own financial circumstances.

If you seek your own original financing, the following shopping list, tables, and the Personal Action Worksheet at the end of this chapter can help you to work out a deal that's best suited to your circumstances.

Where to Shop

The major sources of home financing are savings associations and banks, plus some credit unions and insurance companies. There are also private mortgage brokers in most communities who act as middlemen in finding mortgage loans for home buyers. Mortgage brokers are usually paid by the lenders for their services.

FHA and VA Loans

The difference between fixed interest and adjustable interest loans has already been discussed. There's another broad distinction that should be considered, for it can affect the amount of down payment you'll be required to make. This distinction is between insured loans and noninsured loans.

Lenders don't really want to foreclose on properties if the borrower defaults. Foreclosure is a messy, costly, and aggravating proceeding. A lender would much rather have some form of guarantee that all or a portion of the payments will be made as agreed. Indeed, lenders *can* obtain insurance that will offer those guarantees. There are two main sources of this insurance: the U.S. government and private insurance companies.

The U.S. government offers two types of insurance plans. One is offered through the Federal Housing Administration (FHA), and the other, through the Veterans' Administration (VA). FHA will insure certain mortgage loans if both the buyer and the property meet governmental requirements. The VA will also guarantee loans made to eligible armed services veterans, again providing that all qualifications are met. Because the government is guaranteeing repayment of these loans—at least in part—the lenders are willing to take greater risks with such loans than they would if there were no guarantee. In short, the lenders are willing to make these loans to borrowers with smaller down payments. Check with local lenders for current requirements.

Lenders can also obtain insurance through private companies. As with the FHA and VA loans, the private insurance plan means a lower risk for lenders. Borrowers might have to pay a slightly higher monthly payment as a result of their loans being insured, but the cost can be well worth it if it allows them to purchase a house with a relatively small down payment.

One type of insured loan is the FHA-245, also known as the graduated payment plan. This loan is geared toward younger people who might not be able to meet the high monthly payments currently called for. In the graduated payment plan, the monthly payments for the first few years of the loan are lower than they would be under a regular plan. As the years go by, and as the borrower's income presumably increases, the payments increase accordingly.

Noninsured loans, whether at a fixed rate or adjustable interest rate, generally require a down payment of roughly 20 percent of the purchase price of the property.

Ginnie Mae, Fannie Mae, and Freddie Mac

In most cases, once you have signed your home loan IOU to the lender, the lender will turn around and sell that IOU. A number of entities are chartered by the government to buy loans from lenders. The most well known are the Government National Mortgage Association, the Federal National Mortgage Association, and the Federal Home Loan Mortgage Corporation. Their nicknames, derived from their initials, are, respectively, "Ginnie Mae," "Fannie Mae," and "Freddie Mac." Private entities (such as insurance companies, pension funds, and individual investors) might also buy home loans from lenders.

Here's an example of how this works: You sign a thirty-year home loan agreement (the IOU), payable to XYZ Bank, for $150,000 plus interest. As part of the deal, you pay XYZ Bank $3,000 in points, as well as other processing fees. XYZ turns around and sells your IOU to Ginnie Mae for the face amount of $150,000. XYZ Bank keeps the $3,000 in points as its earnings on the deal, and it now has its $150,000 back to lend to someone else. Ginnie Mae then turns around and pools your IOU along with others like it and sells the whole package to investors. (See chapter 6.) This concept creates a steady flow of money for home loan purposes, which in turn helps our economy grow.

You might never be told that your loan has been sold; it doesn't matter. You continue to make your payments to XYZ Bank, and the bank forwards them to whomever has bought your loan. **Warning:** If you are told to send your payments to anyone other than the original lender, check with all parties involved that this change is legitimate and get confirmation thereof in writing.

Conventional and "Jumbo" Loans

In order to sell loans to Ginnie, Fannie, or Freddie, the loans must meet strict requirements regarding your income, your credit, and the value of the property. The loan also must not exceed a fixed dollar amount, which recently was somewhat over $200,000. That ceiling is usually increased slightly every year for newly written loans.

Loans above the maximum amount are referred to as jumbo loans. Ginnie, Fannie, and Freddie may not buy jumbos, but other investors might. Because lenders can easily sell qualifying conventional loans to Ginnie, and so on, they may charge borrowers a lower interest rate than a jumbo borrower would have to pay. Thus, if the amount of loan you're seeking is at or near the current conventional limit, it could pay you well to structure your finances so that you can qualify for the lower interest rate that likely will come with the conventional loan.

RESPA

What points and other fees will you have to pay in order to get the financing you're seeking? Under the federal Real Estate Settlements Procedures Act (RESPA), lenders are required to give you a copy of a government booklet, *Settlement Costs*, no later than three days after you have made your loan application. The information in this booklet is very important. It describes your rights under the federal law and contains helpful advice on completing your property transaction. The law also requires that the lender give you a good faith estimate of all settlement costs (or closing costs, as they're often called). You should also determine whether the closing costs are to be paid at the closing or whether they can be added into the mortgage and spread out over the life of the mortgage.

Interest Rates

What will be the original interest rate, and what fluctuations might it be subject to in the future? Table 7–2 is a handy guide to help you find the monthly payment for any size mortgage at various interest rates and terms of repayment. Table 7–3 illustrates how different interest rates can affect your actual costs on a mortgage—and those cost differentials can be tremendous, as the table clearly shows.

How Much Down Payment Is Required?

The amount of the down payment required and the amount you have available for down payment may not jibe. If you have more than enough, you're

TABLE 7–2   Monthly Mortgage Payment Finder (Fixed Rate) (Per $1,000)

Annual Fixed Interest Rate	Length of Mortgage			
	15 years	20 years	25 years	30 years
7%	8.99	7.76	7.07	6.66
7½%	9.28	8.06	7.39	7.00
8%	9.56	8.37	7.72	7.34
8½%	9.85	8.68	8.06	7.68
9%	10.15	9.00	8.40	8.05
9½%	10.45	9.33	8.74	8.41
10%	10.75	9.66	9.09	8.78
10½%	11.06	9.99	9.45	9.15
11%	11.37	10.33	9.81	9.53
11½%	11.69	10.67	10.17	9.91
12%	12.01	11.02	10.54	10.29

Example: What would the monthly payment be (interest and principal) on a $90,000 mortgage for 30 years at 9% interest? Find the factor where the 9% line meets the 30-year column. That factor is 8.05. 8.05 times 90 = 724.50. The monthly payment, then, would be $724.50.

in good shape, but then you'll have to decide *how much* of your available funds you want to use as a down payment. If you have less than the required amount, how will you raise the difference? If one lender requires a higher down payment than another, the interest rate may be lower or the other terms may be more favorable. These must be compared.

TABLE 7–3   How Interest Rates Affect Your Out-of-Pocket Costs ($120,000 Mortgage for 30 Years)

Fixed Rate (%)	Monthly Payment	Total Amount Paid Out After			
		5 years	10 years	20 years	30 years*
7	$ 799	$47,940	$ 95,880	$191,760	$287,640
8	881	52,860	105,720	211,440	317,160
9	966	57,960	115,920	231,840	347,760
10	1,054	63,216	126,432	252,864	379,296
11	1,144	68,616	137,232	274,464	411,696
12	1,235	74,088	148,176	296,352	444,528

Example: What would be the difference in cost to you on a $120,000 loan between an interest rate of 8 percent and 9 percent? During the first five years the 8 percent loan would cost you $52,860 (monthly payment of $881 times 60 months) compared with $57,960 for the 9 percent loan—a difference of $5,100. Tax deductibility of interest will also affect your out-of-pocket costs. Calculate accordingly.

*To find the total *interest* paid over the full thirty-year life of the loan, subtract the original amount borrowed ($120,000) from each of the amounts in this column.

TABLE 7–4 **How Down Payment Affects Your Costs (Purchase Price $160,000, 30-Year Mortgage, 9 Percent Fixed Rate)**

Down Payment		Amount of Mortgage	Monthly Payment	Total Payments After		
Percent	Dollar Amount			10 years	20 years	30 years
5	$ 8,000	$152,000	$1,224	$146,800	$293,700	$440,640
10	16,000	144,000	1,159	139,700	278,200	419,100
15	24,000	136,000	1,095	131,400	262,800	394,200
20	32,000	128,000	1,031	123,720	247,440	371,160
25	40,000	120,000	966	115,920	231,890	347,760
30	48,000	112,000	902	108,290	216,480	324,870

Example: What would be the difference in cost to you if you make a 10 percent down payment versus a 20 percent down payment on a $160,000 purchase, with a fixed interest rate of 9 percent for a 30-year loan? With a 10 percent down payment, after 20 years you will have made total payments of $278,200 ($1,159 a month times 240 months.) With the 20 percent down payment, after 20 years you will have made total payments of $247,440. In other words, by making the larger down payment you will save almost $31,000 in payments over 20 years. However, if you did have the 20 percent available and only used half of it as down payment, you would have had $16,000 to spend or invest over the years.

Exercise 7.5

Table 7–4 illustrates how different-sized down payments can affect your total mortgage expense over a period of years. There is no easy solution to the dilemma of how much to pay down. It must be resolved based on your own personal circumstances as they are now and as you expect them to be.

How Long Should the Mortgage Run?

Exercise 7.6

The longer the mortgage, the lower the monthly payment. But that means a higher interest expense over the long term. However, it's unlikely that you'll stay with that mortgage for more than ten or twelve years, for the average American changes houses and moves on within that time. Table 7–5 shows the rate at which your debt is paid off over the years, and Table 7–6 illustrates the different cost factors involved for mortgages of varying terms.

Other Services from Lender

You should try to determine what other kinds of financial services are available to you from respective lenders. Some may offer nothing more than friendly and helpful advice. Don't underestimate the value of this service. Advice can come in handy and may be the deciding factor in your choice of a lender for your home financing.

TABLE 7–5   **Mortgage Reduction Schedule, 30-Year Term, Any Amount**

	Percent of Original Balance Still Unpaid	
Years Elapsed	At 9% Fixed Rate	At 12% Fixed Rate
5	95.9	97.7
10	89.4	93.4
15	79.3	85.7
20	63.5	71.7
25	38.8	46.2
30	-0-	-0-

Example: On a loan of $100,000 at a 9 percent fixed interest rate, after 10 years of making payments, 89.4 percent of the original balance, or $89,400, will still be unpaid. Ouch. On a loan of $120,000 at 12 percent fixed rate, after 20 years of making payments, 71.7 percent of the original debt, or $86,040, remains unpaid. Double ouch. It's not until the last five or so years that the debt is rapidly reduced. Review the earlier section in this chapter on how interest is figured.

TABLE 7–6   **How the Length of a Mortgage Can Affect Your Costs ($120,000 Mortgage at 9 Percent Fixed Interest Rate)**

Length of Loan	Monthly Payment		Amount Paid After				
			10 years	15 years	20 years	25 years	30 years
15 years	$1,218	Int.	$ 84,840	$ 99,240			
		Prin.	61,320	120,000			
		Total	$146,160	$219,240			
20 years	1,080	Int.	$ 94,800	$126,360	$139,200		
		Prin.	34,800	68,040	120,000		
		Total	$129,600	$194,400	$259,200		
25 years	1,008	Int.	$100,200	$140,880	$170,400	$182,400	
		Prin.	20,760	40,560	71,520	120,000	
		Total	$120,960	$181,440	$241,920	$302,400	
30 years	966	Int.	$103,200	$149,040	$188,040	$216,360	$227,760
		Prin.	12,720	24,840	43,800	73,440	120,000
		Total	$115,920	$173,880	$231,840	$289,800	$347,760

Example: On a 20-year loan of $120,000 at a 9 percent fixed interest rate, you will have paid a total of $129,600 in the first 10 years. Of that amount, $94,800 will have been interest and $34,800 will have been principal (reduction of the debt).

Notes Regarding Mortgage Calculation Tables:

- Using Tables 7–2 and 7–5, you can structure "what if" projections for a wide range of possible mortgage terms. These can help you prepare comparisons regarding how the interest rate (Table 7–3), amount of down payment (Table 7–4), and length of loan (Table 7–6) will affect your own specific loan needs.

- Income tax deductions for interest paid are not taken into account, since they will vary from person to person and from time to time. But you should estimate how those deductions will affect your cash flow.

Exercise 7.7

- The calculations do not cover adjustable rate mortgages, since the numbers on those loans can vary widely from year to year. You can, however, estimate an *average range* that an adjustable loan will likely cover, and do your "what if" projections accordingly.

- In the calculations, amounts are rounded off.

APPLYING FOR HOME FINANCING

Exercise 7.8

After you've done your shopping for rates, terms, and other clauses, you will decide which lender you want to make formal application to. Before you do, spend a few dollars to examine your credit file at your local credit bureau to make sure that everything is in order. Erroneous information can find its way into your credit file, and you have rights under the federal Fair Credit Reporting Act to have false information corrected. See chapter 11 for more details on your rights under this law. The lender will do a credit check

---

STRATEGIES FOR SUCCESS

A Shorter Home Loan Is Better, If You Can Afford It

The most common home loans run for a thirty-year term. But if you can afford to make higher monthly payments, you can be much better off taking a shorter term on your home loan. Example: On a fixed rate 8 percent loan of $100,000, the monthly payments on a thirty-year term will be $734. For a fifteen-year term at 7.75% (rates being lower for a shorter-term loan), the payments will be $941—a difference of $207 per month. If you can handle those higher payments, you'll be considerably happier after ten years. After ten years on the original fifteen-year loan, you'll owe about $50,000. But ten years into the thirty-year loan, you'll still owe more than $90,000. Why? On the longer loan, most of your payment goes toward interest, with very little toward actually reducing your debt. Discuss these alternatives with your lender before you make a commitment.

on you. If false information has not been corrected in your file, it will cause delays in processing your application.

In addition to obtaining detailed financial information on you—including your income and your debts—the lender will appraise the property you are buying. A title search will also be called for to assure that the lender can be properly secured if a loan is made. These processing steps can take from a few days to a few weeks and might entail some fees that you will be expected to pay, whether the loan is approved or denied. You should determine in advance just how long the processing will take and what cost, if any, you will have to assume.

If your application is approved, you should obtain a copy of the lender's commitment, in writing, so that there is no mistake about the terms of the arrangement. It's very likely that any commitment will extend for only a limited time at the given interest rate. If the purchase transaction is not completed within that specified time, the lender could back out of the commitment, at least at the quoted interest rate. If you suspect that the transaction will not be completed within the time of the lender's commitment, you should move quickly to attempt to get it extended.

It could happen that a lender will approve your application, but with the contingency that you provide a cosigner; or the loan may be approved for a lesser amount than you had requested. In the event a cosigner is required, the lender is asking you to find someone else who will sign the IOU with you. This shouldn't be taken as an insult. It may merely mean that the lender doesn't feel comfortable with your age, the amount of job experience you've had, or or your credit history. After payments on the loan have been made for a few years, you can request that the cosigner be removed from the obligation. Discuss this possibility in advance with the lender.

CREATIVE FINANCING

When interest rates go up, home loan financing becomes more difficult to obtain. When lenders evaluate a loan application, they compare your income with the amount of monthly payment that would be required to pay the size loan you're seeking. Higher interest rates could boost your monthly payment over the level the lender feels comfortable with, and the lender might decline your loan.

In times of higher interest rates, lenders, brokers, buyers, and sellers have put their heads together to come up with unique ways of accomplishing everyone's desires. These generally fall under the category of creative financing. Following are some examples of creative financing techniques. Before you commit yourself to any such technique, it is essential that you get adequate legal advice. These arrangements can be very complex and can create legal pitfalls that you might not be aware of. Protect yourself before you sign anything.

Ask Lender for "Rate Lock"

If interest rates are moving upward at the time you're looking for a home loan, you could run into a serious problem. A lender might quote you a given interest rate on the day you apply for the loan. But the loan might carry a higher interest rate by the time the transaction is completed, which could be months later. And that higher interest rate could really put you into a bind. When you shop for a loan, ask if the lender will give you a rate lock—a guarantee that the interest rate on the loan will not go above a certain level, no matter when the transaction is completed. It might cost you something to get a rate lock, but it could be worth it if interest rates are on an upward spiral.

Land Contracts

A land contract can be anything that a willing buyer and a willing seller agree to. Example: Sam, the seller, and Bob, the buyer, are negotiating the terms of a potential deal. Sam is asking $180,000 for his house. Bob has no money for a down payment but is willing to pay $190,000—$10,000 more than Sam is asking. Both Sam and Bob know that a normal lender would not consider financing such an arrangement with no down payment. But if Sam is willing to accept Bob's terms, they can enter into a contract accordingly. It's customary in a land contract for the deed not to be delivered to the buyer until an agreed-upon amount of time has elapsed, during which time, presumably, the buyer will have proved his or her ability to make the payments in timely fashion.

The Sleeping Second

Selma, the seller, is asking $120,000 for her house. She wants $50,000 as down payment, and she's willing to carry the buyer's IOU in the form of a first mortgage for $70,000. Bernice, the buyer, has the $50,000 down payment, but she doesn't have enough income to make the monthly payments on a $70,000 first mortgage. She does, however, have enough to make the payments on a $50,000 first mortgage. They agree that Selma will carry a $20,000 sleeping second. Bernice will make the payments on the first mortgage. The second mortgage will have no payments for the first three years—or whatever other time the parties agree to. Interest will accrue on that sleeping second, probably at a higher rate than a normal second mortgage, since Selma is being very accommodating to Bernice. At the end of the agreed-upon time, either the second mortgage has to be paid off, which will mean refinancing the entire deal, or payments must begin on the sleeping second, or whatever else the parties have agreed to.

Buying Down

One type of creative financing, buying down, is more commonly seen in new housing where developers are attempting to sell homes during times of high interest rates. Say, for example, that the current prevailing rate is 9 percent, but buyers cannot afford home loans of more than 7 percent interest. A hungry developer might contribute the 2 percent difference in order to sell the homes. As a rule, the developer would do this for only the first few years of the loan, at the end of which time it would be understood that the buyer would then take over the higher monthly payments. This enables buyers to get into homes at a lower monthly payment, banking on the expectation that after a few years their incomes will have increased enough to allow them to live comfortably with the higher payment.

Shared Appreciation Loans

If a buyer cannot afford either the amount of the down payment or the monthly payments, the seller, or any other third party, might enter into an agreement with the buyer to provide a portion of the down payment or the monthly payments. In return for doing that, the outside partner or seller would share in any future appreciation in the value of the house. This is a shared appreciation loan. This kind of arrangement offers very attractive potentials, but it is not without risks and it requires the assistance of a knowledgeable attorney from the very outset.

TAX COMPLICATIONS

The home financing arena is further muddled by major tax law changes created by Congress in 1986 and 1987. These changes relate to how much of your home loan interest expense can be deductible on your tax return. Limitations on deductibility will come into play, for the most part, if you *refinance* an existing home loan or if you borrow money using your home as collateral (so-called home equity borrowing, in which you give the lender a mortgage as security). The amount of your interest deductions can be affected by the *date* you do such borrowing, the *amount* you borrow, and the *purpose* for which you are borrowing. Professional tax counsel should be sought whenever you borrow using your home as security.

TIMING, TIMING, TIMING

A final word to those who embark on the stormy seas of home loan shopping: A great deal depends on your getting your loan paid out to you at the exact time you need it. Delays in processing loan applications can cause a domino effect with wide repercussions. If you learn that your loan processing is delayed for whatever reason, you might not be able to have your closing at the time you wanted it. Technically, that might give the seller the right to cancel the whole transaction, though most sellers will go along with moderate delays if they are approached properly at the earliest possible time. A delay in your closing means that you'll have to continue living where you are for another month or two. That means added cost and inconvenience. If you are in an apartment and you've already given notice to your landlord that you expect to leave on November 1 and you find that your home loan application won't be completed until December 15, you're in a pickle.

To the best of your ability, make certain that you establish a workable schedule with the lender from the outset. Complete the proper paperwork within the prescribed time frame. Delays may be caused by the lender as well as the borrower, and there's little you can do to prevent that. But the more open and thorough your communications with the lender, the better able you'll be to anticipate and deal with any possible delays.

PERSONAL ACTION WORKSHEET

Financing Comparisons

It's expected that most home financing plans will be based on an adjustable interest rate—a rate that can be adjusted upward or downward from time to time. Since it's impossible to know what future rate fluctuations will be, there's no way a borrower can accurately predict his or her mortgage costs over a long period of time. The dilemma is further compounded by the fact that different lenders use different formulas to vary the rate, thus making a comparison between lenders very difficult. The following worksheet is to help you ask the right questions in evaluating adjustable rate financing plans. The more you know about how the plans work, the more judicious your decision can be.

	Plan A	Plan B	Plan C
☐ What is the starting interest rate?	_____	_____	_____
☐ How often can the rate be changed?	_____	_____	_____
☐ How much can the rate be raised at any given interval?	_____	_____	_____
☐ How much can the rate be raised over the life of the loan?	_____	_____	_____
☐ How much can the rate be lowered at any given interval?	_____	_____	_____
☐ How much can the rate be lowered over the life of the loan?	_____	_____	_____
☐ By what outside index are the rate changes to be measured? (Consumer Price Index? Cost of funds? Prime rate?)	_____	_____	_____
☐ Is there a prepayment penalty? If so, how much?	_____	_____	_____
☐ If the rate is increased at any given interval, do you, the borrower, have the option of keeping the monthly payment the same (in which case the final maturity of the loan will be extended)?	_____	_____	_____
☐ If your answer to the above question is yes, what limits, if any, are there to the option?	_____	_____	_____

CONSUMER ALERT

Be Well Prepared for Loan Application Process

Exercise 7.9

In the late 1980s an excess of bad loans were made all across the country. (See chapter 11.) Since then, lenders have become stricter in the information they require from loan applicants. Because home loans involve many legal and technical matters, loan applicants must be ready to present a burdensome amount of documentation. It's wise to ask in advance for a list of all the items your lender might want. Then check off each item as you acquire it, and note the full list of items in a covering letter that you send to the lender along with your application. That will help you make sure you've supplied everything needed, which will speed up your application process.

Bank of America, for example, has asked home loan applicants to provide the following:

Your last two years' W-2 (wage and earnings) statements; your last month's current pay stubs; your most recent three months' bank statements (to verify funds for down payment); your most recent monthly mortgage statement *and* either the last full year-end mortgage statement or canceled checks for the last twelve months' mortgage payments (this is for those who already own a home); your federal income tax returns for the last two years; your most recent loan statements for all other debts, charge accounts, and credit cards.

There are additional requirements for those purchasing, for those refinancing, and for those who are self-employed. All told, plan to spend several hours digging through all your records before you even start filling out the application.

UPS & DOWNS   *The Economics of Everyday Life* ———————————————

Exercise 7.10

The Frenzies of Home Loan Interest Rates

Before you read this segment, please read the Ups & Downs segments in chapters 12 and 13. They will provide a necessary introduction to interest rate movements in general.

The interest rate phenomenon in home loans can best be expressed as weird. Consider: With adjustable rate loans, the *starting* rate for a loan will be pegged to current *long*-term rates. But the up and down rate adjustments that are made periodically (usually every six months) are pegged to *short*-term rates (such as U.S. Treasury Bill rates or comparable measures). So you have a long-term (15 to 30 years) debt that is constantly being rearranged as short-term (3 to 12 months) interest rates move up and down. This protects the lender if interest rates trend upward and protects the borrower if rates fall.

With fixed interest loans there's an even more bizarre situation. Banks must keep a "spread" between the interest they earn from the loans they make and the interest they pay to their depositors. This spread provides money for the bank to operate and, hopefully, make a reasonable profit. When a bank makes a fixed rate home loan for thirty years, at, say, 8 percent, it is committed to earning only that 8 percent on that money for that time period. If, at that time, the bank is paying 5 percent (on average) to its depositors, it has a spread of 3 percent. But that payment to depositors is based on *short*-term trends, such as certificates of deposit for one or two years. A few years go by, and interest rates in general move up, so that the banks are paying 6 or 7 percent to their depositors. But they're still only earning 8 percent on the fixed rate loans they made years earlier. So they could be losing money on those particular loans. New loans will, of course, be made at higher rates, but it can be unhealthy for lenders to be making money on some loans and losing it on others—particularly if they loaned heavily while rates were low, and got caught in a competitive free-for-all for depositors when rates later turned higher. In this fixed rate scenario, as opposed to the adjustable rate one, borrowers are happier when interest rates go up (they're protected with their lower fixed rate), and lenders are happier when rates go down (they can pay less to their depositors and thus increase their spread).

The intervention of Ginnie Mae and her cousins (see the discussion in this chapter) as buyers of loans has helped to moderate the risks involved. But the ups and downs of home loan interest rates remain a puzzle for both borrowers and lenders.

? WHAT IF . . . ?

How would you deal with these real-life possibilities?

1. You've applied for a home loan of $120,000. Your credit rating is fine, and your income status is secure. But because of a lower-than-expected appraisal, the bank is willing to lend you only $110,000. You definitely want to buy the house. How can you proceed to your desired end?

2. You've worked out a home-buying budget that has virtually no breathing room, considering all the costs of financing, furnishing, utilities, and other obligations that go with homeownership. Your home loan application is approved, but at a higher interest rate than you had expected. (Rates went up between the time you applied and the time the loan was paid out to you, and you didn't have a rate lock.) The higher interest rate will mean an extra $80 per month out-of-pocket. How will that impact on your life? What are your options?

3. Your home financing has been approved: you'll get the purchase money mortgage from a local bank, and the seller will take back a second mortgage of $25,000. However, at the last minute the seller tells you he'll carry your IOU for only one year. This matter hadn't been discussed before. You had assumed that he'd carry the IOU for a much longer, though unspecified, period. What problems does this pose? How can you resolve them?

NUMBER CRUNCHERS

Do the calculations to make decisions in these real-life possibilities.

1. See exercise number 1 in Number Crunchers in chapter 6. Using the mortgage tables in this chapter, take the calculations some steps further: Using the same housing prices and down payments, calculate the dollar amount of down payment and monthly payment using 7 percent and 12 percent fixed interest rates for a 30-year term. Of all the resulting possibilities, pick one at random, and calculate how much of the loan would be paid off after making payments on it for 5 years, 10 years, and 15 years.

2. You're shopping for a home loan of $100,000. Using current rates as a starting point, calculate what your monthly payments would be if your interest rate increased by one-half percentage point each year for 5 years. What if rates decreased by one-half percentage point each year for 5 years? Compare the results with the current rates on a fixed rate loan.

FOR BETTER OR FOR WORSE

Things beyond our control often impact our personal and financial well-being, for better or for worse. Some are more predictable than others. How could you be affected if the following real-life phenomena happened? Could you have seen it coming? What steps could you have taken to minimize damage or maximize advantage? The better able you are to anticipate and recognize these forces, the better equipped you are to deal with them.

1. Believing that you have a good credit history, you apply for a home loan. But your credit report comes back with some information that causes your application to be rejected. You could lose the deal.

2. You've spent twenty hard hours of drudgery preparing all of the documents and applications for a home loan at Bank A. Then Bank B announces home loans—for which you would qualify—at an interest rate one percentage point less than Bank A.

3. At the closing of your home purchase you are told of about $2,500 in miscellaneous loan costs that you had not expected—at least, you couldn't recall being told about them.

Exercise 7.11

Housing Costs
and Regulations

A home is no home unless it contains food and fire for the mind as well as the body.
Margaret Fuller

The cost of maintaining a dwelling does not end with writing your monthly mortgage or rent check. Home or condo owners, in particular, feel a constant drain on their budget from such expenses as property taxes, property insurance, utilities, and maintenance. All these items must be properly anticipated if you are to keep your financial affairs on an even keel.

In addition to costs, your dwelling situation can be affected by local rules and regulations that must be complied with.

This chapter is designed to assist you in planning sensibly to meet your overall dwelling costs and to alert you to the legal rights and responsibilities that pertain to dwellings. You'll learn how to

- Choose the right type and amount of property insurance
- Take action to cut your property taxes if they are wrongfully too high
- Get control of your utility and maintenance costs
- Protect yourself and your property if neighbors or landlords violate housing rules and regulations

PROPERTY INSURANCE

Property insurance provides two forms of protection. First, it reimburses you for loss or damage to the building, the contents, and the furnishings. Second, it protects you in the event that harm comes to other people or to the property of other people. This latter form of protection is known as public liability insurance. As an owner or tenant of property, you can be responsible if others are harmed as a result of your negligence. The law does not require you to maintain public liability insurance on your house or apartment, as it does on automobiles in most states. But the law will require you to pay damages should a court find that you were responsible for injuries suffered by another. Lack of proper insurance either on the building or for public liability can prove financially catastrophic.

In general, homeowner's insurance will reimburse you in the amount needed to replace or repair lost or damaged property, based on its value at the time of loss. Some kinds of property, such as a house or jewelry, tend to increase in replacement cost. Other types of property, such as furniture and carpeting, tend to decrease in value. These changes in value are known as *appreciation* and *depreciation*. Your insurance should be adjusted periodically to reflect these changing values.

For those who rent, there is a special type of policy called the tenant's policy. It provides protection against loss or damage to furnishings and personal items as well as public liability protection.

The cost of your homeowner's or tenant's insurance will depend on a number of factors: the company you deal with, the risk rating of your property, and the amount of protection you seek.

The Company You Deal With

Exercise 8.1

As with all other forms of insurance, property insurance is competitive. Rates for similar coverage can differ from company to company. The cheapest protection is not necessarily the best. You must try to gauge the extent of service you'll get from the company, their response to claims, and the possibility of increased premiums when claims have been submitted.

The Risk Ratings of the Property

Each property insured will be rated by the insurance companies according to relative risk factors. These factors can include location of the building and proximity to fire stations and fire hydrants, construction of the building (for example, brick as opposed to wood frame), proximity to other buildings, and fire and crime statistics in the neighborhood in which the building is located. Check with your agent to determine what precautions you might take to keep your property insurance premiums as low as possible. Such precautions might include installation of fire extinguishers and fire retardant materials, cleanup of attics and basements, installation of security devices such as smoke detectors and burglar alarms, and secure locking mechanisms.

The Amount of Coverage You Desire

If you have a mortgage on your house, the lender will require you to carry at least enough insurance to pay off your debt if the house is destroyed. You might not care to pay for any more protection than that minimum amount. Or, if you desire, you can carry much broader coverage. (Even flooding can be insured against under existing federal programs.)

THE TYPES OF POLICIES AND COVERAGE

Exercise 8.2

Homeowner's insurance comes in three primary forms: the basic form, or "Homeowners 1"; the broad form, or "Homeowners 2" (the tenant's form is similar to the Homeowners 2 and is known as Homeowners 4); and the comprehensive form known as "Homeowners 5." A special form, "Homeowners 3," combines the broad form (HO2) coverage on personal property with the comprehensive form (HO5) coverage on the dwelling itself.

The Basic Form (HO1)

With HO1, your premises are protected against the most common risks. These risks include:

- Fire
- Lightning
- Windstorm
- Hail
- Explosions
- Riots
- Aircraft
- Vehicles
- Smoke damage
- Vandalism, malicious mischief
- Theft (except for certain items, among which are credit cards)
- Breakage of glass in the building
- Loss of, or damage suffered to, personal property that you removed from endangered premises (e.g., the building next door to you is on fire and you flee into the night clutching some private possessions that are later lost or damaged—they are covered under your basic form policy)

The Broad Form (HO2)

The broad form (HO2) and the tenant's form (HO4) provide protection against additional risks at a nominal extra cost. These include:

- Falling objects
- Collapse of the building
- Damage to the building due to the weight of ice or snow
- Certain damage caused by escape of steam and water from a boiler, radiator, or similar device
- Certain accidents involving electrical equipment, such as an over-loaded circuit that blows out an appliance

The Comprehensive Form (HO5)

The comprehensive form is sometimes referred to as an *all risk* policy. But it will generally exclude certain risks from coverage, such as earthquakes, tidal waves, sewer backups and seepage, landslides, floods, war, and nuclear radiation. See each specific policy to determine what exceptions are listed. Even though flood may be excluded from coverage, the federal government has acted to make flood insurance more easily available to homeowners in flood-prone areas. Your agent can give you details on this coverage. The added cost of the comprehensive protection may not be worth it to many homeowners; examine your own circumstance to determine what kind of protection is best for the dollars available.

Protecting Other Property

Exercise 8.3

The typical homeowner's policy also provides extended coverage for other forms of property. For example, garages and storage sheds will customarily be covered for 10 percent of the full value of the main building. In other words, if the main building is covered for $80,000, the auxiliary buildings will be covered for a total of $8,000. Your personal property within the home, such as furniture, appliances, and bedding, may be covered for as much as 50 percent of the coverage on the house itself. Other types of personal property, including jewelry, chinaware, paintings, and furs, will be covered under your basic policy for loss due to fire but will have to be separately covered for theft or loss. (See the section "Valuables.")

If your home or apartment suffers damage and you are required to live elsewhere while the damage is repaired, the typical homeowner's and tenant's policies provide you with additional living expenses—usually 10 percent on the basic HO1 policy and 20 percent on the broad and comprehensive policies—with the percentages calculated on the total primary value. In addition, your trees, plants, and shrubs will be covered for up to 5 percent of the primary value in the event they are damaged.

Public Liability

Homeowner's policies also contain public liability protection. Commonly, the homeowner's policy provides up to $100,000 liability protection per occurrence, $1,000 in medical expenses payable to others, and 50 percent of your home's coverage in property damages. For example: A guest in your house slips on a banana peel that you have negligently left lying in the hallway. X-rays reveal that she has fractured her hip and has also broken her wristwatch in the fall. The homeowner's policy provides up to $1,000 in medical expenses and reimburses the injured party for the broken watch. The injured party then learns that she will be unable to work for a number of months and makes a claim against your homeowner's policy. The public liability provision would pay up to $100,000 in damages—loss of income—as a result of the accident.

If you live in an apartment or a condominium, the issue of public liability protection is a bit more complicated. You should maintain coverage to protect yourself for anything that may occur within *your* premises. The apartment building owner or the condominium owner's association should also maintain adequate coverage to protect all interested parties in the event of an injury in a *common area,* such as a parking lot, a hallway, or an elevator. You, as a tenant or condo owner, should make certain that the coverage on the common areas is adequate to protect you if someone is hurt in a common area and sues everyone in sight for as much as possible.

Much higher limits for public liability can be obtained at a fairly modest increase in premium, and a wise homeowner might do well to consider obtaining a much higher level of protection than the basic policy offers.

Valuables

Valuable personal property may *not* be adequately covered for theft or loss under your homeowner's or tenant's policies. Valuable personal property can include such items as jewelry, paintings, sculptures, china, silver, cameras, computers, collections (stamps, coins, medallions), golf clubs, furs, securities, cash, and credit cards. In order to be fully covered for loss of these items—whether at home or away—you may have to obtain a separate *personal floater.* The cost of this added insurance can be considerable. You should seek the assistance of your agent in determining exactly what personal property is covered under your homeowner's policy and under what circumstances you may wish additional protection for your valuables.

The Deductible

Exercise 8.4

The cost of your policy will vary in relation to the deductible you choose. The deductible is the amount you pay out of pocket for any losses before the insurance company becomes responsible. Some policies have a no-deductible clause, which means that the insurance company is responsible for the first dollar onward. A $50 deductible means that, in any given occurrence, you must pay the first $50 worth of expense before the insurance company becomes responsible. Deductibles can be as much as $250 or $500. In choosing a higher deductible, you are exposing yourself to more potential risk in return for a lower premium. The premium will not be lowered as much as the risk will be increased. For example, the difference in cost between a $50 deductible and a $250 deductible may be only $20 or $30, but you're exposing yourself to $200 more potential risk. However, the higher premium is an actual out-of-pocket cost that you can save, whereas the added risk is only a possible expense that you might never incur.

The Coinsurance Clause

This can be extremely important. The coinsurance clause states generally that, if you wish to receive full replacement value for any damage to the premises, you must insure the premises for at least 80 percent of its replacement cost. For example, a house has a current replacement cost (not counting the land and foundation) of $80,000. That means that at current going prices, it would cost $80,000 to duplicate the house, in its depreciated condition, on the existing foundation. (The land and the foundation are not included in figuring costs for insurance coverage because theoretically they would not be destroyed.) But the owner had insured the building for only $56,000, which is $8,000 shy of the 80 percent level of $64,000. The owner has a fire in the house that results in an actual loss of $16,000. But because he has not insured up to the 80 percent coinsurance level, the company will pay him only $14,000 instead of the full $16,000. Why? Because the owner's coverage was only seven-eighths of what it should have been under the coinsurance clause ($56,000 is seven-eighths of $64,000). Thus, the owner will receive only seven-eighths of the actual damages ($14,000 is seven-eighths of $16,000). If the owner had insured the property for the full 80 percent coinsurance value, or $64,000, he would have recovered the full $16,000 on the loss. The difference in premium between the full 80 percent value and the lesser value would have been so relatively small that the owner could be accused of being woefully imprudent for not obtaining the balance of the 80 percent coverage.

Keeping Up with Change

Prudent homeowners or tenants will make a careful inventory of all furnishings, appliances, and personal property and evaluate current market or replacement costs of those items in order to determine whether they are adequately covered by a basic homeowner's policy. The owner or renter will also be aware of the effects of inflation in most areas of the country. Many policies offer clauses that automatically increase the amount of coverage in line with inflation, for as the replacement value of the house increases, so must the amount of coverage if the owner is to be adequately protected. Policies may also be available that will pay you the full amount needed to rebuild your home, no matter what the cost.

If a homeowner or tenant acquires new personal items, or disposes of old items that have been insured, the owner must notify the insurance company so that the new acquisitions can be properly covered and the old dispositions properly deleted. When the insurance company is notified, it will issue an endorsement amending the policy, which should be checked for accuracy and then attached to the policy.

Filing a Claim

Exercise 8.5

In the event you do suffer a loss or damage, notify your insurance agent immediately. The agent may require that you obtain estimates of the proper repair or replacement of damaged items. If a burglary or theft has occurred, it

STRATEGIES FOR SUCCESS

Be Wise About Home-improvement Costs

Adding major improvements to your home can increase the value of the home accordingly. But take care not to overdo it, or you won't be able to recapture the expense when you later sell. Two prime problems: improving the house so much that you price it out of the range of similar homes in the neighborhood; and improvements that are too personalized, which a prospective buyer might find frivolous or unnecessary. For example, new kitchen cabinets and bathroom fixtures are reasonably safe bets: you'll probably get back most of the cost of them when you sell. But building an observatory in your attic or installing a waterfall in your yard might not appeal to a buyer. Chances are you won't get your money back on such highly personalized items. Consider the items in Table 8-1.

TABLE 8–1   Payback Time

If you spend money remodeling or adding on to your home, how much of that money are you likely to get back when you later sell the home? Numbers can vary widely, depending on your location, the quality of the work, and when it is done, but here are some general guidelines that might influence you to go ahead, or not bother with, a specific project. Figures are national averages. Return is the percentage of the original cost that you're likely to get back on resale.

Item	Average Cost	Payback	Return
Attic bedroom	$22,840	$19,084	84%
Bathroom addition	11,645	10,593	91
Bathroom remodel	8,423	6,480	77
Major kitchen remodel	21,262	19,190	84
Minor kitchen remodel	8,057	8,030	94
Master suite addition	36,472	30,530	84
Refinish basement	16,665	8,499	51
Built-in media center	4,353	2,699	62
Hard-wired security system	1,303	756	58
Home office	8,706	5,423	67
Replace siding	5,458	3,983	73

Pools: Returns averaged 31% for vinyl-lined, 44% for concrete (gunite), and 45% for fiberglass.

Sources: Remodeling Magazine, Dec. 1996.

may be necessary to obtain copies of the police report. If someone is hurt on your property, you should also report this immediately to your agent, for a public liability claim may arise. Under the public liability provisions of your homeowner's policy, the insurance company is obliged to provide legal defense for you against such claims as well as to pay any claims that are found to be valid. Delay in reporting to your agent could jeopardize your rights under your homeowner's policy.

PROPERTY TAXES

Property taxes (also called real estate taxes) provide the money that allows your city government to operate. A portion of the property taxes may also be allocated to the county and state within which your city is located to enable them to provide their respective services.

How are property taxes calculated? In order to meet the expenses of city services, the city must generate income from taxation. Representatives of the assessor's office review each property in the city periodically to determine the actual value of each parcel. When the current value of every property is known, the assessment rate is applied. For example, a given city may determine that residential property will be assessed at 20 percent of market value, while commercial property will be assessed at 25 percent and industrial property at 30 percent. (Business and industrial areas frequently contribute to a heavier share of tax dollars because they are using the property for income-producing purposes.) Thus, a house with a market value of $150,000 may be assessed at $30,000. In theory, all properties of the same type with equal market values are assessed equally.

They then determine the tax rate. Based on their budgetary needs, they may determine that the tax rate for a given year will be $100 for each $1,000 of assessed valuation. Thus, the house with the $150,000 current value, which has an assessment of $30,000 (20 percent of the current market value according to the formula) will pay taxes of $3,000 for the year.

The tax rate is adjusted annually to keep the city's income and expenses as close to equal as possible. Periodically all properties in the city, or a selection of properties in the city, may be reassessed to make sure they are in line with the prevailing market values.

Commonly, homeowners are billed for their property taxes in two installments six months apart. Tenants also indirectly pay a share of the tax because some of their rent is applied by the landlord to the tax bill on the property. If a property owner fails to pay property taxes, the city can sell the property at public auction to satisfy the unpaid taxes due.

Protesting Your Assessment

Exercise 8.6

Local laws allow owners to protest the assessment on their property and, if successful, reduce the assessment and thereby the taxes. Tenants can also take steps to have the assessment reduced in conjunction with the landlord, in the same way that individual property owners can.

STRATEGIES FOR SUCCESS

Energy Audit Can Save $$$$$

Your local utility company—gas, electric, water—may be willing to examine your home to see how you might be wasting energy. And wasted energy is wasted money. In addition to hints and tips that utilities publish from time to time, they may send representatives to your home to make an inspection that can result in money-saving suggestions. An energy audit can be particularly worthwhile if you are thinking of installing new major energy-using devices, such as water heater, furnace, air conditioner or refrigerator.

Although each local assessor's office attempts to value equal properties equally, errors can occur. Equal properties are those comparable in size, location, and date and quality of construction. Example: Your house and your next-door neighbor's house are identical. They were built at the same time by the same builder, and have the same size and room layout. They are virtual twins—with one exception: your house is assessed for $38,000 while your neighbor's house is assessed for only $30,000, with an annual tax bill roughly 20 percent lower than yours.

If an error exists concerning property you own or occupy, nobody other than you will take steps to correct that error. An improper assessment can mean hundreds of dollars lost each year, so it behooves any property owner to examine the local assessment rolls every few years to determine that the property is, in fact, being properly assessed.

The steps are relatively simple. Visit your local assessor's office and compare the assessments of the buildings in your immediate neighborhood. If you determine that your property is appraised too high, ask the assessor to explain how to file a protest. It's not necessary to have an attorney, but it might be wise if there is enough at stake. Regulations will differ from one community to the next, but it is common for there to be a cutoff date each year, after which assessments cannot be protested until the following year.

Exercise 8.7

Figure 8–1 illustrates a typical neighborhood. Assume that all houses were built at the same time and are equal in size and condition. Houses A and C are assessed at $20,000 each; house B is assessed at $25,000; houses D and E are each assessed at $30,000. Why the discrepancy? Since A, B, and C are indeed equal, it is likely that house B is overassessed by $5,000. House D might be rightfully assessed at $30,000 since it is a corner lot and in many communities a corner lot is considered more valuable than an interior lot. House E might be properly assessed at $30,000 if the street on which it fronts is considered to be a "better" street, such as a cul-de-sac, than the street on which the other houses front. But if you owned house B, D, or E, you'd be wise to make an inquiry of your local assessor.

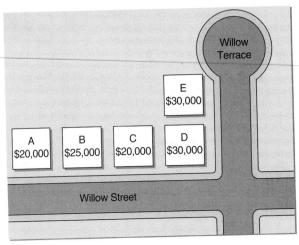

FIGURE 8–1   Property tax assessments

UTILITIES

The owner of a house makes arrangements with the local utility companies for them to provide water, gas, electricity, and telephone service. Utility bills, particularly for heating, can vary considerably throughout the seasons. Some utility companies offer budget payment plans in which the estimated annual cost is broken down into relatively even payments, allowing homeowners to even out their overall budgets.

The importance of energy conservation cannot be overstated. In addition to keeping your energy usage at a minimum—in line with your personal comfort needs—look into the tax credits and rebate plans offered by many states as well as the federal government for conservation improvements to your property. Explore these possibilities with your local utility companies.

MAINTENANCE AND REPAIRS

Human nature being what it is, we seldom get around to doing preventive maintenance on a house—such as seasonal lubrication and servicing of a furnace—until we hear the creaks and rattles warning that it is about to self-destruct. Unexpected maintenance costs can be a severe jolt to any budget.

To the homeowner, a periodic inspection is cheap insurance, alerting you to potential dangers and expenses. In addition to paying for ongoing maintenance costs, wise homeowners will set aside a reserve for replacements—a fund to take care of these costs without having to borrow, or dip into savings, or otherwise disrupt their normal budgets.

LAWS REGULATING HOUSING

A number of laws can affect the rights and obligations of both property owners and tenants. These laws differ from state to state and from city to city, so you should make inquiry in your own locality as to any laws that might affect you.

Zoning

Cities specify that certain areas may have only certain kinds of uses permitted in them. The city will be divided into zones according to the uses allowed in those zones. The broad categories in zoning regulations are residential, commercial, industrial, and agricultural. Within each category there may be subcategories. For example, within a residential category, there may be zones for just single-family housing, and zones in which multiple housing is permitted. Each zone may have regulations applicable to that zone. In a commercial zone, for example, there may be a requirement that so many off-street parking places are available for each thousand square feet of building space.

Generally, zoning regulations are like a pyramid: higher uses are permitted in any of the lower use zones, but lower use of zones may not be permitted in the zones above them. Figure 8–2 provides an illustration: In most cities, the highest use is for single-family homes, often designated as R (for

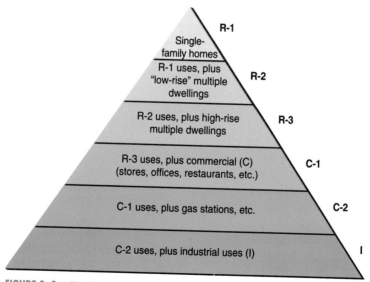

FIGURE 8–2   Zoning use

residential) -1. In areas zoned R-1, therefore, only single-family homes will be permitted. The next zone down may be designated R-2. These zones would permit R-1 uses (single-family homes) plus "low-rise" multiple dwellings. The next zone down might be called R-3, and it would permit all R-2 uses, plus high-rise multiple dwellings.

Zoning laws exist to maintain the quality of your neighborhood. For example: You wish to set up a beauty parlor in your home. You hang a sign on your front porch and accept clientele. If your home is in a zone that prevents businesses from being operated in the home, neighbors could have your business stopped because it is in violation of the zoning ordinances.

Residents of any municipality should make themselves aware of current zoning regulations and be on the alert for any change in the immediate vicinity that could affect the value of their residence. Zoning hearings are usually open to the public, and customarily appeals can be taken from unfavorable zoning rulings. If many people are affected by the possibility of a zoning ordinance change, they can group together and hire an attorney to represent all their joint interests.

Nuisances

One of your neighbors keeps a rooster that crows at dawn each morning; another plays a stereo at high volume every night; still another permits dangerous conditions to exist. These practices, and others like them, are known as nuisances. If you're located in an apartment house or a condominium, you may be able to get assistance from a sympathetic landlord or from the condominium owners' association. If you're a homeowner, you may have to resort to the local police or to your own attorney to get satisfaction. Nuisance laws exist in almost every city, but enforcing them can involve feats of diplomacy that the local magistrates may be incapable of carrying out to your satisfaction. If you can't resolve a nuisance problem with a neighbor by simple diplomacy, consider arbitration before getting involved with lawyers. Many communities offer free or low-priced arbitration services.

Eminent Domain

The law of eminent domain permits a government to acquire private property when the government can prove that the need exists for the public welfare. The process is generally known as condemnation, and it occurs where new highways and bridges are to be constructed, where urban renewal programs take place, and where other public uses are called for. Owners of property threatened by condemnation are entitled to fair payment for their property. Procedures vary as to how property owners are compensated.

There may be a hearing at which property owners present their claims for fair compensation. If the owners aren't satisfied with the offer, they may appeal, and if the appeal does not satisfy, the owners may take the matter into the courts. The aid of a lawyer and a competent real estate appraiser is advised in any condemnation situation.

The law of eminent domain can also affect your property indirectly, without actually taking any portion of it. For example, a new highway nearby may create noise and pollution problems for your house. None of your property has actually been taken, but the value of the property may suffer as a result. You may be entitled to some claim for damages as a result.

Anyone who is either buying or already owns any property should be aware of any possible eminent domain that could take place within proximity to your property. Knowledge of an impending condemnation might discourage you from buying certain property, and that knowledge can also permit you to take early action to protect your interests if a condemnation threatens currently owned property.

Rent Control and Condominium Conversion Regulations

If you live in a multiple-dwelling unit, rent control ordinances and condominium conversion regulations can have a very important effect on your rights. These laws will be discussed in more detail in the following chapter on renting.

PERSONAL ACTION WORKSHEET

Insurance Inventory

Whether you're a renter or an owner, it's important that your valuable personal possessions be adequately insured against damage or loss. Insurance coverage is advisable if the damage or loss would cause you financial distress. (Insuring items of sentimental value may be an unwise expense.) Too little or too much coverage can be costly. This checklist will help you determine the right amount of coverage. A color photo of each item can be very helpful if you ever have to file a claim.

Items	Current Protection	Replacement Cost	Cost to Insure Fully	Most Recent Appraisal
❑ Jewelry	_____	_____	_____	_____
❑ Collections	_____	_____	_____	_____
❑ Art	_____	_____	_____	_____
❑ Chinaware	_____	_____	_____	_____
❑ Silverware	_____	_____	_____	_____
❑ Cash, securities	_____	_____	_____	_____
❑ Musical instruments	_____	_____	_____	_____
❑ Electronic items (TV, stereo, VCR, computer)	_____	_____	_____	_____
❑ Sports equipment	_____	_____	_____	_____
❑ Furniture and furnishings	_____	_____	_____	_____

CONSUMER ALERT

Mortgage Insurance Can Be Confusing

There's one kind of insurance related to home ownership that really doesn't insure the property itself. Rather, it insures that your mortgage payments will be made in the event of the death or disability of the primary bread-winner in the family.

Since your mortgage debt is the largest you'll probably ever face, and since your payments represent a major obligation, it's wise to protect yourself against a catastrophe that could affect your ability to pay this debt.

Life insurance on your mortgage is generally of the "decreasing term" variety. The coverage decreases monthly as the amount of your debt decreases. Depending on your age, you might want to explore a level term or ordinary life policy instead of the decreasing term. Those might provide better long-term protection without greatly increasing your cost.

On the death of the breadwinner, proceeds of mortgage life insurance are commonly paid directly to the lender. This may not be best for you. It might be preferable to obtain a policy that would pay your named beneficiary (spouse, children) to do with as they please. Rather than have the mortgage paid off, they might prefer to continue making payments or to sell the house with the original mortgage intact. If the interest rate on the mortgage is lower than the current rate, it could prove costly later if the survivors needed to refinance the property at a higher interest rate.

Disability policies make your monthly payments for you if you are unable to work due to illness or accident. Many have a thirty- or sixty-day waiting period before payments commence. Compare the terms and costs of such policies, bearing in mind other sources of income that might be available to help you make your payments during a spell of disability. Your own insurance agent might be able to provide better coverage at lower cost than the lender can.

UPS & DOWNS   *The Economics of Everyday Life*

Why Utility Costs Fluctuate

As with food and travel prices, the seasons again are the main culprit for changing utility prices. You'll spend more on heating in the winter and more on cooling in the summer. Lawn watering boosts water bills in spring and summer; shorter days mean higher electric bills (for lighting) in fall and winter. Many of these fluctuations can be evened out: Most utility companies have budget plans that can offer you a level monthly payment throughout the year.

But other factors can also impact on your utility budget, and when they do you might have to increase your conservation vigil to keep costs down.

Commodity prices   You no doubt use gas or oil for heating, and your local electric company may burn oil to turn its generators. Worldwide fluctuations in the prices of these commodities will influence what you pay to warm your house, heat your water, or turn on your lights.

Mother Nature   Natural forces can play cruel tricks, such as shutting off the water supply. Recently, California suffered through a prolonged drought. Homeowners faced heavy penalties if their water usage exceeded certain levels. Farmers were also deprived of their full supply of water, which cut down the size of the crops, which in turn boosted food prices.

Competition   Telephone utilities didn't have any competition until the mid-1980s, when American Telephone and Telegraph (AT&T) was broken up into separate regional units, and a number of long-distance telephone companies emerged to challenge AT&T's historic monopoly. Today you have your choice of many long-distance carriers and local carriers. This change, together with the emergence of cellular phones, has transformed what once was a simple one-page telephone bill into a massive computer printout.

Regulation   With rare exceptions, suppliers of water, electricity, heating fuels, and telephone services are regulated by a state agency, the Public Utilities Commission (or a name similar to that). These agencies see to it that the utilities charge rates that are fair to consumers, but they still allow the utilities enough income to maintain and expand their facilities, and to attract investment capital. But mistakes can happen: nuclear power facilities were built across the nation in the 1970s that would supposedly reduce electricity costs. However, many of those expensive projects failed to meet their targets, and local consumers had to bear much of the excess costs.

?
?

WHAT IF . . . ?

How would you deal with these real-life possibilities?

1. You would like to do some work out of your home. Examples might include dealing in baseball cards or other collectibles; setting up a beauty salon; becoming a mail order distributor; or providing services to the public, such as tax returns or piano lessons. Each of these activities might violate a local zoning ordinance or might otherwise upset neighbors. What can you/should you do in advance to minimize any problems?

2. In chatting with neighbors you learn that your property taxes are much higher than those of comparable dwellings in the immediate neighborhood. One neighbor suggests to you that if you try to get your taxes lowered, that effort could backfire and cause everyone else's taxes to go up. Where do you go from here?

3. You have some valuables that would be covered on your property insurance policy only if they were separately "scheduled." Your insurance agent tells you that the cost of doing so would be very high. What options do you have that would be cost-effective?

NUMBER CRUNCHERS

Do the calculations to make decisions in these real-life possibilities.

1. There are many ways to cut your utility costs, including better insulation, weather-stripping on doors and windows, and awnings and shades to reduce the need for air conditioning. Calculate the actual installed costs of any such devices that you think can be cost-effective. Estimate as closely as possible (with the help of your utility companies) what savings you can realize. What net benefits, if any, are there? How will the installation of any of these devices affect the value of your property when you want to sell it?

2. How much can you save on property insurance premiums if you increase your deductibles? How much financial risk does this expose you to? How much can you reduce your risk by reducing your deductibles?

3. Based on your existing property insurance policy (either as an owner or as a tenant), calculate how much you'd receive from your insurance company if you suffered specific damages: (a) Fire damages the building—reconstruction cost of the building is $30,000, and replacement cost of personal property is $10,000. (b) Smoke damages personal property—cleaning and replacement cost is $3,000. (c) A burglar breaks in and steals the TV set, VCR, computer, and golf clubs—replacement cost total $4,000. If you can't calculate the answers on your own, ask your insurance agent to help you.

FOR BETTER OR FOR WORSE

Things beyond our control often impact our personal and financial well-being, for better or for worse. Some are more predictable than others. How would you be affected if the following real-life phenomena happened? Could you have seen it coming? What steps could you have taken to minimize damage or maximize advantage? The better able you are to anticipate and recognize these forces, the better equipped you are to deal with them.

1. It's party time! Saturday night, and you're expecting thirty guests for a rousing birthday party. As the first guests arrive you remember that you forgot to renew your dwelling insurance policy the day before, the last day of the grace period.

2. A fire in your apartment building causes smoke damage to your furniture and all fabrics (clothes, linens, towels, drapes, etc.) They stink, and it will cost about $1,000 to clean and deodorize everything. You don't have tenant's insurance because you thought it cost too much.

3. A neighbor's home is burgled. A few days later you're visited by a home security company selling burglar alarms.

Renting

Many a man who pays rent all his life owns his own home. And many a family has successfully saved for a home, only to find itself at last with nothing but a house.

Bruce Barton

Tens of millions of Americans rent their dwellings. Many do so because they've not been able to accumulate enough money to purchase a house or condominium. Others do so because they prefer the freedom and flexibility that comes with renting. Renting entails many important legal and financial considerations. This chapter will make you aware of those considerations and will help you resolve common problems that come with renting. They include:

- What factors you should evaluate in deciding whether to rent or to buy
- How to understand the terms of a lease and how to negotiate a rental arrangement that's best for you
- How you may be able to obtain the right to buy the place you've been renting or want to rent
- What to do if your rights as a tenant are violated

If you are a renter, you are paying another person a fee for the privilege of living in his or her property. You might rent a person's house, or you might rent a multiple-unit dwelling, such as a duplex, a condominium complex, or an apartment house. Mobile home rentals are also not uncommon.

A renter occupies a dwelling in one of two ways: on a month-to-month basis or on a fixed-term basis. On a month-to-month basis, both the land-lord and the tenant have the right to terminate the arrangement upon giving 30 days' notice to the other party. Commonly, the landlord expects the tenant to comply with certain rules and regulations, which are often spelled out in a written agreement. On a fixed-term basis, the landlord and tenant agree in a written document that the tenant has the right to occupy the premises for a specific time, such as one year or two years. The agreement between the two parties is referred to as a lease.

PROS AND CONS OF RENTING

Exercise 9.1

Many people, particularly in larger cities, are dyed-in-the-wool renters. They simply prefer the apartment mode of living—being close to other people and free of the cares that often go with ownership. To them, rental is a way of life, and they don't think about buying a home.

Other people have no choice: They don't have the money to make a down payment on a home, and thus they must be renters. This group is further broken down into two categories: (1) those who prefer to spend their money on other things rather than accumulate it for a down payment, and thus will probably remain permanent renters, and (2) those who desire to become owners eventually and who structure their budget so as to accumulate the necessary down payment. As they struggle to accumulate those funds, they often wonder: Is it worth it to own a home, or should we just be content as renters?

Traditionally, homeownership has been considered a wise step financially. Over the long run, that probably remains true. But ownership is not the right choice for everybody.

To help you make the decision best suited to your needs, desires, and abilities, let's examine the pros and cons of renting, as illustrated in Figure 9–1.

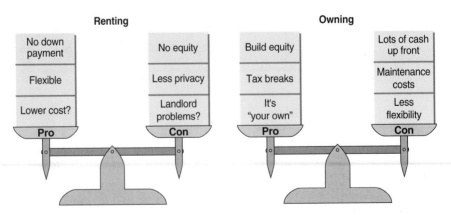

FIGURE 9–1   Renting versus owning

Flexibility

One of the primary advantages of renting—whether it's a house or an apartment—is flexibility. When a lease expires, the tenant is free to move on or renew. There are none of the time-consuming, expensive concerns of selling one home, buying another, and trying to dovetail the two transactions. The flexibility is even greater where furnished units are rented, for the chores of physically moving are considerably minimized. Renting is often preferred by people who have not yet settled into their chosen lifestyle or career and by those whose work or interests dictate frequent moves. The same is true for persons at or near retirement who might wish to be able to come and go as they please without the concerns of ownership.

No Money Tied Up

With few exceptions, ownership requires that a substantial sum of money be tied up in the property. When you buy a house or condominium, it's necessary to make a down payment. Moreover, as you make your monthly mortgage payments, a portion of which goes to reduce your mortgage debt, those additional sums are effectively tied up in the property. Money that's tied up in property is money that could otherwise be earning income for you if it were invested. Until you sell, borrow against, or refinance the property—all of which could be time consuming and costly—you cannot get at your money. In a rental, there's no need to tie up large sums of money beyond your security deposit, which usually is about two months' rent.

Income Tax Implications

Ownership provides certain income tax advantages that are not available to renters. Tax laws allow owners to take deductions for the interest they pay on their mortgage and for the property taxes they pay. This can mean a substantial saving in taxes. Furthermore, if you sell your home and realize a profit, that profit is subject to favorable tax laws. (See chapter 10 for a more detailed discussion.)

These tax advantages have often been the deciding factor for many people in purchasing a home rather than renting. But a closer look at the situation reveals that in many cases the advantages are not necessarily as attractive as they seem on the surface.

For example: The Alpers have saved $20,000 to use as a down payment for the purchase of a house. Considering the interest they pay on their mortgage, their property taxes, and their tax bracket, the ownership of the home results in an income tax saving of $2,000 a year. Had the Alpers *not* bought a home but had instead invested the $20,000 at 10 percent interest, they would have earned $2,000 per year—before income tax considerations. In this particular case, careful arithmetic indicates that they may not be that much better off financially on a year-to-year basis as a result of buying instead of renting their dwelling and using their available funds for investment. It can be a very close call.

In deciding between owning and renting, this income tax factor should be calculated based on your own tax situation. The numbers differ from person to person, from deal to deal, and from year to year. The more costly the house and the higher the interest rate, the more favorable the tax advantage can be to an owner.

No Chance of Profit (or Risk of Loss)

Exercise 9.2

One of the attractions of ownership is the lure of profiting on a resale. Tenants have no such chance for profit, but they also face no risk of loss.

Indeed, the lure of profit often bears fruit. But profit is often the direct result of inflation, and although you may profit on the sale of your existing home, you'll soon realize that you have to live somewhere, and the cost of acquiring new housing will have risen in step with the price of your old housing. Thus, your profit can be easily absorbed by the simple change from one dwelling to another.

Profit can also be reduced by two other factors: real estate commissions and income taxes. In all likelihood, you will use a real estate agent to help you sell your house, and a commission of 6 or 7 percent of the selling price goes to the agent. Furthermore, if you sell your house at a profit, that profit might be subject to federal income taxes. (If you sell your house at a loss, that loss is not deductible.) See chapter 10 for further details.

No Protection Against Inflation

Neither owning nor renting can fully protect against inflation. For a month-to-month tenant, the rental can be increased on 30 days' notice. For a tenant on a lease, the rent can be increased upon renewal of the lease (subject to any rent control ordinances that may apply). Homeowners can expect increasing expenses for property taxes, property insurance, maintenance, repairs, and utilities. And if homeowners are making payments on variable rate mortgages, their monthly payments can be subject to increases as well. Homeowners with fixed interest rate mortgages have much greater protection against inflation because their payments for interest and principal will remain constant for as long as they own their property.

Overall, homeowners do have a better chance to protect themselves from inflation, because as prices rise over the years, so will the value of their homes. The only problem with this, as noted earlier, is that the prices of all other homes will have risen comparably, so that any profit they realize on the sale may turn out to be illusory when they purchase new homes.

This particular advantage of homeownership is based on the assumption that housing values will continue to rise. But that phenomenon is by no means guaranteed. Housing markets are definitely subject to up and down fluctuations. If your timing is unfortunate enough to find you buying when the market is high and wanting to sell when the market is low, this inflation-proofing advantage of homeownership will not exist. Indeed, you might have been better off renting.

No Building Equity

"Why rent and collect worthless rent receipts when we can own and be building a hefty equity in our home?" Fact or myth? Although it's true that rent receipts have no tangible value, the other side of the question can be misleading. The average stay in a dwelling by a typical American family is from seven to ten years and, during those early years of the common thirty-year mortgage, the reduction of mortgage debt is very small indeed.

Equity is the difference between what your house is worth and what is owed on it. Part of each mortgage payment you make reduces your debt and, theoretically, when you later sell the property, you recapture that sum, plus any appreciation in the value of your house.

Chapter 7 discusses in more detail how interest is figured on mortgages. For the moment, note that during the first ten years of a 9 percent thirty-year mortgage, the reduction of debt on the mortgage is only about 10 percent of the total original mortgage.

For example, during the first ten years of a $150,000 mortgage that is set to run for thirty years at a 9 percent interest rate, you will have reduced your mortgage indebtedness from $150,000 to just $135,000 (see Table 7–5).

Added Expenses

If you're a tenant, the cost of certain repairs may be borne by the landlord, depending on the terms of the lease. If you are an owner, you'll usually have to bear most of these costs yourself. As a tenant, you're probably limited in the number of alterations and modifications you can make to the premises. As an owner, you are free to do as you please—paint your house or condominium walls purple and pink if you like—as long as you're aware of the implications of such modifications when it comes time to sell it. You run the risk of overpersonalizing your premises and scaring away would-be buyers. You also run the risk of overimproving the premises and thus pricing the dwelling out of the market for comparable units within that neighborhood. But bearing those factors in mind, the freedom of modifying your dwelling is vastly greater in an ownership situation than with a rental.

TO BUY OR TO RENT: A CASE HISTORY

Exercise 9.3

Let's examine a situation in which a family is debating buying versus renting. This example does not presume to answer the dilemma. It's merely intended to serve as a guide to help you know what arithmetic you should consider.

The Browns have found a condominium, and they can either buy or rent it. The purchase price is $82,000; the monthly rental would be $900, which would include all utilities, maintenance, and association dues.

If they buy, they have $12,000 in cash to use as a down payment, and the property has an existing $70,000 mortgage with an annual interest rate of 12 percent. The mortgage can be assumed. Monthly payments on interest and principal total $720. Property taxes are $120 per month, property insurance is $40 per month, and utilities and maintenance total $100 per month. Thus, if they buy, their total monthly cash outlay would be $980.

The Browns estimate that, based on their current tax bracket, ownership will result in tax savings to them of $2,000 in the first year, or $166 per month.

On the other hand, if they decide to rent and they invest their $12,000 at 10 percent return, they will take in $1,200 during the first year (before income taxes), or $100 per month. After taxes, they estimate that the $100 per month would shrink to $76 per month. Thus as Table 9–1 shows, they are looking at a difference of $10 per month net savings if they buy instead of rent. This alone might convince them to buy, particularly if they felt that they'd have an opportunity to reap a profit upon a later sale.

TABLE 9–1   The Browns: Renting versus Owning

Monthly Costs			
As Owners		**As Renters**	
Mortgage	$720	Base rent (including utilities)	$900
Property tax	120	After-tax earning on invested $12,000	76
Property insurance	40		
Utilities and maintenance	100		
	980		
Tax savings	166		
Out-of-pocket cost	$814	Out-of-pocket cost	$824

But the Browns know their own circumstances very well: they suspect that within a year Mr. Brown's job might require them to move to a different city. They've also examined the local housing market and have found that prices are flat and seem likely to remain so for at least many months. Looking one year ahead, they realize that if they have to sell the condominium and find themselves without a buyer for just one month after they've been transferred, they will be out more than $900. That would more than wipe out the monthly savings they'd have realized during that year by being owners instead of renters.

The Browns, it appears, are almost in a "toss the coin" situation. Table 9–1 illustrates the arithmetic of the Brown's dilemma. Resolving the matter can depend on personal circumstances. How long might they stay in a given dwelling? How wisely will they invest their funds if they decide to rent instead of buy? Which way will the housing market turn? The case of the Browns is not intended to convince you to become a renter or a buyer, but merely to show you the arithmetic and the crystal ball gazing that you must do in order to reach a conclusion best suited to your own circumstances.

SHOPPING FOR RENTALS

Exercise 9.4

Many of the same considerations apply when you are looking for a dwelling to rent or to buy. How close will it be to your place of work, to shopping, to schools, to entertainment? What is the condition of the building and of the neighborhood? How large are the premises and will they suit your foreseeable needs for the time you'll be living there?

Additional matters need to be considered if you are looking for an apartment. You should talk to other tenants in the building and try to determine the level of service and care provided by the landlord. Are reasonable requests by tenants taken care of promptly and courteously? Is the building well maintained, both aesthetically and mechanically? What has been the history of rent increases? Are there any local rent-control ordinances that apply to the building?

The Personal Action Worksheet at the end of this chapter will help you in your quest for an apartment.

Depending on your community, the classified ads in your local newspaper may be all you need to direct you to available apartments. In larger communities, you might find it desirable to seek the services of a rental agent. It's not uncommon for a rental agent to charge the tenant a fee for finding an apartment. Before you contract with a rental agent, determine what fees will be expected from you and get personal references from other individuals who have used that rental agent.

When you buy a house, you can reasonably expect that a real estate agent who is working for you will escort you from one house to another.

STRATEGIES FOR SUCCESS

How to Compete for Rental Space

You want to rent an apartment, and it's your bad luck that there are more lookers than apartments on the market. The competition for a good apartment in your price range is tough. How can you win? Assume that any prudent landlord will want to check your credit and see references, particularly from your current landlord and from your employer. Get a copy of your credit history from your local credit bureau. Get copies of those references and have them in hand to give to the landlord when you apply. This will save the landlord time and trouble. Also, offer to give the landlord a cash deposit on the spot—maybe $50 or so—to take the apartment off the market while he or she checks you out. Make it refundable if he doesn't accept you, nonrefundable if you bow out. You're putting some money at risk, but if you're sure you want the unit, this strategy can help assure you of getting it.

But don't expect the same kind of service from a rental agent. In all likelihood, you will be given the address and instructions on how to view the apartment, and you'll be on your own.

Depending on the supply of apartments in your community, and on the demand for them, you might find it necessary to leave a deposit with the landlord immediately if you find a place you like. If the demand is high and the supply low, a landlord will rent to the first interested party who puts up the necessary deposit. On the other hand, if the demand is low, the landlord might be willing to "hold" a given apartment for you for a day or two, perhaps even longer. In such a case, it would be to your advantage to get that promise in writing from the landlord.

When you examine an apartment, determine whether the landlord expects you to rent on a month-to-month basis or to sign a lease. Examine the premises carefully and determine that everything is in proper working order (appliances, plumbing, electrical outlets). If you have children or pets, or expect to have them, make sure they will be acceptable to the landlord. And in addition to finding out what the monthly rental will be, find out what kind of deposits the landlord expects.

THE LEASE AND ITS KEY CLAUSES

Exercise 9.5

Renting a dwelling—be it a house, a mobile home, or an apartment—involves numerous rights and obligations between landlord and tenant. Those rights and obligations may be spelled out in a full-fledged contract called a lease. A lease is not of the same financial magnitude as the mortgage that corresponds to the purchase of a house, but it can entail many thousands of dollars, and you want to make sure you're getting what you bargained for.

Basically, the lease entitles you to occupy certain premises for a certain period of time at an agreed-on price. Here are some of the key clauses that could affect the nature and cost of your occupancy.

Expenses

The lease should set forth exactly who is responsible for what expenses including utilities and real estate taxes. If the tenant is responsible for utilities, will the tenant be separately metered so that the true utility costs can be exactly measured? If the tenant is paying based on a certain percentage of the total building occupancy and is not separately metered, will the tenant be getting a fair shake?

Repairs

Who will be responsible for *making* which repairs? And perhaps more important, who will be responsible for *paying* for the repairs that are made? The landlord may be responsible for seeing to it that repairs are made, but some repairs may be done at the tenant's expense, others at the landlord's. Generally, the landlord is responsible for repairing structural defects and for keeping the central heating unit in proper working order. The tenants may be responsible for attending to their own repairs on minor items within the premises, including but not limited to plumbing leaks and defective appliances. Examine the premises before you sign a lease to determine what possible repair bills you might be facing during your occupancy. If you determine that you would be more than normally vulnerable to repair costs, you might want to renegotiate the repair clause of your lease with the landlord before you sign.

Quiet Enjoyment

Quiet enjoyment is a legal term that assures you of the right to privacy and quiet in your occupancy of the premises. If the landlord fails to deliver quiet enjoyment—that is, fails to keep the neighbors from playing their stereo next to your bedroom wall at four o'clock in the morning—you will have the right either to withhold your rent payment or to get assistance in court in upholding your rights.

Extra Fees

Does your monthly rental include all the features of your occupancy, or will added costs be hidden in the small print on the back page of the lease, such as parking fees, use of recreational facilities, and assessments for improvements in the common areas? All rental costs and fees should be clearly understood prior to the signing of any lease.

Renewal Options

Will you have a right to renew your lease on the expiration of the original term? Not all leases contain this privilege, and it may be one worth bargaining for. Without a renewal option, the landlord can ask whatever the market will bear when the original lease term expires. If the tenant is not willing to pay what the landlord is asking, the landlord has the right to make the tenant move out. A renewal option is for the protection of the tenant: he or she has the right either to stay on at the agreed-on rental or to move out. It's reasonable to expect that the rental rate will be higher on a renewal than on the original term so that the landlord can be protected against rising costs. Even at a higher rent, however, the renewal option does offer the tenant flexibility and choice, things often worth paying for.

Some leases may contain an automatic renewal clause. When such a clause exists, the lease may automatically renew for another term unless the tenant gives written notice to the landlord that he or she does not wish to have the lease renewed. If you are involved in such a lease and you fail to give the proper notice, you could become responsible for lease payments for an additional term. For example, if the original term was for one year and the automatic renewal clause goes into effect, you could become responsible for an additional year's rent.

Sublease Privileges

You may be subleasing *from* another party, or you may wish to sublease *to* another party. If you are subleasing from the original tenant, you will be subject to the terms of his or her lease. Prior to subleasing from another party, you might want to determine whether in fact that party has the right to sublease to you and, if the landlord has given his consent, if such consent is called for in the original lease. If you sublease from another party and that party does not have the legal right to sublease to you, the landlord technically could evict you, and perhaps the main tenant as well, for violation of the lease.

On the other hand, if you wish to have the right to sublease to other parties while you are the main tenant, you must make certain that the lease contains this privilege. In the sublease clause, the landlord may or may not reserve the right to approve of any sublessee, generally for reasons of creditworthiness. Unless the landlord consents, the fact that you subleased to another party will not relieve you of your obligation to pay the rent.

A sublease privilege is one that favors the tenant. It gives the tenant the flexibility of being able to move out before the lease has expired and to defray obligations by allowing another party to live in the apartment or house. If you do sublease to another party, you must make certain in advance, by way of a credit history and references, that the party is creditworthy and reliable.

Security Deposits

There are three possible types of security deposits you might be required to pay: deposits to ensure the payment of the rent, cleaning deposits, and damage deposits. The rental deposit is usually designated to cover the last month's rent of the lease. This gives the landlord some protection in the event you move out early. Moving out early does not necessarily relieve you of your remaining obligations under the lease. Technically, if you move out after eighteen months of a twenty-four-month lease, you'll be liable for the remaining six months. The landlord will apply the one month's deposit you have paid toward that six months' obligation and will be able to commence legal proceedings to collect the remaining five months' rent from you.

STRATEGIES FOR SUCCESS

Good P.R. with Landlord Can Pay Off

Relations between landlords and tenants are seldom all sweetness and light, but they can be more positive than negative if you, as a tenant, maintain good public relations with your landlord. You're not obliged to do so, but it can pay off for you. Paying your rent promptly leads to smooth relations and can win a good credit reference for you—which can be of value. If minor repairs or replacements are needed, do them yourself, which is usually a lot better than going through the aggravation of reporting minor problems and waiting for the landlord to correct them. It's appropriate for you to ask the landlord to reimburse you for for any out-of-pocket expenses the landlord would normally incur. And you can try to arrange for some payment for your labor. Landlords appreciate your handling small repairs, just as they appreciate prompt reports of leaks or any other problems that can escalate into expensive repairs. If you and your landlord understand each other's point of view, chances are you'll be able to negotiate a more favorable renewal.

If the premises need cleaning, he landlord can be expected to apply the cleaning deposit to that task, and the tenant might not receive any of the deposit back. If damage has occurred, the damage deposit will be applied to making the necessary repairs, but the tenant's obligation might not be limited to the amount of the deposit. If the damage exceeds the amount of the deposit, and the lease stipulates that damages aren't limited to that amount, the landlord can pursue the tenant for the excess needed to make the appropriate repairs.

For the fullest protection of the tenant, both parties should closely examine the premises before the tenant takes occupancy to determine the condition of the unit. For example, there may be a crack in a wall that would normally be covered by a piece of furniture or a wall hanging. If it's there when the tenant takes occupancy, the fact should be noted on the lease so that no one can claim that you caused the damage during your occupancy. The tenant and the landlord may trust each other implicitly, but the tenant has to remember that on moving out, there may be a different landlord who will not remember that the crack was there at the time the tenant moved in. Color photos of the premises can be particularly helpful in this regard.

Improvements

The tenant of an apartment or a house may wish to make certain improvements on the premises during the term of occupancy. Normally, if improvements are easily removable, such as curtains, they would remain the property of the tenant. Some improvements, however, may not be quite so portable. For example, a tenant may install built-in bookcases or a wet bar. Unless the tenant and the landlord have agreed otherwise in advance, improvements of this sort might be claimed by the landlord as part of the property. If any improvements are to be made in the premises, the landlord and the tenant should agree, *before* the improvements are made, who will have the benefit on termination of the lease.

Amending the Lease

Even though a lease is a binding legal contract, it can be amended in writing at any time by mutual agreement of the landlord and tenant. (The same holds true in a purchase contract for a house or condominium.) Any amendment should be signed by both parties. Any such changes could be inserted into a lease agreement even after the agreement has originally been signed and occupancy has been taken. Legal advice should be sought on the specific consequences of amendments.

Insurance

Landlords must insure themselves against damage to the building, such as fire damage. But you, as a tenant, will be responsible for insuring your own possessions. See chapter 8 for a discussion of tenant's insurance. If the building is extensively damaged by a fire or other catastrophe, you may not be able to occupy your apartment. In your tenant's insurance, determine how much payment you'll receive for temporary quarters until your building is again available to you.

MONTH-TO-MONTH TENANCY

Not all tenants have a written lease. Many people occupy dwellings on a month-to-month basis without the benefit of any written documents. This, in effect, is a one-month lease, which allows the landlord to alter the terms by giving one month's notice and allows the tenant to vacate by giving one month's notice. Laws may differ from state to state on precisely what the rights of the parties are on a month-to-month lease. Generally, a landlord wishing to raise rents or a tenant wishing to move out must give at least one month's notice from the start of any month of their respective intentions to do so. For example, if a tenant wishes to vacate on March 1, he or she should give proper notice to the landlord not later than the preceding February 1. If this is done, the rental obligation will cease after February, as will the right to occupy the apartment. If, however, notice isn't given until say, February 10, the tenant might be legally bound to pay the March rent.

COMBINATIONS OF LEASING AND BUYING

In some situations you might become a tenant and then an owner. You may have a lease with an option to buy or a lease with a first refusal to buy.

A Lease with an Option to Buy

A lease with an option to buy puts the parties in this status: tenants have the right to occupy the premises for the stated time and for the stated rent. At any time during their tenancy, they have the right to notify the owner of their intent to purchase the property at a previously agreed-on price. During the period of tenancy, the owner cannot sell the property to any other party unless the tenants agree to release their option to buy.

Here's an example. The Greens lease a house at $1,000 per month with an option to buy the house for $100,000. They may exercise their right to buy at any time during their tenancy but at least thirty days before the end of the lease. If they wish to exercise their option, they give the owner the proper notice and enter into a sales agreement. If they fail to give the proper notice within the allotted time, their option will expire and they will no longer have the right to purchase at the agreed-on price.

By entering into a lease with an option to buy, the owner of the premises is taking the property off the market for at least the term of the lease. The owner has no assurance that the tenant will in fact buy the property and may be forgoing an opportunity to lease or sell the property to others at a better rental or purchase price. Thus, the owner can be expected to charge a price for giving a purchase option to the tenant. That price might be a higher than normal rent or purchase price, or a flat sum up front that would not be refundable if the option were not exercised, and that might be applied (in whole or in part) against the purchase price if the option is exercised.

A Lease with a Right of First Refusal

A lease with a right of first refusal to purchase is another alternative that should be considered. Under a lease with a right of first refusal to purchase, the owner will still be free to offer the property for sale to others during the term of the tenancy, subject, however, to the right of the tenant to meet any bona fide offer the owner may acquire. Here's how such an arrangement might work. The tenant and the owner agree on a $1,000 per month rental. During the period of the tenancy, the landlord has the right to offer the property for sale to anyone at all. A would-be buyer offers $105,000. The tenant then has the express right to meet that $105,000 offer within a period of, say, three days after receiving notification by the landlord of the offer. Or the tenant can pass on the offer, and either have to move out or become the tenant of the new owner.

In the case of a lease with a first refusal to purchase, the landlord is not taking the property off the market, as in a lease with an option to purchase. Thus, the landlord might be less inclined to charge a premium price for either the rental or the purchase.

RENT LAWS

Virtually every city has ordinances pertaining to health and safety measures in multiple-residence dwellings. These ordinances require landlords to maintain proper levels of sanitation, structural soundness, adequacy of plumbing and wiring, and precautions against fire. Such ordinances vary considerably from city to city. Tenants who think their rights have been violated with respect to these health and safety ordinances should notify the landlord. If a violation of an ordinance is not corrected, the appropriate city offices should be notified. Rent-control laws and condominium-conversion laws have proliferated in recent years. These laws are designed to protect the interests of tenants, and you should become aware of any such laws that exist in your community.

Rent Control

Rent-control laws protect tenants by limiting the rental increases that a landlord can seek. The laws may also prohibit discriminatory leasing practices and may protect tenants against wrongful eviction. These laws can differ widely from city to city—with some cities having none at all—so you should determine what specific ordinances apply in your own case. Where rent-control laws do exist, they will generally spell out how tenants can seek relief from landlords who may have violated the law.

Condominium-conversion Laws

Leonard, the landlord, owns a four-unit apartment house, which he wants to sell for $300,000. But the economy is weak, and he has a hard time finding anyone who wishes to make the investment. Leonard then has a clever idea. Instead of looking for a single buyer for the whole building, why not convert the building into condominiums and sell each unit separately for $100,000 each? It may take some additional paperwork, but he will probably be able to dispose of the building faster and at a much better price: $400,000 instead of $300,000. This is an example of what is known as condominium conversion: apartments being converted into individual condominiums.

This can be bad for some tenants, particularly if they don't have the necessary down payment, and are thus forced to move. On the other hand, many tenants find it an attractive opportunity, enabling them to convert their non–tax-deductible rent into substantially tax-deductible mortgage payments.

Condominium-conversion laws were passed to protect the former type of tenants, those who found themselves dispossessed of their living quarters, often because of inconsiderate and greedy landlords.

Condominium-conversion ordinances typically require at least a majority approval of existing tenants before a landlord can convert the property into condominiums. The ordinance may also require approval of the city.

If you are a tenant, you may someday have to face the possibility of your apartment being converted into a condominium. If that time arrives, you should consider the advantages to becoming an owner and the advantages in remaining a tenant, even if it means having to move. The chapters in this book on buying and financing a house can help you make a prudent decision.

TERMINATING A LEASE

As far in advance of your leaving as possible, read your lease carefully. Be certain that you know when the lease terminates. Watch out for any clause that would create an automatic renewal of the lease. Such a clause may read, "Unless either party gives notice to the other in writing of his intention to cancel this lease, the lease will automatically renew for another year upon [date]." This means that if you don't want the lease to renew automatically, you must give proper notice to the landlord in writing before a certain date. If you fail to do this, the landlord can technically hold you liable for another year's rent.

If you have given the landlord a security deposit, what does the lease state about getting it back? Many state laws stipulate when, and under what conditions, a landlord is to return a tenant's rental deposit. Know in advance what your rights are so that you won't have to forfeit any money.

If you're planning to move before your lease has expired, does your lease give you the right to sublet the apartment? If you do sublet, you should be certain that the subtenants are responsible. They should sign an agreement assuming all your obligations under the lease, including the obligation to repair at their own expense any damages they cause.

If you wish to move far in advance of the termination date and either you don't wish to or cannot sublet, you should discuss a settlement price with the landlord. You can, of course, simply move out, continue to pay your rent, and hope that the landlord will rerent your apartment quickly. Generally, the law puts some burden on the landlord to try to rerent as quickly as possible, but you can't always depend on the landlord to be diligent in this respect.

If you are renting any appliances or furniture or have any services under contract for an apartment or a rented house, be certain to examine the rental documents. For example, if you have leased the furniture or large appliances, you'll want to be certain that you can terminate those contracts concurrently with leaving the apartment.

If you are paying your own utilities, arrange well in advance to have all utility meters read as of your final day of occupancy. Ask the utility companies—telephone, electric, gas, water—to bill you for the final reading, and be sure that the meters are returned to the landlord's name following your departure.

If you suspect that there may be *any* question whatsoever regarding the condition in which you are leaving the house or apartment, settle it with the landlord *before* you leave. Go over the property with the landlord and be certain that he agrees that everything is as it should be. Then ask the landlord to sign a brief letter stating that everything is in the proper condition.

Renters are entitled to the same tax deductions for moving expenses as homeowners are, provided they meet the same distance and work tests. The cost of settling your lease obligation with your landlord if you move before the end of the lease may be included as one of the deductible expenses.

✓ ***PERSONAL ACTION WORKSHEET***

A Guide for Renters

If you're comparing rental dwellings, this checklist will help you determine the respective advantages and disadvantages of various sites. The cheapest rent doesn't necessarily mean the best dwelling. If you choose one place and find you're unhappy with it, bear in mind the cost, energy, and aggravation involved in finding another place and making a move.

	Dwelling A	Dwelling B	Dwelling C
❑ Monthly rent	_____	_____	_____
❑ Month-to-month, or lease? If lease, for how long?	_____	_____	_____
❑ If lease, do you have options to renew? At what rental?	_____	_____	_____
❑ Total amount of deposits required (security, cleaning, damage)	_____	_____	_____
❑ Will deposits earn interest? At what rate?	_____	_____	_____
❑ Estimated miles traveled per month to work, school, routine shopping	_____	_____	_____
❑ Estimated travel cost per month	_____	_____	_____
❑ Is there a resident manager to handle problems?	_____	_____	_____
❑ Other tenants' opinions of building management	_____	_____	_____
❑ General condition of building, grounds, your specific unit	_____	_____	_____
❑ Are pets allowed?	_____	_____	_____
❑ Is the building governed by any local rent-control ordinance? If so, what is the extent of your protection?	_____	_____	_____
❑ Extra amenities available: pool, rec room, parking, laundry, storage area	_____	_____	_____
❑ Security provisions: doorman, access to entryway, lighting?	_____	_____	_____

⚠️

CONSUMER ALERT —————————————————————————————

Look Before You Lease

Renting an apartment (or house) on a month-to-month basis does not constitute a heavy commitment on your part. If things don't work out, you can leave on giving thirty days' notice in the proper fashion.

But signing a lease for a year or two can involve thousands of dollars, and if things don't work out, you could be caught in a costly hassle or have to endure considerable inconvenience. Take these precautions before you sign a lease:

- Determine whether there are objectionable noises from adjoining apartments. There might be little you can do to silence a tuba-playing neighbor once you've moved in. It might be a sign to look elsewhere.
- Check with other tenants in the building to learn how the landlord adjusts complaints, makes needed repairs, and otherwise fulfills the obligations specified in the lease.
- A rapidly growing phenomenon is the rental of condos. You rent a unit from an individual owner rather than a landlord who owns the whole building. In many cases, the owner of the unit has bought it as an investment and is renting it out until he or she can sell it at a profit. The owner may reside in another city and may not be concerned with the ongoing welfare of the tenants. In situations like this, overall management of the building is diluted, and there can be considerable difficulty in maintaining tenant satisfaction. A committee of absentee owners simply cannot maintain the same level of efficiency as can an on-premises landlord or management company. If you're faced with these possibilities, be forewarned accordingly.
- Learn the landlord's policies with respect to returning security deposits. If he or she is reputed to be slow, nit-picking, or argumentative, be prepared to exert your legal rights to ensure getting back whatever you're entitled to within the proper time limits set forth in your state's (or city's) laws.

UPS & DOWNS   *The Economics of Everyday Life* ───────────────

Why Rental Costs Go Up and Down

Being a tenant does not necessarily mean that your dwelling costs will forever spiral upward. If you're willing to take extra time in seeking a rental and if you're willing to make some compromises, you might find ways to lower your costs, or at least keep them reasonably stable. Consider the following:

Local laws   Different cities can have very different laws regarding rent control, property taxation, trash removal, police and fire protection, and so on. All of these elements can mean widely differing costs to landlords, who in turn pass those costs onto tenants. Main Street is the boundary between City A and City B. Comparable rental units on either side of Main Street may have widely different rental prices because City A and City B have widely different local laws.

New competition   Landlords of new apartment buildings often offer steep rental discounts to new tenants. This competitive pressure can cause landlords in comparable nearby buildings to drop their rents accordingly—at least until the competition subsides.

Furnishings   The more a rental unit is furnished, the higher the rent will be. If you have your own furnishings, particularly stove and refrigerator, you can keep your costs down. If you don't have furnishings and the landlord can provide them (at a somewhat higher rent), you might be better off making a deal with the landlord than buying or renting the furnishings from someone else. The landlord can get a nice tax break by buying and providing you with furnishings; take this into account in your negotiations with him.

Changing neighborhoods   As local conditions change, so do rental rates. Run-down areas have been renovated into trendy "where-it's-at" parts of town, and once-trendy places have become derelict. When pride of ownership becomes fashionable in a given area, you can expect rentals to rise. When you start seeing graffiti, rents will be stable or falling.

One-on-one negotiations   Simple negotiations that can affect the ups and downs of rental costs are as follows: (1) If a landlord is having vacancy problems, he or she will be much more flexible on the rental price for a tenant who has good character and credit references. (2) If a landlord wants you to sign a one-year lease and you're willing to commit to a two-year lease, you might well get a better price. (3) If you're willing to do your own repairs, the landlord might bless you, in addition to lowering your base rent. Those who don't ask don't get.

? **WHAT IF . . . ?** _____

How would you deal with these real-life possibilities?

1. You have an opportunity to rent a delightful condominium. The owner is moving and is keeping the condo as an income property. But since it is a condo, and your landlord lives in a faraway city, you won't have the same relationship to other residents of the building that you would have in an apartment with local management. What are the pros and cons of such an arrangement? What can you do to protect yourself?

2. You find a terrific apartment, but no sooner have you moved in than you find out the landlord is an ogre. He's very unpleasant, slow to remedy problems, and of no help when it comes to resolving disputes among tenants. What would you do in such a case?

3. An apartment looks great to you, and you sign a lease and move in. Within a few days you realize there are problems that didn't appear during those few glowing minute when you first fell in love with the place. The traffic noises from the street are very annoying; there are musty odors; the water pressure is too low. All these problems are beyond the landlord's ability to fix. What would you do in such a case?

▦ **NUMBER CRUNCHERS** _____

Do the calculations to make decisions in these real-life possibilities.

1. You're moving into a new apartment that has no stove or refrigerator. You don't own either of those appliances. Evaluate the numbers in each of these cases: (a) The landlord provides appliances of low quality, but adequate for your needs, for an extra $20 per month. (b) You can buy good-quality units for $1,000 and take them with you when you leave. (c) You can buy cheap units for $600 and worry when you move out about what you'll do with them. Which option will work best for you?

2. Moving into an apartment, you have a choice of a month-to-month tenancy starting at $800, with a high probability of frequent increases, or a one-year lease at $750 per month, followed by an option for a second year at $850 per month. You're not sure how long you'll be there. What do the numbers dictate to you?

3. You're leasing a house that you might want to buy at a later time. The owner offers you a lease with a right of first refusal to buy, with a monthly rental of $1,200. Or you can have a lease with an option to buy at a set price: the same monthly rental, but a $5,000 option fee that you lose if you don't buy and that applies to the price if you do buy. Evaluate your alternatives.

FOR BETTER OR FOR WORSE

Things beyond our control often impact our personal and financial well-being, for better or for worse. Some are more predictable than others. How could you be affected if the following real-life phenomena happened? Could you have seen it coming? What steps could you have taken to minimize damage or maximize advantage? The better able you are to anticipate and recognize these forces, the better equipped you are to deal with them.

1. You are renting, and your lease gives you a right of first refusal to meet any bona fide outside offer to buy the place. Soon after you've moved in, but before you've really had a chance to settle down, such an offer is presented and you have seven days to meet it, or you'll have to move out.

2. You move into an apartment knowing that rent-control laws prohibit your landlord from raising your rent more than 2 percent a year. Then the city does away with the rent-control laws.

3. You sublet your apartment to a friend of a friend. You don't know him, but your friend vouches for him. There's no written agreement. The subtenant trashes the place.

Selling Your Home

The super-salesman neither permits his subconscious mind to "broadcast" negative thoughts nor gives expression to them through words. For he understands that "like attracts like," and negative suggestions attract negative action and negative decisions from prospective buyers.

                                                        Napoleon Hill

Perhaps the only transaction more complicated than buying a home is selling a home. Indeed, many people find themselves doing both simultaneously. When selling a home—or even when vacating a leased dwelling—there are so many personal details to attend to that many of the important financial aspects of the matter are overlooked. This can be a costly error. This chapter will point out these important financial aspects and will prepare you to deal with them. They include:

- Setting the proper price and terms for the sale of your home
- Getting your money's worth from your real estate agent
- Investing the necessary time and money to bring the best possible offers from would-be buyers
- Taking advantage of tax laws that apply when you sell your home and when you move
- Getting out of a leased dwelling in the proper fashion

Exercise 10.1

Selling your home—be it a house, condominium, or cooperative—can be a leisurely activity or a hectic one. It's leisurely if you have all the time in the world; if you have not made a commitment to move to another dwelling until you've sold your existing one; if you're not under pressure to start a new job in a different location. These situations are the exceptions rather than the rule. Most often, selling a home is hectic: You're already committed to a new dwelling, and you feel that you must sell your home by a certain date or risk having to make payments on two dwellings.

Time can be a costly pressure. Under the crush of a deadline, you are likely to accept a lower price than the house might otherwise bring. And you're liable to make other mistakes—financial or legal—that you could later regret. It's easy to say that you should allow yourself ample time to sell your house. But it's not always that easy, particularly when a job transfer occurs.

If a job transfer causes you to move, your first step should be toward your personnel office to find out what assistance your employer will offer you with respect to the sale of your home and your moving expenses. Many employers provide financial and legal assistance in such cases. But you might have to ask for it. If you are changing jobs to go with a new employer, determine what relocation assistance the new employer will offer.

WHAT'S YOUR HOME WORTH?

Your home is worth just what a willing buyer is prepared to pay for it. Not one penny more.

It's easy, however, to get caught in a trap of thinking your home is worth much more than it really is. Example: Your next-door neighbors recently put their house on the market, with an asking price of $150,000. Your house is identical to theirs, if not actually bigger and better. So if they're asking $150,000 for their house, then your house must be worth at least that much, if not more. Right? Wrong. That they're asking that much for their house doesn't mean they'll get it. In fact, their house might be worth only $120,000, or maybe even less. And yours might be worth no more than theirs in the final analysis.

Overpricing your house can be costly, because it can delay a sale of the house. And every month that goes by during which the house is not sold means mounting costs to you: your mortgage payment, your property insurance, your maintenance and upkeep. There will also be anxiety, security problems, concern over vandalism, and other dilemmas associated with being an absentee owner. Reread the discussion on the anxious seller in chapter 6.

Therefore, setting a realistic price for your home is the first and most important order of business. A realistic price is a factor of many things, some of which are not easy to calculate.

Factors to Consider

Exercise 10.2

The major factors to consider are the condition of the home itself, the condition of the neighborhood, how much "paper" you are willing to carry, how anxious you are to sell, whether or not your existing mortgage is assumable, and the availability of new financing at the time you are selling.

Condition of the House

Are you trying to sell what real estate people call a *move-in gem* or a *fixer-upper*? You must put yourself in the shoes of would-be buyers and see the house as they see it. Is it visually appealing? Is it structurally and mechanically sound? The more positive the answers to these questions, the higher the price you can ask and get.

Condition of the Neighborhood

Is the neighborhood in a state of improvement or decline? There's not much you can do about it if it's in a state of decline except to be ready to accept a lower price than you had otherwise hoped for. You have to anticipate that prudent buyers will recognize the trend of the general neighborhood and structure their offers to you accordingly. What about the immediate vicinity of your home? If your neighbors' houses are eyesores, that can have a negative effect on the value of your home. It might be worth a diplomatic chat with any such neighbors to urge them to correct the eyesores. It might even be worth your chipping in to help them do so in order to help you get a better price on your house.

How Much "Paper" Are You Willing to Carry?

If a potential buyer does not have as much cash down payment as you're asking, you might consider taking his IOU (in the form of a mortgage) in order to get your asking price. This will be discussed in more detail later in the chapter, but it must be considered as an element in setting your price in the first place.

How Anxious Are You to Sell?

In this respect, price and time work hand in hand. The more time you have, the higher the price you can afford to ask, with the knowledge that you can always lower the asking price as your ultimate deadline gets closer. When time is of the essence, you can't afford the luxury of overreaching on your price. The more critical the time factor, the closer to the actual market your pricing must be.

Is Your Existing Mortgage Assumable?

An assumable mortgage, particularly one whose interest rate is lower than the current market rate, can be one of the most attractive features of the deal you are offering. The assumability of any mortgage depends on the creditworthiness of the party who wishes to assume the mortgage. Furthermore, the lender may have reserved the right to alter the interest rate if the mortgage is assumed. You should find out what the terms and conditions would be to allow a buyer to assume your mortgage.

Is Financing Available?

It could be to your advantage to visit with local mortgage lenders to determine what kind of financing they would offer on the sale of your house. Not only can this help you set a realistic price, but it can also help facilitate a sale to a buyer who is seeking new financing.

Seeking Components

After taking into account all the factors just listed, perhaps your best guide to determining a proper price is to seek comparable sales in the past few months. Try to find houses similar to yours that have recently sold and determine the selling price. Your best source of information on this point will be local real estate brokers. Any information you can gather on your own from friends and neighbors will also be helpful. But be certain that you determine the actual *selling* price of any comparable properties, not the *asking* price. As noted earlier, there can be a big difference between the two.

Exercise 10.3

When you do seek comparables, make sure the houses you're comparing are truly comparable. They should be as similar as possible in size, configuration, age, condition, and amenities. Table 10–1 will help you evaluate comparables in your neighborhood.

TABLE 10–1   Comparable Housing Sales

	Comparables			
	Your Home	House A	House B	House C
Location (midblock, corner, cul-de-sac, etc.)				
Traffic (light, medium, heavy)				
Access to mass transit				
Access to freeways				
Access to shopping				
Lot size				
Square footage (house)				
Bedrooms, baths				
Year built				
Condition				
Extra amenities (pool, etc.)				
Asking price (original)				
Selling price				
Time on market				
Other pros, cons				

Should You Refinance Before You Sell Your Home?

Dilemma: You plan to put your house on the market, with an asking price of $150,000. You owe only $60,000 on your home loan. Your loan can be assumed by a creditworthy buyer. Would it pay to refinance your home loan up to, say, $125,000, in order to make it easier for a would-be buyer to make a deal with you? Refinancing can cost a few thousand dollars. Can you recoup that money in your selling price? If your home doesn't sell very soon after you refinance, you'll have to be making payments on that much larger loan. Can you recoup those expenses in your selling price? Seek the advice of your real estate agent and lender. If the housing market is brisk, refinancing before you sell can help get a buyer into the fold, at relatively little risk to you. In a slow market, the reverse might be true. Know the costs before you proceed.

Condominium and Cooperative Restrictions

If you are selling a condominium or your interest in a cooperative building, you may be restricted in your ability to sell. Any such restrictions would be contained in the condominium or cooperative master agreement. You may, for example, be required to offer your unit back to the other owners at a fixed price, or at a price to be agreed upon, before you can offer it to the public at large. Examine the master agreement closely, with the help of a lawyer if necessary, to determine what restrictions, if any, you must comply with.

USING A REAL ESTATE AGENT

Exercise 10.4

Does it pay to use a real estate agent to sell your house, or should you try to sell it on your own and save the commission costs? Real estate commissions on the sale of a house average about 6 percent. On a $100,000 sale, the commission would be $6,000.

If time and money are no object to you as a seller, you might want to try, for a limited time, to sell it on your own. But at some point, except in rare cases, time and money will be of concern to you. If you've made arrangements to move and you haven't sold your old home before you take occupancy of the new one, you'll be faced with the double payment mentioned earlier. It takes only a few months of these double payments to equal what the real estate commission might have been.

If you try to sell your home on your own, give yourself a time limit: If you haven't received any acceptable offers within that time limit, it might be best to turn to real estate professionals for assistance.

What an Agent Can Do

What can a real estate agent do for you as a seller?

Market and Pricing

A good agent knows the condition of the market in your general neighborhood and can help you set a realistic price in accordance with the pricing criteria mentioned earlier.

Financing

A good agent is familiar with financing capabilities in your community at the time you are interested in selling. The agent, who has regular contact with mortgage lenders and knows what kind of down payments, interest rates, and other conditions currently apply, should also be able to assist a potential buyer in obtaining financing.

Advertising

Are you prepared to write—and pay for—effective advertising that will lure buyers to your home? Those are among the duties of the real estate agent, and you can test their effectiveness in creating good advertising by scouring the classified ads in search of advertising you find particularly appealing.

Showing Your Home

A real estate agent should be ready, willing, and able to show your home to prospective buyers at any time. You might not be able to do this because of your work commitments. Moreover, the agent should be able to separate casual lookers from serious buyers and save you time accordingly.

Sales Force

Not only is the individual agent working for you, but so are all the other members of the sales force of the firm. Thus, you multiply the number of potential sources of buyers.

Multiple Listing Service

Most real estate firms belong to a local multiple listing service, which publishes a directory of all houses for sale through real estate agents in the community. If your home is listed in the multiple listing directory, virtually every agent in town will be capable of acting as a salesperson for you. If a firm other than the one with whom you've contracted brings in a buyer, the commission will be split between the firms, with your own agent getting a specified share of the commission.

Negotiating

As you read in chapter 6, both buyers and sellers who are working with real estate agents have skilled negotiators at their sides. You may be skilled at whatever you do, but not at the fine art of negotiating a price on the sale of a house. In this respect alone, a good agent can prove worthwhile.

Objectivity

It's only natural for homeowners to become emotionally involved in their homes. The decor, the furniture layout, the traffic patterns of your home—all these are your own creation and are important to you. But to a would-be buyer, it might all look like a hodgepodge. It's much easier for a real estate agent to take an unbiased view of the property and convince a buyer that everything can be altered to suit the buyer's own tastes and needs. You can't be your own best salesperson if you take offense at potential buyers turning up their noses at your own creations. The real estate agent can overcome this problem.

Finding a Good Agent

Exercise 10.5

As in seeking any other kind of professional help, it's important that you determine the reputation and integrity of real estate agents, as well as the firms they work for. Gather personal references from other people who have used the services of that individual or firm. How were they to deal with professionally? How would former clients rate their performance with respect to creativity and placement of advertising; their availability to show houses; their negotiating skills; their access to financial markets; their willingness to stick to their guns even if a particular property doesn't seem to attract potential buyers? You should also check with the local county Board of Realtors to learn whether the individual and the agency are in good standing. Check also with the state board of licensing that controls real estate brokers and sales agents to determine that their license requirements have been met and maintained.

As you interview potential real estate agents, you will discuss the price that they think they can obtain for your house. When you do, beware of a practice known as highballing. An agent, overanxious to get the listing, might lead you to believe that he or she can deliver a buyer at a much higher price than you might have expected. You could thus be lured into signing a long-term exclusive agreement with an agent whose actual performance might be far less than what you would have wanted. The real estate industry has a code of ethics designed to protect the public, but, as in any industry, abuses occur. And once you've signed a listing contract with a real estate agency, you have little recourse if they don't live up to your expectations.

The Listing Contract

Normally, real estate agents will require you to sign an exclusive listing contract that will bind you to their firm for as long as the contract states. Six months is a normal minimum term in many communities. In addition to the length of time the agreement is to run, the contract will set forth your asking price. But there is no assurance whatsoever that the agent will be able to deliver a buyer willing to pay that price. Thus, the asking price stated in the listing contract is not binding on anyone. It's merely a target toward which the agent will be shooting.

In a standard listing contract, you, the seller, will be responsible for paying a commission to the agent if the agent brings in a buyer ready, willing, and able to pay your asking price. If such a buyer is brought in, and you have changed your mind and don't want to sell to that buyer, you may still be responsible for paying the commission to the agent. If a firm other than the one you're dealing with brings in the ultimate buyer, your own agent will still get a portion of the commission.

Negotiating the Commission

Generally, real estate agents state what commission they expect to receive, but it can be worth your while to negotiate for a lower commission. Nothing ventured, nothing gained. If it appears that the house will be easy to sell—because of its condition, location, asking price, or other factors—the agent might be willing to accept a lower commission. On the other hand, if it appears that the house will be difficult to sell, the agent might seek a higher than customary commission. Whatever commission is decided on, it will be due and payable upon the final closing of the transaction. If a listing contract expires without the agent having brought in a buyer, you are free to contract with any other agent or to renegotiate an extension of the contract with the original agent.

Preparing Your Home for Sale

If you want to sell your home as quickly as possible and at the best possible price, spend some money and energy putting the house in the best possible condition to attract buyers. Some of these expenses can be deducted from any profit you realize, thus cutting your tax liability. Consider the following:

The Exterior

The exterior appearance of the house and grounds is vitally important. Many potential buyers will cruise around the area, and their first impression of the outside will stick in their minds. Even a house that is elegant inside can scare away buyers if the outside looks shabby. Keep your lawn, hedges, bushes, and other foliage properly trimmed. You might want to plant seasonal flowers to give the property a better appearance. Be sure your gutters and downspouts are all properly placed. A few gallons of paint to touch up exterior trim can be very important. Homeowners often neglect to notice signs of wear and tear because they have become accustomed to them. Ask some friends to give you their honest opinion of what might need improvement. Get rid of unsightly matter around the house. Winter and northern climates add a visual problem to any house. Be certain that snow is shoveled and that icicles are removed from overhangs. If winter days tend to be gray and dull in your area, consider some lighting that can improve the appearance of the exteriors, particularly in the late afternoon hours when many prospects are likely to call.

If there are any indications that you aren't keeping the outside of the house in good shape, a prospective buyer might suspect that there are problems lurking inside as well.

Step Inside

A would-be buyer entering your house should get the impression that it is bright and cherry, light and airy. To give a bright and cheerful impression during the daylight hours, raise the shades and open the blinds and curtains. If there is a room, such as a den or study, that you want to have appear particularly cozy, the reverse might be true. Try various combinations of natural and artificial light to achieve the best effect for each room. Keeping the windows clean will brighten the house and give a cared-for-impression.

The Kitchen

The kitchen might be the most important room to would-be buyers. Do all you can to make it sparkle. Stock a supply of kitchen deodorant: We often fail to notice odors in our kitchens because we're accustomed to them, but they could be displeasing to a prospect.

Touching Up

Any buyer examining a house will be constantly thinking. "How much will we have to spend to put the place in the shape we want it to be in?" Your real estate agent can help you determine where touching up might improve the salability of the house. For example, some rooms could benefit from painting, particularly if they are now painted with a very strong color. Light, neutral colors please more buyers. Dirt smudges on the woodwork or torn window screens, which make a decidedly negative impression on buyers, are simple to correct.

Closets and Storage Space

Cluttered closets, basements, and attics discourage buyers. Before you begin showing your house, scour these areas thoroughly. Get rid of everything you don't need. Give whatever you can to charities—you may get a handsome income tax deduction by doing so—and throw away anything you can't give away. Otherwise, you'll end up paying to move it to your new location.

Mechanicals

Assume that any serious buyer will sooner or later check to see that everything in the house is in proper working order. To minimize troubles in this regard, make sure that everything works properly: electrical circuits, light switches, plugs, doorbells, plumbing, windows, furnace, air conditioning, and so on. Call a plumber to correct any rattles, knocks, or other annoying noises that ring through the house when water is running. Oil any creaking doors and loosen any stuck windows.

Design

Examine the major rooms in the house to see how minor changes of furniture or lighting might improve the room's appearance. You may be able to enhance the appearance of the house with throw pillows, scatter rugs, and other decorative pieces that you can acquire at reasonably low cost.

Leaks and Other Damage

A prospective buyer who sees signs of leaking—on the ceilings or around sinks, toilets, tubs, or showers—will immediately start tallying up many hundreds of dollars in repair bills to correct problems that are naturally assumed still to exist. If a leak has long since been repaired but evidence of it still shows on the surface, get it covered up. If the leak still exists, get it corrected. If nothing else, any sign of a leak gives a would-be buyer a better bargaining position.

What Financing Is Available?

The availability of financing is as important to the buyer as is the asking price.

If interest rates are high at the time you put your house on the market, you should be prepared to explore a wide range of creative financing possibilities, always with the advice of a good real estate agent and a lawyer. Chapter 7 explores some of these creative financing possibilities.

Is Your Mortgage Assumable?

As noted earlier, you should determine as quickly as possible whether your mortgage can be assumed and under what conditions. If your mortgage is not assumable, you should inquire of local lenders what types of financing plans are available to a creditworthy buyer. Take these steps before you start showing the house; let your real estate agent be your guide.

Will You Take Back "Paper"?

Whether by choice or necessity, you may find yourself having to take a buyer's promise to pay rather than cash. This will be in the form of a first or second mortgage, which should be drawn up by a lawyer. If it is necessary for you to carry the buyer's promise to pay, negotiate an interest rate close to the current going rate charged by conventional lenders. It is also advisable to keep the duration of such mortgages to a minimum. Try to get the buyer to accept a term of three years or less. At the end of that time, the buyer would be responsible for obtaining new financing independently. If a buyer insists on a longer repayment program, you should negotiate a higher interest rate as consideration for granting extra time.

All these negotiations will, of course, depend on your level of anxiety to sell. The more anxious you are to sell, the less room you'll have to negotiate the terms of any paper you may be taking back.

TAX IMPLICATIONS WHEN YOU SELL YOUR HOME

The Taxpayers Relief Act of 1997, while otherwise known as "mind-numbing complexity," (*The Wall Street Journal*) did make one aspect of taxation much easier to deal with. Unlike a confusing mess of possibilities prior to 1997, the new law states relatively simply that couples who sell their principal residence do not have to pay taxes on the first $500,000 worth of profit. For singles the tax-free profit is up to $250,000. In order to qualify for this tax break you must have lived in the home for at least two of the last five years. Sales of vacation homes are still subject to taxation. This law is effective for all home sales from May 7, 1997, onward.

STRATEGIES FOR SUCCESS

Good Timing for Your Move Can Save Money

If you're lucky enough to choose the time you want to move, you can save money in the process. Most moving takes place during the summer months—school's out, etc. That can mean a tougher (and more costly) time in getting movers to meet your schedule or in renting move-it-yourself vehicles. Moving in winter, especially in northern climates, poses extra hazards such as icy roads and snowstorms. If you have the luxury of choosing, spring and fall are the best times. What about taking the kids out of school? If they're young enough, it might not matter. In their teens, it could pose some problems. Discuss the situation with teachers at both the new and old schools. If you *can't* choose your own moving time, at least try to book the moving companies as far in advance as possible. That way you have more time to schedule other aspects of your move in the most economical way.

MOVING EXPENSES

Exercise 10.6

Moving involves many important considerations. Whether you hire a moving company or do it yourself will probably depend on the amount of household goods you'll be moving, the distance, and the time of year.

If your move is within the boundaries of your state, the moving company will not be controlled by the Interstate Commerce Commission. Customarily, such moves (intrastate) are charged on an hourly basis, plus time and materials for any packing that the mover does for you.

Generally, interstate moves of equal weight and equal distance will cost roughly the same with most moving companies. There may be important differences in the overall cost of the move based on the amount of packing and unpacking you wish the movers to do. These rates will vary from company to company. You may wish to pack your own nonbreakables and have the moving company pack the more fragile items, such as glassware, china, and lamps.

Representatives of moving companies can give you the estimates on the cost of your move, but bear in mind that these are only estimates and not firm bids. The actual cost can't be determined until the van is loaded and weighed prior to its departure. Moving companies are required to give you Interstate Commerce Commission information that spells out your rights. Be certain to read that document, for it informs you of the recourse you have if something goes wrong.

TAX DEDUCTION OF MOVING EXPENSES

Exercise 10.7

A major portion of your moving expenses (for which you are not reimbursed by your employer) may be tax-deductible. Because moving expenses can amount to a considerable sum of money, you should keep a careful record of all such expenses and take advantage of whatever the law allows. In order to deduct moving expenses, you must meet two tests: the distance test and the work test.

The Distance Test

As illustrated by Figure 10–1, measure the distance between your former home and your former place of work. Let's call the distance A and say it's ten miles. Now measure the distance between your former home and your new place of work. Let's call that distance B and say it's sixty miles. The law requires that the difference between distance B and distance A be at least fifty miles. If it is, you pass the distance test. Note that the distance does not refer to the location of your new *residence* but rather to the location of your new *place of work*.

The Work Test

During the twelve months immediately following your move, you must be employed full-time for at least thirty-nine weeks in order to pass the work test. If you are self-employed, you must be employed full-time for at least thirty-nine weeks during the first twelve months immediately following the

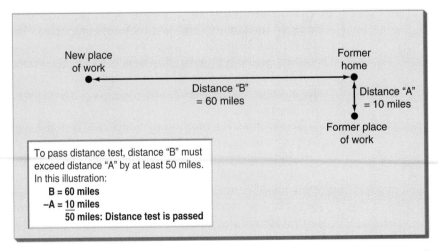

FIGURE 10–1   The distance test

move and you must also be employed full-time for at least seventy-eight weeks of the twenty-four months immediately following the move.

If you meet both the distance test and work test, the following expenses of your move may be deductible, in whole or in part. Check current IRS regulations to determine the limits to these deductions: travel expenses, including meals and lodging while en route from your old residence to your new residence; the cost of moving your household goods; the cost of house-hunting trips; the cost of temporary quarters at your new location, if needed; and some of the costs involved in selling your former residence or settling your lease at your old location.

PERSONAL ACTION WORKSHEET

A Guide for the Home Seller

This worksheet should help you *set* and *get* the best possible price for your home. It will cost money to complete some of the items, but the expense may return itself many times over in a better price and in a faster sale. You may need the assistance of your real estate agent. Some of the information can be found at your local tax assessor's or county recorder's office.

❏ What has been the actual selling price of three *comparable* homes in your area within the past few months? A ＿＿＿＿＿＿＿ B ＿＿＿＿＿＿＿ C ＿＿＿＿＿＿＿

❏ How long were those homes on the market before they sold? A ＿＿＿＿＿＿＿ B ＿＿＿＿＿＿＿ C ＿＿＿＿＿＿＿

❏ Based on these comparable sales, what do you realistically think your home should sell for? ＿＿＿＿＿＿＿

❏ How will your home appear to a would-be buyer? ＿＿＿＿＿＿＿＿＿＿＿＿＿＿

Ask two friends, and your real estate agent, to give you an honest opinion of:

❏ The exterior (paint, trim, landscaping) 1 ＿＿＿＿＿＿＿ 2 ＿＿＿＿＿＿＿ 3 ＿＿＿＿＿＿＿
❏ The entry (lighting, odors, a sense of clutter or of orderliness) 1 ＿＿＿＿＿＿＿ 2 ＿＿＿＿＿＿＿ 3 ＿＿＿＿＿＿＿
❏ The kitchen (cleanliness, odors, does everything work the way it should?) 1 ＿＿＿＿＿＿＿ 2 ＿＿＿＿＿＿＿ 3 ＿＿＿＿＿＿＿
❏ Closets, other storage areas (cluttered, or clean and spacious-looking) 1 ＿＿＿＿＿＿＿ 2 ＿＿＿＿＿＿＿ 3 ＿＿＿＿＿＿＿
❏ Bathrooms (squeaky clean a *must*) 1 ＿＿＿＿＿＿＿ 2 ＿＿＿＿＿＿＿ 3 ＿＿＿＿＿＿＿
❏ Other rooms (lighting, odors, traffic flow, condition of flooring and walls) 1 ＿＿＿＿＿＿＿ 2 ＿＿＿＿＿＿＿ 3 ＿＿＿＿＿＿＿
❏ Mechanical elements, such as heater, appliances (Does everything work properly? Are there noises, odors, etc., that would be offensive?) 1 ＿＿＿＿＿＿＿ 2 ＿＿＿＿＿＿＿ 3 ＿＿＿＿＿＿＿

It's difficult to see your own home as others see it. Prospective buyers can be persnickety, and first impressions—such as the items listed here—can make the difference between "Thanks but no thanks," and "Let's talk about the price."

CONSUMER ALERT

Moving-day Headaches

Selling a home or leaving an apartment invariably involves one activity that many people regard with fear and loathing: moving day.

All major moving companies offer abundant literature on how to take the pain out of moving: how to do your own packing, how to complete a proper inventory of your goods, how to get the children out of your hair, and so on. Helpful though this literature may be, it may not prepare you for some of the common pitfalls of moving. These include:

- **The lowball estimate**   An overzealous sales representative from a moving company may give you an estimate on the cost of the move that is much lower than what you've received from other companies. This could be due to an honest error on the part of the salesperson; it could be due to your failure to disclose everything you had planned to move; or it could be an intentional ploy by the salesperson to win your business. Remember: An estimate is just an estimate. The total cost of the move won't be known until everything is packed and the van is weighed. Which leads us to:

- **"Bumping"**   The term *bumping* describes the practice whereby four burly 200-pound moving men sit in the back of the moving van while it's being weighed. And you pay for it. It may be a rare occurrence, but it can be costly. Interstate Commerce Commission regulations clearly state that you, the shipper, are entitled to be at the weighing of the truck. That can be a money-saving precaution to take.

- **Schedule demolition**   Despite the best intentions, the day of pick-up of your goods can be missed. And the day of delivery at your new destination can also be off-target. These missed dates can cause chaos, not to mention considerable cost, if you have to live in a motel for a few days waiting for the van to arrive. Moving companies generally can't guarantee pick-up and delivery dates unless you reserve exclusive use of a van. Your best protection against these scheduling problems is to anticipate that the worst will happen. Then if everything goes off smoothly, you'll be that much happier.

UPS & DOWNS   *The Economics of Everyday Life*

Why Housing Costs Go Up and Down—Part II (Continued from Chapter 6)

Trendiness   As a rule, newer homes with more modern decor and more up-to-date appliances can command higher prices than older homes that are otherwise equal in size, location, and quality of construction. As a seller, you're competing with houses that are newer than yours, all other things being equal. You may be able to ask a higher price for your home if you update it. But will the higher price offset the cost of the updating?

The "in" neighborhoods   Areas come and go in popularity, and prices for homes in those neighborhoods will fluctuate accordingly. There may be better buys in other parts of town, but if you feel compelled to be in the "in" area, you'll pay more to get in. And then you'll have to hope that it's still "in" when you want to sell.

Land-use changes   If there is a major change in how nearby land is used, the value of homes in that area can move up or down sharply. Heavier traffic patterns, construction of busy commercial uses, and spreading urban decay can blight home property values. Homeowners in such areas usually fight bitterly against any such impending changes. Development of parklands, reduction in traffic, and creative design controls in an area can be a boon to home values. Sellers should try to anticipate any such trends and time their sales accordingly. Local zoning laws limit some land-use changes, but zoning laws can always be changed, particularly if a developer holds out the promise of creating new property tax revenues for the community. Which brings us, directly, to:

Property taxes   Property taxes can have a major long-term effect on housing prices. Two examples can be found in the U.S. Northeast and in California. In the Northeast many older cities were faced with huge costs to keep their infrastructure (roads, bridges, public buildings, etc.) in repair. They had to boost property taxes to get the money to do that work. Higher property taxes clobbered the budgets of lots of families, many of whom sold out as quickly as they could (thereby putting more downward pressure on housing values) and moved to California, where they were willing to pay higher housing prices so that they could live without fear of rising property taxes. In 1978 California established a law that put a strict limit on property tax increases. State and local revenues increase as newcomers move in.

All these factors are interrelated. It's tough to second-guess them, but you have to try.

? WHAT IF . . . ?

How would you deal with these real-life possibilities?

1.   In planning to sell your house, you interview a number of real estate agents. They range from passive to pushy, and the prices they think they can get for your house covers a wide range. They seem to be flexible on the length of time of the listing agreement, and you sense that the amount of the commission may be somewhat negotiable. What steps do you take to sort out of all the differences so that you can make the best choice?

2.   Your house has been on the market for three months, and you've had no offers. The time is rapidly approaching when you have to move to your new place. The real estate agent suggests you lower your asking price by around 15 to 20 percent. What are your options?

3.   You've received two offers on your house. One is on the very low side, but it's all cash. The other is what you've been hoping for, but the buyer will need time—probably six weeks—to get a firm commitment on getting financing. And there's no guarantee that he'll get the financing. During that time, the cash offer will have been withdrawn. How would you resolve this dilemma?

NUMBER CRUNCHERS

Do the calculations regarding these real-life possibilities.

1.   You bought a new house before you sold the old house. Your monthly outgo (mortgage payments, property taxes, insurance, up-keep, etc.) is $1,800 on the new house and $1,100 on the old house. Until you sell the old house—for which you're asking $120,000— you're in a bind. The real estate agent tells you that if you drop your asking price on the old house to $100,000, it will sell quickly. If you hang in there at $120,000, you might get it eventually. You want to hold out for the best possible price, but that extra $1,000 a month outgo is starting to hurt. Evaluate how much and when you should drop the asking price.

2.   Your real estate agent tells you that by putting some money into your house, you can command a higher price. Calculate what you can do and the cost thereof. How much higher a price will these improve-ments bring, and how quickly?

FOR BETTER OR FOR WORSE

Things beyond our control often impact our personal and financial well-being, for better or for worse. Some are more predictable than others. How would you be affected if the following real-life phenomena happened? Could you have seen it coming? What steps could you have taken to minimize damage or maximize advantage? The better able you are to anticipate and recognize these forces, the better equipped you are to deal with them.

1. You've sold your house and moved out, but the closing hasn't taken place yet. Before the closing there's a thunderstorm, and the new buyer tells you of some serious roof leaks that you had been totally unaware of.

2. You're going to sell your house to take a job in another city. The biggest employer in your current city announces layoffs of 30 percent of its work force.

3. You went to the Big City to make your fortune, but things didn't work out. You're close to broke. You reluctantly realize that your best tactic, at least until you can replenish your bank account, is to move back in with your parents. But they've just signed a contract to sell their home and will be moving into a small condo.

11

Financial Institutions

That's where the money is.

       Notorious bank robber, Willie Sutton, on being asked why he robs banks.

Sutton's involvement with banks was a lot more clear-cut than yours will be. Dealing with banks and other financial institutions—savings associations, credit unions, and so on—can be complicated in these rapidly changing days. But the dealings can be worthwhile in terms of handling your money matters and making your money grow. This chapter is designed to acquaint you with how financial institutions work, what they can do for you, and what your rights are as a user of their services. You'll learn about such matters as

- Which institutions offer what services
- How checking accounts work, and the advantages and pitfalls in using them
- How to shop for the services you'll need
- What laws protect you with regard to financial matters, and how to pursue your rights if they are violated

YOUR CHOICES

Suppose you have some money and you have no immediate need or desire to spend it. What can you do with it? You have many choices. You can put it in your pocket, in the cookie jar, or under your mattress until you do need it. Or you can entrust that money to one of many financial institutions for a variety of purposes.

If you wanted to use that money to pay some of your debts, you could open a checking account at a financial institution. Then instead of having to deliver cash to each of your creditors, you could simply mail them a check to satisfy the debt. The check, in effect, allows the creditor to receive money from your checking account. You may wish to invest the money so that the total sum will assuredly increase until such time as you need it for other purposes. In such a case, you could establish a savings plan at a financial institution.

You might wish to speculate with the money in the hope that it might increase in the future. In this case you could establish an account with a stock brokerage firm—one type of financial institution. Or you might wish to put the money away for a very long time so as to provide an assured fund for yourself in later years or for your survivors upon your death. In such a case, you would contract for a life insurance policy with an insurance company, yet another type of financial institution.

On the other hand, suppose you need money—to buy a car or a house, to pay your taxes, to go on a vacation, or for any other purpose. If you couldn't borrow the money you needed from your friends or relatives, you would approach a financial institution for the appropriate type of loan.

THE MIDDLEMEN

Financial institutions play an important middleman role in the nation's economy and in your own personal financial situation.

At any given time, countless individuals (and businesses and governments) have more money on hand than they need for their immediate purposes. At the same time, countless others do not have the money they need for specific purposes.

Financial institutions act as middlemen by providing a safe place for those with excess money to keep it until they need it. At the same time, they supply services and loans to those who seek to borrow at a fair and reasonable cost.

Middlemen view this activity as a business. They must acquire their raw material (other people's money) at the lowest possible price (competition considered). And they must lend it out on the most prudent basis, taking into account the ability of the borrowers to repay the money at the agreed-on time. In order for middlemen to survive, they must make a profit. Thus, they must charge the borrowers more for the use of the money than they pay to the investors entrusting them with their money.

Some middlemen act not as a business but as a service to members of an association. The members band together to pool their excess money and provide for the needs of borrowers. Although it isn't important for the association to generate a profit, members must still generate enough income within the operation to pay for personnel and other overhead. This type of financial situation is typified by credit unions, which commonly represent employees of a specific company or members of a particular trade union.

THE INSTITUTIONS

This chapter concentrates on institutions offering banking and lending services. Stock brokerage and insurance companies will be covered in chapters 14, 15, and 17.

Commercial Banks

Commercial banks are often referred to as full-service institutions. They offer a broad range of services, including checking accounts, savings accounts, trust facilities, and virtually all types of loans.

Commercial banks are generally limited to doing business within their state boundaries. They may be chartered by the state government or by the federal government to operate within a particular state. If a commercial bank is state-chartered, it will be controlled and regulated by the state banking commission. If a commercial bank is federally chartered, it will be controlled and regulated by the Comptroller of the Currency. (If a bank is federally chartered, it will have the word "national" in its name—such as First National Bank. Or it will have the initials N.A.—National Association—after its name.) Most major banks, and many smaller banks, are also members of the Federal Reserve system, which exerts additional controls and regulations on the nation's banking industry.

Exercise 11.1

Deposits in commercial banks are insured by the Federal Deposit Insurance Corporation (FDIC) (see Figure 11–1) for up to $100,000 per account in the event of the bank's failure. Congress can modify the amount of insurance and the number of accounts that can be covered by it; check the current limits. The FDIC is a federal agency that constantly scrutinizes the operations of all banks it insures for the protection of the depositors and the community. All federally insured banks pay an annual premium to the

FIGURE 11–1 Logo for Federal Deposit Insurance Company (FDIC)

FDIC, and the total is set aside as a reserve to be used to pay off the depositors, should a bank be liquidated. In addition to its own funds, the FDIC can call on the U.S. Treasury for additional money to back up its guarantee to depositors. The strength of the FDIC lies not just in its funds but also in its constant surveillance and its expertise in determining when banks are in trouble, intervening as swiftly as possible to prevent financial loss.

In addition to FDIC examination, banks may also be examined by state or federal authorities, depending on their charter. They are also examined by their own internal auditors and by outside independent auditors on orders from the bank's own board of directors. Examinations are generally by surprise and are very rigorous. All cash is counted. All loans are scrutinized in detail, including original credit information, current payment status, and prospects for ultimate full payment. If an excess of loans seem to be in jeopardy, the examiners will instruct the bank to take steps to correct the situation. The results of examinations are kept confidential between the examiners and the bank's officials. But examiners will follow up to determine whether the bank has taken necessary corrective steps to keep the operation in healthy condition.

Mutual Savings Banks

Mutual savings banks are state-chartered and are insured by the FDIC, which examines them as it does commercial banks. The major part of the business of mutual savings banks is savings plans and loans on real property—mortgages and home-improvement loans. Deregulation in the financial industry, however, has allowed mutual savings banks to extend their scope of business to include checking accounts and various types of consumer loans.

Savings and Loan Associations

Traditionally, savings and loan associations concentrated their business in savings plans and home loans, but the era of deregulation has given them powers to offer checking accounts and various consumer loans. Savings and loan associations are insured by the FDIC (see Figure 11–1).

In recent years, many savings associations have begun to call themselves banks, as permitted by law—thus the further blending in the public's eye of the various types of financial institutions.

Credit Unions

Because credit unions don't advertise the way commercial banks and savings and loan associations do, they're not as familiar to the public as those other institutions. But credit unions are playing an increasingly important role in the U.S. financial system. They are associations of individuals who have a common bond—they work for the same employer, they belong to the same religious order, or they are members of the same union or trade association. Credit unions are not operated for profit; furthermore, they are tax-exempt. They are operated solely for the benefit of their membership, which is generally open to all individuals who meet their requirements.

Exercise 11.2

Credit unions offer checking accounts and accept savings accounts that may pay slightly higher interest than other institutions. This is possible because they do not have the profit motive, generally are located in modest quarters, and do not have to pay any federal income taxes. Credit unions in some areas make installment loans to their members of a rate slightly more favorable than that charged elsewhere.

Insurance on credit union accounts is available through the National Credit Union Administration (NCUA).

Consumer Finance or "Small Loan" Companies

These are private businesses, generally operating under state licensing, that make small loans available to creditworthy seekers. Consumer finance companies do not accept public deposits. They obtain their money by borrowing from larger institutions such as banks and insurance companies. A small number of these companies have branches throughout the entire country, but most are limited to individual states or cities in their sphere of operation.

Merchant Lenders and Credit Card Companies

Technically, these are not financial institutions in the same sense as banks and savings and loan associations are. But they do provide a financial service to many millions of Americans: making credit available virtually at the request of the customer. Generally, a merchant lender is a retail or service establishment that accepts a customer's IOU as payment for goods sold or services rendered. In other words, rather than pay cash, the customer can *charge it*.

In effect, the merchant lender is lending the money to the customer to enable the customer to buy the product. Many merchants do this strictly as a convenience for their customers and to be in line with services that their competitors offer.

Some companies—such as gasoline companies, hotels and motels, and airlines—issue charge cards to creditworthy applicants. Thee cards allow users to charge their purchases, thus creating a loan from the issuing company. The loan is repayable based on the terms contained in the original credit agreement.

Another form of quasi-financial institution is the credit card company: American Express, Diners Club, and Discover card are prime examples. They have made arrangements with many thousands of businesses across the nation and around the world to accept their credit cards in lieu of cash. When a customer makes a purchase on a credit card charge, the credit card company makes payment to the specific merchant and then seeks repayment of the amount borrowed by the customer. The credit card company is thus acting strictly as a middleman between the merchant and the customer. Most commercial banks also issue various forms of credit cards—VISA and MasterCard. When a purchase is made with a bank credit card, the banks pays the merchant and seeks repayment directly from the customer.

Insurance Companies

Insurance companies (life, health, property, and so on) act as financial middlemen in that they hold your money for you and invest it, waiting until such time as stated risks occur (death, illness, fire, and so on). They also offer some forms of investments, such as annuities. Their specific roles are explained in more detail in the respective chapters on insurance.

Financial Planners

A new type of financial "institution" has emerged in recent years: companies and individuals who perform financial planning services. Some are independent. Some are associated with insurance, brokerage, and accounting firms. Some perform services on a fee-only basis. Some earn commissions from products (insurance policies, mutual funds, etc.) they sell to their clients. Most are reputable; some are not.

The swift rise of financial planning as a profession has been accompanied by an equally swift rise in abuses. Throughout most of the nation, there are few laws governing or licensing financial planners. Virtually anyone can call himself or herself a financial planner, with or without credentials, education, or scruples. If a consumer gets involved with an unscrupulous so-called planner, there may not be any governmental agency with which to register a complaint. There may not be any recourse for lost money. There could be, in short, a disaster.

Exercise 11.3

Many major universities offer programs in financial planning. Two entities specialize in the field: The Institute of Certified Financial Planners (ICFP), based in Denver, offers a course leading to a Certified Financial Planner (CFP) designation, and American College in Bryn Mawr, Pennsylvania, offers a course leading to a Chartered Financial Consultant (ChFC) designation. These designations are not sanctioned by governmental licensing

STRATEGIES FOR SUCCESS

What You Should Know about a Financial Planner

Exercise 11.4

The strategy to use in choosing a financial planner should be similar to the methods you'd employ in choosing any professional in whom you must put a great deal of trust. As with a doctor or lawyer, you'd want to know the person's training, experience, and credentials. You'd want impeccable personal references from reliable sources. And you'd want to make sure that there is the right "chemistry" between you and the planner. Make certain you can distinguish personal rapport from a smart sales pitch. The two can easily be confused. If the planner earns a commission from selling, determine up front just what it is he or she does sell, so you'll know when you're being pitched. Be sure that the planner won't object if you seek second opinions on the recommendations he or she gives you. If the planner works on a fee basis, understand from the outset exactly how those fees will be charged.

agencies, rather they are in the form of a degree issued by the school. Another entity is the International Association for Financial Planning (IAFP), based in Atlanta.

Many who call themselves planners may be licensed or registered in a related field, such as insurance, real estate, stock brokerage, or accountancy. As noted, many have no governmental licensure or registration of any kind. If a planner works on a fee-only basis, you must determine what you get for that fee. If a planner earns a commission on products he or she sells you, you must determine how objective the planner really is: are you being sold something that's in your best interest or in the planner's best interest? In all cases, you must shop around, get personal references, compare services, and, when in the slightest doubt about the advice or sales pitch you've received, get a second opinion, preferably from someone who isn't selling anything.

SERVICES AVAILABLE AT FINANCIAL INSTITUTIONS

Exercise 11.5

The following financial services are those commonly found at larger commercial banks. They may also be available at smaller banks, savings and loan associations, mutual savings banks, and credit unions.

Checking and savings accounts	Special checks
Safe deposit facilities	Notarial services
Trust services	Electronic banking
Loans and credit cards	Collection services
Mortgages	Investment departments

Let's now take a closer look at what these services consist of. *Note:* Savings accounts (passbook accounts and certificates of deposit) are briefly noted here and are discussed in greater length in chapters 13 and 14. Installment, credit card, and business loans are dealt with in chapter 12, and mortgages are discussed fully in the chapters on housing, especially in "Financing a Home," chapter 7.

Checking Accounts

It would be both inconvenient and risky if we had to conduct all our financial transactions with cash. Checks, simply stated, act as a substitute for cash. Checks are more convenient, and the risk of loss is virtually eliminated.

The efficiency of our checking systems is founded on a combination of mutual trust and law. We have grown accustomed to accepting these money substitutes as having the value represented. In those rare cases when the documents prove invalid, there are laws that can punish those who have violated the law and the trust between the parties.

How Checking Accounts Work

Bob lives in Phoenix, Arizona, and works for the Ajax Supermarket. Each day, the supermarket gathers up all the money it has collected from its customers and deposits the money in its checking account at the Arizona National Bank. The store will then issue checks to its employees for their wages, checks to the landlord for the rent on the building, checks to suppliers for the food it obtains from them, and so on.

The checks order the bank to make payment to the holder of the check. That's the essence of the words "pay to the order of" that appears on all checks. The check—the order to pay—must be signed by a properly authorized representative of the store. The bank will have obtained copies of all the authorized signatures permitted on the checks and can compare those signatures with the signatures on the checks if they wish to determine the validity of the order to pay.

Bob's weekly paycheck, after all deductions have been taken out for income taxes, Social Security, and fringe benefits, looks like the one in Figure 11–2.

"Negotiating" a Check

Bob now holds a piece of paper that is worth $400 to him. The piece of paper is a legal document in which the Ajax Supermarket instructs the Arizona National Bank to pay to the order of Bob Rosefsky the sum of $400. The check is thus known as an order instrument. How can Bob then translate that piece of paper into real money? He can cash the check, he can

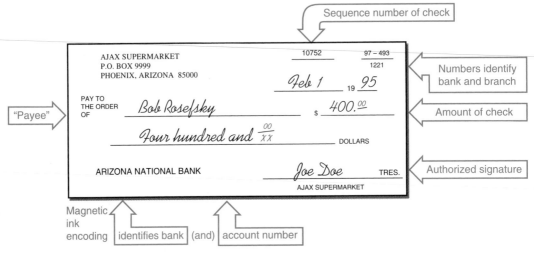

FIGURE 11–2   Sample check

deposit the check into his own account, or he can use the check to pay a debt or pay for a purchase.

Cashing the Check

Bob takes the check to a branch of the Arizona National Bank, identifies himself, and asks for cash in exchange for the check. Before the bank will give Bob the cash, it will want him to acknowledge that he has in fact received the money. The bank must do this to prove that it has fulfilled the order given it by the supermarket. Bob acknowledges that he receives the cash by signing his name on the back of the check in the area indicated. (See Fig. 11–4.) This is known as a blank endorsement. Bob receives his money; the bank has proof that it has properly fulfilled the order given it. As the check is processed internally, the supermarket's account with the bank will be reduced by $400 as a result of cashing the check.

Note this important precaution with respect to a blank endorsement: A blank endorsement converts the check from an *order* instrument into a *bearer* instrument. A check containing a blank endorsement can theoretically be cashed by anyone who is the bearer or holder of it. In other words, if Bob endorsed the check in blank when he received it, and it dropped out of his pocket on the way to the bank and was found by a dishonest person, that dishonest person could probably cash the check, and Bob would be out $400. A check should be endorsed in blank only at the time the money is received.

Depositing the Check

Bob can deposit the check to his own checking account at the Citizens Bank of Phoenix. To do so, he must properly <u>endorse</u> the check and fill out a deposit slip. He may endorse the check in <u>blank</u>, as if he were cashing it. Or, more prudently, he can put a <u>restrictive endorsement</u> on the check. A restrictive endorsement would read, "For deposit only to acct #007-085844," followed by his signature. A restrictive endorsement simply restricts what can be done with the check. In this particular case, it can only be deposited to Bob's specific account. If a restrictive endorsed check were lost, a finder would have a very difficult time doing anything with it. Restrictive endorsements should always be used on checks mailed to banks for deposit.

Figure 11–3 is a sample illustration of a deposit slip. Deposit slips are commonly preprinted with the name and address of the account holder. The person making the deposit writes the identifying number of the bank on which the check is drawn—in this case 97-493—and the amount of the check being deposited, $400. In this particular case, Bob is taking $50 in cash out of the check, as noted on the deposit slip, so the actual amount of the deposit is $350. When the deposit is processed, the receiving bank will encode its own identifying number as well as the identifying number of Bob's account, as shown in the illustration.

Clearing the Check

If Bob does deposit the check in his own bank, his bank technically doesn't know whether the check is any good. It has no way of knowing whether the Ajax Supermarket has money in its account at that time to honor the check.

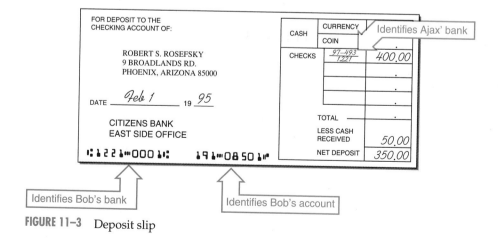

FIGURE 11–3   Deposit slip

It could thus say to Bob, "Technically, we can't permit you to take money out against this check until we're sure that it has *cleared*, that is, been honored by the bank on which it's drawn, Arizona National."

Bob's bank will actually send the check to the store's bank, where it will be processed. The Arizona National Bank does not notify Bob's bank that the check was good. Bob's bank will know that the check was good and was honored only if it does *not* get it back from the Arizona National Bank. If, in fact, the supermarket did not have enough money in its account to clear the check, the Arizona National Bank would return it to Bob's bank with a note that it was dishonored, or had *bounced*, in this case for lack of sufficient funds.

Because both banks are in the same city, it customarily takes only one or two days for the check to go from one bank to the other. Thus, Bob's bank can be reasonably sure that the check has cleared if it hasn't heard otherwise within two or three days—the time it would take for a check to go round-trip, if in fact, that was its fate. In common practice, Bob's bank knows that he has been depositing these checks from the Ajax Supermarket for many years and that there has never been a problem. Thus, they would probably allow him to draw against those funds without waiting for the check to be cleared by the originating bank.

While a check is in the clearing process—which can be many days if it was written on a bank in a distant part of the country—the funds are considered *uncollected* by the bank. Example: Bob receives a check for $1,000 from his cousin Bernie in Binghamton, New York. Bob deposits it to his account at the Citizens Bank of Phoenix. Bob's bank knows that it could take three or four days for the check to return to Bernie's bank in Binghamton. If the check is to bounce, it will take another three or four days before Bob's bank finds out about it. Or, if the check does not bounce, Bob's bank will still want to wait extra days to be assured that it hasn't in fact bounced. Bob's bank thus regards that $1,000 as uncollected funds for a period of six to eight days. But Bob thinks he has $1,000 in the bank, and he writes a check for $700 to a local used-car dealer as down payment on a car. The car dealer takes Bob's check into Bob's bank the next day, where it bounces. Bob has drawn a check against uncollected funds and the check is not honored. Not only does this cost Bob $20 for the bounced check fee, but it also causes him considerable embarrassment.

Federal law requires banks to clear deposits within a few days. To be on the safe side, particularly if you are depositing large checks or out-of-town checks, ask your bank how long the clearance time will be.

Using the Check to Pay Debts or for Purchases

Bob owes $400 to his friend Gary in Taos, New Mexico. He wants to use his paycheck to settle his debt to Gary. He thus puts a special endorsement on

BLANK	RESTRICTIVE	SPECIAL
ENDORSE HERE	ENDORSE HERE	ENDORSE HERE
Bob Rosefsky	*For deposit only*	*Pay only to*
	to acct. # 98765	*Gary Smith*
	Bob Rosefsky	*Bob Rosefsky*

FIGURE 11–4 Types of endorsement

the back of his check , which reads, "Pay to the order of Gary Smith," followed by his signature. A special endorsement gives only the named party the right to collect the amount of the check or to negotiate the check on to a subsequent holder. When Gary receives the check, he endorses it by signing his own name below Bob's signature, and the check eventually comes back to the original bank where, presumably, it will be honored.

Although Bob can pay off his debt in this fashion, it might be unwise for him to do so. It would be better for him to deposit the store's check into his own account and then draw his own check payable directly to Gary. He would ultimately receive back his canceled check and would thus have proof that Gary had received the payment and that the debt was paid. With a special endorsement, the store will get the check back, and Bob might have to seek the store's help in verifying that Gary received the money. Figure 11–4 shows samples of blank, restrictive, and special endorsements.

Following are some additional aspects of checking accounts.

Stopping Payment

The treasurer of the Ajax Supermarket learns that the computer has erroneously issued a check to one of the store's meat suppliers. The check is for $500 more than it should be, and the treasurer is concerned that the meat supplier will cash the check and will refuse to refund the excess $500 because there had been an ongoing dispute between them over a previous bill. The treasurer wants to stop the check before the meat supplier can cash it at his bank.

It's literally a race against time. The proper course for the treasurer is to go to his bank, Arizona National, and issue a stop-payment order. He must inform the bank in writing as to the number and amount of the check, the date it was issued, and to whom it was paid, and then sign the order. This done, the bank will then refuse to allow payment on the check when it is presented. But if the meat supplier gets to the bank first and is able to cash the check, he will have the money in hand, and it will then be a hassle between the supplier and the store as to who is entitled to the money.

Once a proper stop-payment order has been filed with the bank, the bank might be responsible to the store if it makes payment on the check in error. Thus, once a stop-payment order has been signed, the bank alerts all its tellers and the appropriate bookkeeper on the Ajax account to refuse payment, should the check be presented. If a stop-order is conducted verbally and the proper documents haven't been signed, the bank might not be responsible if it does pay the check. Banks customarily charge for the processing of a stop-payment order.

Overdrafts

We previously noted the problems that can arise when a checking account customer writes checks against uncollected funds. The same costs and embarrassments can occur if you write checks when there simply isn't enough money in the account to cover the check. This is a case of being overdrawn. Customers who frequently overdraw their accounts jeopardize their credit standing with the bank. In some instances, a bank may pay a check even though it would overdraw the account. This may occur because the customer is in good standing, rarely has overdrawn, and is overdrawn by a relatively small amount. The bank isn't worried about getting its money, and, rather than put the customer to any inconvenience, the bank will allow the check to be paid.

In other cases, banks offer overdraft privileges to their customers. If a check overdraws an account, the bank automatically lends the customer at least enough money to cover the overdraft and deposits that loaned money into a customer's checking account. The loan must then be repaid at a specified rate of interest. This program can be convenient and eliminate embarrassment, but it can also be very costly. It may also act as too great a temptation for a customer who lacks the discipline to keep a checking account in proper balance.

Keeping Track of Your Account

The register, or stub, is where the checking account customer keeps a record of all deposits and checks. The register should be updated immediately with each transaction. One of the most frequent causes of overdrawn accounts and other errors is customer failure to enter deposits and checks. If you neglect to enter a check transaction in your register, you run the risk of forgetting that transaction and subsequently overdrawing. Registers come in several forms. Figure 11–5 shows some sample registers, indicating how transactions are noted in them.

a.

CHECK #	DATE	CHECK ISSUED TO (or description of deposit)	AMOUNT OF CHECK	AMOUNT OF DEPOSIT	BALANCE 139.90
143	2/21	To Joe's Gas Sta For Gas	7.75		CHECK OR DEP. 7.75 BAL. 132.15
Dep	2/27	To (Net Paycheck) For		200.00	CHECK OR DEP. 200.00 BAL. 332.15
144	3/5	To Electric Co. For Feb. bill	28.10		CHECK OR DEP. 28.10 BAL. 304.05
145	3/5	To Savings & Loan For March pmt.	242.00		CHECK OR DEP. 242.00 BAL. 62.05

b.

CHECK # 144 DATE 3/5	
To Electric Co. Feb. bill	
BALANCE	332.15
CHECK	28.10
DEPOSIT	
NEW BAL.	304.05

CHECK # 145 DATE 3/5	
To Savings & Loan March pmt.	
BALANCE	304.05
CHECK	242.00
DEPOSIT	
NEW BAL.	62.05

FIGURE 11–5   (a) Sample checkbook register; (b) sample checkbook stubs

The Statement and Reconciliation

The bank sends a monthly statement to each of its checking account customers. This statement contains an itemized listing of all transactions made on the account and includes all checks written and cleared during the previous month, as well as all deposit slips. In this way, the customer has written verification of every transaction. The bank also makes a microfilm record of all items, which the customer can refer to if necessary.

The statement also contains instructions for determining that the balance shown by the bank matches the balance shown in the customer's account. This is known as *reconciling* the account. Figure 11–6 presents an example of a monthly account reconciliation.

				CHECKS NOT YET PAID		

1. Arrange canceled checks and deposit slips by number or date.
2. Check them off in your check book, verifying each amount as you proceed.
3. Add to your checkbook any deposits or other credits recorded on this statement that you have not already added.
4. Subtract from your checkbook any checks or other charges recorded on this statement that you have not already subtracted.
5. List at right each check you have written that is not yet paid by bank (does not show on statement). Total them, and enter total on line 10.

CHECKS NOT YET PAID		
DATE	#	AMOUNT
3/8	149	52.50
3/9	150	7.50
3/10	151	10.00
TOTAL		70.00

6. List any deposits you have made that do not show on statement, and enter total on line 8.

DEPOSITS NOT YET CREDITED	
DATE	AMOUNT
3/10	100.00
TOTAL	100.00

7. Ending balance as shown on statement.
8. Add total from line 6.
9. Subtotal
10. Subtract total from line 5.
11. This total should be the same as the balance in your checkbook.

$	182.00
+	100.00
	282.00
−	70.00
$	212.00

FIGURE 11–6   Sample reconciliation of checking account

Shopping for Checking Accounts

The distinction between checking accounts and savings accounts has been blurred in recent years. Formerly, checking accounts did not pay interest; only savings accounts did. Now we have checking accounts that pay interest, and savings accounts that allow check-writing privileges. The Personal Action Worksheet at the end of this chapter will help you to decide which plans offer you the lowest cost (or highest income). The important matters to consider in shopping for the best account are: the minimum required balance in order to earn interest and offset service charges, the number of checks you customarily write each month, and the overall convenience you can enjoy and beneficial relationships you can establish by dealing with a particular institution.

Savings Accounts

Savings accounts are available at commercial banks, mutual savings banks, savings and loan associations, and credit unions. Generally, they take one of three forms: passbook accounts, saving certificates of deposit (CDs), and money market accounts.

Unlike checking accounts, where money flows in and out constantly, savings accounts are relatively inactive. They're used as a device to accumulate money over a long period of time.

Financial institutions are willing to pay savings account customers for the use of their money. The payment is referred to as *interest*. In effect, customers are lending their money to the institution, and the institution is paying interest for the loan.

Passbook Accounts

The old standard type of savings account is the passbook account. A passbook account may be opened with any amount of money, and the customer may make deposits to, or withdrawals from, the account as desired. (Some institutions may limit the number of withdrawals permitted in a month or in a quarter, and if that number is exceeded, the institution may levy a service charge.) Passbook savings account customers will usually receive a small booklet, or *passbook*, in which each deposit and withdrawal is entered and in which the interest earned on the account is added to the customer's balance. (A variation of the passbook account is the statement account, in which a monthly or quarterly statement is mailed to the customer. The statement reflects all transactions in the account for the preceding period.)

Certificates of Deposit (CDs)

A certificate of deposit is a contractual agreement between customer and institution whereby the customer agrees to leave a certain sum of money with the bank for a fixed period of time—perhaps as short as seven days or as long as ten years. CDs generally pay a higher rate of interest to the customer than passbook accounts because the institution is assured that it will have the fixed sum of money available for lending for a known period of time. CD customers who withdraw funds before the agreed-on date suffer a penalty. Check current penalty regulations before you open a CD account.

Money Market Accounts

This type of account is, in a sense, like a super passbook account. Money market accounts pay a higher rate of interest than passbook accounts but usually require a fairly substantial initial deposit—perhaps $1,000 or more.

Many such accounts impose a service charge if there are too many deposits or withdrawals in a given period of time.

Competition is keen among institutions for savings accounts of all types. Careful shopping is essential if you are to obtain the best deal available at any given time. Because many consider savings accounts as a form of investment, they are treated more fully in chapter 14.

Safe Deposit Facilities

Safe deposit boxes provide the best security for valuable items and documents that cannot be replaced or duplicated. Financial institutions that rent safe deposit facilities make boxes of varying sizes available, generally on a yearly rental basis. The amount of the rent depends on the size of the box. The person or persons renting safe deposit facilities must sign a signature card at the time the box is rented, and they are given a key to the box. Then, only those persons who have signed the cards and who can present the key are permitted access to the box. It takes a combination of two keys—the one given the customer and the one held by the institution—to allow entry into a box. If the customer loses a key, the likelihood is that the institution will have to drill the door open, probably at the customer's expense. Naturally, access to the box is available only during normal banking hours.

Some institutions may offer safe deposit box facilities at a reduced charge for customers who utilize other services.

Trust Services

Trust departments are usually found in larger commercial banks. The basic function of a trust department is to act as a trusted custodian of money or property for customers who require such services.

One frequent use of trust services arises when an individual directs that, after his or her death, property go to survivors "in trust." The customer has thus established an agreement with the bank to act as trustee of the stated money and property. The trust department will then be responsible for investing the money prudently, for managing property (such as real estate), for selling any securities or properties it deems proper to sell, for assisting with the necessary tax returns and other accounting matters on behalf of the trust, and for distributing the proceeds in accordance with the wishes of the individual who established the trust. Charges are levied for trust services based on the total value of assets in the trust and the complexity of the instructions the trust department must follow. For further discussion of trusts, see chapter 19.

Special Checks

Traveler's checks provide a safe and convenient means of having funds available when you are traveling—in the United States, where personal checks may not be acceptable outside your own home community, and particularly in foreign countries, where neither personal checks nor American dollars may be acceptable as exchange. Traveler's checks can be purchased at most financial institutions in denominations of $10, $20, $50, and $100. The common charge is $1 per $100 in traveler's checks. If lost, traveler's checks can be replaced at offices of the issuing agencies, or by mail, as directed in the institutions included with each packet of traveler's checks. Keep a list of your traveler's check numbers to expedite replacement of lost or stolen checks.

Money orders are a form of check purchased at financial institutions (and from the U.S. Postal Service), usually for payment of bills or for any other personal needs. Money orders can be purchased in any denomination. They generally cost more than checks, and one must go to the institution in order to buy one; thus, they aren't nearly as convenient as a checking account.

If you're entering into an important transaction—such as the sale of your home—and you want to be absolutely certain that the check you receive from the other party is good, you may require that the party give you a cashier's check or certified check instead of a personal check. A cashier's check is drawn on the bank's own funds. A certified check is an individual's check, but the bank has certified (in effect, guaranteed) that the funds are indeed in the account and are set aside for payment of the certified check. If you are required to present a cashier's check or certified check, your bank can accommodate your request quickly and at little or no fee, depending on your status as a customer.

Notarial Services

We often have to sign documents requiring that our signature be notarized. This service is performed by a notary public, and most financial institutions have a notary public available to serve their customers. The purpose of notarization is to verify that the signature is indeed that of the person indicated. When a signature is to be notarized, the document must be signed in the presence of the notary, and the notary must be certain of the signer's identity. Many institutions do not charge for notarial services for their customers. Notarial services can also be obtained through law firms, governmental offices, and insurance agencies.

Electronic Banking

Exercise 11.6

Most institutions throughout the nation have installed electronic tellers. These automatic teller machines (ATMs) offer twenty-four-hour service on a variety of transactions: withdrawals, deposits, loan payments, and transfers from one account to another. Customers wishing to utilize these services are generally issued a plastic card with a secret code number assigned to it, thus preventing anyone except the authorized user from using the card. Be certain you know what fees your bank charges, if any, for use of its ATMs. If you use an ATM that is not your bank's, you can be charged additional fees.

Collection Services

Business and commercial accounts are more likely to make use of this little-known service. For example, a landlord who lives in a distant city may find it more convenient for tenants to make their payments to the local bank, which in turn deposits the payments into the landlord's account in that bank. The landlord might think that the rent gets paid more promptly if the payments are made to a local bank. Charges are made in accordance with the volume of services rendered.

Debit Cards

The newest popular product offered by banks is the debit card, which is somewhat the reverse of a credit card. When a debit card is used by a customer to pay for a purchase, the amount of the purchase is immediately deducted from the user's checking account. In effect, it replaces writing a check. Debit cards look like credit cards, and merchants accept them as readily as credit cards. Indeed, some merchants will allow users to get extra cash, over and above the amount of the purchase. If the amount registered by a debit card exceeds the balance in the customer's account, a debt is created, which must be repaid plus interest. There might be a charge each time a debit card is used; and there's always a danger of forgetting to deduct the amount of a debit card use from your checking account. So care is called for when making use of this service.

Investment Departments

What banks don't lend out to the public or keep in reserve, they invest, usually in high-quality government and corporate bond issues. Many investors who seek such securities find it more convenient and less costly to acquire them through their bank investment department than through stock brokerage firms. Inquire at a local bank to see whether the investment department can provide service comparable to, or better than, local brokerage firms.

STRATEGIES FOR SUCCESS

It Pays to Have a Friend at Your Local Bank

Banking can be a very impersonal matter. More and more people are banking with automatic teller machines, telephone/computer hook-ups, and mail. Most of your deposits, withdrawals, and other ordinary banking needs can be handled in this manner. But it's a sound strategy to have a friend at the bank—preferably an officer—who knows you and who can lend a hand if you have any problems or questions. For instance, you might have a foul-up with a credit card statement or a checking account balance. Or you might need a loan in a hurry. A friend at the bank can help you in such circumstances. Prepare a financial statement to help expedite loan requests, and discuss your financial status with your banking friend once a year or so. And be ready: Someday your friend will be transferred to another branch of the bank. Have another friend waiting in the wings.

LAWS THAT GOVERN FINANCIAL INSTITUTIONS AND THEIR TRANSACTIONS

Financial institutions, and the transactions that emanate from them, are governed by a complex system of state and federal laws. As noted earlier, each institution is given its original license to operate either by the state in which it is located or by the federal government. The respective government then generally oversees and regulates the operation of the institution, including periodic audits and examinations to ascertain whether the institution is complying with governmental guidelines.

The State Laws

State regulations that institutions must comply with include laws of negotiable instruments (an important aspect of which is the concept of the "holder in due course"), laws of usury, and laws regarding secured transactions.

Negotiable Instruments

The negotiable instruments laws refer to instruments—such as checks and promissory notes (IOUs)—that are negotiated—sold, exchanged, and otherwise passed from hand to hand. Each state has its own laws of negotiable instruments, but they all tend to be similar. In essence, negotiable instruments laws determine what constitutes a valid negotiable instrument and what does not. A check is a good example of a negotiable instrument. It carries an unconditional order to pay a fixed sum of money to the holder; it's dated; and the person who has drawn the check has signed it. If a check does not contain any of these elements—such as the signature of the drawer—it could be construed as being nonnegotiable. In short, it may be returned to the person who drew the check, and, thus, the intended transaction does not occur.

Another example would be a promissory note: You buy a TV set from a local appliance dealer, and, instead of paying cash for it, you sign a promissory note in which you agree to make payments over a specific period of time. The promissory note is payable directly to the dealer. The dealer, in turn, sells your promissory note to a local bank or finance company. You then end up making your payments to the bank. The bank has become a *holder* of your negotiable instrument *in the due course of business*, assuming that the instrument has been properly created and executed. If you had neglected to sign it, the TV dealer would not have been able to sell it to the bank. If the TV dealer had not properly endorsed it, the bank would not have bought it.

Assuming that all the paperwork was done properly, what would happen if you got the TV set home and found out that it didn't work? You'd want to refuse to make payments to the dealer, but the dealer would simply tell you that he had sold your IOU to the bank. Could you refuse to make payments to the bank? Federal Trade Commission regulations state that, in general, if you, a buyer, would have a valid claim or defense against the original dealer, you have the same claim or defense against a party that had subsequently bought your promissory note. In other words, if you could legally have refused to pay the dealer because the TV set was defective, you could just as legally refuse to pay the bank for the same reason. Before you sign any promissory notes be sure you understand contractual terms that could have a strong bearing on your obligation to pay.

Under these regulations, most consumer credit contracts must contain a notice stating that the holder of the contract or promissory note will be subject to the same claims and defenses that the buyer could have asserted against the seller.

Wary consumers should thus become aware of the protections the law allows and should promptly assert their rights if there is the least suspicion that these rights are being violated.

Usury Laws

Exercise 11.7

Each state has its own laws of <u>usury</u>. The usury laws dictate the maximum rate of interest that can be charged for various types of loans.

You should determine what the maximum interest rates allowable for various categories of loans are in your own state.

Lenders charging usurious rates of interest on any kind of financing may be subject to penalties. Borrowers in usurious transactions should determine what their rights are and take appropriate action.

In most states, the laws of usury apply to individuals only. Corporations do not have the same measure of protection when they borrow.

Secured Transaction Laws

You purchase an automobile and arrange for financing through your local bank. In the typical transaction, you sign documents that give the bank the right to take back your car if you fail to make the payments as promised. As a result of your signing these documents and the bank's recording in the appropriate government office, the bank has what is known as a *security interest* in your new automobile.

By recording the security agreements, the bank has put all other parties on notice that it has a first lien on that particular property. When you pay off the loan, the bank should release that security interest by completing and filing the appropriate papers.

Secured transaction laws are slightly different in each state. These laws describe how lenders can protect their security interest in properties and how they must release that security interest when the loans are eventually paid off. The law does not dictate when or if a borrower must put up security for a given loan or how much security should be put up. That's between the borrower and the lender. The law does, however, describe how each party is protected in such a transaction.

The Federal Laws

Federal laws with which institutions must comply include the Truth in Lending Law, the Truth in Savings Law, the Fair Credit Billing Law, the Fair Credit Reporting Act, the Equal Credit Opportunity Law, and the Fair Debt Collection Practices Act.

Truth in Lending Law

The main purpose of the Truth in Lending Law is to inform borrowers and consumers of the exact cost of credit so that they can compare costs offered by various credit sources.

The Truth in Lending Law applies to virtually all issuers of credit, including banks, savings and loan associations, credit unions, consumer finance companies, residential mortgage brokers, department stores, automobile dealers, furniture and appliance dealers, artisans (such as electricians and plumbers), and professionals (such as doctors, dentists, and lawyers). If these parties, or any others issuing credit to the public, extend credit for personal, family, household, or agricultural uses, or for real estate transactions, they must comply with the Truth in Lending Law.

The main objective of the Truth in Lending Law is to establish a uniform means of quoting credit costs. The law dictates that any granter of credit must clearly set forth the *total finance charges* that the customer must pay, directly or indirectly, in order to obtain the desired credit. The finance charges can include any of the following costs: interest, loan fees, finder's fees, service charges, points (commonly, the added fees charged in a residential mortgage transaction), appraisal fees, premiums for credit life or health insurance, the cost of any investigation or credit reports.

In addition to stating the total dollar amount of finance charges, the credit granter must also express the cost in terms of a percentage. This is known as the *annual percentage rate* or *APR*. The APR formula requires all lenders and credit granters to quote credit costs using the same mathematics. APR, then, is the pure way of comparing credit costs between different lenders.

The Truth in Lending Law does not fix the interest rates that may be charged on credit. That's between the lender and the borrower within the limitations of state usury laws.

Figure 11–7 is a drastic simplification of a disclosure statement as required by the Truth in Lending Law. The real form can be very confusing, but this will give you a general sense of what a real disclosure statement attempts to do. Before you sign a real disclosure statement be certain that you understand every item listed on it.

If you have to put up your home as collateral for a loan, the Truth in Lending Law requires that the lender give you a three-day period in which you can cancel the transaction by sending proper notice to the lender. The purpose of this three-day cooling off period is to protect borrowers who may have second thoughts about a transaction, particularly if they have received a high-pressure sales pitch or misleading promises. If you do elect to cancel such a transaction and if proper notice is given to the lender, you are entitled to a return of any down payment you have given the lender or merchant.

The Truth in Lending Law also sets forth regulations regarding the use of credit cards, the liability for their unauthorized use, and the means by which credit may be advertised.

Truth in Savings Law

The Truth in Savings Law requires banks (all covered institutions that accept deposits) to quote the interest rates they pay on deposits in a uniform fashion. This will help customers shop for the best rates.

1. (A)   Amount you are borrowing: $ _____
   Charges to be added to amount borrowed
   - Insurance costs (credit life, credit health, etc.) $ _____
   - Recording fees $ _____
   - Lien fees $ _____
   - Licensing, title, and registration fees $ _____
   - Loan fees (points, commitment fees, rate lock,
     appraisals, credit reports, notary, document
     preparation, etc.) $ _____

   (B)   Total of extra charges $ _____

   Total amount financed (A + B) $ _____

2. Annual Percentage Rate: _____ %

3. Dollar amounts of finance charges:
   - Simple interest at _____ % per year $ _____
   - And/or add-on or discounted interest $ _____
   - And/or flat charges $ _____
   - Other $ _____

   Total finance charges $ _____

4. Monthly payments: $ _____ per month for _____ months. Note any balloon
   payments, if any, that are to be paid.

5. Prepayment privilege or charge: If the loan is paid in advance of the above
   schedule, what rebates will the borrower get, or what charges will the
   borrower have to pay?

6. Security: What collateral is being given for this loan? Describe:

7. List separately any charges that are to be paid separately by the borrower
   or are to be withheld from the loan proceeds and paid by the lender:
   $ _____ $ _____ etc.

FIGURE 11–7   Simplified Disclosure Statememt

The main feature of the law sets forth the Annual Percentage Yield (APY) as the standard method of quoting rates paid on deposits. The APY tells you, most simply put, how many dollars you'll earn if you deposit your money for one year. If you're depositing $1,000, and the APY is 5.3 percent, you'll earn $53 if you leave your money in the account for one year. This is meant to eliminate the confusion that arises when banks calculate interest in different ways (see chapter 14).

Other aspects of the law: Banks must pay interest on all funds in interest-bearing checking accounts; some banks had been excluding a portion of each account from earning interest. Banks are restricted on how much interest they can dock you if your balance slips below a certain minimum amount; some banks had been overdoing that. In advertising their accounts banks may not call an account "free" or "no cost" if you are required to maintain a minimum balance to avoid fees; however, signs in bank lobbies do not fall under the rules for advertising, so consumer vigilance is still needed.

Fair Credit Billing Law

The Fair Credit Billing Law was designed to put an end to the frustration that credit customers experience when they receive a bill that contains an error and they cannot get the error properly corrected. It pertains to open-end credit—credit arising out of revolving charge accounts, checking overdraft plans, and credit card obligations. It does *not* apply to normal installment loans or purchases that are paid in accordance with a set schedule of installments.

The Fair Credit Billing Law covers only billing errors on your periodic statement. Billing errors are those that arise from the following: charges you did not make or charges made by a person not allowed to use your account; charges billed with the wrong descriptions, amount, or date; charges for property or services that you did not accept or that were not delivered as agreed; failures to credit your accounts for payments or for goods you have returned; mistakes in computing finance charges; billings for which you request an explanation or written proof of purchase; and failures to mail or deliver a billing statement to your current address, provided you gave at least ten days' notice of any change of address.

The Fair Credit Billing Law requires that open-end creditors give a notice summarizing the dispute settlement procedures to all customers who have active accounts. After the first notice, additional copies must be provided to customers every six months.

The dispute settlement procedures regarding a billing error, as outlined by the Federal Trade Commission, are as follows:

- **How you notify the creditor of a billing error**   If you think your bill is wrong, or if you need more information about an item on your bill, here's what you must do to preserve your rights under the law. On a sheet of paper separate from the bill, write the following: your name and account number; a description of the error and an explanation of why you think it's an error; a request for whatever added information you think you need, including a copy of the charge slip; the dollar amount of the suspected error; and any other information you think will help the creditor identify you or the reason for your complaint or inquiry.

Send your billing error notice to the address on the bill listed after the words: "Send inquiries to" or similar wording indicating the proper address.

Mail it as soon as you can but, in any case, early enough to reach the creditor within sixty days after the bill was mailed to you.

Do not simply notify the creditor by telephone. This will not necessarily protect your rights under the law.

- **What the creditor must do**   The creditor must acknowledge all such letters within thirty days, unless the creditor is able to correct your bill during the thirty-day period. Within ninety days after receiving your letter, the creditor must either correct the error or explain why the bill is correct. After explaining the bill, the creditor has no further obligation to you even if you still believe there is an error, except as provided in the fifth item of this list.

- **How you are protected from collection and bad credit reports**   After the creditor has been notified, neither the creditor not an attorney nor a collection agency may send you collection letters or take other collection action regarding the amount in dispute. But periodic *statements* may be sent to you and the disputed amount applied against your credit limit. You cannot be threatened with damage to your credit rating or sued for the amount in question, nor can the disputed amount be reported to a credit bureau or other creditors as being delinquent until the creditor has answered your inquiry. However, you remain obligated to pay whatever portion of your bill is not in dispute.

- **What happens if the dispute is settled?**   If it is determined that the creditor has made a mistake on your bill, you will not have to pay any finance charges on any disputed amount. If it turns out that the creditor has not made an error, you may have to pay finance charges on the amount in dispute, and you will have to make up any missed minimum or required payments on the disputed amount.

- **What happens if the dispute is not settled?**   If the creditor's explanation does not satisfy you and you notify the creditor in writing within ten days after you receive that explanation that you still refuse to pay the disputed amount, the creditor may report you to credit bureaus and other creditors and may pursue regular collection procedures. But the creditor must also report that you do not think you owe any money, and the creditor must let you know to whom such reports were made. Once the matter has been settled between you and the creditor, the creditor must report this to all those who were notified that you had been delinquent.

- **How the creditor can be penalized for not following the procedure**   If the creditor does not follow these rules, the creditor is not allowed to collect the first $50 of the disputed amount and finance charges, even if the bill turns out to be correct.

- **When can you withhold payment for faulty goods or services purchased with a credit card?**   If you have a problem with property or services purchased with a credit card, you may have the right not to pay the remaining amount due on them if you first try, in good faith, to return the item or give the merchant a chance to correct the problem. There are two conditions on this right: (1) You must have bought the item or services in your home state or, if not within your home state, within 100 miles of your current mailing address; and (2) the purchase price must have been more than $50. However, these two conditions do not apply if the merchant's business is owned or operated by the creditor or if the creditor mailed you the advertisement for the property or services.

In brief, the Fair Credit Billing Law gives you the right of extensive protection against alleged errors in billing. But you must exercise your rights as they are stated in the law. If you fail to do so, you may have waived them.

Fair Credit Reporting Act

The Fair Credit Reporting Act is designed to give you access to any information that may be on file at local credit bureaus regarding your individual credit history. It also enables you to take steps to correct erroneous or outdated material that may be in your file.

It should be noted, contrary to what many people think, that credit reporting agencies are *not* governmental agencies. They are generally private firms, operating either on their own or as a cooperative of various merchants and lenders within the community. Their job is to accumulate appropriate credit information on individuals and make it available to their respective participating members. Easy access to credit information makes it more convenient for credit to be granted to creditworthy people. To this extent, the local credit bureau, as a clearing-house of information, serves a most valuable purpose. But there have been abuses within that industry, and the Fair Credit Reporting Act was designed to correct those abuses.

Exercise 11.8

Under the Fair Credit Reporting Act, you can, on presenting proper identification, learn the contents of your file at your local credit bureau. The identification requirements are for your own protection, to minimize the chance that a stranger may walk into a credit bureau, claim to be you, and view your credit file.

Regarding erroneous information, you can request the bureau to reinvestigate any items you question. If the information is found to be inaccurate or cannot be verified, it will be deleted. If the reinvestigation doesn't resolve the problem, you can write a brief statement explaining your position, and the statement will be included in all future credit reports. If an item is deleted or a statement added, you can request that the bureau so notify anyone who has received regular credit reports on you during the last six months.

You may be able to get free copies of your credit file periodically. If you seek copies more frequently, you may have to pay a fee for the service.

Information in your credit file that is unfavorable to you may not be disclosed to creditors after seven years have elapsed—unless you have had a bankruptcy in your past. That information may remain in your file and be available to inquiries for up to fourteen years.

In late 1997 some additional consumer rights were added to the Fair Credit Reporting Law:

If you've ever wondered why you get unsolicited offers in the mail for credit cards or insurance plans, it may be because your local credit bureau has sold your name and relevant data to a credit card company or an insurance company. You can prevent this from happening by notifying your credit bureau accordingly. Notifying them by telephone will get your name off the lists for two years; notifying them in writing will get you off permanently. This is a highly advisable step to take. Not only will it remove unneeded temptations. It will also cut down on the chance that a scam operator will intercept a mailed solicitation and apply for a credit card in your name.

Also, credit bureaus must now also offer toll-free telephone lines so that you can talk to a real person about a possible credit bureau error, and any credit bureau mistakes must be corrected within 30 days. And other businesses (banks, merchants, finance companies, etc.) who supply information to credit bureaus are legally bound to clear up any misinformation on you that they have in their files. FTC enforcement powers were also expanded by the new law changes.

As with the other laws, the Fair Credit Reporting Act gives you rights, but it's up to you to exercise those rights.

Equal Credit Opportunity Law

The Equal Credit Opportunity Law is designed to prevent any discrimination on the basis of the gender or marital status of any person applying for credit. In the most general sense, this law was designed to correct abuses that often prevented creditworthy women from receiving credit for reasons relating specifically to their gender and marital situations. Highlights of the law include the following:

- Creditors must not discriminate against any applicant on the basis of gender or marital status in any phase of a credit transaction.
- Creditors must not make any statement to any applicant that would discourage a reasonable person from applying for credit because of gender or marital status.

- Creditors must open separate accounts for husbands and wives if requested and if both are creditworthy.
- Creditors must consider alimony and child-support payments as they would any other source of income in assessing creditworthiness if the applicant wishes to rely on those means of income.
- Creditors must allow applicants to open or maintain accounts in their birth-given name if they so desire.
- Creditors must give the reason why credit has been denied or terminated when asked by the applicant.

Fair Debt Collection Practices Act

The Fair Debt Collection Practices Act prohibits abusive, deceptive, and unfair debt-collection practices. The law covers personal, family, and household debts, including loans, charge accounts, and medical bills. Here, in brief, is how the law works:

- Debt collectors may contact you in person, by mail, telephone, or telegram, but not at unusual places or times, such as before 8 A.M. or after 9 P.M. Debt collectors may *not* contact you at work if your employer disapproves. Debt collectors may contact any other person for the purpose of trying to locate you but may not tell the other person anything other than that they are trying to contact you. If you have an attorney, they must contact only your attorney. The debt collector must not tell anybody else that you owe money; should not talk to any person more than once; should not use a postcard; and should not put anything on an envelope or in a letter to others that identifies the writer as a debt collector.
- Within five days after you are first contacted by debt collectors, they must send you *written notice* telling you the amount of money you owe, the name of the creditor, and what to do if you think you do not owe the money.
- If you think you do not owe the money, you must inform the debt collectors, in writing, within thirty days after you were first contacted. The debt collectors may then not contact you again except: (1) if they send you proof of the debt, such as a copy of the bill, in which case they can begin collection proceedings again, or (2) to notify you that certain specific action will be taken but only if, in fact, they usually do take such action. In short, you can stop the debt collectors from constantly harassing you if you properly notify them in writing to stop.
- A debt collector may not use false, deceptive, threatening, or abusive statements to induce you to pay and may not threaten to take any legal action that in fact cannot be legally taken.

PERSONAL ACTION WORKSHEET

Earnings and Costs of Checking Accounts

This is designed to help you compare the costs of various checking account plans—particular those that pay interest. As with so many other of our day-to-day concerns, the lower price is not always the best price.

	Plan A	Plan B	Plan C
❏ How much do you have to keep in the account in order to earn interest; in order to avoid charges for your checking account?	_____	_____	_____
❏ Are these minimums *averages* per month (or quarter) or fixed dollar minimums?	_____	_____	_____
❏ Can you keep the minimum balance in an account other than the checking account, such as a savings certificate?	_____	_____	_____
❏ What charges will you incur if your required minimum balance drops below the set level?	_____	_____	_____
Basic monthly charge?	_____	_____	_____
Charge per check written?	_____	_____	_____
❏ Based on your past history (if you've had a checking account previously), what type of average balance would you expect to keep in your account?	_____	_____	_____
How many checks would you write per month?			
❏ If you've not had a checking account before, estimate your average balance.	_____	_____	_____
❏ Based on these estimates, how much do you expect you'll earn (interest income less monthly charges) with this plan?	_____	_____	_____
❏ Business hours of institution?			
Open Saturdays?	_____	_____	_____
Automatic teller machine available?	_____	_____	_____
❏ Convenience in getting to and from the institution?	_____	_____	_____
❏ Personal feelings about the institution: helpfulness of staff, other services offered, etc.	_____	_____	_____

CONSUMER ALERT

A Flood of Plastic

Today some banks do nothing but offer credit cards. They don't have branch offices. They don't have checking accounts or savings accounts. They just offer credit cards. Actually, *offer* is not the correct word to describe what they do: "aggressively solicit customers" would be more like it.

Maybe you've received mail from some of them: "Congratulations! You have been *PRE-APPROVED*[1] for our new **TITANIUM** Card, which gives you an unlimited[2] line of credit, NO ANNUAL FEE,[3] a **LOW, LOW**[4] interest rate on your unpaid balance and $1 million worth of travel insurance.[5] All you have to do is tell us a little about yourself, and your *PRE-APPROVED* **TITANIUM** Credit Card will be on its way to you.[6]

The BIG PRINT GIVETH, the small print taketh away:

[1]Pre-approved? Does that mean you've been approved before you've been approved? No. It means that they got your name from some mailing list they bought.

[2]Unlimited? Yes, but subject to the limits we decide to put on once we've suckered you into sending us an application and have you salivating for this new credit card.

[3]No annual fee for the first week. Thereafter, an $89-a-year fee will be pro-rated and charged against your first month's bill.

[4]Low, low interest rate of 29.7% APR, which you'll have to admit is lower than 35.7%.

[5]Your life is covered, absolutely free, for a cool mill if you are killed while flying over the South Pole in a helicopter. See policy for other limitations and restrictions.

In a recent year, banks of all sorts sent out some 2.7 *billion* "pre-approved" credit card solicitations. That amounts to about seventeen offers to every American between the ages of 18 and 64, which translates into roughly $130,000 worth of available credit per household!

In addition to the danger of taking on more debt via plastic, many lenders now are increasing the interest rate on existing credit card debts when they learn that those borrowers have applied for extra credit. In other words, just by making an application for a loan or credit card you never accept, you risk having a higher rate of interest on your existing loans.

Stop and think: all these banks offering all these credit cards—they'd stop doing it if people didn't gobble up their offers. 'Nuf said.

UPS & DOWNS   *The Economics of Everyday Life*

Why the Health of Financial Institutions Changes

Prior to 1980, banks and S & Ls were limited as to how much interest they could pay on deposits. But the federal government was not limited as to how much interest it could pay to investors. When Uncle Sam went on a borrowing binge in the late 1970s to pay for various government programs, he offered higher interest rates to investors than could be obtained at local banks and S & Ls.

Not surprisingly, huge numbers of investors pulled their money out of local institutions to invest it with Uncle Sam. The banks and S & Ls cried, "Foul! The government limits the interest *we* can pay, then goes ahead and offers higher rates. We'll lose all our deposits and go bust! Unfair competition!"

Congress listened and cut out the interest rate controls to enable the local institutions to compete more freely. S & Ls were also given vastly broader lending powers: office buildings, hotels, shopping centers, oil rigs, you name it.

The S & Ls then found themselves in a very enviable position: they were able to attract deposits from the public because the federal government was insuring those deposits; and they were able to pay any rate of interest on those deposits they wanted to, because the limits had been taken off. Furthermore, they could now venture out into more exciting lending activities: "Why bother with dull, boring, safe single-family mortgages when we can lend our money to build skyscrapers in Peoria . . . or ritzy resort hotels in Fargo . . . or mega-maxi shopping malls (550 stores! 22,000 parking spots!) in Shinbone, Wyoming." So they made loans on projects like that.

All of this went hand in hand with the "greed" mentality of the 1980s. "I want *that* and I want it *now!*" "Debt is good because it lets us buy things!" "The economy will always grow, and we will always get richer."

Then—speaking of ups and downs—a funny thing happened. Nobody wanted to rent space in all the new shopping centers in all the Shinbones of America, and the high-flyers starting crashing to earth.

The debacle that resulted was unparalleled in our nation's history. As one of every three S & Ls folded, their insured depositors had to be protected. This cost hundreds of billions of dollars, most of which added to our national debt and annual budget deficit. In other words, the taxpayers paid the price of Congress's deregulation of the thrift industry.

Can it happen again? Commercial banks have been pleading their case to Congress, asking for broader powers that could include selling insurance, acting as stock brokers and being able to take an ownership (stockholder) position in nonbank corporations. This latter item has long been common in Japan, and has been blamed for the economic troubles Japan suffered throughout the 1990s. There's a potentially lethal conflict of interest between a *lender to* and an *owner of* a corporation. If Congress lets this happen, we could see the S & L catastrophe all over again.

?

WHAT IF . . . ?

Test yourself: How would you deal with these real-life possibilities?

1. A stranger telephones you, stating that she is a financial planner. She offers to give you an analysis of your financial situation at no cost. What opportunities and/or pitfalls might such a meeting present? What homework could you do before scheduling such a meeting?

2. Your request for a car loan at your bank has been refused. This amazes you, because you have always had an excellent credit rating. The loan officer says the loan request was denied because your credit history shows a delinquency on a debt to a local hospital. You've never had any dealings with that hospital. What might have gone wrong, and what can you do to correct the problem?

3. You've paid off your car loan promptly, and you have all the canceled checks to prove it. You're trading in the old car for a new one, and the dealer checks and finds that public records still show a loan against the old car. Showing him your canceled checks does not satisfy him. What has happened? How can you rectify the matter?

4. Your credit card bill shows a charge that you didn't make. What steps can you take to have the erroneous charge removed?

NUMBER CRUNCHERS

Do the calculations to make decisions in these real-life possibilities.

1. How much will it cost you per month for the following checking account plans, assuming that you write ten checks per month and make four deposits per month: (a) basic monthly service charge of $2, plus 10¢ for every check written; no charge for deposits made. (b) no monthly service charge; 20¢ per check and 10¢ per deposit. (c) no service charges at all if you keep a minimum of $500 in the account, and you will earn 3 percent interest per year on your average balance; if your balance falls below $500 in any month, there's a $3 charge, plus 15¢ per check and no charge for deposits. Which is the best account for you? How can you alter your checking account habits to improve your cost situation?

Exercise 11.9

2. You open a checking account with $100. After the following transactions, what is the balance in your account: (a) paycheck deposited— $444.85; (b) cash withdrawn—$50; (c) birthday gift check deposited— $100; (d) groceries—$32.90; (e) tax refund deposited—$379.58; (f) charge for new checkbook—$8.50; (g) paycheck deposited (net, after taking out $50 in cash)—$397.85; (h) rent (your share)—$420; (i) interest earned on balance in account—$1.41; (j) birthday gift check bounces; (k) charge for bounced check—$5.00.

FOR BETTER OR FOR WORSE

Things beyond our control often impact our personal and financial well-being, for better or for worse. Some are more predictable than others. How would you be affected if the following real-life phenomena happened? Could you have seen it coming? What steps could you have taken to minimize damage or maximize advantage? The better able you are to anticipate and recognize these forces, the better equipped you are to deal with them.

1. Your wayward brother-in-law finally pays you back the $4,000 he owes you. You deposit the check in your account and write out a number of checks against it for money that you owe. Then your brother-in-law's check bounces.

2. You sign a contract for home improvements, realizing that you have to give the contractor a second mortgage on the house as collateral for the loan. A week later you learn that the contractor has a very bad reputation.

3. You write a check for $500 as down payment on a used car. An hour later you change your mind but the seller of the car says "a deal is a deal." You phone your bank to stop payment on the check. The bank tells you over the phone that they will do so. But they don't, and the check is cashed by the seller.

12

Credit and Borrowing

There can be no freedom or beauty about a home life that depends on borrowing and debt.

Henrik Ibsen

Imagine what would happen to our economy if it weren't possible to borrow money. Everything would grind to a halt: People couldn't buy cars, houses, or appliances until they had accumulated enough cash to do so. Similarly, businesses and governments would be hard pressed to create new facilities, purchase needed equipment, and expand ongoing programs.

We live in a credit (borrowing) society. Making wise use of your ability to borrow can enhance your life. Abusing your credit can be very harmful. This chapter will explore the wise and unwise uses of credit and will guide you in the ways that credit techniques work. You'll learn:

- How to evaluate how much borrowing you can afford to do and under what circumstances
- Where to seek the credit you need and how best to ensure you'll get the money you need
- How to structure your borrowing to suit your ability to repay your loans
- How to avoid the dangers of credit abuse
- Where to look for help if you have credit problems

BUY NOW, PAY LATER

Most of us take the "Buy now, pay later" aspect of our economy for granted. But it was not always so.

It wasn't until about 1916, with the development of a phenomenon called the Morris Plan, that the individual working person could borrow from banks and other financial institutions. Prior to that, business, governments, and wealthy individuals were the predominant borrowers. Their loans were generally on a "demand" or "time" basis. A demand loan would be repayable in its entirety on the demand of the lender. A time loan would be repayable after the passage of the stated amount of time. If the borrower wished and the lender was willing, such loans could be renewed for an additional period of time, once the borrower had paid the interest due. It was generally felt that if plain working folk borrowed on such a basis, they would not be able to repay the lump sum at the agreed-on time.

Then a banker named Arthur Morris devised a plan that would enable the individual worker to borrow money that was needed for immediate purposes. Today, Mr. Morris's plan seems commonplace, but it was a revolutionary concept when it was originally devised.

The key to his idea—which came to be known as the Morris Plan—was that a loan could be repaid in monthly installments over a fixed period of time. The Morris Plan was the origin, and grandfather, of the installment loan, the time payment plan, the revolving charge account, the credit card loan, and all the other forms of borrowing that we are accustomed to.

Morris's reasoning was simple enough: although it might be difficult for the typical worker to repay one large lump sum, if individuals were prudent and well employed, they should be able to set aside a fixed amount each month to apply to the debt. This type of debt would command a higher rate of interest from the borrower, and the lender would have a constant inflow of money as payments were made each month on the loans, thus enabling the lender to keep putting the available money back to work on a constant basis.

From an initial institution in Virginia, the Morris Plan proved itself. Within a few years scores of Morris Plan institutions were in operation around the country.

Commercial banks soon saw the advantages and profits in making such loans, and merchants began to accept the installment IOUs of customers for many products. The buy now, pay later years were on their way.

The Morris Plan, and all that developed from it, proved successful on more than one level. By putting borrowing power into the hands of millions of American workers, more goods could be manufactured and sold. This, in turn, helped to create more jobs which, in turn, created more income for more people. This then enabled a much larger segment of the population to borrow and buy.

Today, there are very few adults in the United States who do not carry one of the descendants of the Morris Plan with them in their wallets or purses—the credit card. The credit card, in effect, allows holders to write personal installment loans—within limits—whenever and wherever they choose.

Understanding the workings of credit and borrowing is essential to all those who want to manage their personal and financial affairs wisely. Let's now take a closer look at their workings and how they can be put to proper and sensible use.

WHAT IS CREDIT?

Credit—the ability to borrow—is not a right. It's a privilege earned through careful planning and faithful performance. Good credit, properly used, can be a most valuable asset. Wise borrowers have studied their own financial situation with great care. They know the difference between needs and luxuries. They know within pennies their ability to repay. They know how to approach the lender, what to ask for and what to expect. They can resist the temptations that scream, "Buy me now!" and "Easy credit!"

They have carefully defined their *access to credit, credit needs*, and *credit capacity*. And they can keep each in proper perspective and balance. Let's take a closer look at these three important elements of credit.

Access to Credit

Access to credit refers to the amount of credit readily available to you through such means as charge accounts, credit cards, and installment loans. Access to credit, of course, is directly related to lender and merchant willingness to grant credit. That, in turn, depends on your past performance, income, other debts, work, and the purposes for which you wish to borrow.

Credit Needs

Credit needs refer to the various needs you may have that can be fulfilled through borrowing. Common needs for borrowing include purchasing an automobile; revolving charge accounts at department stores so that a large clothing purchase, for example, can be paid for over an extended period of time, thus making it easier on the monthly budget; home improvements; and personal emergencies. *Note:* We are referring to *needs*, not luxuries. Using credit to acquire luxuries, as opposed to using credit to fulfill needs, can be dangerous. If your available credit is used excessively to obtain luxuries, you can cut off your access to credit for the more important needs.

Credit Capacity

Capacity for credit refers to the amount of borrowing you can realistically handle, considering both your current and future income and expenses.

People often find that they have access to more credit than they realistically need. For example, Charlie and Charlotte estimate that they have access to roughly $15,000 worth of credit. Based on past experience, they are confident that their bank would lend them up to $5,000 without collateral, if necessary. The sum total of all their credit cards and charge accounts would allow them to go into additional debt of about $5,000. And a representative of a lending firm has told them that the equity in their house would allow them to borrow another $5,000—if, naturally, they were willing to give a second mortgage on the house. Their current credit *needs* are much more modest. Their automobile is paid off, and next year they'll need a new one. They estimate that they might need about $8,000 for this purpose. Over and above that, their credit needs don't exceed $1,000—to be used in their charge accounts to even out the monthly cost of clothing and home necessities.

Currently, then, their *capacity* for credit exceeds their credit *needs*. However, in a few years, Charlie and Charlotte's oldest child will be starting college, and they expect to have to borrow quite heavily to meet those costs. At that time, their credit *needs* may exceed their credit *capacity*. They should begin making plans to ensure that they'll be able to borrow what they need when they need it. They would be wise to visit a lending officer at their bank and review their *access* to credit, their *needs* for credit, and their credit *capacity* now and for the next three to five years. Such a periodic review is wise for anyone who wants to maintain good control over the wise use of credit.

Credit Sources

Installment loans for a variety of purposes are available at banks, savings and loan associations, credit unions, and consumer finance (small loan) companies. As a general rule, the cost of borrowing tends to be highest at the consumer finance companies. Interest rates at credit unions tend to be equal to, or slightly lower than, those at banks and savings and loan associations.

Exercise 12.1

Dealer financing is another common source of credit. When you purchase such items as automobiles, furniture, and appliances, the dealer may be able to arrange financing for you. The dealer may extend the loan to you directly or may place your loan with one of the financial institutions mentioned earlier. A dealer who places financing with another institution usually gets a fee for doing so. Before you accept a dealer financing arrangement, you should compare the cost of doing so with what you'd be charged if you dealt directly with a lender of your choice.

Charge accounts are frequently used as a source of credit. Department stores, for example, will approve open-end credit arrangements with credit-worthy customers. This will allow you to charge purchases at the store up to a certain limit. You'll be expected to pay at least a minimum amount each month toward your debt. If you don't pay your charge account debts in full each month, you'll be charged interest for the balance left owing. This interest charge is usually based on the average amount outstanding in your account during the prior month.

Credit cards have become one of the most popular sources of credit. The most common types of credit cards are those offered by banks: MasterCard and VISA. These cards are honored extensively throughout the United States and in foreign countries. These cards have also been offered through nonbanking entities, such as AT&T and affinity groups (airline frequent flyer plans, fraternal organizations, and the like). Dean Witter offers the Discover card. "Travel and entertainment" cards (American Express, Diners Club) are commonly used for business purposes at hotels and restaurants. Airlines and gasoline companies also issue charge cards for use in obtaining their specific products and services.

Applicants who are deemed creditworthy are granted a line of credit by the credit card company. That is, a maximum amount is established that these individuals can charge against the card. The card user is then expected to pay at least a certain monthly minimum and any debt unpaid will be charged interest.

The manner in which interest on credit card debts is calculated can be very complex. The best way to avoid the matter entirely is to pay your credit card debt in full each month so that no interest at all accrues against you. Most issuing institutions will also charge an annual fee for the use of the credit card. Interest costs on credit card usage tend to be higher than interest costs on a direct installment loan made at a bank.

Undisciplined use of credit cards and charge accounts can create serious financial problems. It's much easier to pay the minimum monthly amount than to pay off the entire month's charges. But this adds heavy interest costs to your debt, and those costs keep mounting over the months (and perhaps even years) that you take to pay off the debt. And the ease of using credit cards compounds the problem by adding new debts to your existing debt. If you pay off the full month's charges immediately, you

STRATEGIES FOR SUCCESS

Beware Low-rate Credit Cards and High Loan-to-Value Home Loans

In the highly competitive world of selling credit cards, one common ploy is to offer a lower interest rate on your debt than what you now might be paying. "Pay off all your high interest debts with our low rate card. . . ." You don't have to look too far to read that this low rate is "introductory," and you therefore must assume that after the introductory period your rate will be kicked up to a higher level, and you'll be back where you started from. Or worse. Is it worth it? Proceed with caution.

Another come-on is the so-called high LTV mortgage, offered mainly by nonbank lenders. LTV stands for loan to value: If the value of your home is $100,000 and you have $70,000 in loans against it, your LTV is 70 percent. High LTV lenders—seeking to woo the millions of overanxious, overextended homeowners—offer loans of up to 125 percent of the value of their homes. As in the above example, a borrower could get an extra $55,000 on top of the current debt of $70,000 in a 125 percent LTV loan. This is DANGEROUS! Although you might lower the interest rate on some of your debt, you risk losing the house if you default on a high LTV mortgage. And if you sell before you've paid down the high LTV mortgage, you could end up still owing money after you no longer own the home. Or you might not be able to sell at all without paying off the loan.

should not incur any interest costs at all. But if you take the line of least resistance, paying only the minimum monthly amount, you'll sooner or later find yourself looking at a mountain of debt that can be very difficult indeed to pay off.

Credit Reporting

The promptness with which you pay your existing debts affects your ability to borrow in the future. Your performance is known as your credit history. Information that makes up your credit history is compiled by a credit bureau. Credit bureaus exist in every community for the purpose of gathering information on the credit performance of individuals in that community. See the discussion in chapter 11 on the Fair Credit Reporting Act, which controls what credit bureaus can and cannot do, and what your rights are with respect to your credit history.

Figure 12–1 illustrates a typical credit report in abbreviated form.

Date of report _____

Name and address of Credit Bureau _____

Name and address of company for whom the report has been created _____

Name and address of person whose credit is being reported _____

Social Security # _____ Spouse's name _____

Present employer _____ Since _____ Position _____

Date employment verified _____ Monthly income _____

Date of birth _____ Own or rent _____

Former address _____ From _____ To _____

Former employer _____ From _____ To _____

Spouse's current employer _____ Since _____ Monthly income _____

<u>Credit History</u>

Business Reporting	Date Opened	Last Pmt.	Highest Credit	Present Status		Times Past Due		
				$ owed	Past Due	30–59 days	60–90 days	90+ days
ABC Bank	06/17/98	01/17/99	$2,500	$1,970	-0-	1	-0-	-0-
XYZ Car Dealer	08/11/97	01/03/99	12,500	9,644	-0-	-0-	-0-	-0-
Credit Card	07/27/95	12/18/98	6,000	4,280	-0-	1	-0-	-0-

Public Record: Small Claims Court 11/16/97. Subject was sued for $300 by TV Repair shop. Subject claims repairs were incomplete. Case was dropped.

FIGURE 12–1 Credit History Report

Note: This is an abbreviated version of the typical report as created by the Associated Credit Bureaus, a national trade association of credit bureaus. It is meant to highlight only the most pertinent information relevant to this chapter.

HOW THE COST OF CREDIT IS FIGURED

Simple Interest

The fee you pay for the use of someone else's money is called interest. Interest rates are expressed as a percentage of the amount borrowed and for a given period of time. For example, if you borrowed $1,000 for one year and the interest rate was 10 percent a year, you would pay a fee of $100 (10 percent of $1,000) for the use of the money for a period of one year. If you were borrowing $1,000 and the interest rate was expressed as 1 percent per month, you would pay a fee of $10 per month (1 percent of $1,000 equals

$10), or a total over the year of $120 in interest. In these examples, you would have the use of the entire $1,000 for the full period, be it one year or one month. This calculation is what is commonly known as simple interest.

Loans calculated on a simple-interest basis are generally repayable in one lump sum at a specific time, such as 30, 60, 90, or 120 days from the date of the loan. Or the loan may be repayable on the demand of the lender. Businesses generally borrow on a simple-interest basis, and some individuals may also be able to borrow on that basis. (The expression *prime rate* refers to the simple-interest rate that banks charge their most creditworthy borrowers. Prime-rate loans, in theory, are the safest and lowest risk loans that lenders make. Thus, the prime rate is the lowest interest rate a lender will offer. Borrowers who do not have the financial strength and creditworthiness of prime-rate borrowers pay a higher rate of interest. As the prime rate moves up and down, as it tends to do regularly, other interest rates usually follow.)

Of more concern to the average individual is the mode of calculating interest on installment and open-end credit. Installment loans are those that are repayable in equal monthly installments; open-end credit refers to debts generated through charge accounts, credit card accounts, and checking account overdraft accounts. In an open-end account, you will be billed for a minimum monthly payment, based on the total amount of the current balance you owe.

Add-on Interest

Probably the most common way of calculating interest in an installment loan is the add-on method. Here's how it works. Say you want to borrow $1,000 for twelve months, and the rate is 6 percent add-on per year. Your rental fee for the use of the bank's money will be 6 percent of $1,000, or $60. The lender will then add the $60 on to the $1,000 worth of principal, making a total of $1,060.

That sum, $1,060, is divided by twelve, giving you twelve equal monthly payments of $88.33 each. Thus, with the add-on loan, you receive the $1,000 in cash and, over the course of one year, you will repay $1,060. It sounds like simple interest, but it is really quite different. In the simple-interest loan, you have the use of the full $1,000 for the full one year. Under the installment method, such as add-on, you have the use of the full $1,000 during only the first month of the loan, at the end of which you make your first payment. During the second month, therefore, you have the use of only 11/12 of the money and proportionately less each month until the final month, when you have the use of only 1/12 of the money. In effect, then, you are paying $60 rental, but you don't have the use of all the money all the time, as you would in the simple-interest loan. However, you do have the use of whatever it is you obtained with the money you borrowed—a car, an appliance, or whatever.

What if the loan is for more than one year? In the add-on method, the interest rate would be multiplied by the number of years. For example: if you are borrowing $1,000 for two years at a 6 percent per year add-on rate, your total interest obligation would be $120 over the full two-year period. (Six percent per year, or $60 per year, times two years equals $120.)

Discount Interest

Another way of figuring interest on installment loans is the discount method. A loan that nets the borrower $1,000 for twelve months at a 6 percent discount per year rate works like this. Working from a prefigured chart, the lender notes that 6 percent of $1,064 equals $63.84. Let's round that off to $64 for ease in figuring. A promissory note is signed for $1,064, and the lender *discounts,* or subtracts, the interest from that, leaving you with $1,000 in cash. The $1,064 is divided by twelve, giving you twelve equal monthly payments of $88.66. You receive $1,000. You repay $1,064. Comparing the discount with the add-on method, you can see that the discount results in a slightly higher cost to the borrower and a slightly higher return to the lender. In other words, in these examples, the 6 percent discount method costs the borrower $4 more a year than the 6 percent add-on method.

How Interest Costs Are Expressed: APR

If you were shopping for a loan, and one lender quoted you a 10 percent add-on rate, another quoted you a 10 percent discount rate, and still a third quoted you a 10 percent simple-interest rate, you'd be very confused. But, thanks to a federal law, the Truth in Lending Law, the confusion is removed. Under the Truth in Lending Law, lenders and granters of credit may *calculate* their interest rate and other finance charges any way they want (within the limitations of the state's usury laws). But no matter how those rates are calculated, they must be *expressed* in terms of annual percentage rate (APR). The Federal Trade Commission has prepared extensive tables by which any lender can convert add-on or discount rates to APR terms. Table 12–1 shows the conversion of add-on rates for common installment loans to APR, based on the FTC Tables.

For example, a 6 percent a year add-on rate for a 24-month loan is equal to an APR of 11.13. A 6 percent a year add-on rate for a 36-month loan is equal to an APR of 11.08.

Under the Truth in Lending Law, all lenders are required to quote their rates only in terms of APR, even though many of them may still calculate their rates on an add-on or discount basis.

TABLE 12–1   **Converting Add-on to APR**

Term (Months)	Add-on Rates (Percentages)			
	5½	6	6½	7
12	10.00% APR	10.90% APR	11.79% APR	12.68% APR
18	10.18	11.08	11.98	12.87
24	10.23	11.13	12.12	12.91
30	10.23	11.12	12.00	12.88
36	10.20	11.08	11.96	12.83
48	10.11	10.97	11.83	12.68
60	10.01	10.85	11.68	12.50

Open-end Credit

In the typical installment loan, the borrower receives a lump sum of money and pays it back in equal installments. In open-end credit, that's not necessarily the case. If, for example, you have a credit card account and you have not paid all your charges, you will be carrying an *open-end loan*. *Open-end* means that you can add to that debt by making additional charges or diminish it by making payments. Because the total balance you owe at any given time can fluctuate, the APR is normally calculated on the average balance owed throughout the monthly billing period.

The APR rate will be expressed on the billing statement each month as required by the Truth in Lending Law.

Figuring Your Installment Loan Costs

The APR gives us the means to compare true interest rates on various loan quotations. The actual dollar cost of any loan will be set forth in the disclosure statement provided you by the lender. See Figure 11–7 for a sample disclosure statement. Other financing costs can be included in the disclosure statement; so, for your best protection in comparing loan costs, you should have a complete tally of all the costs involved in any given quotation, expressed in dollar terms on the disclosure statement. Use that as your ultimate comparison.

Insuring Your Installment Loan

Many lenders suggest that you obtain credit insurance as a part of your installment loan transaction. There are two common types of credit insurance:

Exercise 12.2

life and health. If you obtain credit life insurance as a part of the transaction, the insurance will pay off any remaining balance on the loan if the borrower dies before the loan is paid off. The borrower's survivors need not, therefore, pay the remaining balance on the loan.

If you obtain health insurance on your loan, the insurance will make your payments if you become unable to work for an extended period of time because of illness or accident. Credit health insurance will differ regarding the initial waiting period involved before the insurance takes effect. For example, if a waiting period is fifteen days, you must be unable to work for fifteen days before the insurance takes effect. In such a case, if you're out of work for, say, twenty-five days, the insurance will protect you for the last ten days. Some credit health plans may protect you in case of partial disability.

Another form of credit insurance is unemployment insurance. It makes your payments for you if you lose your job for specific reasons.

If you wish to obtain any of these forms of insurance, you can pay the lender separately, or the cost of the insurance can be added to the amount you're borrowing, which would increase your interest cost and payments accordingly.

Paying Off an Installment Loan Ahead of Schedule

Loan officers frequently have to resolve a perplexing dispute that arises when customers wish to pay off their installment loans ahead of schedule. Here's a typical situation. Charlie had borrowed $5,000 for a thirty-six-month term. The interest cost for three years was $900, which, when added to the $5,000, gave Charlie a total debt of $5,900 and monthly payments of $164. Eighteen months have elapsed, and Charlie has accumulated some unexpected funds and wishes to use them to pay off his installment loan. Against the original debt of $5,900, Charlie has, during these first eighteen months, made payments totaling $2,952. That would reduce his debt to $2,948.

Charlie then figures that since he's halfway through the loan, he should pay half the interest he originally committed to, or $450. Subtracting the $450 from the $2,948, Charlie calculates that he owes the bank $2,498 to wipe the loan off the books. But the bank figures differently. They figure that Charlie is entitled to get back only 25.7 percent of the original $900, or $231. In other words, of the $900 Charlie was originally committed to pay, the bank is charging him 74.3 percent of that amount, or $669. In effect, then, $231 of his original interest commitment would be "rebated" to him. This would make his payoff figure $2,717. Charlie is enraged to learn that he owes the bank $219 more than he had expected to. What happened to that $219? The Rule of 78s happened.

The Rule of 78s

It was noted earlier that in the typical installment loan borrowers have the use of the full original amount borrowed only during the first month of the loan. Then, as borrowers make periodic payments, they have the use of progressively less and less of the original amount of the loan. That's the basis for the so-called Rule of 78s, which is used to determine how each month's payment is broken down into interest and principal.

In an installment loan, the borrower commits himself to pay a certain amount of interest over the term of the loan. If he pays off the full balance of the loan before the full term elapses, the borrower is entitled to get back a portion of his interest cost, plus a portion of any other rebatable charges such as insurance. But the borrower does not get back an amount directly proportional to the amount of time the loan has run. As in Charlie's case, if you pay off a thirty-six-month loan at the end of eighteen months, your interest rebate does not equal one-half of the original amount of interest, even though half of the loan has elapsed.

Here's an example of the Rule of 78s in action.

Exercise 12.3

On a twelve-month loan, a borrower has the use of all the money during the first month. She then makes her first payment. During the second month, she has the use of only 11/12 of the money. For the third month, it becomes 10/12. And so on until the last month, when she has the use of only 1/12 of the money.

Because the borrower has the use of more money in the earlier months, she has to pay proportionately more for it. Actually, the borrower has the use of twelve times more money in the first month than in the last month.

In the Rule of 78s, the sum of the number of months in a twelve-month loan equals 78 (1 + 2 + 3 + 4 . . . to 12 = 78). During the first month of a twelve-month loan, you're charged with 12/78 of the total interest. During the second month, you're charged with an additional 11/78 of the total interest. During the third month, you're charged with an additional 10/78 of the total interest. The last month, you'd be charged with 1/78. The total of the twelve fractions is 78/78, or 100 percent of the total interest.

If, therefore, you paid off the loan at the end of six months, you'd be charged for 57/78 of the total interest owed (12 + 11 + 10 + 9 + 8 + 7 = 57). Your rebate would be the remaining 21/78, or about 27 percent of the original interest charged to you. If the original interest has been $60, you'd thus be rebated about $16.

For loans of other than twelve months' duration, the key number becomes the sum total of the number of months.

For example, in a 24-month loan, the sum of the numbers 1 through 24 equals 300. During the first month of such a loan, you'd be charged for 24/300 of the total interest. During the second month, you'd be charged for 23/300 of the total of the interest. And so it would go throughout the term of the loan. Table 12–2 converts all these fractions into percentages to enable

TABLE 12–2 Rebate Schedule from the Rule of 78s (Showing Percentage of Finance Charge to Be Rebated). This Schedule Applies to All Interest Rates.

Number of Months Loan Has Run	Original Term of Loan (Months)				
	12	18	24	30	36
1	84.6	89.5	92.0	93.5	94.6
2	70.5	79.5	84.3	87.3	89.3
3	57.7	70.2	77.0	81.3	84.2
4	46.1	61.4	70.0	75.5	79.3
5	35.9	53.2	63.3	69.9	74.5
6	26.9	45.6	57.0	64.5	69.8
7	19.2	38.6	51.0	59.3	65.3
8	12.8	32.2	45.3	54.4	61.0
9	7.7	26.3	40.0	49.7	56.8
10	3.8	21.0	35.0	45.2	52.7
11	1.3	16.4	30.3	40.9	48.8
12	-0-	12.3	26.0	36.8	45.0
13		8.8	22.0	32.9	41.4
14		5.8	18.3	29.2	38.0
15		3.5	15.0	25.8	34.7
16		1.7	12.0	22.6	31.5
17		.58	9.3	19.6	28.5
18		-0-	7.0	16.8	25.7
19			5.0	14.2	23.0
20			3.3	11.8	20.4
21			2.0	9.7	18.0
22			1.0	7.7	15.8
23			.33	6.0	13.7
24			-0-	4.5	11.7
25				3.2	9.9
26				2.1	8.3
27				1.3	6.8
28				.65	5.4
29				.22	4.2
30				-0-	3.1
31					2.2
32					1.5
33					.90
34					.45
35					.15
36					-0-

Note: To calculate rebates for longer loan periods, halve the time frames. Example: To find the amount to be rebated after 24 months have elapsed on a 48-month loan, look for the number where the column "loan has run—12 months" meets the row "Original term of loan—24 months." That number (26 percent) is approximately the same as you'd find after 24 months have elapsed on a 48-month loan.

you to calculate the rebate on loans ranging from twelve to thirty-six months at six-month intervals.

For loans set to run for other terms than those shown in the table, your banker can give you a precise rebate breakdown. A good working knowledge of installment loans and how rebates are figured can be most important in determining when, how, and why you should consolidate loans, refinance them, or pay them off. Here's how you can figure the rebates on any loans included in the table.

1. Determine the total interest you have been charged for the loan.
2. Decide at what point you want to figure the rebate—say, after nine months of a twenty-four-month loan. Locate the factor on the rebate chart where the column "loan has run—9 months" meets the row "original term of loan—24 months." That factor is 40 percent, which is the percentage of your interest charge that you will get back or that will be credited to you if you pay off the loan after nine months.
3. Multiply your original interest cost by the rebate percentage to get the actual dollars to be rebated.
4. From your original total debt, subtract the amount of payments made so far. Then subtract the dollar amount of your rebate. The final total is your payoff figure.

Figuring Payoff

Here's an example using this formula. You had originally borrowed $2,000, repayable in thirty months. The interest cost was $250, making your total debt $2,250. Monthly payments are $75. You want to pay off the balance due after nine months. What will your rebate and your payoff amount be? (*Note:* The rebate schedule is the same for all interest rates.)

1. The percent of your total original interest that will be rebated to you is 49.7 percent. That's where the 30-month column (original term of loan) meets the 9-month row (number of months loan has run).
2. Your rebate is $124.95 (49.7 percent of $250).
3. Your payoff figure is $1,450.75. From the original total debt of $2,250, you subtract $675, representing the nine payments you made at $75 each. From that sum you further subtract the $124.25 that is your rebate. In other words, your payoff figure is your *original debt* less *payments made to date* less *rebate due you*.

Other rebatable charges, such as insurance premiums, are figured on the same basis. Thus, if you had a life insurance premium charge on the loan of $30, you would receive a rebate of that charge of $14.91 (49.7 percent of $30).

Does it make sense to pay off an installment loan early? In the preceding example, the borrower presumably found himself with a windfall of $1,450. Even though his loan was only 30 percent paid off (9 months out of 30), more than half the total interest he was committed to pay had been used up. If he uses the $1,450 to pay off the loan, he'll save about $125, representing the remaining interest he's obliged to pay. If, instead, he invests that $1,450 at a 5 percent annual percentage yield (APY), it will earn roughly $150 over the next two years.

Refinancing an Installment Loan

Having the money to pay off an installment loan is a pleasant dilemma rarely faced. Much more frequent is the desire to refinance the loan to reduce the monthly payments. The Rule of 78s applies in this situation just as it would in an early payoff. Following the preceding example, an individual may wish to refinance the original $2,000 loan after nine of the thirty months have elapsed. As the formula indicates, he will have a balance owing of $1,450. Assume that he wishes to refinance that balance for a new thirty-six-month term at an 11.08 APR (6 percent add-on). He would have to obligate himself for an additional $261 in interest for that new loan. The $261 added to the $1,450 remaining payoff figure would give a new debt of $1,711 and monthly payments (interest and principal) of $47.53. He thus reduces his monthly payments by almost $30, but in so doing, incurs added interest expense and an ongoing debt for fifteen additional months. Refinancing a debt in such a manner should be done only after counseling with a loan officer. To extend the debt could create a bottleneck years down the road when other credit needs arise.

Increasing an Installment Loan

As with refinancing, individuals frequently want to borrow more money on their credit line. For example, in the preceding situation, assume that the borrower wants another $1,000. He does not wish to take out a separate new loan but wants to add the $1,000 to his existing installment loan to run for a period of thirty-six months. His payoff balance on the original loan is $1,450. To that the lender adds the $1,000 new money, plus interest. Assuming an 11.08 APR (6 percent add-on), the additional interest would be $441. This gives him a total debt of $2,891 with monthly payments of $80.30. For roughly $5 more than he is now paying each month, he has another $1,000 cash in hand. But, as with refinancing, he has stretched his payment schedule out fifteen months longer than the earlier payment period. As with refinancing, adding on to debt in this manner should be done only after counseling with a loan officer.

SHOPPING FOR LOANS

Interest Rates

A slight difference in the interest rate on an installment loan can have a considerable impact on the overall cost for the term of the loan. Table 12–3 illustrates the effect of varying interest rates on a sampling of different loans.

The Effect of Down Payment Size

To the extent that you borrow to buy anything, the cost of borrowing can add as much as 10 to 30 percent to the cost of the item. The less you borrow, the less interest you'll be paying, and the lower your monthly payment.

The question may arise as to whether you are better off financing the whole amount of a purchase and putting the available down payment dollars into savings where it can earn interest. Generally, when you're starting from scratch with an installment loan, before the Rule of 78s

TABLE 12–3   Comparing Interest Rates

APR (Percentage)	Add-on (Percentage)	Total Interest	Total to Be Repaid	Monthly Payments
On a Loan of $1,000 for 12 Months				
10.00	5.5	$ 55	$1,055	$ 87.92
10.90	6	60	1,060	88.33
11.79	6.5	65	1,065	88.75
12.68	7	70	1,070	89.33
On a Loan of $2,000 for 24 Months				
10.23	5.5	$220	$2,220	$ 92.50
11.13	6	240	2,240	93.33
12.12	6.5	260	2,260	94.16
12.91	7	280	2,280	95.00
On a Loan of $3,000 for 36 Months				
10.20	5.5	$495	$3,495	$ 97.08
11.08	6	540	3,540	98.33
11.96	6.5	585	3,585	99.58
12.83	7	630	3,630	100.83

comes into play, you probably wouldn't do as well going for the larger financing. Because a savings account pays less than what you must pay a lender for a loan, you'd probably be better off applying your available cash toward the purchase price and reducing the amount of the loan accordingly.

Table 12–4 illustrates the dollar effect of varying down payments on a specific loan.

How Long Should Your Loan Run?

The amount of time, or term, of an installment loan can affect overall costs considerably. The longer the term, the lower the monthly payments and the higher the interest costs. Do the lower payments make up for the higher interest costs? Table 12–5 illustrates the effect of different terms on loans of varying sizes.

Other basic guidelines are helpful in determining how long an installment loan should run. Generally speaking, the life of the loan should not exceed the expected life use of the product or service you're borrowing for. Also, when you borrow for a recurring need, the loan should be paid off before the need occurs again. Examples of recurring loans include those for taxes, vacations, and cars.

For example, say you borrow $600 on June 1 for a summer vacation. With a twelve-month loan, you'll be all paid up by the next summer. But with an eighteen-month loan, you'll be paying for this year's vacation until the end of next year. If you were to borrow again in June of next year for that year's vacation, you'd have a few hundred dollars of this year's loan still unpaid if you had taken the longer plan. If you then combined the remaining old bal-

TABLE 12–4   Effect of Down Payment on Loan Costs on a $3,000 Purchase, at 11.08 Percent APR (6 Percent Add-on), for a 36-Month Loan

Down Payment	Amount of Loan	Total Interest Cost	Total to Be Repaid	Monthly Payment
$ 0	$3,000	$540	$3,540	$98.33
300	2,700	484	3,184	88.44
500	2,500	450	2,950	81.94
800	2,200	396	2,596	72.11
1,000	2,000	360	2,360	65.55
1,200	1,800	326	2,126	59.05
1,500	1,500	270	1,770	49.16

TABLE 12–5   **The Effect of Different Terms on Loan Costs**

Amount Borrowed	Term of Loan (Months)	Total Interest Cost	Total to Be Repaid	Monthly Payment
$1,000	12	$ 60	$1,060	$ 88.33
1,000	18	90	1,090	60.55
1,000	24	120	1,120	46.67
1,000	30	150	1,150	38.33
1,000	36	180	1,180	32.77
2,000	12	240	2,240	93.33
2,000	18	300	2,300	76.67
2,000	24	360	2,360	65.55
2,000	30	420	2,420	57.62
2,000	36	480	2,480	51.67
3,000	12	360	3,360	140.00
3,000	18	540	3,540	98.33
3,000	24	630	3,630	86.42
3,000	30	720	3,720	77.50
3,000	36	900	3,900	65.00

ance and the new loan for yet another eighteen-month loan, you could still be paying for part of the year's vacation three years from now. This is an example of *pyramiding,* and it can be a dangerous practice.

Car loans should be geared to the time you expect to retain the car. If you trade every two years, for example, your loan should be paid off within that period. Running the loan longer than the life of the car makes the borrower prone to the risk of pyramiding.

Major household items, such as large appliances, might not need replacing for a decade or more. But they should not be financed for as long as they will last. These debts should be eliminated as quickly as your budget will allow in order to make room for other borrowing needs and to keep your interest expenses down. Most lenders won't exceed a few years for such loans anyway, but avoid the temptation of becoming involved in longer plans that might allow for lower monthly payments. The interest cost will be that much higher, and you could still be paying off a loan when you'd rather have that credit capacity available for some other purpose.

One-shot loans, such as those for special events (weddings, etc.), special trips, and other nonrecurring personal needs should also be paid up as quickly as your budget will allow. The needs won't recur, but taking such a loan for too long a term can clutter up your future borrowing capacity and have you paying more interest than is wise.

Home improvements, particularly major additions such as patios, pool, and extra rooms, can get a bit tricky. These items can easily run into many thousands of dollars, and common installment financing plans run to five years, occasionally longer. For the most part, these improvements become a part of the house—you won't take them with you when you move. You may recapture all or most of the cost when you sell the house.

When these improvements are integral to the house, you might find it better to add the cost on to your mortgage if you can. Check with your mortgage lender to evaluate cost and feasibility. For example, a $4,000 home-improvement loan for five years could entail monthly payments of roughly $83. If you added that same amount to a mortgage that had twenty years left to run, the monthly payments would be about $35. If you expect to be selling the house within ten years or less, it could be better to add the home-improvement costs to your mortgage.

Home Equity Borrowing

Exercise 12.4

With home equity financing, you give the lender a mortgage on your home as security for the loan. The attraction of this type of financing is that the interest on a loan secured by a mortgage can be tax-deductible, whereas interest on other types of consumer debt is not deductible. (Check the most recent tax regulations for current conditions.)

Offsetting the advantage of tax deductions for the interest are the costs of acquiring home equity financing. Since a mortgage is involved, you should expect to pay for an appraisal, for title insurance, for recording fees, for document preparation, for points, and other related costs. (See chapter 7 for more details.) You should determine what these costs will be before you apply for the loan and compare them with the benefits of the tax deduction. You might find it cheaper in some cases to borrow directly rather than via the home equity route. Needless to say, if you don't own a home you can't use home equity financing.

There are two basic types of home equity financing: the home equity *loan,* and the home equity *line of credit.* With the loan, you apply to the lender for a specific amount, and if your application is approved you get that lump sum of money and repay it in accordance with a set formula. With the line of credit, you apply for the right to borrow up to a certain sum of money. As you need that money you take it from the lender, and you only pay interest on whatever amount you owe at any given time. Home equity financing might be available with either fixed or adjustable rates of interests. Costs will differ from lender to lender and from time to time.

DOS AND DON'TS WHEN YOU APPLY FOR A LOAN

The following list of dos and don'ts can help you communicate more effectively with your lender and help get your loan application processed more efficiently.

- **Do** all your shopping and homework beforehand. Whenever possible, know exactly what you're going to borrow for, how the money will be used, and what the total needs will be.

- **Do** make sure all your other credit accounts are up to date before you apply for credit. If necessary, check with each creditor and with your local credit bureau. A credit history showing late accounts may not kill your chances of getting a loan, but it can certainly cause delays and aggravation.

Exercise 12.5

- **Do** get an idea of the rates charged by various lenders. This can be done quickly, discreetly, and, if you wish, anonymously. Be certain that any quotes you receive are expressed in terms of APR (annual percentage rate), and determine what the total dollar charges are for interest and any other fees the lender may impose.

   You might be able to obtain a more attractive interest rate if you make a larger down payment or if you are a customer of the institution in other departments. Service and convenience must also be considered.

- **Do** prepare a list of all your other debts, including the name of each creditor, purpose of the loan, original amount borrowed, current amount owed, and monthly payment. This will make the loan officer's job much easier and your application simpler to process. Divulge all pertinent credit information, even if you think it might not look good. The lender will probably discover it anyway, and, if you haven't mentioned difficult accounts, the lender will wonder why.

- **Do** inquire in advance whether the lender has any specific requirements or taboos. Some lenders have strict requirements regarding a borrower's years on the job and period of residence in the community as well as the minimum down payment for specific purchases.

- **Do** be sure to tell the loan officer clearly and specifically just what the money is for. The more concise you are, the more the officer will be able to advise you if you appear to be going overboard on a certain debt.

- **Do** make sure that your requested time for loan repayment does not exceed the use period of whatever you're borrowing for. If you let the lender know you've considered this, it will demonstrate your prudence and could enhance your relationship with the lender.

- **Do** be prepared to discuss your budget in detail. The loan officer wants assurance that money will be available to pay off the loan, and if there is no room in your current budget for the repayment, your request may be declined—and perhaps wisely so. If you plan to trim other expenses to make room for this debt, or if you are anticipating a higher income in the future, discuss these factors with the loan officer.

- **Do** bring your spouse, if you have one. Granted, under the federal Equal Credit Opportunity Law it is no longer necessary for both spouses to sign credit agreements, but debt is still a family responsibility morally, if not legally—and both partners should have a full understanding of their involvements in each other's financial matters.

- **Do** seek the loan officer's specific advice on related financial matters. It's part of the job, and the officer may be able to discover and solve other money problems in ways you aren't aware of.

- **Don't** try to get a better interest rate by telling a loan officer that you can do better elsewhere. Chances are you'll be told to go ahead and do so. And if you can do better elsewhere, you might as well.

- **Don't** caution the loan officer not to check a certain credit reference. If there is a problem or a dispute with one of your creditors, clear it up in advance. If you raise suspicions, the loan officer will undoubtedly take steps to find out what it's all about.

- **Don't** be disturbed if the loan officer asks you to do your other banking business, such as your savings or checking account, with that institution. This is part of the job. Often, loan applicants are upset by such suggestions, and this can destroy an otherwise good relationship. A simple "I'll be happy to consider it" should suffice if you don't want to change at the moment.

- **Don't** fret if the loan officer starts "selling" life or health insurance for your loan. If, after you understand their program, you still don't want it, merely decline politely.

- **Don't** expect the loan officer to tell you whether your intentions regarding your borrowing are wise. If you aren't sure of the wisdom of your loan, maybe you shouldn't be asking for it.

- **Don't** be surprised, however, if the loan officer does question your wisdom. Loan officers are in the business of evaluating personal financial decisions, and their professional knowledge may help correct or amplify your thinking, or point out something you overlooked. Perhaps the officer can suggest alternatives, some of which may provide a better solution than the one you're seeking.

- **Don't** wait until the last minute to apply for a loan. Anticipate your needs far enough in advance to take care of all the details. If other matters hinge on whether you get the loan, keep the other parties informed of your progress. Careful and thoughtful planning in this regard can prevent serious problems.

- **Don't** demand an answer to your application within a certain time. You have a right to have your papers processed promptly, assuming that everything is in order. The lender will make every effort to do so. But delays, such as receiving an incomplete report from a credit bureau, can happen.

    Often, too, applications have to be considered by the loan committee. Loan officers aren't "passing the buck" when they refer applications to the loan committee. Requests might be for more than the loan officers have authority to approve, or they might just want to get other opinions on a puzzling point in the application. The committee can often be helpful simply by giving borrowers the benefit of all its best collective thinking.

    When you make your application, the officer should be able to give you a fairly good idea of how long it will take to process. Perhaps the officer can speed it up a bit for you if circumstances warrant. But a dead line or an "or else" will probably cause antagonism.

Exercise 12.6

- **Don't** balk if the loan officer asks you for a cosigner or collateral to support a given loan request. The officer is trying to help you get your loan, but lending policies require security. You might not want to comply, but rather than argue about it (which won't help matters), ask for an explanation.

    There is often room for compromise. A request for collateral or a cosigner doesn't necessarily mean your credit isn't good. There just might not be enough of it—because of your age, job tenure, and so on. Remember that the loan officer doesn't have to ask you for the extra security—she can turn you down flat. It doesn't hurt to inquire if the request for collateral or a cosigner can be altered so that the cosigner is obliged for only a part of the loan or the loan is only partly collateralized.

CREDIT ABUSES

Pyramiding

As noted earlier, pyramiding occurs when a loan for a recurring purpose has not been paid off by the time the purpose recurs. Let's look at a specific example.

Otto buys a new car and finances $10,000 for three years at an interest rate of 6 percent add-on (11.08 percent APR). His interest cost for the three years will be $1,800, which, added to the amount financed, gives him a total obligation of $11,800. This will require monthly payments of $328 (rounded off).

Two of the three years go by, and Otto falls in love with a brand-new car. He must have it. His credit is good—he has paid his $328 per month on

time without fail, and he has no qualms about financing $12,000 over and above his trade-in for the new purchase. But if he looked carefully at the arithmetic, he might develop some serious qualms.

Here's how it looks. After paying $328 a month for twenty-four months, he has paid in a total of $7,872, leaving $3,928 still owing on the original loan. If he refinances now, he'll be entitled to a rebate of some of the interest from the original loan—$210. (See Table 12–2: after 24 months of a 36-month loan, you get a rebate of 11.7 percent of the original interest charge; 11.7 percent of $1,800 is $210.60.) So Otto's payoff on the first loan is $3,718.

That amount is added to the new financing: $3,718 plus the $12,000 needed for the new car totals $15,718. Interest (same rate, same term) of $2,829 brings the total IOU to $18,547, which will mean monthly payments of $515! To satisfy his yen for the new car, Otto must increase his monthly payment by $187, and he's obliging himself to paying more than $2,800 in additional interest. He's still paying for part of the original car five and six years after he first bought it.

If he had waited to buy a new car until he had paid off the first loan—that is, the full three years—then he could finance a new $12,000 loan for about $395 per month.

As Otto's case illustrates, pyramiding can be costly, whether it originates innocently or as a result of lack of financial discipline. Otto took undue advantage of his access to credit, and exceeded both needs and capacity to borrow.

The pyramiding trap is equally dangerous, if not more so, as it affects credit cards and charge accounts. For example, Esther runs up $50 in gasoline bills for her car during a month. She charges them on a credit card. At the end of the month, the bill comes in and, rather than pay the full $50, she decides to send in only the minimum payment, say, $10.

The same thing happens the next month: $50 worth of gas bills and a $10 payment. And so on throughout the year. Unless Esther comes to her senses, she could still be paying for her January gas in December and even well into the following year.

The simple way to avoid pyramiding is to remember that an installment loan or an open-end credit debt should be paid off before the need to borrow for the same purpose occurs again.

Ballooning

Which is more appealing, a twelve-month loan for $1,000 with monthly payments of $88.33, or the same loan with monthly payments of only $60? The temptation is to take the loan with the smaller monthly payments, but obviously there's a catch—with the smaller monthly payments, there will be one very large payment at the end of the loan, for the loan is to run for only twelve months. In this particular case, after making payments for eleven months at $60 each, the borrower will still owe roughly $400 in the twelfth month. This is what's known as a balloon payment, and it can be dangerous. If the borrower can't make the large payment, it may be necessary to refinance and incur additional interest costs. Although the Truth in Lending Law requires lenders to disclose the annual percentage rate and the total costs involved in making the loan, there may not be adequate disclosure regarding the size of the monthly payments. Any borrower should know whether there are balloon payments at the end of the loan. Unless there are compelling circumstances for a balloon payment program, prudence dictates sticking to the repayment plan with equal monthly payments.

Oversecuring

If you were borrowing $1,000 to pay for your summer vacation, it would not seem wise to have to put up your car, your house, your bank account, and all your other assets as security for that loan. Reputable lenders would certainly not require such collateral. But some lenders may seek more security than is reasonable for certain loans. This security may include a general assignment of your wages and your personal property. If a borrower pledges those assets to obtain a loan, the lender can take action to recover them should the loan become delinquent. The borrower should determine exactly what collateral is being given to the lender, and if more is being required than seems necessary, the borrower would do well to shop around at other lending institutions.

Loan Sharks

Despite all the consumer-protection laws and publicized warnings, there will be loan sharks as long as there are people willing to pay exorbitant fees for borrowed funds. Loan sharks operate outside the limits of the law. Their interest rates are far above what the state usury laws allow, and their collection techniques can be brutal. If anyone becomes involved with a loan shark, he or she can expect to bear extremely severe consequences. Consult a banker or an attorney to seek out better ways to alleviate your debt problems.

Loan Consolidation

The appeal is almost irresistible: "Why suffer with all those big monthly payments when you can consolidate all your debts into one loan with a much smaller monthly payment?"

Exercise 12.7

If you have accumulated too much debt, loan consolidation seems a logical and convenient way out of the crisis. It's a line of least resistance too often taken by borrowers not aware of the potential pitfalls. Poorly planned, a consolidation loan can cause more troubles than the original loans did. Sound planning may provide more suitable alternatives. Using the following example of a loan consolidation and consulting the interest finders and rebate formulas in this chapter you can plan any consolidation and judge its value.

Charlie and Charlotte have the following loans:

- A car loan, whose original total amount was $3,540, including interest of $540. The loan has run for twenty-four months and has twelve months to go. Monthly payments are $98.33.
- A home-improvement loan that originally totaled $2,480, of which interest was $480. The loan has already run for thirty months and has eighteen months to run. The monthly payments are $51.67.
- A personal loan, originally totaling $1,090, of which interest was $90. Twelve months of the loan have already expired, with six months still to run. Monthly payments are $60.55.

Table 12–6 illustrates Charlie and Charlotte's debts and how much they would need to pay them all off.

Charlie and Charlotte need roughly $2,330 to pay off their existing debts. At an interest rate of 11.08 APR (6 percent add-on), they can obtain a loan of that amount for three years, which would entail an added $419 in interest, giving them a total new debt of $2,749. Their thirty-six monthly payments would be $76.30 each, compared with the $210.55 they're now paying.

It seems like an easy way out of what has become for them a serious jam.

TABLE 12–6   **Loan Consolidation: Charlie and Charlotte's Debts**

Loan	Current Balance	Monthly Payment	Months to Run	Payoff Figure Now
Car	$1,180	$ 98.33	$12	$1,117
Home Improvement	930	51.67	18	860
Personal	363	60.55	6	352
Total		$210.55		$2,330

But is it wise? Is it worth it? If they wait just six more months, the personal loan will be all paid off, reducing their monthly payments to $150. In twelve months, the car loan will be paid off, reducing their payments to $51.67. And in eighteen months, the home-improvement loan will be paid, eliminating their monthly payments altogether.

The consolidation loan will have cost them an additional $419 in interest and will require payments of $76.36 for thirty-six more months. During the next three years, Charlie and Charlotte will, in all likelihood, have new reasons to borrow. Rather than consolidating their loans, they might be better off if they simply tighten their belts and continue with their current debt load. It will be lightened considerably in just six months.

Careful communication with a lending officer is necessary to arrive at a sensible consolidation plan. If proper loan planning is done in the beginning, the need for a consolidation loan will never occur.

CURES FOR OVERINDEBTEDNESS

Charlie and Charlotte could be candidates for a severe case of overindebtedness. This problem, if not promptly treated, can seriously damage their credit history and can impair their ability to obtain credit for many months or possibly years. Eventually, it might force them to obtain credit through sources that specialize in higher-risk situations and that charge higher interest rates accordingly.

The first symptom of overindebtedness is late payments. Not only do late payments entail late charges, which can be as much as 5 percent of the amount of the payment (the law varies from state to state), but they can also result in a bad credit rating.

Borrowers who *anticipate* that they might be running into a delinquency problem should act *before* the actual delinquency occurs. Borrowers in such straits should visit *in person,* not by phone or by mail, with the creditors in question and explain the overall circumstances. It might be possible to arrange a different payment date that would be more convenient, or remake the loan on favorable terms, or get a temporary reduction in payments. It might even be possible to have late charges waived if your reason for delinquency is acceptable to the creditor.

It's up to the borrower to keep the lender informed of the circumstances. If the lender doesn't know what the borrower's problems are, he could rightfully assume that the borrower is being willfully delinquent.

If the borrower is in default, the lender can commence whatever legal remedies have been reserved in the loan agreement. If collateral has been pledged for the loan, the lender can take steps to recover the collateral and sell it to pay off the loan. If a cosigner is involved in the loan, the lender can look to the cosigner for payment. In some instances, the lender may be able to attach, or garnishee, the borrower's wages.

Debt-counseling Services

Exercise 12.8

In many communities, lending institutions cooperate to create a debt-counseling service to assist people in financial trouble. In many communities, this is known as the Consumer Credit Counseling Agency. See your banker for more details on such services available in your community. The agency usually contacts your creditors and gets them to hold off on their collection procedures while you make an effort to reorganize your financial matters. You'll have to show good faith by making some regular periodic payments. If the counselors have been successful, those payments will be smaller than what your normal payments would have been.

If a reputable debt-counseling service is not available to you or not capable of helping you, the next step might be to consult an attorney, who can arrange for an Assignment for the Benefit of Creditors. This is similar to the services offered by debt counselors in that it tries to convince creditors to accept a smaller monthly payment until the full debt is paid off.

Bankruptcy

Exercise 12.9

The ultimate way out of overindebtedness is bankruptcy. If you reach this point, you should seek the aid of an attorney. Bankruptcy is a last resort for solving debt problems; it can remain on your credit history for as long as ten years.

Many lenders attempt to rehabilitate a bankrupt family or individual, particularly if the reasons for bankruptcy were beyond their control. But an ex-bankrupt can still find it difficult to obtain the kind of credit needed for his or her lifestyle. Indeed, bankruptcy often reduces the quality of people's lives dramatically for an extended period of time.

Bankruptcy laws are federal laws, though state laws may apply in determining the property that can be exempted from bankruptcy proceedings.

Credit Repair Clinics Can Be Costly Mistakes

You're up to your neck in debt, and the walls seem to be caving in. How can you get out of this jam? You see an ad that promises to help you get rid of your debts and restore your credit to A-1 condition. All these advertisers want is an up-front fee of $300, or $500, or however much they can get from you. They tell you to send them the amount of your monthly payments, and they'll parcel it out to your creditors, putting you back on a good footing with them all. You go along with them and within a month, your creditors are hounding you again. Didn't the credit repair clinic pay your creditors the money you gave them? You call them. The operator tells you that that number is no longer in service. Is your money gone for good? Probably. This is how some of these outfits operate. Be on guard for other, more subtle ways they can separate you from your money. You're most susceptible when you're having credit panic attacks.

There are two basic bankruptcy proceedings for individuals: Chapter 13, otherwise known as the wage-earner plan, and Chapter 7, often referred to as straight bankruptcy.

Chapter 13

Under Chapter 13, the debtor, under the supervision of a referee and the federal bankruptcy court, works out a plan for the repayment of outstanding debts. In effect, this wage-earner plan keeps creditors from getting at your wages and your property while giving you time to work out a timely payment of outstanding debts. (A similar plan for businesses is known as Chapter 11, in which owners of businesses attempt to reorganize their affairs to satisfy their debts while their creditors are kept at bay.)

A Chapter 13 proceeding generally carries less stigma than a Chapter 7 proceeding.

Chapter 7

In a Chapter 7 proceeding, your debts are discharged, or eliminated altogether. Under a Chapter 7 declaration, certain of the debtor's property can be exempted from creditors' claims. A debtor can choose whether to take the exemption allowed under federal law or exemptions that may be allowed under state laws. The Chapter 7 bankruptcy can be filed only once every six years. (A debtor can file a new Chapter 13 proceeding once he has completed payments based on a prior Chapter 13 proceeding.)

Sometimes personal catastrophe requires an individual to undergo bankruptcy proceedings. Sometimes, however, it is nothing more than the undisciplined use of credit that leaves an individual with little choice but to declare bankruptcy. The public at large has little sympathy for individuals who spend their way into bankruptcy. Know before you proceed that the specter of bankruptcy will haunt you for years to come.

DISCIPLINE

Making wise use of your ability to borrow can enhance your life. Imprudence can result in financial and emotional disaster. The lure of easy money—through charge accounts, credit cards, and other "cash-in-a-flash" enticements—can become addictive. Younger people, less experienced in the complexities of handling a budget, can easily be trapped in the credit bind. It's at the earliest stages of using credit that a firm sense of discipline must be self-imposed. Only you can determine the debt you're comfortably able to carry, considering your other financial needs and desires. But there is one unshakable rule that will apply to your use of credit: For every dollar you borrow (or charge) you will be adding ten to thirty cents a year to the cost of your credit purchase. It can be difficult enough to make ends meet without adding such a heavy burden.

PERSONAL ACTION WORKSHEET ───────────────

Comparing Loan Costs

It *can* pay to shop around for the best interest rate available on loans—such as car loans, home-improvement loans, and any other personal or business borrowing needs. Loan sources include not only banks and savings associations but also credit unions, dealers, and some insurance companies. Employers, relatives, and friends might also be sources. Answering the questions in this checklist will aid you in comparing the pertinent terms of most common personal loans.

	Lender A	Lender B	Lender C
❏ Down payment required	_____	_____	_____
❏ Collateral required	_____	_____	_____
❏ Cosigner required (If so, when can cosigner be released from obligation?)	_____	_____	_____
❏ Annual percentage rate (APR)	_____	_____	_____
❏ Monthly payments	_____	_____	_____
❏ Total interest cost for life of loan	_____	_____	_____
❏ Late charges, if any	_____	_____	_____
❏ Will a better APR be offered if you maintain other accounts with the lender? (You may have to ask, but it can be worth it.)	_____	_____	_____
❏ Cost of credit life insurance	_____	_____	_____
❏ Cost of credit health insurance	_____	_____	_____
❏ If you pay off the loan early, are rebates of interest based on the Rule of 78s?	_____	_____	_____
❏ For credit cards and charge accounts, how is the APR calculated?	_____	_____	_____

CONSUMER ALERT

Credit Traps Can Be Costly

Aside from ignoring the temptation to sign up for every credit card offering that comes in the mail, the cautious consumer should be on the alert for these abuses that can hit you with hidden costs.

The Myth of "E-Z" Credit   The ads look so appealing, particularly if you've had credit problems in the past: "EASY CREDIT . . . NO MONEY DOWN . . . PAST PROBLEMS FOR YOU ARE NO PROBLEMS FOR US . . ." The reality is that if credit is that easy to get, it can be very hard to repay: high interest costs and harsh collection procedures if you don't repay on time. One couple fell for an E-Z credit offering from a furniture store. After two years of making their payments like clockwork to the store, they thought they'd have an excellent credit reference that they could use to borrow from the bank on better terms. But they found that the store did not, and would not, divulge their good payment record to the credit bureau. The store wanted to keep this couple—and others like them—as captive borrowers.

Bumping   Get in the habit of keeping the copies of your credit card charges. If a disreputable merchant sees you throw away the copy, he'll know that he has a good chance of "bumping" the amount of your charge—increasing the charge by changing the numbers on the charge slip that goes to the bank. It's easy to bump a 3 up to an 8, or a 1 up to a 4, thus turning a $30 charge into an $80 charge, or a $15 charge into a $45 charge. If you don't check your monthly statement closely—and lots of folks don't—you might never realize you've been stung.

Giving Your Credit Card Number to Strangers   Don't do it. Ever. For any reason. That goes double for people who call you on the phone to sell you something, or to tell you that you've won a free vacation, or anything of that sort. DON'T DO IT. EVER. FOR ANY REASON.

UPS & DOWNS   *The Economics of Everyday Life*

Why Your Consumer Interest Costs Go Up and Down

Aside from the general movements of interest rates (discussed in other chapters), the cost of consumer interest can fluctuate widely because of a number of factors.

Changes in calculations   This is particularly the case with credit cards, and it can be maddeningly complex. The lender may simply change the interest rate on the unpaid balance of your account, and it may be one change for balances owing from cash advances and another for balances owing from purchases. The lender may alter the formula for determining exactly what balance will be used for calculating that interest. The lender may change the grace period during which no interest is charged, or may alter the annual fee that you pay for the card, or any combination of these two methods.

Tax considerations   You might switch your consumer debt into home equity financing—as discussed in this chapter—and thereby gain tax deductibility for the interest you pay, which in turn can cut your overall cost. But, as noted earlier, it's essential that you calculate the costs involved in obtaining home equity financing versus the benefits you derive from the tax deductibility.

Charging habits   No one has ever seen a credit card jump out of a wallet or purse, lay itself down on the stamping machine, and ring up a sale. If you blame your credit cards for the debt burden you're carrying, you're aiming in the wrong direction. Look into the mirror and say to the person there: "Change your ways pronto!" As your charging habits change, so will your credit costs. Tighten up, and watch those costs come down. Lose your sense of spending discipline, and get ready for sleepless nights. Here are some simple techniques that can help you bring your charging habits in line with good sense:

- Pay off your balance in full each month. Easier said than done, you say? No. It *is* easy, if you don't charge more than you can afford to pay. Set an affordable charing limit for yourself each month. Write it bold and put it on the door of your fridge. Each time you charge, write it down on the tally and keep a running total. When you hit your monthly limit, put your credit card *into* the fridge and leave it there until next month.

- At all costs, avoid paying just the "minimum payment required this month." The monthly statement highlights that amount, and you're easily lured into paying just that much. Note well: If that's all you pay, and you never use the card again, it might take two to four years of those minimum payments to bring your balance to zero. And you'll be paying a huge amount of interest for taking the line of least resistance.

?

WHAT IF . . . ?

Test yourself: How would you deal with these real-life possibilities?

1. You go shopping on a Friday evening for a new stereo set. You fall in love with one that you absolutely must have right away. It'll set you back $600. (a) The store offers you a finance plan that will lock you into monthly payments at a high rate of interest, but you can go home with the new set. (b) You can use your credit card—it's the same high rate of interest, but there's more flexibility on the payments. And you can take the set home with you. However, charging $600 on your card will put you right up to the card's limit. Or, (c) for the best terms, you can go to your own bank or credit union. But you can't do that until Monday, which means you can't take the set home with you. And you're not sure that the bank will approve your loan request. What choice will you make? Why?

2. You've fallen two months behind in your debt payments, and it looks like you won't be able to make most of the payments for the third month. State the pros and cons of the following actions: (a) Confessing to your creditors that you're in deep trouble and don't see a way out. (B) Answering an ad from a company that promises to erase your credit problems. (c) Talking to a bank about a consolidation loan or any other solution it can offer. (d) Visiting a bankruptcy lawyer. (e) Asking someone close to you to lend you the money to bail you out.

NUMBER CRUNCHERS

Do the calculations to make decisions in these real-life possibilities.

1. Using the tables in this chapter, calculate the monthly payment on a $9,000 car purchase: (a) Down payment (or trade-in value of your old car): 15 percent; interest rate: 10.2 APR; term of loan: 36 months. (b) Down payment: 20 percent; interest rate: 12.91 APR; term of loan: 24 months.

2. Two years ago you borrowed $4,000 on a 36-month installment loan. The interest on the loan was $720, making your total IOU $4,720. Monthly payments, rounded off, have been $131. Now, after 24 months of making payments, you have come into a windfall of $2,000. You're thinking of using the money to pay off the balance due on your loan. Using the Rule of 78s, what will be your payoff figure? Instead of paying off the loan, what if you invested the $2,000 for one year at a 5 percent return? Which is the better option? By how many dollars?

3. What were the finance charges on your most recent credit card bill (or, if you don't have any, check someone else's)? What formula was used to calculate the charges? (rate of interest used and amount on which the interest was imposed)? Were the charges correct?

FOR BETTER OR FOR WORSE

Things beyond our control often impact our personal and financial well-being, for better or for worse. Some are more predictable than others. How could you be affected if the following real-life phenomena happened? Could you have seen it coming? What steps could you have taken to minimize damage or maximize advantage? The better able you are to anticipate and recognize these forces, the better equipped you are to deal with them.

1. Out of the blue you get what looks like a check in your mail, payable to you for $2,500. It's from a finance company, and the letter with it says that all you have to do is endorse the check and deposit in your bank account, and *abracadabra*, you've got a loan for $2,500.

2. You're told you'll need a co-signer for a car loan you've applied for. You ask a friend to do so, she agrees, and the bank agrees to accept her. At the last minute she changes her mind, and says she won't co-sign.

Exercise 12.10

3. You're deep in debt, and a so-called debt-counseling service offers to bail you out. You have to send them $300 to open the service with them. The next day their phone is disconnected and they've moved out of their offices.

13

Making Your Money Grow: An Overview

The expectations of life depend on diligence. The mechanic that would perfect his work must first sharpen his tools.

Confucius

If a man empties his purse into his head, no one can take it away from him. An investment in knowledge always pays the best interest.

Benjamin Franklin

The ads, the magazine covers, and the sale pitches shriek at you: "10 Hot Stocks That Will Double Before Sunset!" "5 Super Mutual Funds That Will Let You Retire at 40!" "Let *The Wall Street Psychic Newsletter* Turn Your Constant Worries into Instant and Permanent Wealth!"

What's a person to do?

A person with good common sense will ignore all of these get-rich-quick come-ons. They're after your money. That's how *they* get rich quick.

Putting your money to work wisely requires knowledge, and that takes study. It requires patience, and that takes saying no to the fast-buck lures. It requires vigilance, and that takes discipline. It requires knowing the difference between risk and safety, and that takes learning. And it requires working toward predetermined goals, as discussed in chapter 2, and that takes planning and prioritizing. If you think it's easy, you could be in trouble.

If you want a quick surge of excitement when you put your money to work, go to the casino or the track, knowing that you could walk away empty-handed. If you want to build long-term security and comfort for yourself and your family, give heed to this chapter, which will build a foundation by teaching you

- How to evaluate different types of investments
- How to measure the impact of taxes on your investments
- How to locate specific investment information and guidance

It will also give you the foundation for understanding more specific investment techniques discussed in subsequent chapters.

TODAY DOLLARS AND TOMORROW DOLLARS

An essential part of your financial program involves putting away dollars you don't need today so that they can be available to you in the future. There are many different ways you can go about accumulating Tomorrow Dollars. Some involve a high degree of risk; others involve relatively little risk. Some methods offer a comfortable measure of protection against inflation, whereas others provide little or no protection. Some ways may seem simple, others complicated; some require luck, others prudence.

The challenge is to find the right program, one that will enable you to accumulate the needed amount of Tomorrow Dollars safely, comfortably, and in such a manner as not to interfere with your ability to pursue today's needs and desires.

The importance of your future needs and desires will be a major factor in shaping which accumulation techniques you choose. In the opening of this book, we discussed the importance of establishing goals, and you were urged to set specific targets, subject to the inevitable changes that occur as we mature and as our needs and objectives change. Now let's examine the specific vehicles you can use to help reach your specific destinations.

Automatic Accumulation

In shaping our long-range accumulation program, we must remember that some Tomorrow Dollars are being created automatically as a result of other transactions we are making. For example, a homeowner makes monthly payments on a mortgage. A portion of those payments applies to interest on the debt, and a portion applies to debt reduction. Eventually, when the house is sold or refinanced, that portion of the payments that had been applied to the debt may be recaptured in cash. This recaptured money is commonly referred to as *equity*. It's a form of automatic accumulation.

Another form of automatic accumulation can occur with life insurance. Here a breadwinner is putting away Today Dollars to be used by the survivors after his or her death. In whole life insurance policies, the policy will also build values that allow the policy owner to either cash in the policy, or borrow against it, or convert the values into other forms of insurance. The insured is building these future values as an automatic part of paying the life insurance premium.

Deductions from our paycheck represent another form of accumulation of Tomorrow Dollars. Social Security taxes are automatically deducted from the paycheck of everyone covered by the system, and, in many cases, pension and profit-sharing plan contributions are also deducted. Thus, we are joining with our employers and our government to create a pool of Tomorrow Dollars.

Active Accumulation

Active accumulation of Tomorrow Dollars can take two broad forms. First, we can lend our dollars to another person or institution with the understanding that they will pay us a fixed amount of interest for the use of our money. This type of accumulating is referred to as fixed income investing; a savings account is perhaps the most familiar form of accumulating dollars within this category.

A savings account is, in effect, a loan to a financial institution, accompanied by an agreement stating that the institution will pay us "rent" for the use of our money—interest.

We may also make loans to governments and corporations. A U.S. savings bond (series EE bond) is an example of one of the many kinds of loans that we can make to the federal government. Loans made to cities and states are referred to as municipal bonds. Loans made to corporations are referred to as corporate bonds.

These forms of accumulating Tomorrow Dollars normally carry a high degree of assurance that we will get all our money back plus the agreed-on interest at the agreed-on time. We receive a contract from the debtor that promises to pay us what we are due, regardless of whether the debtor operates efficiently or profitably. If the debtor should fail, the interest and principal due us might be in jeopardy. Although there have been instances of corporations and municipalities defaulting on their debts, defaults by the federal government have never happened, nor have insured accounts in federally insured banks and savings institutions ever lost money as a result of the failure of the institution.

The other broad form of active accumulating of Tomorrow Dollars is to buy something we hope will generate income and also possibly increase in value while we own it. As owners, either in part or in whole, we have a stake in another entity—an equity.

We buy a portion of ownership in a company, hoping that the company will be profitable and that it will distribute a portion of its profits to its owners. We also hope that the value of our ownership interest will increase, allowing us to sell it at a profit in the future.

We may invest in real estate, hoping to operate that property so that it generates income and increases in value so we can reap a profit when we sell. Similarly, we may invest in our own business where, in addition to earnings and profits, we may also be able to pay ourselves a living. When we invest our money in owning a piece of another entity, there are many outside forces that can shape the destiny of our Tomorrow Dollars.

The distinctions between lending and buying are critical. When we lend, we have a binding legal contract that promises us the return of our money, plus interest. When we buy something, we are the owners, and we have to take our chances that we can get our money back at any time we wish. In addition, what our money will earn for us as owners is always questionable. Remember the distinctions when you make any plans regarding the accumulation of Tomorrow Dollars.

INVESTMENT CRITERIA

Safety: The Reward/Risk Rule

We'll now examine the main criteria you must evaluate when you embark on a program of accumulating Tomorrow Dollars. These criteria include safety (the reward/risk rule), liquidity, yield, pledge value, hedge value, and income tax implications.

STRATEGIES FOR SUCCESS

Investing Versus Speculating: All the Difference in the World

The words *investment* and *investing* are used commonly to describe putting your money to work. That's the generic sense. For purposes of this Strategy I want you to think of investing differently: as distinguished from *speculating*. Indeed, the single most valuable lesson you can learn from this course—or from a lifetime's worth of financial experience—is the critical difference between investing and speculating. It's a two-word vocabulary drill that can literally alter your life.

When you *invest*—in the sense we're using here—*you know with assurance* how many dollars you're going to have X or Y or Z years from now. You *know*. It's not a guessing game or a "hope so."

When you speculate, *you do not know, you cannot know, and no one can tell you* how many dollars you'll have X or Y or Z years from now. You might have a lot more than you'd expected. Or you might have a lot less. There is no way of knowing until that day arrives.

Investing means putting your money into *assured* plans: savings, money market instruments, and good quality bonds, and/or mutual funds that put their money into these types of securities. Speculating means the stock market, commodities, most real estate, and/or mutual funds that put their money into these types of securities.

To the extent that it is important to you to know how much money you'll have at any time, concentrate on investing. If it's not that important to you, speculate with your money. Know the difference before you write that check. Finding out later can be too late.

Exercise 13.1

The reward/risk rule is as simple and as powerful as the law of gravity: The bigger the reward you seek, the higher the risk you'll take. The more conservative individual may look at this a bit differently: The safer my money, the less return I'll have to be satisfied with. And yet a third, and perhaps more elemental viewpoint: In planning a program of savings and investments, much depends on whether you'd rather eat well or sleep well.

The various investment and speculation vehicles discussed in this chapter will be explained in greater detail in the following chapters.

Liquidity

Liquidity refers to how quickly and conveniently you can retrieve your money and at what cost.

For example, in a regular savings account, you can get all your money plus accrued interest immediately, simply by making the request in the proper fashion to the institution. With a certificate of deposit, or CD—in which you have placed your money with the institution for an agreed-on minimum amount of time—you might have to forfeit a portion of your interest and principal if you want to get your money out right away. But generally the certificate will pay you a higher rate of interest than the regular passbook savings account.

In other words, the passbook savings account is more liquid than the savings certificate, but at a price. The passbook account offers a lower rate of return in exchange for your ability to get your cash out more readily.

The need for liquidity varies from case to case. If you are confident that you won't need your money for an extended period of time, you can afford to give up liquidity in favor of higher return. On the other hand, if you think you'll need the money sooner, you should forgo the higher return for quicker access to your money. The amount of liquidity you need, or are willing to forgo, depends on the nature and timing of your own goals.

Yield

Generally, yield refers to how much money your savings or investments will earn for you. For example, if a savings account is paying 6 percent interest per year and you put $100 into the account, you will receive $6 interest for the year on that $100. Your yield may be expressed a "6 percent" or as "$6 per $100 per year." The term *yield* is often used interchangeably with *return* and *return on investment* (see chapter 11: "Truth in Savings Law").

In making any form of investment, you should determine not only what yield you can expect immediately but whether that yield will continue, for how long, and to what degree of fluctuation it might be subject.

If you put your money into long-term corporate, government, or municipal bonds, you are assured of a constant yield for the amount of time you own the bonds, assuming that the debtor continues to pay the interest promised. The actual face value of the bond may fluctuate up and down during the time you own it, and you may sell the bond for more or less than what you originally paid for it. But the actual income you receive for the term of your ownership will remain constant. If you buy a government bond for $1,000 that promises to pay 8 percent a year, you will receive $80 for each year you own the bond, regardless of whether the market value of the bond increases or decreases.

Passbook savings accounts are subject to minor fluctuations in yield over the years.

If you buy a share of ownership in a company—stock—and that company distributes a portion of its profits to its owners—dividends—your yield, or return, is expressed as the amount of dividend dollars you receive. If you pay $100 for a stock and during the first year of your ownership the company pays you $5 in dividends, your yield can be expressed as 5 percent, or $5 per $100, per year, based on your purchase price.

Many companies have long histories of dividend payments, and many also increase their dividends from time to time. Even more companies have erratic dividend payment histories, and some companies pay none at all. If a company runs into hard times, dividend payments may suddenly halt. On the other hand, if a company suddenly has a surge in business, it might start to pay dividends unexpectedly. The stock market, then, offers a broad range of yield possibilities.

In choosing among various investments you will want to compare their yields relative to the amount you are investing. Bear in mind the likelihood of a yield continuing at a particular level. For example: $1,000 invested in a long-term government bond may pay you interest of $80 per year, and there is the highest degree of certainty that that yield will continue without interruption. At the same time, $1,000 invested in a given stock may pay you $90 in dividends. That would appear to be a better yield on your $1,000, but there's no way of knowing whether that dividend will continue, or be reduced, or be eliminated, or be increased. Then you must also consider the possibilities of gain or loss.

"Total Return"

It's important to keep a clear distinction between yield and "total return." For example, you buy stock for $100 and, during the first year of ownership, it pays a dividend of $5. But, at the end of the year, you sell the stock of $120. You have realized a gain of $20 on your investment, plus a dividend of $5, for a total overall increase in your fund of $25. Would this be considered a yield of 25 percent? Technically, no. It is indeed an overall gain of 25 percent, but it comes from two different sources: the dividend yield of 5 percent and the increase in value of 20 percent. Similarly, if you sold the stock at year-end for $80, you still would have had a dividend yield of 5 percent, but you would have suffered a loss of $20, or 20 percent of your original investment.

Some forms of investment, such as mutual funds, announce their past performance in terms of "total return," which takes into account both the dividends and the gain/loss factor. This can represent an accurate picture of performance if, in fact, an investor bought and sold on the precise dates represented. But few fit that mold. Marketing strategies dictate that total return be trumpeted loudly for periods in which it would have been high; the number is muted, if not ignored, for periods when the total return would have been low, or negative.

In building toward a specific future goal, a relatively predictable yield can be far more useful than the relatively unknown total return. Prudent investors should structure their programs accordingly.

Pledge Value

From time to time, you have an unexpected need for money: to take advantage of a once-in-a-lifetime bargain, to pay pressing bills, to help out someone in need, to pay for expensive repairs. You may not have the cash on hand, and it thus becomes necessary for you to borrow the needed money. The quickest, and sometimes the cheapest, way to borrow money is to pledge your investments as collateral for such a loan. The pledge value of any investment is a measurement of what percent of the value of the investment you can borrow, how quickly you can get the money, and how much it will cost you.

Savings accounts—both passbook and certificate—have the highest level of pledge value among the common types of investments. Most depositors can usually borrow virtually all the money in their savings account at favorable rates, without any delay. This can be an excellent device for obtaining short-term funds in a hurry and may be preferable to actually invading the savings account or cashing in the certificate.

Because stocks are prone to fluctuation in value, they have a somewhat lower pledge value than savings accounts. The amount you can borrow from your banker against any given stockholdings will depend on the quality of the stock itself. You can also borrow from your broker on a margin account. In either case, of course, you have to surrender the certificate as collateral for the loan.

Good-quality real estate has a high pledge value but, because of the nature of the documentation required in borrowing against real estate, the process can be costly and time-consuming. This, in effect, detracts from real estate's otherwise good pledge value.

Hedge Value

Investors must be concerned about the ability of their investments to withstand the effects of inflation. The common expression is "hedging against inflation." This aspect of investing, then, may be called the hedge value of an investment.

This investment criterion is often discussed in terms of "the future value of money." In short: The spending power of your money erodes over the years as inflation nibbles away at it. Investment advisers might admonish you that because of this, you must invest larger amounts now than you might have thought necessary so that your *future* spending power can keep pace with your *current* spending power. Balance such precautions with the likelihood of your earning power increasing as well (thereby enabling you to create a bigger pool of future investment dollars), and that your future spending (such as in retirement) might be much more modest than it is now, thus not requiring as proportionately large a nest egg. The tightrope you have to walk is between maintaining a comfortable lifestyle now and providing adequately for your future. Too much investment for the future can crimp the present, and vice versa.

Many investors have theorized that the stock market should be a good hedge against inflation. The theory is that as prices rise, so should the profits of companies and, thus, so should the value of the stock of those companies. However, the paths of stock prices and inflation are not always parallel. Even if the stock market is a good hedge against inflation, that would be of no help to the individual investor who chooses stocks or mutual funds that do not follow the general trend of the stock market.

Savings accounts have long been accused of offering no protection against inflation because the principal amount invested doesn't grow except for periodic additions of interest to the account. There is actually some protection against inflation because interest rates paid on savings plans tend to rise in line with rising costs. By the same token, interest rates paid on savings plans may also decrease in the face of decreasing costs.

Real estate has long been considered a good hedge against inflation, but this depends on the nature of the property, the management of the property, and the trend in the community in which the property is located.

In short, no form of investment or speculation is a guaranteed hedge against inflation. But there is one very important caution to note regarding the psychology of inflation. Over the years, as inflationary trends have come and gone, thousands of small investors have let wily salespeople convince them that inflation was destroying their life savings. The salesperson offered a "better deal." But that better deal has frequently been a very risky, if not downright fraudulent, transaction in which the frightened investors have lost all or a portion of their life savings. Thus, the *fear* of inflation caused them to lose much more money than they might have lost through inflation itself.

Tax Implications

Tax regulations are constantly changing. Investors must factor in the tax implications of the various types of investments available to them. Tax implications divide investments into three broad categories:

- **Taxable investments**   Taxable investments are investments in which, except as noted later, all your income will be taxed in the year in which it is earned.
- **Tax-deferred or tax-sheltered investments**   With tax-deferred or tax-sheltered investments, the payment of taxes on income earned can be delayed until some future time.
- **Tax-exempt investments**   All, or a substantial portion of, your income from tax-exempt investments is tax-free.

Taxable Investments

Interest earned on savings plans and corporate bonds is taxable at both the federal and state levels. Interest earned on U.S. Treasury securities is taxable on your federal return but not on your state return. Dividends received on stocks are taxable on both your federal and state returns. If you receive income from mutual funds in any of the above categories, that income is generally taxed in the same way as if you held the specific investments directly.

Congress often changes its mind about how investment income is taxed. The tax rate on capital gains (derived when you sell stocks or real estate at a profit) has gone up and down like a yo-yo over recent decades. You must determine the current (and likely future) tax status of any investment before you take the plunge.

Tax-Deferred and Tax-Sheltered Investments

U.S. savings bonds are probably the best-known form of tax-deferred investment. Another example of a tax-deferred investment is the Individual Retirement Account, or IRA, which allows workers to invest money each year for their retirement. The amount they invest in the plan each year may be a form of tax deduction, thus reducing their immediate tax obligation. Furthermore, the earnings on these funds are not taxed each year. However, when the money is withdrawn, the taxes on the withdrawn money must then be paid. The presumption is that when money is withdrawn on retirement, the individual investor will be in a much lower tax bracket than at the time the contributions were made. Thus, there can be a considerable tax break. Moreover, all the money has been allowed to work without being subject to taxation, which can make a substantial difference in an overall nest egg over the long term. The Keogh plan, for self-employed individuals, is another example of a tax-deferred investment. IRA and Keogh plans, and their close cousin, the 401(k) plan, plus changes made to those plans by the 1997 Taxpayer Relief Act, will be discussed in more detail in chapter 18.

The most common form of tax-sheltered investment is real estate. Because buildings physically depreciate, tax laws allow real estate investors to deduct a *depreciation* factor from their income. This depreciation factor does not represent an actual loss in value on the building, but rather, a paper loss. Indeed, the buildings may be increasing in value even while the owners are deducting depreciation on their tax returns. The depreciation factor offsets income that the building may be earning, thus reducing the amount of taxable income the owner has to pay. When the building is sold, however, the tax payable by investors on any profit will be affected by the amount of depreciation they have deducted in earlier years. (Depreciation does not apply to one's residence.) This aspect of investing is discussed in more detail in chapter 16.

Tax-Exempt Investments

When local governments, such as cities and states, borrow money, investors do not have to pay federal income taxes on the interest they receive. These investments are known as municipal bonds, and the income the investor receives is referred to as tax-exempt.

There are some exceptions, however:

* As a result of some of the intricacies in the 1986 Tax Reform Act, some municipal bonds are now taxable. Investors should check on this before buying municipal bonds.
* If you invest in municipal bonds and sell the bonds at a profit, the profit itself is taxable, even though the interest you earned while you owned the bonds may not be.
* If you invest in municipal bonds issued by a government unit outside your state of residence, the interest earned will be subject to any state income taxes you have to pay. For example, if a California investor buys a municipal bond issued by the city of San Diego, the interest earned is exempt from both federal and California income taxes. But if that same investor buys a municipal bond issued by the city of Houston, the interest earned is exempt only from federal taxes. The investor has to pay California income taxes on that interest.
* The laws are always subject to change by Congress or by the Supreme Court.

Tax-exempt investments will be discussed in greater detail in chapter 14.

INVESTIGATION

"Investigate before you invest" is one of the essential maxims to remember when putting your money to work. An equally important statement all too frequently overlooked is "investigate before you un-invest." Do your homework before you place your funds in any kind of situation. But don't stop doing the homework after you've made the investment.

Knowing when to get out of a situation is as important as knowing when to get in. "But," many say, "I don't want to become a slave to my investments. I don't want to have to worry about it. I just want to be able to put it away and have it grow and deliver what I'm seeking without the worry or the constant checking."

All well and good—but such a course may result in a diminished nest egg compared to what it might have been. The decision is up to each individual; you don't have to become a fanatic. But investing can be likened to planting a grove of trees. For it to bear the most and the best possible fruit involves care, nurturing, and an awareness of all the steps you can take to improve your crop. In short, your ability to prosper will depend largely on your willingness to work.

Sources of Information

More literature is published every year on investments than on any other subject, with the possible exceptions of dieting and sex. It's impossible to keep up with the outpouring: hundreds of books, thousands of magazine and newspaper articles, tens of thousands of reports and analyses published by stock brokerage firms and investment advisory firms. Where is one to begin?

Books

Exercise 13.2

Books run the gamut from the "doom and gloom" variety to the "how to get rich overnight" type. The former tend to preach that the end of the world is rapidly approaching and that unorthodox investments are called for to cope with the calamity. The latter lure investors toward highly speculative types of portfolios. Between these two extremes are a number of worthwhile books published each year on basic money management and investment programs. Sample them at your local library or bookstore, and read one or two a year to give yourself some diversity of views and tactics. In general, the problem with books—including this one—is that a considerable amount of time elapses between the writing and the publication, and many of the ideas presented can be outdated before the book is in the stores.

Magazines

Exercise 13.3

Time, Newsweek, and *U.S. News & World Report,* all weeklies, contain good current information and informative columns on finance and investing. *Forbes* is published every other week and is directed to an audience of businesspeople and investors. It is most highly recommended as a source of specific information and general guidelines on a wide variety of investment techniques. *Financial World,* a weekly, contains in-depth articles on specific stock opportunities and much statistical information. *Fortune* (published every two weeks) and *Business Week* are both examples of excellent financial journalism, directed more to the businessperson than to the relatively inexperienced investor. If any of these periodicals prompt you to be interested in a specific investment situation, check with your stockbroker for more detailed information. Also worthwhile are *Money* and *Kiplinger's Personal Finance.*

Newspapers

Exercise 13.4

The Wall Street Journal, read daily and thoroughly, is the best of all possible tools to keep you alert, not only to specific investments but to the state of the economy as well. *Investor's Business Daily* is a relative newcomer, but is also an excellent source of financial data. *Barron's* is a weekly financial newspaper. The business pages of your local newspaper are a necessary supplement to these newspapers.

Seminars and Courses

Local community colleges, universities, and financial firms often conduct programs geared to the investor's needs. Such programs will normally be announced in the school catalogs and in newspaper articles or advertisements. Many seminars conducted by private firms and financial institutions are designed primarily to attract clientele or to sell specific investments to attendees.

Television

Exercise 13.5

Your television set can be the source of some very good, and some very bad, investment advice. The national Public Broadcasting System (PBS), Cable News Network (CNN) and CNBC offer a variety of worthwhile programs on money and investments. Some television channels offer stock market reports intermingled with advisories in which the host touts a particular form of investment disguised as an objective news presentation. Be certain that you understand the difference between an objective presentation and one that is designed to sell something.

STRATEGIES FOR SUCCESS

Investment Objectives Should Suit Your Age

A 25-year-old has more flexibility in investing than a 55- or 65-year-old. If younger people make mistakes, they have more time and more psychological resilience to recover than older people do. Thus, younger people can more easily afford to take risks than older people can. As investors get older, risk-taking should gradually decrease. For these reasons, you should define your investment objectives clearly in line with your age. All investment plans should start out with building a solid, risk-free foundation. During a person's twenties and thirties, a moderate amount of prudent risk can be taken to generate income and capital growth. In the forties and fifties, the objectives should tend more toward safeguarding income and preserving capital. By the time investors are in their sixties, preservation of capital, along with reliable income, should be the primary, if not exclusive, objective. That's a conservative approach. If you choose to differ, know the risks of doing so.

The third variety of investment information available on television can be more dangerous than beneficial. This is the "seminar" in which the host attempts to sell an expensive home study course, suggesting that you can learn all the secrets of successful investing in real estate, the stock market, commodities, you name it. This does not mean to say that you won't get some information for your many hundreds of dollars if you buy these courses. But if these were truly the secrets of success, then everybody who bought them would know them and they would no longer be secrets. It must be, therefore, that these pitchmen are making more money selling you the secrets than they could make by putting the secrets to use. Let the buyer beware.

The Internet

The Internet is the newest source of information on investing, but it is fraught with danger for the novice. Newspapers, books, and broadcast material have editors who screen material before it is distributed. Analysts for stock brokerage firms have their opinions scrutinized by someone in authority. But on the Internet, anyone can put out anything they want. There are no editors, no gatekeepers, no quality control systems to separate the worthwhile from the worthless. Even material from presumably credible sources can be altered by hackers, unbeknownst to you.

The overwhelming preponderance of investment material on the Internet is designed to sell you something. If someone is trying to sell you something, they can't be objective. A great deal of investment material on the Internet smacks of potential fraud, misleading sales pitches and possibly illegal touting of various securities.

In due time the Internet might have more credibility as a source of investment information. But as of now, it would be prudent to use the Internet only as a source for verifiable statistical information. There can be decent material out there on the Web. But the dangers of being waylaid by sharp operators while on your way to the good stuff offset the benefit of cyber-researching.

Information Overload

There's an obvious hazard in the world of investment information: there's just too darn much of it. There are thousands of stocks, thousands of bonds, thousands of mutual funds, and all of them fluctuate second by second. Who can keep track of more than a few dozen at a time? There aren't enough hours in a day—or in a week or a month, if you've got a life to live—to do more than barely scratch the surface of all that's out there. And every brokerage firm and mutual fund company is clamoring to get their hands on your money, proclaiming that they have the best answers. They can't all be right, can they?

So what's a poor novice to do? Here are some tips from experience: Stay away from the "let me tell you about how I made a bundle" chit-chat. Turn a blind eye and a deaf ear to the sales pitches. Don't envy the boasters. Don't go riding on a band-wagon unless you know where it's going (and you never really can.) Don't send your money out to work for you unless you know where to go looking for it in case it doesn't come back when you expected it to. Know your goals and priorities (when, how much, what's most/least important) and stick to them.

Finally, learn well the basic concepts in this course. The knowledge you gain will then lead you to the resource materials most appropriate for you.

SOURCES OF INVESTABLE FUNDS

Exercise 13.6

All sources of investable funds must be accurately evaluated. You may have little control over the inactive investment activities you're now engaged in, such as building the equity in your home, your life insurance policies, your pension or profit-sharing programs, or your Social Security. But these funds can become actively investable at some future time, and you must determine how much will be available and when. Reasonable estimates, periodically revised, will be needed to help assure that you reach your goals. Check periodically with your employer and with your local Social Security Office to determine what you can reasonably expect from those respective sources.

Discretionary Income

The major source of active investment funds is your discretionary income—the difference between what you take home in earnings and what you currently spend for your needs. "But," say the majority, "I'm just living hand to mouth as it is. By the time everything is deducted from my paycheck and I keep up with rising costs and make some modest improvements in my lifestyle, there's barely a penny left to put away."

Or, as is also said: "There's too much month left at the end of the money." True enough, and in many cases there's little you can do about it. However, a close examination of your current living style, in comparison with your *desired future* living style, is in order. Investable funds can be created by cutting down on current expenditures or by increasing current income. Simply translated, this means additional work and/or belt-tightening. Whether you wish to do either depends on how closely your *existing* investment program meets your targeted goals. The alternative, of course, is to cut down on future goals. But that, perhaps, is the most dangerous course of all.

Consider that the most critical goal for most people is to have enough income to live in the desired style when work ceases and retirement begins. If, when that time rolls around, you don't have what you had hoped to have, *you don't get to do it over.* You're locked in. Again, it's up to each individual: How much, if anything, are you willing to sacrifice in your current lifestyle in order to assure a future lifestyle? When you can answer that question, you'll be able to determine what adjustments you want to make in your current discretionary income.

Inheritances and Gifts

Other sources of investable funds can include inheritances and gifts. This is a touchy area that must be handled delicately but nevertheless must be faced. A great many people will receive inheritances from parents and other family members; the amount may be token or considerable. It may occur soon, or it may not occur for many, many years. The amount ultimately received can have an important bearing on your overall plans. If you know or can determine what can be reasonably expected in the way of an inheritance, you may want to adjust your existing investment program or your current lifestyle accordingly.

WHO CAN HELP YOU?

Financial Planners

Help is available from a number of sources in structuring a long-range investment program. Financial planners, as noted in chapter 11, can provide assistance over a wide range of financial matters. Some may even have the expertise (and licensing) to help you in other areas, such as accounting and insurance. Learn in advance their reputation and credentials.

Mutual Fund "Families"

Many investors are finding good assistance in handling their money through "families" of mutual funds. Many of the larger mutual fund companies operate a number of different specific funds, each geared toward different investment objectives. They range from the rockbound conservative to the wildly speculative and all points in between. Mutual fund companies provide ample literature explaining what each of the various specific funds can provide. The attractive feature of the fund "families" is that it's easy for investors to switch all or part of their money from one fund to another quickly and at little cost.

You, the Investor

Nobody cares more about your financial well-being than you do, and you have to be able to sort out all the jargon, analyze all the proposals, evaluate all the opportunities, and make the final decisions. *You have to take responsibility for your own future,* and that requires obtaining the necessary information to know when the advisers are right or wrong.

In the chapters that follow, we'll examine the most common types of investments available: what they are, how they work, and their respective features regarding yield, liquidity, safety, hedge value, pledge value, taxation, and investigation.

There are no specific rights or wrongs in structuring an investment portfolio. Each must be tailored to the needs, both current and future, of particular individuals or families. And each must be structured with the thought that those needs can and probably will change over the years. Thus, although the discussions are presented from a relatively conservative viewpoint, there's ample room for disagreement.

PERSONAL ACTION WORKSHEET

Planning Your Future Income

Where will the money come from to allow you to meet your future goals? This exercise will help make you more aware of the potential sources of your Tomorrow Dollars. For the sake of this exercise assume that you plan to retire in 10 years (or that there is some other defined goal that you hope to accomplish at that time). Evaluate the following possible sources of money, and see how close you come to meeting your estimated needs. If there is a shortfall, how will you make up the difference?

	Lump Sum Available	Monthly Income, If Lump Sum Is Invested at 5 and 7 Percent Annual Interest
❐ Pension proceeds	_____	_____
❐ Profit-sharing plan	_____	_____
❐ Social Security	_____	_____
❐ Equity in your home (after setting aside enough to provide satisfactory living quarters)	_____	_____
❐ Cash or loan value in your life insurance policies	_____	_____
❐ Existing investment programs (savings, bonds, etc.)	_____	_____
❐ Existing speculative programs (stocks, metals, commodities, etc.)	_____	_____
❐ Inheritances realistically expected	_____	_____
❐ Discretionary income (excess of current income over current expenses that could be put to work to create a source of Tomorrow Dollars)	_____	_____
❐ Miscellaneous: collections, works of art, and so on, that could be sold	_____	_____

CONSUMER ALERT

All the Economists in the World . . .

There's an old saying, "If you laid all of the economists in the world end-to-end, they still wouldn't reach a conclusion." Economists grouse about that. They think that their science (called *the dismal science* by some) is much maligned.

Exercise 13.7

In order to make wise decisions about putting money to work, the help of an economist would seem worthwhile. You can't afford your own private economist, but megabillion-dollar financial institutions can. Twice each year *The Wall Street Journal* does a survey of close to sixty of the nation's top economists to seek their opinions on important trends.

At the time of one such recent survey the interest rate on U.S. Treasury three-month bills was 4.15 percent; on thirty-year Treasury bonds it was 7.61 percent, the rate of inflation as measured by the Consumer Price Index (CPI) was 2.7 percent, and you could buy 98.5 Japanese yen for one U.S. dollar. The economists were asked to predict where each of these numbers would be one year in the future. Their estimates: three-month Treasury bills ranged from a low of 2.85 percent to 7 percent. The Treasury bond: low: 5.75 percent, high, 8.4 percent—22 of the economists predicted 7 percent or less; 14 predicted 8 percent or higher. For the CPI: low 2.0, high, 4.3. For Japanese yen per dollar the estimates ranged from 90 to 127.

If economists can't reach a conclusion, don't feel too bad if you are sometimes confused about all this.

UPS & DOWNS *The Economics of Everyday Life*

What Makes Interest Rates Go Up and Down?

The availability of money is to our economy—national and personal—as food is to our bodies. As the price of money (interest rates) fluctuates, so does the economy. Low interest rates encourage borrowing: we buy more cars, houses, computers, and so on, and that means more jobs for more people. That's a good thing. But as people have more money to spend, they tend to pay more for many items, and then inflation sets in. That's a bad thing.

High interest rates discourage borrowing, which can mean a slowdown in economic activity. That's a bad thing. But investors who earn interest much prefer higher levels, which gives them more money to spend, which can mean more jobs for more people. That's a good thing.

Yes, it's complex and confusing. No matter which way interest rates move, some people can benefit and some people can suffer. What, then, does cause these movements?

The Federal Reserve System The Federal Reserve, our nation's central bank, dictates moves in short-term interest rates. It does so by manipulating the *discount rate*. That's the interest rate that regular banks are charged when they borrow from the Fed, which they often do. Those higher or lower borrowing costs are passed along to the bank's customers, and the rate change thus works its way through the nation's economy.

The banking industry Banks can act on their own to move rates up or down. When they want to stimulate borrowing, they lower their rates. If borrowing demand is high, and banks sense they can make more profit they raise their rates. The *prime rate*, which is the rate banks charge their most creditworthy borrowers, is the key. As the prime rate moves up or down, all other rates soon follow, such as car loan rates, home loan rates, and the rates the banks pay on deposits.

Speculators Those who bet in the futures markets (see chapter 16) on which way interest rates are headed can cause rates to fluctuate. Speculators play in the government bond market, hoping for profits if bond prices go up. Heavy buying or selling of bonds by speculators can influence the prices of those bonds. As the bond prices move up or down, the interest rates that can be earned on those bonds move down or up. (See the discussion in chapter 14 on how bond prices and interest rates move in opposite directions.)

International events Global occurrences can influence interest rates. To keep U.S.-made goods competitively priced in other nations, the international value of the dollar must be at certain levels. Tweaking interest rates up and down can influence the value of the dollar accordingly.

No one can predict with certainty which way rates will move, or how far, or for how long. But it is an absolute certainty that interest rates will change, and knowledge is your best defense against uncertainty.

?

WHAT IF . . . ?

Test yourself: How would you deal with these real-life possibilities?

1. Your employer offers a retirement/investment plan. The money that will be credited to your account can be put to work in a number of ways: (a) a fixed income plan that will pay interest at a guaranteed level for one year, after which the rate will be adjusted in keeping with current trends; (b) a mutual fund that invests in the stock market, seeking long-term growth (see chapter 15); or (c) stock in the company you work for. All earnings on the plan will be tax-deferred until the money is withdrawn. You have no other long-term investment program at the moment. The money that goes into this account can be divided up in any combination, and the combination can be changed once each year. Based on your own current circumstances, how would you allocate the money for the coming year? Why?

2. You have $1,000 to invest, and you have no specific plans as to how you'll use the money, now or later. But for safety's sake, you want to keep it in a savings plan. You can earn two percentage points more in a three-year plan than you can in a six-month plan. Considering your own needs for liquidity, which plan would you choose? Why?

3. You've received a windfall of $10,000. Based on your own needs and desires, how would you put that money to work, considering the ultimate purpose for which you'd spend the money—hedge value, pledge value, yield, and safety?

NUMBER CRUNCHERS

Do the calculations to make decisions in these real-life possibilities.

1. Your employer offers a retirement/investment plan. You can put up to 5 percent of your annual salary into the plan each year. For every dollar of your own that you put into the plan, the employer contributes 50 cents. The amount you put in on your own each year will not be subject to income taxes in that year. And all earnings from the plan will be tax-deferred. If you went for the maximum contribution, how much could you put in this year? What would be your employer's matching amount? How would that impact on your income taxes for the year? Do the same calculations based on putting in one-half the maximum.

Exercise 13.8

2. You have $10,000 to invest, and you're debating between taxable and tax-exempt securities. Right now you can earn, say, 7 percent on a one-year taxable savings certificate, or 5 percent on a 10-year tax-exempt bond. (Assume they are equally safe.) What will be your actual earnings on each, after tax considerations, assuming the income from the savings certificate will be taxed at 15 percent? At 28 percent? What concerns, if any, do you have about the difference in term between the two?

3. What's the cheapest rate you can get on a subscription to *The Wall Street Journal*? *Money*? *Forbes*? Do they offer student discounts? How does the subscription rate compare with the newsstand price?

FOR BETTER OR FOR WORSE

Things beyond our control often impact our personal and financial well-being, for better or for worse. Some are more predictable than others. How would you be affected if the following real-life phenomena happened? Could you have seen it coming? What steps could you have taken to minimize damage or maximize advantage? The better able you are to anticipate and recognize these forces, the better equipped you are to deal with them.

1. A salesman convinces you to invest in gold, telling you that it's a perfect hedge against inflation: As prices go up, so does the value of gold. A year later, prices have gone up by 5 percent, but gold has gone down by 10 percent.

2. You subscribe to a magazine that promises to deliver money-making tips on the stock market. A few months later you are inundated by phone calls from stock brokers tempting you to buy all kinds of stocks you've never heard of.

3. You apply every penny you can against your mortgage. Objective: cut interest cost and build equity quicker. You're confident that if you ever need cash in a hurry, you can borrow it using the house as collateral. One day you need cash in a hurry. The bank tells you it will take four to six weeks and $3,400 in costs to process a second mortgage loan for you.

14

Making Your Money Grow: The Money Market

Certainly there are many things in life that money won't buy. But it's very funny. . . . Have you ever tried to buy them without money?

Ogden Nash

Not too many years ago, the average person had few safe choices for investing money. The most common methods were passbook savings accounts and government savings bonds. Today, however, the choices are many and varied. New techniques are constantly emerging. But you need *not* be perplexed by all the different offerings. You *can* distinguish clearly what each of them offers you. And you *can* choose which is best for you. That's the purpose of this chapter:

* To describe how different savings techniques work
* To help you evaluate the opportunities available to you in certificates, bonds, mutual funds, and other situations
* To acquaint you with certain tax-favored plans
* And, overall, to help you shape your own investment program, using these various devices

Chapter 13 described the two basic ways of making your money grow. One way is to lend it to others, in return for which you receive a fee known as interest. The other way is to buy something (such as stock or real estate) and hope that you can sell it later for more than you paid for it. During the time you own such an entity, you may also receive a share of the entity's profits if, in fact, it is profitable.

There is a critical distinction between the two basic techniques. With the former—lending—you have an agreement with the borrower (financial institution, corporation, government) that states that you are entitled to have all your invested money returned, either on demand or at some specified future time. The agreement also states the amount of interest you are to receive. That amount of interest either is fixed at a certain level or is subject to variation. If the interest rate is variable, there may or may not be limits as to how high or how low the rate may go. In summary, you are *assured* of getting all your money back (assuming that the borrower remains healthy) and of getting at least some interest.

When you *buy* something, you do *not* have assurances of getting all your money back or getting any return on your money during the period of ownership. If you are fortunate, your investment may increase many times in value. If you are unfortunate, your investment could wither and even disappear altogether. But there is no way of knowing for certain when you make the investment what the future will hold. This is the essence of *risk.*

A conservative investment philosophy dictates that you safeguard your future by using assured techniques. Once you have embarked on a well-disciplined plan to create such a foundation for your future security, you might then want to consider using the risk techniques. If you are fortunate, the risk techniques could later enhance your future; if you are unfortunate in your choice of risk investments, your future could suffer.

Let's now explore the various ways of lending your money so as to assure your future security. In the broad sense, the arena in which you find these opportunities is known as the money market.

WHAT IS THE MONEY MARKET?

The money market is not a place but a concept. In a general sense, when IOUs and money change hands, money market transactions have thus taken place. When you open a savings account or buy a savings bond, you have entered into a money market transaction: you have loaned your money to a bank or to the government and you have received their promise to repay you. (In a more technical sense, the money market refers to certain transactions involving short-term government and corporate bonds. See the later discussion on money market mutual funds for more detail.)

A wide selection of money market investments is available. Some plans are open-ended: there is no fixed time period, money can be deposited and taken out at will, and the rate of interest earned can fluctuate from day to day. Other plans have fixed interest rates and fixed maturities, which can range from as short as a few days to as long as thirty years and all the points in between. With these types of plans the investor might be limited in making additional deposits or withdrawals, and withdrawals prior to maturity could mean a penalty for the investor.

How Is Interest Figured?

As noted, interest is the fee a borrower pays in order to have the use of someone else's money. Interest is normally expressed as a percentage of the total amount borrowed, calculated on a yearly basis. In other words, if you make an investment of $1,000 at a 6 percent annual interest rate, you receive $60 in one year. If you were to remain with that investment for only half a year, you would receive $30 in interest. If you stayed with it for two years, you would receive $120. That's the simple part.

Aside from the rate of interest, two other aspects involved in calculating your true return can have a distinct effect on your overall investment: the compounding of interest and the crediting of interest to your account.

Compounding of Interest

The compounding of interest means that the interest you earn stays in your account and begins to earn interest itself. Following the preceding example, if you earned $60 in interest during the course of one year (on a $1,000 investment at a 6 percent annual rate) and you left that $60 in the account, you would then have $1,060 to work for you during the second year. During the second year, your $1,060 would earn $63.60. And so it would go for future years. You have an ever-increasing amount of money working for you because the interest is left in the account to compound.

In many types of accounts, interest is compounded more frequently than once a year. Quarterly compounding is very common, as is daily compounding. WIth quarterly compounding, the interest you earn during each quarter of the year is added to your original principal balance. Table 14–1 illustrates this method. During the first quarter of the year, with your $1,000 investment at 6 percent, you earn $15 (that is, one-fourth of $60). At the start of the second quarter, you have $1,015 working for you, which will earn $15.23. That $15.23 earned during the second quarter is added to the $1,015 of principal; thus, you have $1,030.23 at work for you during the third quarter. As Table 14–1 illustrates, more frequent compounding means a higher return to the investor.

Passbook savings accounts are the most common type of investment in which compounding takes place. But some investments do not offer com-

TABLE 14–1 **Comparisons of Compounding Methods—$1,000 at 6 Percent Annual Rate**

	Quarter	Quarterly Compounding	Annual Compounding
	1st	$1,000.00 earns $15.00	
First year	2nd	1,015.00 earns 15.23	
	3rd	1,030.23 earns 15.45	
	4th	1,045.68 earns 15.69	$1,000 earns $60
	Balance at work, end of first year	$1,061.37	$1,060
	1st	$1,061.37 earns $15.92	
Second year	2nd	1,077.29 earns 16.15	
	3rd	1,093.44 earns 16.40	
	4th	1,109.84 earns 16.64	$1,060 earns $63.60
	Balance at work, end of second year	$1,126.48	$1,123.60

pounding: corporate bonds, for example, will pay you interest twice a year by check directly from the company. If you don't reinvest that interest on your own, it will not be working for you.

Crediting of Interest to Your Account

Savings plans can differ with respect to the manner in which interest is actually credited to your account. Many institutions will credit you with interest from the day a deposit is made until the day the deposit is withdrawn. For example, if you made a deposit in such an institution on January 15 and withdrew the total balance on December 15, you would earn interest for the full eleven months the money was in the account. However, some institutions use different methods of crediting the interest to your account. For example, an institution might require that the money remain in your account for a full caldendar quarter in order to earn interest. Thus, if you made a deposit on January 15, you would not earn any interest until the beginning of the second quarter, April 1. Also, if you withdrew the money on December 15, you would forfeit interest for the entire fourth quarter of the year since you withdrew it before the end of the full calendar quarter. In such a case, even though your money was with the institution for a full eleven months, you would be earning interest for only six months—the second quarter and the third quarter.

Another method of crediting interest uses the low balance in any quarter as the amount on which interest is computed. For example, you start the first quarter of the year with $1,000 in your account. On January 15 you

TABLE 14–2   **How Does Your Money Grow? No. 1**

If You Invest $1,000 a Year at This Interest Rate	You'll Have This Much After This Number of Years			
	5 Years	10 Years	15 Years	20 Years
2 percent	$5,289	$11,044	$17,398	$24,414
4 percent	5,464	12,065	20,097	29,868
6 percent	5,980	13,970	24,570	38,990
8 percent	6,340	15,650	29,320	49,420
10 percent	6,710	17,530	34,960	63,000

Note: This table does not take into account income taxes on interest earned. Investments are presumed to be made at the start of each year.

Exercise 14.1

withdraw $600 to pay bills; on February 15 you put the money back into your account. During that first quarter of the year, you will be credited for interest on only $400, even though you had $1,000 in the account for the majority of the time. In a day-of-deposit to day-of-withdrawal account, the interest would be calculated on the balance in your account each given day of the quarter, and you wouldn't forfeit as much as you do in the low-balance type of calculation.

Determining the true yield on a money market investment requires more than just examining the rate of interest being paid. You must examine the frequency of compounding and crediting of interest to the account as well. The Truth in Savings Law (see chapter 11) restricts how banks may calculate and advertise such plans.

Tables 14–2 and 14–3 illustrate how your money will grow over various period of time at different rates of interest, compounded annually.

TABLE 14–3   **How Does Your Money Grow? No. 2**

If You Make a One-time Investment of $1,000 at This Interest Rate	You'll Have This Much After This Number of Years			
	5 Years	10 Years	15 Years	20 Years
2 percent	$1,104	$1,219	$1,346	$1,486
4 percent	1,217	1,482	1,803	2,193
6 percent	1,340	1,790	2,400	3,210
8 percent	1,470	2,160	3,170	4,660
10 percent	1,610	2,590	4,180	6,720

Example: To understand the power of compound interest, look at where the 20-year column crosses the 6 percent line: $1,000 will have grown to $3,210. In other words, your investment will have increased by $2,210 over 20 years, or an *average per year* of $110.50. That means, in effect, that you have had an *average* annual growth of 11.05 percent.

Note: This table does not take into account income taxes on interest earned.

TYPES OF MONEY MARKET INVESTMENTS

The variety of investment opportunities is staggering. As borrowers compete ever more aggressively for investors' dollars, new techniques and new twists on old techniques are emerging at a rapid pace. The selection of opportunities available to you today might be still broader and more varied than the selection that follows.

Passbook Savings Accounts

A passbook savings account is an open-end agreement between the customer and the financial institution. The customer can put in or take out as much money as desired at any given time. While the money is in the account, it will earn interest in accordance with the agreement between the institution and the investor. The institution may reserve the right to alter the interest rate being paid, on giving proper notice to its investors. The form of notice should be set forth in the rules of the passbook account. Some passbook accounts require a minimum balance—say, $100. If the balance falls below the minimum, the account stops earning interest *and* may be charged service fees.

Some institutions offer special types of passbook accounts that are a cross between a passbook and a time certificate. These accounts will have a fixed maturity, but the customer may be able to add or withdraw certain sums from the account periodically.

Financial institutions also offer money market accounts. These accounts generally require a fairly high minimum deposit—perhaps as much as a few thousand dollars—whereas passbook accounts have little or no minimum requirements. The money market accounts pay a higher rate of interest than passbook accounts, but they may limit the number of withdrawals you can make in a period without penalty. Federally insured institutions protect both types of accounts—as well as checking accounts—up to $100,000. Check with your institution for complete up-to-date details on how your account is insured.

- **Yield**   Passbook savings accounts have traditionally given the lowest yield of all money market instruments. To determine the true yield, it's important for the investor to be aware of the annual interest rate payable as well as the frequency of compounding and crediting of interest to the account.

- **Liquidity**   Passbook savings accounts and money market accounts are as liquid an investment as one can make short of storing the money in a cookie jar. You can withdraw your entire principal at any time. If interest is not credited daily to your account, you could sacrifice some interest if you withdrew funds prior to the end of the month or quarter.

- **Safety**   Savings accounts insured by the federal government have the highest degree of safety.
- **Hedge value**   The interest rate payable on passbook accounts and on money market accounts can rise as inflation boosts costs generally. That doesn't necessarily mean that they will rise. If an inflationary trend sets in, investors must pay careful attention to the possible earnings on their savings plans and move to those that offer the best return, all things considered.
- **Pledge value**   Savings accounts have a very high degree of pledge value. You can normally borrow up to 90 percent or more of the total amount in your account at favorable rates by presenting your passbook to a loan officer and signing simple documents.
- **Tax implications**   Interest earned on passbook accounts and money market accounts is fully taxable. Check the latest tax regulations.

Certificates of Deposit

Certificates of deposit (or CDs) are fixed contracts for a specific amount of money to run for a specific length of time and to pay a fixed interest rate. A CD may be contracted for as short a period as seven days or for as long as ten years, perhaps even longer. The interest rate payable on any CD will depend on general interest rate conditions at the time the investment is made.

Once a fixed-interest CD investment is made, the interest rate agreed to will be in effect throughout the life of the CD, even though the general rates may change subsequently. For example, on Monday, you obtain a thirty-month CD from a local bank with an interest rate set at 6 percent per annum. You are guaranteed that 6 percent rate for the life of the CD. On Tuesday, the same bank announces that it will pay 5 percent on all thirty-month CDs. That change will not affect you. It will only affect people who obtain CDs from Tuesday onward until any other change in the interest rate is made. By the same token, if on Tuesday the bank should announce an increase in the CD rate, you will not be able to take advantage of the higher rate since you committed to a firm contract on Monday at the 6 percent rate.

Exercise 14.2

Some institutions offer CDs with a variable rate of interest. This may entitle you to a higher rate of interest if rates go up during the life of your plan. If rates turn down, however, and the plan does not have a downward limit, it could mean that you will earn a lesser rate of interest than you started with.

As a general rule, the longer the life of the CD, the higher the rate of interest you'll earn. In other words, if a one-year CD was paying, say, 5 percent, a two-year CD might pay upwards of 6 percent, a three-year CD close to 7 percent, and so on. Bear in mind, however, that while the longer CDs earn a higher rate of interest, you are tying up your money for that much longer and thus losing some flexibility in your overall financial structure.

Penalties

Since CDs are firm contracts for a set amount of time, you will be penalized if you withdraw money from your CD before the maturity date. Government regulations have changed from time to time with respect to the total penalty that can be charged.

Check with your own bank to determine the penalties currently in effect on early withdrawals.

Renewal

Commonly, when a CD reaches its maturity, the institution will renew it for another term at the interest rate then prevailing. For example, you have a six-month CD that was obtained at a 6 percent interest rate. Today the CD is maturing, and the current interest rate on such CDs is 5 percent. Unless you instruct the institution to the contrary, it will automatically renew your CD at the 5 percent rate. Some institutions, however, will not automatically renew CDs: they may instead place the funds in a passbook savings account, lacking your instructions to the contrary. In such a case, you would likely earn a much lower rate of interest than a renewed CD would have paid.

Here is a common problem that arises when investors fail to pay attention to the renewal provisions of their CDs. Your six-month CD will mature on May 15. At the end of a seven-day grace period—May 22—it will automatically renew for another six months. You have every intention of getting to the bank on or before May 22 to take the money out so that you can put it to some other use. But you get distracted and don't get around to doing this until May 23. By that time the CD has already renewed, and if you now want to take out the money, you will have to pay a penalty.

Choices

Exercise 14.3

Institutions offer a huge assortment of CDs. With a myriad of choices at hand, making the right decision becomes a complex matter.

The Certificate of Deposit Shopping List (Figure 14–1), used in conjunction with the Personal Action Worksheet at the end of this chapter, will help you locate the best deal for your money. As you shop, be certain you know the extent of insurance on your deposit. If it's anything less than the full Federal Deposit Insurance, you must determine exactly what protection, if any, you actually have.

Certificate of Deposit Shopping List

	Institution		
	A	*B*	*C*

☐ *Fixed or variable interest rate?*
There's no way of knowing which will be better for you over the long run. The fixed rate is a sure thing. The variable rate is a guessing game: it could do better for you than the fixed; it could do worse.

☐ *Frequency of compounding?*
Given two plans with identical *rates*, the one that compounds more frequently will give you a higher return.

☐ *Minimum deposit required?*
How much must you deposit in order to earn the desired rate of interest? Minimum will differ from place to place.

☐ *Size breaks?*
At many institutions, larger deposits will earn higher rates of interest. If you can come up with a larger sum of money, you might be able to get a higher return.

☐ *Add-on privileges?*
Will you be able to put additional sums of money into your certificate account? This might involve a blending of interest rates: combining the original rate with the new rate in effect at the time you make your additional deposit. Add-on privileges offer an extra measure of convenience, particularly for such accounts as IRAs.

☐ *Borrowing privileges?*
If you need the money before the certificate matures, you'll have to face a penalty for early withdrawal. It may be much cheaper for you to borrow against your certificate, rather than cashing it in. Compare borrowing costs with penalty costs.

☐ *Intangibles*
Difficult to judge, perhaps, but could be important. What other services might the bank offer you? Are you pleased with their manner, their way of doing business? Are they conveniently located and open at convenient hours? Are their personnel friendly, helpful?

FIGURE 14–1   Certificate of deposit shopping list

Investment Criteria

- **Yield**   You are certain to receive the yield you bargained for by virtue of your contract with the financial institution. Regardless of the interest rate offered, the Truth in Savings Law (see chapter 11) requires all banks to quote the annual percentage yield (APY). That's the best criterion for accurately comparing various offerings.

- **Liquidity**   The liquidity of CDs is somewhat impaired as a result of the penalty provisions for early withdrawal. It is possible, however, to borrow against a CD rather than cashing it in if you have an immediate need for some of the money.

- **Safety**   As with passbook savings accounts, CDs at federally insured institutions are protected by the federal insurance programs up to $100,000 per account. Thus, CDs are considered to be at the highest level with respect to safety.
- **Hedge value**   None, with fixed rate CDs. Variable rate CDs can have attractive hedge value.
- **Pledge value**   As with passbook savings accounts, CDs can be used as collateral for borrowing. Many institutions will guarantee a fixed interest rate, should you wish to borrow against a CD. Such an interest rate might be 1 percent over what you're receiving on your CD. In other words, if you are receiving 6 percent interest and you wish to borrow against your CD, you would have to pay 7 percent a year for borrowing any of your funds. As noted, this could be a cheaper way of getting to your funds than cashing in the CD prematurely and suffering a heavy penalty.
- **Tax implications**   Interest income on CDs is fully taxable.

INVESTING IN THE BOND MARKET

What Are Bonds?

Just as you often borrow money—to buy a car, to fix up your home, to pay your bills, or to refinance existing older debts—business and governments likewise borrow money for similar needs. They may borrow for a long term, upward of forty years, or for a short term, a few years or even a few months. When they borrow for a long term, the IOU they issue is referred to as a bond. Short-term IOUs may be referred to as bills, notes, and, in the case of corporate short-term IOUs, commercial paper.

There are three major categories of bonds—corporate, federal government, and local government. And there are three ways an investor can get involved in bonds: directly, semidirectly, and indirectly.

You can buy bonds *directly* through a stockbroker and, in some cases, through the investment department of major banks. You can invest in bonds *semidirectly* through mutual funds that specialize in various bonds. The mutual funds pool the investments of many individuals and spread them out over a wide assortment of different issues. This is something the ordinary investor can't do individually.

Although you may not be aware of it, you *already* have *indirect* investments in the bond market. If you have a bank account, an insurance policy, or pension fund, it's very likely that some of your money is already invested in the bond market—and that in itself is a good reason for you to become familiar with the workings of bonds.

Corporate Bonds

Under the overall heading of corporate bonds are included the IOUs issued by railroads, public utilities (such as local electric and gas companies), and industrial firms (manufacturers, service companies such as airlines, retailing firms). Broadly speaking, there are two classifications of corporate bonds: straight and convertible. The straight bond is a simple long-term IOU of the issuing company in which the company agrees to pay the investor a fixed interest rate. The convertible bond carries with it the right of the holder to convert the bond into shares of that same company's common stock. Convertible bonds, or convertible debentures as they're sometimes called, are discussed in more detail later in this chapter.

Corporate bonds can usually be bought in denominations of $1,000, and the commission payable to a stockbroker is generally less than when buying stock. If you hold a bond until maturity, and it's redeemed directly by the issuer, there'll be no commission to pay.

How to Read Bond Quotations

Many major local newspapers carry bond quotations, as does *The Wall Street Journal* and *Investor's Business Daily*. *Barron's*, a financial newspaper issued weekly, also contains a full listing of traded corporate bonds.

In bond price quotations, the number quoted is the selling price of the bond expressed as a percentage of its face value. Thus, if a $1,000 bond is currently selling for $950, the quotation would appear as 95, which is 95 percent of its face value. Similarly, a bond selling for $985 would be quoted as 98½, which is 98.5 percent of its face value.

Exercise 14.4

An example: in 1978 the XYZ Company borrowed some money from public investors and issued bonds as IOUs. These bonds contained a promise to pay 6 percent interest per year for thirty years to everyone who bought the bonds, issued in $1,000 denominations. The bonds would thus mature in the year 2008, at which time the XYZ Company would pay all holders of the bonds $1,000 for each $1,000 bond. Over the years, investors traded the bonds back and forth among each other. Owing to market conditions, that bond today sells for $950. The quote in the newspaper would look like this, on a day when there was no fluctuation in its price:

Bond	Hi	Low	Last
XYZ 6s 08	95	95	95

This bond would be referred to as the XYZ Company 6s of 08. The 6s refers to the original interest rate that the company agreed to pay, or 6 percent; the 08 refers to the year of maturity, 2008; the three 95 figures refer to the high, low, and closing prices for the day. (Remember, we said that the price didn't fluctuate on this particular day.)

How Bond Yields Are Figured

Bonds have three different yields, and the difference must be clearly understood. The following description does not take into account brokerage commissions or income taxes payable on bond interest received.

COUPON YIELD   Referring back to the earlier example of the XYZ 6s of 08, we find that the 6 percent interest the company originally agreed to pay is known as the coupon yield. In other words, the company guarantees that it will pay $60 each year (usually in semiannual installments) to each holder of each $1,000 bond. The bond may fluctuate in price up and down, but the holder will continue to get $60 a year for each $1,000 bond held, regardless of the price of the bond.

CURRENT YIELD   We noted that the bond was quoted at $950 on a given day. If an investor purchased a $1,000 bond for $950 and received $60 per year in interest from the company, the actual current yield is 6.3 percent ($60 on $950, which is your actual investment). If, on the other hand, you had paid $1,050 for the bond, your *current yield* would be roughly 5.7 percent ($60 is 5.7 of $1,050, which is your actual investment).

YIELD TO MATURITY   The third concept of yield is called the yield to maturity, and it's a bit more difficult to understand. Say that you buy a $1,000 face value bond for $950, and you buy it exactly one year before its maturity date. It's paying 6 percent per year. When the bond matures one year after your purchase date, you get back the full face amount, or $1,000. That's $50 more than you paid for it, and that $50 is considered a capital gain. Also, you're going to get the $60 in interest during the year you hold the bond. Altogether you will receive $110 in one year for your $950 investment, or a *yield to maturity* of just over 11.6 percent ($110 is 11.6% of $950).

Exercise 14.5

If, however, you purchased the bond five years before maturity date, that $50 gain would be prorated over the remaining five years. Thus, you would be getting the $60 each year in interest plus an eventual extra $50 on redemption, which is equal to an extra $10 on average each year, assuming that you hold the bond until maturity. Your annual *average yield to maturity* would then be approximately $70 each year, or about 7.4 percent of your initial $950 investment.

How Bonds Fluctuate in Value: A Most Important Concept

If you buy a good-quality bond with a face value of $1,000, you will get your $1,000 back from the borrower—the government, the corporation— on the maturity date of the bond. But between the day you buy the bond and the maturity date, the market value of that bond *can and will* fluctuate. In other words, on any given day, the bond might be worth more or less than you paid for it. If you find yourself having to sell a bond before it reaches maturity, you might have to sell it at a loss. Or you could gain a profit. When people talk about the safety of bonds, they are referring to the *full value redemption at maturity date.* In the intervening years, however, the safety factor is subject to two main influences: interest rate movements and the financial condition of the issuing entity.

As a general rule, the market value of a bond moves in the *opposite* direction of interest rate trends. (The market value of a bond is what you can get for it if you were to sell it at any given time.)

Why is this so? Let's look at another example of the XYZ Company. When XYZ borrowed the money in 1992, conditions were such that it had to pay an interest rate on those bonds of 6 percent or $60 per $1,000 per year. Let's say that you bought one such bond at that time. Nine years have elapsed, it's 2001, and conditions are such that if XYZ were to borrow now, the company would have to pay 8 percent interest per $1,000, or $80 per $1,000 per year. When you originally bought the XYZ bond, you intended to hold onto it for the full thirty years, earning interest as the years went along. But in 2001, you face a financial emergency and find it necessary to sell the bond. You come to me and say, "Bob, I have here a perfectly good $1,000 bond from the XYZ Company, paying 6 percent interest per year. I'd like to sell it to your for $1,000."

I reply, "Why should I pay you $1,000 for that bond when I can buy a brand-new bond from a company of comparable quality that will pay me 8 percent or $80 per year? If I can earn 8 percent on my money today, why should I settle for 6 percent, which is all I would earn if I bought your bond from you for $1,000."

I can see that you're dismayed. You had invested in this bond in good faith, being told that it was perfectly safe, and now you can't sell it for what you paid for it. I'm a good sport, though, so I make you an offer. "I'll buy your $1,000 bond from you for $750. I'll earn $60 a year, which means that on my investment of $750 I'll be earning 8 percent, which is what I can get in the open market by buying a brand-new bond today (8 percent of $750 equals $60)."

Now you are shocked. In order to sell your bond, you have to take a $250 beating. But now you understand the workings of bond values. It's not a cheap lesson, but it's a worthwhile one. If interest rates had moved *down* during the same period of time, you would have been able to sell your bond at a *profit.*

The reality is this: We never know in which direction interest rates will be moving, or how far, or for how long. Thus, there is always an element of risk in investing in bonds, whether you do so directly or indirectly.

The other factor that can affect the market value of a bond is the financial status of the issuing entity. If a company falls on bad times or if a local government runs into financial difficulties, the marketplace may evaluate the bonds of those entities as being worth less because of the problems. For example, the question might arise: Will the company be able to earn enough money to pay the interest it owes on its bonds? If the marketplace deems that payments of interest or principal are in jeopardy, then the value of those bonds will fall. It's a repeat of the reward/risk rule: investing in this company is now riskier because of its impaired financial condition. Thus, the market value of its bond falls.

As bonds get to within a few years of maturity date, they are less susceptible to these various fluctuations.

Sinking Fund

When corporations borrow money, they often do something most individuals and families would be well advised to do. They set up what is called a sinking fund, out of which they will eventually pay off the bond. They put aside so much money each year toward the eventual redemption of that bond and actually use that money to pay off the investors, either at maturity or in advance of maturity if market conditions so dictate.

Call Privileges

A company has issued a bond paying 7 percent interest per year. After the passage of a number of years, the interest rates prevalent throughout the economy have dropped to 6 percent. The company sees an opportunity to refinance the existing IOUs and drop its interest rate from 7 percent to 6 percent, thus cutting its interest expense considerably. In order to take advantage of such opportunities, many bonds have written into them a call privilege, which means that the company has the right to call in the existing bonds and pay off the holders at an agreed-on price. Investors are then faced with the problem of having to reinvest the money at a lower interest rate than they had been earning.

A would-be investor in corporate bonds should determine what call privileges or protection exists. Because a bond is usually a relatively long-term investment, it would be to the investor's advantage to know that the company can't call the bond for at least five to ten years.

Corporate Bond Ratings

Thousands of corporate bonds are available to investors at any given time. How is one to determine the relative quality of so many bonds? Corporate bonds are rated according to quality by two companies: Standard & Poor's and Moody's. Both rating systems are very similar, taking into account the basic financial strength of the corporation and its ability to pay the interest on its debts. The highest rated bonds offer the lowest rate of interest and the lowest risk to investors. Following is a brief summary of the Standard & Poor's ratings:

Exercise 14.6

AAA	Highest grade obligations
AA	High-grade obligations
A	Upper-medium-grade obligations
BBB	Medium-grade obligations

BB	Lower-medium-grade obligations
B	Speculative obligations
CCC-CC	Outright speculations, with the lower rating denoting the more speculative
C	No interest is being paid
DDD-D	All such bonds are in default, with the rating indicating the relative salvage value

Generally, institutional investors—banks, insurance companies, pension funds and the like—will focus their bond investments in the AAA and AA ranges, and to a lesser degree in the A range. These are known as the *investment quality* ratings. Rarely, if ever, will they dip below A ratings. You might be guided according in your own choice of bonds, or of mutual funds that invest in bonds.

The ratings companies keep a watch on the financial status of all bond issuers, and if there is a change in the financial strength of a company, its rating will be changed accordingly. For more specific details on the ratings, refer to the monthly rating books published by the two companies, available at stock brokerage firms and at most local libraries.

Junk Bonds

Bonds had historically been considered a safe haven for investors' money. But hundreds, perhaps thousands of companies found the door to the bond market closed to them. They weren't able to raise funds by issuing IOUs because they weren't creditworthy enough.

In the mid-1980s, a concept emerged that enabled many of these companies to borrow money in the bond market, albeit at higher rates of interest than their more creditworthy peers. The higher rate of interest was due to the higher level of risk involved in lending money to less "proven" corporations.

For the most part these bonds were rated BBB or lower. Because of the low ratings they became known as *junk bonds,* even though many of the corporations issuing them were of reasonably good quality. The higher yields appealed to speculators, and a gambling-like atmosphere surrounded junk bonds for many years. Abuses were rampant, and many investors and brokerage firms were badly hurt. By the mid-1990s the tumult had subsided. But high-risk bonds still exist and can still pose problems for unsophisticated investors.

Investment Criteria

- **Yield**   With higher-rated companies you have a very high assurance of receiving the yield (interest payment) you have bargained for. With lower-rated companies the yield may be in doubt.

- **Liquidity**   The major bond exchanges (New York and American) maintain a market for buyers and sellers of bonds. But depending on the issue and the number of bonds being bought or sold, it could take from a few minutes to a few days to effect a transaction.

- **Safety**   The higher the rating of the bond and the closer it is to maturity, the safer your investment. As noted, bond prices fluctuate in value, moving in the opposite direction from interest rates.

- **Hedge value**   If a bond is bought at or near face value, there is little protection against inflation. As prices move upward—interest rates being among those prices—bonds are likely to decrease in value, as noted earlier. Thus, the hedge value might be considered negative. If, on the other hand, a bond is bought below face value and maturity is approaching, the bond price will move upward as maturity nears, thus offering a measure of protection against rising prices.

- **Pledge value**   The amount that one can borrow against bonds and the interest rate paid on such a loan depend on the quality of the bond as determined by the rating services. Generally, well-rated bonds provide ample opportunity for pledging at reasonably favorable interest rates. However, if a bond has decreased in value, the amount that can be borrowed against it will decrease proportionately.

- **Tax implications**   Interest earned on corporate bonds is taxable.

U.S. Government Bonds

The federal government is the biggest borrower of all. Federal IOUs range from the common savings bond for as low as $25 to the multimillion-dollar obligations issued frequently by the U.S. Treasury. The federal government even borrows from itself. For example, the Social Security Administration invests its own funds in U.S. Treasury IOUs. Federal government obligations are further broken down into three subcategories: U.S. Treasury borrowings, federal agency borrowings, and savings bonds.

U.S. Treasury Borrowings

The U.S. Treasury borrows frequently on a short-term, medium-term, and long-term basis. Short-term obligations are called Treasury bills, and their maturities range from three months to one year. Medium-term obligations are called Treasury notes, with maturities ranging from 2 to 10 years. Long-term issues are called Treasury bonds, with maturities ranging form 10 to 30 years. Any of these Treasury debts can be obtained at a nominal commission through a stockbroker or the investment department of a bank, or directly from the Federal Reserve Bank at no commission. The prices and yields (before commissions) of all U.S. Treasury obligations are listed daily in *The Wall Street Journal* in a column titled "Treasury Bonds, Notes, & Bills."

Exercise 14.7

Federal Agency Borrowings

A number of federal government agencies are frequent borrowers of large sums of money. The money they borrow is generally pumped back into the economy to subsidize such things as mortgage loans for home buyers and farm loans for the agricultural industry. Investments are available in a wide range of maturities. Short-term obligations, usually for a year or less, are commonly called *notes.* Medium-term obligations, which may run from one to five years, are commonly referred to as *debentures.* Long-term obligations that run from five to twenty-five years are referred to as *bonds.* Some of the more popularly traded federal agency obligations are issued by the Federal National Mortgage Association, the Federal Home Loan Bank, Banks for Cooperatives, Federal Land Banks, and Federal Intermediate Credit Banks.

The prices and current yields (before commissions) of Treasury obligations and agency obligations are quoted daily in *The Wall Street Journal* under the heading "Government Agency, and Similar Issues."

Savings Bonds

Savings bonds are the most commonly known and popular forms of bonds issued by the federal government. They are currently called EE and HH bonds. (Savings bonds sold prior to 1980 are E and H bonds.) EE bonds sold since November 1, 1982, offer a fluctuating rate of interest. This is designed to keep the bonds more competitive with savings programs offered by financial institutions.

Here's how the fluctuating-rate EE bonds work: If you buy and hold the bonds for at least five years, you will earn the fluctuating rate of interest or the guaranteed minimum, whichever is greater. The fluctuating rate is adjusted every six months, and it's based on 85 percent of the average yield on five-year U.S. Treasury securities. If that yield is 7 percent, the EE bonds will pay 5.95 percent for that six-month period.

Exercise 14.8

One particular advantage of E and EE bonds is that the interest you earn is not taxable on your federal income tax return until you cash the bonds in. The interest is also tax-exempt on state and local income tax returns. E and EE bonds continue to pay interest for forty years from their date of issue. Once they have reached forty years of age, they stop paying interest and should be cashed in. Taxes will be due on the accrued interest at that time.

HH bonds may be acquired in exchange for E or EE bonds. In thus exchanging your E and EE bonds, you can further defer taxation on the accumulated interest until the HH bonds are cashed. But interest earned on the HH bonds is taxable in the year you receive it. Check with the nearest Savings Bonds Division of the U.S. Treasury for full details on the current rates and terms of savings bonds.

Zero Coupon Bonds

As noted earlier, bonds typically pay interest twice a year, and the face amount is then paid to bondholders on the maturity date of the bonds. With zero coupon bonds, no interest is paid until maturity. The bonds are bought at one price and then redeemed in the future for a much higher price. In short, these bonds have a coupon yield of zero. The most commonly traded zero coupon bonds are derived from U.S. Treasury issues and have been nicknamed by various brokerage firms as CATS (Certificates of Accrual on Treasury Securities) and TIGRs (Treasury Investment Growth Receipts). Corporations also issue zero coupon bonds.

Zeros, as they are also called, have proved popular because they offer a guaranteed return for a set period of time, and there is no need to bother with reinvestment of your interest earnings. However, the IRS has ruled that although you are not receiving interest *in hand* each year, you must pay taxes on the accrued interest each year. Thus, zeros might not be advisable for personal accounts that are subject to taxation. But they could be appropriate for IRA and Keogh plans or for any other tax-deferred portfolio. Get full details from your stockbroker before you invest.

Inflation-Proof Bonds

Since 1997 the U.S. Treasury has been offering five- and ten-year bonds that have built-in "inflation-proofing." Here's how they work. You invest $1,000 in one of these bonds. During the first year the Consumer Price Index (CPI), which is the common measure of inflation, moves up by 4 percent. That means that a product that cost $1.00 a year ago will now cost $1.04. Your inflation-proof bond will automatically increase in value by 4 percent, from $1,000 to $1,040. Thus, the purchasing power of your money is protected. This adjustment will take place each year in keeping with the changes in the CPI. That's the good news.

The bad news is that the rate of interest you'll earn on such a bond will be a lot less than on a standard U.S. Treasury bond of similar duration. You can't have it both ways. What you gain in inflation protection you lose in current income. The best use of these bonds would be as a minority portion of your retirement portfolio to insulate you from the effects of long-term inflation. In the short term you can live with a 2 or 3 percent rise in the CPI, which has been its track record in recent years. But over a few decades, that constant edging upward of costs can clobber you if you've not taken some protective steps.

Some major mutual fund companies are now also offering similar inflation-proof funds. The same precautions apply, but with an added dose of care if the investments are of any lesser quality than that of the U.S. Treasury.

Investment Criteria

- **Yield**   On regular government, and zero bonds, you are certain to get the yield you are promised. The yield on EE bonds, as noted, fluctuates, with a minimum guarantee if you hold the bonds for five years. HH yield can be modified by the Treasury Department.

- **Liquidity**   There is an active market for government, agency, and zero issues, which allows you to cash in your holding prior to maturity at the going market price, subject to commissions. EE and HH bonds may not be cashed in until six months after date of purchase.

- **Safety**   Government issues are considered to be in the highest safety category. To the ultimate skeptic, it's safe to presume that before the government falls, everything else will have long since fallen.

- **Hedge value**   As with corporate bonds, an investor in *long-term* government issues has virtually no protection against inflation, assuming that interest rates go up as inflation increases, which is likely. The rate of income is fixed, and higher interest rates will mean lower market values for the bonds, as discussed earlier. Short-term investors are better able to guard against inflation. If inflation has boosted interest rates, short-term investors can move into higher-yielding issues as their older ones mature. The fluctuating-rate EE bonds do offer good protection against inflation.

- **Pledge value**   E, EE, and HH bonds cannot be pledged as security for a loan; thus, they have no pledge value. Other government issues can be pledged, usually at a very high percentage of their face values. Generally, government issues would have higher pledge value than corporate issues of comparable size and maturity.

- **Tax implications**   Government and agency bonds: federally taxable but exempt from state and local income taxes; E and EE bonds: tax-deferred for federal returns, tax-exempt on state and local income tax returns; H and HH: interest earned each year is federally taxable for that year; zeros: interest earned (even though not received by you) is taxable each year; tax-deferred if in IRA or Keogh accounts.

Municipal Bonds

States, cities, towns, water districts, school districts, sewer districts, highway authorities, and a variety of other local entities have periodic needs to borrow funds. The interest these bonds pay has been deemed exempt from federal income tax obligations. This, of course, benefits the local taxpayers. It makes the cost of building and maintaining schools, roads, sewers, or whatever, cheaper. If the bonds were not tax-exempt, they would have to be issued at higher interest rates, resulting in higher interest costs, which would be passed along to taxpayers.

The two major types of municipal bonds are general obligation bonds and revenue bonds. The general obligation bonds are backed by the taxing authority of the locality. The revenue bonds are backed by the revenues produced by the entity, such as toll roads on a highway authority bond or water usage fees on a water revenue bond. As a rule, general obligation bonds have a higher level of quality than revenue bonds because the power to tax citizens is a more reliable source of income than the ability to raise revenues from toll roads, city-run hospitals, and the like, some of which can be risky.

The 1986 Tax Reform Act put limits on the purposes for which municipalities can issue tax-exempt bonds. Many had been using their tax-exempt borrowing status to attract investment funds and then turning the money over to private developers to build housing projects. Congress felt that this was a potential abuse of the tax-exempt borrowing privilege, and it created quotas on how much of that type of borrowing was tax-exempt. Municipalities will still continue to borrow for such purposes, but the interest they pay to investors may not be tax-exempt. In other words we have municipal bonds that are *tax-exempt* and a small number of municipal bonds that are *taxable.*

Tax Exemption

The most notable aspect of tax-exempt municipal bonds is that the interest they pay investors is exempt from the investors' federal income taxes. Interest earned is also exempt from state income taxes if the investor lives in the state in which the bond is issued. However, if you buy a municipal bond and later sell it at a profit, that profit is subject to full federal and state income taxes.

Exercise 14.9

In comparing a tax-exempt investment with a taxable investment, you must determine how many dollars are left in either case after paying any applicable taxes. Table 14–4 compares tax-exempt and taxable yields. Example: A taxpayer in the 28 percent tax bracket invests $1,000 in a tax-exempt security paying 7 percent, or $70 per year. If that same investor put $1,000 into a taxable security paying 9.7 percent a year, he would earn $97 before federal income taxes. If the $97 was taxed at the 28 percent rate, he'd owe a tax of roughly $27, reducing his *after-tax* yield to $70. In that case, a taxable yield of 9.7 percent would be the same as a tax-exempt yield of 7 percent. Numbers were rounded off, and state income taxes and commission costs are not included in the example.

Although tax exemption of municipal bonds is attractive, municipal bonds are not for everyone. Taxpayers in higher brackets can benefit considerably, but taxpayers in lower brackets might not be better off with municipal bonds than with taxable securities.

TABLE 14–4   **Comparing Tax-Exempt and Taxable Yields**

If You Are in This Tax Bracket:	A Tax-exempt Yield of				
	3%	4%	5%	6%	7%
	Will Net You the Same as a Taxable Yield of:				
15%	3.5%	4.7%	5.9%	6.9%	8.2%
28%	3.7	5.5	7.0	8.3	9.7
33%	4.5	6.0	7.5	8.8	10.4%

Municipal Bond Quotations

Quotations on the prices and yields of municipal bonds are not available in daily newspapers. An investor would have to contact a stockbroker for specific details on the prices and yields of any municipal bonds.

Municipal Bond Ratings

Municipal bonds are rated by the same two services that rate corporate bonds, Standard & Poor's and Moody's. As with the corporate bonds, these ratings services examine the financial status of the municipalities, and the ratings compare the relative qualities of the various issues. The formats in both ratings systems are similar. Following is a brief summary of the Standard & Poor's ratings.

AAA	Highest quality
AA	High grade
A	Good grade
BBB	Medium grade
BB	Speculative-grade
B	Low grade
D	Default

As with corporate bonds, if the financial condition of a municipality changes, so will its rating. Higher ratings mean a lower return to investors and a lower risk. Check with the rating services for more specific details.

Investment Criteria

- **Yield**   In higher-rated municipal bonds, you are assured of receiving the yield you bargained for. Lowest-rated bonds are subject to termination of interest payments and even possible loss of principal.
- **Liquidity**   Trading in municipal bonds is not as active as trading in stocks and corporate bonds. Thus, an investor wishing to sell municipal

bonds may have to wait many hours or days (or possibly even weeks in the case of smaller issues) until a willing buyer comes along. A seller anxious to get a quick trade may have to settle for a lower price.

- **Safety** As with corporate bonds, the higher the rating of a municipal bond, the higher the safety level. Municipal bonds, like corporate bonds, are subject to the same fluctuations and call privileges. Long-term investors in municipal bonds must be concerned about getting caught in a long-term downswing in the value of their holdings if interest rates move upward from the time they bought the bonds.

   Some private companies offer insurance on municipal bonds, which will cost you a small portion of your return. Note well, though, that this insurance is to guarantee you full payment on maturity. It will not protect you against the day-to-day market value fluctuations of the bond.

- **Hedge value** Municipal bonds offer rather indirect protection against inflation. Although the bond itself pays a fixed rate of income for as long as one holds it, the tax-exempt factor can be translated into some protection against inflation for the investor whose income is on the rise. As your income increases, you move into even higher tax brackets. The higher the tax bracket you're in, the greater the tax advantage the municipal bond affords you.

- **Pledge value** Holders of municipal bonds should be able to borrow against their holdings without much difficulty. The percentage of the total value they can borrow and the interest rate they'll have to pay depend on the quality of the issue, as well as its current price level. The higher the quality, the higher percentage of face value you may be able to borrow.

STRATEGIES FOR SUCCESS

Compare Yields Along with Maturities

One basic rule of money market investing is clear: all other things being equal, a security that promises a higher yield also carries a higher risk. But what if all other things are *not* equal? What if they are equal in quality (such as federally insured deposits or U.S. Treasury obligations), and the only difference is their maturity—that is, how long they have to run. That can also affect the yield. Generally, the *longer* the term, the *higher* the yield. But the longer term doesn't always produce enough improvement in yield to warrant tying up your money for those extra years. Here's a simple example at one point in time. A three-year obligation of the U.S. Treasury offered a yield of 5.9 percent. At the same time, a ten-year Treasury obligation offered a yield of 6.7 percent. Is it worth tying your money up for seven extra years to gain less than one extra percentage point in yield? Ask yourself before you take the plunge.

MISCELLANEOUS MONEY MARKET INVESTMENTS

Over the last decade, the ingenuity of the financial marketplace has been particularly bright with respect to the creation of new and unusual forms of fixed income investment. Some of the concepts outlined here have long been the domain of big-money investors. But as the competition for investment dollars has heightened, the concepts have been enlarged to allow the small investor access to these techniques. Over the years, some will capture the public attention, some will fail to, and new techniques will continually emerge.

Mutual Funds

The mutual fund concept has found great favor with the public at large. Mutual fund companies and stockbrokerage firms pool the investments of many small investors and put that money to work in a variety of ways.

The most common types of mutual funds invest in the stock market. These funds are discussed in more detail in chapter 15. But mutual funds in the money market have grown rapidly in popularity; these funds encompass corporate bonds, municipal bonds, U.S. government bonds, and money market instruments. Before examining each specific type of fund, let's examine some of the main distinctions among mutual funds in general.

- **Closed versus open**   The vast majority of mutual funds are open-ended. The managers of the fund are continually buying and selling securities at whatever pace they see fit. Thus, the composition of the overall fund is constantly changing. The ability to buy and sell allows the fund managers to adjust to changing market conditions. It also expands the possibility of the managers' making *wise* decisions *and un*-wise decisions. Open-end funds are also often known as managed funds.

  There are also a small number of closed-end funds. These function in much the same way as the open-end funds with respect to buying and selling securities on a continuing basis. To invest in a closed-end fund, however, you buy shares in such funds on the stock market rather than dealing directly with the mutual fund company itself.

  Yet another type of pooled investment is the unit trust. Unlike investment funds, which are constantly buying and selling securities, the unit trust buys a group of securities and holds them until maturity. Thus, the income is more certain with a unit trust than it is with a managed fund, but the value of each share is susceptible to the ups and downs of the market—remember, interest rates and bond prices move in opposite directions.

- **Load versus no-load**   This refers to the commission price an investor pays to buy shares in a mutual fund. A load can be as much as 8 or 9 percent of the initial investment. In other words, in a typical 8½ load fund, 8½ percent of the investor's initial investment will go to pay the brokerage commission. On a $1,000 investment, $85 goes toward commissions and only $915 goes to work for the investor. A no-load fund implies that there is no commission to pay when acquiring the investment. But other charges may be incurred over the life of the investment with both load and no-load funds.

- **Maintenance and service charges** In addition to the loading commission, mutual funds will charge some kind of monthly or annual service fee. Commonly, the service fee is based on a percentage of the fund's assets. Some funds may also take a fee based on the earnings of the fund during the year. These fees may be deducted from the total fund assets or directly from each individual account. Either way, they are an added cost that can affect your yield.

  Some mutual funds charge a redemption fee when you cash in your shares. Before making your initial investment, you should determine any and all charges that may occur.

- **Fund objectives** With fixed income mutual funds, the most common objective is to generate maximum income for the investors. (With common stock mutual funds, the objectives fall into a broader spectrum ranging from income to speculative growth.) But there can be a distinct difference in the level of income and safety sought by various funds. How will a fund invest the money? Some funds will go for the highest quality investments available. This will mean the highest possible level of safety for investors but a lower level of income. It's necessary to determine the broad makeup of the portfolios of a number of funds before making an investment decision.

- **Minimum investment required** On average, the minimum initial investment required in fixed income mutual funds is $1,000. After the initial investment, investors may make additional investments in smaller amounts.

- **Extra privileges** Many mutual funds are a part of a family of other mutual funds. The owners of shares in such funds may therefore have the privilege of exchanging all, or a portion of, their shares for shares in another fund managed by the same investment advisory group. For example, you might switch from a corporate bond fund into a common stock fund or vice versa, at a minimal charge. Reinvestment privileges—whereby your earnings are automatically reinvested in additional shares of the fund—are commonplace, usually at no extra charge. Withdrawal privileges—taking out a fixed amount each month or each quarter—are also available, with some minimal restrictions as to the amount that can be withdrawn.

- **Investment criteria** The investment criteria of a given fixed income mutual fund are approximately the same with regard to yield, liquidity, safety, hedge values, and pledge values as for that specific type of instrument in which the fund is investing. In other words, a mutual fund that concentrates exclusively on long-term corporate bonds has the same investment criteria as comparable individual corporate bonds. There is one important difference, however. The value of the investment criteria depends largely on the investor's own individual ability to interpret changes, trends, and concepts. Theoretically, professional money managers are better able to do this than individuals. It follows, theoretically, that an investor who is seeking high income may do well, but a professional money manager may be able to do better.

The mutual fund concept allows investors to spread the risk over many securities rather than place all their eggs in one basket. But a careful evaluation of the objectives, the management, and the overall risks involved is as necessary with a mutual fund as it is with a single investment and a specific issue. Investors are advised to read a number of prospectuses of various mutual fund offerings so as to distinguish among the various criteria noted in the previous discussion. Following is a summary of major types of fixed income mutual funds.

Corporate Bond Funds

These funds invest in a wide variety of corporate bonds: high-quality, low-quality, long-term, short-term. The range of possibilities is vast, and it is essential to examine the prospectuses to determine the level of risk and income an investor can expect.

Tax-Exempt Municipal Funds

These mutual funds invest predominantly in municipal bonds—those whose income payable to investors is exempt from federal income taxes. Some funds invest in bonds issued from a single state. Residents of those states who invest in such funds will receive their interest free of state and local income taxes. The range of quality and risk is not as wide as with corporate bonds, but a range does exist. As with municipal bonds, investors should be aware that not all the income will necessarily be exempt from federal income taxes. If, for example, a mutual fund buys a bond and sells it later for a profit, that portion of the profit that is distributed to shareholders will be considered taxable. Furthermore, interest income from a mutual bond fund can be taxable on the local level (state and city). As the prospectuses for these funds disclose, many funds do not invest 100 percent of their assets in tax-exempt municipals. They reserve the right to invest a small portion in other types of instruments that may be taxable. On the whole, however, the major portion of income on such funds would be tax-exempt. It's wise to check with your tax adviser to determine if tax-exempt mutual funds make sense in your situation.

Government Bond Mutual Funds

One of the fastest-growing segments of the mutual fund industry has been funds that invest in U.S. government securities, including bills, notes, bonds, federal agencies, and the government-backed mortgage pools. (See the discussion in chapter 16 on these mortgage pools.) As a rule, these government funds involve relatively high-quality securities, which means a relatively low rate of return to investors but a high level of safety and the peace of mind that goes with it. Investors must always be aware, however, that bond-market prices and interest rates move in opposite directions. Thus, even though these mutual funds are touted as being the ultimate in safety, the unavoidable risk of market fluctuation exists. The bonds in the fund are safe, but that means that they will pay 100 cents on the dollar *at maturity*. In the interim, there is always the risk of fluctuation that can send the value of an investment down suddenly if interest rates rise, and vice versa.

Money Market Mutual Funds

Exercise 14.10

Money market mutual funds have been very popular with investors. They give small investors access to higher rates of return that might not otherwise be available. And they provide a good "parking place" for investment dollars while investors wait for better opportunities to appear. Note one important distinction between money market *mutual funds* and money market *accounts* that are available at banks and savings institutions: Money market accounts are protected by the Federal Deposit Insurance programs. Money market mutual funds do not have that same protection. Otherwise, the accounts function in a similar way. It's best to compare the current rates of return of the funds versus the accounts before making an investment choice. Here are some of the main features of money market mutual funds:

- They are flexible. Investors can get out at any time without penalty.
- The return on these funds varies from day to day, as interest rates fluctuate. Thus, an investor will never know what the actual return will be in the long run. (With certificates of deposit, investors are assured a fixed rate for a fixed period of time.)
- Fees are reasonably low compared with other types of mutual funds.
- In virtually all money market mutual funds, the investor will be dealing with a salesperson or stockbroker. Sooner or later that investor should expect to receive a call from the salesperson or broker suggesting that the investor get out of the money market fund and into something else. An investor who isn't prepared for that sales pitch may agree to a switch that could prove profitable or unprofitable. In short, an investor may be wooed away from a highly secure position into a speculative one. This is not necessarily bad, but the investor should be aware of the potential before making the investment.

- Shares in money market mutual funds are not insured like bank accounts, but the bulk of money market fund investments are in highly secure instruments such as government issues and bank certificates.
- Many large brokerage firms will offer to tie in money market investments with checking accounts and credit card availabilities. In effect, the portion of your checking account balance that isn't needed for immediate use can be invested in the brokerage firm's money market fund, where it can earn a high rate of interest. Prospective investors should carefully examine the minimum deposits required for such services and the cost of these services.

Following are some other types of money market investments that may be available to individual investors directly or that may be included in a mutual fund portfolio.

Banker's Acceptances

Say a U.S. company sells a product to a Japanese company for $200,000. The Japanese company gives the U.S. company a written promise to pay for the goods on delivery, which is expected to be in six months. The U.S. company doesn't want to wait for its money, so it goes to a bank with the Japanese company's promise to pay. The bank examines the credentials of the Japanese company and agrees to buy its promise to pay from the U.S. company at a certain price. The bank has thus, in effect, "accepted" the Japanese promise to pay. The bank may then turn around and sell this IOU to investors. The instrument is known as a banker's acceptance. In effect, the investor is buying a foreign company's promise top pay. The investor is secured to the extent that a bank or other financial institution is willing to take the risk itself. Banker's acceptances tend to pay an attractive rate of interest for short-term investments.

Commercial Paper

When corporations borrow for a long term, as discussed, their promises to pay are called corporate bonds. Often, corporations borrow for a short period of time—such as a few months. Short-term corporate borrowings are referred to as commercial paper, and their quality tends to follow the quality of the corporation's bonds. As the bond is rated, so is the commercial paper commonly rated. Money market mutual funds frequently carry sizable amounts of commercial paper in their portfolios.

Floating-rate Bonds

As discussed previously, interest rates and the market value of bonds move in opposite directions. To recap briefly: If you invest in a bond that is paying, say, 8 percent interest a year, or $80 per $1,000 invested, and interest rates in general move upward, then the market value of your bond will shrink. This is because an investor in a higher interest rate environment can buy a brand-new bond yielding, say, 9 percent. So why should anyone pay you full face value for yours, which yields only 8 percent?

One type of investment gets around this problem: the floating-rate bond. If the interest rate on a given bond is permitted to move up and down, the principal value will not fluctuate. Example: using the same original 8 percent investment, if interest rate trends move upward to, say, 9 percent, and your bond is allowed to pay you the higher rate of return, your principal value will remain intact. By the same token, if interest rates move down, your principal will remain at the $1,000 face value level and you'll receive a lower yield. In other words, you can't have it both ways: in bond investments, you have to accept either a floating rate of interest or a floating market value.

Floating-rate bonds are available in both the taxable and tax-exempt categories. The most popular ones have been issued by banks.

Convertible Bonds

These issues (sometimes called convertible debentures) are corporate bonds that give the owner the right to convert the bonds into common stock of the issuing company. Here's an example: XYZ Corporation issues a convertible bond with a selling price of $1,000. The bond pays an interest rate of 10 percent—$100 per year. That rate is fixed for the life of the bond. Owners of the bonds have the right to convert their bonds into fifty shares of XYZ common stock, which is now selling for $20 per share and paying a $2 per share dividend. Thus, the income from fifty shares of the common stock is $100 per year, the same as the bond. At this point, the $1,000 bond and the fifty shares of common stock are equal in value. There would seem to be no point in converting from the bond to the stock. However, an investor may be hopeful that the dividend on the stock will increase, say, from $2 to $3 per share. If, in fact, that happens and the investor has converted from the bond to the stock, the yield will increase from $100 per year to $150 per year. The interest rate on the bond is fixed, but the dividend rate on the stock is not. Therefore, an investor who is willing to speculate on increased dividends might find convertible bonds profitable.

On the other hand, the bond is eventually going to be worth $1,000 at maturity. The investor knows that for sure. The stock could drop to a much

STRATEGIES FOR SUCCESS

A Formula for Safe Retirement Investing

How should your Individual Retirement Account, or 401(k) plan, or any other retirement money be invested? To the extent that you will be depending on this money for retirement living, it's not wise to take much risk with it. Take risks with money you don't need for retirement, but not with this important stash. It *must* be there at retirement time, and if you take risks it might *not* be there. Then what?

Consider this simple formula: Add your age plus forty. That's the percentage of your retirement money that should be risk-free. The rest can be put to moderate risk. So if you are thirty, your age plus forty equals seventy. Thus, 70% of your must-be-there retirement money should be risk-free. If you are fifty, 90 percent of your must-be-there retirement money should be risk-free. The older you are, the less risk you can afford to take, because there's less time and less resilience to recover from mistakes.

This is a very conservative formula. Take greater risk at your own risk. See Strategies for Success on page 353 for added views on this subject.

lower level than its conversion value. An investor who converts is taking a chance that the stock may decrease in value and result in a considerable loss and vice versa.

During the holding period, prior to a decision to convert, the bond and the stock will tend to move up and down on a fairly parallel course. Once investors have converted from the bonds to the stocks, they are stuck. They can't automatically convert back to the bonds again if their expectations don't work out.

PERSONAL ACTION WORKSHEET ───────────────

Comparing Returns, After Costs

The true return on any given investment can only be calculated after all costs have been taken into account. These costs include commissions (when both buying and selling), ongoing fees (such as those charged by mutual funds), and income taxes. To get a clear comparison of various types of money market investments, calculate the return, after costs, of the following securities. Use actual current returns now available. For the "Tax" column, use your own current tax rate. If you're not in a taxable situation, use the lowest current tax rate.

	Return Before Costs	Commissions to Buy	to Sell	Ongoing Fees	Tax	Total Costs	Return After Costs
❏ 12-month bank CD	_____	_____	_____	_____	_____	_____	_____
❏ Bank money market account	_____	_____	_____	_____	_____	_____	_____
❏ Broker money market fund	_____	_____	_____	_____	_____	_____	_____
❏ Corporate bond mutual fund (low-risk, full-load)	_____	_____	_____	_____	_____	_____	_____
❏ Government bond mutual fund (low-risk, full-load)	_____	_____	_____	_____	_____	_____	_____

What Is the Secret to Financial Success?

A friend asked me a fascinating question recently. "Is investing wisely the ultimate secret for financial success?"

My answer, and I hope you'll agree, was "No."

My questioner, thinking that he had hit upon a formula long sought by humankind, was puzzled by my answer.

I explained my brief but firm reply: Certainly investing wisely is something to strive for. But all the wise investing in the world won't help you a whit if you spend it all willy-nilly. And all the fat dividends and huge profits you can reap aren't worth a hoot if you are miserable day to day because of a dead-end job or marriage or social life.

Money can buy toys, but it can't buy self-esteem. Money can buy power, but it can't buy good health. Money can glamorize your exterior, but it can't uplift your interior. Money might provide the image of happiness, but not the spirit of happiness.

Everyone must find their own equilibrium, their own sense of balance between the material things they seek and the simpler pleasures of life. You should not feel beholden to anyone—it's your life to live as you choose it, subject to your responsibility to those who depend on you. But at the end of the day it's you who must say to yourself, "Way to go!"

Wise investing is only part of financial success. Wise spending, wise prioritizing, and wise risk management are the other prime elements of financial success. And financial success is only one part of overall personal success.

The friend who asked me the question was sixty-one. He hadn't learned yet. You may be a lot younger. I hope you learn a lot more a lot earlier than my friend.

UPS & DOWNS *The Economics of Everyday Life*

How Stock Market Ups and Downs Affect Money Market Ups and Downs

You say you're *never* going to have anything to do with the stock market; you're just going to stick with safe and simple savings certificates and other money market types of investments discussed in this chapter. Be careful: You can never escape the ripple effects on the stock market. (See chapter 15.)

When the stock market moves sharply upward, for whatever valid or fanciful reason, it attracts money out of the money market like a super-magnet. Conservative money market investors see big gains being made in the stock market, and they abandon their lower yielding but *safe* accounts to take a plunge in the risky waters of the stock market. Greed, naiveté, lack of discipline—all are part of human nature. All of this money pouring into the stock market keeps the rally going, and that attracts still more money market investors. And so it goes until gravity reasserts itself and the stock market tumbles.

If such a stock market rally occurs when the nation's economy is strong and banks need depositors' money to lend to meet borrowers' demands, then banks will react to the outflow of deposits by increasing the interest rates they pay to depositors to lure them back.

If such a stock market rally occurs when the nation's economy is weak and banks aren't being hounded by would-be borrowers, then banks will let the interest rates they pay to their depositors drift—probably downward.

Why? Because lower rates will eventually stimulate borrowing, which will stimulate the economy, which will prod interest rates upward, which will create more profit opportunity for the banks. It's a cyclical thing.

Then there's always "the other hand." When the stock market tumbles—as it inevitably does after each rally—investors will flee Wall Street to the safe harbor of money market securities. If this happens at a time when the economy is strong and banks are competing for deposits, money market interest rates can go up. If it happens when the economy is weak and banks are not competing for deposits, money market interest rates will likely remain flattish.

The internal tie-ins between these markets are devilishly intricate. But it's worth the effort to understand them, so that you can make your own decisions more effectively.

? *WHAT IF . . . ?*

Test yourself on the concerns of this chapter. How would you deal with these real-life possibilities?

1. You want to put away money for the following purposes: (a) college tuition for your children; (b) a super vacation traveling through Europe; (c) retirement. However little or however much you may really have to salt away, what percentage of it would you put into the money market for each of these three purposes? What types of plans would you favor for each?

2. An investment adviser suggests that she can put your money to work in a mutual fund specializing in high-yield corporate bonds and that the fund will give you a return five percentage points higher than what you could earn by investing in U.S. Treasury securities. What more should you ask of this adviser? What might be the pros and cons of making such an investment?

3. The company you work for is issuing bonds—borrowing money— from the public at large. You feel that it might make a good investment for you. The bonds are well rated, and the interest rate is two percentage points higher than what you're earning in your savings account. You plan to cash in the bonds in about five years. What would happen to your investment if interest rates five years from now had dropped from today's levels? What if they had risen? Why?

NUMBER CRUNCHERS

Do the calculations that are needed to help you make decisions in these real-life possibilities.

1. Grunt arithmetic, but worth the exercise: You invest $1,000 in a savings plan that pays 8 percent interest, compounding annually. You invest another $1,000 in a corporate bond that pays 8 percent interest per year, payable annually, with no compounding. You'll deposit the interest from the bond in a savings account paying 5 percent interest, compounding annually, but only if there is $500 or more in the account—otherwise it pays no interest. How would your money grow in either of these plans over five years? Ten years? (Forget income taxes for purposes of this exercise, but not in real life.)

2. A bond is quoted in the newspaper as follows: "ZYX 7s 04 Closing price 92." If you bought that bond at today's closing price, what would be your coupon yield? What would be your current yield? What would be your yield to maturity if you held the bond until maturity? (Assume that the maturity date of the bond is on the anniversary of the date you buy the bond.)

3. You're comparing two money market mutual funds. One has a load charge of 8½ percent plus annual fees totaling 3/4 percent of the value of your account. The other has a load charge of 4 percent, plus annual fees totaling 1½ percent of the value of your account. Assume you have $10,000 to invest and that both funds will grow by 7 percent per year. Where will you stand with each fund after one year? Three years? Five years?

FOR BETTER OR FOR WORSE

Things beyond our control often impact our personal and financial well-being, for better or for worse. Some are more predictable than others. How would you be affected if the following real-life phenomena happened? Could you have seen it coming? What steps could you have taken to minimize damage or maximize advantage? The better able you are to anticipate and recognize these forces, the better equipped you are to deal with them.

1. You want total complete safety for your retirement kitty, so you put it all into long-term government bonds. Five years later something urgent comes along, and you need to cash in those bonds. In the interim, interest rates have gone up, so if you cash in the bonds you'll have a loss of more than 20 percent.

2. You've invested a lot of money in a top-rated corporate bond, and you rest easy knowing that your income from it will be steady and reliable. One day you see that the value of the bond has fallen considerably. On checking, you find the rating on the bond had been dropped from AA to C.

3. You shop around for the highest yielding one-year CD. A year later you are happy to let the CD renew for another year, until you learn that the rate has fallen by two percentage points.

15

Making Your Money Grow: The Stock Market

If stockbrokers are so smart, where are all their customers' yachts?

Anonymous

This chapter continues our exploration of ways you can make your money grow—we hope. The stock market involves aspects of risk not found in money market investments. The nature of those risks is not always understood by would-be investors/speculators. If the risks aren't understood, serious damage can be done to your financial well-being. To help you understand and evaluate those risks, we'll examine:

- What makes the stock market tick
- How to understand the language and the numbers of the stock market
- What motivates various kinds of people to put their money to work in the stock market, the better to help you identify and understand your own motivations
- Which specific techniques you can use within the arena of the stock market
- How to evaluate the professional help available to you through stockbrokers

A PERSPECTIVE

From 1982 until late 1987, the stock market enjoyed one of the longest and most powerful run-ups in its history. For six years, nothing seemed to be able to dampen the enthusiasm of stock market players. Speculative fever ran amok, not just in the United States but in most of the other major stock exchanges around the world. Then, on October 19, 1987, the earth shook under Wall Street. The Dow Jones Industrial Average plummeted 508 points, its worst single day up to that point. It was the unthinkable, the incredible, the impossible, all rolled into one. In the space of just six and one-half hours, roughly one-half trillion dollars' worth of what could have been spendable wealth disappeared. That market crash, and its long-term after-effects, served as a grim, but real and healthy, reminder that speculation has its comeuppance.

To anyone who might think that that was a one-time-only phenomenon, another quake rocked Wall Street almost ten years to the day later. On October 26, 1997, the Dow Jones Industrial Average plummeted nearly 530 points. This wasn't as drastic a drop percentage-wise as the one in 1987 because the DJIA was much higher in 1997 than it had been 10 years earlier. But it could foreshadow even further turbulence for a gravity-defying stock market throughout the late 1900s. (Superstitious investors might want to be wary come October 2007.)

This chapter is a primer on how the stock market functions. It's not intended to predict the future. But there certainly is a new dimension in the stock market's future: As with earthquakes, until one *does* happen, you can always choose to believe that one might *never* occur. Once an earthquake *does* occur, it becomes etched in your brain permanently. From that moment on, you always know that it can occur *again*. Thus it is with the stock market: until a crash occurs, you can always pretend to believe that one might never occur. But once it has occurred, there's no denying that the "impossible" can happen again. Bear this in mind as you consider the basic functions of the stock market as outlined in the balance of this chapter.

STOCK OWNERSHIP AS A FORM OF INVESTING

In the previous chapter on money market investing, we explored the possibilities of creating future wealth by "lending" your money to another entity and receiving in turn a promise to pay a fee (interest) for the use of your money, plus the promise to return it at an agreed-on time. These promises are legally binding obligations of the debtor.

Stock ownership as a form of investment is quite different. With stock ownership, investors become part owners of a business enterprise and have no promise (legal or otherwise) that they will receive any fee for the use of their money or that anyone will be obliged to pay them any or all of their money back at any future time.

Lending versus Buying, Debt versus Equity

What's the difference between lending our money to a business (investing in a corporate bond) and buying a portion of ownership in the business (buying stock)? Businesses often need money to develop new products, expand their facilities, buy new equipment, modernize, and pay for other job-creating activities. Some of the money needed may come from the profits the business generates, but this isn't always enough. In order to acquire large sums of money relatively quickly, a business will either borrow from investors (issue corporate bonds) or will sell a portion of itself to investors (issue stock). The former route is frequently referred to as the debt market, and the latter as the equity market.

Regarding its debt, the company has a legal obligation to pay interest to the investors and to return the principal sum at the agreed-on time. With equity, or stock, the company has no such legal obligation. *If* profits are in fact generated, the company *may* distribute a portion of the profits to the stockholders. The company is under no obligation to buy the stock back from a stockholder. If stockholders want to sell their stock, they hope to find buyers willing to pay an attractive price.

The important priority to note in comparing debt with stock ownership is that debt service (interest) *must* be paid *before* profits are tallied. Profits are the dollars left over after the business has paid all its obligations, among which are the payments due on its debts.

The same holds true when a business is terminated, either voluntarily or otherwise. In such a procedure, commonly called a *liquidation,* everything the company owns is converted into cash. Out of that pool of cash, all the company's debts are paid, including any bonds that may be outstanding. What's left over is split up between the stockholders. In other words, creditors have priority over stockholders in liquidation as well as in the day-to-day operation of a business.

The profitability of any kind of business venture depends on a great many factors, including the management of the business, the nature of the competition, overall ups and downs in the nation's economy as well as in the particular industry, and the totally unpredictable quirks and whims of the investing public. It's this last element—the whims and quirks of the investing public—that makes the stock market an unending series of dilemmas. In the stock market, you are not just betting on how profitably the company can perform; you are also betting on how *other* people think the company might perform.

Primary versus Secondary Market

Distinction should be made between the primary, or new issues, market and the secondary market. The primary market is that aspect of stock trading in which companies raise money from the investing public. Once the money has been raised and shares of ownership in the companies have been issued to the investors, the stock is traded in the secondary market. Only a tiny percentage of all stock transactions are primary market transactions; the vast majority are on the secondary market. New issues are called *initial pubic offerings,* or I.P.O.s. They are often extremely speculative.

The primary market serves a critically important purpose in the economy of the nation: it provides ready access for companies to raise money for expansion, research, and other worthwhile purposes. The secondary market is often looked on as little more than a gambling casino. There is, however, an important purpose for the secondary market: without the secondary market, the primary market could not exist. Businesses could not raise money by selling stock if investors did not know they could readily sell their stock at a fair price. Thus, despite the often speculative aspect of the secondary market, our economy would flounder without it.

Possibilities versus Probabilities

Virtually every transaction in the stock market, every purchase, and every sale of every share, is essentially a disagreement. Sellers want to get out because they don't think the stock offers them satisfactory income or potential any longer. Buyers want to get in because they think the stock *does* offer satisfactory income or profit potential. In other words, the two parties disagree about the potential of the stock.

The stock market offers a vast spectrum of possibilities. The challenge is to find that small cluster of possibilities that can help achieve your stated objectives.

In your own life, you have a spectrum of future needs and desires: some probable and some possible. It's *probable* that you're going to retire someday and will need adequate money to live on. It's *possible* that someday you might be in a position to enjoy a trip around the world. Goals that are probable or fixed or certain need appropriate techniques if they are to be achieved. Those techniques tend to fall into the fixed income investment spectrum. You can't afford to take chances that you will or will not achieve those fixed and necessary goals. You have to be certain, or at least as certain as you can be, that they will be reached.

Exercise 15.1

Other goals that are less certain may be appropriately sought by the *less certain* investment techniques, principally the stock market, *but not until after you have established a disciplined program that you feel confident will put you on the path to achieving your fixed goals.*

In other words, get a reasonable program under way that will take you to your fixed destinations. If you still have funds available to invest after you've put enough away toward those top priorities, you may want to consider the more speculative techniques to help you achieve lower priority goals—goals that if not achieved will not cause you real suffering.

For a more vivid comparison of the difference between fixed income investing and "ownership" investing, let's look at the following scale, which represents the likelihood of achieving stated objectives. The *objective:* to put away X dollars today and know that you will have Y dollars at some future date.

1	Almost totally certain
2	Fairly certain
3	Highly probable
4	Probable
5	Highly possible
6	Possible
7	Relatively uncertain
8	Totally uncertain

The better-quality ranges of the fixed income types of investment fall into the top half of the scale, from 1 to 4. The better-quality range of stock falls in the middle, from 3 to 6. The majority of investments in the stock market fall in the 4–7 range, and a considerable number are in the 6–8 range.

For the balance of this chapter, we'll examine in greater detail some of the inner workings of the stock market. In no way should any of the discussion be construed as recommendations to buy, sell, or hold any types of securities; the purpose is to help you determine whether the stock market offers the opportunities that will help you meet your goals, to understand how the mechanism works, and to motivate you to do further independent research to find those specific areas that will provide you with the returns you're seeking.

Cautions

As you read and discuss the material on the stock market, bear in mind the following cautions:

- Aided by sophisticated computers, millions of work hours are spent every day studying every movement, jiggle, and quiver of the stock market. Yet no one can predict with any degree of certainty what direction the market as a whole, or any individual stock, is liable to take even a minute or two from now.
- There have probably been more statistics compiled on the stock market, and more books written about it, than any other phenomenon on earth. Yet it continues to be one of the most confusing, mystifying, and frustrating subjects in our experience.

- The stock market touches our day-to-day lives in more ways than we can imagine, yet we are powerless to control it in even the slightest way. Even though you may never have had anything directly to do with the market and don't intend ever to have anything to do with it, it can still affect you. If the company that employs you is traded on the stock market, swings in the value of the stock can affect the future profitability of the company and possibly the future of your job. If your employer or boss is a stock market trader, his or her success or failure in the market on a day-to-day basis can affect his or her personality and attitude, which in turn can affect yours. If your pension fund or profit-sharing fund has money invested in the stock market, the investment expertise of those who manage those funds can have a profound bearing on your future.

- There is no person, no book, no system, no computer, that can assure you of making money in the stock market. The stock market can play an important function as an integral part of establishing your future security. But unless you approach it in the proper frame of mind, with the proper expertise, and with the proper degree of skepticism, its traps and pitfalls can play havoc with your aspirations.

How a Business Operates

A brief look at how a corporation functions will assist you in understanding the workings of the stock market.

A corporation is a legal entity in its own right. Each separate state has its own laws governing how a corporation may be created and run. Like a person, a corporation can own, buy, or sell property; it can be taxed; it can sue and be sued; and it can conduct business.

A corporation is owned by its stockholders. The stockholders determine what they wish their corporation to do. But it is cumbersome for the stockholders to meet and consult over every item of corporate business. Thus, the stockholders elect representatives who will act on their behalf in setting basic policy for the corporation. This group of representatives is referred to as the *directors*. The chairman of the board of directors controls the flow of the board's meetings, and as such can be the single-most powerful person in the corporation.

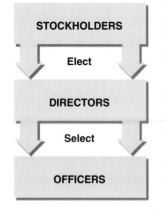

In turn, the directors select individuals to carry out the day-to-day operations of the business. These people are called the *officers* of the corporation. The chief officer of a corporation is usually called the president or chief executive officer (CEO). Answering directly to the president may be an array of vice presidents, each with their own areas of tasks, obligations, and responsibilities. Other officers of the corporation commonly include the treasurer, the secretary, and the comptroller, and each of these may have an additional hierarchy of assistants.

The stockholders generally meet once each year, at which time they are informed of the progress and potential of the corporation. It's at the annual meeting that the stockholders elect the directors, who in turn select the officers. Stockholders who are unable to attend this annual meeting can send proxies, authorizations on which they indicate their selection of directors and their choices on issues on which they have been asked to vote.

It is the rule rather than the exception in most large corporations that the stockholders comply with the recommendations of the board of directors. In recent years the annual meetings of many major corporations have been enlivened by sharp discussions between ownership and management regarding corporate responsibility in the fields of discrimination, pollution, and political practices. As a result, many corporations have adopted policies in keeping with stockholders' wishes regarding these highly visible public issues.

HOW THE STOCK MARKETS OPERATE

An individual's share of ownership in a corporation is represented by the stock certificate, which stipulates how many shares the individual owns. The value of each share is determined by a number of factors: profitability of the company, future potential for the company, amount of dividends the company is paying, and, broadly, what the public at large thinks the stock is worth. Stockholders wishing to sell their stock must find buyers willing to pay the asking price. Investors wishing to buy stock must find willing sellers. In small local corporations, word of mouth may be all that's needed to find the respective buyer or seller. But with large corporations, particularly those with millions of shares outstanding, this would be impractical. If would-be investors in stocks did not feel confident that they could sell their shares quickly and efficiently, they would probably be discouraged from making investments in the first place.

Thus, throughout the nation and the world, exchanges long ago came into being to provide a ready marketplace for both buyers and and sellers. The most familiar is the New York Stock Exchange, located in lower Manhattan, in an area commonly referred to as Wall Street. Other major exchanges include the Nasdaq, the American Stock Exchange, and the Pacific Stock Exchange.

Exercise 15.2

The stock exchanges are basically a clearing house where buyers and sellers try to get the best buying or selling price. An investor who wishes to buy or sell stock places an order with a local stockbroker who works for a firm that owns a *seat* on an exchange. The order is relayed from the local broker's office to the firm's facilities on the floor of the exchange. In some cases, the brokerage firm may fill the order itself. In other cases, the order may be referred to a specialist on the floor of the exchange. Each individual stock traded on any given exchange is represented by a specialist, whose job it is to match buy and sell orders and to keep an orderly marketplace for the stock. In order to do so, specialists may be required actually to buy or sell stocks from their own account.

When the order is filled, word is relayed back to the local brokerage firm, which informs the customer of the results. Written confirmation of the transaction follows shortly thereafter.

The Prospectus

Exercise 15.3

Before a stock can be publicly traded on an exchange, it must comply with certain governmental regulations. If a stock is to be sold only to the residents of the specific state in which the company is located, the company must comply with local state regulations. If it is to be traded nationally, it must comply with requirements of the federal agency that oversees such matters, the Securities and Exchange Commission (SEC).

Federal regulations require that a company disclose a variety of facts relating to its operation, including the identity and experience of its management, its debts, its legal affairs, its overall financial status, and the potential risks an investor might face in investing in the company. All this information—usually spelled out at great length in cumbersome legal jargon—is contained in a document called the prospectus.

A prospectus is required when a company initially sells its stock, or when it issues subsequent securities, including stocks or bonds. Once the initial prospectus has been issued, a company need not issue subsequent ones unless it offers additional securities at a later date. Thus, while the prospectus is an important tool for the investor, if it is substantially out of date (as most are), its value is diminished. Yet it still serves as important background material and should not be ignored.

Corporations do issue annual reports for the stockholders and for the SEC that contain more up-to-date information than the prospectus. A would-be investor should examine the annual reports, and it would be wise to compare these reports with the original prospectus, if for no other reason than to determine how well the company has met its originally stated objectives.

Mutual funds also must issue a prospectus when they seek investment dollars from the public. The existence of a prospectus for either a mutual fund or a stock can mislead an investor into thinking that the government has somehow given its blessings to the validity and value of the given investment. Nothing could be farther from the truth. On the front cover of each prospectus is this often overlooked statement:

> **These securities have not been approved or disapproved by the Securities and Exchange Commission, nor has the Commission passed on the accuracy or adequacy of this prospectus. Any representation to the contrary is a criminal offense.**

That statement means exactly what it says: The government does not in any way stand behind any of the statements made in the prospectus. If the prospectus is misleading or inaccurate, the corporation or mutual fund can be subject to criminal prosecution. The prudent investor will make wise use of the prospectus but will not be misled by it or by any sales pitch that implies governmental approval when none indeed exists.

Investors' Insurance

Exercise 15.4

The government does offer one measure of protection to investors, through the Security Investors Protection Corporation (SIPC).

When scores of banks folded as a result of the Great Depression in the 1930s, the government acted to create an insurance program that would prevent a recurrence of such a disaster. The Federal Deposit Insurance Corporation came into being to insure bank depositors against the institution's failure. But, until 1970, there was no comparable protection for investors who entrusted their funds to stock brokerage firms. A severe stock market collapse in 1969–1970 caused a number of brokerage firms to fail. Many more, on the brink of failure, were absorbed by larger and healthier firms. As a result of the near panic that ensued, the government, in conjunction with the securities industry, took steps to create the SIPC, which would insure investors' accounts for the value of any securities or funds held by their brokerage firm in the event of a failure of such a firm. Most major firms currently provide this protection to their customers, but some smaller firms do not. (*Note:* The insurance does *not* protect against the value of any stock going down.)

Keeping the Records

The shares of most major corporations are traded by the hundreds or thousands every business day. It's not uncommon for more than 500 million shares of stock to change hands in a single day on the New York Stock Exchange alone. This total volume is made up of many thousands of individual transactions, representing handfuls or major blocks of shares. Smaller corporations whose shares are seldom traded may hire clerical workers to do the bookwork involved in amending the list of stockholders. But most major corporations hire transfer agents to take care of this burdensome task. Transfer agents are usually affiliated with major banks.

When you buy or sell shares of a stock, the transfer agent is notified accordingly, and your name is either placed on, or removed from, the list of stockholders of that corporation. As dividends become payable, the transfer agent sees to it that the dividend is transmitted to you or to your account with the stockbroker.

When you buy stock, you have the choice of obtaining the certificate registered in your own name (or in the name of whatever parties you choose as owners, such as husband and wife jointly) or of having the broker retain custody of the stock. In the latter case, the stock would be listed in <u>street name</u>—technically, it is in the broker's name and possession, but the broker is holding it for your account. Some investors prefer to have the certificate in their own hands, aware that they should make proper safekeeping arrangements for it. Other investors prefer the convenience of having it remain in the broker's custody, in which case the investor receives a monthly statement from the broker indicating the status of the account and detailing the securities being held in the investor's name.

Each buy and sell transaction is followed up by a written <u>confirmation</u> that indicates the date of the transaction, the price for which the security was bought or sold, the amount of the broker's commission and any appropriate taxes, and the net amount due to the broker or to the investor from the broker. These confirmation slips should be retained by the investor; they contain information helpful in determining future gains or losses on the stock. The confirmation slips also indicate the settlement date, which is the day by which payment must be made and the stock delivered.

Executing an Order

Once you have opened an account with a broker by signing the necessary papers, you can execute orders, that is, instruct your broker to buy or sell on your behalf. Most orders to buy and sell stock are handled by telephone. It's important, therefore, to make certain that your broker has followed your instructions explicitly, particularly concerning the number of shares you're selling or buying, the price at which you wish to buy or sell, and the specific type of order you're giving. These specifics should be repeated between you and the broker, and you should make immediate written note of them.

Orders to buy or sell stock can take many different forms. Here are the major types.

Market Orders

What is a <u>market order</u>? If you instruct your broker to buy or sell "at the market," the broker will then buy or sell your shares at whatever the going market price is, trying, of course, to get the best possible price, though it may not be exactly what you had in mind. For example, XYZ is currently selling at $50 per share, and you instruct your broker to buy 100 shares "at the market." At the moment your order reaches the floor, the best possible price for those shares may have risen to $51 per share. That's what you would end up paying. On the other hand, if you instruct your broker to sell 100 shares "at the market," the best possible price available when your order reaches the floor might be $49, and that's what you'll get. It could also work the other way around. You might be able to buy at a lower price than you had anticipated or sell at a higher price.

Limit Orders

A <u>limit order</u> sets a maximum or minimum price on the sale or purchase of shares. For example, you purchased 100 shares of XYZ at $50 per share. You have made up your mind that if it reaches $55 per share, you want to sell and take your profits. You can place a limit order at $55 per share, and that order will be executed only when the stock can be sold at $55 per share. If the stock never reaches that level, the limit order will never be executed. If you want to buy stock, a limit order can also be used. Say you wish to buy 100 shares of XYZ if the price drops to $45 per share. You place a limit order with your broker, and if and when XYZ hits $45 per share, your order will be executed. If the stock never does hit that price, your order won't be executed.

Time Orders

A <u>time order</u> can be attached to a limit order. It adds a time deadline to the limit order. A time order may be for a day, or for any number of days. One common type of time order is called a *good this week* (GTW) order. This order will remain in effect until the end of the calendar week. Example: You would like to buy 100 shares of XYZ for $45 per share, but only if XYZ hits $45 per share before the end of this week. You thus instruct your broker to enter a combined limit order and time order. If XYZ does hit $45 per share before the end of the week, your order will be executed. If not, then you will not have bought the stock. Another form of time order is called the *open order,* or *good till canceled* (GTC) order. It is a standing order to buy or sell at a fixed price until you, the investor, cancel the order or until it is executed at that price.

Fill or Kill Orders

A <u>fill or kill order</u> is an order to buy or sell at a fixed price immediately. Example:You wish to sell 100 shares of XYZ at $55 per share. With a fill or kill order, if your broker cannot execute immediately for al the shares you wish to buy or sell at that price, the order will be canceled.

WHO INVESTS IN THE STOCK MARKET, AND WHAT ARE THEY SEEKING?

The vast diversity of stock market investors can be broken down into three broad categories: by objective, by size, and by type.

Investors by Objective

What are investors seeking when they buy stocks? It could be any one, or a combination, of the following: short-term growth, long-term growth, income, and "no foggy idea." Let's look at each in turn.

Short-term Growth

This objective might be best described as "out to make a fast buck." If this is your objective, you might be as well served by your nearest racetrack or gambling casino as by the stock market. Humorist Will Rogers had some good advice for those who dive into the stock market looking for the fast buck: "It's easy to be successful in the stock market. You just buy stock, and when it goes up, you sell it. And if it don't go up, don't buy it."

Long-term Growth

This more prudent objective is more likely to reward the patient investor who has done the necessary homework. Investors whose objectives are long-term growth analyze industries and specific companies whose long-term future looks healthy and profitable and select investments accordingly. If such investors select wisely and luckily and are willing to wait long enough, they may well realize their objectives.

Income

Many investors get involved in the stock market with the primary objective of receiving income in the form of dividends. Although the dividends they earn may not be as rewarding as what they could have earned in money market investments, there is also the secondary hope that the stocks will increase in value over a period of time.

Investors whose objectives are balanced between growth and income are perhaps the ones who approach the market most intelligently. They are the investors who set targets for upside potential and downside potential. They might, for example, define their objective as a 15 percent annual return (after brokerage commissions) on investment—perhaps 7 percent might come through receipt of dividends and the other 8 percent through increase in the value of shares. Say that XYZ Company is selling at $50 per share and is paying $3.50 per share divided per year. That's equal to a 7 percent return in the form of dividends. If, during an investor's first year of ownership of XYZ, the price moves from $50 to $54 per share—an 8 percent increase during the year—the investor has realized his or her 15 percent objective. By the same token, the investor would also set a downside limit. If XYZ drops to $45 per share, the investor would get out at that price and thus be sheltered from any further losses. There re no strict rules of thumb as to what a desirable balance is. Many of your objectives in this area must relate to what can assuredly be attained with the same investable dollars in the money market.

"No Foggy Idea"

This well may represent the majority of stock market investors. In short, they haven't the foggiest idea what their objectives are. They're not sure why they bought what they bought when they bought it. And they have no notion as to when or why they should sell. Their only hope for success in the market is good luck.

Investors by Size

Individual investors generally trade in small blocks of stock. Blocks of 100 shares are referred to as round lots; blocks of less than 100 shares are referred to as odd lots, which usually carry a slightly higher brokerage commission, called the *odd lot differential*.

The large investors, such as pension and profit-sharing funds, mutual funds, trust funds, large corporations, and insurance companies, often trade in very large blocks—many thousands of shares at a time. Large block trades can disrupt the normal flow of supply and demand of shares and can thus cause considerable fluctuations in the price of a given stock at the time such an order to buy or sell is placed.

Sharp fluctuation can also be caused by extremely sophisticated computer programs that investors use to tell them when to buy or sell shares of stock. This is known as *program trading*. It kicks in when certain criteria are met by a given stock and/or market conditions in general and/or a variety of specific technical indicators. Computers can react to these signals much more quickly than a human can, so a buy or sell order can easily catch mere mortals by surprise. There is no limit as to how much program trading can take place, and since this kind of electronically stimulated trading usually involves huge blocks of stock, it can have an extremely disruptive effect on the normal ebbs and flows of daily trading. All the more to muddle up anyone's attempts to analyze the stock market.

Investors by Type

The following are brief descriptions of eight broad categories of investors representing individuals or institutions. They are all in the market at the same time, all expressing a constant flow of opinions that may be in total accord or total discord with those of their colleagues. Let's take a closer look at the cast of characters.

Novices

Novices aren't really sure what they're doing. Their obvious motivation is to "make money," but they're not really certain how, or if, they will. If they have done any studying at all, it's probably been only superficial; probably they have become involved in the market because of the suggestion of someone else, and they're probably following the suggestion at its face value.

Insiders

There are three types of insiders: the way-insiders, the fringe-insiders, and the pretend-insiders. The way-insiders are people on intimate terms with the day-to-day operation of the corporation—officers, employees, directors or major stockholders. They are privy to information not yet available to the public that, when released to the public, can have a good or bad effect on the stock of the company. A way-insider may know, for example, that a potentially profitable deal is about to be completed or that a sharp loss is about to be announced. If the information is accurate and the announcement has the anticipated effect, the way-insider can reap a substantial profit, or avoid a sharp loss by selling out existing holdings.

Because of a business or personal relationship with a way-insider (such as being a stockbroker, lawyer, accountant, or supplier of the way-insider), the fringe-insider may have indirect and usually delayed access to the intimate information available to the way-insider. Perhaps the fringe-insider will get the information in time to benefit from it; perhaps not.

The pretend-insider is another step removed from the fringe-insider and is in the "friend of a friend" category. By the time the pretend-insider gets the information, the upswing or downswing may have long since occurred. Beware of pretend-insiders.

Trading on inside information is illegal. It's not supposed to happen, but it does, and the Securities and Exchange Commission admits that enforcement of their insider-information rules is extremely difficult. Even though certain insiders are required to report their buy and sell transactions, it is still very difficult to discover and prove wrongdoing. Illegal though it may be, and successful or unsuccessful though it may be, it does exert a distinct effect on specific stocks and, to a lesser extent, on the market as a whole.

Hunch Players

Often active seasoned veterans of the stock market, hunch players may be convinced that all the study in the world is for naught because the quirks and whims of fellow investors are imponderable and have a greater effect on the value of any given stock than the true value of the company itself. Hunch players listen avidly to tipsters. Much of their trading is based on gut reaction, a voice in the night, an omen.

Theory Traders

Theory traders base their transactions on specific theories that may be directly tied to something as tangible as governmental statistics or as intangible as international currency fluctuations. Theory traders can be very influential when their theories prove correct; however, they also have a way of disappearing temporarily when their theories prove incorrect. Many theory traders are often found reading stock market advisory newsletters, generally the wellspring of their information and decisions. Because they paid a steep price for these advisory letters, they assume the information has to be correct—otherwise it wouldn't be so expensive.

Sentimentalists

This well-intentioned group of investors place their money in stocks of companies that they work for or that are located in their hometowns. Sentimentality or loyalty will be their primary reason for investing. Emotionally, it's like rooting for the home team, but rationally this can amount to nothing more than total speculation.

Technical Analysts

Technical analysts (sometimes called *chartists*) are serious students of the stock market. Technical analysts closely follow and chart short-, medium-, and long-term trends in individual stocks, in groups of stocks, and in the market movement as a whole. They have come up with a dazzling array of indicators that supposedly give signals to buy and sell. There are market peaks and market troughs; there are bellwether stocks that purportedly lead the way to one direction or another; high ratios and low ratios; moving averages; overbought and oversold indexes; and charts that plot every conceivable squiggle a given stock may be subject to.

But, in spite of all the information available, the problem is that the meticulously plotted signals of the analysts are often invalidated by the actions of other traders who pay no attention to these signals. Furthermore, the analysts don't necessarily agree with each other as to which signal means what, and often come up with conflicting conclusions.

Fundamentalists

Fundamentalists are serious investors who have done their homework and are willing to continue to do the necessary homework: Analyze profit-and-loss statements, dividend-payment records, the amount a company has earned on its invested capital, profit margins, the ratio of a company's assets to its liabilities and debts, and the trends in the company's overall performance over recent years, as well as the health and growth trends of the industry as it relates to the economy as a whole. Fundamentalists have learned how to evaluate the financial statements of the companies they are interested in, and how to seek out the basic value of each company. Fundamentalists are not necessarily frequent traders; they are willing to wait years for the value of a stock to prove itself in terms of price appreciation and dividend payments. They realize that market decisions are subject to the actions of all the other types of investors but feel confident that their prudent and rational analysis of the facts at hand will survive the whims and flutters caused by other types of investors.

Fundamentalists know that there's no such thing as a sure thing in the stock market but they are willing to take the time necessary to find the best things available.

Fundamentalists shun advice from tipsters, don't rely on hunches, aren't seduced by sentimentality, and won't subscribe to any theories not borne out by accurate financial analysis of the specific companies of interest.

Prudent Investors

Prudent investors are the fundamentalists-plus. Plus what? Perhaps a bit of technical analyst, for many of the analytical devices can be helpful in the fundamentalist approach. Perhaps also a bit of the hunch player, for even the most prudent investor occasionally needs the guts that is second nature to the hunch player to survive unexpected turns for the worse. Prudent investors also have most of the following attributes.

- Prudent investors have a clear understanding of their current financial situation and overall investment objectives. They convey this understanding to their stockbroker and make a joint commitment with the broker to stick with the stated objectives. If prudent investors want the benefit of the broker's expertise, they must give the broker proper instructions. Without that basic understanding between investor and broker, both may be groping in the dark. Periodically, with a broker's aid, prudent investors review their objectives and determine whether they are still reasonable in view of the unpredictable nature of the stock market.

- Prudent investors clearly define their own roles. Are they investors or traders? Investors, broadly speaking, are putting their money to work and are willing to let it do the job over the needed span of time. Traders are working their money and must have the know-how to cope with weekly, daily, and hourly fluctuations and trends. Prudent investors can be a little bit of both, but to perform this balancing act, they must keep their more prudent investment funds and more speculative trading funds strictly segregated. When the two start to mingle, objectives can swiftly get derailed.

- Prudent investors do their homework. Investment decisions are ultimately the investor's, not the broker's. There are thousands of securities, no two alike, and no human being can keep track of the fine points of more than a few dozen at a time. A broker can give the investors research tools and an opinion, but investors must reach their own conclusions. And sound conclusions require work.

- Prudent investors avoid the quirk of human nature that drives people to want to recover losses as quickly as they have occurred. This can lead an investor out of one speculative situation into another.

- Prudent investors learn from past mistakes. Why did they buy or sell too soon or too late? Did they listen to a tip? Did they play a hunch? Did they panic? The ability to recognize one's own mistakes and benefit from them is a rare quality, one worth cultivating by the prudent investor who doesn't already possess it.

- When prudent investors invest in a stock, they determine, at that time, when they will be likely to sell. They set limits for themselves and stick to them. They have determined how great a loss they are willing to take in order to acquire a certain gain. They are well acquainted with that old maxim of the investment community: "Take your profits when you can, and cut your losses when you can."

- Prudent investors are well aware of the value of a good night's sleep. Or, for that matter, of a good day's work. Distractions and frustrations caused by involvement in the stock market can detract from one's productivity and pleasures.

- Prudent investors do not waste time or money chasing after systems that purport to "beat the market." There are none. And there aren't any books, brokers, newsletters, analysts, chartists, economists, or tipsters who know anything more about where the market is headed than you do. If there were, we'd have heard about them long ago.

STRATEGIES FOR SUCCESS

Put Your Money Where Your Knowledge Is

You want to take a fling in the stock market, but you don't know where to begin in choosing stocks. How about picking companies that specialize in an area of your own knowledge? Your field is chemistry—why not choose chemical company stocks? Your hobby is photography—consider photographic companies. You have a good background in Asian matters—maybe you should invest in a mutual fund that specializes in Asian companies. That's the basic idea: Put your money where your knowledge is. As somewhat of a specialist, you're better equipped to evaluate the potential of a company, or of a group of companies, that deal in a subject you're familiar with. It can make sense, can't it? At least you have a better chance of success than you might if you knew nothing at all about the company whose stock you chose to buy.

BASIC STOCK MARKET INFORMATION

The daily trading activity of all the major stock exchanges is contained in alphabetical order in fairly complete detail in *The Wall Street Journal* each day.

Price Quotations

Exercise 15.5

Many local daily newspapers also carry extensive listings, though many are abbreviated from the full listings used in *The Wall Street Journal*.

Figure 15–1 shows a sample New York Stock Exchange listing. Let's examine the details more closely. The listing is "AbtLab," which stands for Abbott Laboratories, a major manufacturer of various health-care products. (All companies traded on the exchange carry an abbreviation or trading symbol. Abbott's is ABT.)

- **52 Weeks High/Low**   This listing indicates that during the previous fifty-two weeks, Abbott Laboratories sold at a high of 68 ($68) per share and a low of 42.2 ($42.20) per share. The purpose of the high/low listings is to give you some idea as to the stock's recent trading history. This recent trading range may reflect the likely pattern of the next few months. But beyond that short-term outlook the past history offers no assurances as to the price of the stock over the longer haul.

- **Dividend (Div.)**   The <u>dividend</u> column indicates the rate of dividend paid based on the most recent quarterly dividend. It is not necessarily an indication of dividends that will be paid in the future. Abbott Laboratories paid a dividend in the prior year of 1.08, that is, $1.08 per share. An investor would have to dig more deeply to determine the likelihood of any company's continuing its indicated rate of dividend for the near future.

- **Yield % (Yld)**   This listing indicates the yield, in percentage terms, that you would receive if you bought the stock at its current price (64) and received the dividend of $1.08; $1.08 is roughly 1.7 percent of $64.

52 weeks		Stock	Div.	Yld. %	P.E. Ratio	Sales 100s	High	Low	Close	Net Chg.
High	Low									
68	42.2	AbtLab ABT	1.08	1.7	2.5	12209	65	63	64	+1

FIGURE 15–1   Sample newspaper listing of stock quotation

Convertible Preferred

Like convertible bonds, noted in chapter 14, convertible preferred stock may be converted into shares of the company's common stock at an agreed-on ratio. And, as with convertible bonds, the price of convertible preferred stock tends to fluctuate in tandem with the common stock, but the fluctuations are generally not as great as with the common stock. Thus, convertible preferreds are considered to offer attractive advantages: a relatively high rate of return on one's investment (from the dividends paid on the preferred stock); a chance to convert into the common stock if the common stock starts to rise rapidly; and a downside cushion of protection since the preferred stock will tend not to drop as rapidly or as deeply as the common stock might if prices begin to fall.

Convertibles are a sophisticated area of investing that require further study. Ample literature is available from most brokerage firms.

Warrants

On occasion, when a company is issuing bonds or new shares of stock, it may offer warrants to purchasers as an extra inducement to get them to invest. The warrant entitles them to purchase shares of common stock at a fixed price for a set period of time. In other words, if the common stock is selling at $20 per share at the time the bonds or new shares are issued, the warrant might entitle the holder to acquire a share of common stock at $25. The issuing company will fix the life of the warrant, which may be a few months or a number of years.

Warrants are totally speculative. Owners of warrants have no ownership in the corporation unless or until they exercise the warrants—that is, trade them in for the shares of stock to which they are entitled. Owners of warrants receive no dividends and have no voting rights in the company.

XYZ has issued warrants to buy its stock at $25 a share. You like XYZ, but you don't have $2,500 with which to buy 100 shares. You watch XYZ stock move to $27 a share, and you're confident that it will climb to $35 a share within the next twelve months. You buy 100 warrants at $2 per share for a total investment of $200. As the stock of XYZ climbs, so will the value of the warrants. Essentially, for every $1 increase in the value of the stock itself, the warrants will also increase by $1. Thus, if XYZ does reach a higher level, such as $35 a share, the value of the warrant may have increased from your $2 buying price to $8. You will have reaped a gain on the stock without having had to purchase the stock itself. The warrants did the job for you. However, there is an ultimate danger with warrants: they expire at a designated time. Once they expire, they are worthless. If the stock doesn't rise as you had hoped it would, neither will the warrant. The stock you can keep owning forever. But the warrant becomes worthless at its expiration date. Trading in warrants is highly speculative. There are comparable opportunities in trading in stock options, which are explained in the next section.

Stock Option Trading

Trading in stock options is a sophisticated form of investing that can range from highly speculative to staunchly conservative. We will now examine the basic concepts of stock option trading, and readers who find the technique appealing will want to seek further information from stockbrokers about specific option-trading possibilities.

Placing a Bet

There are two main ways to gamble at the racetrack. First, you can buy a horse and enter it in races. If your horse wins, you receive the winner's purse. If the horse never wins, you can recoup some of your investment by selling it or using it for breeding purposes. In other words, even if your initial gamble never pays off (the horse never wins), the horse still has some residual value.

Second, you can place bets on other people's horses. The life of your bet will be approximately two minutes—the time it takes to run the race. If the horse you bet on wins, you win. If the horse you bet on loses, your betting ticket is instantly and permanently worthless. In short, there is no residual value on the bet.

The situation is very similar in the stock market: there are two basic ways you can gamble. First, you can buy stock and hope that it increases in value. If it does and you sell the stock, you have won. If the stock does not go up, there is still some residual value in the dividends you will receive and in the selling price you get for it at some later date.

Second, you can place a bet that the stock will increase in value. You can do this without actually having to buy the stock itself. You place your bet by buying what is known as an *option*. An option, in effect, is a bet on the stock. And like a bet on a horse, the option has a limited life, after which it will become worthless.

Option trading is to stock trading what horse betting is to horse owning. Let's take an oversimplified look at how it works.

Calls and Puts

The most common type of option trading is betting that a given stock will increase in value. Technically, this is known as a call option. It is also possible to bet that a stock will decrease in value. You can place such a bet by buying what is known as a put option. For purposes of this discussion and for the sake of clarity, we'll restrict the material to call options.

Buying Call Options

Table 15–4 is a simplified sample of a call option quotation in the newspaper.

This quotation refers to call option trading in the stock of the XYZ Company. As the columns on the far left indicate, the actual price per share of XYZ common stock closed the preceding day at $41 on the New York Stock Exchange. The rest of the quote illustrates nine potential "bets" that can be placed on the future of XYZ's stock.

Look at the bottom line under Strike Price—the entry is 45. Let's assume that we are now in late November. You have a hunch that XYZ will rise from its current level of $41 per share to $45 per share by next January. You'd like to bet on your hunch. You can do so by buying the stock itself, but buying 100 shares will cost you $4,100.

Or, you can buy a call option. A call option gives you the right to buy the stock at a given price (known as the *strike price*) by a certain date, which is usually the third Friday of the month indicated. The price you pay for a call option is known as the *premium*. As Table 15–4 indicates, you can buy a call option that gives you the right to purchase XYZ at $45 per share any time between now and the third Friday of next January for $2 per share. Contracts are sold in 100-share lots, so a 100-share option contract would cost you $200.

Your objective here is not necessarily to buy the stock (although you do have that right). What you are really hoping for is to sell the call option contract at a profit. As the stock moves up (or down) the value of the call option moves accordingly.

If you bought 100 shares of the stock for $4,100 and it moved up to $4,500 by January, you'd have reaped a profit of $400 (before commissions). If you bought a 100-share call option contract for $200 and XYZ moved to $45 per share by, say, December, the value of the option would have increased by $4 per share, or $400 for 100 shares, to roughly $600, and you'd have a $400 profit (again before commissions) on a bet of only $200.

TABLE 15–4   Call Option Trading: Sample Quotation

Stock	NY Close	Strike Price	Jan. Premium	Apr. Premium	July Premium
XYZ	41	35	7	8	9
XYZ	41	40	3½	4½	5
XYZ	41	45	2	3	4

But note this critical difference: If you had bought the stock and the price did *not* rise, you would *still own* the stock *indefinitely*, and you'd still be entitled to any dividends the stock paid. However, with the option, if the bet doesn't work out, the option expires at the established date and you own nothing after that time.

Let's say you weren't quite as optimistic about XYZ going to $45 per share by January, but you thought it might reach that level before the following April. In that case, you could buy an option for a premium of $3 per share, or $300 for a 100-share contract. If you wanted to have until July to see whether the price moved up, a 100-share contract would cost $400. The longer the life of the option, the higher the price. This is because you have more time for the stock to reach the desired level. In effect, you're paying an added premium for the extra time.

Buying call options is highly speculative. Once you've bought an option, you receive no dividends on your invested money and the clock is running against you: The option becomes valueless at the expiration date. It's like the betting ticket on the horse that didn't finish in the money.

Selling Call Options

Who do racetrack bettors buy their bets *from*? They buy them from the racetrack owners, who have very carefully calculated that they will keep a portion of every bet for their own overhead and profit (not to mention taxes). For every dollar that is bet, the racetrack may pay back only about 80 cents in winnings to the bettors. Over the days and months and years, the track knows that it can't lose. That's why it's better to own a racetrack than to bet at one. The same philosophy holds true with call option trading: it's better to sell call options than to buy them.

From whom do option buyers buy their contracts? They buy them from option *sellers*—people who already own the given shares of stock and who are willing to sell them to buyers at a specific price.

Referring back to the quotations, let's assume that you had purchased 100 shares of XYZ some time ago for $35 per share. You've been happy with the stock and with the dividends it has paid, yet you'd be willing to part with the stock if it hit $45 per share. That would mean a $10 per share profit to you.

The option exchanges offer you intriguing possibilities. As the quotations indicate, you, as the owner of XYZ, can sell someone else the right to buy your 100 shares any time between now and next January, and you'll receive a $200 premium in exchange. Or you can sell an April contract for $300 and a July contract for $400. If you sell a call option and it is never exercised, you get to keep the whole premium. You also get to keep any dividends that are paid on the stock during the life of the option. That's like the racetrack keeping a portion of each bet for its own purposes. If the option is exercised, you must give up your stock at the strike price—$45 per share in the current example. But you have expressed a willingness to do that—to take a $10 per share profit—as part of your overall investment philosophy. If the option is not exercised, you can sell yet another one and keep the premium. If the option is exercised and you give up the stock, you have the $4,500 to reinvest as you see fit. (None of these examples takes brokerage commissions into account.)

As this example indicates, selling call options can be a sound and secure way for owners of stocks to increase their return substantially without increasing their risk. As long as you are willing to let go of your stock at a fixed higher price than you paid for it, you literally have everything to gain and nothing to lose by selling call options on stocks you already own. If you plan to make new investments on stocks for the purpose of selling options against those stocks, you of course take on yourself the basic risk inherent in any stock investment: the potential fluctuations in value that could work for or against you. Since this discussion was intended as nothing more than a brief overview of option-trading possibilities, interested investors should seek further information on specific techniques from their stockbroker.

Rating the Stocks

Like bonds, stocks are ranked and rated by both Standard & Poor's and Moody's. The following excerpts from the Standard & Poor's explanation of their rating system not only is informational but also serves as a guide to the prudent investor in quest of the relative value of stocks within the broad selection available.

> *Earnings and dividends rankings for stocks: The relative "quality" of common stocks cannot be measured, as is the quality of bonds, in terms of the degree of protection for principal and dividends. Nevertheless, the investment process obviously involves the assessment of numerous factors—such as product and industry position, the multifaceted aspects of managerial capability, corporate financial policy and resources—that make some common stocks more highly esteemed than others.*
>
> *Earnings and dividends performance is the end result of the interplay of these factors, and thus over the long run the record of this performance has a considerable bearing on relative quality. Growth and stability of earnings and dividends are therefore the key elements of Standard & Poor's common stock rankings, which are designed to capsulize the nature of this record in a single symbol. The rankings, however, do not pretend to reflect all other factors, tangible and intangible, that also bear on stock quality.*

The Standard & Poor's rankings for common stocks are as follows:

A+	Highest
A	High
A−	Good
B+	Medium

B   Speculative

B−   Highly speculative

C   Marginal

D   In reorganization

Refer to the respective ratings themselves for more detail and information on this important aspect of evaluating one's investment alternatives.

Dividend Reinvestment Plans

Dividends are usually paid to stockholders quarterly. If you own 100 shares of XYZ and it is paying a dividend of $5 per share, you will receive a total of $500 in dividends during the year, in quarterly checks of $125. That money is yours to spend or to reinvest. But many investors get lazy about reinvesting their dividend earnings and spend the money on nonessentials. This can erode the potential size of their nest egg.

Exercise 15.9

Many companies offer an alternative to sending quarterly dividend checks. They offer automatic dividend reinvestment plans in which your dividend is used to purchase additional shares of stock in the company. If an investor wishes to acquire additional shares at no out-of-pocket cost the dividend reinvestment plan is an ideal way to proceed. There are some special advantages to the automatic dividend reinvestment plans, depending on the specific company. Brokerage commissions are very low or nonexistent. If your dividend check is not sufficient to buy a full share of stock, fractional shares can be purchased. And some companies even offer a discount on the purchase price as compared to the going market price.

Companies that offer automatic dividend reinvestment plans notify stockholders of the availability. To sign up, the investor merely fills out the form sent by the company. From that point on, dividends are reinvested automatically, and customers receive a quarterly statement of the account. The company retains the actual additional shares purchased, and the investor can cash them in at any time by notifying the company.

Here is how a dividend reinvestment plan can work. You own 100 shares of XYZ with a value of $50 per share and an annual dividend of $5 per share. Assume, for the sake of this illustration, that the price of the stock and the amount of the dividend do not vary over the years. As you can see (Table 15–5), in the first year, your 100 shares will earn $500 worth of dividends. Those dividends in turn will buy ten additional shares of stock, giving you a total of 110 shares going to work for you at the start of the second year. In the fourth year, you would have earned $665.50 in dividends on your original investment of $5,000. Your return has increased because you have more shares working for you earning dividends. The automatic dividend reinvestment plan does for your stockholding what compounding interest does for your money market investments.

TABLE 15–5   **Dividend Reinvestment Plan**

| | 100 Shares of XYZ, Value $50 per Share, Dividend $5 | | | |
Year	Shares Owned Start of Year	Dividend Earned	Buys This Many New Shares	This Many Total Shares by Year End
1	100	$500	10	110
2	110	550	11	121
3	121	605	12.1	133.1
4	133.1	665.50	13.31	146.41

Following is a brief list of some of the many hundreds of companies that have offered dividend reinvestment plans. Check with a stockbroker to determine the current status of available plans.

Allied Chemical	Exxon	PepsiCo
AT&T	General Electric	RCA
Bristol-Myers	General Motors	Sears
CBS, Inc.	Goodyear Tire	Texaco
DuPont (E.I.)	IBM	USX
Eastman Kodak	Mobil Corp.	Xerox

PRICE AND VALUE: WHAT CAN AFFECT THE WORTH OF A STOCK?

The distinction between *price* and *value* is as important in the stock market as in any other form of commerce. A patch of barren land in the middle of the desert may sell at a very low price, say, $10 an acre, because it seems to have no value. But if there is oil hiding under that patch of land, the *value* can be astronomically high, even though the price was very low.

On the other hand, that same barren patch may have absolutely no value—no oil or anything else hidden beneath it. But a fast-talking pitchman can sell the land to a gullible investor as the site of a future oil well. In that case, the price may be astronomically high in comparison with the value.

Whenever we spend money we try to make sure that we're getting good value for it; that value and price are compatible.

In the stock market, we have to maintain the same vigil, for the price and value of a stock can very easily take off in opposite directions. We might speculate on a stock with little intrinsic value, but, because of a speculative fever, the price of the stock may jump and reap a bonanza. Or we may invest in a stock with sturdy and dependable values only to find that a reverse form of speculation has condemned the stock to a severe plunge, and our money with it.

Many factors can have a direct effect on the *value* of a given stock as well as on the *price.*

Value

The underlying value of a stock is related to the profitability of the company in selling its product and services to its customers. The essential factors involved are the expertise of management; the cost of its raw materials (which can be affected by weather conditions, labor costs, strikes, and delivery problems); its efficiency in producing its finished product from the raw materials (which can likewise be affected by the foregoing elements of labor, weather, and gremlins); and the efficiency with which it delivers the finished product to the market, at a price and in a package the public is willing to accept.

With a great many of our major companies now involved in global commerce, international factors must also be considered. These can include fluctuations in currencies between various nations, international politics, trade and tariff regulations, and the same unpredictability regarding weather and labor strife that we have in the United States, but compounded by distance and difficulty in communicating.

Price

Following are some of the important elements that, although they do not affect the underlying *value* of the company, can have a distinct bearing on the *price* of the stock.

- When a new issue of stock is being offered to the public, the salesmanship of the brokerage firm can have a bearing on the price of the stock. Persuasive salespersons can boost the price of new issues far beyond the true value of the stock. If a new stock is issued when the market is not receptive, even the best salesperson may not be able to prevent a sharp downturn in the value of the stock.

- The general health and outlook of the national economy can give a boost to the market as a whole, and sometimes to specific stocks, or it can have a depressing effect if the news is bad.

- Financial analysts periodically examine major listed companies to try to determine the true valuation of the company. Optimistic reports can have a positive effect on the price of a stock, and pessimistic ones can have a depressing effect. Minor errors or misstatements in these reports can also have a dramatic effect on the price of the stock.

- A large investor may be persuaded to make a substantial investment in a company. A major investment could inspire optimism in other investors. On the other hand, if a major investor pulls out of a situation, for whatever reason, this could result in pessimism. Either action can affect the price, at least for the short term.

- One of the great imponderables is competition. The threat of formidable competition can have a depressing effect on the stock of a given company; the fading of competition can have a buoyant effect.

- Merger mania can have a powerful effect on the prices of many stocks. XYZ, an electronics firm, announces that it plans to buy, or merge with, PDQ, a telecommunications firm. This signals that PDQ might be up for grabs—*in play* is the term Wall Streeters use—and that a bidding war may take place for PDQ, boosting its shares' prices. If investors think that such a merger would be good or bad for either XYZ or PDQ, the prices thereof can rise or fall sharply as a result. A not-infrequent side effect to the XYZ–PDQ merger is that investors might sense that other telecommunications firms will also become buyout targets, and the stock prices of those companies can be affected accordingly.

- The rumor mill is a potentially troublesome source of information (or misinformation) that can affect the price of a stock. Wall Street is a tight little community, and word gets around fast. The day-to-day ebb and flow of rumors is perhaps one of the most prevalent forces in shaping the daily fluctuations of the market.

MUTUAL FUNDS IN THE STOCK MARKET

Stock market mutual funds pool the dollars of many small investors and place them in a broad portfolio of various stocks. Thousands of mutual funds offer a wide variety of choices to the investor. The objective of *performance* funds is to create as rapid a growth pattern as possible. These funds tend to be more speculative, taking chances on stocks that fund management sees as having a quick short-term potential rise. *Growth* funds are geared more to long-term steady growth, with less emphasis on dividend income. *Income* funds are designed to generate maximum current dividend income. *Growth/income funds* attempt to achieve a balance between growth and income factors.

The primary task of the investor seeking mutual funds as a vehicle is to determine whether the fund's objectives are in line with his or her own: short-term growth, long-term growth, income, or a combination of these. These objectives are spelled out in the fund prospectus, which should be read before any investment decision is made.

See the discussion of mutual funds in chapter 14, in which some of their major features are described in detail.

Once a group of appropriate funds is selected, investors must review the factors that can shape their investment future: costs involved in buying into the fund, annual charges for management or maintenance, the history of the fund in meeting its stated objectives, and so on.

Sales costs (loading fees) vary considerably with stock mutual funds, from as much as 8½ percent of the investment to as little as zero (no load). Similarly, annual or monthly maintenance and management fees vary considerably. In many cases, load funds (those with a sales charge) may charge smaller annual fees than no-load funds do, and proponents of the load funds claim that this difference over the long pull offsets the initial commission factor. There is heated debate over which is better— load funds or no-load funds. Proponents of each side can find specific groups of funds over specific periods of time in which their viewpoint prevailed. There is no simple answer. Like the stock market itself, there's an element of speculation even in choosing one *type* of fund over another.

Mutual funds are quoted daily in *The Wall Street Journal* and *Investor's Business Daily,* as well as in many local daily newspapers, weekly in *Barron's,* and annually in *Forbes* magazine. *Forbes* devotes an entire issue (usually in August) to the mutual fund industry. It rates the funds based on their performance in general up and down markets, giving a perceptive analysis of how various funds have performed during periods of boom and adversity. Other good rating services are "Investment Companies," by A. Weisenberger and Morningstar.

The daily listings of mutual funds quote the net asset value (NAV), the offering price, and the net asset value change. The net asset value of a mutual fund is the actual value per share. It's arrived at by dividing the total assets of the fund by the total number of shares outstanding. If a fund has $10 million in total assets and 1 million shares outstanding, the net asset value per share will be $10.

The offering price is the price an investor would have to pay for shares in a particular fund. If the fund is a no-load fund, "N.L." may be indicated in the offering price. If the fund is a load fund, the offering price will be higher than the net asset value price, with the difference being the commission charges. For example, a fund may show a net asset value (NAV) of $12.68, and an offering price of $13.86. The investor pays $13.86 for each share, currently carrying an actual market value of $12.68. The difference of $1.18 represents the loading charge; $1.18 is 8½ percent of $13.86. But as a percentage of your money that's actually going to work for you, it is 1.18/12.68, or 9.3 percent.

Another fund shows a net asset value of $7.70 and an offering price of $8.28. The difference is the loading charge, which is equal to 7 percent of the dollars invested. A no-load fund will sell at the same price per share as the net asset value.

Mutual Fund Advertising

There have been abusive advertising and selling techniques in the mutual fund industry. In order to try to discourage inflated and misleading claims as to how a fund has performed, the Securities and Exchange Commission, in mid-1994, approved Truth in Advertising regulations for the mutual fund industry. Now, if a fund's performance ranking is being touted, the ad must also describe all the criteria on which the ranking was based (type of fund, number of funds in that category, and the time period of the rankings). Some funds had not counted their load charges when illustrating their performance, and some had waived certain fees or deferred certain expenses during a ranking period. Those practices could make the fund's performance look much stronger than it really was. Those practices are now prohibited. But the burden is still on the investor to discern the facts. And the most overpowering fact is this: Past performance of any mutual fund gives *absolutely no assurance as to how that fund will perform in the future.*

Mutual Fund Mistakes

Here are the most common mistakes made by mutual fund investors.

1. The investor does not know how much of the investment will go toward the selling commission. Given too high a commission, the prudent investor might prefer to shop for a comparably performing fund that has a lower commission or no commission at all.

2. The investor does not have a clear idea as to how the money will be invested. In short, the investor has not examined the mutual fund's objectives and does not know clearly whether the given fund is speculative or conservative.

3. The investor does not keep close account of the monthly statement. Unaware from month to month of how the investment is performing, the investor may not know when it would be a good time to sell the fund or to buy more of it.

Mutual Fund "Families"

As noted in the previous chapter, most major mutual fund companies operate a number of individual funds. These funds run the gamut from the conservative U.S. government securities type to the highly speculative types that invest in options, commodities, and risky stocks. The attractive feature of the fund families is that you can switch from one type of fund to another simply, quickly, and at very little cost. Thus, in shopping for a mutual fund, you should shop for the families as well as for the specific funds within the families, and you should understand clearly the terms and conditions of switching funds before you make a commitment.

CHOOSING YOUR BROKER: A GUIDE THROUGH THE INVESTMENT JUNGLE

All these dilemmas are difficult enough for the advanced investor to cope with, let alone the novice. The right broker can be an invaluable aid in your evaluation of the various factors that face an investor. There is no assurance that the broker will know the truth or falsity of any given rumor or will be able to evaluate the long-term implications of a new competitor entering the market or an old one leaving it. And a broker can't spend as much time on your account as you might want. But a good broker, wisely chosen, can direct you to sources of information that can assist you in making a proper decision and can steer you away from unreliable sources.

Choose your broker carefully, remembering at all times that *you* must make the ultimate decisions based on the broker's recommendations and advice. A good broker can be a valuable ally in helping you meet your financial objectives, but only if you and the broker take the time to spell out those objectives clearly and only if the broker steadfastly assists you in meeting them.

Remember that a broker, with rare exception, earns a living by executing trades, getting a commission on each trade whether you are winning or losing. In other words, if your broker's going to eat, you've got to trade. If you invest a given sum of money in a given stock and instruct the broker to

STRATEGIES FOR SUCCESS

How to Resolve Problems with a Broker

The best way to solve a problem with a broker is to avoid getting into any difficulties at the outset. Every time you place an order you'll get a printed confirmation of the details. Be certain that the order has been placed precisely as you requested. If there are any mistakes on the confirmation, contact the broker immediately! If a broker seems to be uncooperative in resolving a dispute, go *in person* to explain the problem to the branch manager, and do so immediately! Send the details of your dispute in writing to the firm's Complaint Resolution Department (or office of similar name). If matters really get sticky, filing a written complaint with the National Association of Securities Dealers and/or the Securities and Exchange Commission and/or your state's office of securities regulation may be helpful. Most agreements with brokerage firms call for problem resolution by arbitration, if you haven't been able to nip the problem in the bud.

stash it away and forget about it for five or ten years and announce that that's all the market investing you plan to do, it's no wonder the broker doesn't regard you as a favored customer. Granted, the broker makes a commission on your initial investment, and if he or she is still around when you cash it in, the broker will make another commission on the sale. But meanwhile your money is sitting idle as far as your broker is concerned, with no further commissions in sight.

Naturally, brokers want their customers to do well. Each satisfied customer enhances the broker's professional image and is like a walking, talking billboard.

Many brokers do not keep close tabs on all their customers' various accounts and may neglect to advise them to buy or sell at an advantageous time. They may be too prone to listen to unfounded rumors and to pass them along to customers. They may not be making adequate use of research materials available through their firm and through other sources. They may be spending too much time hustling and too little time learning. On the other hand, a dedicated and conscientious broker can help you build and maintain an investment portfolio that can help you achieve short-term goals and long-term prosperity.

Consider these criteria in evaluating brokers: how closely their investment philosophy parallels yours; their reputation for integrity and hard work, which you can learn from other customers who have used their services; the amount and continuity of their schooling, scholarship, and research; their willingness to spend time helping you to set and achieve your goals; and, finally, chemistry—something that can't be described, shopped for, or cataloged. It's just got to be there and you'll know it when it is or isn't.

PERSONAL ACTION WORKSHEET

Playing the "Paper Game" with Mutual Funds

The "Paper Game" is a harmless—and free—way to acquaint yourself with the ups and downs, the trials and tribulations, of mutual funds. Play the Paper Game for six months or a year, and you'll have gained a good idea of whether it's the kind of place you want to send your money off to.

The rules of the Paper Game are very simple:

1. To simplify the Paper Game, we're just going to be concerned with the change in net asset value (NAV) of each fund. Select any five mutual funds whose shares are listed in your daily newspaper. Pick funds that you think have the best chance of appreciating in value (as opposed to generating income.) Make believe you buy 100 shares at today's price. We'll call this Group A.

2. Write the names of twenty-five other growth-type mutual funds on separate slips of paper. Pick five at random, and make believe you buy 100 shares of each at today's price. We'll call this Group B.

3. Use the tally sheet below to keep track of your purchases. You may sell Group A mutual funds whenever you like, but you must then pick a replacement. You can also sell Group B funds whenever you like, but must replace it by picking another one of the slips at random.

4. At the end of the designated time—you choose, six or twelve months—tally how you have done. Compare your Group A results with your Group B results. What has this exercise taught you about putting real money into mutual funds?

	Purchase Price and date*	Selling Price and date*	Gain or Loss in $	Gain or Loss Annual %**
Group A Funds				
1.				
2.				
3.				
4.				
5.				
Group B Funds				
1.				
2.				
3.				
4.				
5.				

*List the price paid or received for 100 shares less all commissions, redemption fees, etc. **List the annualized percentage gain or loss: If your investment was, say $1,000 and you realized a gain of $100 in twelve months, your annualized gain would be 10 percent. If you realized a $100 gain in six months your annualized gain would be 20 percent, and so on.

CONSUMER ALERT

Choose Your Mutual Funds Wisely

For many years I had a phone-in show on the ABC network station in Los Angeles. One of the most frequent questions I had from listeners boiled down to this: "Should I invest in mutual funds?" I would usually answer—not meaning to be a wiseguy, but to make an important point: "That's like saying, 'I'm hungry. I want to go to the market to buy some food.' What kind of food will you buy? Filet mignon or Twinkies? Caviar or Pop-Tarts?"

I never ceased to be amazed that so many people were so unaware of the incredibly vast array of choices to be made among mutual funds, from the raging speculations to the conservative dull-but-you'll-sleep-well variety. And beyond that, I was just as amazed when people told me they had bought mutual funds because of an advertisement or a sales pitch that boasted of a high rate of return, without giving the faintest attention to whether their choice matched their personal objectives.

And then there were those poor folks who had bought the wrong fund and had seen their nest egg waste away, and all they could say was, "But the salesman told me that it should go up, not down." Ah, the word *should*. Of course it *should* go up. But it didn't.

These days billions of dollars are flowing into mutual funds for 401(k) plans and IRA plans and all sorts of other retirement and investment programs, and the marketing people with the mutual fund companies are targeting these investors with all the power at their disposal. It's easy to sell mutual funds when the stock market is booming, as it has been through most of the 1990s. People begin to think they are mutual fund geniuses, when in fact they're just lucky to be in a rising market. When the law of gravity reasserts itself, which it will do with regularity, a lot of the fortunes that have been made during the 1990s' bull market will fast disappear. And what will you have learned from the experience?

The criteria for making wise mutual fund choices have been discussed in this and the preceding chapter. Add to those criteria some numbers regarding specific mutual fund costs:

Most mutual funds charge customers annual 12b-1 fees, which can amount to about .25 percent of your balance in the fund. 12b-1 fees cover the funds' costs of marketing their product (that's right—you're helping to pay for the advertising that they use to lure you in as a customer) and at .25 percent that means that $2.50 of every $1,000 you have invested goes toward these fees.

In addition to the 12b-1 fees there are other management fees charged against your account—over and above any sales commissions you pay when you invest, and any redemption fees you pay when you cash in your chips. The total average mutual fund expenses, including 12b-1 fees, are about 1.27 percent a year for mutual funds that invest mainly in stock, and about .97 percent for bond funds, according to Lipper Analytical Services, a major mutual fund tracking company.

Say you invested $10,000 with a load charge (sales commission) of 6 percent. That means that only $9,400 of your money is working for you, the other $600 (6 percent of $10,000) going as sales commission. If your $9,400 grew by 8 percent in a year—or $752—you'd have a total in the fund of $10,152 (the initial $9,400 plus the $752 growth). If the fund then took away 1.27 percent of your total of $10,152, or about $129, you'd be left with $10,023. Remember that your original investment was $10,000. Your *net earnings* in the above year came to $23. That's a return of just one one-fourth of one percent for the year on your original investment.

Take it from there and crunch those numbers with all your might before you take the plunge. No, I'm not against mutual funds. But neither am I selling anything.

UPS & DOWNS   *The Economics of Everyday Life*

What Makes Stock Prices Go Up and Down?

Most of the other Ups & Downs segments in this book describe matters of relatively reasonable predictability: weather conditions will impact on food prices, wars can frighten oil prices, and so on. But the stock market can defy any crystal ball. Here are some examples of stock market behavior in recent years.

Bad news   The nation's economy is in a tailspin, which, you would think, would send the stock market into retreat. To stimulate the economy the government lowers interest rates. This is supposed to encourage borrowing by business and by individuals, all of whom will go out and buy things and thus put an end to recession. Lower interest rates scare investors out of low-yielding but safe securities and into what seems to be a more promising stock market. The huge inflow of investment dollars causes a spurt in the stock market. So much for bad news.

Good news   The economy is booming. Employment is up. This should bode well for the stock market: more workers means more people can buy more things, which should give companies a shot at better profits. But the stock market sees it differently. As industry demands more workers, workers will bargain for higher wages. Higher wages means lower profits, and in anticipation thereof the stock market takes a tumble. So much for good news.

"Discounting" of expected news   Some events and trends can be anticipated with reasonable accuracy: car sales, unemployment, changes in tax laws, Federal Reserve policies on interest rates, and so on. The stock market doesn't usually wait for the events to happen. It will react *in anticipation* of the events, up or down, days or even weeks before the event. When the event does occur, the market has already factored it into the price of stock. This is referred to as the market having *discounted* the news in advance. The trick is to figure out when that discounting will occur. No one really ever knows.

Profit taking   After every rally there is a fallback. There's never any way of knowing when a mass profit-taking selloff will occur. It's usually a mob psychology function, and, if you can figure out mob psychology, you'll make more money at that than you ever will in the stock market.

Frenzy   There are buying frenzies and there are selling frenzies. Both are motivated by the absolute loss of common sense. Call it temporary insanity. You get a hot tip on a stock. For one brilliant moment in time, you actually believe that you're the only person on earth with this knowledge. Then, when you and the millions like you who share the information buy or sell on the tip, you are part of a frenzy. It's sheer madness. But in a way this is what makes the stock market more interesting than root canal surgery.

?   WHAT IF . . . ?

Test yourself: How would you deal with these real-life possibilities?

1. The stock market is going through a protracted downturn. Nothing seems to be able to stabilize it. You hear rumors that your company's pension fund is heavily invested in the stock market and that it is suffering considerable losses. What steps can you take to learn the facts? What steps *will* you take to learn the facts? If you find that the rumors are true and that your future pension benefits might be in jeopardy, what, if anything, can you do about it?

2. Reverse of the above: The stock market is going up with a vengeance, and your pension fund is making a handsome profit. What, if anything, can you do to share in that good fortune here and now, rather than waiting until retirement? If you can't do anything on your own, with whom can you ally to get something done?

3. A mutual fund sales pitch indicates that the fund has had an annual average total return of 17 percent for the last three years. That's double what you've been earning in your current mutual fund. What further information should you get about this fund before you make an investment decision?

4. You become privy to information about a company which, when made public, will sharply influence the price of that company's stock. Or at least, so you believe. What options do you have? What option(s) will you choose?

NUMBER CRUNCHERS

Do the calculations to help you make decisions in these real-life possibilities.

1. You buy 100 shares of XYZ at $40 per share. XYZ pays an annual dividend of $2. The company offers an automatic dividend reinvestment plan. Assume that the dividend will remain constant over the next five years and that the stock will increase in value by 5 percent each year. How much will your XYZ investment be worth after five years if you partake of the dividend reinvestment plan? How much will your XYZ investment be worth after five years if you spend all the dividends as you receive them? (For purposes of this exercise, don't worry about commissions or taxes.)

2. You embark on a long-term plan to accumulate stock in National Pripichik and Gumball (NP&G). Your initial investment is $4,000, which buys 200 shares. Every year for the next five years you will spend another $1,000 buying NP&G. The prices you pay per share each year are $18 in the first year; $16 the second year; $19 the third year; $21 the fourth year; $20 the fifth year. How many shares (including fractional amounts) of NP&G will you own after five years, and what will they be worth? (Forget dividends and commissions for purposes of this exercise.)

3. You have $10,000 to invest. Half goes into a savings plan that will pay 6 percent interest per year, compounding annually. The other half goes into 100 shares of a stock that pays no dividends. How much will the stock have to appreciate each year, on average, in both dollars and percent, to equal what you'll have in the savings plan after five years? (Forget commissions and taxes for this exercise.)

FOR BETTER OR FOR WORSE

Things beyond our control often impact our personal and financial well-being, for better or for worse. Some are more predictable than others. How would you be affected if the following real-life phenomena happened? Could you have seen it coming? What steps could you have taken to minimize damage or maximize advantage? The better able you are to anticipate and recognize these forces, the better equipped you are to deal with them.

1. You shop around for a mutual fund that invests in stocks, seeking one with the best winning track record possible. A year later the stock market has gone south by 8 percent, but your fund has dropped 24 percent.

2. The government creates very attractive tax breaks for companies that do a lot of genetic engineering research and development. The market reacts most positively, and you jump in yourself. A year later the government revokes the tax breaks and gives them instead to the home-building industry.

3. All of the stock market commentators and pundits are predicting a huge rise in the Dow Jones Industrial Average over the next year. You take a big plunge, as does your pension plan. The next day war breaks out in the Middle East and the oil supply to the United States is severely threatened.

16

Making Your Money Grow: Real Estate and Other Opportunities

Character and personal force are the only investments that are worth anything.
                                                                    Walt Whitman

Beyond the money market and the stock market, there is a whole galaxy of opportunities for making your money grow—or shrink. Some can be relatively simple, and even fun—such as collecting coins, stamps, sports cards, and autographs. Others are much more complex—real estate, commodities, or investing in precious metals or gems. Many of these "opportunities" are aggressively sold by smooth-talking pitchmen. The naive investor who does not do the necessary homework can end up in trouble. The serious investor who studies hard and realistically evaluates all risks can be successful. After reading this chapter, you should be able to

- Distinguish between the various types of real estate investments
- Understand the time and expertise needed to manage real estate investments properly
- Recognize the pros and cons of speculating in such areas as commodities, precious metals, and gems
- Evaluate the true risks and tax implications in any of these methods of making your money grow

MYTHS AND FACTS ABOUT REAL ESTATE INVESTING

Property values sometimes increase at a rapid rate throughout much of the country, and as those values increase, the mystique about investing in real estate grows, too. Fostered by myriad get-rich-quick books and seminars, and by the proud boastings of investors who claim to have "made a killing" in real estate, the mystique takes on dangerous proportions for the uninformed would-be real estate investor. Let's first examine some of the myths and some of the facts about investing in real estate.

Myth: Real estate is easy; anybody can make money at it.

Facts: Successful real estate investing always has and always will require a considerable amount of expertise. As in any kind of investment, there will always be a handful of lucky ones who make it look easy to others. But those are the exception. Real estate is a fast track: experts profit at the expense of novices. The experts know when to buy, when to sell, how to finance, and how to manage property properly. And even the experts can make mistakes. Expertise in real estate investing can take years to achieve. It requires the ability to deal efficiently and profitably with tenants, tax assessors, lenders, insurance agents, contractors, lawyers, appraisers, and other prospective buyers and sellers. The novice real estate investor, lured by the myth of fast and easy money, is apt to make serious mistakes and incur serious losses.

Myth: Real estate offers an assured return on your investment.

Facts: Real estate investing is very much like the stock market in that there is no assurance of profit: A tenant defaults, seriously decreasing your income. Your furnace or central air-conditioning unit self-destructs, leaving you with a multithousand-dollar repair bill. The taxes on real estate double in a short period of time. A visitor to your building trips on a piece of broken flooring material and sues you for five times the amount of your public liability insurance. The neighborhood in which your building is located begins to deteriorate seriously. An unexpected rerouting of traffic makes your building far less attractive to good-quality tenants.

Events such as these can greatly reduce your expected return. Any would-be investor in real estate must approach any project with a keen awareness of the potential unknowns.

Myth: Property values always go up.

Facts: Real estate is cyclical. There are up periods, there are flat or down periods, and it's impossible to predict the cycles in any community at any given time. Real estate is also subject to the "greater fool" theory. That theory states that if you buy something at whatever price, eventually a greater fool than yourself will come along and buy it from you at an even higher price. This theory fails when property values have gone too high too quickly and the community runs out of greater fools. Then you're stuck.

Always be aware that in any time of investment, winners always boast, but losers are never heard from. This contributes to the myth of profitability in real estate. Winners not only boast; they exaggerate. Losers keep their mouth shut. Thus, you'll hear an excessive amount of good news and a sore lack of bad news from people who have tried their hand in real estate.

Myth: You don't need any money to invest in real estate. You can buy property with "no money down."

Facts: Perhaps more money has been made selling books and seminars on this subject than will ever be made in real estate itself. The simple facts are: sure, you can buy real estate with no money down, if you can find a seller who is willing to part with property for no down payment. Or, you can try to find a lender who is willing to lend you 100 percent of the purchase price. In either case, you're liable to be paying a higher price than the property is worth or a higher interest rate than would be called for in a normal deal. And once the hefty monthly payments begin, you could really be behind the eight ball. The novice real estate investor who tries these techniques is on very risky ground.

The Good Points

Despite these pitfalls, real estate can provide an attractive investment to individuals willing to do the homework and put forth the energy to maintain their investments. If the local marketplace is properly researched, if the premises and legal documents are properly scrutinized, and if the required amount of time is devoted to the project, real estate can be very productive over the long run. One of the most attractive aspects of some real estate investment is the tax deduction allowed for the physical depreciation of the building. This factor can not only render the income from the real estate investment free of income taxes but can also shelter some of the investor's other income from taxes. This will be discussed in more detail in the section on income-producing real estate.

A World of Opportunities

There are four major categories of real estate investments, plus one category that allows you to invest as part of a group. The categories are as follows:

- **Income-producing real estate**   You purchase a building with the intent of renting it out to tenants, thereby realizing income. You may also realize a profit when you sell the building.
- **Vacant-land investing**   You buy unimproved land with the intent of either developing it, renting it out, or selling it at some future date at a profit.
- **Turnover investing**   You buy a property with the intention of reselling it as soon as possible at a profit. Income is a secondary consideration.

- **Mortgage investing**   You lend other people money, with the loan being secured by real estate. You don't actually acquire an ownership interest in the property at the time you make the investment, but you might if the borrower defaults. Thus, it's essential that you know the values that apply to the underlying real estate that is collateral for the loan you've made.

- **Group ventures**   You pool your money with that of other investors in any or all of the preceding categories. Group ventures can include real estate investment trusts, syndications, and partnerships.

The whole world is made up of real estate, and opportunity exists in every country in which the free enterprise system is at work. Common sense, however, dictates that the closer to home you invest, the more knowledge and control you have with respect to your investment. Let us now examine the basic categories of real estate investment.

INCOME-PRODUCING REAL ESTATE

The primary objective in investing in <u>income-producing real estate</u> is to earn income on your investment and, to the extent possible, obtain tax sheltering of that income through the depreciation deduction. But, as noted earlier, many factors can affect the flow of income. Here are some of the main factors that must be considered.*

Factors Affecting Income-producing Property Investments

Quality and Type of Tenants

Consider the problems involved in an apartment complex that rents primarily to young, single people. An owner can expect a relatively high rate of turnover. With each turnover comes the chance of a vacancy and the possible need to refurbish the apartment. On the other hand, an apartment complex catering to older persons might have a low rate of turnover. Applying the reward/risk rule, which relates as much to real estate as it does to any other form of investment, the properties with the highest chance of turnover and higher refurbishing costs should carry a higher rent than the more stable properties.

In commercial properties, a broad spectrum of possible tenants can occupy any given space. Consider, for example, uses that are possible in a small neighborhood shopping center—a popular type of moderate real es-

---

*If you expect to be a tenant running your own business—as discussed in detail in chapter 21—much of the following material will also be important for you.

tate investment for small- to medium-sized investors. A given space might be occupied by a business such as an insurance agency. It will have relatively little traffic and will need no special plumbing, electrical, or drainage installations. The same property might be occupied by a coffee shop, which could have a high level of traffic that can contribute to the more rapid deterioration of the premises; in addition, such installations need specialized plumbing, electrical, and drainage connections. Moreover, these uses can generate smoke and grease and are possible fire hazards that could increase the insurance rates for both the building and the adjoining tenants.

The creditworthiness of tenants should not be overlooked. When entering into a lease, landlords should check with the local credit bureau to determine a tenant's creditworthiness. A sloppy credit history suggests a number of possible actions that landlords should consider: They might want to decline renting to such a tenant altogether; they might feel that the credit problems justify asking a higher rent; they might seek a cosigner to ensure payment of the rent; and they might request a substantial rental deposit from the tenant.

A tenant who is tardy with rent can cause more than one problem. In addition to the headaches and aggravation landlords must endure in collecting overdue rent, landlords might have to dip into their own funds to meet *their* monthly payments as they fall due.

Nature and Quality of the Building

The potential risks and rewards for the landlord are directly related to the quality, location, and nature of the building itself. As in buying a house (chapter 6), the investor in income-producing real estate must pay attention to all the mechanical and structural details of the building. It is wise to hire a construction specialist to make a detailed inspection and provide a report on the building. A building with hidden defects can cause serious problems for the unsuspecting landlord; a building in good physical condition will keep risk at a minimum and cut down problems of maintenance, repairs, and replacements. Many investors in real estate are content to take the seller's or realtor's word concerning the condition of the building. More prudent investors discover, with professional assistance, whether the building measures up to their standards.

Location is important to the investor, who must determine whether traffic patterns or changes in adjoining neighborhoods can have an effect on the investment. An attractive gas station, motel, shopping center, or restaurant on a heavily trafficked thoroughfare might seem most appealing. But if a new highway diverts all the traffic away from the street, the result can be disastrous. A neighborhood shopping center might seem to offer attractive possibilities; but when a bigger and better shopping center is constructed a few blocks away, the unaware investor may regret ever having signed the down payment check.

Prudent investors check with the local zoning board to determine what uses are permitted in areas near their property. They check with the traffic and highway agencies to determine what possible changes in traffic routings are anticipated. And they check with other real estate firms to learn what new developments are pending within the trading area of the property they're buying.

The nature of the building must also be considered. Many buildings are limited by their size, shape, and type of construction as to the uses to which they can be put. Food franchise buildings often fall into this category; they might prove unadaptable to other uses. On the other hand, some buildings are easily converted to suit different purposes. The more limited the use of a given building, the more difficult it may be to find tenants.

Property Taxes

Prudent investors also check with the local tax assessor to determine the current and probable future trends with respect to property taxes. If property taxes are likely to be moving upward sharply in the years ahead, prudent investors will want to know if they can still meet their financial projections. Can they expect their tenants to absorb a share of increased property taxes? How will the long-term trend in property taxes affect their ability to sell the building profitably in the future?

Utility Costs

All other things being equal, it's better for the landlord if the tenants pay their own utility and fuel costs—water, electricity, gas, heating oil. That can take a lot of financial pressure off the landlord, particularly in areas of climatic extremes, where heating or air-conditioning costs can demolish the most carefully planned budget. If a building, either residential or commercial, is not already separately metered for such utilities, the prudent investor will think twice about making the investment. If a landlord does pay the utility costs, he or she can require tenants to pay a pro rata share of any such costs beyond a certain agreed-on base amount. Lacking such protection, the landlord is at the mercy of broken thermostats, leaky faucets and toilets, and other costly energy wastes.

Management of the Property

Perhaps the biggest shock to the novice real estate investor is how much time and aggravation it takes to manage the property. When you call your doctor in the middle of the night with a mysterious pain, you may be told to take two aspirins and call back in the morning. When a tenant calls you in the middle of the night to complain of a leaking toilet, you can't just tell him to throw two aspirins into it and call you back in the morning. Management takes time, patience, skill, diplomacy, expertise, and a sense of humor. If you're not a good handyman yourself, you have to find people in the trades on whom you can depend: plumbers, electricians, painters, carpenters, and so on. When you have a vacancy, you must be prepared to refurbish it to get it up to standard, and you must show it to prospective tenants, many of whom will not show up at the agreed-on appointment time.

If the property generates enough income, it might be advisable to hire a professional manager who can deal with all these matters. A good management firm will cost you between 5 and 8 percent of your rental income. A good management firm can be the landlord's best ally; a shoddy management firm can be the landlord's worst enemy. Get personal recommendations before you hire a management firm. If the management firm is also acting as rental agent, be certain that it will screen prospective tenants to your strict standards. Otherwise, the management firm could rent the premises to tenants unacceptable to you in order to generate a rental commission in a hurry.

Financing

The mechanics of financing income property are generally the same as financing one's own home. The investor (unless paying all cash) gives a down payment to the seller of the property and either assumes an existing mortgage or obtains a mortgage loan from outside sources.

The prudent investor seeks a good return on invested capital (the cash down payment) and to that end attempts to structure the mortgage so that there is adequate cash flow to meet objectives. If there are interest rate escalation clauses, the owner must be prepared to adjust rents accordingly if he or she wants to maintain a constant rate of cash flow.

The real estate investor may also need large sums of money at indeterminate dates for major renovations and repairs. The investor should negotiate with the lender to obtain such funds by adding them on to the existing mortgage at the best possible terms.

When lenders are considering mortgage loan applications on income property, they examine not only the owner's credit but also the caliber of tenants. The owner's ability to pay the mortgage is directly related to the ability of the tenants to make their rental payments. The better the tenants, the more favorable terms the borrower can negotiate with the lender. Better quality tenants, as noted earlier, may be able to bargain for a lower rent from the landlord. The landlord can make up this difference by seeking the most favorable terms on the mortgage payments.

The Lease

At the heart of any real estate investment is the lease: the agreement between the investor/owner and the tenant/user. Whether the property is commercial, residential, or a combination, the specific terms of the lease have an important bearing on the investor's success. Residential leases tend to be shorter and simpler, usually running for a period of not more than one or two years. Commercial leases are more complex. In either case, the prudent investor sees to it that an attorney prepares a lease best suited to the investor's interests.

Following are some of the more important terms that should be evaluated, particularly in commercial leases.

LENGTH OF THE LEASE   In commercial leases tenants want to know that they have the right to use the property for as long as the business is profitable. If it ceases to be profitable, a tenant will probably want to leave.

A preferred situation for a commercial tenant would be to have a medium-term lease—say, three to five years—with options to renew at an agreed-on rent. This option offers the tenant both flexibility and fixed overhead. But this might not be to the landlord's advantage. By giving a tenant the privilege of renewing, the landlord is effectively taking the property off the market for the length of the original term and possibly the period of renewal.

Where renewal clauses exist, the tenant must give notice of intention to renew prior to the expiration of the lease. Technically, the landlord does not know until notice is given whether the space will be vacated. The landlord can make inquiry, but tenants are legally not obliged to express their intentions to renew or depart until the time stated in the lease agreement. Where there are no renewal privileges, the landlord knows exactly when to expect the premises to be vacated and can begin seeking new tenants, certain of when they can take occupancy. Or the landlord can renegotiate the lease with the existing tenant and hope that conditions permit an equal or better rent on the renewal term.

The landlord should bear in mind that because a tenant has a right of renewal at an agreed-on rent, this does *not* guarantee that the tenant *will* pay that rent. The renewal date may roll around, and the tenant may want to continue in the space, but at a reduced rental. This can cause a predicament for the landlord, who now has a relatively short period of time in which to try to find a better tenant for the premises. Working out such problems often comes down to nothing more than plain old hard-nosed bargaining. If there's a surplus of tenants looking for space, the landlord is in a better position, and vice versa. There's no way of knowing what these conditions will be like years in advance, so the parties just have to be prepared to cope with situations as they arise.

Another factor to consider, particularly in a commercial building, is that a long-term lease with a good-quality tenant can translate into a lower interest rate on the financing.

THE RENTAL RATE   In most cases, market conditions and the tenant's creditworthiness will determine the probable amount of rent a given tenant will pay. In residential rentals, the rent is quoted as a flat rate: "Apt. 106 rents for $875 per month." In commercial rentals, the rent is often expressed in terms of square feet. A space of 1,000 square feet that rents for $1,000 per month, or $12,000 per year, will be quoted as "$12 per square foot per year" or, in some cases, "$1 per square foot per month."

Commercial rentals are also referred to as "gross" or "net." In a gross lease, the landlord is responsible for virtually all operating costs on the property, including real estate taxes, utilities, maintenance, cleaning, and generally servicing the premises. The tenant in a gross lease pays a higher rent, in return for those services. In a net lease, the tenant is responsible for those expenses.

The landlord who wants a minimum of involvement in the management of the building will prefer a net lease. Some tenants may prefer a net lease because they can more directly control the operating expenses in the building. Whether a lease is gross or net, the building must still be properly maintained. A landlord, even with the most perfect net lease, must still see to it that the tenant performs all the proper management, maintenance, and repairs required under the lease.

Rental payments may be fixed for the term of the lease, or they may escalate in line with rising prices or simply by agreement between the parties. In addition to the basic flat rent, commercial leases often have percentage clauses.

A percentage clause states that the tenant must pay additional rent to the landlord in an amount equal to an agreed-on percentage of the volume of business the tenant does. For example: The tenant may be required to pay 6 percent of all gross income in excess of, say, $100,000 per year. In such a case, if the tenant's business does not gross over $100,000 in a year, the percentage clause does not go into effect. But if the tenant generates

$150,000 of volume, the percentage lease requires the tenant to pay 6 percent of $50,000 or $3,000 in additional rent for that year. The existence and terms of a percentage clause are a matter of negotiation between the parties. If a landlord feels that a tenant's business prospects are good, the landlord may prefer a lower base rent with a percentage clause. A more conservative landlord may simply prefer a higher base rent and no percentage clause. A percentage lease allows the landlord the right to look at the books and records of the tenant so that the correct amount of the payment can be determined.

USE OF THE PROPERTY   The lease stipulates the purposes for which the premises can be used.

In addition, particularly in a shopping center, the tenant may request a *noncompetition* clause. This would prevent the landlord from allowing other spaces in the center to be rented to competitors. The landlord has to evaluate such a request in light of current market conditions, eagerness to rent the space, and the rent the tenant is willing to pay.

REPAIRS AND RESTORATIONS   The lease should stipulate who is responsible for every kind of repair. Customarily, the tenants are responsible for making minor interior repairs, and the landlord is responsible for structural repairs and matters affecting mechanical equipment, such as the heating plant and the air-conditioning unit. Of course, the parties can agree to any combination of who does what and who pays for what.

A restoration clause is also subject to negotiation between the parties. This clause can require tenants to restore the premises to their original condition at the time they first took occupancy. If tenants have made renova-

STRATEGIES FOR SUCCESS

Choose Tenants Wisely for Best Returns

As with any investment, the higher the quality, the lower the risk—and the lower the return. That's as true in real estate as it is in the stock market. Higher-quality tenants in your building mean less risk to you: they'll pay their rent on time, and their checks won't bounce. Knowing those conditions, you might be willing to take a slightly lower rent in return for fewer headaches. Some wise steps to take before signing on a new tenant: get an up-to-date credit check; verify employment; get personal references, including the current landlord; and meet with the prospective tenant personally. If you're a good judge of character, you'll be able to spot a trouble-free tenant. And remember: the responsible tenant will leave the premises neat and clean. That's less expense for you down the line.

tions within the premises, they will have to see to it, at their own expense, that the property is brought back to its original condition unless the landlord later agrees otherwise. If a restoration clause is agreed on between the parties, it is necessary to obtain a careful description of the premises at the time of the start of occupancy (including color photographs as an added precaution.)

DEFAULT   What if tenants don't live up to the agreement? They may damage the property and not repair it. Or the tenant may leave in the middle of a lease and try to escape making further payments. As a measure of protection against default, a prudent investor insists on a rental deposit and a breakage and damage deposit from a tenant. The rental deposit, usually designated as the last month's rent on the lease, ensures that the landlord will have at least some cash in hand should the tenant skip. The breakage and damage deposit protects the landlord to some extent in the event the tenant neglects to make repairs. But it should be clearly understood that the amounts of the rental deposit and the breakage and damage deposit are not the limit of the tenant's obligation. The tenant should still be obliged to make whatever payments are due over and above the amount of the deposits.

"Compounding" Your Income

In fixed income investments, your earned interest can be automatically reinvested in your account and go to work for you. This is known as compounding interest. The same ends can be accomplished in the stock market through either a dividend reinvestment plan or a mutual fund that pumps your earnings back into additional shares of the fund. But can you compound your earnings in a real estate investment? Yes, prudent real estate investors realize that a portion of their income should be reinvested back into the property, by way of refurbishing and modernization. The net effect of this *should* be to generate higher income from tenants of the property.

It's not as simple or as automatic as the compounded interest on your savings account, and it requires some expertise to know which dollars can generate additional rent. The investor may prefer to take all income out and invest it in some other fashion, or spend it. But the investor should examine the possibilities of reinvesting the money in the property before making an ultimate decision.

For example, a tenant might agree to an increase of $20 per month if the landlord repaints the premises. The paint job might cost $1,000, but the landlord will be getting an additional $240 per year for the balance of the lease period. That's a 24 percent return on the $1,000 investment—an attractive situation, indeed. The prudent investor is continually on the alert for ways to increase and compound income by plowing profits back into the property.

Real Estate Investing and Taxes

Before we proceed to analyze how a real estate investment works, it's necessary to understand one of the basic principles of income tax law. Suppose that your taxable income in a given year was $35,000. All that income came from work. (Taxable income is what's left after all your deductions and exemptions have been subtracted from your gross income.) You are married and filing a joint return. You are in the 28 percent tax bracket. If you could come up with another deduction of, say, $1,000, that would reduce your taxable income from $35,000 to $34,000. At a 28 percent tax rate, that means that you would reduce your tax bill by $280. The $1,000 deduction reduces the amount of tax you have to pay to Uncle Sam by $280. This is an example, in very oversimplified fashion, of a tax shelter. It's a deduction generated from some outside source that allows you to reduce the tax you would have to pay on the income you earned from work.

For many investors, ample opportunity to reduce taxes by this means is available in real estate. *If your adjusted gross income is under $100,000, you can still use deductions from real estate investments to offset as much as $25,000 per year worth of income from work.* (If your adjusted gross income is between $100,000 and $150,000, you can still achieve a partial deduction. The concept of adjusted gross income is explained further in chapter 20, on income taxes.)

Let's now study an example of how such a deal can work.

The Depreciation Deduction

You own and actively manage a small apartment house. Your purchase price was $150,000. You made a down payment of $10,000 and obtained a mortgage of $140,000, payable over twenty years at a fixed interest rate of 13 percent. Your monthly payments on that mortgage will be $1,640. See Table 16–1.

Your operating figures are set forth in Table 16–2: your annual income is $26,400. Your annual expenses are $25,680. This leaves you with a net income, after expenses, of $720. You invested $10,000 of your own cash, so you are receiving a return of 7.2 percent on your invested money. That's a decent return, but you could earn as much by putting your money into bonds and not have all the hassle of managing a building. So where's the attraction? It comes from the depreciation deduction.

Tax laws permit investors to show a loss on their income tax forms to reflect the supposed physical deterioration of their property. Obviously, this

TABLE 16–1   **Purchase of Real Estate Investment**

Purchase price	$150,000
Down payment	10,000
Mortgage	$140,000

13% fixed rate for 20-year term = monthly payments of $1,640

TABLE 16–2   Operating Income and Expenses

	Per Month	Per Year
Rental income	$2,200	$26,400
Expenses		
Interest	$1,600	
Taxes (approx.)	100	
Insurance	100	
Maintenance	200	
Misc.	140	
	$2,140	$25,680
Net income	$60	$720

Exercise 16.1

loss is not a real out-of-pocket loss, particularly if the building is appreciating in value. An investor who owns an income-producing residential property can claim those losses over a period of 27½ years. An investor in commercial property can claim the losses over a 39-year period.

The tax law states that only the building portion of a property, not the land portion, is depreciable. For purposes of the depreciation deduction, you must separate out the cost basis of the building itself. As Table 16–3 indicates, the value of your building is $110,000. That's the depreciable portion of the total investment. Dividing 27½ years into $110,000, we get a $4,000 per year depreciation deduction.

Here's how the arithmetic works: You are entitled to an annual depreciation deduction of $4,000. Assume you're in the 28 percent tax bracket on your federal income tax return. The depreciation deduction of $4,000 erases the tax liability on the $720 you earned from the building. Assuming you've been actively involved in managing the building and otherwise qualify, the rest of the depreciation deduction will erase the tax liability on $3,280 worth of your income from other sources, such as work. A total of $3,280 worth of income that is not taxed currently means a tax savings for the year of $918. (That is, 28 percent of $3,280 is $918.)

So your actual income, as Table 16–4 indicates, amounts to $1,638, which represents a return of 16.38 percent on your cash investment of $10,000. In addition to that, you will be building equity in the property as you pay

TABLE 16–3   Depreciation Breakdown

Land (not depreciable)	$ 40,000
Building (depreciable)	110,000

Depreciation period of 27½ years

$110,000 ÷ 227½ = $4,000 depreciation per year

TABLE 16–4   **Return on $10,000 Cash Investment**

Operating profit	$720
Taxes saved in current year on nonbuilding income as a result of depreciation deduction	918
	$1,638

down the loan each month and as the value of the property (hopefully) increases over the years.*

Now the Bad News

You paid $150,000 for the building. Say that you own the building for ten years and you take depreciation of $4,000 for each of those years, for a total of $40,000 in depreciation deductions. At the end of ten years, you have the opportunity to sell the property for $250,000. Naturally, you'll have to pay a tax on your profit.

What is the extent of your profit? You paid $150,000 and received $250,000 for an apparent profit of $100,000. But you'll have to pay income taxes on more than $100,000. Because you claimed $40,000 in depreciation deductions while you owned the building, the tax law requires that your cost basis be reduced by that amount. In other words, in calculating your profit on the building, you must calculate your cost (for tax purposes) as the original price you paid for the building *minus* any depreciation deductions you had claimed. The original price was $150,000 and you claimed deductions of $40,000. Thus, your cost basis for tax purposes would be $110,000. The gain that is subject to income taxes is, then, the difference between your selling price and your cost basis, $250,000 minus $110,000; or $140,000. In other words, some of the tax advantages you enjoyed while you owned the building are taken away at the time you sell the building. Again, it is necessary to make a careful analysis of tax laws in effect at the time of sale to structure the best terms and the best time for a sale.

INVESTING IN VACANT LAND

Investing in vacant land can be one of the most extreme forms of speculation. We do hear of "killings" made in land by investors; and we hear statements, such as the one Will Rogers made, "You ought to buy land, cuz they ain't gonna print no more of it." But success in vacant land investment, for

---

*Tax laws affecting real estate investments (and all other types of investments) change frequently. The tax implications in the preceding example may be different by the time you make an investment in real estate. It's absolutely essential that you check current tax laws and get professional assistance in analyzing how the laws affect any investment you plan to make.

the most part, remains the province of the skilled professional, who has the expertise, the capital, and the selling skills needed to turn a profit most of the time. *Note:* We said *most of the time.* Even the skilled professional will have setbacks.

Other forms of investment pay some income to investors—interest on fixed income investments, dividends on stocks, rentals on income properties. But vacant land requires investors to be constantly *paying out* money: real estate taxes, liability insurance and security. Investors in vacant land have also put their capital beyond reach until the land is actually sold. It is difficult and costly to borrow against vacant land.

Factors Affecting Vacant-Land Investments

Whether you are buying land for future building purposes or in hope of profit on a fast turnover, you should take into account the following factors:

"Known" Land

There's a much better chance for success if you're dealing with known land—that is, land in a community with which you're familiar and on which you can get estimates from real estate professionals on probable future value. Known land also implies that you are certain of the availability of utilities, sewers, roadways, and other necessary facilities.

"Unknown" Land

Uncounted millions of dollars are lost every year by people who sign contracts and checks to buy parcels of unknown land—generally, land in distant places that is being sold as part of a development program for the creation of a "new city," a resort, or a retirement village. Although there are legitimate developments in all parts of the country, the abuses, intentional or otherwise, that have arisen have been all too frequent.

Anyone considering investing in vacant land for future personal use, particularly if it's unknown land, must observe the following cautions.

SEE THE LAND   View the land and walk it from corner to corner before you sign any documents. The majority of people who have been bilked on such deals haven't done this.

CONSULT AN ATTORNEY *BEFORE* YOU SIGN ANYTHING   The attorney can determine whether the land you saw is the land you'll actually be buying. He will also scrutinize the other documents involved and help you ascertain exactly what you can expect for the money you're paying.

READ THE PROPERTY REPORT   If a developer is selling land on an interstate basis—to buyers in many states—federal law requires that a Property Report be provided. It must contain information prescribed by the In-

Exercise 16.2

terstate Land Sales Act, a federal law. If a developer fails to provide the Property Report within the prescribed time limits, the buyer may be entitled to revoke the contract and obtain a refund.

Appraisal

Get professional help in order to determine the true value of vacant land. The seller's asking price and the true current market value may be far apart, and you don't want to pay more than you should. A professional appraiser can assist you in learning the true current market value. The appraiser will take into account recent comparable sales of similar property, existing and future potential traffic patterns in and around the land, future population trends and the stability of the tax base.

Tests

Whether you're planning to build on the land or hoping to sell it to someone else who will, certain physical tests will have to be done. These tests are the soil test and the percolation test. You should know the results of these tests before you buy any vacant property.

The soil test determines the bearing capacity of the soil. In other words, how much of a building load can the soil withstand? Percolation tests determine the drainage capacity of the land—how much rainfall and moisture the land can absorb without turning into a swamp or a sea of mud.

Surveys

The boundary survey and the topographical survey assure a would-be buyer/builder of the true boundaries of the property and of the precise slopes that may exist on the property. If there is, for example, too much slope to the property, a prospective builder might be faced with expensive earth-moving costs, and those costs could affect the price a buyer is willing to pay for the property.

Dollars and Cents

If a parcel of vacant land doubles in price within the short space of five years, an investor might only break even. Here's the arithmetic. Assume that an investor pays $10,000 cash for vacant land, forgoing a return on the money of, say $600 per year by simply investing the money in insured savings. In addition, the investor may have the following typical expenses: property taxes, $500; insurance (mainly for public liability, to avoid lawsuits if anyone is hurt while crossing the property), $200; signs, advertising, and security, $200. Total annual expenses (including lost interest) are thus $1,500, or a total over five years of $7,500.

Assume that five years later the investor is able to sell the property for $20,000. If the investor has used a real estate agent to find a buyer—which is likely—the commission to the real estate agent will be 10 percent of the selling price, or $2,000. In addition, there will probably be expenses related to the sale, particularly legal fees and recording costs, which can easily total $500. The total expenses then are $10,000—$1,500 per year for five years, or $7,500, plus $2,500 at the time of sale. The selling price of $20,000 thus results in a net of $10,000. Over a five-year span, the property has doubled in value, and the investor has broken even.

This example is intended to provide you with the kind of "what if" arithmetic you face before making a decision. The time to evaluate this risk is before making any commitment to invest in vacant land. Once the commitment is made, you can't get out of it as you could selling stock or cashing in a savings certificate. You're stuck with it until a buyer comes along, and if that buyer isn't willing to meet your price, you may have to take whatever is offered. And the longer you hold on, the more it costs.

"TURNOVER" INVESTING

Probably somewhat more speculative than higher quality income property investing, and probably less speculative than vacant land investing, is the purchase of existing homes for subsequent resale: "Turnover" investing. It's a tricky business, requiring expertise, hard work, and patience. But many small investors have found handsome profits in such endeavors.

Many opportunities are attractive to investors with talents for making repairs. Such talents allow you to make accurate estimates of what renovations might be needed, how much they'll cost, and how much they can boost the potential selling price. A few hundred dollars wisely spent on paint, paneling, or flooring can increase the potential selling price by a thousand dollars or more.

The procedure involves seeking out houses that have good underlying basic value but can be bought for less than the normal market price, usually because the owners are anxious to get out.

The success of any venture depends on the investor's ability to buy wisely and to finance wisely.

Buying Right

Buying right requires careful evaluation of the neighborhood as well as of the physical structure itself. A rundown house in an area of better homes can command a handsome price if it's spruced up and put on a par with its surroundings. Another rundown house might offer little or no profit potential regardless of how much you do because the neighborhood isn't that desirable. Remember that your buyers are looking for location as well as a house, and the selling price is affected accordingly.

There are three major ways you can seek attractive situations. You can scout around for people who are hard pressed to sell, because of either time or money pressures. Word of mouth and simply driving around looking for "For Sale" signs are ways of discovering such opportunities. Advertising is another way. The seller may place a classified ad with a tip-off that indicates a good buy; or you, as the investor, can advertise in the "Homes Wanted" or similar classifications of the want ad pages.

A second source: real estate agents in your area. Make it known to a number of them that you're in the market for such houses, and ask them to contact you if they spot any. Often, agents might be reluctant to take a listing on rundown houses from the seller, but if they know they have a possible buyer, they could put you into a number of opportunities.

A third source: banks and savings and loan institutions that have delinquent property loans. This deserves particular attention because you might have a source of automatic financing when you later sell to another party.

Financing Right

If you've bought right, and if you've refurbished correctly, your chances of finding a willing buyer will be greatly enhanced if you can offer the property fully financed. This means that a creditworthy buyer can step right into a mortgage for which you have made prior arrangements. In order to make such arrangements, it will be necessary to develop a relationship with a lender who will be willing to cooperate with you in such transactions. As part of the negotiations involved in setting up such relationships, you may have to guarantee all or part of any loan that is arranged for your buyer. Although this can improve your potential profitability in the sale of the house, it does put you on the hook for an extended period; you should be careful that the buyer makes an adequate down payment and that his or her credit history justifies your assuming that risk. As noted earlier, mortgage lenders in the community may have an inventory of used homes that they'd be willing to sell at attractive prices to investors willing to fix them up and offer them for resale. In such cases, they may be willing to make advance commitments for long-term financing to creditworthy buyers.

The Profit Margin

Perhaps the biggest challenge in this kind of investment is building a big enough profit margin into the deal to cover all the initial expenses, as well as continuing expenses, and yet not price the property out of the market. Investors must be aware that once renovations are completed and the property is on the market, time can start working against them. Every month that goes by in which the house remains unsold means added costs—interest, taxes, insurance, advertising, and so on. As these costs mount, investors, for lack of buyers, may drop the price. As the expenses rise and the asking price drops, investors may succumb to feelings of panic. That's the worst danger. Carefully estimate the difference between what you will pay for the property, the renovations, and the continuing expenses, and what you'll receive in the sale.

A well-structured deal offers the opportunity for substantial profit if a buyer is found in the early months, but, as time goes by, profitability rapidly erodes. Anyone investing in homes for resale purposes must give careful consideration to this risk.

INVESTING IN MORTGAGES

Mortgages are not actually real estate investments, but many people think of them as such. These investments fall more into the fixed income category: You're buying someone else's IOU with a piece of real estate as security. But because you could end up owning the real estate if the borrower defaults on the payments it should be considered a real estate investment.

Prudent investors must scrutinize the value of property just as they must scrutinize the creditworthiness of a borrower. They must exercise the same precautions that a bank would in making a mortgage loan: appraising the property, determining the credit status of the borrower, and getting adequate protection regarding title and property insurance. An attorney is needed to prepare all the required documents, and the cost of the legal service must be taken into account. It's not unusual in private mortgage investing for the costs of legal matters and related documentation to be passed along to the borrower. In addition, the private mortgage lender might be able to impose extra fees or points in much the same way institutional lenders do.

Before you become an <u>investor in mortgages</u>, it would be valuable to meet existing mortgage brokers in your community and determine what the current going prices and interest rates are. You might even, as a would-be investor in mortgages, prefer to deal through such brokers before you set out on your own. The mortgage brokers will place your money for you in mortgages and will take a fee for their service. Most communities have many mortgage brokers who are always looking for funds they can invest, content to take a service fee for their efforts. You can find them listed in the Yellow Pages.

If you do choose to use a mortgage broker, make sure that the broker is reputable. If you turn your money over to a disreputable individual, you might never see it, or the person, again.

"Taking Back" a Mortgage

If you sell property and agree to accept the buyer's IOU in full or partial payment, this is known as "taking back" a mortgage. The buyer becomes obligated to you to make the payments called for in the mortgage agreement. Many people who sell their homes or business properties don't have immediate use for the full proceeds and might prefer to let the money stay in the property as a form of investment.

Initiating a New Mortgage

This involves making a new mortgage loan to people who are buying someone else's property. The interest rate, costs, and added fees that you, as an investor, can generate are subject to negotiation between the parties. Some important cautions are in order if the deal is to be structured to your best advantage.

First, you must determine why the people are not able to obtain conventional financing through a normal lending institution. If it's because the borrowers' credit status is weak, you might be asking for trouble. In such a case, you might be able to command a higher interest rate (subject to state usury laws) because you are taking on a higher than normal risk. Or the property buyers may simply not have enough down payment to meet the requirements of the institution, even though the credit status is perfectly acceptable. This is a lesser risk but one that you should evaluate nonetheless.

Second, protect yourself in setting the number of years the loan will run. Banks measure their mortgage loans in decades, but it's not wise for an individual to tie up money for that long. You can establish a payment program that is based on a thirty-year payout, for example, but you should reserve the right to have the full amount payable in a much shorter time, say five years. This is subject to negotiation between the parties. The borrowers might not like the prospect of having to refinance the loan at the end of five years, but they may be willing to go along with it if there's no better deal elsewhere.

Your documents should state that the buyers cannot sell the property without your express permission. You would not want the property to be sold to a person whose credit status is unacceptable. You might permit the property owners to do so if they remain liable for the debt in case the new buyer defaults.

In establishing the interest rate on a new mortgage or a taken-back mortgage, you might also want to consider what many institutional lenders are doing: putting in clauses that permit them to alter the interest rate when and if interest rates in general change.

Buying Mortgages at "Discount"

Some years ago, Murphy bought Johnson's house, and Johnson took back a mortgage from Murphy at a 10 percent interest rate. Today Murphy still owes Johnson $40,000 on that mortgage, and payments are to run for another ten years. Johnson needs money now. He can't wait ten years to collect what is owed him. Johnson approaches you to sell you Murphy's IOU. You know that Murphy is very creditworthy and that the value of the property is more than ample to cover your investment. But comparable investments are available today that will give you a yield of 14 percent. So why would you buy Murphy's IOU, which pays only 10 percent?

You might offer to buy Murphy's IOU at a *discount;* that is, for less than the face value. Depending on how anxious Johnson is to get cash, he might be willing to sell you the $40,000 IOU for, say, $30,000. If such a deal is made, you will receive 10 percent on the amount of capital you have at work, and you will also, over the ten-year period, receive $10,000 over and above what you invested. The attractiveness of this kind of investing depends on the original interest rate on the mortgage, the amount of discount you can negotiate, and the true yield that results from the combination of the interest rate and the discount.

Mortgage Pools

Instead of just investing in a single mortgage, you can also pool your money with that of other investors in an assortment of numerous mortgages. The most popular program for this type of investing is offered through the Government National Mortgage Association (GNMA, or "Ginnie Mae"), an agency of the U.S. government. Ginnie Mae buys mortgages from lenders (banks, etc.), packages a few dozen into a pool, and then offers certificates to investors. Each certificate represents a share of ownership in a specific pool of mortgages; the minimum purchase price for a new certificate is $25,000. Ginnie Mae certificates are guaranteed by the U.S. government, which has made them very attractive to investors.

As a Ginnie Mae investor, you receive monthly checks, just as if you owned a single mortgage. The problem of return of principal, as discussed below, also exists with Ginnie Mae investments: if you don't reinvest each monthly payment as you receive it, it ceases to work for you. However, there are many mutual funds that invest in Ginnie Mae certificates. Shares in these funds can be obtained for as little as $1,000, and they do offer automatic reinvestment of your monthly income.

Other government-related programs offer similar forms of mortgage pool investing: the Federal Home Loan Mortgage Corporation ("Freddie Mac") offers participation certificates (PCs) and collateralized mortgage obligations (CMOs), and the Federal National Mortgage Association ("Fannie Mae") offers mortgage-backed securities (MBSs). Get full details on these plans from stockbrokers. And be certain to shop around, since prices and terms can differ from place to place.

Pitfalls: Return of Principal and Early Payoffs

There's one catch to investing in mortgages. Each monthly payment you receive contains some interest and some of your own investment that you're getting back. (Review the section on mortgage financing in chapter 7 to refresh your recollection of how this aspect of mortgages works.) Since you're receiving a small part of your investment back each month, that means that you have less and less of your original investment working for you as the months go by. Unless you take steps each month to reinvest your principal, your ultimate return won't be as much as you might have thought it would be.

For example, you invest $10,000 in a mortgage paying 12 percent interest for ten years. You will receive monthly payments of $143.50. Over the full ten years, those payments will total $17,220. You will have received, therefore, $7,220 more than you had invested. Divide that figure by 10 (for 10 years), and you come up with an average annual return of $722, which is equal to a 7.22 percent return on your original investment of $10,000. What happened to the 12 percent return that you were expecting? Each month, as you received the checks from the borrower, your original $10,000 investment dwindled because you were getting some of it back. In short, the whole $10,000 wasn't working for you all the time. In order to have kept it working for you, you would have had to reinvest the principal portion of each monthly payment as you received it. In all likelihood, the only way you could invest such small monthly sums safely would be in a passbook savings account, where your return would be far lower than 12 percent.

Another problem can arise when mortgages are paid off by the borrowers earlier than anticipated. Many investors in mortgage pools got soaked in 1993 because of this. Interest rates on home loans had reached a twenty-year low in 1993—under 7 percent for thirty-year fixed-rate loans. This prompted millions of homeowners to refinance their existing loans, which carried rates of 8 percent, 9 percent, 10 percent, and higher. This was a bonanza for the homeowners, but it was a bomb for those who had invested in the higher-yielding mortgage pools. Instead of having their investments run for ten to fifteen years at high rates, the investors were paid off early and then had to reinvest their money at much lower rates. They may have received all of their principal, but their income was cut substantially. This happens every time home loan interest rates take a dramatic plunge.

GROUP INVESTING

Small investors can pool their money with that of other small investors in real estate to take advantage of the depreciation laws discussed earlier.

Syndication and Limited Partnerships

Usually a promoter will embark on a project such as an apartment complex or a shopping center. Shares will be parceled out in denominations of $5,000, $10,000, and so on, to investors who wish to become involved. The promoter will take a fee for efforts in organizing the syndicate and may also share in the profits of the project. These syndicates are usually structured so that the promoters reserve all control of the money and the property, and the investors have no say in the matter.

Real estate syndications often take the form of a limited partnership in which individual investors are known as limited partners and the promoters are known as general partners. Syndications and limited partnerships are not without risks. Often, unwary or gullible investors believe grossly exaggerated profit potentials on such deals, only to find that such rewards never materialize. The prudent investor in a syndication will take every precaution, including viewing and appraising the property, making certain that all legal documents are in order, and determining the reputation and reliability of the organizers.

Real Estate Investment Trusts (REITs)

Exercise 16.3

These are investment programs set up under the federal tax laws to allow small investors access to the real estate investment market. A REIT is like a mutual fund. It will pool the money of small investors to acquire a variety of real estate investments and, as long as it adheres to tax regulations, it can pass its profits, income, and depreciation deductions along to individual investors. REITs tend to be much larger and more broadly based than syndicates. Since REIT shares are sold on stock exchanges, not only is the value of REITs affected by the income and profitability of the real estate interests they own, but they are also subject to the whims of the stock market. Because of this, REITs lose much of their element of certainty for prudent investors.

Potential investors should carefully examine the prospectus of a REIT to determine the nature and type of investments it is making and what the potential returns are.

Private Partnerships

Because so many real estate investments require a large down payment, an individual might seek partners in a particular venture.

But there can be problems. All the individuals involved must be firmly committed to the same long-term objectives. For example, investment partners must determine how much of the income will be pumped back into the property for refurbishing. They must determine who will be responsible for managerial duties, bookkeeping, tenant problems, and all other matters relating to the investment.

If one partner wants to sell out, will she be required to offer the share to the other partners first and, if so, on what terms? What kind of vote will it take to determine whether the property should be sold or refinanced?

The natural human tendency is not to worry about such matters until they arise. This can be foolhardy, for nothing can stand between friends and business associates more harmfully than disagreement over money. All possible items of dispute, including these noted here, should be reduced to a binding contract among the parties at the inception of the deal. A contract can't eliminate disputes, but it can minimize them.*

INVESTING IN SMALL BUSINESSES

Many people come across opportunities to invest in local businesses, becoming involved either as silent partners, active partners, or proprietors. An existing business may be seeking fresh capital for expansion or renovation or for the purchase of equipment. The owner may prefer to seek private financing rather than bank financing. The owner may prefer to offer a share of the profits to an investor rather than having to pay interest on a loan. Or an owner may wish to sell for a variety of reasons: retirement, illness, or simply a desire to move on to something else. On the other hand, the owner may be trying to get out from under a bad situation.

In any case, a would-be investor in a going business must do extensive and detailed investigation and will need the assistance of a lawyer and an accountant. Here is a brief checklist of matters the prudent investor must examine with the aid of those professional assistants.

- **Use of funds**   If the business is seeking funds for expansion, renovation, or new equipment, how specifically will the funds be put to use?

---

*The previous discussion offers only rudimentary guidelines on real estate investing. If you contemplate becoming seriously involved in real estate investing, it would be advisable for you to take the courses and exams given in your state leading up to the licensing of salespeople and brokers. Check with your local county Board of Realtors to determine how these courses of instructions can be obtained.

What are the prospects of the new capital being able to generate added profits?

- **Reason business is being sold**   If a business is being sold, you must determine the reasons for the sale. Is it a genuine case of retirement, illness, dissatisfaction with an associate, or lack of a successor? Or is there some problem that might not be visible on the surface?

- **Goodwill**   If you will be replacing the existing owner, either totally or partially, in the day-to-day operation of the business, you'll want to determine how much of the business's success (or lack thereof) is due to the owner's presence.

- **The lease**   Your attorney should review the lease on the premises to determine how well protected you are. How long does the lease run, and what kind of renewal options do you have? What provisions are there for increases in the rent or utilities, property taxes, and maintenance? To what extent will you be responsible for repairs? Will there be any percentage clauses requiring you to pay a portion of your gross business volume to the landlord as additional rent?

Working for Yourself

Chapter 21, "Working for Yourself," was created to help you evaluate the pros and cons, the dollars and cents, of going into business on your own, either by investing in an existing entity or starting one from scratch. Whether you are looking for self-employment or just for an investment opportunity, chapter 21 will help you do the analysis and arithmetic needed (with the help of the appropriate professionals) to make sound decisions.

GAMBLING IN COMMODITIES

Like vacant land and new business ventures, the commodities market represents a form of pure speculation. It's one of the most volatile, unpredictable, and high-pressure gambles yet devised. Next to a commodities exchange, a Las Vegas casino seems tame.

A commodity transaction is a bet on how much a given item will be worth at some date in the future. All of the items on which the bets can be placed (see Table 16–5) fluctuate wildly in value, moment to moment and day to day.

There's an old saying, "If you want to make a small fortune in the commodities market, start with a big fortune." That's not a joke. Horror stories abound from investors—some sophisticated, but most naive—who have been lured into the commodities market with the hopes of fast profits. Part of the extremely speculative nature of the commodities market involves the

TABLE 16–5   **Commodities and Exchanges**

Commodities	Exchanges
Grains and oilseeds (corn, oats, soybeans, wheat, etc.)	Chicago Board of Trade
Livestock and meat (cattle, hogs, pork bellies, etc.)	Chicago Mercantile Exchange
Food and fiber (cocoa, coffee, sugar)	Coffee, Sugar & Cocoa Exchange
Metals (copper, gold, silver, platinum, paladium)	New York Commodity Exchange, New York Mercantile Exchange, Chicago Board of Trade
Petroleum products (crude oil, heating oil, gasoline)	New York Mercantile Exchange
Foreign currencies (British pound, Canadian dollar, Japanese yen, German mark, U.S. Treasury Bonds and notes	Chicago Mercantile Exchange
Stock market indexes (Standard & Poor's 500 Index, New York Stock Exchange Index)	Chicago Mercantile Exchange, New York Futures Exchange

fact that your "bet" has a time limit to it. If you make a bet on a given commodity, there's a time limit on that bet. In effect, if your horse hasn't finished in the money within the set period of time, you lose your bet altogether. In the stock market, you can own a stock as long as you like, waiting for it to hit whatever target price you have in mind. You can live with the stock for years and years as it goes through its ups and downs. But, with commodities, when the expiration date arrives, your betting ticket becomes worthless.

Your bet can be won or lost because of many exotic and unpredictable influences, including weather conditions, crop blights, national and international politics, major shifts in the world's economy, minor shifts in the economy of any given nation, consumer boycotts, wars and insurrections, and even subtle shifts in popular opinion.

Exercise 16.4

Table 16–5 lists a small sampling of some of the items that can be bet on in the commodities market, as well as the exchange where the betting can be done. Any student interested in learning more about speculating in the commodities market can obtain abundant material through a stockbroker or through individual exchanges.

Commodity Funds

If the commodities market intrigues you, but the high level of risk frightens you, you might find commodity funds more to your liking. Commodity funds pool small investors' money and bet it on a diversified selection of commodities. In effect, commodity funds act like mutual funds, but technically they are a form of limited partnership.

Commodity funds can be somewhat less risky than direct speculations in commodities because of the diversification that is not available to individuals speculating on their own. Furthermore, at least it is hoped, professional management of the fund should be capable of making better decisions than an individual can.

Commodity fund investors should be wary of the costs they can incur by investing in the fund. It's not unusual for total costs, including management fees, brokerage commissions, and incentive fees, to total as much as 20 to 30 percent per year. That means that the investor won't make any money at all until after the fund has earned enough to cover those fees.

The prospectus of any commodity fund should be read thoroughly before an investment decision is made. In examining the prospectus, you should determine the extent of diversification of the fund's assets, the experience of the portfolio manager, and your ability to get your money out when you want it.

FOREIGN EXCHANGE AND DEPOSITS

Foreign Investing

In addition to speculating on various foreign currencies in the commodities market (see Table 16–5), there are many other ways that people can invest and/or speculate in the economic facets of other nations.

Bank Accounts

U.S. investors often open bank accounts in other nations, particularly Canada and Mexico. They may be lured by attractive interest rates, or they may be planning to spend time in those other nations and want the convenience of having accounts there. The latter reason makes more sense. If you're simply hoping to earn a higher rate of interest abroad than you can at home, then you must take into account a number of factors that can be unpredictable: the future exchange rate of the U.S. dollar versus the other currency; the tax laws of the other nation; and the ever-present possibility of the other currency's being devalued. In order to open a bank account in the currency of another nation, you have to convert your dollars to, for example, pesos. Then, when you want to retrieve the money to spend it back at home, you have to convert it from pesos back to dollars. These exchanges will cost you something, which could offset much of the seemingly attractive rate of interest you had hoped to earn. Tax laws in the other nation might require that a portion of your earnings be withheld to pay taxes in

STRATEGIES FOR SUCCESS

Beware of Unregulated Businesses

Stock markets and banks are strictly regulated by the government. If something goes wrong, you *might* have an ally in the state or federal government who can help you unravel the problem. But in many other areas of investment opportunity, governmental regulation ranges from slim to none. Simply stated, this means that if something goes wrong, you're on your own. You may have no recourse to any official agency. Generally speaking, franchising, distributorships, investments in precious metals, and limited partnerships are subject to relatively little governmental regulation. Even where regulation does exist, the road to recovery can be long and tortuous. Before you send away your money, know who's out there to help you get it back if things go wrong.

that nation. With respect to the possibility of devaluation, your investment can be immediately diminished in value if the other nation unilaterally declares that its currency is worth less per dollar today than it was yesterday. Another overriding concern: Your bank deposits in the United States enjoy the protection of the Federal Deposit Insurance programs. Would you enjoy the same protection if you invested in the banks of other nations?

Stock and Mutual Funds

Exercise 16.5

A small number of stocks in foreign companies can be bought and sold on United States stock exchanges using the device called American depository receipts (ADRs). In effect, a major U.S. bank buys a supply of shares of those particular companies and holds them in an escrow account for the benefit of American investors who purchase the ADRs. As an owner of the ADRs, you're subject to the same market fluctuations as you would be if you owned the stock directly.

Most major U.S. mutual fund companies offer a variety of funds specializing in foreign regions or specific nations. By investing in these funds, you get the benefit of supposedly expert analysis and advice in choosing particular stocks.

PRECIOUS METALS

Gold, silver, and platinum are extremely risky speculations. This was made clear at the start of the 1980s, and matters aren't likely to change for the rest of the century. Witness: In the early months of 1980, gold soared to more than $825 an ounce from the previous year's level of about $250 an ounce. At the same time, silver reached $50 an ounce from its level a year earlier of about $10 an ounce. In early 1982, gold had plummeted to less than $330 an ounce—a loss of more than 60 percent to those who had bought it at its peak. And there were many who had done so. The silver debacle was much swifter. One wealthy Texas family, the Hunts, had virtually cornered the silver market in early 1980, borrowing heavily to do so. When their ability to repay those debts came into doubt, the price of silver plunged by 80 percent within just a few months. Many small investors were wiped out.

Would-be investors in <u>precious metals</u> should remember the reasons why gold and other metals became tarnished: Widespread abuses and fraudulent dealings scared many people away from buying metals. Metal prices no longer seemed to respond to the signals that had set price moves just a few years earlier, signals such as world crises, inflationary trends, and interest rate movements. Many of the so-called gold bugs—commentators and analysts who touted the metals—began to lose their loyal followers because of bad advice. The speculative fever could return at any time, and when it does, many more innocents will get burned.

If you must speculate in precious metals, it is imperative that you deal only with firms whose reputations are totally reliable. Particularly avoid dealing with strangers over the telephone or through the mail. Whomever you deal with, use the following standards of measurement to be certain that you're getting what you bargained for.

Gold and silver are weighed in troy ounces. There are 31 grams to a troy ounce, and there are 480 grains to a troy ounce. It can be dangerous to confuse grains and grams and ounces.

What is referred to as pure gold is known as 24-karat gold. Anything less than 24-karat gold means that gold is mixed with another metal. Thus, 18-karat gold is $^{18}/_{24}$ (or 75 percent) real pure gold and 25 percent other metal; 12-karat gold is 1/2 pure gold and ½ other metal. Similarly, what is referred to as sterling silver is not pure silver but, rather, roughly 92.5 percent silver and the rest other metal.

The commonly quoted prices for these metals do not refer to a single ounce but to a much larger quantity. The price is known as the spot price; gold is quoted in 100 troy-ounce lots and silver in 5,000 troy-ounce lots. You would, then, expect to pay a higher price per ounce for quantities under the spot level.

Where to Speculate

- **Commodity exchanges** You can bet on the future value of precious metals on a number of commodity exchanges. Gold is traded on the

New York Commodity Exchange. Platinum is traded on the New York Mercantile Exchange. Silver is traded on the New York Commodity Exchange and the Chicago Board of Trade. Most major stock brokerage firms can place these bets for you.

- **Mining companies** Rather than buy the metals themselves, you can buy stock in the companies that mine them. Again, stock brokerage firms can handle the transactions for you. Mining stocks can be every bit as speculative as the metals themselves, but many do pay dividends, so your money is earning something for you as long as you own the stock.

- **Coins** Many nations, including the United States, have minted gold coins over the years. Some of them are older and, if in good condition, may have collector value over and above the gold value itself. To determine the true value of any such investment seek the assistance of a reputable coin dealer. All coins are subject to counterfeiting.

- **Jewelry** All gold jewelry manufactured in the United States is by law required to have the correct karat content stamped on the piece. But this law is not rigidly enforced. The best protection is to deal with reputable jewelers. Speculating in gold by way of jewelry purchases is probably the least feasible in terms of making money, for you will pay the dealer's markup plus the cost of any artistry that has gone into making the piece. It's unlikely that you'd be able to recapture those costs unless the value of gold triples or quadruples within a fairly short period of time.

One final caution: Trading in gold and silver—except on the commodity exchanges—is virtually unregulated. That means you'll have no governmental agency to turn to for help if you find you've been bilked.

STRATEGIC METALS

Strategic metals, in the broad sense, include cobalt, manganese, iridium, molybdenum, and chromium, among others. These metals are considered important to our national defense and industrial production, but we must import them from other countries in large quantities. Advances in technology could render some currently strategic metals not so strategic in the future; conversely, other currently insignificant metals and chemicals could become very important in the future.

As with the precious metals, the strategic metals are often touted as easy paths to getting rich quick by the same kinds of promoters who push gold and silver. As with gold and silver, the strategic metals investments are highly speculative.

GEMSTONES

The most popular form of gemstone speculation has been in diamonds. But speculation in colored gemstones (rubies, emeralds, and sapphires, primarily) has also been popular.

Gemstones are as unique as snowflakes. They vary not only in size and color, but also in basic quality, from priceless to pure junk. If you buy any gemstone sight unseen, you could be getting the junk. To buy any gemstone without first having it appraised by an independent certified gemologist is extremely hazardous.

Whether it's your intent to speculate in gemstones or to acquire them as jewelry pieces, you should be aware of the characteristics that contribute to their value or lack thereof. Diamonds are considered to be the most easily appraised of all gemstones. Colored gemstones are more difficult to appraise accurately because of the wider range of colors and chemical compositions in them. But, even with diamonds, experts can vary by as much as 10 to 20 percent in their estimates of value.

Exercise 16.6

Diamonds are evaluated in accordance with the four "Cs." Colored gemstones use similar formulas. The four Cs are color, cut, clarity, and carat weight.

- **Color**   Diamonds can range in color from the highly regarded "pure blue-white" to murky yellows. The better the color, the higher the value. Gemologists can grade the color of a diamond by use of a spectroscope. Even slight differences in the color grade can make a substantial difference in the value of a given stone.

- **Cut**   Raw diamonds (in the rough) will be cut into various sizes and shapes. The more highly valued cuts are those that permit the maximum brilliance of light to refract through the stone. The depth of the stone and the faceting contribute to brilliance or lack of it. The shape of the finished stone can also bear on its value. Gemologists can measure the precision of the cut of any diamond and grade it numerically.

- **Clarity**   When a diamond is looked at under a magnifying glass or microscope, impurities appear. (Some may even be visible to the naked eye.) The highest-clarity diamonds are those with the fewest flaws. Clarity is also rated numerically by gemologists.

- **Carat weight**   There's a lot of confusion between *karat* and *carat*. *Karat,* as noted earlier in the discussion on gold, measures the percentage of pure gold in a given item. *Carat* is an actual unit of weight. Thus, a diamond might weigh—on an actual scale—one carat, or two carats, and so on. A carat is divided into 100 points. Thus, a 25-point diamond is equal to one-quarter of a carat. Of two diamonds equal in color, cut, and clarity, the heavier one (carat weight) is the more valuable. But a one-carat stone of high quality in terms of color, cut, and clarity could be worth vastly more than a three-carat stone whose cut, color, or clarity is poor. Also, a single stone is worth more than an aggregate of smaller stones of equal quality and total weight. Thus, a single one-carat stone will be worth more than four 25-point stones of equal quality.

COLLECTIBLES

The possibilities are limitless: from old comic books to Chinese jade, from antique buttons to hubcaps, and everything in between. Whether prudent investment or wild speculation, the field of collectibles offers a measure of personal satisfaction in the hobby aspects of the endeavor. Thus, it is difficult to evaluate the financial considerations of collecting. If you get enough pleasure out of accumulating beer cans, movie posters, or original Picasso oil paintings, then perhaps the money doesn't matter.

But whether your objectives in collecting are personal, financial, or any combination of these, you need to observe some basic precautions lest you be separated from too much money needlessly.

- Coins and stamps are the most established forms of collectibles. Abundant information has been published on both, and the novice should take advantage of that literature. Both before buying and before selling, the latest price lists should be consulted. If major transactions are contemplated, an outside appraisal can be inexpensive insurance to protect a large investment.

- Many forms of collectibles cannot be readily converted into cash. The more exotic the items, the fewer potential buyers there may be. Finding a buyer for a collection may require considerable time and expense—such as advertising in specialized publications that deal with those types of items.

- Art collectors may have to turn to dealers to convert their collectibles into cash. A dealer is likely to pay only half the item's retail value, and that could mean a loss to the collector. On the other hand, some dealers are willing to take an item on consignment and take a commission on a sale. The commission may range from 10 to 25 percent. If the dealer is not successful in selling it, you take it back.

- Many collectibles go through fads. They may be hot one year, cold the next. If you get involved in a fad collectible that is on the wane, you could end up a big loser, but if you're lucky enough to get in on the rise, you could be a big winner.

- All collectibles require some level of expertise. Much of that expertise can be acquired by studying; much of it only by trial and error. Before embarking on a program of collectibles, therefore, do whatever studying you can and then proceed with caution until you are confident of when and what to buy, and when and what to sell.

TELEVISION "INVESTMENT OPPORTUNITIES"

Hardly a day goes by in which the average television viewer, flipping through the channels, doesn't find yet another get-rich quick scheme being offered on the tube in the form of a seminar, a lecture, a classroom full of "eager students," or some other such sales gimmick. Popular subjects for these spiels have been real estate, the stock market, mail-order distributor-ships, and a variety of cleverly disguised pyramid schemes. If anyone makes money from these so-called investments, it's the cable TV operator and the promoter—not the person who spends many hundreds of dollars for the "learn-at-home self-study kit." Valid information may be contained in those kits, whether it's on audiocassette or in printed form. But putting the information to use is never as easy as the TV pitchman makes you think it is. Nor are the "students" in the TV seminar classroom as honest or as ea-ger as they seem to be. They are probably hired actors performing a role for a day's pay rather than satisfied investors who have already gotten rich from the product. These self-promoting television programs prey on the naive and gullible individual trying to to find a new career or investment opportunity. They should be approached with the utmost caution. And note well: The money-back guarantees that are generally offered are worthless if, in fact, the company does not honor those guarantees. That has been the case all too often, leaving customers out many hundreds of dollars, with no recourse to anyone to get their money back.

PRIVATE LENDING

While not generally thought of as such, lending money to individuals or businesses is a form of investment. Whether they approach you or you ap-proach them, the same precautions are in order: Establish terms (interest rate, repayment date) that will be fair and reasonable. Check the credit of the borrower to determine the level of risk you are undertaking. If you think that the borrower's signature alone on the promissory note does not adequately protect you, seek either collateral or a cosigner for the loan. Be certain that you know the borrower's financial status: What other debts does the borrower have? What kind of income sources does he or she have? And, all things considered, from what sources will the borrower be able to make repayment on the loan? Have a promissory note properly drawn up by a lawyer, setting forth all the appropriate terms, including your rights should the borrower default on the payments. Have the borrower (and cosigner, if any) sign the note.

In short, take all the same precautions a bank would take when making a loan. If you find yourself faced with the prospect of making a private loan, a chat with your banker could be helpful to make sure you protect yourself adequately. In addition to having the banker show you the specifics of the loan procedure, it might be wise to inquire whether the banker would be willing to make the loan himself or to buy the loan from you should you later wish to sell the borrower's IOU. A banker who balks at either prospect probably sees some flaw in the loan that you might want to know about. Are you willing to take a risk that the bank would not?

KNOWLEDGE

Whether you're investing in the money market, the stock market, the real estate market, any of these assorted miscellaneous investments/ speculations, or any new activities that may come along, the best investment of all is your own investment in knowledge. The world of money is changing at an increasingly rapid pace: taxes, interest rates, governmental regulations, the emergence of new techniques, are all in a state of flux. Your own individual circumstances are also changing. You can't afford to ignore this outpouring of new information. If you want to make your money grow, you must fertilize it. And knowledge is the best fertilizer.

PERSONAL ACTION WORKSHEET

Income Property Evaluator

Before undertaking an investment in income property, make a careful analysis of both the cash flow and the condition of the property. The following analysis sheet will help you get started. Further analysis as to the specific investment advantages should be done with the help of your accountant and real estate agent.

	Prop. A	Prop. B	Prop. C
❏ What is the general condition of the building, including foundation, walls, roof, landscaping?	_____	_____	_____
❏ What is the specific condition of "working" aspects, including plumbing, heating, air conditioning, electrical system, elevators, appliances?	_____	_____	_____
❏ What is the current rental income (all sources)?	_____	_____	_____
❏ Are there any controls on raising rents?	_____	_____	_____
❏ What is the potential rental income within 12, 24, and 36 months?	_____	_____	_____
❏ What are the current operating expenses?	_____	_____	_____
❏ Do leases provide that tenants absorb any portion of operating expenses?	_____	_____	_____
❏ What are the potential total operating expenses within 12, 24, and 36 months? (Allow for likely increases in property taxes, insurance, maintenance, etc.)	_____	_____	_____
❏ What is the general condition of the immediate neighborhood, and what are the future trends?	_____	_____	_____
❏ Are nearby traffic patterns likely to remain stable, or might they be changed?	_____	_____	_____
❏ Can the existing mortgage be assumed by the buyer? At what interest rate?	_____	_____	_____
❏ What is the cost of interest for new financing, if needed?	_____	_____	_____

❏ What type of secondary financing
   will be needed?   _____   _____   _____

❏ Will the seller make secondary
   financing available? At what
   interest rate? Terms?   _____   _____   _____

❏ What is the estimated management
   time and money needed to run the
   property efficiently (in hours and
   dollars per week)?   _____   _____   _____

CONSUMER ALERT _____

If You're So Rich, How Come You're Not Smart?

Pardon the reversal on the old saying. It used to be that if you were smart you should also be rich. Nowadays, there's growing evidence that just because you are rich doesn't necessarily mean you're smart, too. If you have all the money in the world to hire the best talent and pay for the best research, how far wrong can you go, particularly if the players are the Rockefellers in the United States and the Mitsubishi people from Japan? And if players like that can goof horrendously, what's the poor novice investor to do? Here's what happened to these heavy hitters:

Mitsubishi bought an 80 percent interest in Rockefeller Center for about $1.4 billion, of which $1.3 billion was a mortgage owed to the sellers, Rockefeller Center Properties, Inc. But despite having such major-league tenants as General Electric, NBC, Simon & Schuster, and Radio City Music Hall, there wasn't enough rental income to make the mortgage payments. Attempts to renegotiate the mortgage failed, so Mitsubishi threw the property into bankruptcy, which could take years to unravel.

But don't pity the poor Rockefellers. They had the good sense to lay off their bet with a Real Estate Investment Trust (REIT), which took in money from some 40,000 small investors to cover the Rockefeller exposure. Shares in the REIT plummeted from $20 to $5. How far wrong can you go with names like Rockefeller and Mitsubishi? Ask the REIT 40,000.

But that sad deal pales by comparison with the experience of Dr. Sasaki, a Japanese investor who saw his net worth go from $4.7 billion to *minus* $2.4 billion in just a few years. *The Wall Street Journal* dubbed Dr. Sasaki the *poorest person in the world*. Here is what happened to the good doctor:

In the 1980s speculation was rampant in real estate in Japan, due largely to the government opening up the lending spigots full blast at the banks. Dr. Sasaki took advantage of the cheap and easy borrowing and accumulated ninety buildings! With all that money chasing a finite amount of property (the classical definition of inflation), property values soared out of sight.

Then in 1990 the erstwhile clueless Japanese government began to worry about the high property values. If borrowers couldn't pay their loans, the defaults could bring down the entire economy. So, to curb the speculation, the government forced the banks to raise interest rates on existing loans and curtail new lending. Guess what? The real estate market crashed, and Dr. Sasaki ended up owing $2.4 billion more than the buildings were worth. Don't you hate it when that happens?

Could U.S. lenders do the same thing? Not only could they. They did! It was called the Savings and Loan debacle. And yes, it could happen again.

UPS & DOWNS   *The Economics of Everyday Life*

Why Collectibles Go Up and Down in Value

Collecting things can be fun. If you can have fun and make money too, all the better. With this kind of attitude imbedded in the minds of many people, a collectible "industry" has emerged, making things for people who want to have fun and make money. The fun part is easy; the money part can be quite tricky. Originally, collectibles meant stamps and coins. While governments printed and minted millions of each, there was a known limit to the number created, and each had the legitimacy of a government behind it. And governments are nonprofit entities.

When private companies make *collectibles,* there is concern as to how their profit-making motives will impact on the future value of the items they make. Those items include huge numbers of plates, dolls, figurines, souvenirs, toys, sports cards, lithographs, and comic books. The following techniques can be used to manipulate values.

Fad   Clever marketers will spot fads and be ready for them with a supply of collectibles to sell. Olympic pins were all the rage at the Atlanta games in 1996. Sports memorabilia come and go with the popularity and incomes of our athletic heroes. (On a morbid note, when Magic Johnson announced that he was HIV-positive, a run began on his memorabilia and prices went sky-high.) When the fads fade—and they always do—so do the prices.

Questionable advertising   Collectibles are worth more if they are made in limited number—and still more if each one is numbered—and still more if each one is signed by the artist—and still more if the mold or engraving plate is destroyed after the limited number is made, which assures that no more can ever be made. Many ads may say that they are *limited editions,* but that can mean anything: "limited to how many we can make in the next twelve months" or "limited to the number of orders we get." A true limited edition must state a specific number. Legitimate manufacturers will stick to that number, and the long-term value of the object will be reflected accordingly.

Secondary market   One way to artificially boost the price of *new* collectible items is to manipulate public opinion as to the value of *older* items in the series. Say that each year a company makes a porcelain doll of that year's Oscar-winning director. They are marketed as *collectibles,* with hints that they will increase in value each year. The 1993 doll was issued at $100, and later models went up by $25 each year. When the newest model is announced, collectors salivate when they hear that the market value of the 1993 model is now $500! But it can all be a sham. To manipulate the secondary market (the price of the older dolls), a few ads can be placed in catalogs that collectors read, offering to buy the 1993 doll for $500. Word travels fast. When you call to sell them yours, you'll be told they've already bought all they can afford. Sorry. Similar gossip can also be spread at collectible shows and on the Internet. The new models sell out, and the game begins anew the next year.

? WHAT IF . . . ?

Test yourself: How would you deal with these real-life possibilities?

1. There's yet another crisis in the Middle East. A shooting war seems likely. You get a phone call from a stranger pitching gold: "The price will go through the roof because of international uncertainties." He may be right. Evaluate the pros and cons of dealing with this person.

2. You are on the Building Committee of your synagogue or church. Money is being pledged by members to build a day school. It's expected that it will take two to three years for the money to come in, and another year after it's all in before construction is ready to proceed. In the meantime the money has to be invested. Other members of your committee include a commodity broker and a mortgage broker. They both offer plans to invest the money through their own channels. In each case they will relinquish their normal commissions if the investments flow through them. You are asked for your thoughts on those modes of investing. What would you say?

3. On a visit to Mexico you learn that Mexican banks are paying five percentage points more to savers than are banks back home. You're intrigued, and you consider shifting most of your savings there to boost your earnings. If millions of Mexican citizens are doing it, why shouldn't you? What further information do you need in order to make a sound decision?

NUMBER CRUNCHERS

Do the calculations to make decisions in these real-life possibilities.

1. Some friends are urging you to chip in with them to buy a vacant parcel of land on the outskirts of your city. They feel there's a good chance to make a tidy profit as the city grows in that direction. A one-fourth interest would cost you $10,000. Total annual expenses on the property are $2,200 (including property taxes and insurance). When the property is sold, assume that you'll have to pay a real estate commission of 10 percent of the selling price and that income taxes on any profit will be 15 percent of the profit. If the property is sold after three years, how much will it have to sell for so that you can reap an average annual net return of 10 percent on your $10,000 investment?

2. You're thinking of investing in real estate. You look at a residential property priced at $175,000 and find that 35 percent of that price represents the land value. A commercial property is priced at $240,000, and 68 percent of that price represents the land value. Based on the depreciation periods noted in this chapter, how much of an annual

depreciation deduction would you be entitled to on each of these buildings, if you paid the asking price?

3. You invest $500 a year for five years in stamp collecting. That money could have earned 6 percent per year, compounding annually, in a savings plan. At the end of five years, how much would the stamps have to be worth to be equal to what you would have had in the savings plan (not counting income taxes)?

FOR BETTER OR FOR WORSE

Things beyond our control often impact our personal and financial well-being, for better or for worse. Some are more predictable than others. How could you be affected if the following real-life phenomena happened? Could you have seen it coming? What steps could you have taken to minimize damage or maximize advantage? The better able you are to anticipate and recognize these forces, the better equipped you are to deal with them.

1. You invest in a small apartment building. Even though the rental income in the first year will be offset by your expenses, the expected 10 percent annual increases in rent will produce a nice profit for you. Shortly thereafter, the city passes a rent control ordinance limiting rent increases to 2 percent a year.

2. A broker convinces you to bet a lot of money on the future value of the British pound. If the pound is strong against the dollar, you're a big winner, and the British government looks certain to succeed economically. Along comes a three-month dock strike against British shippers. The British economy is crippled, and the pound plunges against the dollar.

3. A late-night TV infomercial is selling a course on how to get rich in real estate by buying property with no money down. For $499 you can buy the course, with a money-back guarantee within thirty days if you're not satisfied. After twenty-nine days you're not satisfied, and you call the company to ask for your money back. You're told that you didn't use the right technique to buy the properties, and that you should "try it this way for another month and see if it doesn't work out for you."

17

Life, Health, and Income Insurance

This is a world of action, and not for moping and groaning in.
                    Charles Dickens

Part Five is titled "Protecting What You Work For." In order to do that, you must take steps to minimize the risks that everyone faces in day-to-day life: loss of life, serious medical problems, and loss of income. All the best financial planning in the world can come to naught if you do not take these steps to protect yourself.

This chapter isn't going to try to sell you any insurance; rather, it's designed to enable you to

- Understand how life, health, and income insurance policies work
- Distinguish among different types of policies, their benefits, and their costs
- Gain a working knowledge of the language and jargon of insurance policies so that you can communicate clearly with sales personnel
- Determine how much of what type of insurance you actually need as part of your overall protection plan
- Be aware, and take advantage, of insurance programs available through various governmental agencies

COPING WITH RISK

Life is full of surprises—risks—that we don't always anticipate or prepare for. Some of these risks we accept willingly: driving a car, taking on a new job, investing or betting our money. Others may be strictly a matter of fate: illness, natural disaster, an employer going bankrupt.

In earlier chapters, we examined automobile insurance and homeowner's (and tenant's) insurance. Those types of insurance reimburse us for damages suffered to our cars and our dwellings and also reimburse people who suffer losses arising from automobile accidents that involve us and accidents to others on our property. We may never suffer losses in connection with our cars or our homes, but we still need the insurance to protect us against the *possibility* of such losses.

Likewise with health and income insurance: We may never be ill, and we may never suffer loss of income from extended illness, accident, or other unforeseen cause. But we still need insurance to protect us against the *unforeseen*.

Life insurance is designed to provide money to the survivors of an insured person when that person dies. Death is certain to occur, but we never know when. If the breadwinner of a young and growing family dies prematurely, life insurance will, in effect, reimburse the survivors for lost earnings, thus enabling them to continue to live in relative comfort and security. If an insured person dies at or after the normal life-expectancy age, the proceeds of the insurance may be needed to pay estate taxes, to provide support for a surviving spouse, to allow the insured's business to continue, or simply to add to the wealth of the survivors. Let's take a look at insurance in general as a device to protect us against loss. Then we'll examine the basic mechanics of life insurance.

Insurance Is Protection Against Risk

That is what insurance is all about. Example: On an average day, 1,000 skiers will run a slope and one will end up in the hospital. The cost of hospitalization may be $5,000. You never know whether that injured skier will be you or one of the 999 others. If it is you, your injuries will cost you $5,000. But if each skier chipped in $5 to cover the cost of that day's accident—whomever it might happen to—you have eliminated your risk at a very insignificant cost. For the price of $5, you may have saved yourself $5,000. You may run the slope 1,000 times and never be hurt, but experience indicates that that's not likely.

If all the skiers don't chip into a kitty to protect themselves, some enterprising person may make the arrangements for them: point out the risks each skier faces, arrange to collect and hold all the money in safekeeping, and pay the proceeds to the injured parties as injuries occur. For this

service, the entrepreneur is entitled to a fee; thus, instead of charging $5 per skier, the charge may be $5.10 or $5.20. In so doing, the entrepreneur is acting as a one-person insurance company.

That, in a nutshell, is how the insurance industry operates. The insurance company determines the probability of loss in many given situations, such as a house burning down, an automobile crashing, a person dying before the normal life expectancy, and so on. The company further determines how much money it must collect from each individual to insure protection for all the individuals, should the stated loss occur. (These calculations are known as the actuarial phase of insurance.) That money, or premiums, paid by the insured is invested prudently, so that the fund, or reserve, can grow until it comes time to pay benefits to people who have suffered losses.

When one enters into an agreement with an insurance company the parties sign a contract that sets forth all the specific rights, duties, and obligations of the parties. This contract is called an insurance policy. Its details are discussed later.

WHY LIFE INSURANCE?

Victor is forty years old with a wife and two teenage children. He's in good health and makes about $45,000 per year with good prospects for improvement. He wants his children to have a good college education, but meeting his mortgage payments hasn't allowed him to put much money aside for college. Even though Victor's life expectancy is about an additional thirty-five years, he's very much aware that he could die tomorrow. Contemplating this possibility, Victor thinks, "If I died suddenly, where would the money come from to keep my family reasonably comfortable and provide for the college educations? I'd need an immediate nest egg of about $300,000. If they invested that wisely, the income and some of the principal could take care of their needs for quite a long time. But right now I'd have trouble raising the price of a new suit, let alone $300,000."

Instant Solution?

How can Victor resolve this dilemma? He might be lucky enough to beat multimillion-to-one odds and win a lottery. Or he could stash money in a savings plan; at the rate of $300 per month, he'd meet his goal in just under twenty-five years. These aren't very satisfactory solutions.

To solve his problem, Victor needs an *immediate* and *guaranteed* way to create protection for his family. That is the main purpose of life insurance.

Life insurance can be created instantly (or, more correctly, in the few weeks it takes to process an application). Rather than take chances on a lottery ticket or wait decades for a savings fund to build up, Victor can immediately create the level of protection he wants through life insurance.

STRATEGIES FOR SUCCESS

Insure Before It's Too Late

The single most important lesson in this chapter, and perhaps even in the whole book, is that *you never know when you might become uninsurable!* Whether for life, health, disability income, or long-term care insurance, you can become uninsurable as a result of unexpected medical problems. A slightly less worst-case scenario is that a medical condition might cause you to have to pay a lot more for the coverage you want, compared with if you were in good health. Further, the older you are, the more costly the insurance can be. When it comes to insurance, playing the waiting game can definitely be a losing proposition.

The protection is guaranteed as long as the premiums on the policy are paid. Victor may also consider the desirability of life insurance for his wife and children. If his wife works and if the family also depends on her income, she should consider insuring her life so as to replace the income that would be lost in the event of her premature death. Insurance on the life of a nonworking spouse can pay the costs of treating a terminal illness or paying for child care now provided by the nonworking spouse. If the spouse's estate is subject to estate taxes, life insurance can be used to pay those taxes in lieu of having to sell other assets to pay the tax. The *primary* objective of a family's life insurance portfolio should be the replacement of income in the event of a breadwinner's death.

On learning how the dilemmas can be solved, Victor (and you) are likely to ask, "Can I afford to do it?" But a more appropriate question might be, "Can I afford *not* to do it?" The material that follows will give you guidelines that will be useful in establishing any life insurance program suitable for your own needs.

THE BASIC ELEMENTS OF LIFE INSURANCE

A life insurance policy is a contract between an individual and a life insurance company. The individual agrees to pay premiums, in return for which the company guarantees to pay a certain amount to the beneficiaries named in the contract at the death of the insured party. But life insurance policies are as different as snowflakes. There are more than 1,800 life insurance companies in the United States, and all of them offer many different types of policies. Furthermore, the mathematics of life insurance differ widely, depending on the age of the insured at the time the policy is purchased, the amount and type of coverage, and the specific terms of the contract. The most visible common thread in all life insurance contracts is that the younger you are when you initiate a contract, the lower your costs will be. Let us now examine some of the major diversities in life insurance.

Kinds of Companies: Stock and Mutual

There are basically two different kinds of life insurance companies: stock companies and mutual companies. Stock companies are owned by stockholders, in much the same fashion as stockholders own such companies as General Motors and AT&T. If the company is run profitably, the stockholders will receive dividends on their stock in much the same way as stockholders of industrial companies.

Mutual companies are owned by their policyholders. In a mutual company, when the premium income exceeds the expenses (benefits paid and other expenses) by a certain amount, the policyholders/owners will receive back a portion of the excess. These sums are also referred to as dividends, but they are technically not the same thing as dividends received on common stock.

Par and Nonpar Policies

The kinds of policies issued by mutual companies, for which dividends are paid to policyholders, are referred to as participating policies—the policyholders participate in a distribution of excess income over expenses.

Stock companies generally do not pay such dividends to their policyholders. These policies are referred to as nonparticipating policies. In some instances, however, stock companies do issue participating policies.

Participating and nonparticipating policies are commonly referred to as par and nonpar.

The difference between stock and mutual companies may be better understood by referring back to the earlier example of the skiers. The skiers who banded together on their own to chip in $5 for each day formed a kind of mutual company. The skiers who declined to do this on their own but entrusted the matter to an outsider took part in a stock company.

Premiums on par policies will customarily be higher than premiums on nonpar policies, all other things being equal. But the owner of a par policy has the hope of receiving dividends each year that may be used to offset the cost of the policy. The dividends on a par policyholder could reduce the out-of-pocket cost of insurance to less than that of an equal nonpar policy. For example, two policies of equal face value, one par and one nonpar, have annual premiums of $300 and $250. If the par policy pays a dividend of $60 per year, then the par policy will end up being less expensive than the nonpar policy. But insurance companies cannot give any guarantee of what dividends will be paid in any given year. It will depend on their actual experience of premium dollars received and expense and benefit dollars paid out.

How Is Life Insurance Acquired?

Life insurance is generally acquired in one of three ways: group plans, private plans, and credit plans.

Group Plans

Group life insurance is designed for groups of people in similar circumstances. Your employer, for example, may provide a plan for all employees. Group insurance may also be issued to members of social organizations, professional organizations, and unions. The insured individuals may not be required to take physical examinations to prove the state of their health. The group insurance policy will cover all eligible persons, and each will receive a copy of the master policy, or an outline of it. In some cases, the employer or union may pay the premiums for all the individuals; in other cases, such as professional associations, individuals make their own payments.

When an individual ceases to be a member of the group, his or her insurance may terminate. But, in many cases, it's possible for the individual to continue the coverage by paying the necessary premiums personally.

Because administration costs on a group policy can be much lower than those on individual policies, the premium cost to those in a group plan is generally lower than what it would be in a private plan.

Private Plans

Private insurance is contracted for directly between the individual and the insurance company. Depending on the issuing company and the amount of insurance involved, a physical examination of the insured may be required.

Credit Plans

When you borrow money, the lender may offer you life insurance that will pay off any balance on the loan should you die. This is available in mortgage loans and in installment loans, such as for an automobile or home improvements. The amount of the insurance decreases as the balance on the loan decreases. (This is known as decreasing term insurance.) In short-term installment loans, the insured will generally pay the full premium in one lump sum at the inception of the loan. In long-term loans, the amount of the insurance premium is frequently added to the amount of the loan and is included in the payments.

Types of Life Insurance

Life insurance policies are generally either permanent or temporary. Permanent insurance is designed to run permanently: that is, for the life of the insured individual. This type of insurance is known as ordinary, straight or whole life insurance.

Temporary insurance is designed to run for a specific period of time, such as one year, five years, or ten years. This is known as term insurance. At the end of the term, the insurance ceases. With renewable-term policies, the insured can renew for an additional term, but at a higher premium cost. Term policies may also be convertible to ordinary policies.

Universal life insurance offers a variety of flexible features: Within limits, the face amount of the policy and the amount of annual premium can be adjusted by the owner of the policy.

Another type of life insurance contract is the annuity, in which the insured is guaranteed a fixed monthly payment, which will begin at a specified time and will last for the agreed-on length of time. Let's take a closer look at these various types of life insurance.

Permanent Insurance

Permanent insurance is a lifetime contract. You agree to pay a fixed premium, and the insurance company agrees to deliver a stated sum of money at your death or, in certain cases, at some earlier time. If the money is to become payable prior to death, the insured may elect to receive it in a lump sum or in periodic installments, plus interest. The company can also hold the money (paying interest on it) for as long as the insured lives and then pay it to the beneficiaries. The rate of interest payable on money held for the insured or survivors will be set forth in the contract.

A permanent policy builds up *cash values*, also referred to as conversion values or nonforfeiture values. These values permit the insured to terminate the policy and obtain either cash or some other form of insurance at some later time. These values are discussed in more detail later.

Examples of permanent insurance include:

- You agree to pay the stated premiums for, say, twenty years. At the end of that period, the policy will be *paid up*—the full face value will be payable on death, and you don't have to pay any more premiums. This policy would be referred to as a Limited Pay Plan or, in this case, Twenty-pay Life: Twenty years of payments pays it up in full.

- You agree to pay the stated premiums for the remainder of your life. At your death, the full face value will be payable. This policy would be referred to as a Whole Life Policy.

- You agree to make certain premium payments, and the full face value is then paid at a stated age, say, 65. If you don't elect to take the cash, you can exercise other options such as receiving installment payments or having the company hold it for you for later payment to you or your beneficiaries. Such a policy may be referred to as *endowment at age 65*.

The amount of the premiums for these various policies varies considerably. For example, in the Twenty-pay Life policy, the insurance company has only 20 years in which to accumulate the money needed to pay the benefits, even though the life expectancy of the individual may be much longer. So the company must charge a higher premium than it would for Whole Life, for it has fewer years in which to accumulate the needed funds.

In the endowment policy, the full face value becomes payable at a specific age. Again, the company has fewer years in which to accumulate the needed money than it would on a Whole Life policy, so it must charge more accordingly.

Term Insurance

Term insurance is "pure" insurance. You obtain a fixed amount of protection at a fixed annual price for a fixed amount of time. For example, a 25-year-old might obtain a term policy for $25,000 for five years at an annual premium of $100 per year. In most term policies policyholders can renew for an additional term but at a higher annual premium, since they are older. Thus, the 25-year-old, on reaching age 30, might find that his $25,000 worth of protection will now cost $120 per year. To renew for another five-year term at age 35, the annual premium might go to $150 per year. As the insured gets older still, the cost will increase at greater rates on each renewal.

With rare exceptions, term insurance policies do not build up any of the cash or conversion values found in permanent policies.

Many term insurance policies contain a right to convert to a permanent insurance policy at stated times. Depending on the company and the amount of insurance, the insured may or may not have to take a physical examination, either on initiating or renewing the term policy or on converting it to a permanent policy.

Because term insurance does not have any cash value buildup as a rule, it is the least expensive for initial out-of-pocket premium expenses. But as term insurance is renewed at ever-increasing ages—and thereby at increasing rates—the ultimate out-of-pocket expenses can exceed those of permanent life insurance.

As indicated earlier, another, and still cheaper, form of term insurance is decreasing term insurance, which accompanies mortgage loans and installment loans. Such insurance is cheaper because the amount of actual insurance decreases each year as the balance on the loan decreases.

Universal Life Insurance

Universal life insurance is a variation of whole life insurance. In general, the universal policy allows the owner to make periodic adjustments in the amount of coverage and the amount of premium to be paid. Universal life mixes investment features with insurance features. When interest rates are high, universal policies can be very attractive because your premium dollars are invested at higher rates of return, and those returns are, in large part, credited to you. When interest rates are lower, the universal policies are not as attractive. For the relatively unsophisticated individual, the complexities and variabilities of universal life may render it not the best product for your needs.

Annuities

An annuity provides income for an individual who purchases such a contract. This individual is called the *annuitant*. The buyer of an annuity contract pays money to the insurance company either in one lump sum or in periodic payments over a number of months or years. The insurance company then agrees to pay back to the contract holder a sum of money each month for an agreed-on amount of time.

That sum of money may be fixed in the contract (a fixed-dollar annuity) or may vary (a variable annuity), but there is a guaranteed minimum. With a fixed-dollar annuity, the funds are invested conservatively—predominantly in government and corporate bonds as well as mortgages.

With a variable annuity, a substantial portion of the money may be invested in the stock market. The theory is that the stock market can provide protection against inflation. If the theory works, the annuitant may get more back than might have been received under a fixed-dollar annuity.

Here's a brief description of the common types of payment programs available with annuities.

- **Straight life annuity**   Once you have made your payments, you will begin to receive the agreed-on monthly sum at the agreed-on date. The payments last for as long as you live. Whenever an annuitant dies the payments cease. If the annuitant lives far beyond the normal life expectancy, she will continue to receive the monthly payments as long as she lives. The company, in effect, is taking the risk that the annuitant will live no longer than the life expectancy.

- **Annuity with installments certain**   This provides monthly payments for a fixed period of time—perhaps ten or twenty years. If annuitant dies before the time has elapsed, the named beneficiary receive the payments until the term finally ends.

- **Refund annuities**   If an annuitant dies before receiving back money paid in, the beneficiary will get back the balance may be in installments or in one lump sum.

- **Joint and survivor annuity**   This type can cover two a husband and a wife. When one dies, the other con the payments until the agreed-on fund or the length exhausted.

- **Single premium annuity**   Rather than make an annuity, you can make a single lump-sum accumulate until your payout plan begins. As with cash values on straight-life insurance, the earnings on annuities accumulate on a tax-deferred basis. That is, no income taxes are payable on those earnings until the earnings are withdrawn. Because of this the single premium annuity is often regarded as a form of investment rather than as a form of insurance. Indeed, it is heavily marketed as such.

Single premium annuities may offer a fixed or a variable rate of return. The single premium annuity will also have a penalty provision: you forfeit some of your original investment if you withdraw any of it during the earlier years of the contract. (If the rate of interest being paid on the annuity drops below a certain level, you might be able to withdraw your money without penalty. This is known as the bailout provision.)

The Parties to an Insurance Policy

As many as five parties can be involved in an insurance policy contract: the insured, the owner, the beneficiary, the contingent beneficiary, and the company. The roles of each of these parties are important to understanding life insurance. Let's take a closer look at each.

The Insured

This is the person whose life is insured by the policy. It is on the death of the insured that the proceeds are paid. The insured may also be the owner of the policy, but it is possible for the insured and the owner to be different parties.

A fairly new product is the second-to-die policy, in which two people—usually husband and wife—are insured in the same policy. In these policies, the death benefits are paid only when the second of the two insured parties dies. Because two parties are insured, the company has a longer time span before it has to pay death benefits. Thus, the cost to the insured parties can be much less for a given face amount than if only one party were insured.

The Owner

The owner is the most important person in the policy, for it is the owner who has the power to exercise various options including naming and changing the beneficiary, making loans against the policy or cashing in the policy.

Consider Harold and Esther. Harold applies for a life insurance policy on himself and retains ownership in his own name. He names Esther as the beneficiary. In this case, Harold is both the insured and the owner. Harold can later transfer ownership to Esther.

Here are other examples of the owner and the insured not being the same party. Lillian is a valuable employee, so her boss pays for a policy on

Lillian's life payable to the company. This is to protect the company in the event of Lillian's death—it would alleviate, for example the expense of getting along temporarily without Lillian's services. This is known as *key employee* insurance. The company is the owner of the policy, and Lillian is the insured.

Jim needs a loan from his bank. The bank may offer Jim a life insurance policy, with the proceeds payable to the bank in the event of Jim's death. As discussed in chapter 12, this is known as credit life insurance. In such a case, the bank is the owner of the policy and Jim is the insured.

The owner has exclusive powers regarding a life insurance policy. The owner can assign the policy to a creditor. For example, Jim, instead of buying a new credit life policy, assigns an existing policy to the bank to protect the bank in the event of his death. Should Jim default on the loan, the bank can take whatever cash values exist in the policy. (An assignment is valid only if the insurance company has been properly notified and has accepted the assignment.)

The owner can change the beneficiary of the policy, provided that that right has been reserved in the original policy.

The owner can transfer ownership to another party, and this might be wise in certain instances of estate planning.

The owner can exercise the conversion provisions in the policy.

The owner can dictate the manner in which the face amount will be payable to the beneficiary, where a choice exists.

Only the owner can make these changes, and they must be done in accord with the insurance contract. The insured cannot exercise these powers unless the insured is also the owner. If Harold conveys a life insurance policy on his own life to Esther as the owner, then it is Esther, and Esther only, who can exercise the rights granted in the policy. As long as Harold retains ownership, only he can exercise those rights.

The Beneficiary

The beneficiary is the one who receives the payments to be made on the death of the insured. The choice of the beneficiary is up to the owner of the policy, who, as noted earlier, may be the same party as the insured. The beneficiary may be one or more persons, a charity, a business concern, or the estate of the insured.

The Contingent Beneficiary

There is always the possibility that the originally named beneficiary will die before the insured. The owner of the policy can name a contingent beneficiary, who will take the place of the original beneficiary if that person dies before the insured. If no contingent beneficiaries are named, the policy will set forth how the proceeds will be distributed.

The Company

The company is, of course, the insurance company with whom you are entering into the contract. You, as the insurance buyer, will deal with a representative of the company—either an agent connected directly with the company or an independent agent who may represent a number of various companies. The agent is the party to whom the insured should turn when any question arises.

The Life Insurance Contract and Its Clauses

A life insurance policy is a legally binding contract once it has been properly signed by the owner and the company. The policy sets forth all the rights, duties, and obligations of the parties. The only way the contract can be amended is by written agreement between the parties. Changes to a life insurance policy—or any other kind of insurance policy—are called endorsements or riders.

The Application

The application is the questionnaire the applicant for insurance must fill in to have the policy issued. The application contains pertinent information about the individual applying for insurance, including medical data. If the application contains false or misleading information, the policy may later be voided if the insurance company does learn the truth. For example, an individual applying for life insurance may have recently had a severe heart attack but states that he is in perfectly good health. If the policy is issued, he has entered into the agreement on false premises, and the policy may be voided if the company learns of the circumstances within the stated time limit.

Insurance companies go to considerable lengths to avoid being defrauded. Physical examinations are conducted, and neighbors may be interviewed to learn an individual's personal habits. All doctors the applicant has seen in the past few years may be questioned.

The Medical Information Bureau assists the insurance industry in minimizing fraudulent applications. When people apply for life, health, or disability insurance, they sign a statement giving the insurance company permission to relay all health information to the Medical Information Bureau (MIB) and seek out any information that may exist there relative to the individual's health.

Of all applications for life insurance in the United States, only 3 percent are declined. Eighty-five percent have policies issued at the standard risk levels, and 4 percent of the applications have policies issued at extra risk levels. Where there is an obvious health problem but one not so great that the company will refuse coverage, the policy may be issued, but at a higher premium.

Face Amount, or Face Value

The face amount is the amount of money due the beneficiary on the death of the insured. It is set forth on the policy, and it is what we usually refer to when we talk about the amount of an insurance policy. For example, if we say a "$10,000 life insurance policy," we're talking about the face value of the policy.

It is possible that the beneficiary could receive more or less than the original face value. The beneficiary may receive more than face value if a double indemnity clause was activated in the policy. The beneficiary may also receive more than the face value if the owner had applied dividends that had been received toward the purchase of additional insurance.

If the owner has borrowed against the policy and has not paid off these loans the beneficiary will receive the face value minus any unpaid loans (and accrued interest owing on those loans).

Double Indemnity, or Accidental Death Benefit

A double indemnity clause, which is available at an additional premium, provides for the payment of double the face amount in the event of accidental death, as opposed to natural death.

Incontestable Clause

The insurance company has a set time, usually two years, during which it may contest any suspected false information in the application. During that period, a company can void the policy if improper statements were made. But once the two years have elapsed, the company can no longer contest any statements.

Guaranteed Insurability

Some policies will, for an additional premium, guarantee you the right to increase the face value regardless of your health. The cost of obtaining this guarantee should be carefully evaluated.

Premium and Mode of Payments

The policy contract will spell out how much the premiums are on the policy and how they can be made. The policyholder may elect to pay premiums annually, semiannually, quarterly, or monthly. Monthly or quarterly payment plans might cost slightly more due to increased bookkeeping.

Lapse, Grace Period, and Reinstatement

The company will pay the face value to the beneficiary as long as the policy remains in force. The term *in force* means that the owners have paid their premiums on time. If a policyholder does not pay on time, the policy can lapse. When a policy lapses, it is terminated. There is no more insurance.

It can be most imprudent to let a policy lapse. Money paid in up to the date of lapse will be forfeited, and if you wish to obtain life insurance at a later time, it will cost more because of increased age. In some cases physical problems may prevent you from being able to get the insurance at all.

The insurance industry has structured the typical life insurance policy so that a lapse does not occur that easily or that automatically.

If a premium is not paid by the stated due date, policyholders will have a grace period of usually thirty-one days, during which they can still make payment and continue the policy in force without any penalty.

If payment still has not been made by the end of the grace period, many permanent policies have an automatic cash loan provision. If cash values have already begun to build up in the policy and there is enough to cover the payment of one premium, the company automatically borrows against those values and uses the proceeds to pay the premium, thus continuing the policy in force for another period.

Even after a lapse has occurred, policyholders have a limited time within which to reinstate the policy. They may have to take a new physical examination or sign a statement about health conditions. If the company is satisfied about the state of the insured's health and all back premiums and any interest owing thereon are paid, the policy can be reinstated.

Waiver of Premium

This is available at a slight additional cost on most life insurance policies. It provides that if the insured is totally disabled, the need to make premium payments will be waived. It's like a miniature income disability policy built into the life insurance policy. Note that the definition of *totally disabled* differs from policy to policy. It might, for example, be defined as "unable to work in a job for which you were trained" or "unable to work at all." The difference can be important.

Conversion Values

Conversion (or nonforfeiture) values become available to policyholders under permanent life insurance policies. The values build up as you pay premiums over the years, but the rate of buildup varies from policy to policy. In shopping for life insurance, you should carefully compare the rate of growth and relative size of these values. Policy A may have a lower premium than policy B for the same face value. Thus, policy A may seem to be the better value. But policy B may have higher conversion values, which could be of considerable importance years later. Thus, what you get for your premium dollar isn't just the face value of the policy. These values must be considered most carefully.

Here's how conversion values work. If you cease paying your premiums by choice or otherwise, these conversion values will allow you to convert your policy into a number of alternative plans.

CASHING IN You can cash in the policy. You then receive the amount of cash set forth in the cash value table, and the policy terminates.

BORROWING You can borrow against the policy up to the amount in the loan value table, at a rate of interest set forth in the policy. It might be a very attractive rate compared with what one would have to pay at a bank.

Borrowing is simple: notify the company of your wishes and receive a check shortly thereafter. Repayment is up to you: you need not repay the principal at all; but you must pay interest annually. If you do not repay the principal, the face value will be diminished by the amount of the outstanding loan at the time of the insured's death. For example, if the face value on a given policy was $10,000 and the owner borrowed $1,000 against it and then died before repaying the loan, the beneficiary would receive only $9,000.

From time to time, it might pay to borrow against your life insurance values. For example, if you can borrow against your policy at 8 percent, and you can invest at, say, 10 percent, the 2 percent differential is profit. If you invest conservatively, you will still be protecting your family, since the investment itself would be available to them in the event of your death. However, if you speculate, you are jeopardizing the well-being of your survivors.

If you borrow against your life insurance policy for consumer debt purposes (to buy a car, to pay off debts, etc.), the interest you pay on the debt will not be tax-deductible. If you borrow for business purposes, or for investment, the interest might be deductible in full. Check with your tax advisor for most current regulations.

CONVERTING TO EXTENDED TERM INSURANCE You can convert your existing program to extended term insurance. With such insurance, you will be covered for the same original face value of the policy, but only for a *limited period of time* rather than for the rest of your life.

CONVERTING TO PAID-UP INSURANCE You can convert to paid-up insurance. If you cease paying premiums, you can still be covered for a *portion* of the face value for as long as the original policy would have protected you.

AUTOMATIC PREMIUM LOAN This provision, as noted earlier, will allow the company to borrow against your loan values automatically in order to make premium payments you have neglected to make.

Conversion Tables

Each policy contains a table of conversion, or nonforfeiture, values. Table 17–1 is an abbreviated sample. Values are based on the age of the insured at the time the policy is taken out. Values will vary from company to company and from one type of policy to another.

TABLE 17–1   Conversion Values, Sample Policy, $10,000 Face Value

End of Policy Year	Cash or Loan Value	Paid-up Insurance	Extended Term Insurance
5	$1,590	$1,410	14 yr. 48 days
10	1,340	2,900	20 yr. 310 days
15	2,100	4,130	22 yr. 288 days
20	2,890	5,180	22 yr. 303 days

Here's how the tables work. The face amount of the insurance policy is $10,000, and the age of the insured at the time the policy was taken out was 25. At the end of the tenth policy year the policyholder will have $1,340 worth of cash/loan values. That means he or she can stop making payments, cash in the policy, terminating the insurance altogether, and have $1,340 cash in hand. Or the policyholder can borrow that much against the policy and continue the policy in force by paying the annual premiums.

If the policyholder converts to paid-up insurance, at the end of the tenth policy year he or she will have a permanent policy with a face value of $2,900. There are no more premiums to pay, and protection is guaranteed for life for $2,900 in face value. Or at the end of ten years, this individual could convert to extended term, in which case he or she would be covered for the full face amount ($10,000) for 20 years and 310 days. At the end of that time, the coverage would cease altogether. Table 18–4 (chapter 18) illustrates how values can build up over longer periods.

In order to do any of the conversions, the insurance company must be notified. It would be advisable to discuss such a move with your insurance agent before you actually proceed.

Dividend Options

If you own a dividend-paying policy, you'll have choices as to how those dividends are paid. You can get a check to do with as you please; you can apply the dividends toward the next premium due on the policy; you may let the dividend "ride" with the company, where it will earn interest; or you can use the dividends to purchase additional life paid-up insurance. This last option increases your protection at no out-of-pocket cost to you.

An annual statement from the company will indicate what dividends are payable and will instruct you how to choose the way dividends will be applied. If you have any questions, discuss the matter with your agent.

Settlement Options

Settlement options may include paying the entire face amount in one lump sum to the beneficiaries; paying periodic payments, including interest, to the beneficiaries; paying interest only to the named beneficiary, with a lump sum payable to a subsequent beneficiary on the death of the primary beneficiary. As a rule, the owner of the policy can choose the settlement option. In some cases, a beneficiary might also be able to select an option. Each policy will spell out exactly what options are available and how to go about choosing them and changing them.

BUYING LIFE INSURANCE: WHO NEEDS IT, AND HOW MUCH?

When we're hungry, we go to the market and buy the food we need; we don't have to wait for someone to tell us that our stomachs need refilling. Not so with life insurance; the need is not as clear-cut. Indeed, contemplating the need for life insurance reminds us of our own mortality, and it's no surprise that human nature would short-circuit such thoughts.

Sound personal financial planning demands that life insurance be carefully investigated. Not everyone needs life insurance, but everyone should at least examine how life insurance can function with respect to their long-term needs and objectives.

Who needs life insurance? In short, if you want to protect or enhance the well-being of anyone who is dependent on you, and your existing assets aren't adequate to provide that protection, life insurance can get the job done quickly and assuredly.

Premature Death

Exercise 17.1

If a young breadwinner dies unexpectedly, how will his or her family survive? For example: You have two children, ages 10 and 12. You want to be sure that there is enough money for your spouse and children to live comfortably, and for college for the children. Term insurance designed to run for fifteen or twenty years can provide the protection that's needed.

Or you might prefer permanent insurance, which will cost more at the outset but is likely to cost less many years down the road. A combination of the two might work best for you. Remember: Your family is unique. What's right for other families might not be right for yours. Evaluate the financial exposure your family has in the event of the premature death of a breadwinner, and act accordingly.

Normal Life Expectancy

Once the children are grown and most major obligations have been taken care of, the need for life insurance diminishes. Many families, though, continue their life insurance in order to provide an inheritance for the survivors.

Tax and Business Purposes

Chapter 19 will help you determine whether your heirs are facing the prospect of federal estate taxes on your death. If they are, life insurance can be used to pay that tax. Lacking the needed cash, survivors might be faced with having to sell other assets—house, investments—in order to pay the tax. Having to sell off those other assets could provide a hardship for survivors. Life insurance eliminates the need to sell off other assets.

Similarly, business interests can be protected by life insurance. If you are the sole proprietor in a small business, your death could cause the business to have to terminate. If, however, there is life insurance payable to the business, those proceeds, which are not taxable to the recipient, could be used to keep the business running, or they could buy time to allow for an orderly liquidation of the business. Either way, your survivors can be protected by that immediate infusion of cash into the business.

How Much Insurance Is Needed?

The first task is to determine who is going to be protected by the insurance and to what extent. For example, do you want to ensure that the children will have at least half of their college tuition guaranteed in the event of your premature death? 75 percent? 100 percent? Are they on their own after that? Or do you want them to have a nest egg to help get them started in their chosen careers? These are individual questions that only you can answer.

Now comes the time for some thoughtful arithmetic. You must determine, as accurately as possible, the following:

- What might be the possible extent of "final" expenses, which can include uninsured costs of a terminal illness, burial or cremation expenses, estate taxes, and money to help survivors get through the early difficult time of adjustment. (If you're amply protected against terminal illness costs through your health insurance you may exclude them from your life insurance planning.)

- How much existing debt—mortgages, personal loans, and so on—might the survivors have to pay? If you don't want the family to sell assets to pay off the debt, you can cover such contingencies through life insurance.

- How much per year will the survivors need to maintain themselves in a suitable style of living? Consideration must be given to the possibilities of the spouse remarrying, of a previously nonworking spouse going to work and the child-care expenses that might entail, of children going to work, and of other potential sources of income that might materialize. Elimination of the deceased's own cost of living—food, clothing, recreation, and so on—must also be evaluated.

- What extraordinary expenses will the survivors face, and what part of those expenses do you want to ensure them of being able to meet? Such expenses might include education, weddings, a stake to go into business on their own, and so on.
- For how many years would you want the survivors to continue their particular lifestyle on a worry-free basis?
- What benefits will be provided by Social Security? A visit with your nearest Social Security office can provide this information.
- Inventory all assets at current market value, potential future value, liquidity and their earning potential. Determine when assets could, or should, be converted to cash to meet family needs, and which non-earning assets might be converted to earning assets.
- What other sources of income might there be in the future, such as in-heritances or scholarships? You can't count on these sources, but you should be aware of the possibility.
- Evaluate current life insurance policies. Determine what the proceeds could earn annually if they were conservatively invested (see Tables 14–2 and 14–3) and how long the proceeds would last if the principal were invaded by a certain amount each year (see Table 18–5, chapter 18). Evaluate all your other assets in the same manner. This informa-tion may not be easy to compile, and you may want the impartial help of an accountant or your insurance agent. This information is es-sential to forming an intelligent plan.

A Case History

Exercise 17.2

When you've surveyed your data, the gaps can be measured and the alter-natives for filling those gaps can come into focus.

Let's examine a fairly simple case. This exercise illustrates the type of analysis you should make to estimate your own life insurance needs.

Phillip is married, has a 12-year-old child, and earns $3,000 a month after taxes. His wife does not work but is capable of doing so should the need arise.

Phillip's current financial status is as follows:

- He owns his home, which has a current market value of $150,000. He owes $60,000 on a mortgage with monthly payments of $620.
- He has $5,000 in a savings plan.
- He has $10,000 in the profit-sharing plan at work. This could be payable immediately to his survivors in the event of his death.
- He owns two cars, both used, with a current total value of $8,000.
- He has a life insurance policy, with a face value of $45,000.

Phillip has estimated what his family's financial status would be if he were to die suddenly. His existing health and burial insurance would take care of all his final expenses. His assets are not high enough to make him liable for estate taxes. His wife and child would need approximately $1,720 a month for living expenses (mortgage payment, $620; other living expenses, $800, taxes and miscellaneous, $300).

If he died now, Phillip would not want his wife to sell the house. She could, however, make use of the savings account, the profit-sharing plan, and the life insurance proceeds, all of which would total $60,000.

Phillip and his insurance agent, using Table 18–5 in this book, calculate very conservatively that if the $60,000 were invested at 7 percent per year, before income tax considerations, it would generate earnings of $360 per month. If Phillip's widow were to embark on a ten-year program of dipping into principal, the $60,000 could generate an income of $696 per month, as indicated in Table 17–2. A fifteen-year dipping plan would give her an income of $538 per month. In order to provide enough for his wife and child to be comfortable, Phillip needs an additional $100,000 in life insurance. That amount, if invested in accordance with the program in Table 18–5, would provide an additional $1,160 per month, for a ten-year period, at the end of which time the sum would be depleted. But the total of the $696 from the existing $60,000 nest egg, plus the $1,160 per month from the new insurance to be acquired, will provide Phillip's survivors with a grand total of $1,856 per month.

After ten years, when the entire nest egg is gone, the child will have completed college. The house will have increased in value considerably, and the mortgage on the house will have decreased considerably. Phillip's wife will be left with a substantial equity in the home, which she can sell to create a sizable nest egg for her living expenses.

These calculations do not include earnings of Phillip's widow and child from work. And it does not take into account estimated Social Security benefits of $1,110 per month until the child reaches the age of 16. Furthermore, Phillip's widow can resume receiving Social Security benefits when she reaches the age of 60. All this income can be banked to create an even greater security blanket. Phillip's wife might choose to return to work herself and embark on a fifteen-year dipping plan, which would give her an income of $1,434 per month. That, plus her earnings from work, might be a more satisfactory program for her.

Phillip's situation is a *relatively* uncomplicated one. If he were concerned about such matters as paying estate taxes, creating a substantial college

TABLE 17–2   **Income Sources**

	Interest Only[a]	10-Year Payout	15-Year Payout
From existing $60,000	$360	$ 696	$ 538
From extra $100,000	585	1,160	896
Total income available	$945	$1,856	$1,434

[a]Principal amount always remains intact.

tuition fund, protecting a business interest, or any other matter beyond the ordinary, his need for insurance would be much greater. Now, having solved the puzzle of how much insurance he needs, Phillip must tackle the far more perplexing matter of what kind of insurance to buy.

What to Buy

Buying life insurance is a lot like buying a car. You can choose a subcompact with no frills, or you can go lavish and splurge on a fancy sedan with all the trimmings. The sticker price isn't always the determining factor in what you buy. If you need a car just to hop back and forth to the office or the shopping center, the subcompact might make the most sense. But if you're a traveling salesman and expect to be driving thousands of miles every week, it may well be worth the added price to buy the luxury car so that the physical comfort of the automobile reduces the wear and tear on your body. There's no easy answer.

Exercise 17.3

Life insurance is just as complicated. You, or Phillip, could go for the stripped-down term policy or for a "loaded" Whole Life policy. Both have pluses, both have minuses.

The cost of life insurance has long been the subject of debate between advocates of term life and advocates of whole life. SInce whole life insurance builds up conversion values within the policies, those who favor such policies feel that the real cost of the insurance should take into account what those values are in future years. This is generally referred to as the "cost adjusted" method. Whole life insurance costs more than term life at the inception of the policy, but years later, for example, if a policyholder cashes in a whole life policy, the total cost of premiums, offset by the cash-in value, could be much less than the out-of-pocket cost of a term policy of equal face value. Term advocates prefer to measure cost strictly on an out-of-pocket basis.

The debate will rage on, and it would take a huge book to list all the possible costs of all the possible combinations of policies. It's a jungle out there for price shoppers. As a rough guideline, the following tables illustrate the range of costs you might find for various types of policies. The prices are from surveys conducted in recent years and represent the better values among those companies and policies surveyed. Note well that all prices are subject to change.

Exercise 17.4

Table 17-3 illustrates price ranges for various types of term policies for non-smokers age 35 and 45. Term policies are for $250,000 face value. Annual renewable policies will increase in cost each year. Ten- and 20-year level term policies have a fixed cost for the first 10 and 20 years, respectively, and after that premiums will increase considerably. (There are also term policies available with 5 years and 15 years of level payments. An agent can quickly provide you with costs for those plans.)

TABLE 17–3   **Costs of Term Policies, $250,000 Face Value**

Age	Gender	Annual Renewable First Year	10-Year Level Premium Per Year, 1st 10 Years	20-Year Level Premium Per Year, 1st 20 Years
35	Male	$195–$238	$210–$230	$273–$350
35	Female	188–248	185–210	265–330
45	Male	260–348	360–430	535–675
45	Female	250–275	285–343	398–505

Source: Consumer's Digest, Sept./Oct. 1996.

Table 17–4 illustrates both low and high ranges of whole life policies with face values of $100,000. Policies in the higher ranges might have higher conversion values. Neither dividends nor conversion values are taken into account in these examples. See Strategies for Success on page 521, which compares rates for smokers.

If you have questions about the stability of any life insurance company, refer to *Best's Insurance Reports* and *Best's Recommended Life Insurance Companies,* both of which are available in most libraries. Your state's insurance department can help too.

The Insurance Agent

Exercise 17.5

There is no such thing as a typical insurance agent. An agent's training might range from minimal to the rigorous demands of the courses leading to the CLU (Chartered Life Underwriter) designation. His or her experience might encompass weeks or decades. His or her income level can range from paltry to six figures. And personality, sales techniques, and sense of ethics can run the full human spectrum.

Many agents will seek you out. If you can find the right agent, you've made a valuable catch. But how do you know what to look for? Before we get into a shopping list, let's take a quick look at some of the dilemmas in the industry.

TABLE 17–4   **Costs of Whole Life Policies, $100,000 Face Value**

Age	Gender	Low Range	High Range
35	Male	$ 634–$1,052	$1,280–$1,300
35	Female	634–897	1,069–1,098
45	Male	1,178–1,514	2,425–4,504
45	Female	1,140–1,178	2,055–2,070

Source: Consumer's Reports, August 1993.

- **Dilemma No. 1**   Insurance agents make their living by selling insurance policies. Proper counseling may be of equal or greater value to you than the policy itself, but agents don't make a penny unless they make a sale. Needless to say, good counseling can produce a good sale, but it might not.

  Agents, therefore, take a calculated risk on how much time they can spend with any given prospect in counseling sessions. This can result in counseling and selling efforts becoming intermingled, to the point where you might not be able to tell them apart.

  If an agent is not willing to take the time needed to understand your goals, you might not be getting the service you need. And agents might not take the time if they are not confident that there will be a sale as a result. This dilemma is perhaps best resolved by frank communications at the outset: "Agent, this is what I have to learn from you before I will even consider doing business with you. If you're willing to teach me what I think I have to know, I may well be a customer, but there's no guarantee. If you're willing to proceed on those terms, fine. If not, perhaps it would be best if we didn't waste each other's time."

- **Dilemma No. 2**   With rare exceptions, richer people have better access to more sophisticated insurance counseling than poorer people. This, for better or worse, is the way of our world.

  It might take an agent the same time to sell a $10,000 policy to a working family as it would to sell a $100,000 policy to an executive. The rewards to the agent are drastically different. Moreover, the agent who is going for the big sale will probably be better equipped to handle the more sophisticated problems wealthy prospects will have. People with lower incomes also need sound advice, but it may be more difficult for them to get it.

  The more you learn about life insurance, the better able you will be to take advantage of any advice given, and the better you understand the more sophisticated advice that could be of greater value.

- **Dilemma No. 3**   Each of us has so many dollars to spend. Some of those dollars will be spent on our current needs, and some will cover future needs and desires. Many institutions would like to take care of our future dollars for us—insurance companies, mutual funds, banks, savings institutions, stockbrokers. They all make their living by putting our future dollars to use until we need them, and the competition is keen to get access to these dollars.

  Each of these giant industries has become envious of the others. Some segments of the life insurance industry have reacted, for example, by putting mutual funds in the same attaché case as their insurance policies. The funds might be good; so might the policies. Mixing them together too much may not be.

  With all these financial industries competing with each other for our future dollars, it's essential that we keep a clear distinction between insuring and investing. Each has its separate set of purposes and goal-fulfillment abilities. Insurance offers certainty; some forms of investment offer a measure of certainty, whereas others offer little more than possibility.

Evaluating the Agent

Keeping these dilemmas firmly in mind, what then do you look for in an insurance agent?

As in choosing all professional advisors, you must have trust in their ability, confidence in their training, and knowledge of their integrity. You don't usually get these on a hunch or a first impression, although it's not impossible. Personal familiarity, recommendations from others, and reputation in the community are indicators. The individual who comes on with a hard sell after the first "How do you do?" may have the same program to offer you as the agent who holds fire until after the proper rapport has been established. The choice is up to you.

What are the agent's credentials, background, training, and prior experience? Does the agent represent only one company or, as is the case with independent agents, a number of different companies? These are important factors to determine and evaluate. It is, of course, possible for a novice who is eager to get established to serve you just as well as an old pro. But the perennial job hopper is liable to leave you with some loose ends hanging.

THE CLU   Chartered Life Underwriters (CLUs) are insurance agents who have been through rigorous courses of instruction. Only a small percentage of agents are CLUs. The time and educational requirements may scare off many from pursuing the credential. These educational requirements include courses on economics, taxes, estate planning, corporate law, contract law, pensions and profit-sharing plans, accounting, and the technical aspects of life insurance.

Each course requires about sixty hours of classroom work, as well as abundant outside homework. On completing the courses, each agent must pass a four-hour written exam in each of five subject areas.

A CLU doesn't have any product or secret policies to offer you that other agents don't have, but a CLU does possess the education that might enable her to make the best determination of your needs and find the best policies to satisfy those needs. (Certainly, there are many fine agents without the CLU designation who can serve your needs most adequately.)

In dealing with a CLU, you are working with an individual who has invested hundreds of hours becoming more expert in the insurance field. That fact alone might induce many insurance shoppers to lean toward doing business with a CLU.

Remember that any insurance agent, CLU or not, can make a living only by selling policies. The amount of time an agent can give to counseling a client is limited. But the *quality* of counseling is important, perhaps more so than the amount of time given it. And that might well be where the CLU has another edge.

IT'S YOUR CHOICE The difference between *choosing* an agent and *being chosen by* an agent can be very important. The selection process is up to you. Remember that you are not buying a simple product that you'll use today and be done with tomorrow. You're striving to build a structure that will shelter you and your dependents for many years. If it's built right, it will last, it will perform, and it will have been worth the time and the money involved.

INSURANCE WHEN THE RISK MIGHT NOT OCCUR

There is a very important difference between life insurance and the other common forms of personal insurance. With life insurance, as long as the policy remains in force, the company must pay the benefits to the beneficiary at a fixed date: the death of the insured. There is no question that the loss being insured against—the death of the insured—will occur. The insurance company is able to make a reasonably accurate estimate as to when that date will probably be, and it knows precisely how much it must then pay.

With the other common forms of personal insurance—health, income, property, and public liability—the risk that is being insured against may not occur. If it does, it might occur tomorrow or ten years from now. When it does occur, the company may have to pay a token amount to the insured, or a moderate or substantial sum. There may be a dispute as to whether or not anything should be paid.

With life insurance, you know for certain that a fixed sum of money will be available to you or your beneficiaries. With the other forms of insurance, the money you pay out may never be seen again. Human nature may lead us to think—dangerously so—that serious illness will come to others but never to us. We would thus never be out of pocket as a result of such occurrences, and therefore we should keep our costs for such insurance to a minimum.

In many respects, the losses that can be suffered as a result of risks relating to health, income, property, and public liability can be far more devastating than the death of a breadwinner who leaves no life insurance. Vague and unpredictable though these risks may be, it would be careless not to acquire protection against financial disaster.

The basic mechanics are generally the same for life insurance and the other forms of personal insurance. A contract (policy) is entered into between the insured party and the insurance company. The contract sets forth all the rights and obligations of the parties.

But the claim procedures with these other forms of personal insurance can be much more complicated than with life insurance. When an insured individual dies, the company is notified of the death and makes the payment. But in the other forms of insurance, there may be many questions about the status of the insured or of the injured parties, and the extent of damages suffered may be subject to question.

Don't Smoke, Don't Age, Be a Female

Smokers pay through the nose for life insurance. And smoking can also mean much higher premiums for health, disability income, and long-term-care insurance. Look at the difference in costs for a smoker and a nonsmoker from a mass-market term-life insurance company. For $100,000 worth of term coverage, here are the annual costs for nonsmokers and smokers, male and female, at varying ages. Costs are just for that one year and will differ from company to company.

Age	Nonsmoking Male	Smoking Male	Nonsmoking Female	Smoking Female
30	$150	$ 200	$150	$ 200
40	155	270	151	210
50	205	445	165	345
55	275	730	215	495
60	480	1,180	295	795
65	625	1,644	505	1,245

These numbers speak incredibly well for themselves. Not only do they show the added cost of smoking—and the added cost of waiting to buy life insurance, if you haven't become uninsurable in the meantime—they also give you some clear ideas about the longevity of smokers versus nonsmokers.

Presenting a claim for payment with these types of personal insurance may require filling out extensive forms. The information you submit is subject to investigation by the insurance company to determine the validity of the claims.

Although the vast majority of all claims are paid in accordance with the company's obligations, the insured must see to it that the full measure of the claim is clearly stated and paid for.

HEALTH INSURANCE

In order to know where we're headed it can often be helpful to know where we're coming from. Follow along, then, for a perspective on this important subject.

Of every dollar spent in the United States each year, roughly fourteen cents goes into health care in all its many forms, including the cost of health insurance itself.

Prior to the 1990s, despite rapidly rising health care costs, the whole proposition was relatively easy to understand and deal with, if for no other reason than that we had gotten used to a decades-old system. Roughly 85 percent of the nation's population was covered by health insurance policies, either through a group policy at work or a privately purchased policy, most or all of the time. (A person between jobs, for example, might have been temporarily not covered, though that need not be the case today, as will be discussed later.)

Almost all health insurance policies had a number of common characteristics:

1. You could see the doctors of your choice. This was the one feature the U.S. citizens seemed to care most about.

2. You had to pay a *deductible* before the insurance would kick in on your behalf. The deductible is a set amount per person and/or per family per year, such as $250, $500, $1,000 or more. Those who had private policies could choose the deductible they wanted. Those covered by group policies usually had no choice; the employer would pick one deductible that everyone was subject to.

3. After you had paid the deductible amount—out of your own pocket—the policy would then pay a set percentage of all your covered medical expenses. Commonly, policies would pay 80 percent of those expenses and you'd be responsible for paying the difference.

4. All policies had limits as to what they would pay for and how much. These limits would vary from policy to policy, but in general they would include how much a policy would pay for a hospital room, a specific surgical procedure, a visit to a doctor's office, and so on. There would also be limits on the total amount a policy would pay during the course of one year and over a lifetime.

5. For the most part, most people were familiar enough with their policies to be able to get along with them. Yes, there were inequities and abuses and overcharges and underpayment of claims from time to time. Yet the system functioned, and as the old saying goes, "If it ain't broke, don't fix it."

But then it broke.

We Needed a Fix

Forces in the economy took hold of the health care industry, and it's been chaotic ever since. Review chapter 1 to familiarize yourself with how forces beyond our control can affect our economic well-being. The health care industry is a perfect example.

The first fracture came in 1988. People had been complaining long and loud about rapidly rising health care costs, but the 1988 incident began to prompt many people to do something about all these complaints. That incident was a change in the income tax laws that took a lot of money away from a lot of people. The law was enacted in 1986, to take effect in 1987. So the first time most people were impacted by the law was when they filled out their 1987 tax returns in 1988.

Here is how the tax law changes took away a lot of money from a lot of people: Prior to the income tax law change, if people spent money on health care for which they were *not* reimbursed by insurance, they could get a fat income tax deduction as a result. It wasn't so bad having to pay for medical costs out of pocket as long as you could get a tax deduction for them. But the tax law change took away that deduction for most people.

For example, prior to 1987, if a family had an adjusted gross income of $30,000 and unreimbursed medical expenses of $2,000, they would be entitled to a tax deduction of $1,400. The deduction was allowed for the amount that unreimbursed medical costs exceeded—on a rough average—2 percent of adjusted gross income (2% of $30,000 is $600). The deduction is for the difference between the $2,000 expenses and the $600 limitation, or $1,400.

From 1987 onward, the deduction was allowed for unreimbursed medical expenses in excess of 7.5 percent of adjusted gross income. The same family, therefore, would have no deduction at all during a year in which their adjusted gross income was $30,000 and their unreimbursed medical expenses were $2,000. Seven and a half percent of $30,000 is $2,250. Their expenses were less than $2,250. Therefore, no deduction was allowed. Ouch!

Medical costs were rising rapidly, and taking away the deduction rubbed salt into the uninsured wounds. The media got on the case. The politicians got on the case. Health care costs had become the demon spirit of our land.

The second fracture came in 1992 with the election of a Democrat to the White House—the first such since 1980, when health care concerns were far secondary to skyrocketing gasoline costs and hostages in Iran and nuclear weapons in the USSR.

The Republican economic philosophy has always been *"Hands off:* the private sector can take care of the economy better than the government can." The Democratic philosophy has always been *"Hands on,* particularly if the economy seems to be going haywire." Then governmental intervention can be more effective in solving the problem than the private sector can, the argument goes.

In 1993, the Clinton administration began a project to overhaul the entire health care system in America. *Entire.*

A Case of Overkill

After almost two years of meetings a plan was finally presented to the media and the public. It was gargantuan in scope and mind-boggling in complexity. Perhaps the single most negative aspect of it was that it seemed to threaten that Americans might have to give up one of their most cherished freedoms: the right to choose their own doctors. The media did an about face: "Yes, we felt that the health care dilemma was an awful one, but this overhaul plan is overkill."

The public and the politicians agreed, and the overhaul proposal died swiftly in Congress. But while all of this was going on, there was one segment of the economy that was actually doing something about it all: the health care industry. They said, in a nutshell, "If we don't get our act together, and soon, we're going to end up being regulated by the government. The government will tell us how much we can charge and how much treatment we can offer and how much we'll get reimbursed from certain insurance programs. Better we regulate ourselves than let the government do it for us."

The Dawn of Managed Care

Thus began the era of *managed care*. We're just a few years into this new era, and the dust of confusion may not settle for many more years. So this portion of this chapter is, of necessity, a work in progress, a transitional essay on one critical aspect of personal finance going through enormous change.

The essence of managed care is that instead of each doctor/hospital/lab/out-patient surgical center/running its own facilities and personnel, groups of these health care deliverers have banded together to form organizations with the hope that one central management for the organization can be more cost-efficient than a whole lot of individual management arrangements. Think of the cost-savings that can be achieved by combining twenty doctors' offices into one: lower administrative costs, lower paperwork costs, lower rent, lower personnel costs, lower purchasing costs, and so on.

Further, all specialty work can be referred within the organization rather than losing it to outsiders. And by having central management instead of each doctor having to worry about payrolls and computer programs and form-filling-out-by-the-ton, life will become more pleasant, and the doctors can concentrate on doing what they're trained to do best: doctoring.

Costs to consumers will come down. To some extent, the freedom of choice of doctors can be retained (life, after all, is a series of compromises) and the government will leave the industry relatively alone.

All well and good. Is it working? Sort of. When massive change comes to any entity, particularly one as gigantic as the health care industry, there are going to be glitches and bad publicity, consumer complaints and lawsuits, and the continuing nightmare of possible governmental intervention. Then energies have to be directed toward putting out the fires and reassuring the public, and that can cost a lot of money.

A lot of hospitals and older doctors have seen their incomes plummet, particularly as the government cuts back on reimbursements from treating governmentally insured patients on Medicare. At the same time, a lot of hospitals are cutting costs by merging, and a lot of younger doctors are entering the profession with an eye toward living a more ordered life, even though at a lower income level than their older colleagues.

The core of all this is that you as a health care consumer (and we all are, or will be, whether we like it or not) must be ready to change as the industry changes. And the changes are already momentous. Before the 1990s, about 70 percent of all health care payments were made by regular insurance plans, either private or group, and the balance was through managed care facilities. Today those numbers are reversed: 70 percent of health care is through managed care facilities, and the balance is through regular insurance. One educated guess: By 2010, if current trends continue, close to 90 percent of all health care will be through managed care facilities.

The vast majority of workers covered by group plans are having to pay for an increasing portion of their health care coverage—whether through regular insurance plans or managed care plans. In 1986, about 40% of workers with single coverage were paying for part of their coverage. A decade later, 85% were. How much have those workers been chipping in over the same time frame? Worker contributions have increased from about $360 per year in 1986 to almost $500 per year a decade later (that's before deductibles, co-payments and the like). And here again the trend is upward, even though the inflation of medical costs has somewhat stabilized.

So What Do We Do Now?

One unavoidable conclusion to all of this is that individual choice of doctors has been severely curtailed. Yet we seem to be getting along all right. We gripe at different things for different reasons. But our life expectancy rates and our general health conditions seem to be surviving the changes without harm. We are adapting, but we must be vigilant, protective of our rights, and, above all, well informed. With that in mind, let us survey the health care industry in these changing times, with an eye toward helping you get the best medical care that circumstances will allow.

If You Don't Have Choice . . .

. . . Don't give up hope. Many people who have health plans at work are more or less stuck with whatever the company has decided to provide for them. Some workers fear leaving their jobs because they might lose their health coverage. That should no longer be of concern. The Health Insurance Portability Act of 1997 allows workers to change jobs without putting their coverage in jeopardy. This will be discussed in more detail later in the chapter.

Many employers offer Cafeteria Plans as a part of their overall fringe benefits program. These plans allow you—as in a real cafeteria—to pick and choose from a number of benefits available. Such a plan might enable you to improve your health insurance coverage. This might involve giving up some other benefit, but you've certainly nothing to lose by researching the plan in full. Flexible Spending Accounts are another form of benefits that can allow you to set aside some of your earnings on a tax-free basis to use toward unreimbursed medical expenses. This, too, should be explored. (See chapter 2 for more details on Cafeteria and Flexible Spending Plans.)

It costs employers between $3,000 and $5,000 per employee per year for typical health plans. Employers want to keep good workers, and a good health plan is a way of doing so, despite the healthy price tag. Most workers shopping for private coverage on their own would likely find that it would cost a lot more because of the savings involved in insuring a group as opposed to an individual. But not all employers are diligent in researching health plans for their workers. If stimulated to do so by a group of workers, or by a union, or by an aggressive health plan salesperson, a new and better program could emerge, to the benefit of all concerned. So if you don't like your current plan, don't give up hope. A job change or a concerted effort to get your employer to improve the existing plan are clear possibilities.

Some people might have a choice of health plans one day, and not have a choice the next day. How can this happen? Some unforeseen medical problem can crop up that can render them uninsurable, not just for health coverage, but for life, disability income, and long-term-care insurance as well. See the Strategy for Success on page 499.

If You Do Have a Choice . . .

. . . You have a lot of homework to do. Here are the general guidelines of the types of plans available, and checklists to help you determine the relative value of each. First, let's look at the spectrum of possibilities. That spectrum ranges from complete freedom of choice to very limited freedom of choice. The former is what's known as *fee for service.* You choose your own doctor, hospital, clinic, or any other facility. You get the service you seek, and your health insurance policy pays the fee, subject to limitations in the policy and deductibles, as described earlier.

Limited freedom of choice is characteristic of managed care. *Health maintenance organizations* (HMOs) are the strictest example. You join an HMO for a set annual fee. You are assigned a *gatekeeper*—a family doctor who will act as your first contact. Whatever specialists may be needed will be assigned to you by this primary care doctor, and those specialists will be affiliated with the HMO. The HMO will also have its own lab and other related facilities, and may have its own hospital. In most cases, all of your care takes place at the HMO facility. In short, you pretty much do what the HMO tells you to do, and your annual fee covers all, or most all, of your expenses. If you're not happy with your HMO gatekeeper or specialists, you can request different ones. Circumstances will dictate whether you can get a change. As a general rule, HMOs cost less, perhaps a lot less, than comparable fee for service care through an insurance policy.

In between these two ends of the spectrum, there are a number of shades of grey. Most common is the *preferred provider organization* (PPO). In a PPO, numerous doctors and care facilities have signed a contract to care for covered individuals at fixed rates, which are usually discounted from normal rates. For example, if your health plan at work offers you PPO services, you can choose your own doctors—primary and specialists—from among the PPO's list of members. The same goes for hospitals, labs, and other facilities. You see the doctors at their own offices. So your freedom of choice can be much broader than with an HMO. Your plan will pay agreed fees to the PPO, which may be all or part of the set PPO fee. If the plan doesn't pay it all, you make up the difference. You can also choose non-PPO providers, but you'll have to pay more out of pocket for that privilege.

Two other similar facilities are independent physicians associations (IPAs) and point-of-service (POS) plans. Both of these allow you some broader choice than the HMO, but likely at extra cost to you. IPAs are made up of doctors who maintain their own private practice but are linked into a broad network of specialists. You can choose your own primary care doctor from among those participating in the IPA, and then that doctor will refer you to specialists—perhaps a choice of specialists—as the need arises. POS plans allow you to see out-of-network providers for an extra fee, not unlike the PPOs.

Go Figure

Confusing? Without a doubt. To make matters more so, not all of these plans will cover or pay for the same services. For example: some plans will cover you only in your home city or state, with you having to pay extra if you need medical attention when you're away from home. Some will only prescribe certain drugs for certain conditions—presumably from a pharmaceutical company that offers them a fat discount if the plan gives them an exclusive on a specific drug. Plans can also differ widely on coverage for emergency room visits, mental health services, rehabilitation services, and more. The fact that a lot of facilities that used to be nonprofit are now for-profit muddies the water even more.

It is appropriate to say a few words about nonprofit versus for-profit, since that is a critical element in the emergence and ultimate success or failure of managed care. Many nonprofit medical facilities—such as community hospitals—are heavily subsidized by taxpayers. Critics of nonprofit institutions allege that they are not efficiently run. They lose money as a result, and the ripple effect is a compromise in the quality of service they can render. Those who favor the for-profit concept maintain that free enterprise can run any business—hospitals among them—more efficiently than nonprofits. They can even turn a profit, and if some of that profit is plowed back into the institution, the quality of service can improve. That's a big if. Critics of for-profit institutions say that they are interested only in making money and in rewarding the stockholders (many of whom might be doctors affiliated with the facility), and that service to patients is of secondary concern. Indeed, for-profit hospitals have been accused of fraud, mismanagement, and more, all in the interest of lining the pockets of investors.

Remember: This is all in a state of flux. There might even be significant differences in the health care scene between the time this book was printed and the time you read this chapter. Private enterprise continues to play an increasing role in the health care industry by way of mergers, acquisitions, and technological developments (lasers, scanners, etc.). Fifty state legislatures have bills before them that would create more regulations of various players in the industry. Biotech and pharmaceutical companies are hard at work developing new treatments and medications that can revolutionize overnight how health care is delivered. And there will always be the shadow of the federal government lurking over the industry, waiting to pounce if abuses seem to become too frequent, or the quality of the nation's health seems to be deteriorating.

HEALTH CARE CHECKLISTS

Insurance

If you already have a health insurance policy (as opposed to a managed care plan), the most important thing you must do is to see if it is up-to-date with today's actual costs. If your policy is more than two or three years old, you might be shocked to learn that the benefits promised in the policy are far less than today's real-world costs. That includes all aspects of coverage under the policy: physicians, surgeons, hospitalization (how much will they pay for what types of rooms and for how many days, intensive care, emergency room service), prescriptions, and so on. Your policy may have an inflation rider that would boost coverage based on the actual rise in costs. Don't assume that that's the case. Determine exactly what your coverage is. If you deem it necessary to increase your coverage, discuss that with your agent.

Now comes the homework to see if your health insurance plan is as healthy as you need it to be. Needless to say, the extent of coverage you have—or need—will affect the cost of your policy.

Hospital Coverage

_____ Does your insurance policy cover the hospital you're likely to use if the need arises? Not all policies provide coverage for all hospitals.

_____ Must you be an in-patient to be covered? What coverage is there for out-patient care?

_____ Are you covered for anything that puts you into the hospital? Are any conditions excluded from hospital coverage?

_____ When does the hospital coverage kick in—on the very first day, or is there a waiting period of, say, six or seven days?

_____ What limitations are there, if any, for miscellaneous services such as x-rays, scans, radiation treatment, lab tests, nursing care, anesthesia, oxygen, traction gear, plasma and other blood supplies, ambulance costs, drugs, medications?

Surgical Insurance

_____   Are the surgical schedules in your policy in line with today's actual surgical costs? Most surgical procedures are limited as to how much they will pay you for the main surgeon, assistant surgeons, anesthesia, surgical nurses, operating room fees, and the like.

_____   Is your coverage limited to surgery done in the hospital, or are you also protected for procedures done in the doctor's office or in ambulatory-care facilities?

_____   Is your schedule of surgical benefits tied to your room rate? In other words, if your policy pays more for your hospital room, will they also pay proportionately higher surgical fees?

Physician Insurance

_____   How much will the policy pay for visits to the doctor's office, and does that represent a satisfactory portion of what the doctor actually charges today? Is there a limit as to how many visits the policy will pay for, per person and/or per illness?

_____   What limits are there as to the practitioners who are covered? For example, are you covered for visits to chiropracters, osteopaths, podiatrists?

Miscellaneous Insurance Items

_____   What are the deductibles in your policy—per person, per family, per year, per illness? Once the deductible is met, how much above that amount will the insurance company pay?

_____   What are the policy limits—the total amount the policy will pay per person, per family, per illness, per year, per lifetime?

_____   Do you need maternity benefits, and if so, are they included in the policy, and with what limitations? If you don't need maternity benefits and they are in your policy, you are paying for coverage you can do without. (Better make sure before you cancel it, though.)

_____   To what extent are your dependents covered? When will coverage cease for dependents, especially children?

_____   If you are shopping for a new policy and you have any preexisting conditions, will those conditions be excluded from coverage, and if so, for how long? Will any current health conditions cause you to be excluded from protection altogether, or can you have the desired coverage if you pay a higher premium? (This is called a *rated risk*.)

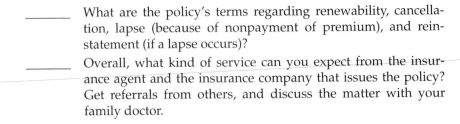

What are the policy's terms regarding renewability, cancellation, lapse (because of nonpayment of premium), and reinstatement (if a lapse occurs)?

Overall, what kind of service can you expect from the insurance agent and the insurance company that issues the policy? Get referrals from others, and discuss the matter with your family doctor.

Managed Care

The selling of managed care plans—to those who have the luxury of being able to choose—is an aggressive marketing phenomenon not unlike the selling of cars and trucks, soda pop, and beer. The commercials and ads for HMOs are more sedate, but the come-on is no less feverish: "We want your money, and we'll give you the best value for your money!" Some initial precautions are in order:

Don't mistake the sizzle for the steak. Advertising for managed care plans may tout such things as "satisfied patient surveys" and "most for the money" analyses. Patient satisfaction and lowest cost do not necessarily translate into *best patient care.* That's a much harder thing to gauge, but it's what you really must be most concerned about. It's easy to "satisfy" a big percentage of an HMO's patients, particularly those who aren't really sick. Give them TLC, keep their appointments punctually, point out "how much this would have cost you elsewhere," and you can have them purring like a kitten. But have they been given the right treatment? The patients don't necessarily know. But they are "satisfied," and will say so if asked in a Patient Satisfaction Survey. Not all such surveys would be so devious, but the possibility exists. The better course would be to do your own survey of a given HMO. Talk to people who are members. Ask them tough, straightforward questions about their experiences. On any given day you can find dozens of them in the HMO's waiting room. Be discreet, but assertive. It's your health you're worrying about.

More specific questions to answer regarding HMOs:

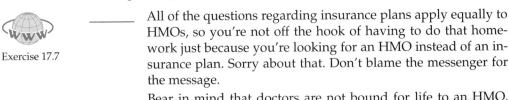

Exercise 17.7

All of the questions regarding insurance plans apply equally to HMOs, so you're not off the hook of having to do that homework just because you're looking for an HMO instead of an insurance plan. Sorry about that. Don't blame the messenger for the message.

Bear in mind that doctors are not bound for life to an HMO. Once you find a good gatekeeper and satisfactory specialists, they can move on and leave you in the lurch. Ask each and any of them that you're liable to encounter how long they've been with the HMO and how long they intend to stay. There are no guarantees, of course, but you'll get some signals that can be of value. In an older and more established HMO you're less likely to find a lot of turnover—the doctors are presumably happy there. Newer ones that have not settled in for the long run might be more susceptible to turnover. But remember, too, that private-practice doctors can also retire, move, quit, die, or become otherwise unavailable. The more you're concerned about this particular issue, the more likely you are to be happier with a PPO instead of an HMO, even though it might cost you more.

_____   If you already have *any* conditions, take *any* medications or need *any* specific treatments, find out if the HMO will cover you in full, in part, or not at all.

_____   Find out how large a roster of primary care doctors and specialists the HMO carries. Are there enough to suit the needs of the clientele and the community? Find out how long a wait there is to see various specialists—cardiologists, OB-gyns, orthopedists, pediatricians, allergists, ophthalmologists, and so on. Inquire particularly about any you think you or your family might be needing.

_____   Locate the HMO's treatment facilities. Is there a facility within easy reach of you, or will you have to travel long distances?

_____   Spending an hour or so in its waiting room will tell you a lot about the efficiency of normal service at an HMO.

_____   Learn what coverage limitations there are, if any, on emergency room care, prescriptions, mental illness, reproductive problems, maternity matters, and treatment needed when you are out of the HMO's jurisdiction. Do not take any of these matters lightly.

_____   Find out what you have to do if you want to switch doctors, either primary care or specialist. Is it quick and easy? Or a pain in the neck? Ask the HMO administrators for their versions, then ask some of the friends you'll be making in the waiting room.

_____   Find out when, and at what cost, you can see doctors outside the HMO or PPO system. You should know whether you have to get permission first, and if so under what circumstances.

_____   Check on the HMO's facilities. As in any business, neatness counts. If a building, or any of its facilities, are unkempt or poorly maintained, that's a sign that someone isn't managing something as well as possible. That could extend to patient care.

Other Forms of Health Care Protection

Some relatively minor sources of health care protection can be available to you. You should know the extent of coverage from all of the following:

_____ Workers' Compensation insurance pays benefits if you are injured or become ill as a result of your work. Benefits can include medical expenses, income reimbursement, and rehabilitations costs. The amount of benefits is fixed by each state.

_____ Medical coverage in your homeowner's and automobile insurance policies can provide some protection to reimburse you or guests when injury occurs in your home or car. The amount of this insurance can be negotiated with your insurance agent.

_____ If harm comes to you through the fault of another, such as in an accident in a car, home or business, the party at fault may be liable for all or part of your medical expenses, as well as lost wages and mental anguish. This is the legal route, which you may have qualms about taking if the circumstances arise. Do as your conscience dictates, but bear in mind that the other party would probably expect reimbursement from you if the situation were reversed.

_____ Governmental assistance can help defray some costs arising from poor health. At the federal level, Social Security can provide benefits in some cases of death and disability. These benefits are paid to surviving spouses and/or children. Supplemental Security Income (SSI) is another aspect of the Social Security program designed to help lower-income people. It provides benefits for disability and blindness for qualifying children and people over 65. At the state or local level Medicaid can pay for a wider range of medical costs for qualifying lower income people.

_____ Medicare is a rather large program and so will be covered in greater detail in the following section.

Medicare

Exercise 17.8

Medicare is a health insurance program administered by the Social Security Administration designed to protect citizens sixty-five years of age and over. The costs of and the benefits provided by Medicare are amended from time to time, and anyone currently eligible for Medicare, or soon to become eligible, should check with the local Social Security office to determine what current costs and benefits are.

There are two aspects of Medicare: hospital insurance (the basic plan), and medical insurance (the supplementary plan). These are referred to as Part A and Part B, respectively.

Persons eligible for Medicare must pay an initial deductible amount with Part A, and a monthly premium in order to be protected by the medical insurance coverage, Part B. Part A, after the deductible has been paid, covers the bulk of the cost of hospital services and extended-care facilities, including rooms, meals, nursing, and certain drugs and supplies. Part B is designed to defray the cost of doctors' services, as well as related medical expenses for such things as x-rays, various equipment, and laboratory fees. Medicare will cover a major percentage of these various expenses, but the insured may be responsible for a certain percentage as well. Part A, the hospitalization insurance, is also limited to a specific number of days.

Exercise 17.9

Many older citizens have the mistaken belief that Medicare is the ultimate protection for them against health-care expenses in their later years. Although Medicare does cover a substantial portion of normal medical expenses, many people may still be burdened by the cost of nursing care and other costs not covered by the program. A number of supplemental programs are available through major insurance companies, and any existing or prospective Medicare recipients should explore the advisability of obtaining some supplemental protection.

Before 1992, buying supplemental Medicare insurance—or Medigap coverage, as it's often called—involved tracking through a jungle of confusing and often misleading policies issued by hundreds of companies. In 1992 Congress passed a Medigap law that standardizes all such policies into one of ten formats. The types of policies range from A to J, with A being the stripped-down version offering minimal supplemental protection, and J being the top of the line, offering a much broader range of protection. Although this may make it easier to sort out the levels of coverage available, you still must compare costs carefully. Not all A policies cost alike, and the same goes for B through J. Careful shopping is still required to get the best value for your money.

INCOME INSURANCE

How long could you get by without any income? One week? One month? Six months? A year? What other sources could you call on for funds to live on? Your savings account? Your investments? The equity in your home? Friends or relatives or institutions who might lend you money?

Income can be lost in one of four ways: quitting your job, being fired, being laid off temporarily, or being laid up as a result of disabilities. With the possible exception of quitting your job, all these occurrences are totally unpredictable.

Loss of work because of disability can mean more than simply lost income. With the disability may come added expenses of rehabilitation, recuperation, medicine and drugs, nursing, and other miscellaneous medical costs. There can also be intangible costs: the depression that the laid-up breadwinner may suffer, the extra demands imposed on other members of the family, the natural worry over what prospects the future holds.

Existing Programs

A number of existing programs give a moderate degree of protection against lost income. But for many people these programs will not be enough, and they will want to examine the opportunities offered by private disability income insurance policies. Before we delve into the specifics of that kind of personal insurance, let's briefly examine some of the other on-going programs that may already be protecting your income.

Sick-pay Plans

Some employers have a set policy on how much sick pay they will provide. Others may play it by ear when an employee is unable to work. You must learn what your employer's program is regarding sick pay, for this is the core of your basic income-protection plan. A private plan, should you acquire one, must be built on the foundation of your employer's sick-pay program.

Worker's Compensation

Workers' Compensation offers a measure of disability income to workers who are injured on the job or who contract a job-related illness. But you could be disabled from causes not related to your work, in which case Workers' Compensation would be of no help to you. Determine what Workers' Compensation benefits for disability income would be, because this, along with the sick-pay plan, is important in structuring any private plan.

Social Security

Exercise 17.10

If you become totally disabled—that is, "unable to engage in any substantial gainful activity," according to the Social Security laws—you may be eligible for monthly benefits under the Social Security system. You can obtain more specific details from your local Social Security office.

Unemployment Insurance

Unemployment insurance offers a measure of income if you are laid off from work. Your state unemployment office can assist you in learning what benefits are payable and for how long. You will be expected to look for work if you are receiving unemployment benefits, and you may waive your rights to the benefits if you do not comply with state regulations.

Waiver of Premium Clauses

Waiver of premium provisions in your life and health insurance policies can protect you, at least to the extent of those obligations. If you are disabled and unable to work, the premiums for those policies would be automatically paid for you. This is only a minimal level of protection, but it would at least assure that those important payments were being met.

Credit Health Insurance

With credit health insurance, if you are disabled and unable to work, loan payments will be made for you during the period of disability. The same protection may be available with your home mortgage. The cost of such insurance, and the benefits payable, will vary from lender to lender.

Evaluating Your Needs for Disability Income Insurance

Exercise 17.11

In order to determine how much disability income insurance you may need, you must evaluate the foregoing sources of protection as well as other personal sources of available income. These latter sources would include the ability of other family members to work; the size of your personal savings and how much you'd be willing to dip into them and for how long; other assets that may be converted into cash such as the equity in your house, the cash values in your life insurance, vested rights in profit-sharing and pension funds that you may be able to get access to; part-time or temporary work that you yourself could do; and loans or gifts from family, friends, and associates.

Once you have made a reasonable determination of outside sources of supplementary income, you can begin to examine the benefits available from private disability income policies.

Private Disability Income Policies and How They Work

Like life and health insurance, disability income insurance is available in a vast variety of sizes and shapes. You may obtain a policy on your own or on a group basis.

Depending on your age, your occupation, and your income, you may be required to take a physical examination for a policy to be approved. The cost of the policy will also vary, depending on your age, income, and occupation.

The Waiting Period

One of the most important factors in shaping a disability income policy is the waiting period—the amount of time you have to be disabled before the insurance will begin to pay benefits. It's possible to obtain a policy that will begin payment of benefits on the very first day of disability due to accident. Or you might obtain a policy with a waiting period of 15, 30, 60, or 90 days, or even longer. Waiting periods may differ for accidental disability and for disability caused by illness (usually a seven-day minimum wait). Obviously, the shorter the waiting period, the higher the premium, for the company will become obliged to pay you that much sooner. This is why it's so important to know what your sick-pay plan is at work. If your sick-pay plan will cover you fully or substantially for, say, thirty days, there's not much point in paying for a disability plan with a very short waiting period. Once your sick-pay benefits have been exhausted, you might want to look to other ready sources of income before you begin the disability plan. If your sick-pay plan will last thirty days and other readily available sources can provide for another thirty days' worth of income, it might make sense to have a plan that begins after sixty days from the date of the disability.

Total and Partial Disability

Disability income policies pay you a flat fixed monthly amount if you are totally disabled. Should you be partially disabled, the company will pay you a portion, usually half, of the full total disability benefit. The definition of total disability is very important. If, in order to receive total disability benefits, you must be totally unable to perform *any kind* of work, it may be more difficult to obtain such benefits. Many people who become disabled are unable to perform their normal job but can perform other jobs or work on a limited basis.

If the definition of total disability states that you are not able to perform *your own specific tasks,* you might be more readily able to obtain total disability benefits. In this case, it would not matter that you could perform other duties. The important distinction is whether you can perform your own normal duties in order to be considered totally disabled.

You should also determine whether the policy requires you to be either bedridden, homebound, or under the care of a physician in order to maintain continuing benefits, whether total or partial. As with all insurance, the more liberal the benefits, the higher the premiums. You're probably getting more protection; therefore, you're paying extra dollars for the desired security.

How Much Protection?

Once the disability payments begin, how long will they continue? One year? Five years? Ten years? Lifetime? Policies differ widely in this respect, as do the costs of the policies. There may also be maximum limitations on how much the policy will pay you over a lifetime. Many income disability policies cease paying benefits or curtail benefits once you have reached age 65, even though you may still be working. Naturally, when you do cease work, it can be expected that the disability income policy will also cease, since it's designed to protect you against lost income from work.

Benefits that you receive from a disability income policy are not subject to income taxes. Thus, it's not necessary for you to try to obtain a monthly benefit that's equal to your actual income.

Some disability income policies offer extra benefits in the event of a loss of a limb or limbs or loss of eyesight. Some also offer death benefits.

Exercise 17.12

All things considered, a sound program of disability income protection is similar to a sound program of medical expense protection. You may prefer to take your own chances on short-term minor disabilities and use the available money to insure amply against major long-term crippling disabilities. As with other forms of personal insurance, the right agent will help you evaluate your needs and illustrate your alternatives for protecting yourself against the probable losses.

Long-Term-Care Insurance

As with matters of retirement and estate planning, this subject might be of greater interest to your parents or others close to retirement age. But remember that the financial well-being of anyone who might become dependent on you is very much your concern as well.

Long-term-care insurance used to be referred to as nursing home insurance. But the coverage available has expanded considerably, and now includes at-home custodial care for those who do not need a nursing home, but do need help in their own homes in order to get along comfortably.

Nursing home care can cost between $40,000 and $70,000 per year—that's for moderate facilities, nothing luxurious. At-home custodial care can cost about $120 per day for one eight-hour shift. That translates to $600 for a five-day week, or more than $30,000 for a full year. You can conservatively expect those costs to increase by about 5 percent per year. In other words, in less than twenty years the costs will have about doubled. Any of those expenses can eat up even a big nest egg in a hurry. Medicare pays for very little, if any, of it.

Long-term-care policies are the cheapest to buy the younger you are. By buying while younger, you avoid the risk of becoming uninsurable because of unforeseen medical problems. It takes some number crunching with a few different policies to come up with the best plan. Here are the main details you will want to evaluate:

Waiting Period

When will the policy begin to pay? From the very first day, or will you have to wait perhaps 30, 60, 90 days, or even longer? The choice is up to you. The shorter the waiting period, the higher the cost. But the difference in cost between no waiting period and a moderate one is relatively small. You might have more peace of mind, therefore, with the shorter waiting period. How much of the possible cost of nursing home or in-home care do you think you can handle on your own without needing insurance help? Therein lies the answer to the waiting period question.

Policy Limits

Policies will typically pay $50 to $100 per day for nursing home facilities, and the amount of at-home care will be pegged to the daily nursing home benefit. Or you can just obtain the nursing home coverage without the at-home benefits.

Inflation Protection

You can opt for no inflation protection, which will be the lowest-cost plan. Or you can choose between a simple and a compounding inflation protection. Example: A policy may offer a simple 5 percent inflation protection, which means that if you start off with a $100 per day room benefit, in the second year that benefit will rise to $105 per day, then $110 per day in the third year, $115 in the fourth year, and so on. In a 5 percent compounding plan, your second year will also be $105, but after that the protection compounds. In the third year your benefit will increase by 5 percent of $105, to $110.25; in the fourth year it will increase by 5 percent of $110.25, to $115.51 and so on. These differences may seem small in the early years—and indeed, they are—but farther down the road it can make a very big difference. After twenty years, the 5 percent simple plan will provide you with a daily room benefit of about $195, whereas the 5 percent compounding plan will provide you with a daily room benefit of about $252. Thus, a person who starts a plan at, say, age 50, will have much more substantial benefits by age 70, when such coverage is more likely to be needed. The at-home benefit should increase at the same rate as the daily nursing home benefit.

The added cost of the simple and compounding plans (the latter being the highest) may prove worth it later on. Having no inflation protection at all affords you the lowest-cost coverage, but you'll have to make up a bigger difference later on if you need the services covered by the policy.

Return of Premium

Some plans offer to refund all or part of what you've paid in to the policy if you never have any claims. This seems attractive on the surface, but you have to pay extra for the privilege. And the amount you have to pay, if otherwise invested conservatively, can grow to an even bigger amount than what you will have paid the insurance company. So crunch those numbers most seriously before you accept this provision.

Discounts

Some policies will offer discounts if both spouses sign up for policies at the same time. And some charitable organizations may make even bigger discounts possible if you join and/or make a contribution to them.

Health Condition

The better your health, the better chance you stand of getting a "preferred" rating, which means a lower cost for the policy. Normal health conditions, even some with slight medical problems, will result in a "standard" rating, and a higher cost accordingly. You don't necessarily have to take a physical for one of these policies, but the companies do scrutinize your medical history very carefully, and problems can easily result in a higher rating or a rejection.

Most major companies that offer these policies have abundant literature that explains all the provisions. Study carefully before you make a choice.

Medical Savings Accounts (MSAs)

This began as an experiment in 1997, to run to 2001. If successful, they will be continued. If not, they will be canceled, but anyone enrolling during this four-year trial period will be able to continue the plan even if the concept is canceled after 2001.

MSAs are designed for self-employed persons and for companies with two to fifty employees. To be eligible you first obtain a high-deductible health insurance plan—that being a deductible between $1,500 and $2,250 per year for singles, and $3,000 to $4,500 for families. Then you can separately invest a large sum of money tax-free, provided that the invested money is only used to pay for medical expenses (or retirement expenses once the investor reaches age 59½). How much can you invest for tax-free earnings? Singles can invest up to 65 percent of their deductible amount, and families can invest up to 75 percent of their deductible amount. In other words, a family with a policy that has a $4,000 deductible can invest up to $3,000 per year in an MSA. If the money is not needed for medical expenses, it can accumulate tax-free until retirement and then be spent at that time.

For younger persons, MSAs offer a most attractive way to build up a long-term retirement fund with an excellent tax shelter. For older persons— say, closing in on age 60—the benefits are not as appealing. The true benefits do take a long time to come to fruition. If you are putting away the money each year to earn tax-free, and you have to take it out each year to pay for medical costs, your tax-free earnings are minimized accordingly. The longer you can let the tax-free earnings stay in the MSA, the bigger the bonanza over the long term.

Health Insurance Portability

The Health Insurance Portability Law of 1997 gives workers the right to continued health care coverage while on the job, between jobs, or when they move to a new job. The law applies to individuals and to businesses with fifty or fewer employees. Here are the basics, with examples as set forth by the U.S. Department of Health and Human Services:

- Small businesses are guaranteed access to health insurance. No insurer can exclude an employee or a family member of an employee from coverage based on health status. Example: The owners of Good Food Cafe have been deterred from buying health insurance for their twenty-five employees. Insurance companies wanted to exclude from any policy one worker, Bill Smith, because he had been diagnosed with cancer. Under the law, all of the employees of the cafe can obtain coverage.

- Once an insurer sells a health policy to a group or individual, they must renew coverage regardless of the health status of any member of a group. Example: Mary Jones, one of Good Food Cafe's employees, develops a heart condition. Under the law, the insurance company must renew the Cafe's policy without dropping Mary or the Cafe from coverage.

- If an individual has previously had health insurance coverage at work, and the job is terminated, or the person moves to another job that does not offer health insurance, that person is guaranteed access to coverage in the individual market without regard to health status, and renewal will be guaranteed. In the alternative, states may develop their own programs to assure that comparable coverage is available to such people. Example: Mary Jones leaves her job at Good Food Cafe to take a new job at Zenith Tool Co., which does not offer health coverage. Under the law, Mary will be able to buy private insurance even if she is in poor health. *Note: The law does not stipulate the cost of such private insurance.* Indeed, it could be quite expensive in Mary's case. But it will be available.

- Coverage cannot be denied for preexisting medical conditions for more than twelve months. Example: Mary Jones's new policy at Zenith can exclude coverage of her heart condition for a maximum of twelve months. And this exclusion may be reduced in relation to the time she was covered for the condition at the Good Food Cafe.

These provisions of the law were quite new at the time this book went to press, so it would be wise to check for more up-to-date regulations and amendments that may have taken place in the interim.

PERSONAL ACTION WORKSHEET

Life Insurance Policy Comparisons

Shopping for life insurance can be very confusing. Companies differ. Specific policies differ. Salespeople differ. Decisions are often made on the basis of the personality of the salesperson or on the "name-brand" reputation of the company. These aren't necessarily improper decisions, but close attention must, of course, be paid to the actual coverage you're obtaining and its cost. The following comparison chart will help you keep a close eye on the numbers themselves.

	Policy A	Policy B	Policy C
❐ Annual premium for a $10,000 straight life policy at your current age	_____	_____	_____
❐ Participating or nonparticipating	_____	_____	_____
❐ If participating, what would have been the dividend paid during the past year?	_____	_____	_____
❐ If participating, what is the company's estimate of dividend for the coming year?	_____	_____	_____
❐ If dividends are left to accumulate with the company, what interest rate will they earn?	_____	_____	_____
❐ Total premium cost over the next 10 years (excluding dividends, since their actual amount won't be known until each year occurs)	_____	_____	_____
❐ At the end of 10 years, what will be your:			
cash/loan value?	_____	_____	_____
paid-up conversion value?	_____	_____	_____
extended term conversion value?	_____	_____	_____
❐ Total premium cost over next 20 years	_____	_____	_____
❐ At the end of 20 years, what will be your:	_____	_____	_____
cash/loan value?	_____	_____	_____
paid-up conversion value?	_____	_____	_____
extended term conversion value?	_____	_____	_____
❐ At what interest rate can you borrow against the policy?	_____	_____	_____

CONSUMER ALERT

An Experiment with Mail-Order Insurance

Health insurance and disability insurance are heavily marketed through the mail, via ads in newspapers and on television. As an experiment, I responded to a number of mail-order insurance offerings. My survey was not scientific, but the results were convincing. You might want to try a survey of your own before you commit yourself to buying health or disability insurance through the mail.

Inquiry No. 1   Eight weeks after sending in the coupon, I had still received no reply. Had I really been in need of the insurance, or had I suffered any malady that could have given rise to a claim, I would have been out of luck.

Inquiry No. 2   I received a policy by return mail, and the bills for it started flowing in. It was a disability income policy, and I compared it in detail with other plans from local agents. The local agents' plans all offered far broader coverage for about the same cost.

Inquiry No. 3   I never received a policy from the company, but I did receive bills urging me to pay the premium before my "valuable coverage" (whatever that may have been) lapsed and left me unprotected.

Inquiry No. 4   In response to the coupon, an agent called on me without an appointment. He was personable and tried to be helpful but would not talk about any of the limitations on the policy unless I asked him directly. He seemed surprised that I knew to ask such questions, and, in some cases, he wasn't sure of the answers. He had no literature to leave with me and said there was absolutely no way for me to see a sample policy unless I signed up with him. Then, he said, I would have ten days to cancel if I wanted to. His main concern was to sign me up on the spot. Can't blame him for trying.

Even with a cancellation privilege, insurance is not a product to be bought sight unseen. All too often, one doesn't exert the effort to cancel an inadequate policy, and the risk is then that you think you're protected when in fact you may be drastically underprotected.

UPS & DOWNS   *The Economics of Everyday Life*

Why Life Insurance Costs Can Vary

Two individuals of the same age are buying the same amount of life insurance. Their costs can vary widely, yet the ultimate payoff for each will be the same. One year later each buys additional policies for the same amount. The one who paid more last year might pay less than the other this year, and vice versa. Why do these costs go up and down?

Smoking versus nonsmoking   Life insurance (as well as other forms of insurance) will cost considerably more for a smoker than for a nonsmoker. The life insurance industry, having recognized the higher risk of paying off sooner to the smoker, has boosted the rates accordingly. See the Strategies for Success on page 521.

Male versus female   Women have longer life expectancies than men. Accordingly, their life insurance costs less.

Underwriting risks   In addition to smoking, some insurance applicants may pose higher risks than others. Known health conditions and participation in hazardous activities are two risk areas that may cause an insurer to charge a higher premium or to reject an application outright.

Type of policy   As noted in this chapter, different types of life insurance—term, whole, endowment, and so on—carry different cost factors, as well as different conversion values.

Actuarial changes   Periodically, the life insurance industry will alter its assumptions as to life expectancy. These are known as mortality tables. As life expectancy increases over the years, insurers have longer to invest the insureds' money. This means that insureds don't have to pay as much to get given benefits as they would have under a previous shorter life-expectancy assumption. These tables are done for the general population, not for individuals. A change in mortality tables will not affect existing policies.

Dividend performance   Participating, or par, policies will pay a sum to policyholders based on the company's performance in taking in money, investing it wisely, and paying it back out in the form of claims. Better performance can mean higher dividends, which can translate into lower out-of-pocket costs for the policy. And vice versa.

Overall company performance   Some insurance companies operate more efficiently than others. Some of the savings they thus realize may be passed on to policyholders in the form of lower premiums. Some companies provide a broader base of service to the public—more offices, more informational literature, more training for agents and staff, and so on. This may result in higher costs to policyholders, who might deem it worth the few extra dollars. Some companies may invest imprudently, thus risking everything for themselves and their insureds.

? WHAT IF . . . ?

Test yourself: How would you deal with these real-life possibilities?

1. You have a whole life par policy for $50,000. Your annual premium cost is $500. You've been paying on the policy for five years. Your annual dividend is now projected to be $40. Up to now you've been lazy, letting the annual dividends stay with the company, which is paying you 4 percent interest on the accumulated amount. But now you want to change things. You can either let the dividend apply against your annual premium, thereby reducing your out-of-pocket cost each year, or you can use the dividend to purchase paid-up additions to the policy each year. This year your dividend will buy you $120 worth of paid-up life insurance, and the amount should grow each year. Which will you choose. Why?

2. The only doctor you've ever known is the old family doctor whom your parents have had you see since you were a kid. He's getting on in years now, and you're on your own. You want to get set up with practitioners your own age. You have a choice between (a) a standard insurance plan that allows you to choose any doctor or any hospital you want; (b) an insurance plan that is tied in with a PPO or (c) an HMO. What homework would you do to make your choice, and which choice will you make?

3. Your company has long had a very liberal sick-pay policy. Now it is shifting to a very rigid plan: five paid sick days per year, period. What can/would you do to protect yourself?

NUMBER CRUNCHERS

Do the calculations to make decisions in these real-life possibilities.

1. Uncle Moe and Uncle Joe each have a $10,000 life insurance policy with double indemnity provisions. You are the beneficiary of both policies. At the time of Uncle Moe's death at the hands of a hit-and-run driver, he had borrowed $4,000 against the cash value of his policy. Uncle Joe had been more prudent, using his annual dividend to buy extra paid-up insurance, which totaled $3,000 at the time of his death from natural causes. How much will you collect from each uncle's insurance policy?

2. You are covered by a $50,000 life insurance policy that happens to have the same conversion values as the one illustrated in Table 17–1. After the policy has been in force for twenty years, how much can you borrow against the policy? How much can you cash it in for? How much paid-up insurance can you convert to? What extended term insurance can you convert to?

3. Your company's sick-pay policy will provide full pay for ten sick days per year, then half pay for ten sick days per year, and that's all. You're evaluating three different disability policies, each of which will pay you $1,000 a month for up to five years in the event of total disability. If need be, you can dip into your savings for $1,000 a month for up to six months to keep you afloat, but you'd rather not touch that nest egg. The policies will cost respectively, $520 per year with a 60-day waiting period, $392 with a 90-day waiting period, and $347 with 180 days. Evaluate your options and pick one.

FOR BETTER OR FOR WORSE

Things beyond our control often impact our personal and financial well-being, for better or for worse. Some are more predictable than others. How would you be affected if the following real-life phenomena happened? Could you have seen it coming? What steps could you have taken to minimize damage or maximize advantage? The better able you are to anticipate and recognize these forces, the better equipped you are to deal with them.

1. Your good health depends on a common prescription drug, which costs $100 per month. You join an HMO and learn, after you've paid, that they don't prescribe that particular medication, but a similar one. The similar one doesn't do the job for you.

2. Your widowed mother has a stroke and can no longer care for herself, but she refuses to go to a nursing home. She needs someone with her for at least twelve hours a day for her to be comfortable. Her total assets are $25,000, and she gets $900 a month from Social Security. She has no long-term-care insurance.

3. You are planning to get a major life insurance policy to protect your family. You develop a very severe cough, which you suspect might be due to your smoking.

Exercise 17.13

Exercise 17.14

18

Financial Planning
for Later Years

Hell begins on the day when God grants us a clear vision of all that we might have achieved, of all the gifts that we have wasted, of all that we might have done that we did not do.

Gian Carlo Menotti

Inside every person there's an echo of years earlier, when the younger self did something very right—or very wrong—that had a very distinct effect on the older self. "If only I hadn't let that fast-talking salesman con me into that bum deal with my whole life's savings." "If only I had started to salt away money for retirement when I was 30, instead of now, when I'm 60." "If only I had paid attention to my pension benefits before I quit that job in a huff." So it goes.

Your years of financial maturity may seem far off, but the planning you do now, and the actions you take now, can have a most decisive effect on your security, or lack of it, when that time does come. This chapter is intended to motivate you to think of the eventuality of that day and to ignite an awareness of

- Your housing needs as your family begins to diminish
- Your sources of income when work ceases
- Your legal rights under your pension plan
- Your capabilities of combatting inflation
- How to take best advantage of the Individual Retirement Account, 401(k), and other tax-sheltered retirement plans

IF NOT FOR YOU, THEN FOR YOUR PARENTS

"Wait a minute," you might be saying now. "This retirement stuff is not for me. I'm decades away from those concerns, so why don't I just skip this chapter?" Not so fast. You may be right about how little these matters apply to your present-day concerns. But your parents, or other people close to you, might be very much involved in these "later years" issues. And your knowledge can be helpful to them. Look at it this way: Wouldn't it be worth it to you if you could help your parents structure their later years so as to reduce the chances of their becoming financially dependent on you? If you answered yes, this chapter is very important to you.

REACHING FINANCIAL MATURITY

Exercise 18.1

There comes a time—and it's different for everyone—when we reach a plateau that we'll call financial maturity. This time, particularly for families, generally is when children have grown up and moved out on their own. It's a period when we look at our personal and financial affairs from a new perspective. Many of our needs have changed, and many previously vague goals now come into focus.

As we reach financial maturity our needs and attitudes are in a state of change regarding housing, investing, insurance, use of leisure time, and the ultimate direction of our working career. Many of the financial decisions we make in our twenties and thirties can have a profound bearing on our ability to fulfill goals during the mature years. Thus, thinking about and making plans for the years of financial maturity should begin at the earliest possible time.

The most dangerous course is to ignore the future totally. We live in an age of instant gratification, constantly urged and teased into buying things for the here and now. If we succumb to such urges excessively, we can end up ruining tomorrow for the sake of today. Tomorrow *will* come, and we must be ready for it.

Let's take a close look at some of the major elements of financial planning for the later years in order to get a broad view of the alternatives. We can present only possibilities and probabilities; specific solutions will be strictly up to each individual and family.

Housing

"This is the old homestead. This is where we raised our family. This is where we feel comfortable. It's almost all paid for—why should we move?"

Or, "Without the children, we don't need this house to rattle around in any longer. Do we sell or do we stay, and what are the ramifications of either choice? If we sell, do we find another place in our community, or do we move to a new community? Do we find another house? A condominium? An apartment?"

Our housing requirements are often drastically altered with the onset of financial maturity, and our personal feelings may easily stand between us and many thousands of dollars that could help provide added security and comfort in the years beyond.

The dilemma is simple enough: retaining the old "family homestead," with its comforts and its memories, or exchanging it for another home that may be more practical and economical.

Many homeowning couples in their fifties and sixties have substantial equity in their homes. In addition to what they have paid in on their mortgage debt, the value of the property itself will probably have increased considerably. But as long as that equity is tied up in the house, it's not working for you—except to provide a roof over your head. You may be perfectly content with that roof. However, by selling or refinancing the house, you could get a large sum of money with which to buy other pleasures.

Moreover, one of the main financial advantages in homeownership—the deductibility of mortgage interest and real estate taxes—may be of far less value to you after you have retired than they were in earlier years.

Let's examine the case of the Johnson family to see what alternatives face them. Mr. and Mrs. Johnson are in their mid-fifties. The large family home they purchased fifteen years ago is far too big for just the two of them now that their children have moved out. They've started to think seriously about retirement—planned for ten years hence—and they realize that their home represents their single biggest asset as well as their single largest monthly expense. Should they keep the house or sell it? And if they sell it, should they rent or buy another?

Their house originally cost them $75,000: they paid $15,000 as a down payment and obtained a thirty-year mortgage for $60,000 at 8 percent interest, with monthly payments of $440. Today, with fifteen years yet to pay on their mortgage, they still owe roughly $48,000.

If they sold their house today, they could get $150,000 after brokerage commissions. Thus, if they were to sell it and pay off their existing mortgage, they

would have a $102,000 tax-free cash-in-hand nest egg to do with as they please. In addition to their mortgage payment of $440, they have real estate taxes averaging $120 per month, property insurance costs of $40 per month, utility costs averaging $120 per month, and maintenance expenses averaging $80 per month. Their total outlay for shelter, is therefore, $800 per month.

Staying As Is

Let's assume that the Johnsons are willing to spend $800 per month for their basic shelter. They realize that inflation will boost their property taxes, insurance, utilities, and maintenance costs. But because they have a fixed-rate mortgage, the monthly mortgage payment will not be affected by inflation. Table 18–1 illustrates the approximate effect of inflation on their future monthly housing costs, assuming that inflation will double these costs in fifteen years. If the Johnsons remain in the house, then ten years from now, when Mr. Johnson plans to retire, their outlay will have crept up to $970. Anticipating that his wages will continue to increase between now and retirement, he has no worries about being able to handle that increased monthly housing outlay. Fifteen years from now, the mortgage will be paid off, and, as Table 18–1 indicates, their monthly outlay will drop to about $720.

Staying put seems to be the simplest course for the Johnsons, but is staying put the *best* course for them? What are their other choices?

Becoming Renters

If they sold the house now, they could rent either an apartment or another house. Instead of spending the $800 per month on the mortgage and housing expenses, they could apply it toward their rental. By selling, they'd also have $102,000 in cash to spend or invest. If they invest the $102,000 they could use some of the income from that investment toward their rental.

If, for example, they invested the $102,000 in a plan that yielded 6 percent after taxes, that would generate $510 per month income for them. That, added to their current monthly housing outlay of $800, would allow them to spend $1,310 per month on rent. And they would always have their

TABLE 18–1 **Monthly Housing Outlay—Existing Home**

	Now	In 10 Years	In 15 Years
Mortgage	$440	$440	$ 0
Property taxes	120	200	240
Insurance	40	70	80
Utilities	120	160	240
Maintenance	80	100	160
Total	$800	$970	$720

$102,000 nest egg intact to do with as they pleased in the future.

If the rental increased on their apartment, and if the yield on the $102,000 investment also increased proportionately, they could maintain a fairly level standard of housing over the long term. Otherwise they would have to adjust accordingly.

Buying Another Dwelling

Another alternative would be to buy another dwelling—house, townhouse, or condominium—with the proceeds of the sale of their existing home. Let's say that the Johnsons find a smaller dwelling with a $100,000 price tag. They put $40,000 of their total $102,000 nest egg toward a down payment on the new house, and sign up for a $60,000 mortgage for fifteen years at 9 percent. The new monthly mortgage payments would be $609. Let's assume that the other costs would be lower in their new dwelling because it's a more modest property: $100 for property taxes, $30 for insurance, $60 for utilities, and $60 for maintenance. This brings the grand monthly total outlay to $859—$59 more than they have currently been paying. Table 18–2 illustrates what their current outlay in a new smaller house would be for the present, and for ten and fifteen years hence.

Remember that the Johnsons have $62,000 left over from the sale of their previous house. Assume that they put that to work in an investment that will earn them 6 percent after taxes, or roughly $310 per month. They can apply that income toward their housing expense and still leave the $62,000 nest egg intact for future use. Table 18–3 shows the net housing cost for the Johnsons in their new home, assuming that they apply the income from their investment toward these costs.

Currently, their net housing costs would be $549 per month. That's $251 per month less than what they now have budgeted for housing. They could, if they wish, begin an additional investment program with that $251 per month and create an even larger nest egg for their retirement years.

TABLE 18–2   **Monthly Housing Outlay—New, Smaller House**

	Now	**In 10 Years**	**In 15 Years**
Mortgage	$609	$ 609	$ 0
Property taxes	100	160	200
Insurance	30	50	60
Utilities	60	100	120
Maintenance	60	100	120
Total	$859	$1,019	$500

Note: Projections are based on an approximate annual inflation rate of 6 percent for property taxes, insurance, utilities, and maintenance costs.

TABLE 18–3   **Net Housing Costs—New, Smaller House**

	Now	In 10 Years	In 15 Years
Base costs (from Table 18–2)	$859	$1,019	$500
Income from $62,000 investment	310	310	310
Net housing cost, after applying investment income	$549	$ 709	190

What About Refinancing?

If the Johnsons decided to stay put for the time being, would it make sense for them to refinance their existing mortgage? Unless the current interest rates are *equal to or less than* the original 8 percent interest rate on their existing mortgage, refinancing at this time would be of relatively little benefit. Assume they were to refinance their existing $48,000 mortgage for a new period of 30 years at 12 percent interest each year. Their monthly mortgage payments would actually *increase* by $54 per month, to $493 per month. Obviously, there's no advantage to such a move. Careful calculations, including all costs involved, will be necessary to determine the value of refinancing at any particular time.

Profit Potential

The Johnsons face yet another perplexity to reach a decision: What profit potential might they be giving up if they sell their existing house? The house has doubled in value in the past fifteen years. Will it double again in the next fifteen years? If they sell now and become renters, would they then be giving up a veritable small fortune? On the other hand, if they sell now, and buy another house, what is the profit potential on that other house? Could it be more or less than the potential on the existing house?

If the Johnsons are risk-takers, they might prefer to hold onto their existing house and take their chances on the future housing market. If they are more conservative, they might prefer to sell now and have a greater sense of security for the years to come.

There is no rule of thumb as to which choice is best for any given family. But there are choices to be made, and those choices should be evaluated clearly, with professional help, wherever uncertainty emerges.

Investing

Our investment attitudes and tactics are likely to undergo a considerable change as we reach financial maturity. Until now, we've been concerned with *generating* capital to meet the heavy expenses of housing, educating the children, and other family needs. Now, with those needs substantially accomplished, we turn to the philosophy of *preservation* of capital. While we were younger, we could afford to make mistakes and still recoup. Now we may be at an age when a financial loss is more alarming: we may have neither the time nor the ability to recoup.

The advantages of fixed income investing, as opposed to more speculative forms, become clearer. Although many are just reaching their peak earning years at this stage, the wisdom of taking risks is diminishing. We simply have less time to recover from a loss. Anticipating that time when work may cease, we begin to realize the importance of preserving our capital so that there will be adequate funds available. This does not imply that all attempts to generate capital more speculatively should be abandoned. But the risk factor must be examined more closely and should be considered with much more respect than it may have been a decade or two earlier.

A portfolio of fixed income investments to preserve capital can take many shapes. Perhaps the line of least resistance is to take whatever lump sum you may have accumulated and just put it into long-term high-yield bonds and leave it there. This minimizes the need to have your nose buried in *The Wall Street Journal* constantly looking for better opportunities. If you're locked into a given situation, you may regret it later if better opportunities do present themselves. On the other hand, nothing better may come along, and you'll be content to ride it out with your locked-in situation.

The prudent investor in the mature years must be aware of the value of liquidity and flexibility. To obtain liquidity and flexibility in the fixed income portfolio, consider the advantages of building a portfolio based on *staggered maturities.*

Staggered Maturities

Instead of investing a lump sum for one long period, you break up the lump sum into perhaps three or four or five nearly equal segments and invest them for different maturities. For example, you have a $10,000 lump sum that you want to put into fixed income securities. Consider breaking it into four equal parts of $2,500 each and investing each of the four segments for a different maturity: one segment for one year, one for two years, one for three years, and one for four years. Within each time span, you can take advantage of the highest yield security available. Then as each segment matures, starting in one year, you can reinvest that money into whatever is best at that time, considering safety and yield.

With a portfolio like this, you'd have one-quarter of your total nest egg roll over every year. In some years you might have to take a lesser yield than you had previously been earning on that segment because of a drop in interest rates. In other years, you might be able to obtain a better return. With a program of staggered maturities (not exceeding a five- or six-year maximum), you're going to have a higher degree of control and liquidity with your nest egg, which could bring you a greater sense of satisfaction and financial return.

Overall, as noted in chapter 14, the fixed income portfolio allows you to predict with reasonable certainty how much money you will have available at any given future point. By sticking to fixed-income investments with shorter maturities, you can avoid the problem of being caught in a long-term downtrend of prices on such fixed-income securities as bonds. If you need to tap your next egg, you will have minimized any worry that the value will have shrunk because of fluctuations in those securities.

Insurance

Financial maturity brings accompanying changes in our insurance program. We may have had a life insurance program designed to protect our family in the event of the premature death of the breadwinner. Now the family is on its own, and we may have far better uses for those dollars.

Life insurance programs begun when you are in your twenties and thirties can have a most important effect on financial status in your fifties and sixties. If, when you're young, you sacrifice a bit of current pleasures for the sake of greater security in the future, you can create a life insurance program that will serve you well in the later years. In chapter 17, we examined some of the alternatives facing young people in choosing various kinds of life insurance programs. Let's now look at the effect of one particular choice decades later.

When Joe was age 30, he bought a straight life insurance policy with a face value of $50,000. His annual premium for this protection was $653. From the very first day the policy was issued, Joe and his family had the peace of mind of knowing that $50,000 would be payable to his family in the event of Joe's death. Joe has lived a full and healthy life, and today, twenty years later, he looks at the conversion values in his life insurance program.

Table 18–4 illustrates Joe's policy. (See chapter 17 regarding how these values work.) When Joe is age 50 and the policy is twenty years old, Joe's life insurance needs are quite different than when he bought the policy. His

TABLE 18–4   Joe's Life Insurance

At Age	Total Premiums Paid to Date	Conversion Values		
		Cash/Loan Value	Paid-up Insurance	Extended Term
50	$13,060	$14,450	$28,550	19 years, 103 days
65	22,855	27,550	39,950	14 years, 160 days

Note: Policies will differ with respect to these values.

children are grown now, and there is little need for immediate cash to take care of his family in the event of his death.

At age 50, Joe will have paid premiums totaling $13,060. The policy now has a cash surrender value of $14,450. In other words, Joe can cash in the policy and receive back *more* than what he paid in. If he invests the $14,450 at 6 percent per year, he will have a return of $867 per year, leaving his $14,450 nest egg intact. The net results: For the past twenty years he has guaranteed his family a substantial lump sum of money—$50,000—in the event of his premature death. Now, instead of being out of pocket $653 for premiums each year, he can have an added income of $867 per year, plus a cash nest egg of $14,450. If he cashes in the policy, the $50,000 coverage will terminate.

Joe may also elect to borrow the $14,450 from the company, to do with as he sees fit, while paying interest on the loan at the rate stated in the policy. If he chooses this alternative, the policy will remain in force, except that in the event of Joe's death, the proceeds payable will be the face value of the policy minus any loans outstanding against the policy.

Joe's other alternatives are to convert the policy to a paid-up or an extended-term status. If he chooses the paid-up method, he can cease paying the annual $653 premium and will have a life insurance policy with a face value of $28,550, paid up for the rest of his life. He doesn't have to pay any more premiums, and, on his death, his survivors will receive that sum. If he converts to extended-term insurance, he will be able to stop paying premiums and still be insured for the full $50,000 face value for a period of 19 years plus 103 days, until he's almost 70.

What if Joe continues to pay on the policy and keep it in force until he reaches age 65? He will have paid in a total of $22,855 in premiums, and he will have a cash value of $27,550. The other conversion values for that age are indicated in Table 18–4.

Another option open to Joe at this time would be to convert the paid-up values in his policies to second-to-die coverage. To do this, he would add his wife to a new joint policy so that both of their lives would be covered. The proceeds would be payable on the death of the second of the two insured parties. Assuming that both Joe and his wife are in good health, converting the paid-up values in the old policy to a second-to-die policy could give them a much higher face value, which could benefit their children or pay off any other debts, including estate taxes.

The important thing is that the 30-year-old Joe did in fact create the program that the 50-year-old Joe or the 65-year-old Joe can now either continue or convert to suit current needs. *The young man created a liquid and flexible package that can benefit the older man.*

Health insurance is also important. Anyone covered by a group medical plan should, at the earliest possible time, investigate what health insurance alternatives are available at retirement, particularly if you plan to retire before reaching Medicare eligibility at age 65. Does your health insurance coverage continue after you retire? If so, at what cost, if any? If not, what kind of supplemental coverage is available to you and at what cost? Long-term-care insurance should also be explored. (This subject is discussed in greater detail in chapter 17.) Careful examination should also be made of eligibility for Medicare, what coverage it provides, and at what cost. Will you want supplemental coverage in addition to what Medicare provide you? The sooner you look into these matters, the better off you'll be.

Activities and Idleness

Our personal activities and pleasures may undergo substantial alteration when we reach financial maturity. Much of our free time in the younger years may have been devoted to family affairs or community activities. We may also find that friends are shifting from old patterns into new ones, and there may be a desire to pursue various interests with those friends.

Very serious problems can arise if you don't develop outside interests that will provide satisfaction and self-fulfillment in later years. In spite of all the money one may have accumulated, the loneliness, boredom, and help-lessness that can attack retirees are overpowering.

To Work or to Retire

As financial maturity begins, we start to think about how long we wish to continue working in our current jobs, whether we wish to take on some new work, or whether we wish to enjoy a leisurely retirement. Our choices, and how we move toward them, can have a critical influence on the quality of our later years.

If you intend to continue working, either voluntarily or out of necessity, what kind of employment might be available to someone with your skills, desires, experience, and needs? If gradual retirement is in your future, when will you begin to taper off, and how quickly? Will you want to try something that you'd always wished you could do?

The earlier you start shaping those thoughts into something tangible, the better. If you anticipate a work activity that will take some investment on your part, the earlier you start setting aside the necessary funds, the better you'll be able to accomplish your desires. If no investment will be needed, you'll have all that much more time to establish extra reserve funds to see you through, should the business venture not work out.

Some Particular Thoughts for the Older Single Person

The single person reaching financial maturity has some different considera-tions from those of the married person. Single people who do not have de-pendents obviously have little need for life insurance and can allocate those dollars elsewhere. To the extent that single people want to leave an inheritance, life insurance does provide a good vehicle for that purpose, as it does for married people.

Many single people may have life insurance policies acquired many years ago. When the original need for insurance has diminished, single people should examine the conversion privileges in the policies, as noted earlier in the case of Joe.

If disability strikes, the single person who is alone can be at a disadvantage—long-term convalescence can be costly and time-consuming. Housekeeping, shopping, nursing care, and the like must be considered, and the costs can run high. It's essential for single persons to maintain comprehensive insurance programs or other alternatives that will protect them in the event of long-term disability.

A single person facing a long-term disability may need a lawyer's help. If you are unable to act on your own behalf, someone trusted should be allowed to step into your shoes and take care of important matters for you. These matters could be as simple as writing or endorsing checks, or as complex as selling a home. The Power of Attorney can be a valuable tool for the single person, particularly in the event of an extended disability.

A Power of Attorney need not be given to a lawyer; it can be granted to anyone you choose. But a lawyer should definitely draw up the documents. A Power can be limited to specifically stated acts or can be general in scope. A general Power of Attorney is very broad and should be entered into only in the most compelling circumstances. Your lawyer can give you more details.

Concerns About Health Care

Preretirement financial planning includes keeping a close eye on health insurance, particularly if a couple's main health plan is based on one spouse's job, with the other spouse being covered as a dependent. To what extent will the dependent spouse be covered when the working spouse retires? Presumably, the retiring spouse will be covered by Medicare and/or a continuation of the employer's group plan. But the dependent spouse might not yet be eligible for Medicare, and the employer's plan might not cover spouses of retirees. If neither kind of coverage is available to the dependent spouse, can that spouse obtain the needed health insurance privately? Would preexisting conditions limit the protection available to such a person? Discuss this with a good agent so that any problems can be minimized while the dependent spouse is still insurable.

FINANCIAL ARRANGEMENTS FOR THE LATER YEARS

Exercise 18.2

How much money will you have to live on when your work tapers off and/or ceases altogether?

Before we take a closer look at planning a retirement budget, we must discuss one very common concern: "Whatever we have to live on, it won't be enough because inflation will eat away at it."

The Specter of Inflation

Inflation can be a specter, particularly if the ability to work has diminished or disappeared. But it can be coped with.

On reaching the later years, many individuals reduce their living expenses and thus blunt the effects of inflation. Moving to smaller quarters, moderating clothing needs and having only one car can sharply reduce financial needs. Many families will have paid off their home mortgages and many will terminate or convert existing life insurance programs, and no longer have those costs.

Beyond what families do unconsciously to meet their diminished needs, they might also take some conscious steps to cut spending. A review of any budget can reveal minor excesses that can be reduced without materially affecting lifestyle.

The effects of inflation can also be blunted on the income side. Social Security payments are scheduled to increase in line with Consumer Price Index fluctuations, and many pensions have escalation clauses tied to rising prices. Furthermore, as costs move upward, so inevitably do yields on fixed income investments, and those higher yields can offset the inflationary bite.

STRATEGIES FOR SUCCESS

Don't Leave Safe Harbors Foolishly

Investing for retirement requires an emphasis on safety: putting a major portion of your money into the safe harbors of federally insured savings plans, government bonds, and high-quality corporate bonds. But even with the best of planning, interest rates might fall, or inflation might rise. Either phenomenon can erode your supply of spendable dollars. When either occurs, Snake Oil Sam is not far behind, offering mystical plans to beat the low interest rates or the high inflation. Don't leave your safe harbors at the beckoning of Snake Oil Sam. He can lead you into risky waters where you can suffer grievous losses. If you stay in the safe harbor, interest rates will eventually go back up, and inflation will go back down, and things will stabilize. More importantly, in the safe harbor your money *will be there when you need it*. With Sam, it *may be gone forever*. Keep your expectations reasonable, and learn to live comfortably on lower yields. Then higher yields, when they come, will be a bonus for you.

Shaping the Budget

Two primary sources of sustenance must be considered in detail: income and principal. Income is money received from all sources such as Social Security, pensions, investments, and work. Principal is accumulated money working for you that may be dipped into for living purposes as the need arises. The prudent course is to attempt to live off income and keep principal in reserve until needed. A careful review of your investment program is necessary. How much principal do you have? How well is it protected? Can you count on the projected income from principal? If not, how can you restructure your investments to offer a more assured income flow?

Income Sources

The younger you are, the more difficult it will be to get specific figures on what retirement income will be available to you. But at least ten or fifteen years before you anticipate retirement, you should begin to estimate what might be expected. As the date approaches, you should check with regularity—at least every second year, tapering down to every year—in order to focus more clearly on the actual income figures. One very sad mistake is to conjure up in your own mind what these income sources may be—those who guess too high can be sharply disappointed. The proper way is to check with the specific sources and get their best estimates as to the actual dollars that will become available, and when.

Income from Social Security

Exercise 18.3

Social Security payments are increased periodically as the Consumer Price Index increases. A visit to your local Social Security office can be helpful; the closer you get to actual retirement, the more closely the Social Security Administration can estimate your income.

Income from Pensions and Profit-Sharing Plans

Visit with your employer's pension or profit-sharing plan administrator to determine what money you may have coming from those sources. What options do you have with those funds? Will you be paid a fixed monthly amount and, if so, for how long? Will you be able to obtain a lump-sum payment, what will it be, and when can you get it? Will payments continue beyond the death of the working spouse and be available to the surviving spouse and, if so, for how long? The Pension Reform Law of 1974 makes many provisions for the benefit of pensions-to-be. That law is discussed later in this chapter; included in the discussion is a rundown of the Individual Retirement Act 401(k) plans and other tax-sheltered retirement plans.

Income from Investments

As retirement nears and the ability to earn income from work diminishes, you'll seek more assurance that a fixed amount will be available to meet your needs. This means, most simply put, that you have to take less and less risk when you put your money to work. Putting your money at risk means that you have less assurance, perhaps none at all, as to how much income or principal you'll have during those years when you must depend upon an assured amount. The stock market may have been fine for you as a capital-building vehicle when you were a few decades younger. But verging on retirement, you can't afford all the risks that go with the stock market. Develop a sound program of fixed-income investments—high rated bonds and savings plans—with perhaps some high quality stocks that pay a good level of assured dividends. Risk means potential loss, at a time you can least afford it.

Income from Working

Many people continue to work long after they are eligible to retire. They may go into business for themselves or take a full- or part-time job out of either choice or necessity. But the younger you are, the more difficult it is to predict how much post-retirement income you might earn from working, or for how long it might continue. With the earning potential from work so unpredictable, it would be prudent not to rely on any such income for your basic well-being. It might be best to consider any such income as "icing on the cake" to provide for extra comforts and leisure activities during retirement.

Owing to peculiarities in the income tax laws and Social Security regulations, it is possible for some people to end up with more spendable income—after taxes—once they have retired as compared with before retirement. For example, when Flora was age 64, she had a total income from her job of $30,000 per year. After all taxes and voluntary pension contributions were taken into account, she was left with a net spendable income of $24,000. The following year, she retired. Just to keep busy, she took a part-time job, from which she earned $10,000 during her first year of retirement. She received an additional $8,000 for that year from a pension plan and $10,000 from Social Security. The Social Security income was not taxable. Considering all taxes on her sources of income, Flora ended up with a net spendable income of $25,000 during her first year of retirement, even though her actual income from work was a fraction of what it had been during her working years. In other words, she had more spendable money after retirement than she did while she was working.

Post-retirement income from work can also be affected by Social Security regulations, which can reduce your benefits if you earn more than a set amount during a given year from work. Anyone planning to work after starting to receive Social Security benefits must determine what effect the earnings will have on benefits. There are three ways that Social Security laws can reduce your postretirement income.

1. If you earn income from work, that income will be subject to the same Social Security taxes you've been paying all through your working years.

2. Once you start receiving Social Security benefits, up to 85 percent of what you receive can be subject to income taxes if your overall income exceeds a certain level. That overall income includes earnings from work and from investments. So working can push your Social Security benefits into a taxable level.

3. If you are receiving Social Security benefits, those benefits are reduced by income you receive from work. The latest regulations on this matter are that Social Security recipients under age 70 will forfeit one dollar's worth of benefits for every three dollars they earn at work over a certain threshold. That threshold for 1999 is $15,500. In other words, if Robin Retiree earned $16,500 from work in 1999, Robin's Social Security benefits will be reduced for the year by $333. (Earnings from investments do not count in this matter.) The threshold is scheduled to rise in the following years to $17,000 for the year 2000, $25,000 for 2001, and $30,000 for 2002. From age 70 to onward these forfeits no longer apply.

All of these Social Security regulations are subject to change at any time, so you must check the current ones as they pertain to you.

The Principal Sources

The principal sources of future spendable dollars may be easier to estimate than income sources, particularly if an investment portfolio is in fixed income situations. The potential principal sources are the following.

Equity in Your Home

As noted earlier, many people refinance or sell their homes to get access to the dollars they've been paying on their mortgage. This equity can represent a substantial portion of anyone's ultimate nest egg and should be estimated as carefully and as far in advance as possible.

One technique for tapping the equity in a home is known as a reverse mortgage. Instead of borrowing a lump sum and then making monthly payments to the lender, the lender sends you a monthly payment, and the debt (plus interest) builds up over the years. The accumulated debt must be paid off when the homeowners move, sell, or die. Very few lenders offer such plans; they are complicated and need careful study. The American Association of Retired Persons (AARP) offers literature on the subject. Another equity-tapping technique is a sale-leaseback, which is usually done between parents (the homeowners) and their children. The parents, in effect, sell the house to the children, who in turn give a lifetime lease back to the parents. The parents thus get cash up front. The children get monthly rent plus some possible income tax breaks. The advice of a lawyer and an accountant should be sought before embarking on these techniques.

Life Insurance Values

Individuals with conversion values in their life insurance policies should determine precisely what those values currently are and what they will be in future years. Personal circumstances will dictate whether to continue the protection of the life insurance in full, convert it to one of the other forms of life insurance, or retrieve the cash that's available.

Pension and Profit-Sharing Funds

If lump-sum distributions are available instead of monthly payments, these should be counted in your overall sources of principal. See the discussion later in this chapter on lump-sum pension and profit-sharing distributions.

Business Interests

If you have an interest in a business, either wholly or partially, how might that be converted into investable funds, and at what time? How can you best sell out your business or professional practice and on what terms?

Anyone in these circumstances must recognize when a business or professional practice is at peak potential and reach a decision as to how much energy should be devoted to the business compared to other pursuits. A common problem arises when a business owner begins to feel a diminution in energy regarding operation of the business. As energy diminishes, so can profitability and, in turn, the opportunity to reap the best possible price on a sale of the business. The sad end result can be that the business falls far short of being able to provide for the needs of the owner at the time of retirement because the ability to sell it has been so negatively affected.

Prudent planning dictates that when business owners or professionals recognize the peak potential, they should immediately begin a phaseout plan. This generally would involve selling the business to a younger successor, turning over the reins to a family member, or putting the enterprise on the market.

Existing Investment Portfolio

This includes all money you now have invested. Some of it currently may not be offering any return—you are hoping for a gain in value to realize your ultimate rewards. As retirement approaches, you may deem it wiser to convert such nonearning assets into earning ones, so you can specifically gauge how much will be available to you in the future.

Potential Inheritances

Realistically, try to estimate inheritances from family members in the foreseeable future. Will the funds be in cash, securities, property, or some other form? Will they be earning assets or nonearning assets, and what would be involved in converting them into situations best suited to your personal needs? For example, you might inherit a parcel of income-producing real estate. Although this could generate an attractive measure of income, you might not want to continue ownership of the building. It might be a great distance away from where you live or you may simply not have the desire or expertise to deal with income-producing real estate. What are the prospects of selling the building? What taxes would have to be paid on such a sale? How much income could the net proceeds generate? These considerations apply to any inherited assets.

Nest-Egg Dipping: How Much and for How Long?

Most of us face this ultimate dilemma in the later years: to have enough money available to live within a desired framework for an *indeterminate* time, always having enough money to take care of virtually any contingency. Life expectancy and health factors are unknowns, but the amount of money available should be known. If, after work has ceased, you can live comfortably on income alone, your later years should be relatively worry-free. The dilemma is compounded in those many situations where principal has to be invaded, minimally or substantially, to provide for necessities and contingencies.

In many cases, it's necessary for a lifestyle to be trimmed in order to conserve enough principal to guarantee future comforts and necessities. Temptations to dip into principal should be examined carefully. When your principal is reduced, so is your earning power.

Let's say that you have a nest egg soundly invested, and you want to dip into it to increase your monthly spending money. How much, and for how long, can you dip into the next egg before you deplete it? As Table 18–5 shows, starting with a lump-sum nest egg of $30,000, you could withdraw $269 per month for fifteen years. At the end of fifteen years, you would have depleted the nest egg. Or you could withdraw $179 per month indefinitely and always have the original nest egg intact. (In this latter case, you are withdrawing only the interest earned by your investment.) Table 18–5 is based on an interest rate of 7 percent per year, compounded quarterly, before income tax considerations.

TABLE 18–5 Dipping into Your Nest Egg

Starting with a lump sum of . . .	you can withdraw this much each month, for the stated number of years, reducing the lump sum to zero . . .				or you can withdraw this much each month and always have the original nest egg intact
	10 Years	15 Years	20 Years	25 Years	
$ 10,000	$ 116	$ 89	$ 77	$ 70	$ 59
15,000	174	134	116	106	88
20,000	232	179	155	141	118
25,000	290	224	193	176	142
30,000	348	269	232	212	179
40,000	464	359	310	282	237
50,000	580	448	386	352	285
60,000	696	538	464	424	360
80,000	928	718	620	564	467
$100,000	1,160	896	772	704	585

TAX AND PENSION LAWS: HOW THEY AFFECT THE RIGHTS OF WORKERS AND RETIREES

The Effect on Retirement Age

Exercise 18.4

The Tax Reform Act of 1986, in conjunction with Social Security regulations, affects the time at which retirees will be entitled to full benefits from their pension plans. The law states that employees must be at least 65 years of age before they can receive 100 percent of their pension benefits. If they want to retire earlier, the formula for the payout must be the same as that used by the Social Security Administration. For example: Social Security regulations say that workers are entitled to 80 percent of full benefits if they retire at age 62. Thus, if employees wanted to retire at age 62, they would be entitled to only 80 percent of what otherwise would be forthcoming from the employer's pension plan at age 65. So, as with Social Security, early retirees get a lesser pension amount, though they start getting it at an earlier time.

The law also sets forth a gradual increase in the minimum retirement age, again in line with the Social Security formula. For individuals born Dec. 31, 1937, or earlier, the retirement age at which you are entitled to full benefits is 65. If you were born Jan. 1, 1938 or after, and before January 1, 1945, the retirement age is 66. And if you were born after December 31, 1944, the retirement age is 67. Check current Social Security regulations to determine how this will affect you.

The Pension Reform Law (ERISA)

In September 1974, Congress passed the Employee Retirement Income Security Act of 1974, more commonly known as the Pension Reform Law, or ERISA. The purpose of the law was to correct abuses that occurred in the administration of pension funds that resulted in pensioners being deprived of money that was due them.

The administration of the law is under the jurisdiction of two governmental agencies: the Internal Revenue Service and the U.S. Department of Labor. The following discussion is intended to acquaint you with the overall concepts. Persons accumulating pension benefits subject to ERISA should determine from their employer exactly what their benefits will be and what their rights are under the law.

The law is aimed at those pension funds that are "qualified" under the Internal Revenue Service regulations. Qualified pension funds, generally, are those that allow the employer tax deductions for the cost of contributions, and that permit the employees receiving the benefits not to have to report those contributions as income until the money in the fund is later withdrawn. About 60 million Americans are covered by this law.

Exercise 18.5

The Law does *not* require any company to start a pension plan. But if a company does begin one, it must meet the requirements of the law. Furthermore, the law does *not* stipulate how much money an employer should pay in pension benefits for employees, nor how much, if any, an employee should contribute. But the law does establish that once promises are made regarding pension contributions, those promises must be kept.

If your employer does not have a pension or profit-sharing plan, you should still be aware of the benefits available under the law. You may change jobs and go to a company that does have a pension plan, or people close to you may be affected by the law, and your awareness of its benefits can be helpful to them.

The Pension Reform Law attempts to correct abuses in these main areas: vesting, funding, folding, reporting, and managing.

Vesting

Vesting refers to that time when your benefits are *locked up* or guaranteed as a result of the time you've spent on the job. The law is designed to eliminate the problem of when you are entitled to how much money. To understand what this means, let's follow the basic steps involved in obtaining pension benefits from a company.

First, you must become *eligible* to participate in the plan. The law states that any employee who is at least 25 years old with at least one year on the payroll must be taken into the pension plan if the company has one.

Once you become eligible, the company *credits* a certain sum to your pension or profit-sharing account each year until you either leave the company or retire.

The next step in receiving the benefits is *vesting,* or locking up whatever benefits have been set aside in your name.

The law gives an employer two choices with regard to vesting programs for employees who are covered by the employer's pension plan.

GRADUAL VESTING The first choice is a gradual schedule, which requires that workers who are eligible for the plan be 20 percent vested after three years, then an additional 20 percent vested per year after the third year, which would get them 100 percent vested after seven years. Table 18–6 illustrates this plan, assuming that the employer is contributing $500 per year to the eligible employees' pension fund.

Example: The employee must be 20 percent vested after three years of eligibility in the plan. At the end of three years, the employer has put $1,500 into this employee's plan. Being 20 percent vested means that 20 percent of the $1,500 that has been contributed to the plan, or $300, is now *vested* for that employee. In other words, at some future time, the employee will be entitled to receive at least that $300 unconditionally. If that employee quits after three years of service, nothing further will be contributed to his or her plan. If the employee remains on the job, vesting will grow year by year in accordance with the table.

ALL-AT-ONCE VESTING The second vesting choice is an *all-at-once* vesting. After five years of eligible service, an employee is 100 percent vested in whatever money has been contributed to the plan. If that employee quits the job after 4 years 11 months and 29 days, he or she will not become vested at all.

Employers may choose more rapid vesting schedules if they wish. Union pension plans can have ten-year vesting schedules.

These vesting choices do not mean that you're entitled to a full pension once you've achieved full vesting. You may have to wait until you actually retire before any of the funds are available. In certain cases, an employer may be willing to pay the vested funds to an employee in the event of an

TABLE 18–6   Gradual Vesting

Year	Total Amount Contributed	Percent Vested	Dollars Vested
1	$ 500	—	—
2	1,000	—	—
3	1,500	20	$ 300
4	2,000	40	800
5	2,500	60	1,500
6	3,000	80	2,400
7	3,500	100	3,500

earlier termination. This must be determined directly with each employer in any specific individual case.

Note also that these vesting requirements refer to the *employer's* contribution to the pension fund. If you are making your own contribution, either directly or through payroll deduction, you are fully and immediately vested regarding those contributions.

An employer's plan must state which vesting alternative is being used. The employer must keep records of every employee's service and vesting. Each employee is entitled to *a yearly statement* from an employer concerning vesting and accrued benefit status.

Funding

Funding refers to putting enough money into the pension fund to meet the future promises to pay the benefits.

Say that XYZ Company has ten employees in its pension plan. By reasonable estimates, the ten employees will receive pension benefits of $50,000 each over their lifetimes after retirement. Let's assume that all ten employees retire on the same day and that they all request a lump-sum distribution of their benefits. On this mass retirement day, therefore, the XYZ pension fund should theoretically have at least $500,000 in it.

But what if the XYZ pension fund has only $200,000 in it? Why might this be so? Perhaps through some bookkeeping shenanigans or perhaps due to a simple shortfall in the amount it was contributing, the company has missed the mark considerably. What, then, happens to the ten employees? They split up the $200,000 into lumps of $20,000 each and sit there in amazement wondering what happened to them.

The Pension Reform Law attempts to correct this possible abuse. It imposes very stringent requirements on managers of all pension funds to put away the amount that they, according to reasonable expectations, will need to meet the targeted promises.

Despite the rigid requirements of the Pension Reform Law, a company may still violate the law and not properly fund enough money to meet its obligations. You may not discover this until the time for your retirement, at which point, of course, it's too late.

Folding

A company for whom you've worked could fold after you've started receiving your pension benefits, thus putting those benefits in jeopardy.

Exercise 18.6

The Pension Reform Law has created an insurance program that will guarantee retirees at least a *portion* of their benefits if their company folds. The law established the Pension Benefit Guarantee Corporation (PBGC) to administer this program.

This insurance program is intended to provide for benefits that are *vested*. The benefits you're entitled to under PBGC are related to your earnings with the company and your age. If your plan was terminated in 1997, the maximum monthly amount you could get from PBGC would have been $2,761 if you were age 65; $2,181 if you were 62; $1,795 if you were 60, and $1,243 if you were 55. Note again: these are the maximum amounts you can get per month, based on what your benefits with the terminated plan would have been. The amounts are adjusted for inflation every year.

In effect, the PBGC is like a safety net under the overall pension programs throughout the United States. But don't rely on it to the exclusion of any other safety nets you might provide on your own through individual initiative and planning.

Reporting

The law has created these benefits and protections, but how is the average individual supposed to learn about them and keep up to date with them?

The law has seen to that, too. Every eligible participant in a plan must be given a description of the plan, plus a periodic summary of the plan "written in a manner calculated to be understood by the average plan participant." This summary must explain in detail the participant's rights and obligations under the plan. In addition, the company must maintain open access to the latest annual report on the plan, and related documents must be available for examination by participating employees.

The written explanation shouldn't be treated lightly. You should study the booklet when you get it and ask questions if you don't understand. Sound financial planning requires that you know the exact status of your pension rights at all times.

Managing

The law sets stringent guidelines for the management of pension funds. It sets forth fiduciary duties, the punishment for their breach, prohibited transactions, and steps to avoid conflicts of interest between the respective parties. In short, the investment philosophy of pension funds should be conservative enough to comply with this requirement of the law.

Employees have a stake in how their pension money is invested, although they may not have a very strong voice in those decisions. If you think that your company's pension plan is taking too many risks in its investment philosophy, you and your co-workers can voice your opinion to management accordingly. If you belong to a union, your union might be able to do this for you. A pension plan investment manager who makes serious errors may be punished under the law. But that will not satisfy you if, as a recipient of that pension plan, you're getting less than you had been entitled to. The time to voice your concerns is before the mistakes are made, not afterward.

DO-IT-YOURSELF PENSIONS: IRAS, KEOGHS, 401(k)

There is no one—no company, no government, no union—who can take as good care of your future as you can. The sooner you begin taking care of your own financial future, the better off you'll be. Pension and profit-sharing plans may hold the promise of future security. But you might leave the company; the company might fold; the plan might suffer losses as a result of unwise investment strategies. As for Social Security, it is unwise for people born in the 1960s or later to rely on Social Security as more than a token portion of their overall retirement income.

Do-it-yourself retirement planning is enhanced by a variety of plans that offer attractive advantages to those who participate. These plans are the Individual Retirement Account (IRA) and the 401(k) plans for employed individuals, and the Keogh plan for self-employed individuals.

Individual Retirement Accounts (IRAs)

Along with the 401(k) the IRA is the most common do-it-yourself plan. In order to be eligible for a standard IRA, you must have income from work. Income from investments or pensions does not qualify. If you have less than

$2,000 income from work in a given year, the amount you can put into an IRA investment is equal to the amount of income you had from work. In other words, if you earned $1,500 from work in a given year, you would be eligible to invest as much as $1,500 that year in an IRA. If your income from work is more than $2,000 in a given year, then the most you can put into an IRA for that year is $2,000. If each spouse in a family has more than $2,000 income for work in a given year, then the couple can invest up to $4,000 each year in their IRAs. You can put in less than these amounts if you wish. Or you can put in nothing in a given year if you wish. There's no minimum requirement, only a maximum limitation.

Effective for tax years 1998 and onward, if you have a nonworking spouse who does not participate in an IRS-qualified pension plan and the couple's adjusted gross income is not more than $160,000 for the year, that nonworking spouse can put up to $2,000 into an IRA, even if the working spouse does participate in a plan.

Something Old, Something New

The Taxpayer Relief Act of 1997 created new forms of IRAs, which will be discussed after the features of the standard IRA concept have been described. The 1997 law, described by *The Wall Street Journal* as "mind-numbing complexity," will require more study and planning than had previously been the case. But if fully taken advantage of, these new elements of the IRA law can be most beneficial.

Tax Deferral of the Standard IRA

There are two major income tax advantages to the standard IRA. The first advantage is that the earnings in your plan are tax-deferred. You don't pay income taxes on your IRA earnings until you cash in your plan. That means that every dollar your IRA earns goes back to work for you. None of it goes to pay taxes. This tax-deferred feature applies to *all* IRA accounts.

Tax Deductibility of the Standard IRA

The second major advantage to the standard IRA plan is limited to certain individuals. The advantage is that the amount you invest in an IRA each year is tax-deductible to you. Say, for example, you are a married taxpayer filing a joint return, and your income is $30,000. That would put you in the 28 percent tax bracket. If you invest $2,000 in an IRA, that reduces the amount of your income that is subject to income taxes by $2,000. In other words you'll be taxed on $28,000 instead of $30,000. In the 28 percent bracket, that means an immediate cash-in-hand tax saving to you of $560 for that year. The attractiveness of this advantage is clear enough.

If you are *not* covered by a retirement or profit-sharing plan at work, you can claim the deduction for your IRA investment each year. But if you are covered by such a plan at work, your right to claim the annual deduction is determined by how much you and your spouse earn.

Table 18–7 illustrates how this works. For tax year 1998, for example, a couple filing a joint return has an adjusted gross income (AGI) of between $50,000 and $60,000. (See chapter 20 for a definition of adjusted gross income.) If the AGI is $50,000 or less, the couple can claim a tax deduction equal to 100 percent of their standard IRA investment. So, if they had invested a total of $1,500 in their standard IRA, their tax deduction would be $1,500. For every $1,000 in AGI over $50,000, the size of the deduction is reduced by 10 percent. So, if they had an AGI of $51,000, the deductible amount on a $1,500 IRA investment would be 90 percent of $1,500, or $1,350. If they had an AGI of $55,000, the deductible amount on a $1,500 IRA investment would be 50 percent of $1,500, or $750. And so on, until they had an AGI of $60,000, when there would be no deduction.

As you can see in Table 18–7, the phase-out level of the deduction is scheduled to increase every year until 2007.

Penalty for Early Withdrawal from Standard IRAs

In general, if you withdraw money from a standard IRA before you reach the age of 59½, you must pay a penalty to the IRS of 10 percent of the amount withdrawn. You must also pay income taxes on the amount withdrawn for the year in which you made the withdrawal. (You might also have to pay a penalty to the bank or mutual fund where your money was invested if it has penalty provisions for early withdrawals in the contract.) The law also requires you to begin withdrawing from your IRA no later than age 70½.

TABLE 18–7   Standard IRA Deducation Limits

Tax Year	Joint Return AGI	Single Return AGI
1998	$50,000–$60,000	$30,000–40,000
1999	51,000–61,000	31,000–41,000
2000	52,000–62,000	32,000–42,000
2001	53,000–63,000	33,000–43,000
2002	54,000–64,000	34,000–44,000
2003	60,000–70,000	40,000–50,000
2004	65,000–75,000	45,000–55,000
2005	70,000–80,000	50,000–60,000
2006	75,000–85,000	50,000–60,000
2007 and beyond	80,000–100,000*	50,000–60,000

*For every $2,000 increment between $80,000 and $100,000, the amount of the deduction is reduced by 10 percent.

Avoiding the Penalties on Early Withdrawals from Standard IRAs

If you take out standard IRA money before you reach 59½, you can avoid the penalty by arranging for your bank or mutual fund to pay out the money to you in equal, periodic installments over your lifetime. (Some standard IRA withdrawals may also be penalty-free if they are made after death or disability of the IRA owner has occurred, or for certain deductible medical expenses.)

The 1997 Taxpayer Relief Act has added a number of important new provisions to allow penalty-free withdrawals from standard IRAS:

There is no penalty to the IRS if withdrawals are used for the benefit of children, grandchildren, spouse, or yourself for the purpose of higher education expenses or first-time homebuyer expenses. The penalty-free withdrawal is unlimited for educational expenses, but there is a lifetime limit of $10,000 for homebuyer expenses. Note that your bank or mutual fund may have penalties of their own for early withdrawals. Those are not affected by the federal law. And note also that on any withdrawals from standard IRAs for whatever purpose, income taxes must be paid on the withdrawn amount for the year in which the withdrawal is made.

The New IRAs

Effective starting tax year 1998, there are new IRAs that are distinctly different from the standard IRA that has just been discussed.

First, and most intriguing, is the Roth IRA, named after the senator who first introduced the concept. It's also been referred to as the "Plus IRA," and the "American Dream IRA." Which name will stick only time will tell. For now we'll stick with the Roth designation. It's essentially the opposite of the standard IRA. Here's how it works: The maximum you can invest each year is $2,000 per person. (If your adjusted gross income is between $150,000 and $160,000 for couples, or between $95,000 and $110,000 for singles, the amount you can invest each year is phased out in a fashion similar to that of the standard IRA, as earlier described and illustrated in Table 18–7.)

Unlike the standard IRA, the Roth IRAs are *not* tax deductible. You get no tax deduction at all for the amount you invest. However, *all* of your earnings are tax-free. The earnings while the plans are in effect are tax-free, *and* when you withdraw the money it is tax-free—Tax-free, not tax-deferred. Tax-free means no taxes ever. Tax-deferred, as is the case with the standard IRA, means that income taxes will come due at some future time, such as when you withdraw the money from the plan. Furthermore, there is no 10 percent penalty to the IRS for a withdrawal before age 59½. (Again note that your bank or mutual fund may impose an early withdrawal penalty that is not affected by this new federal law.)

So, what's the catch? In order to enjoy these tax-free earnings and penalty-free withdrawal ability, you must not make a withdrawal until five years have passed since you first invested in the plan, *and* the withdrawal must be used to buy a first home for yourself or a family member (child, grandchild), *or* you are in a long-term unemployment situation, *or* upon your disability or death, *or* you are over the age of 59½. In summary, you have to let the money ride in the plan for at least five years, and then to get the full tax-free benefits you must meet any one of the four requirements. If you don't meet the requirements at the time you withdraw, *and* you are under age 59½, the 10 percent penalty kicks in and income taxes are due on the withdrawn amount.

Exercise 18.7

The Roth IRA should be very attractive if you can afford to put the money away for the minimum five years before you can get it back later completely tax-free. What about having a standard IRA versus a Roth IRA? If you can afford it, you can have both. And the more money you can shelter from taxes —either deferred or exempt—the better off you'll be down the road, *provided* you invest the money prudently. A fully taxable prudent investment can end up better than a wildly speculative tax-free investment that falls apart on you. Remember the old reward/risk ratio: The bigger game you're going after, the higher the risk you're taking. Choosing between the two is a very iffy proposition, since you don't know what tax rates will be in the future. The standard IRA gives you tax breaks now; many folks would rather have them in hand than wait a decade or two or three for the breaks. In any case, the wisdom of Solomon may guide you best: divide whatever IRA money you can invest in half and have a go at both.

Bear in mind the description of the 1997 Taxpayer Relief Act of 1997 by *The Wall Street Journal: Mind-numbing complexity*. Many facets of this new law might undergo modifications and interpretations until well into the twenty-first century. As with all other major financial steps that you take with tax ramifications (and they all do) you should check the most current regulations to make certain you're getting the benefits you expect.

Converting Standard IRAs to Roth IRAs

Here's a bit of that mind-numbing complexity we referred to. If you have money in a standard IRA, you can convert it to a Roth IRA if your adjusted gross income is under $100,000. You have to pay income taxes on the amount you withdraw from the standard IRA, but that tax can be spread over four years if you do the conversion before January 1, 1999. The 10 percent IRS penalty does not apply to a withdrawal that's made for conversion purposes.

Does it pay to convert? Not even an accountant can tell you for sure. You're converting money that will some day be taxable (the standard IRA) into money that will come back to you completely tax-free (the Roth IRA). The key to a decision: Will the taxes you have to pay on the withdrawal now be higher or lower than the taxes you'd have to pay when you cashed in your standard IRA? If you think your tax rate will be higher at withdrawal time, the Roth IRA may be your best bet. If you think you're better off taking the tax breaks now and having to pay the taxes on withdrawal at a relatively low rate, then the standard IRA might be better. Or going half-and-half might give you the best results.

The Education IRA

This is a spin-off of the new Roth IRA in that your investments are not tax-deductible, but the money earns tax free and can be withdrawn tax free. Here are the conditions:

The account must be for the benefit of someone under the age of 18, and the maximum that can be put into the account each year is $500. (If your "modified" adjusted gross income exceeds $160,000 for couples, or $110,000 for singles, the Education IRA is not available.)

The account must have a bank as custodian or trustee, which basically means that you must set up the account through a bank. If need be, you can change the beneficiary to another family member with no income-tax consequences.

In order for the withdrawals to be tax-exempt, the proceeds must be used to pay post-secondary (after high school) education expenses of the designated child. These expenses can include room, board, and tuition. If in any given year the withdrawals exceed the education expenses, then income taxes and the 10 percent IRS penalty must be paid on that excess. Any family member (parent, grandparent, aunt, uncle) who qualifies under the income limits can set up an Education IRA for a child. Education IRAs are separate and apart from your own personal standard IRAs or Roth IRAs.

401(k) Plans

Only employees of companies that offer the plans can participate in 401(k) plans. In a 401(k) plan, a certain portion of your wages will be placed in an investment program offered by the employer. Those wages will not be taxable to you until you later withdraw the funds. The earnings will also be tax-deferred. You generally have a choice of investment programs. Common choices include a guaranteed income plan, similar to a savings program; a mutual fund type of plan that invests in a variety of stocks; and a plan that invests in the stock of your company. It's generally possible to mix and match among the different plans, and you can usually change your mix at certain intervals. It's also common for your company to chip in a certain amount of its money for your benefit. For example, for every dollar you put in of your own, the company might put in another 25 cents or 50 cents. The amount you can put into a 401(k) plan was about $8,000 per year in the late 1990s, with increases allowed each year for inflation. Your employer can contribute over and above that amount to your account, subject to the limits of the law.

The withdrawal restrictions for a 401(k) plan are similar to, but slightly more liberal than, those for IRA plans. It might also be possible to get your funds out at an early age in the event of death, disability, or financial hardship. Withdrawals from 401(k) plans are controlled both by the employers' plan and by tax regulations.

A 401(k) plan can be advantageous, particularly if the employer is contributing money on your behalf over and above what you are putting in. Similar plans are available to employees of schools, tax-exempt organizations, and governments.

SEP Plans

A relatively uncommon form of do-it-yourself retirement program is the Simplified Employee Pension (SEP). This concept was designed for small companies that did not want the trouble of all the paperwork involved in a major pension or profit-sharing plan. A SEP operates similarly to a standard IRA. The employer can make contributions to the IRAs that the workers maintain on their own. And the workers can also make their own contributions. If your employer does not have a pension plan, she might be intrigued with the idea of setting up a SEP. It can work to the benefit of both employer and employees.

Keogh Plans

Keogh plans are available to self-employed individuals. The maximum amount of an annual Keogh investment is $30,000, or 25 percent of income from work, whichever is less. The 25 percent is calculated on the amount left after the Keogh investment has been made. Example: a self-employed person earns $60,000 in a year. Her maximum Keogh investment will be $12,000. Why? Her 25 percent limit is based on $48,000 (the $60,000 income less the $12,000 Keogh investment): 25 percent of $48,000 is $12,000. Another self-employed individual earns $200,000 in a year. The maximum Keogh investment allowable is $30,000 for that year. Keogh investments are tax-deductible to the participant. If self-employed individuals have employees, they must make contributions on behalf of certain of those employees. Earnings on Keogh plans are tax-deferred. Withdrawals from Keogh plans are similar to those of IRAs: There's a penalty for withdrawals made before age $59\frac{1}{2}$, and a withdrawal program must begin by age $70\frac{1}{2}$. Keogh plans do have further complexities involving the types of plans that can be set up and how much can be contributed to each one. It's advisable for individuals contemplating a Keogh plan to get professional assistance from their own tax adviser or from the institution in which they're opening the plan.

Setting Up Your Plans

IRAS, Keoghs, and SEPs can be set up relatively simply at banks, savings institutions, stock brokerage firms, mutual fund companies, and insurance companies. The Keogh plan will require more paperwork than the IRA. An IRA or Keogh participant should shop around to determine what types of plans are available. Stock brokerage firms offer IRA and Keogh plans that can be self-directed by the participants. That is, you can instruct the broker how your money is to be put to work. But be aware that if undue risk is taken, it can have a hazardous effect on your retirement nest egg.

Relocating Your Plans

You do not have to keep your IRA or Keogh investments with the same institution forever. The law allows you to move these accounts from one place to another periodically without penalty.

If you do wish to relocate your IRA or Keogh investment, be aware that it can take the bank or brokerage firm weeks to complete the paperwork. Thus, plan in advance to give notice to them so that the paperwork will be ready in time. Also, if you do relocate your funds, keep copies of every document connected with the transfer. If the Internal Revenue Service ever asks what happened to your IRA money, you can prove that you simply transferred it to a different institution rather than withdrawing it to spend it, in which case the IRS would expect you to pay taxes on it, and possible penalties.

How to Invest Your IRA, 401(k) and Keogh Money

There are no hard and fast rules. There is abundant counsel given in this book to assist you. Let's recap the most important points.

1. As noted earlier in this chapter, all the tax breaks in the world are for naught if the investments themselves aren't prudent. A fully taxable but wise investment can work better for you than a speculative venture that is tax-sheltered. The bigger reward you're going for, the bigger risk you're taking. If you risk the money, you chance losing it.

2. Retirement money is money you can't afford to take undue risk with. You don't want to discover at retirement time that you don't have enough to retire on in comfort. You can't go back twenty or thirty years—you don't get a do-over.

3. It's never too early to start stashing money away for your later years. They will be here sooner than you think.

4. If you wander off blindly into "mutual fund land" you're liable to get lost, and so is your money. There are thousands of mutual funds from which to choose, and they range from extremely speculative to very conservative. If the stock market has been hot—as was the case for most of the 1990s—that doesn't mean the same trends will continue.The law of gravity has a way of asserting itself every so often. People who generally say they're going to put their retirement

money into "mutual funds" are speaking too broadly. You must narrow your search. You must find funds whose objectives and investment philosophy match your own. And if you don't yet have any objectives or investment philosophy, you'd better get some real soon.

5. The Age + 40 Rule noted earlier can be of some help. To quickly review it: For that portion of your retirement money that MUST be there, come what may, when you need it, it should be invested in safe securities, such as well-rated bonds and insured savings plans, in a proportion equal to your age plus 40. In other words, if you are 30 years old, 70 percent of your must-be-there retirement funds should be invested safely. The other 30 percent can be put to some speculation. This is admittedly a very conservative course to take. Vary from it as you will, and at your own risk.

PENSIONS AND TAXES

When you receive your pension, all, or a portion of it, could be subject to income taxes. The portion your employer contributed on your behalf is likely to be taxable. Some money that you contributed may have already been taxed in the year in which you earned it and thus won't be taxable when you receive it in your pension check. It would be nice to think that tax matters became easier upon retirement, but taxation of pensions is regrettably complex and must be planned for accordingly.

Lump-sum Payout versus Monthly Payments

You may have the choice of receiving pension or profit-sharing benefits in either a lump sum or a long-term program of monthly payments.

If you are given such a choice, some very careful arithmetic is required—perhaps with the help of an accountant—to determine what is best. How you handle such a decision can mean the difference of many thousands of dollars in your pocket or the tax collector's.

The lum-sum payout means exactly that: you get all you're entitled to in one check. The monthly payout plans can take a variety of forms: You might choose one fixed amount per month for as long as you live, with payments ceasing at your death; or you might choose a plan that provides you with a smaller amount per month but with continuing benefits payable to your survivors after your death.

The first choice that has to be made is between the lump-sum payout and the monthly plan. Each choice will differ, but here is the type of arithmetic you can do to help determine the best choice. Let's assume that you are given a choice between a $50,000 lump-sum payout (after taxes) or $400 per month until your death, after which payments cease. If you choose the lump-sum payment, and if you invested the $50,000 at an 8 percent annual rate of return, you would receive an income of $333 per month (before income taxes.) And you would always have the $50,000 nest egg available to you. On the other hand, if you choose the $400 per month (again, before income taxes), you will indeed be receiving a slightly higher monthly income, but there is nothing at all left after your death; and while you're still alive, there is no nest egg into which you can dip, should the need arise. Based on this example, which is reasonably typical of the choices people have, you might find that if you are ready, willing, and able to handle your own investment of this money, you could do better over the long run by taking the lump-sum instead of the monthly payout. Get professional assistance before you make your choice.

Minimizing the Tax Bite

If you do choose the lump sum payout, there are two devices that can minimize or delay the income taxes payable on that lump sum, the IRA rollover and forward averaging.

The IRA Rollover

With the IRA rollover, if you receive a lump-sum payout from a pension or profit-sharing plan, you can, within sixty days of receipt of the money, reinvest that money in an account designated as your IRA rollover account. By so doing, you postpone the payment of income taxes on the lump sum until such future time as you withdraw the money to spend for your own purposes. By putting the money into an IRA rollover account, the investment will earn interest on a tax-deferred basis until such a time as you withdraw it. The IRA rollover account is generally preferable for those people who do *not* need the funds for current spending purposes.

Forward Averaging

This device is generally preferable for people who *do* need the money to spend currently. By using the forward averaging formula, you pay your income taxes on the lump sum you received in the year in which you receive it but at a much lower rate than normal income taxes. Forward averaging reduces your tax by calculating the tax as if you had received the lump-sum payout over a five-year span. You must meet current IRS eligibility formulas in order to claim the forward averaging device.

ONE FINAL CAUTION

The laws referred to in this chapter can be of great assistance to people who are covered by pension and profit-sharing plans at work. But roughly half the U.S. work force is not covered by any kind of pension or profit-sharing plan. These workers must depend on their own discipline to put away money for the future. They are on their own, and as noted earlier, if they are in the younger generations, they should not expect much from Social Security. They should take advantage of the IRA and 401(k) concepts as much as possible, as well as any other new do-it-yourself programs that may be created by Congress. For those who are not covered by an employer or union pension plan, it's worth repeating the admonition stated earlier in this chapter. *No one can take better care of you than you can yourself. And if you don't take care of yourself, no one else will do it for you.*

PERSONAL ACTION WORKSHEET

Estimating Retirement Costs

Even though retirement may be a long way off for you, this exercise can help you envision changes in your financial situation once your working career has ceased. Assume you'll be retiring within the next few years. Estimate the changes in your income and expenses once that occurs. This will help you shape a workable budget for your retirement—something that most people don't do until it's too late.

	Now	Then
❏ After-tax income from work	_____	_____
❏ After-tax income from investments	_____	_____
❏ Social Security income	_____	_____
❏ Pension, profit-sharing, IRA, 401(k) or Keogh income (assume lump sum is invested at 7 percent annual income, and you're taking out only the income)	_____	_____
❏ Lump sum from any of the above, on hand for whenever you need it	_____	_____
❏ Housing expenses, assuming you stay where you are	_____	_____
❏ Housing expenses, assuming you move to smaller quarters	_____	_____
❏ Extra income resulting from net gain on sale of home, after setting aside any down payment needed for purchase of new home	_____	_____
❏ Transportation expenses (consider particularly that the "going-to-work" car may no longer be needed or will be used much less)	_____	_____
❏ Clothing expenses	_____	_____
❏ Food, both at home and out, considering work lunches	_____	_____
❏ Entertainment	_____	_____
❏ Insurance premiums (life, health, disability; retirement and Medicare often change one's insurance program considerably)	_____	_____

CONSUMER ALERT

Excerpts from a Survey of Recent Retirees

"When I was 30, my employer told me that my pension plan would provide $511 per month at age 65. That, plus my Social Security, seemed enough to meet all my needs and allow my wife and me to have a leisurely and comfortable life at retirement. I left it at that and didn't make any other plans. We spent what we earned and lived well.

"Then came the blow. I was made to retire at age 62, at a $405 per month pension benefit. And times have changed! Not only am I getting more than $100 less than I expected, but the money I am getting doesn't go very far at all. If I had my life to live over again, I'd have anticipated this possibility and would have salted away some of my earnings in an investment program."

• • •

"I retired from my dental practice ten years ago, at age 62. We had no children and, quite honestly, I never became involved in any hobbies or activities. Now I'm paying the price. . . . The worst part of retirement is too much time on your hands. Retirees should have hobbies or sports interests consistent with their health. The worst habit is getting bored and turning to the bottle."

• • •

"Think young and resolve to be independent as long as you're able. Neither your children nor any organization owes you anything. If you think you've reached the age where now someone will take care of you, you're sadly mistaken. If you haven't long ago accepted the fact that only you are responsible for your future, then you're in for a rude awakening."

• • •

"Don't expect to be missed for long by former business associates, and don't visit them unless invited. You should be realistic and accept the loss of clout gracefully."

• • •

"The best advice is for a couple to get as mentally close together as when they were first married, and to remember that they cannot enjoy leisure without doing some work, nor can they enjoy pleasure without having some pain."

UPS & DOWNS *The Economics of Everyday Life*

Why Living Costs Go Up and Down During Retirement

For most folks, retirement means living on a fixed income from pensions, Social Security, and investments. If costs go up, expenses have to go down accordingly; or work has to be resumed (which is often not possible); or principal must be tapped (which is often not desirable).

Basic inflationary trends   Inflation will still have its impact, but less so for retirees than for those raising families. Retirees will have less money to spend, but there will be fewer things that they will have to be buying.

Automobiles   During the working years, a couple might have needed two cars, and those cars might have been fancier and traded in more often in order to maintain a certain image. On retirement, one car will often be adequate, and it can be a more basic model and kept for more years. The annual difference in auto insurance for just one car instead of two can mean a big savings, not to mention the end of commuting.

Clothing   The working wardrobe (and the dry-cleaning and laundering thereof) may have imposed quite a cost burden. (Again, the cost of maintaining an image enters the picture.) The retiree can get by with lower cost and less formal clothing, which doesn't have to be replaced with every change in fashion trends.

Taxes   Those 65 and older get some breaks on their income taxes. At the same time, what they paid in for Social Security over the years provides them with continuing increases in monthly allotments as the cost of living goes up.

Senior citizen discounts   These are available in movie theaters, airline fares, restaurant specials, hotels and motels, insurance plans, barber and beauty salons—the list goes on and on. Many stores offer senior discounts on certain days of the week. And senior organizations such as AARP offer a wide variety of cost-saving plans.

Activities   These are the years to enjoy all that's been put off during the working years: the books that have remained unread, the hobbies that weren't given a fair chance, the videos that were put on the shelf to be viewed "later." "Later" is now, and there's much to enjoy that doesn't involve spending money. Attitudes change: A social life that used to be tumultuous (and costly) may now become *serene* (and inexpensive).

Housing   As noted in the text, there are many alternatives that can reduce the cost of housing—from refinancing a mortgage to moving into smaller quarters. In addition, the lower-cost quarters bring with them lower-cost operating expenses (utilities, maintenance, etc.).

For some, reducing expenses may be a necessity; for others, it may be by choice. Either way, it can be painless and, in the long run, satisfying.

?

WHAT IF . . . ? ———————————————————————————

Test yourself: How would you deal with these real-life possibilities?

1. Your parents (or your spouse's parents) are thinking about moving to a retirement community. Would you be interested in buying their home? How important is it to you that they be close by (say, within an hour's drive)? Are they being realistic about the price they think they can get for their house? Will they have enough to live comfortably in their new home? Is there a chance that they might become financially dependent on you, and if so, are you prepared to help them? If you have siblings, will they be happy with the proposed changes, or will there likely be a lot of family static over the issue? Evaluate all of these matters as they would apply to your own personal situation.

2. An unexpected disability forces you to take a long leave of absence from work. It could be as long as twelve months. As the days go by, you begin to get glimmers of what it might be like to be retired. How do you think such an event might influence you to prepare for your eventual real retirement?

3. You have a choice between a job that offers no pension plan and one that does. The job without a pension will give you 10 percent more take-home pay than the other job, which would stash away that 10 percent toward the pension. Which would you prefer? Why? Would you feel differently if you were ten yers older? Why?

NUMBER CRUNCHERS

Do the calculations to make decisions in these real-life possibilities.

1. Using the examples of the Johnsons in this chapter, and other tables throughout the book, calculate the following: A retiring couple plans to stay in their home for the duration. There's a $70,000 balance left on their mortgage. Monthly payments are $1,660, and the interest rate is 11 percent. If they continue making their current payments, the mortgage will be all paid off in about six years. They can refinance today at 8 percent, for 15, 20, 25, or 30 years. What will their numbers look like with each choice, including not refinancing and just continuing on with their current payments?

2. Your pension plan at work offers the gradual vesting illustrated in Table 18–6. Calculate how much money would be guaranteed to you eventually in the following cases: (a) You and the company each put $1,000 per year into the plan for four years. (b) The company puts in $2,000 a year for five years. (c) You put in $1,500, and the company puts in $500 for seven years.

3. Using Tables 14–2, 14–3, and 18–5, calculate the following: (a) Investing $2,000 per year at 8 percent, how many years would you have to do this to build up a big enough nest egg to allow you to withdraw roughly $900 per month for 15 years? (b) You have $20,000 to invest for the long term. If you stash it away for 20 years at 6 percent, what monthly income can you withdraw starting in 20 years without ever dipping into your nest egg?

FOR BETTER OR FOR WORSE

Things beyond our control often impact our personal and financial well-being, for better or for worse. Some are more predictable than others. How could you be affected if the following real-life phenomena happened? Could you have seen it coming? What steps could you have taken to minimize damage or maximize advantage? The better able you are to anticipate and recognize these forces, the better equipped you are to deal with them.

1. You have invested all of your 401(k) money in the stock of the company you work for. You know the company, and you're loyal. The boss dies suddenly and the stock plunges when it's announced that the boss's lame-brained son will succeed his dad.

2. The government announces that, as a result of a national survey, almost 15 percent of all pension recipients are not getting all the money they should be getting.

3. You know that you have only one more year on the job until your pension rights are fully vested, but you can't stand the job. Then your boss tells you you're being transferred to the worst post in the company for the next year, like it or not.

Exercise 18.8

19

Estate Planning

A son can bear with equanimity the loss of his father. But the loss of his inheritance may drive him to despair.

Machiavelli

No one ever sat on his deathbed wishing he had spent more time at the office.

Anonymous

One of the most important—and most overlooked—aspects of personal financial concern is estate planning. It's important because it goes right to the heart of your financial structure, both while you are living and after your death. And it's overlooked because people don't like to think about their own mortality, let alone make plans regarding it.

When people do investigate planning for their own purposes, they are often mystified and put off by the strange language and concepts that prevail in the field.

This chapter will examine the jargon and the tools used in the field of estate planning, as well as the many considerations that must be taken into account in establishing a sound and sensible estate plan. After reading this chapter you should know

- What a *will* is, and how it works
- Who are the various parties involved in an overall estate planning program, and what are their roles
- Specific things you can accomplish, and problems you can avoid, with a properly prepared estate plan

IF NOT FOR YOURSELF, THEN FOR YOUR PARENTS

Exercise 19.1

You said it about retirement at the start of chapter 18, and you're saying it again now about estate planning: "This stuff is not for me. I'm decades away from those concerns, so why don't I just skip this chapter?" Hold on. As with planning for retirement, estate planning is best started early—not intensely, but at least gently. Moreover, the knowledge you can gain about estate planning now can be of help to your parents or others close to you. And, as in chapter 18, look at it from this somewhat selfish, but realistic, perspective. If you stand to inherit something from your parents, or others, and they have not done the proper estate planning, wouldn't it be worth it to you to diplomatically guide them toward taking the right steps to assure that their wishes are met? If you answered yes, the importance of this chapter to you increases accordingly.

UNEXPECTED PROBLEMS

Barlow was 37 years old, in good health, and financially self-sufficient. All was well with him. Well, almost all.

Barlow's widowed mother lived with him. She was in failing health, but happy that she could live out her remaining days in comfort, close to her son and three beloved grandchildren. But this arrangement deeply troubled Barlow's wife. The wife was extremely bitter about having her mother-in-law live with them. She thought it was an intrusion on her privacy and a negative influence on the children and, perhaps most important, that the money Barlow had to spend on his mother's care was money that could have been spent by the wife for her own benefit. Barlow and his wife frequently fought over this issue. The wife had often expressed her preference for sending her mother-in-law to the county home for the aged to be done with the whole problem.

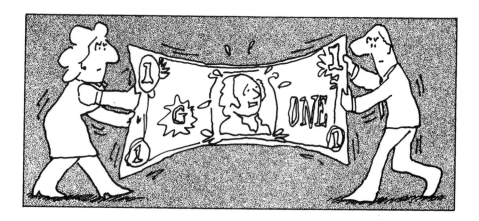

Every Saturday morning, Barlow played three sets of tennis with his friend Murray. Murray was very overweight, and Barlow constantly chided him that their Saturday morning exercise was the only thing keeping Murray from an early grave. On one Saturday, with Barlow leading three games to one in the second set, Murray raced to the baseline to return a high lob. In midstep, he suddenly clutched at his chest, emitted a loud moan, and fell to the ground. He was declared dead on arrival at the emergency room, a victim of cardiac arrest.

It was weeks before Barlow recovered from the shock of Murray's death. But one of the first things he did when order returned to his life was to ask his lawyer one simple question: "Do I need a will?"

"Not necessarily," the lawyer responded.

"But I thought everyone should have a will," Barlow said, perplexed.

"If someone dies without a will," the lawyer responded, "the state in which he lives will determine how his wealth and property are to be distributed. This is what's known as the law of intestacy."

"What would happen to my wealth and property if *I* died without a will?" Barlow asked.

"Under the laws of our state—and each state has its own separate laws on this matter—your wife and children would split whatever there was. Your mother would get nothing," the lawyer noted.

Barlow felt a cold chill go through his body. Under these circumstances, he felt certain that his wife would immediately deliver his mother to the county home for the aged and that his wife would likely embark on a spending spree that could quickly erode the funds he had set aside for his children's college education.

Barlow expressed these fears to his lawyer who, in turn, suggested that Barlow quickly embark on an estate plan.

"Let's begin," said Barlow. "I had thought that such matters were best left to the later years. But I have learned now, the hard way, that it's time to do what's right."

This chapter is intended to acquaint you with the rudiments of estate planning. *It is not by any means a guide to preparing one's own estate plan.* But with the understanding that can be obtained by reading this material, you will be capable of discussing your own estate planning matters with a lawyer who is properly qualified to tend to those matters.

A Minor Device to Aid in Your Reading

One of the most commonly used devices in estate planning is the last will and testament, commonly called a will. To minimize the confusion between a will in this sense and the other uses of the word ("I will follow my lawyer's advice"), *will*, the legal document, is typeset as follows in this chapter: WILL.

WHAT IS AN ESTATE?

While a person is living, his or her estate is all that the person owns, less all that person's debts. On the death of the person, the estate becomes a legal entity in its own right. When John Doe ceases to exist, the "estate of John Doe" comes into existence. This estate becomes the legal machinery that pays the estate taxes, distributes the property and money, and carries out all other legal wishes of the deceased.

If the deceased has executed the proper legal documents, most commonly a WILL, the activities of the estate will be carried out by the executor, a person or an institution named by the decedent to carry out these functions. If the person has died without a WILL, the state in which he or she resided at the time of death will name an administrator, who will be responsible for carrying out the laws of intestacy of that state as they apply to the individual's estate.

WHAT IS ESTATE PLANNING?

Estate planning, simply put, is the development of a program that will ensure that any individual's last wishes are carried out regarding the estate.

We have two primary choices in distributing our estate. The first choice is to take steps on our own to ensure that our wishes are *clearly stated,* that they will be *carried out,* and that they will receive the *full protection of the courts.*

There are many devices to establish the desired program. The most common is the preparation of a WILL. Other devices include life insurance, gifts, trusts, and simply spending it all, leaving nothing behind.

The second choice is to do nothing, in which case the laws of the state of residency at the time of death will determine the distribution of any estate.

Each state has its own laws concerning this, known as laws of intestacy. All state laws are somewhat similar, yet different. You must determine what your state's laws of intestacy are and how they might affect you. Table 19–1 illustrates how the laws of intestacy can vary from state to state.

TABLE 19–1   Who Gets What If You Die Without a WILL (Intestate)?

	If You Are Survived by Spouse and Children, but No Parents:	If You Are Survived by Spouse and Parents, but No Children
State A	Spouse gets ½; children get ½	Spouse gets all; parents get nothing
State B	Spouse get ⅓; children get ⅔	Spouse gets ½; parents get ½
State C	Spouse gets first $50,000, plus ½ of any balance; children get residue	Spouse gets first $50,000, plus ½ of any balance; parents get residue
Your state	?	?

Note: Further differences exist under differing survival conditions. For example, no spouse survives; only parents survive, etc.

THE RIGHTS INVOLVED IN ESTATE PLANNING

Rooted deeply in our legal tradition are the rights of individuals to determine what will happen to their accumulated wealth upon death. Over the years, certain limitations have been placed on the overall freedom to distribute our accumulated wealth as we wish. For example, the federal government and some state governments have a right to tax our wealth. When an estate is required to pay taxes, these taxes are known as estate taxes. The federal government levies estate taxes on a very small percentage of estates. Furthermore, many states levy estate taxes.

In some states, those who *inherit* may become liable to pay taxes to the state. These are known as inheritance taxes.

Our wishes may be limited because they are contrary to public policy. For example, a court may not carry out the wishes of a deceased person who leaves money to an individual on the condition that the individual marry or divorce a certain person, or change religions, or do other things that society at large would deem improper or immoral.

Another limitation exists regarding surviving spouses. Laws differ from state to state but, generally, a surviving spouse has a right to at least a minimum portion of the deceased spouse's estate. If, for example, the laws of a state proclaim that a surviving spouse is entitled to one-third of the deceased spouse's estate, and the deceased spouse has expressed in his WILL that his widow will receive only 25 percent of the estate, the surviving widow has a "right of election against the WILL." In effect, she can disclaim that portion of the WILL that gives her only 25 percent, and, if everything else has been done in proper legal fashion, the widow will then be entitled to the minimum allowed by the state, or one-third.

The overriding limitation on our freedom to distribute our wealth as we wish is that we must do so in accordance with the law. If we want the full protection of the courts, we have to play the game by the established rules.

The most obvious purpose of an estate plan is to determine who will get our money and property after our death. But there are other important purposes. In addition to distributing property, the legal documents of the estate plan can establish who will be responsible for carrying out the wishes of the deceased. If the individual has not named a party to do so, the courts will appoint one.

The proper use of an estate plan can minimize taxes; it can recommend guardians of orphaned children or other individuals previously under the guardianship of the deceased; and it can set forth specific instructions, such as funeral and burial procedures.

The deceased individuals will of course never know the difference, but an estate plan enables them to live with a greater degree of peace of mind knowing that these wishes will be carried out.

THE LANGUAGE OF ESTATE PLANNING

The language of estate planning contains many strange words and phrases. Lawyers bandy these strange words about, not knowing whether their clients understand the meanings. To understand estate planning and to prepare yourself to work with your lawyer on your plan, it's necessary that you grasp the meanings of the most common bits of jargon. Following is a brief glossary of the language of estate planning. (Certain words have a separate feminine form, indicated by the suffix *-trix*. The use of these separate forms for women is declining.)

- A testator, or testatrix, is a person who makes out a WILL. When you ask your attorney to prepare your WILL for you, you are regarded as the testator.
- A decedent is a person who has died. The testator eventually becomes the decedent.
- A beneficiary is one who receives an inheritance in the estate of a decedent. For example, your WILL may say, "I leave my summer cottage to my sister Melba." Melba is thus a beneficiary of a portion of your estate, namely, your summer cottage. But what if Melba should die before you? in your WILL, or in other estate documents, you can name a contingent beneficiary.
- A contingent beneficiary is one who takes the place of a named beneficiary who has already died. For example, "My summer cottage shall go to my sister Melba, and if she dies before I do, it shall go to my other sister, Lucy." In this case, Melba is your beneficiary and Lucy becomes your contingent beneficiary in the event that Melba dies before you do. Had you not named a contingent beneficiary, the summer cottage might have passed through Melba's estate, to whomever she may have named to receive whatever she owned.
- A bequest is the specific property or money given to a beneficiary. In the preceding example, the bequest consists of the summer cottage.
- A life estate is a form of bequest with some strings attached. To create a life estate, the WILL might read: "My summer cottage shall go to my sister Melba for as long as she lives, and on her death it shall go to the Boy Scouts of America, local chapter 123." In other words, Melba has the use of the cottage for her life, but she has no right to pass it on to anyone else on her death, at which time it will go to the local Boy Scout chapter. You have given her a life estate in the summer cottage, and you have further directed who shall get it after her death.
- An executor, or executrix, is a person or an institution named in a WILL to handle the affairs of the estate. Generally, executors will be granted broad powers to allow them to carry out the directions of the WILL. For example, executors commonly will be given the power to buy and sell

properties and securities and to do whatever else may be needed to carry out the wishes of the deceased as closely as possible. Executors may be entitled to receive a fee for their duties, but it is possible to arrange for an executor to serve without a fee. The testator may require that the executor post a bond. This is a form of insurance that will protect the estate from financial harm at the hands of the executor.

The duties of the executor can be considerable. In addition to following the specific wishes of the decedent, the executor may also have responsibilities of a more personal nature to the family members. In all likelihood, the executor will need the assistance of a lawyer and an accountant in fulfilling all the needs of the estate, which can include the payment of estate taxes and income taxes when the estate has earned income on investments or properties prior to the disbursement of the funds to the ultimate beneficiaries. If an executor is unable or unwilling to fulfill his or her duties, the court will generally appoint a successor executor.

- If an individual dies without a WILL, the court will appoint a person or an institution to handle the affairs of the estate. This person is called the administrator. Duties are similar to those of an executor, and the question of fees and bonds will probably be determined by the court.

- Probate is a court proceeding in which the validity of a WILL is established. The term *probate* comes from a Latin word meaning "to prove" or "to examine and find good." If the WILL is properly drawn and executed and no one challenges its terms, the court will direct that the terms of the WILL be carried out. If a challenge arises that can't be settled by the parties, the WILL is thus "contested," and additional court proceedings might be needed.

The laws of probate differ from state to state. Generally, the attorney for the estate, acting in conjunction with the executor, will request that the appropriate court commence the probate proceedings. All potential heirs will have been notified and will be given the opportunity to accept or challenge the WILL as written. Would-be heirs who wish to challenge an otherwise valid WILL will have to do so at their own expense, which can be considerable.

A challenge to a WILL, or a contest, can be a most bitter and costly struggle. Even the most carefully planned and painstakingly drawn estate plan cannot guarantee that an outside party will not challenge it. But the chances of an outside party succeeding in such a challenge will be drastically reduced by virtue of the professional expertise that has gone into creating the plan.

Probate procedures are constructed so that frivolous claims or challenges will be quickly dismissed. In order for a challenge to be successful, the challenging party must have fairly clear and convincing proof that all or part of a WILL was invalid or that the WILL being probated was not in fact the last WILL of the decedent.

THE WILL

Exercise 19.2

A WILL is the most common form of device utilized in the formation of an estate plan. A simple WILL, which is adequate for most individuals, can be prepared quickly and inexpensively.

What Goes into a WILL — the Basic Clauses

Exercise 19.3

In a sense, a WILL is a form of contract: it is a legally binding document that sets forth certain rights and responsibilities of the parties and cannot be changed without the consent of the person who drew up the WILL. If the testator has had a WILL prepared in full compliance with the laws of his or her state, then, on his or her death, the executor has the responsibility for carrying out the wishes stated in the WILL, and the courts of the state are responsible for seeing to it that the rights of the survivors are given the full protection of the law.

The major clauses of a WILL that set forth primary responsibilities and rights are as follows.

The Introductory Clause

This generally is the opening clause of a WILL, and should clearly and unmistakably state, "This is my last WILL and testament," or, "My WILL is as follows." It is essential that this clause establish that you are creating the WILL and that the document is in fact your WILL. If both you and the document are not clearly identified as to who and what they are, it's conceivable that another party might claim that this is not your actual WILL. For example, you might intend to create a WILL by writing a personal letter to your spouse, children, or attorney. You do not clearly identify the letter as being your purported WILL. In the letter, you disinherit one of your children. After your death, the letter is introduced as being your actual WILL. The disinherited child, who would stand to gain considerably if there were no WILL (and the property passed through the law of intestacy, which assures each child a certain percentage of the estate), attacks the letter, claiming that it is not in fact the true WILL of the deceased. The court will probably uphold the disinherited child, thus invalidating the purported WILL and requiring that the property pass through intestacy.

Revocation of Prior WILLS

An individual creating a WILL who has previously made another WILL should clearly revoke the entire prior WILL by stating so clearly in the new WILL. If the testator does not do this, it's possible that the prior WILL, or at least portions of it, might be included in the probate with his new WILL. If there are two WILLS, the later one will generally control, except to the extent that the specific provisions of the two WILLS are consistent with each other. But even this can cause unnecessary complications, which can be avoided by clear revocation of the former WILL.

For example, a testator prepares a WILL in which he leaves $10,000 to each of his grandchildren. At the time he drew the WILL, he had two grandchildren. Many years later, he draws another WILL but does not revoke the earlier WILL. The new WILL contains the same clause giving $10,000 to each of his grandchildren. But now he has eight grandchildren, which means a total bequest to them all of $80,000. This is a very substantial portion of his estate. The question arises as to whether only the original two grandchildren were entitled to the $10,000 bequest or whether all eight are entitled to it. If all eight are entitled to it, other heirs might receive much less. The actual wording of the old WILL and the new WILL, with the court's interpretation of the clauses, will determine who gets what. The example illustrates how confusion can result where there are two WILLS that may convey the same intentions but each with a substantially different effect on the overall estate.

Debts and Final Expenses

Before your survivors can receive their share of your estate, the remaining debts, funeral expenses, and taxes must be paid. Commonly, a testator includes a clause in his WILL instructing the executor to make all these appropriate payments. But even if there is no such clause, the executor is still required to make them.

Each state law sets forth the *priority* of who gets what and in what order. If your state laws require that a "widow's allowance" be paid, that generally is the item of first priority. This is not the widow's ultimate share of the estate but is usually a minimum allowance to enable her to get by for at least a short time. After the widow's allowance, the priorities generally run as follows: funeral expenses; expenses of a final illness; estate and other taxes due to the United States; state taxes; taxes of other political subdivisions within the state, such as cities and counties; then other debts owed by the decedent.

Creditors of the estate must generally file a claim against the estate if they wish to be paid. The executor may determine, or the testator may have instructed the executor accordingly, that certain claims are not valid. A testator cannot invalidate legitimate claims against his or her estate by simply stating in the WILL that those claims are not valid.

If, after all debts, taxes, funeral costs, and final illness expenses are paid, there is enough left to make payments to the survivors, such payments are then made in accordance with the *bequest clauses*. If, however, these expenses consume all the estate, then the survivors receive nothing. In such a case, the estate is considered to be insolvent.

Bequest Clauses

These clauses determine which survivors get how much. Broadly speaking, there are four ways in which property can be left to the survivors: through joint ownership with right of survivorship; through a specific bequest; through a general bequest; and through the residual. (Sometimes the word *legacy* is used in place of *bequest*.)

If property is owned in joint names—such as a home or a savings account—the property will pass to the survivor of the two joint owners. The WILL need not necessarily specify such matters, but it would be wise to note these items in the WILL to avoid misunderstanding.

A specific bequest will refer to a particular item or security. For example, a testator may bequeath to a child "my stamp collection, which is located in safe deposit box 1234 at the Fifth National Bank." The collection will pass to the survivor on the death of the testator, assuming that the testator still owns it at the time of death. If he no longer owns it, then obviously it cannot pass, and the gift will dissolve. The heir will receive nothing in its place unless the testator has specifically instructed the substitution of other items of value, or money, should he no longer own the collection. In addition, if the subject of a specific bequest is not free and clear—it has been pledged, for example, as collateral for a loan—the heir will receive that property subject to the debt against it and will be responsible for paying off the debt unless the testator has instructed that he is to receive it free and clear. For example, the stamp collection may have been pledged as collateral for a loan. The collection is worth $10,000, and the balance on the loan is $2,000. If the testator has not stated that the heir is to receive it free and clear, the heir can be responsible for paying the $2,000 owed. If the testator has instructed that the heir should receive it free and clear, however, the $2,000 debt will be paid out of other estate resources.

General bequests are those payable out of the general assets of the estate. Commonly, general bequests will be in the form of cash, such as "I bequeath to my housekeeper, Marsha Margolis, the sum of $3,000."

After all property has passed through either joint ownership specific bequests, or general bequests, everything that's left is called the residual. Commonly, this will represent the bulk of many estates. A typical residual clause might read as follows: "All the rest, remainder, and residual of my estate I hereby bequeath to my wife and children, to be divided equally among them." There may be further detailed instructions concerning the manner and timing of such distributions, including the possibility of trusts that would parcel out the payments over a specific period of time.

In planning a WILL, it's essential that the testator and attorney discuss all these various provisions for distribution. As individual circumstances change over the years, these clauses should be reviewed to determine that the bequests are still what the testator wishes; and if the subjects of specific bequests are no longer owned by the testator, provisions should be made for the proper substitution.

Other elements of who gets what—and who doesn't—may include clauses of disinheritance; clauses that set forth a preference among various heirs; gifts to charities; and clauses that release individuals from debts owed to the decedent.

Survivorship Clauses

Though rare, it can happen that a husband and wife are killed in a common disaster, such as an automobile accident or an airplane crash. Each of their WILLS should have been created with this possibility in mind, particularly if there are minor children. The couple will want to state their preference as to who will be the guardians of the children in the event of such a disaster. If estate taxes are of concern to the couple, a survivorship clause should also set forth the sequence of the deaths (who is to have been presumed to have died first) in such a way as to minimize the effect of estate taxes.

Appointment Clauses

In this clause, the testator appoints the person or institution who will be the executor of the estate. Where circumstances dictate, a testator may also name an attorney for the estate to act in conjunction with the executor.

If other individuals—such as minor children or elderly parents—are dependent on the testator, the testator should also recommend the guardian for such individuals. The guardian will have the duties and responsibilities, and fee if any, that are specified in this appointment clause.

It's common for one spouse to name the other spouse as executor. The testator wants to know that some one who is deeply concerned with the welfare of the survivors will be in charge of carrying out the duties of the executor. It should be noted, however, that the duties of the executor can be demanding; the more complicated the estate, the more exacting the duties. A surviving spouse may not be equipped to handle many of the duties; thus, many prudent individuals will name an institution, such as a trust department of a bank, as a coexecutor. The institution is fully staffed and capable of carrying out the specific legal and accounting responsibilities of the executorship. Such a move can minimize the burden on the surviving spouse, and adds an element of permanence to the whole matter. Evaluate fee schedules when considering naming a coexecutor.

The Execution

The final clauses of a WILL are very important. They are called the testimonium clause and the attestation clause. In the testimonium clause testators express that they are signing this document as their true last WILL and testament, as of the specific date on which the document is being executed. In the attestation clause the witnesses to the WILL agree that they have witnessed the signing of the WILL in each other's presence and in the presence of the testator on the specific date.

The combination of these two clauses serves as proof that the document is the last WILL and testament of the testator, that the document has been properly signed, and that the witnesses can verify all of this.

The execution of a WILL is a ritual that must follow the letter of the law. Each state's law determines how many witnesses should attest to the signing of the WILL by the testator. It is imprudent for any individual who may receive a share of the estate—either as a family member or as a recipient of a bequest—to act as a witness to the signing of the WILL.

In addition to the signing and witnessing of the WILL, the attorney may have the testator and each witness sign or initial each separate page of the WILL. This may help serve as added proof that the WILL that is finally presented for probate is the true and complete WILL of the testator

Until the WILL is signed and witnessed, it is not valid. Any attempt to shortcut the execution procedure might open the doors to a contest of the WILL if it can be proven that the WILL was not properly signed or witnessed by the appropriate parties.

Changing a WILL

A WILL can be legally changed in one of two ways: it can be totally revoked by a brand-new WILL, in which case the brand-new WILL should expressly state that the former WILL is totally revoked. Or minor changes can be effected by means of a brief document called a codicil.

A WILL *cannot* be legally amended by crossing out or adding words, by removing or adding pages, or by making erasures. A codicil should be drawn up by an attorney and should be executed and witnessed in the same fashion as the original WILL itself. The codicil should then be attached to the WILL. If a WILL is amended in any way other than the creation of a new WILL or the creation of a properly executed codicil, it's all that much easier for anyone to succeed in contesting the WILL. Furthermore, a court might not admit to probate a WILL that has been changed by hand. Such improper changes could conceivably invalidate the entire WILL and could render the estate subject to the laws of intestacy. In short, testators should not destroy all that they have created in the estate plan by making changes unless they are made in the proper, legally prescribed fashion.

Once a will has been drawn and executed, it's common for the attorney to keep the original in a safe or a fireproof file. You should keep a copy or two for your own reference, and if you've named a bank or other institution as executor or coexecutor, the proper people there should also receive a copy for their files.

When Should a WILL Be Amended?

You should review your WILL and overall estate plan at least every three years. Depending on any changes in your circumstances, revisions may or may not be called for. These are the common circumstances that dictate the need to amend a WILL or any other portion of an estate plan:

- If the individual has moved to a different state, the WILL should be reviewed. Remember that the law of WILLS and estate distribution are state laws, and there can be differences from one state to another. You should have your plan reviewed by an attorney in your new state of residence.
- Changes in family circumstances might dictate the need to alter a WILL. A divorce may have occurred. Children may have grown up and moved out on their own. If one child has been particularly affluent and another has suffered economically, you might want to make provision to assist the less fortunate child. You may wish to add or delete charitable contributions, to amend your funeral and burial instructions, to add or delete specific bequests that you have made to individuals—there are myriad possibilities.
- If there have been substantial changes in your assets and liabilities, a review of your WILL might indicate that changes are in order. If you have either acquired greater wealth or suffered financial reversals since the original drawing of the WILL, this may dictate different modes of distribution to your heirs.
- If heirs named in your WILL have died before you, you might want to review the effect that would have on the distribution of your estate.
- If an executor or guardian named in the WILL has died or has become incapable of acting in the desired capacity, or if you simply no longer wish to have that person representing your interests, an amendment to your WILL would be in order.

STRATEGIES FOR SUCCESS

Beware of "Do-it-yourself" Estate Planning Shortcuts

You want to save some money on legal fees, so you buy a book on how to write your own WILL . . . or you copy your cousin Elmer's WILL for your own because you and he tend to think alike . . . or you just buy some blank WILL forms at the local stationary store and fill in the blanks. These moves could be a *big* mistake. Estate planning is complex. Shortcuts can mean that the wrong people can be cut short if you make a mistake in the do-it-yourself process. The proper estate plan, created by properly trained people, can help assure that the courts of your state will see to it that your wishes are carried out. If your do-it-yourself attempt isn't legally proper, chaos could result.

- If tax laws change regarding estates, a review of your WILL would most certainly be in order. The 1976, 1981, and 1997 federal estate tax law changes had a sweeping effect on millions of estate plans already in existence. Virtually all estate plans and WILLS prepared prior to the effective date of these tax laws should be reviewed by an attorney.

It's impossible to know when further changes may come about in the laws, and often court decisions cast slightly new and different interpretations on existing laws. Any of these decisions could affect your own estate, and your attorney should advise you accordingly to make the appropriate changes.

Uncommon WILLS

Occasionally, a court will receive for probate a WILL that has been prepared by the testator in his own handwriting. It may or may not have the appropriate number of witnesses. A WILL that's prepared in the handwriting of the testator is called a holographic WILL. Some states permit the probate of holographic WILLS under certain circumstances, but such WILLS are definitely not substitutes for WILLS prepared under proper legal guidelines. The courts recognize that individuals may be in dire circumstances and unable to acquire the proper legal counsel to prepare a totally valid WILL. Thus, allowances are made for the occasional probate of a holographic WILL.

In more extreme cases, a WILL may be spoken by the dying individual to another party or parties. Such a spoken WILL is referred to as a noncupative WILL. It's allowed only by some states, and then only under strictly defined conditions.

Neither a holographic WILL nor a noncupative WILL should be relied on as a substitute for a properly prepared WILL. A court may find such a WILL invalid and could throw the entire estate into intestacy. Where at all possible, proper legal assistance should be used in creating a WILL.

OTHER DEVICES FOR PASSING ON ACCUMULATED WEALTH

In addition to the common WILL, there are other means whereby you can pass wealth to heirs and other generations.

Trusts

Exercise 19.4

A trust is a "strings-attached" way of passing money or property to another party. For example, you have $50,000 that you would like eventually to pass to your son, who is now 25 years old. But you're concerned that he might run through the money. You thus decide that until he reaches age 40, he should be entitled only to the income that the $50,000 will generate through investments. When he reaches 40, he can have the entire amount. In order to accomplish this, you create a trust.

To be sure that your wishes are carried out without further concern on your part, you make an arrangement with your bank to administer the trust. The bank then becomes the *trustee*. You deposit the $50,000 with the bank, which then agrees to invest it and pay out the income to your son until he reaches age 40, at which time he will be paid the full principal amount.

That's an oversimplified view of the creation and function of a trust, but it's intended to make the point that passing money by trust is not an outright transfer. There are, as noted, strings attached. The trust agreement can stipulate just how much the beneficiary (in this case, your son) will get at what time and under what circumstances.

In the foregoing example, both parties involved in the trust are still living. This would be called an *inter vivos* trust, or a trust between the living.

A trust can also be established in your WILL to take effect at your death. Instead of property passing outright to the beneficiary of your WILL, it may go in trust. For example, you might leave $50,000 in your WILL in trust for your son until he reaches the age of 40, with the full amount payable to him on that date. Where a trust is established in one's WILL to take effect on death, it's referred to as a testamentary trust.

A trust can be revocable or irrevocable. A revocable trust is one that can be revoked or canceled. An irrevocable trust may not be canceled; it is permanent.

Under certain circumstances, trust arrangements may be desirable in place of a WILL or may be used in conjunction with a WILL. There is no fixed rule—it all depends on individual circumstances.

The law of trusts is complicated. A great deal can be accomplished with trusts, both in the control of property and in the minimization of estate taxes. An attempt at a do-it-yourself trust might be even more foolhardy than a do-it-yourself WILL because of the added complexities of the trust laws.

The trustee is the person or firm that has the duty of carrying out the directions of the trust. The trust document, which is a form of contract, spells out the trustee's powers and responsibilities. Many people prefer to use a financial institution as a trustee instead of an individual. Bank trust departments are operated by professionals, and there is assurance of permanence. Such permanence has obvious advantages if a trust is designed to continue for many years. As with naming executors in a WILL, an individual might prefer to name both a corporate trustee (such as a bank) and a person close to the family as cotrustees.

Gifts

Making gifts of money or property is another form of estate planning. Gifts have long been popular with more wealthy individuals as a means of cutting down on their potential estate tax liability. By making gifts prior to death, money or property may escape taxation, wholly or partly. The over-

STRATEGIES FOR SUCCESS

Be Aware of Life Insurance Settlement Options

The common thinking is that when someone who has life insurance dies, the insurance company pays a lump sum of money to the beneficiary of the life insurance policy. That generally is the case, but it need not be. The owner of a life insurance policy has a number of options—called settlement options—that can call for a different form of distribution of the life insurance money. Know what these options are and use them where appropriate. For example: a husband might think that his beneficiaries (wife and/or children) are not capable of handling the large sum of money that the insurance proceeds would be. So he might choose a settlement option in which the insurance company would pay the money out over a period of time, including some interest, rather than one lump sum. Do you know what options your policies offer?

all desirability or feasibility of making gifts a part of an estate plan should be discussed in detail with professional advisors.

Insurance

For many families, life insurance is the main way of passing wealth from one generation to the next. Indeed, in families of moderate means, life insurance may be the only estate planning necessary. But it would be unwise to rely on life insurance policies as a substitute for estate planning. Even the most modest estates should be reviewed with professionals to determine what will occur on the death of each individual. Insurance can pass money from one generation to another, but planning is needed to assure that the parties who need the money most, or are most entitled to it, will get what the testator wishes. For example, a man may have little estate other than life insurance, and if his children are named as beneficiaries, his widow may not receive what she needs for her own survival. If the children aren't willing or able to help her, she could be in dire straits. On the other hand, the widow could be the sole beneficiary of the insurance policies, and the children could thus be deprived of funds their father wished them to have. These matters should be discussed with a life insurance agent, in conjunction with an attorney and accountant.

Joint Names

Putting property in joint names, such as husband and wife, often seems a simple way to ensure that the surviving spouse will receive everything on the other spouse's death. This may be true, but it can subject the estate to taxes that could have been avoided, and it may prevent the money from ultimately going where you had wished it to go. For families of more modest means, a joint-names program might suffice. It's not safe to make any assumptions about the ultimate distribution of an estate in which everything is owned jointly—the advice of a competent attorney is still essential.

HOW TO PROCEED

At the beginning of this chapter, you were introduced to Barlow and his problems. Barlow followed his lawyer's advice and created an estate plan to pass his accumulated wealth and property to those he wished to have it. In addition to the distribution of wealth, Barlow also provided that his mother should remain in his home until it became no longer medically feasible for her to do so. He also established a trust program by which his wife and children would receive their inheritance over a period of years rather than in one lump sum. This arrangement, Barlow felt, would protect the interests of all concerned. Having thus created his estate plan, Barlow achieved a peace of mind that had eluded him for some time.

As Barlow's situation indicates, there are purposes for estate planning other than the distribution of accumulated wealth and property. An estate plan can be utilized to provide care for others, to manage money, to ensure a continued lifestyle for survivors, and to minimize taxation.

If you go about it the wrong way, you may fail to achieve what you want your estate plan to accomplish. Let's take a closer look.

The Wrong Way

Nelson was a wealthy widower with two daughters, Jessica and Rhonda. Jessica had taken over the family business and was dutiful, loyal, and devoted to her father. Rhonda, on the other hand, had had a bitter argument with her father many years before and had run off to Paris. She had been there ever since, earning her living as a jazz guitarist. Nelson had long ago vowed that Rhonda would "never get a penny from me."

One reason for Nelson's wealth was that he carefully watched every penny he spent. Thus it was that, when he was ready to create an estate plan, he shunned the expense of a lawyer. Rather, he went to a local stationery store where, for $2, he bought a blank WILL form and proceeded to fill it out himself, leaving his entire estate to Jessica. The blank WILL indicated that there were to be two witnesses to Nelson's signature. But since Nelson didn't want anyone other than Jessica to know of this WILL, he had only Jessica sign as a witness.

When Nelson died, Rhonda was shocked to learn that she had been disinherited by her father. She asked her lawyer to look into the matter, and, after doing so, the lawyer recommended that Rhonda contest the WILL. If the WILL could be proved invalid, Nelson's estate would be divided equally between Jessica and Rhonda. The lawyer pointed out that there had been only one witness, whereas the state law requires two witnesses. Furthermore, the only witness, Jessica, was the heir to the entire estate, and that threw a further cloud over the validity of the WILL.

Under such circumstances, Rhonda had an excellent chance of having the WILL invalidated, thereby upsetting Nelson's intent to disinherit her. By saving a small sum on legal fees, Nelson allowed half his wealth to go where he had not intended it to go.

The Right Way

There is really only one proper way in which a desired estate plan should be implemented: with the aid of a capable lawyer. Any attempts—repeat, *any attempts*—at do-it-yourself estate planning can be fraught with danger. Last wishes may not be carried out as expressed; taxes may have to be paid when they could have been avoided; and survivors could be left in a variety of predicaments that could have been avoided.

Citizens of the United States have a very precious right: to pass a substantial portion of their acquired wealth to the survivors of their choice. These rights are protected by our courts. For the fullest protection, however, individuals must express their wishes in full accordance with the law.

Each state has its own laws regarding how property passes from a deceased person to survivors. In our highly mobile society, individuals move from state to state and may own property in states other than the one in which they live. Thus, it's possible to be affected by the estate laws of more than one state.

Furthermore, federal laws on estate taxation can have a bearing on the estate of any individual, regardless of which state he or she lives in.

Thus, a lawyer specializing in estate matters, is *the best* qualified party to tend to estate planning. The lawyer may see fit to call in other professionals—bankers, insurance agents, accountants—as the need arises.

The first necessary step in creating an estate plan is a visit with the chosen lawyer. During this initial meeting, you should disclose all your assets, liabilities, and, most important, your estate-planning objectives. The lawyer will then be able to determine what estate-planning documents might be best suited to achieving your stated objectives.

WHAT SHOULD YOUR ESTATE PLAN ACCOMPLISH?

Keep four main objectives in mind when creating or amending any estate plan.

- To establish the proper liquidity and distribution of assets
- To establish a program of sound management of assets

- To provide for the assured continuation of a family's lifestyle in the event of death, disability, or retirement
- To minimize taxation

Three aspects of taxation must be taken into account: the federal gift and estate taxes that would come out of the estate assets; the taxes the heirs may have to pay on inherited property; and the income taxes the estate may have to pay, if it has had earnings before the distribution to the heirs. Let's now take a closer look at each objective.

Distribution and Liquidity

Distribution of assets and the liquidity of those assets go hand in hand. Distribution refers to who gets what. Regardless of the size of your estate, you want to be certain that it will be distributed in the manner you've specified. Liquidity refers to the ability to put cash on the table as quickly as possible and with as little expense as possible. The more liquid one's assets, the easier it will be for everybody to get whatever it is they are to have. The most important reasons for having liquidity are to be able to provide for the immediate needs of one's survivors—spouse, children, and so on—and to be able to pay any estate taxes when they are due.

Mike's case illustrates the dangers in failing to make adequate provision for proper distribution and liquidity in one's estate.

Mike was a good provider, or so he had thought. Twenty years ago, when he was 40, Mike made some major changes in his life. He gave up his job as a plumber, and with a partner, Willy, he opened up a wholesale plumbing supply firm. His only child, Maryanne, was soon to be married, so Mike and his wife, Sybil, decided to sell their home and buy an apartment house. They would live in one of the apartments. Mike also bought a large tract of vacant land fifteen miles outside the city. He was confident that the city would grow in that direction, and that in ten to fifteen years, this land would be extremely valuable as a site for a shopping center and new housing.

All these things accomplished, Mike visited a lawyer to have a WILL prepared. He left the land to Sybil; the apartment house to Maryanne; and his interest in the plumbing supply business to be divided equally between Sybil and Maryanne.

Twenty years later, this is the status of Mike's estate.

- Mike and Willy worked hard at their business, and it prospered. Mike, with an easy and outgoing personality, was the "Mr. Outside" of the business. He took care of the sales, the customer relations, and the goodwill for the venture. Willy, on the other hand, was the "Mr. Inside." He took care of the books, the inventory, and the detail work. Mike was proud that he could draw a salary of $50,000 a year and that his share of the business was now worth $200,000.

- The apartment house also proved to be a good investment. Today, after all expenses, it was generating $20,000 a year income and, if Mike wanted to sell it, he could reap $200,000 after all selling costs. He and his wife continued to live in the same apartment.
- The vacant land didn't fare as well as Mike had hoped, but his potential profit was still substantial. Mike felt that the land could now be sold in various parcels to net him $300,000.
- Mike had no other assets of any consequence. All available income from the business and the apartment house was reinvested back into those entities, and Mike felt that this growing wealth precluded the need for any life insurance.
- Daughter Maryanne's financial situation was constantly in chaos. Mike had given her some financial help, but nothing seemed to change her wasteful, spendthrift ways. Many years ago, Mike had given up. He would no longer help her, and Maryanne felt very bitter and angry toward her parents because of this.
- Mike was a wealthy man—at least on paper. His net worth exceeded $700,000. But in the twenty years since he had drawn his original WILL, he had never taken the time to reexamine it or change it in any way.

A Costly Failure to Plan

In spite of Mike's apparent wealth, after he died his distribution of assets and lack of liquidity resulted in terrible turmoil. The problems Sybil faced were as follows:

- An appraisal of the plumbing supply business verified that, at the time of Mike's death, his interest was indeed worth $200,000. But no buyer could be found. Willy had become very difficult to deal with, and, without Mike's talents, the profitability of the business quickly declined. The income that Mike had been bringing home quickly shriveled to a fraction of what it had been. And that was the money Sybil needed to live on.
- The apartment house had been willed to Maryanne, and she took the opportunity to get her revenge against her parents. She sold the property as quickly as she could and pocketed the profits. Sybil's rent-free days were over.
- In desperation, Sybil looked to the vacant land as her source of salvation. But in her grief and anxiety, she was easily taken advantage of by a buyer. Given enough time and clear-headedness, she could have sold the land for a gain of $200,000. But Sybil found herself accepting half that amount. And, after paying the capital-gains taxes on the profit from the sale of the land, her nest egg was reduced even further.

Alternatives?

Mike's greatest error was his failure to review and update his estate plan. Had he done so periodically, he could have corrected the problems: total lack of liquidity and a distribution plan that gave the wrong things to the wrong people.

What else could Mike have done? He could have worked out an arrangement with Willy whereby Willy would buy out Mike's interest on Mike's death. This could have been accomplished through a *key-person life insurance*. It would work like this: Each partner would have his life insured for an agreed-on amount—say, $200,000 in Mike's case. In the event of either partner's death, the life insurance proceeds would be paid to that partner's survivors, and the other partner would then gain the dead partner's interest in the business. In Mike's case, Willy would have ended up with total control of the business, and Sybil would have ended up with $200,000 cash.

By giving the apartment house to Sybil instead of Maryanne, Mike could have assured Sybil of the continuing rental income, as well as a place to live rent-free.

It would have cost Mike relatively little to implement these or other alternatives. He, of course, is not around to feel the brunt of his planning errors. But his wife will have to live with them for the rest of her life.

Establishing a Program of Sound Management for Estate Assets

The bulk of Marsha's estate consisted of life insurance and stocks. By the time she reached her mid-forties, she had accumulated a large enough estate to provide for her family in a most comfortable style, including education for the children and total peace of mind for her husband, Ned, in the event she should die suddenly, as she unfortunately did.

Her plan had been carefully prepared, but she had made one major miscalculation. Marsha had always handled the bills and other financial decisions. Between Ned's grief and his lack of familiarity with money matters, the estate was wiped out within a few short years.

Marsha had at one time thought that because there was a sizable sum involved, she should arrange to have it flow through some form of managed program whereby the money would be allocated to the family as needed. But because of her faith in Ned and because of the cost involved in a managed program, she didn't do so.

Proper management of assets in an estate is a factor all too often overlooked. Tales are legion of widows and children who have squandered money, been bilked, or were ill-advised.

A thoughtful person planning an estate must be aware of the need for sound management of assets for as long as the survivors will have need of those assets. Management can be accomplished in a number of ways. Assets can flow through a trust whereby income is paid to the survivors, who can have a right to tap the principal as and if the need arises for specific purposes. Insurance policies can be arranged so that the money is paid out over an extended period rather than in one lump sum. Similar extended withdrawal plans can be set up with annuities, mutual funds, and pension and profit-sharing plans. Whether a management program is set up formally, as through a life insurance company or a trust, or whether it's established by common consent among the parties, there is still no substitute for a basic knowledge on the part of family members about the nature of the assets of the estate, an awareness of what can jeopardize those assets, and a cool head to keep things on an even keel, particularly during the difficult early months following the death of the breadwinner.

As with all other elements of estate planning, the matter of management should be reviewed from time to time and amended as needed.

Assurance of Continued Lifestyle

Oliver worked out a fine estate plan, taking into account all the foregoing questions of distribution and management of assets. But his mistake came in viewing the estate plan as something that commenced at the time of death. His primary concern—the concern of many—was to provide ample funds so that his family members could continue to live in their accustomed manner after his death.

But he erred in failing to provide for that same lifestyle while he was still living. When Oliver first fell ill, his business associates continued to pay him full salary for a number of months, even though he was contributing nothing to the business. All his medical expenses were paid by a very comprehensive health insurance program. But after several months, his associates came to him and said they'd have to reduce his salary since the business was hurting from his continued sick-pay benefits and the loss of his energies.

Oliver could understand this and consented to it, feeling that he would soon be on the road to full recovery and at full earnings. But it didn't work out that way. A few months later, his associates told him sadly that they would have to cut his salary down to a minimum level and, a few months after that, it was terminated completely. Even though his medical expenses continued to be paid, there was no income, and Oliver had to start dipping into his reserves.

His illness lingered, and when he died three years later, the bulk of his estate had been used up. His heirs received virtually nothing. Oliver's case illustrates a most tangible problem that has very intangible solutions: an otherwise adequate estate demolished by unforeseen events. In Oliver's specific case, a solid program of life and disability insurance could have provided ample protection and allowed him to leave his estate almost intact. Those are insurable risks, but other occurrences are less insurable. A portfolio of investments can suddenly turn sour. The need to support elderly or disabled family members can drain one's assets suddenly and sharply.

Prudent individuals insure against all foreseeable risks, within reason, without becoming "insurance-poor." And they will further structure their portfolio of investments and business relationships to at least minimize the chaos that could result from unforeseen catastrophes.

Perhaps most important is to communicate with family members about the size of the estate and what they can expect from it. They should be prepared for the contingencies they will face, realizing that the more knowledgeable they are, the better they will be able to cope on their own.

Minimizing Taxes

Carl had no worries about estate taxes. Two years ago, when he had his WILL prepared, his lawyer told him that his estate was not large enough to incur any estate taxes. At that time, Carl's total wealth was approximately $350,000; his house was worth $180,000; his investments, $120,000; his vested rights in a pension fund, $30,000; and his personal property, $20,000. Carl signed his WILL, content that all his wealth would go to his wife and children and that none would go to the government.

But a lot can happen in a short period of time. Carl's wife ran off with Roger, a film critic from Los Angeles, and Carl sued for divorce. His wife didn't contest the divorce—she was content to let Carl keep everything, including the three children. Moreover, and unbeknownst to Carl, his great-aunt Trudy had fallen critically ill and had included Carl in her WILL.

On January 2, 1999 Carl awakened groggily—he had suffered through the previous day with a massive hangover due to overindulgence on New Year's Eve. Now that headache was gone, but his mailbox contained the makings of another one. There were two letters. One was from his lawyer, informing him that the divorce proceedings had become final. The other was from a lawyer in Vermont telling him that his Aunt Trudy had died and that Carl was now the proud owner of one-third of Aunt Trudy's Vermont dairy farm, with his interest worth approximately $400,000. Carl telephoned his lawyer to discuss the inheritance. "Congratulations!" said the lawyer. "The value of the inheritance boosts your total worth to $750,000. However, the divorce means that you can no longer take advantage of the important estate tax-savings device known as the marital deduction. In other words," the lawyer cautioned, "If you were to die today, your estate would owe federal estate taxes of about $30,000."

Carl was dumbfounded. "How can that be?" he gasped. "When I went to bed last night, I could have died in my sleep and not owed Uncle Sam anything."

Carl's lawyer then proceeded to explain to him how estate taxes work.

HOW ESTATE TAXES WORK

Exercise 19.5

Very few estates will be subjected to estate taxes. But as Carl's case illustrates, an obligation to pay those taxes can arise unexpectedly. Or, more usually, the obligation to pay taxes can arise gradually as one's worth increases over the years as a result of inflation (such as in the value of one's house), appreciation in the value of one's investment portfolio, the addition of life insurance and pension benefits to one's net worth, and so on. If you are in your twenties or thirties today, your estate may seem too small to cause you concern about estate taxes. But as you reach your forties, fifties, and sixties your total wealth is likely to increase by many times its current value, thus exposing you to estate taxation.

Sound financial planning dictates that continued attention be paid to one's potential estate tax liability. With proper advance planning, the costly bite of estate taxes can be minimized.

Three Kinds of Taxes

Three possible kinds of taxes can arise when a person dies. They are:

Exercise 19.6

- **Estate taxes**   When a person dies, his or her "estate" becomes a legal entity. If the estate is large enough, the federal government will levy a tax on the value of the estate. The tax is to be paid out of the assets of the estate, generally before anything is distributed to the survivors. It often happens that an estate will have to sell investments or other property in order to pay the federal estate taxes. The federal estate tax is the biggest of all possible taxes arising at one's death.

    Tax laws allow a very big exemption for estate taxes. Through tax year 1997 the first $600,000 of a person's estate (after allowable deductions) was not subject to estate taxes. The Taxpayer Relief Act of 1997 increases the amount of this exemption, as Table 19–2 illustrates.

TABLE 19–2   Amount of Estate Exempt from Federal Tax under Taxpayer Relief Act of 1997

Year of Death	Exemption	Year of Death	Exemption
1998	$625,000	2003	$700,000
1999	650,000	2004	850,000
2000	675,000	2005	950,000
2001	675,000	2006	1,000,000
2002	700,000		

Example: If a person dies in the year 2002, the first $700,000 of the estate (after allowable deductions) is tax-free. Everything over $700,000 is taxable at rates that start at about 20 percent of the taxable amount, up to 50 to 55 percent of the taxable amount.

The most important deduction that can reduce estate-tax liability is the marital deduction, which is what one spouse can leave to the surviving spouse. The amount of the marital deduction is unlimited. Thus, if one spouse leaves his or her entire estate to the surviving spouse, there will be no estate taxes on the estate of the first spouse to die. However, the entire estate of that first spouse will then become part of the estate of the second spouse. And unless the second spouse remarries, there will be no marital deduction on the second spouse's estate. That is where the estate tax trap can catch the unprepared.

Exercise 19.7

There are other ways to cut down or eliminate the federal estate tax. They include reducing one's estate by making annual gifts while living to selected beneficiaries, life insurance trusts, and private annuities. All of these steps involve legal complexities and should be undertaken only with professional counsel.

Further, if you expect an inheritance from someone whose estate might be subject to the federal estate tax, it could behoove you to explore with that other person how the estate tax bite could be minimized so that the government doesn't get any more than it's legally entitled to.

Exercise 19.8

- **Inheritance taxes**   Some states levy an inheritance tax. This tax is paid by those who receive inheritances. The basic difference between estate taxes and inheritance taxes is that estate taxes are paid out of the assets of the estate *before* anything is distributed to the heirs. Inheritance taxes are paid by the heirs *after* the estate has been distributed.

- **Income taxes**   Many months, if not years, can elapse before an estate is distributed to all the heirs. During that time, the assets of the estate may be invested and receive income. In such cases, the income is subject to income taxes. A separate return must be filed for income earned by an estate. An inheritance that you receive is not subject to income taxes. If, say, you receive $10,000 from Uncle Willy's estate, the $10,000 is not considered taxable income to you. If you invest that $10,000 and earn $1,000 a year in interest, however, then the $1,000 income is subject to income taxes on your own personal return. If you receive property as an inheritance and you later sell that property at a profit, the profit is subject to income taxation.

It's Never Too Early

Although estate planning is commonly thought of as an activity for older people, you are never too young to consider the importance and benefits of estate planning. Thought should be given to estate planning when an individual marries and as children are born. Then, as the family grows, further review should be given to a plan at least every few years. As the family changes, so does the need for reviewing the plan. In addition to the financial benefits that can result from sound estate planning, the peace of mind that can be achieved cannot be denied.

PERSONAL ACTION WORKSHEET

Distribution of Your Estate

Estate planning, properly done, should involve an attorney with expertise in the field. The assistance of an accountant and a life insurance agent can also be worthwhile.

Even though federal estate taxes affect only a very small percentage of the population, there are still many important matters that must be resolved: Who will get what? How liquid are your assets? What provisions have you made to take care of the immediate and long-term needs of your survivors?

The following checklist is designed to motivate you to commence a proper program of estate planning. It is based on the assumption that you will die tomorrow. You should acquaint yourself with your state's law of intestacy to learn what would happen if you died without a WILL or other satisfactory distribution arrangements (trusts, for example).

Your Assets	Value	Who Would Get What?
❑ Your home	_____	_____
❑ Your personal possessions	_____	_____
❑ Proceeds of pension or profit-sharing plans	_____	_____
❑ Proceeds of life insurance policies	_____	_____
❑ Any debts owed you	_____	_____
❑ Your investment portfolio, specifically:	_____	_____
Stocks	_____	_____
Bonds	_____	_____
Savings accounts	_____	_____
Real estate	_____	_____
Collections	_____	_____
Other	_____	_____
❑ Any business interests you may have	_____	_____

CONSUMER ALERT

Proceed with Caution on "Living Trusts"

A relatively new device for estate planning has grown in popularity in recent years. It's known as the "living trust" and, for certain families, it can provide a number of advantages. In oversimplified terms, it requires that you transfer your assets now, while you are living, into a trust arrangement. The trust, not you individually, will thus become the technical legal owner of your assets. Since those assets are no longer technically a part of your estate but rather are owned by the trust, they can pass to your designated heirs without having to go through the often costly and time-consuming probate proceedings.

But there can be serious problems. First, living trusts are not for everybody. The initial cost of creating the trust, plus the expense of maintaining it, make it more beneficial for larger or more complicated estates. Second, con artists pitch living trusts to unwitting victims. They use scare tactics. They make misleading claims as to what the living trusts can do. They falsely assert that they have the blessings of such respected groups as the American Association of Retired Persons. They charge more than legitimate local lawyers charge. And in the worst of cases, they build language into the documents that entitles them to horrendous fees upon the death of the person creating the trust.

A living trust should be compared with all other possible alternative methods of estate planning, and you should get the advice of a trusted and objective attorney who is a specialist in estate planning. If you have any doubts about the wisdom of one method over another, seek a second opinion without delay.

UPS & DOWNS   *The Economics of Everyday Life*

How the Liquidity of an Estate Can Go Up and Down

Very few people have to worry about having cash on hand (liquidity) to pay estate taxes. But everyone should be concerned as to how liquid their estates are so as to provide quick and easy access to cash to take care of the immediate needs of survivors. If an estate lacks liquidity, the survivors might have to sell assets at far less than they might be worth in order to generate cash. Or, they might have to borrow heavily, which can erode the value of the estate. The time of death is unpredictable, but the immediate cash needs of survivors can be very predictable. Prudence dictates being aware of these ups and downs of estate liquidity:

Equity in the home   This is often the largest single asset a family has, but converting it to cash can be costly and time-consuming. The house can be sold, but in a weak housing market that could take many months. You can borrow against the existing equity, but that can be costly and can take many weeks. If there is already a second mortgage against the property, it will be quite difficult to borrow further—third mortgages are considered risky, and lenders will charge high fees for the arrangements, both in up-front costs and in the rate of interest.

Pension funds   The ability to get fast cash from a vested pension depends on the terms of the overall pension arrangement, which you should learn about in advance. When can a lump-sum payout be made in the event of the pensioner's death? How much will it be? What are the long-term payout options available to the survivors? What taxes (estate and/or income) will be payable, thereby reducing the amount of cash available?

Investments   If the estate is heavily invested in long-term bonds, the immediate cash-in value of those bonds may be much lower (or higher) than the face value of the bonds. It depends largely on current interest rate levels, compared with what they were when the bonds were purchased. (See chapter 14 for a full discussion.) If the bonds are worth less than face value (because interest rates have gone up over the years), you might have to wait many years before you can sell the bonds for the price that was paid for them. With stocks, though they are liquid, an urgent need to sell might result in losses.

Family business or professional practice   If the deceased operated solo, his or her death might slash the value, and the liquidity, of the business immediately. Any business or practice should take into account the unexpected death of any principal. "Key person" life insurance can be an excellent way to provide instant liquidity. (See the discussion of this insurance earlier in this chapter.)

Windfalls   Inheritances, gifts, insurance proceeds, even lottery winnings can make a big difference in an estate's liquidity. But any windfall has its own built-in "cashability," or lack thereof. The more expected a windfall is, the better you can measure how liquid it might be when you receive it.

?

WHAT IF . . . ?

Test yourself: How would you deal with these real-life possibilities?

1. Who would receive what if you died intestate unexpectedly? Check your state laws to learn the distribution formula. Who would get what if your spouse died intestate unexpectedly? Who would get what if either or both of your parents died intestate unexpectedly? If these intestate distributions don't seem right to you, what can you do to change the outcome?

2. Think of a number of married couples close to you—friends, relatives, and yourself if you're married. If both spouses of those couples were killed simultaneously, what arrangements are in place for the care of their children or any other dependents they might have? Who would handle their affairs? If the results of such unlikely tragedies don't seem right to you, who could each of these couples name now, in a WILL, to become legal guardians in the event of simultaneous deaths?

3. A relative of yours dies. You had expected an inheritance from her of $5,000 to $10,000. You learn that you are not mentioned in the WILL. You also learn that the WILL was improperly drawn. If you contest the WILL, you can have it declared invalid, and a lot of money will be distributed differently from the way the WILL specifies. You still wouldn't get a penny from the WILL, but other heirs might pay you to not contest the WILL. What would you do? What if the stakes were $25,000? $100,000? (Keep in mind that your legal fees will be about 35 percent of anything you collect.)

NUMBER CRUNCHERS

Do the calculations to make decisions in these real-life possibilities.

1. You have the following assets: (a) equity in your house worth $60,000; (b) vested interest in a pension plan worth $80,000; (c) life insurance with a face value of $100,000, (d) other investments worth $50,000. Assume that all these assets are increasing in value, after taxes, by 6 percent per year, compounding annually. (Aren't you lucky!) Assume also that the tax-exempt amount of an estate remains at $600,000. How long will it be before your estate hits a taxable level? Assume that no marital deduction is available to you.

2. Using the same assumptions in #1, assume that Congress today lowered the taxable threshold to $400,000. How long will it be before your estate hits a taxable level? In such a case, how much of your estate will be exposed to the estate tax 15 years from now? That is, by how much will your estate exceed $400,000 15 years from now?

3. Sharpen your awareness of estate distribution: At John's death, he owned his house jointly with his wife; value $130,000, mortgage $40,000. His other assets were worth $100,000, including an antique car worth $25,000, which he left to his son Tom. In his WILL he left $5,000 to "each grandchild." When he drew the WILL he had two grandchildren, but when died he had four. The remainder he left in equal shares to his wife and Tom. All things considered, what will Tom and the widow each get?

FOR BETTER OR FOR WORSE

Things beyond our control often impact our personal and financial well-being, for better or for worse. Some are more predictable than others. How would you be affected if the following real-life phenomena happened? Could you have seen it coming? What steps could you have taken to minimize damage or maximize advantage? The better able you are to anticipate and recognize these forces, the better equipped you are to deal with them.

1. Your father has a sizable estate, but has never drawn a WILL. He and your mother have been estranged for years—they hate each other—but they never divorced. If your dad dies without a WILL, your mother (under the laws of your state) would get half the estate. Dad wouldn't want her to have a penny. You point this out to your dad, and he agrees to have a WILL drawn. The next day he dies of a heart attack.

2. Above facts again, except that Dad does have a WILL prepared, leaving everything to his children and nothing to his wife. After his death the wife contests the WILL claiming that it was entered into fraudulently.

3. A man and a woman are about to be married, the second marriage for both of them. She has a lot of wealth, but poor health. He has the opposite: a lot of health but no wealth. They both have grown children from their first marriages, all of whom are happy for their parents' remarriages. You are one of her children. Everyone has been getting along beautifully, until just before the wedding, when your sister flips out and accuses the stepfather-to-be of marrying Mom for her money.

20

Income Taxes

If we can prevent the government from wasting the labor of people under the pretense of caring for them, they will be happy.

Thomas Jefferson

You can't get away from income taxes. Virtually every facet of your financial affairs is affected in one way or another by the federal income tax: when you borrow, when you invest, when you set up a recordkeeping program, when you plan for your retirement, and when you do your just plain day-to-day budgeting.

To complicate matters, not only will your own finances change from year to year, but tax laws are also in a continual state of flux. Sweeping overhauls of the tax code take place once or twice a decade. And as the tax code changes, the IRS issues new regulations and the courts issue new interpretations. You might have to alter your financial plans if you want to take advantage of what the law allows, or escape any disadvantages that the law may impose.

This chapter is not intended to be a step-by-step guide to filing your tax return. That information is available in a variety of commercial publications. Rather, this chapter is designed to

- Give you a basic understanding of how the income tax laws work
- Illustrate the strategies and decisions you should consider to keep your taxes at a minimum
- Acquaint you with audit procedures and how to deal with them

BE PREPARED

Exercise 20.1

As you read this chapter, you should have at hand the most current copies of the latest 1040 form and the schedules that accompany it. These forms are included in the instruction package the Internal Revenue Service (IRS) mails to all taxpayers each January. They are also available year-round at local IRS offices and during the first few months of each year at most banks, libraries, and post offices.

Examples of tax issues and illustrations of the tax forms are included in this chapter to give you a general understanding of the laws and the forms. For the year in which you are studying this chapter, or doing your return, you must determine the current laws and how they apply to the current forms.

You should complete the Personal Action Worksheet at the end of this chapter *before* you read this chapter.

This chapter discusses federal income taxes. Some states and cities also levy income taxes. State and city tax formats generally follow the federal format, so this chapter will also be helpful to you in understanding your local income tax situation.

THE IMPORTANCE OF KNOWING ABOUT INCOME TAXES

The following stories illustrate what can happen to people who are *unaware* of income tax provisions.

- Ralph and Marcia hired a babysitter to take care of their children while they were at work. Like many people, they hated to do the work connected with filing their tax return. So they went to a low-cost tax preparation service. You get what you pay for: The cheap service neglected to ask Ralph and Marcia if they had child-care expenses. And Ralph and Marcia didn't know enough to mention them. Had they known the facts, they could have cut their tax bill by over $1,000 by claiming the child-care expenses as a credit against their tax!

- Jessica moved from Detroit to Los Angeles to take a better job. When it came time for her to file her tax return, she overlooked the opportunity to claim most of her moving expenses as a deduction from her income. This could have cut her tax bill by many hundreds of dollars— and it would have taken only a few minutes to enter the necessary information on the form.

- Karl was a machinist. His boss required Karl to provide his own tools and work clothes for the job. The boss didn't reimburse Karl for these expenses, but Karl didn't mind the expense. Nor did he pay attention to the tax laws, which allowed him a deduction for part of the unreimbursed cost of the tools and work clothes.

- Brent was a traveling salesman. He returned from the road every Friday afternoon and spent hours sitting at his dining room table doing paperwork associated with his job. Another salesman had once told him that if he did work at home, he could claim a deduction on his tax return for the expense of having an office in his home. Brent thus figured that the use of his dining room table for a few hours each week was worth $2,400 a year in deductible expense, which resulted in a tax savings of over $800. But Brent was dismayed when an auditor for the Internal Revenue Service disallowed it as an *improper deduction,* for it did not meet the guidelines for claiming office-at-home expenses. Brent had to pay up accordingly, *plus* interest and penalty.
- Joel received an inheritance of $2,000. Wanting everything about this windfall to be perfectly legal, Joel included it as income on his return. By doing so, he increased his taxes by $600. But, he figured, he was still better off by $1,400, and the IRS couldn't claim he was hiding income. The IRS gladly accepted the extra $600 from Joel. But if Joel had done his homework, he would have learned that inheritances are *nontaxable income.* He should *not* have reported it, and he should *not* have paid the tax. If he later realized his mistake, he could have filed an *amended return* and gotten back the overpayment.

The Pervasiveness of Taxes in Our Lives

These examples illustrate just a few of the hundreds of common situations involving income taxes. As the examples show, many people pay more than they must. Or they may court costly problems by *not* paying the taxes they do owe. With hundreds, perhaps thousands, of dollars at stake in your own tax return, it's essential that you learn all the possible ways to keep your taxes at the legal minimum. To an extent, a professional tax preparer can help you, but preparers spend only a few hours a year with you. They may not think to ask, and you may not remember, all the transactions you conducted during the year that could have tax consequences.

Your knowledge of the tax laws will help you to be a better recordkeeper and a better manager of your financial affairs. The preparer can only work with the information you provide him. It's up to you to know which transactions have tax implications and to collect the necessary documentation that will enable you to support whatever claims you make on your return.

The income tax structure also requires that you make a number of important choices, such as which form to file, which filing status to choose, whether to itemize your deductions, and so on. Making the wrong choice could mean paying higher taxes than necessary or running into a hassle with the IRS. If you make a choice that favors the government, you *cannot* assume that they'll correct the matter for you. For example, if you choose *not* to itemize your deductions, when in fact doing so would lower your taxes, the IRS will *not* come back to you with the suggestion that you itemize. They'll gladly accept the extra taxes you've paid.

Let's examine the basic workings of the income taxes and how you can make the correct decisions to minimize your taxes legally.

THE BASIC CONCEPT OF INCOME TAXES

Of all the income you receive in a year, only *some* of it is subject to income taxes. There are many ways that the total amount of your income can be *reduced* to find the taxable portion. And once that taxable portion is determined, there are ways to minimize the taxes you owe on that income.

Your assignment, should you choose to accept it, is to find all the ways you can legally reduce your taxable income and the taxes thereon. You might think that this is an impossible mission. It isn't, if you're willing to do some homework, for which you can be amply rewarded.

Following, in brief, are the steps you'll take. We'll examine each one in more detail later.

1. Tally all your income that is subject to taxes. (Do not include income that is not subject to taxes, such as inheritances or life insurance proceeds that you might have received.)

2. Reduce that total by the proper legal methods—adjustments, deductions, and exemptions.

3. Then, figure the lowest possible tax by choosing the right filing status and claiming all proper credits.

Let's look at an oversimplified example of how the income taxes are calculated in accordance with these three steps. Table 20–1 illustrates the case of Glenda and Mac.

Exercise 20.2

TABLE 20–1   **Glenda and Mac's Income Taxes**

1. Income subject to taxation:		$38,000
2. Less: Adjustments	$ 3,000	
Deductions	5,000	
Exemptions	10,200	
Total "subtractions"		18,200
Income on which taxes must be paid:		19,800
3. Tax on $19,800	2,974	
Child-care credit	−330	
Net tax due	$ 2,674	
Withheld during year	3,100	
Refund due Glenda and Mac	$426	

Step 1:

Glenda and Mac had a total of $40,000 in income for the year. Of that, $2,000 was tax-exempt income from an investment and $38,000 was income from work and other taxable sources. This, their total income that is subject to taxation was $38,000.

Step 2:

Calculate all the legal subtractions. Glenda and Mac had $3,000 in adjustments as a result of their eligible individual IRA account investments. Their deductions total $5,000 for the year. In that particular year, each exemption was worth $2,550; Glenda and Mac have two children, so they were entitled to a total of four exemptions, or $10,200. Their subtractions totaled $18,200. That left them with $19,800 of income on which taxes must be paid.

Step 3:

Their proper filing status is as a married couple filing jointly. The tax on $19,800 for the year in question for that filing status was $2,974. Further, Glenda and Mac had paid for child care in order to hold jobs. That expense entitled them to a credit of $330, subtracted from the tax due. That left them with a net tax due of $2,674. During the year, Glenda and Mac had had a total of $3,100 withheld from their pay for federal income taxes. That's $426 more than they ended up owing, so they were entitled to a refund of $426.

We'll now take a closer look at how these specific steps are taken on the tax forms themselves. Bear in mind that the tax laws and forms can change from year to year; thus, this discussion must be general in nature.

If you have not yet completed the Personal Action Worksheet at the end of this chapter, do so now. It's designed to help you to understand how your own personal taxes are to be calculated.

STRATEGIES FOR SUCCESS

Best Bet: Do Your Own Income Taxes

If not every year, then at least every other year, you should do your own income taxes. Because income taxes play such a role in our financial matters, you serve yourself best by being knowledgeable about how income taxes work. And the best way to get that knowledge is to prepare your own returns. Doing so will keep you more aware not only of current tax regulations but also of changes that are slated to occur in the tax laws. By anticipating changes, you can make better decisions regarding such matters as investing and borrowing. If you *don't* do your own taxes at least once every few years, you could make costly *wrong* financial decisions.

Who Must File?

Your first step is to determine whether you are legally required to file an income tax return for the past year.

Depending on your *age* and *marital status*, there are different levels of gross income at which you will be required to file a return. You may not owe any taxes; indeed, you might be entitled to a refund. But you must file a return if you fall within the legal requirements. Determine what the minimum income requirements are for the current tax year. (If you've completed the Personal Action Worksheet at the end of this chapter, you will have obtained this information as well as other specific data that are likely to change from year to year.)

There are a few other circumstances under which you might be required to file a return:

- If you are claimed as a dependent on someone else's tax return, such as your parents', you may be required to file your own tax return if you had a certain amount of *unearned* income during the year. (Unearned income is income from investments as opposed to earned income, which is income from work.)
- Even if your income for the year falls below the minimum levels, you'll have to file a return if you owe certain taxes other than income taxes, such as taxes on a distribution from an IRA account, or Social Security taxes on tips that you didn't report to your employer.
- You will have to file a tax return if you have net earnings from self-employment that exceed a fixed amount. Self-employed persons must also pay self-employment tax on the self-employment income. This is comparable to the Social Security tax that employees have withheld from their wages.

There are some circumstances in which you may not be *required* to file a tax return, but *should* file one. These circumstances include the following:

- You may not have earned enough income to be required to pay taxes, but you did have income taxes withheld from your pay. If you file a tax return, you can get a refund of the taxes that were withheld. If you don't file a return, even though you're not required to, you won't get a refund.
- If you are entitled to the "earned income credit," you must file a return to receive the money that is due you.

Check specific IRS instructions for the current year to determine today's exact filing requirements.

Which Form Should You Use?

Individuals can use one of three forms to file their returns: the 1040EZ, the 1040A, or the 1040. The 1040EZ is the simplest to use, but it can only be used if you are single or married filing jointly and do not claim dependents; are not 65 or older or blind; did not receive any advance earned income credit payments; and had taxable income of less than $50,000 (not more than $400 of which can be from interest income). The 1040A, often called the short form, is available to every filing status but cannot be used if your income is $50,000 or more or if you want to itemize your deductions.

To take full advantage of all the tax-cutting devices available—itemizing deductions, all possible credits—you should use the 1040 form, often called the long form. For the balance of this chapter, we'll be referring to the long-form provisions.

Choosing Your Filing Status

The first important choice you have to make regards your filing status. The segment on the form looks like this:

Filing Status
1 _____ Single
2 _____ Married filing joint return
3 _____ Married filing separate return
4 _____ Head of household
5 _____ Qualifying widow(er) with dependent child

There are five possible choices. Many taxpayers can qualify for more than one status, but choosing the wrong one can result in higher taxes.

Married Taxpayers

Married taxpayers can file separate returns, or they can file a joint return. With few exceptions, it will be to their benefit to file a joint return. If you have doubts as to whether it's better to file jointly or separately, calculate the tax both ways, and choose whichever is the lower tax.

If you were legally married on the last day of the year, you are considered to have been married for the whole year. If your spouse died at any time during the year, you also are considered to have been married for the whole year.

If married persons do file separately, they must do the same with respect to their deductions. Both must either itemize their deductions or use the standard deductions. This is a disadvantage to filing separately.

(There is a possible exception to this general rule if you live with your dependent child apart from your spouse. In order to qualify for this unusual status, you must also meet *all* four tests set forth in the IRS instructions.)

Unmarried Taxpayers

Unmarried taxpayers choose from the other three filing statuses: single, head of household, and qualifying widow(er) with dependent child. Of these three choices, the single status will pay the highest tax, followed by the head of household and the qualifying widow(er). In one recent year, for example, an individual with a taxable income of $27,000 would have paid the following taxes, depending on his or her status.

Single	$4,447
Head of household	4,054
Qualifying widow(er)	4,054

As you can see, choosing the correct legal status can make a considerable difference in the amount of taxes you'll have to pay.

Head of Household

In order to qualify, you have to be unmarried on the last day of the year and you must have paid more than half the costs of keeping up a home that was the principal home for the *whole* year for any relatives whom you can claim as a dependent (see the later discussion on who qualifies as a dependent.) Note that these family members must actually have lived with you.

You can also qualify if unmarried children or grandchildren lived with you, even though they may not technically be your dependents. You can also qualify if your mother or father were your dependents, even though they did not actually live with you.

Qualifying Widows and Widowers

People who qualify for this status pay at the same tax rate as married couples who file a joint return. If your spouse died in a preceding year, you can file as a qualifying widow or widower if you were entitled to file a joint return with your spouse for the year in which he or she died, *and* you did not remarry before the end of the current tax year. You must *also* have a child, stepchild, or foster child who qualifies as your dependent for the year, and you must have paid more than half the costs of keeping up your home, which had to be the principal home of that child for the whole year.

Your Exemptions and Dependents

As was noted earlier, for every exemption you can legally claim, you are allowed to reduce your income that is subject to taxation.

For tax year 1997, each personal exemption was $2,650. After that, it's scheduled to be adjusted for inflation. (High-bracket taxpayers may lose the benefit of all or part of the personal exemptions if their income exceeds certain thresholds established from year to year.) Check current regulations for the year in which you are filing.

The section of the 1040 form looks something like this:

Exemptions

☐ Yourself
☐ Spouse

Total
boxes
checked ☐

Dependents

Name	Relationship	No. of Months lived in your home	If age 1 or older, dependent's Social Security number	Total other dependents ☐
————	————	————	————	
————	————	————	————	
————	————	————	————	
————	————	————	————	

Add numbers entered in boxes above ☐

Obviously, the more exemptions you can legally claim, the lower your taxes will be.

You are entitled to claim one exemption for yourself and one exemption for your spouse. You can claim an exemption for a spouse even if the spouse died during the year. You may claim additional exemptions for every person who is your legal dependent.

Dependents are not limited to children. Other persons may qualify as dependents if all necessary tests are met.

In order to qualify as a dependent, a person must meet *all* of the following five tests:

- The support test
- The gross income test
- The member of household or relationship test
- The citizenship test
- The joint return test

The requirements, in brief are as follows.

- **Support test**   You must provide more than half of the dependent's total support during the calendar year.
- **Gross income test**   Generally, you may not claim a person as a dependent if that person had gross income during the year in excess of the amount of the personal exemption. The gross income test can be

ignored if the person you claim as a dependent is your child and is either under age 19 or is under age 24 and is a full-time student, in accordance with IRS definitions.

- **Member of household or relationship test** A person who lives with you for the entire year and is a member of the household can qualify as a dependent, even though that person is not related to you.

  Certain relatives can qualify as dependents even if they do not live with you, provided they meet all the other tests. These relatives can include children and grandchildren, parents and grandparents, brothers, sisters, stepfamily, and in-laws.

- **Citizenship test** To qualify as a dependent, the person must be a U.S. citizen or a resident of Canada or Mexico for some part of the calendar year in which your tax year begins.

- **Joint return test** If the person you wish to claim as a dependent has filed a joint return on his or her own with a spouse, you cannot claim that person as a dependent.

The tax regulations are very specific about what constitutes support of a dependent. Some expenses qualify, whereas others do not. Check current regulations to be certain that you are proper in claiming your dependents. Note also that you cannot claim a partial dependent.

Declaring Your Income

This is the area in which you must declare all your income that is legally taxable and you must, as noted earlier, take care *not* to report any income that is *not* taxable.

The income section of the 1040 form looks something like this:

Income		
	Wages, salaries, tips, etc.	_____
Attach	Interest income	_____
Copy B of your	Dividends	_____
Forms W-2 here.	Alimony received	_____
	Business income (or loss)	_____
	Capital gain (or loss)	_____
	Pensions, annuities, rents, royalties, partnerships, etc.	_____
	Miscellaneous income	_____
	Total income	_____

The sample income section of Form 1040 does *not* contain all the possible income items. It has been abbreviated to include the more common types of income only. Check current regulations and forms to determine the full extent of reportable income.

Taxable Income

Let's take a more detailed look at each of these items of taxable income.

WAGES, SALARIES, TIPS, ETC.   For most taxpayers, this is the major source of taxable income. Early in the year, employees receive copies of W-2 forms from their employer, which summarize the total income earned during the previous year and how much was withheld to pay income taxes, Social Security taxes, state income taxes, and any other withholdings required or voluntary. The amount of total income on your W-2 form should be inserted on this line, and a copy of the W-2 should be attached to this part of your form when you mail it in.

INTEREST INCOME   On this line, you place the total of all taxable interest you've earned during the year. The current form will dictate whether you are required to itemize on a separate schedule. Taxable interest includes any interest earned on accounts with banks, savings and loans, and credit unions; also interest earned on mortgages, trust deeds, promissory notes, corporate bonds, and U.S. government bonds (except for Series E and EE savings bonds). With Series E or EE bonds, you have the option of declaring the interest earned in a given year and paying taxes on it during that year or of deferring the taxation until you later cash the bonds.

If you own municipal bonds, or mutual funds that invest in municipal bonds, the interest you earn on those investments may be exempt from federal income taxes. If you own municipal bonds that are issued by a local government unit in your state, the interest may also be exempt from state income taxes. However, if you sell municipal bonds or funds at a profit, that profit is fully taxable. Interest earned on U.S. obligations is exempt from state income taxes.

Some types of interest earned are not taxable in the year in which you earned it but will be taxable in some future year. This is known as tax-deferred income. It includes interest earned from annuity plans, IRA and 401(k) plans, Keogh plans, and other pension and profit-sharing programs.

The effects of tax-deferred earnings can be very attractive, since all your earnings remain in your account to work for you. A simple example: Say, you have an account of $1,000 earning 10 percent per year, or $100. In a normally taxable situation, a taxpayer in the 28 percent bracket would have to pay $28 in taxes out of the $100 earned. That would leave $1,072 in the account after one year.

In a tax-deferred account, however, the entire $100 would be added to the $1,000, which would leave $1,100 in the account after one year. Table 20–2 traces a taxable and a tax-deferred account.

TABLE 20–2   **$1,000 Earning 10% per Year**

	Taxable Account	Tax-deferred Account
After		
1 year	$1,072	$1,100
2 years	1,149	1,210
3 years	1,232	1,331
4 years	1,321	1,464
5 years	1,416	1,610

DIVIDENDS   This includes dividends you receive on common stocks, mutual fund shares, and dividends that have been reinvested in shares of common stock or a mutual fund. If the dividends you've received exceeds a certain limit, the form will indicate that you are to itemize all dividend income on a separate schedule.

Any party that pays you more than $10 per year in interest or dividends must prepare a form 1099, which indicates the amount paid to you. Copies of this form are sent to you and to the IRS. Thus, the IRS has a record that you received that money; should you fail to report it on your tax return, expect to be questioned by the IRS.

ALIMONY RECEIVED   This is considered fully taxable income. However, child-support money received is not taxable income. See current regulations for definitions of taxable alimony.

Separately Scheduled Income

If you receive certain other types of income, you will be required to complete additional schedules. These types of income include:

BUSINESS INCOME OR LOSS—SCHEDULE C   If you ran your own business, part-time or full-time, as a sole proprietor, you must complete Schedule C and show the income or loss from that business. (If you operated the business as a partnership or a corporation, you'll have to file the appropriate partnership or corporate income forms.)

CAPITAL GAINS AND LOSSES—SCHEDULE D   Congress has probably changed the regulations on capital gains and losses more often than any other aspect of the entire tax law.

The concept applies to the sale of *capital assets,* which, in general terms, are investments such as stocks, bonds, and real estate. If you sell such items at a profit, you have realized a capital gain. If you sell such items at a loss, you have realized a capital loss. If you hold capital assets for less than the designated holding period, it is a short-term capital gain or loss. If you hold the capital asset for longer than the designated holding period, it is a long-term capital gain or loss.

Both the tax rate on capital gains and the holding period (to distinguish between long- and short-term gains) have bounced around frequently over the last ten or twenty years, making it difficult for investors to anticipate the tax implications of their strategies. Prior to 1987 the maximum tax rate on long-term capital gains was 20 percent. From 1987 to 1990 it was as high as 33 percent. From 1991 to 1997 it was 28 percent. And in 1998 it went back down to 20 percent as a result of the Taxpayer Relief Act of 1997. The holding period has been as short as six months. From 1998 onward the holding period to qualify for the long-term tax rate will be eighteen months. For capital assets purchased after the year 2000, the long-term capital gains rate will be 18 percent if the assets are held for at least five years.

The capital gains tax issue has always been a political football. It is always subject to change, and that must be taken into account in building any kind of investment portfolio.

List capital gains and losses separately on Schedule D. Note, too, that your state may have different requirements on capital gains taxes. This may require more recordkeeping on your part.

If you have net investment *losses,* either short term or long term, you can subtract all or part of these losses from your otherwise taxable income. The maximum amount you can subtract has been $3,000 each year. Example: In 1998 you had investment gains of $2,000 and investment losses of $7,000, for a net loss during the year of $5,000. On your 1998 federal tax return, you can reduce your otherwise taxable income by $3,000 as a result of this loss provision. Assuming that in 1999 you have no investment transactions at all, you can, for that year, subtract the remaining $2,000 worth of 1998 losses from your 1999 income. Check to see what regulations are in effect at the time you file any annual return.

PENSIONS, ANNUITIES, RENTS, ROYALTIES, PARTNERSHIPS— SCHEDULE E   This schedule covers a number of possible income or loss areas, as designated in the heading.

MISCELLANEOUS TAXABLE INCOME

- Fees for services you perform, such as serving as a member of a jury, an election precinct official, a notary public, an executor or administrator of an estate, to name a few, are all miscellaneous taxable income.

- Property you receive through barter. If you receive services or property in exchange for your services, you must include as income the fair market value of the services or property on the date you received it.

- Gambling winnings are taxable income. However, you can deduct gambling losses during the year up to the extent of your winnings. Winnings from lotteries and raffles are considered gambling winnings. If you win property other than cash, the fair market value of that property must be counted as taxable income.

- Prizes and awards received from drawings, television or radio programs, beauty contests, and the like are taxable. So are awards and bonuses you receive from your employer for your good work or your suggestions. Prizes in the form of property must be included in taxable income at their fair market value.
- Unemployment insurance benefits might be taxable income. See the instructions in Form 1040 for the formula that determines how much of your unemployment insurance benefits are taxable.

This discussion includes just a sampling of the most common types of taxable income. Refer to the 1040 instructions to determine whether you have any other form of taxable income.

Nontaxable Income

Nontaxable income should not be reported on your 1040 form. Following is a sampling of the more common types of nontaxable income. Check the 1040 instructions for more specific details.

- **Interest income**   *Some* types of interest income may be nontaxable, including interest received on tax-exempt bonds.
- **Accident and health insurance proceeds**   Payments you receive from the following are exempt from tax: Workers' Compensation; Federal Employees Compensation Act; damages received for injury or illness; benefits from an accident or health insurance policy for which you paid the premiums; disability benefits for loss of income; compensation for loss of a function of your body; and reimbursement for medical care.
- **Gifts and inheritances**   These are not considered income. But if the cash or property you received as a gift or inheritance generates income for you, the income generated is taxable.
- **Life insurance proceeds**   Proceeds paid to beneficiaries are generally not taxable. Possible exceptions: If someone else turned an insurance policy on their life over to you and you paid a price for the transfer of that policy, proceeds payable to you as beneficiary may be taxable to you.
- **Social Security benefits**   Not generally taxable, unless your income from all sources exceeds levels set by law.
- **Scholarships, fellowships, and grants**   Generally, money received in this form is not taxable if you are a candidate for a degree.
- **Prizes and awards**   These may be tax-free if the prize was awarded in recognition of your accomplishments in religious, charitable, scientific, educational, artistic, literary, or civic fields. You must also have been selected as a possible recipient without any volunteering on your part. And you must not be required to perform future services as a condition of receiving the prize. Athletic awards are not tax-exempt.

Total Income

In completing this portion of your 1040 form, you add up all the items that are considered taxable income. From this total income figure, we now begin the subtractions, the first being for *adjustments to income*.

Adjustments to Income

Items included in the adjustments category are often referred to as deductions, but technically they are not deductions. You are entitled to claim these adjustment items even if you do not itemize your deductions.

The most common types of adjustments will appear on your 1040 form in the following manner:

Adjustments to Income	_____
Payments to IRA plans	_____
Payments to Keogh plans	_____
Alimony paid	_____
Total adjustments	_____

Payments to IRA Plans

You might be able to claim an adjustment for money you invest in an IRA plan. (Chapter 18 explains who can qualify for this deduction.)

Payments to Keogh Plans

If you have income from self-employment, you're eligible to take part in a Keogh plan, which can entitle you to an adjustment. (See chapter 18 for details.)

Alimony Paid

Alimony *received* is taxable income. On the other hand, alimony *paid* is an adjustment that can reduce your total income.

Adjusted Gross Income

At this point, total your adjustments and subtract them from total income. The result is the adjusted gross income.

The adjusted gross income is important: the amounts you can claim for some of the itemized deductions are keyed to your adjusted gross income. These formulas will be explained with respect to each deduction to which they apply.

Deductions: To Itemize or Not to Itemize?

Certain types of expenses are deductible from your income. These expenses include those for medical purposes, charitable contributions, taxes you've paid, interest you've paid, casualty or theft losses you've suffered, and other expenses related to your ability to generate income. Some deductions have limits.

Even if you haven't actually incurred such expenses, the law allows you to claim a certain fixed amount of such deductions anyway. This is known as the standard deduction.

The amount of the standard deduction depends on your filing status. Table 20–3 indicates the standard deduction for different filing statuses for 1997. These amounts are subject to change each year due to inflation and/or act of Congress.

Here's an example: Let's assume that during 1997 a married couple did not actually incur one penny's expense for any of the deductible items: they had no medical expenses, had no home loan interest, paid no state income taxes, and made no charitable contributions. Even though they had not incurred *any* deductible expenses, they were entitled to claim a $6,900 standard deduction for that year, which would reduce their taxable income accordingly.

Your Choice

If you have, in fact, spent *more* on deductible items than the standard deduction allows, you are entitled to claim *all* those expenses as deductions. But you must itemize each of them, and you must have proper evidence that you did incur such expenses.

The choice is yours: You can take the easy route and claim the standard deduction, in which case you won't have to keep records of all the particular expenses, and completing your tax form will be that much simpler. Or you can keep all the proper records to prove what you paid for such items. If your true

TABLE 20–3   **Standard Deduction**

Filing Status	1997
Married, filing jointly	$6,900
Married, filing separately	3,450
Head of household	6,050
Single	4,150

deductible expenses exceed the standard deduction amount, it will pay you to itemize. Many taxpayers take the shortcut of the standard deduction when in fact, if they had itemized, they could have saved a lot of money.

How do you decide whether you should itemize? If you are a homeowner, it's very likely that you will have deductible expenses in excess of the standard deduction amount. For most homeowners, the interest on their mortgage and their real estate taxes, both of which are a deductible, will be close to, if not more than, the standard deduction amount.

If you're not a homeowner, you'll have to determine whether your deductible expenses exceed the standard deduction. The following will familiarize you with the types of expenses that are deductible.

To itemize your deductions complete Schedule A of the 1040 form. An abbreviated example of Schedule A is shown here; the actual form is subject to change from year to year. Check current regulations to be certain you are claiming all proper deductions in the proper form.

Schedule A—Itemized Deductions

Medical and Dental Expenses	Casualty or Theft Losses
(Follow formula on current version of Schedule A to arrive at proper deductions.)	(Follow instructions on current version of Schedule A. Complete and attach Form 4684 to your return.)
TOTAL MEDICAL _____	TOTAL CASUALTY OR THEFT LOSSES _____
Taxes	
State and local income _____	
Real estate _____	**Miscellaneous Deductions**
Personal property _____	
Other (itemize) _____	Union dues _____
_____ _____	Other (itemize) _____
_____ _____	_____ _____
TOTAL TAXES _____	_____ _____
Interest Expense	_____ _____
Home mortgage _____	TOTAL MISCELLANEOUS DEDUCTIONS _____
Other (itemize) _____	
_____ _____	**Summary of Itemized Deductions:**
_____ _____	Total medical _____
_____ _____	Total taxes _____
TOTAL INTEREST _____	Total interest _____
Contributions	Total casualty _____
Cash contributions _____	Total miscellaneous _____
Other than cash _____	
TOTAL CONTRIBUTIONS _____	TOTAL DEDUCTIONS _____

Deductible Expenses

Expenses not specifically listed on Schedule A are included under "Miscellaneous Deductions." All deductions are subject to change by law.

MEDICAL AND DENTAL EXPENSES You can claim a deduction for your nonreimbursed medical expenses only to the extent those expenses exceed 7½ percent of your adjusted gross income. In other words, if your adjusted gross income was $40,000, you can claim a deduction for nonreimbursed medical expenses in excess of $3,000.

TAXES You can claim a deduction for any local (state, city) income taxes, real estate taxes, and personal property taxes. Taxes that are *not* deductible include sales taxes, utility taxes, federal income taxes, fines and penalties, and taxes on tobacco and alcohol products.

INTEREST EXPENSES Individuals must keep track of five different types of interest that they pay, and each type is subject to its own rules regarding deductibility.

- **Consumer interest** This includes such items as credit-card debt, charge account debt, car loans, and personal loans. You cannot deduct any of your consumer interest.
- **Home loan interest** See chapter 7 for what is deductible.
- **Investment interest** Interest paid on loans relating to investments is deductible within limitations relative to the amount of investment income you receive.
- **Business interest** If you borrow money for legitimate business purposes, the interest on such loans is deductible.
- **Student loans** Interest can be deductible in accordance with the Taxpayers Relief Act of 1997.

CONTRIBUTIONS You can deduct charitable contributions made to properly qualified charitable organizations. Contributions may be cash or property. If you give property, the deduction would be the fair market value of such property. In order to justify charitable deductions, you must have proper documentation and appraisals. If you are actively involved in a charitable organization, you cannot deduct the value of your time contributed to the organization, but you can deduct out-of-pocket expenses you incur on behalf of the charity.

CASUALTY OR THEFT LOSSES If you suffer a sudden and unexpected loss or casualty, you can deduct the value of the loss if the amount of each separate casualty or theft loss is more than $100, *and* the total amount of *all* losses during the year is more than 10 percent of your adjusted gross income for that year. For example, say your adjusted gross income is $25,000, and you suffer a casualty loss of $2,000. You *cannot* claim that loss as a deduction because it is *less* than 10 percent of your adjusted gross income. But if you had a loss of $3,000 you could claim a deduction. How much? First, you must subtract the $100 just noted; then, you must subtract the 10 percent of your adjusted gross income: $3,000 less $100 less $2,500 equals a deduction of $400.

Deductible casualty losses may result from many causes, including fire, hurricanes, tornadoes, floods, storms, sonic booms, and vandalism.

Nondeductible casualties include car accidents when your own negligence caused the accident; breakage of household items, such as china and glassware, under normal conditions of use; damage done by a family pet; damage caused by termites, moths, plant disease; and damage caused by progressive deterioration of your property.

Theft losses include those arising from burglary, robbery, larceny, and embezzlement. If, however, you simply misplace or lose money or property, that is not a deductible theft loss.

MISCELLANEOUS DEDUCTIONS   The Tax Reform Act of 1986 imposed a formula for calculating these miscellaneous deductions: the 2 percent rule. The rule states that qualifying expenses can be deducted only to the extent that they exceed 2 percent of your adjusted gross income for the year. Example: Your adjusted gross income is $30,000. Two percent of $30,000 is $600. You tally up, say, $1,000 worth of miscellaneous deductions. But on your tax return, you can only claim $400 worth, the extent to which you exceed the 2 percent level, which, in your case, is $600. If your adjusted gross income for the year is $40,000, 2 percent of that amount is $800. In such a case, you can claim miscellaneous deductions only to the extent that those expenses exceed $800.

Here are the major miscellaneous expenses that might be claimed as deductions—subject to the 2 percent rule:

- Fees for investment advice and management
- Fees for administration of trusts
- Legal expenses relating to the collection of income
- Subscriptions to publications on investing
- Rental costs for safety deposit boxes, to the extent the box is used to store investment-related items
- Cost of tax advice and preparation of returns
- Appraisal costs relating to a casualty loss or a charitable contribution
- Unreimbursed employee business expense
- Continuing education expenses
- Business use of your residence
- Literature relating to your job or profession
- Dues to unions or business related associations
- Work uniforms and tools
- Certain costs related to seeking a new job

(If you are self-employed, many of these expenses might be business-related expenses, which may be fully deductible on Schedule C.)

Total all your deductible expenses. If the total exceeds the current standard deduction, you should include that total of itemized deductions on your return. If the itemized deductions do not exceed the standard deduction, then you should claim the standard deduction.

What Is not Deductible

If you claim deductions that aren't legal, the IRS will disallow them, which means that you will have to pay back taxes plus possible interest and penalties. Following is a brief list of some nondeductible items that are often erroneously claimed as deductions.

- Commuting to and from work
- Life insurance premiums
- Property insurance premiums on your home
- Hobby expenses
- Social Security taxes
- Attorney fees (except for producing and collecting income)
- Home-related expenses, such as allowances for children, clothing, utility expenses, school tuition
- Home repair and maintenance expenses
- Losses you might suffer on the sale of your house or personal effects

Computing Your Taxes

Exercise 20.3

We've now reached the point where the actual tax can be calculated. Table 20–4 illustrates what the tax tables in the IRS instruction look like. For those whose taxable income exceeds the limits in the tax tables, there are tax rate schedules to calculate their taxes.

TABLE 20–4   Sample of Tax Tables (In a Recent Year)

If Your Taxable Income is . . .		And You Are . . .			
At Least	But Less Than	Single	Married Filing Jointly[a]	Married Filing Separately	Head of Household
		Your Tax is:—			
30,000	30,050	5,762	4,504	6,197	4,858
30,050	30,100	5,776	4,511	6,211	4,872
30,100	30,150	5,790	4,519	6,225	4,900

[a]A qualifying widow(er) would also use this column.

Example: You subtract from your *total income* all of your *adjustments, deductions,* and *exemptions.* What's left is your *taxable income.* If, in the year illustrated in Table 20–4, your taxable income was $30,027, and you were married and filing a joint return, your tax would have been $4,504. If your taxable income was $30,121, and you were single, your tax would have been $5,790. And so on. Are the taxes different in the current year than in the year illustrated in Table 20–4? By how much?

After calculating the tax due, you then subtract the amount of any *credits* to which you may be entitled. For example: if the married couple in the prior paragraph was entitled to a child-care credit of $300, their tax would be reduced from $4,504 to $4,204.

New types of credits were introduced in the Taxpayer Relief Act of 1997, to take effect in tax year 1998 and onward.

For tax year 1998 taxpayers with children will be entitled to a credit of $400 per child under the age of 17. For 1999 and beyond that credit will be $500 per child under 17. (The child must be 17 at the end of the calendar year to qualify.) The credit is not available to high-income taxpayers: it phases out for couples with incomes of $110,000, and for individuals with incomes of $75,000. The credits are in addition to the personal exemptions.

The so-called Hope credit is available for higher education tuition and fee expenses at colleges, community colleges, and post-secondary (after high school) vocational schools. During the first two years of a student's post-secondary education the credit is $1,500 per student per year. For following years the credit is $1,000 per student per year. Taxpayers may claim the credit for up to two years for each student. (See the following paragraph on the Lifetime Learning credit for further details.) After 2000 the amounts of the credits will be indexed for inflation. There are some technical limits to these credits, such as that the student must be carrying at least one-half of the normal course load. Also, credits may not be fully available in years when the taxpayer takes money out of an Education IRA (see chapter 18) and uses that withdrawal to reduce his or her taxes under the Education IRA rules. This credit phases out for taxpayers with modified adjusted gross incomes of $80,000 to $100,000 for couples, and $50,000 to $60,000 for individuals.

The Lifetime Learning Credit is somewhat of a piggy-back onto the Hope credit. It's available for post-secondary education and for courses that create or improve job skills. It applies to courses that begin after June 30, 1998. The maximum credit is $1,000 per taxpayer per year for 1998 through 2002, and $2,000 per taxpayer per year for 2003 and beyond. Phase-outs for higher income taxpayers are the same as for the Hope credit. The Lifetime Learning credit cannot be taken in the same year that the Hope credit is taken or that deductions for the Education IRA are taken.

The Lifetime Learning credit is available for the third and fourth year of college as well as for graduate school and for adults preparing for new careers.

Note the difference in tax due at the various breakpoints: a single person with taxable income of $30,049 will owe a tax of $5,762, while a single person with a taxable income of $30,051 will owe a tax of $5,776. In other words, with just two dollars more in taxable income an extra $14 in taxes will be owed! On the other hand, the single person with a taxable income of $30,001 pays not a penny more in taxes than the single person with a taxable income $48 higher, or $30,049. This is all the more reason to pay attention to detail in your recordkeeping and tax preparation.

Other Taxes and Payments

Follow IRS instructions on the 1040 form to determine whether you owe any taxes over and above the income taxes. If you had self-employment income during the year, you may owe additional self-employment taxes. If you had more than one employer during the year, more than necessary Social Security taxes may have been paid on your behalf, and you can claim a refund for the excess. The amount of tax withheld from your pay, and the amount of any estimated tax payments you've made on your own, are then either payable by you or refundable to you. This net amount is entered in the section titled "Refund or Balance Due." The return should then be signed and dated by you and by your spouse, if you are filing jointly, and by the paid preparer, if you used one. Mail the return, and a check for any balance owing, to the IRS in accordance with current instructions.

Estimated Taxes

If you have earnings from which there has been nothing withheld for taxes, you may have to pay what is known as the Estimated Tax. This is payable quarterly, in conjunction with filing Form 1040ES. Check current regulations to determine who must pay this tax, and what the penalties are for failing to do so.

Alternative Minimum Tax

The Alternative Minimum Tax (AMT) is designed to make certain that high-income-tax-bracket earners pay at least a minimum amount of tax. Less than one-half of 1 percent of all taxpayers will have to deal with this thorny problem.

TAX-CUTTING STRATEGIES

If you don't claim all the exemptions, adjustments, deductions, and credits to which you are entitled, the Internal Revenue Service won't do it for you. It's your job to keep proper track of all those items and incorporate them into your tax return.

Similarly, you can check out other tax-cutting strategies. The government will not hand them to you. Following are examples of some of these basic strategies.

Tax-Exempt or Tax-Deferred Income

To the extent feasible, take advantage of opportunities to earn tax-exempt or tax-deferred income in your investment program and at work.

Tax-Exempt Income

You can earn tax-exempt income by investing in municipal bonds or in mutual funds that specialize in municipal bonds. (See chapter 14 for a further discussion of these techniques.)

Tax-Deferred Income

Tax-deferred investment income may be available through tax-deferred annuities. In such plans, the earnings on your invested money are not taxed until you withdraw the money.

Some of your income from work may also be on a tax-deferred basis, such as with pension and profit-sharing plans. Your employer may contribute money each year to a pension or profit-sharing plan on your behalf. In effect, he's paying you a form of future income: you won't have the use of the money until some future time, but, in the meantime, you don't have to pay income taxes on it. In addition to pension and profit-sharing plans, some employees might establish a tax-deferred compensation plan that would delay payment for work done until some future year. The object of this is to delay the payment of taxes into a future year when the taxpayer will be in a lower tax bracket, such as during retirement.

One popular device that allows you to earn tax-deferred income is the 401(k) plan. If your employer offers this plan, a portion of your income may be invested instead of being paid to you. That income, and its earnings, will be tax-deferred, as are any contributions your employer makes to the plan. Individual Retirement Accounts (IRAs) and Keogh plans can also be ideal ways to defer taxes. (See chapter 18 for a detailed discussion of these plans.) To the extent you are eligible, you should take advantage of these plans.

U.S. Savings Bonds Series EE also offer the opportunity to earn tax-deferred income. With these bonds you can delay paying taxes on interest earned until you cash in the bonds.

Tax Withholding and the W-4 Form

Suppose someone advised you to embark on an investment plan of $90 per month, and you were guaranteed to earn no interest at all. At the end of the year, you would get back the $1,080 that you had paid in and not a penny more. You'd think such advice was rather absurd, wouldn't you?

The fact is that tens of millions of people do just that.

Of the more than 100 million individual tax returns filed annually, more than 80 percent get a refund from the government. The average refund check is more than $1,000. The reason these taxpayers get a refund check is that they have had more withheld by the employer than was necessary. The government holds these excess payments for the full year and then returns them to the taxpayers in the form of a refund check, once the taxpayers have filed their returns for the year.

Employers are required to withhold from workers' pay only enough to meet each worker's tax obligations for the year. Employers estimate the amount they must withhold based on information the employee provides on a W-4 form. Each employee completes a W-4 form when starting work with an employer. The W-4 form sets forth the number of allowances the employee is claiming. The *more* allowances an employee claims, the *less* is withheld from his or her pay.

What qualifies as an allowance? Most commonly, each exemption you claim on your tax return is equal to one allowance, and if you itemize your deductions, you are entitled to claim additional allowances.

W-4 forms contain a worksheet that will assist you in calculating the correct number of allowances. If you have been having too much withheld from your pay, a proper adjustment in your W-4 form can fatten your weekly paycheck. Then, rather than sending excess money to the government where it earns no interest all year long, you'll have that money to invest or spend as you see fit.

Year-end Strategies

As each year draws to a close, you should estimate your probable tax liability for the year compared to what it might be next year. The reason for doing this is to determine whether it would make sense to shift income or deductions from one year to another in order to cut your tax bill. The strategy behind such moves is to claim deductions in years in which you'd be more highly taxed, and to receive income in years when you'd be taxed less.

For example, if your tax rate or income is going to be lower next year (as is sometimes the case), it could make sense to delay year-end income from December of the current year into January of the next year. A drop in income from one year to the next can occur in many ways: a pay cut is in the offing; a spouse who was working may stop working; or you may have had an exceptionally high income this year due to bonuses, commissions, or capital gains, which are not likely to be repeated next year. Reason? It will be taxed at a lower rate next year, and you'll save money accordingly. It can also make sense to accelerate deductions. This means making deductible expenses this year that you'd otherwise make next year. A deduction is worth more to you in a higher tax year than it is in a lower tax year. Shifting incomes or deductions need span only a few weeks—from late December into early January.

Examples of shifting income include year-end bonuses that can be declared or paid in early January instead of late December; payment for fees or services; sales that result in capital gains. Examples of deductions that can be shifted from one year to the next at year-end include charitable contributions; payment of state income taxes and local property taxes; interest expenses; medical and dental expenses.

Vice versa

On the other hand, it may happen that tax rates are scheduled to go *up* next year, or that your *income* is likely to *increase* substantially next year. In either of those cases, reverse strategies may be worthwhile. In other words, you might want to accelerate income (take it this year instead of next year) and delay paying deductible expenses.

Income Shifting

A family with children can cut their income taxes by making gifts of income-producing assets to the children. The tax saving is based on the assumption that children do not earn as much as their parents and are thus taxed in lower brackets or are not taxed at all.

In a given year, the first $500 of investment income received by each child is free of income tax. The second $500 of investment income received by each child is taxed at the child's tax rate, not the parents' tax rate. If a child is *under* 14 years of age, any investment income over $1,000 received by each child in a given year is taxed at the parents' tax rate (if the parents' tax rate is higher than the child's tax rate). If a child is 14 or over, investment income in excess of $1,000 a year continues to be taxed at the child's tax rate.

Here's an example of how this strategy works: You have a savings account of $6,000 earning 8 percent, or $480, per year. If you make a gift of that account to your child, the $480 of income (assuming it's the only income the child has) will escape federal income taxes. If the account were to remain in your name, you'd have to pay income taxes on the earnings each year of roughly $75 to $150.

Tax Shelters

At any given time, tax advantages may become available in a variety of investments and speculative schemes. It's up to the prudent investor and sensible taxpayer to examine any such opportunities thoroughly; to exercise caution with respect to the enthusiasm of the salesperson; and to proceed with the knowledge that today's tax break could be eliminated tomorrow. If you do claim deductions or credits arising out of a tax shelter scheme, you increase your chances of being audited by the IRS. We'll examine that phenomenon more closely in the remainder of this chapter.

FILING YOUR RETURN

What happens if you are not able to file your return by the due date, or if you discover that a return that you did file was incorrect? The law does allow you an opportunity to get an extension on your filing date, and it also allows you to correct a return already filed if the need arises.

Filing Extensions

Taxpayers can get an automatic four-month extension for filing of their individual returns by filing a form 4868 with the Internal Revenue Service. This form must be filed by April 15 with the IRS center in your area. The extension of the time to file your return is *not* an extension of the time to pay the taxes. Your taxes must be fully paid at the time you file the extension form. You can incur a penalty if you've not paid your taxes by the time you file for the extension. Interest charges on late payments may also be imposed.

If you need more time beyond the automatic four-month extension, you may be able to get an additional extension by sending a letter to the Internal Revenue Service stating your reasons or by filing form 2688.

Amending Your Return

Once you've filed your return you can amend it later if you determine that you owe the government or that they owe you a refund.

The form to use to amend your return is a 1040X. Follow the 1040X instructions carefully, and attach any forms or schedules that are needed to explain the changes.

The law allows you ample time to file an amended return. You have three years from the date you filed your original return, or two years from the time you paid your tax, whichever is later, to file the amendment.

WHAT HAPPENS TO YOUR RETURN? EXAMINATIONS AND AUDITS

For about 95 percent of all individual taxpayers, the year's concerns end with the filing of the return and the payment of any taxes due. But for the other 5 percent, the struggle is not over: about half of them will hear from the Internal Revenue Service with respect to arithmetic errors made on their return, and the other half will be subjected to some form of examination or audit.

Where errors in arithmetic are involved, the taxpayers will hear relatively quickly. But it may be two years, three years, or even longer before some audits are announced and resolved. The Internal Revenue Service generally has three years from the date you filed your return to assess additional taxes. If you have failed to report a substantial item of income, the IRS has six years from the filing of your return to claim back taxes. If someone has filed a return with false or fraudulent information intending to evade taxes, or if someone has failed to file a return at all, there is no time limit as to when the IRS can pursue its claim. But taxpayers are not totally at the mercy of the IRS. The law sets forth clear-cut rights for all taxpayers to appeal and protest decisions that go against them. Let's examine what happens once your return is filed.

The Initial Screenings

All returns are checked to determine that the arithmetic is correct and that any checks attached thereto have been properly completed and signed. If a mistake in arithmetic is discovered, the IRS recalculates the amount of tax due and sends you either a refund for the amount overpaid or a bill for the amount you owe them. If other corrections are needed (for example, you forgot to sign your return), you will be notified accordingly.

A further screening will be conducted to determine whether there are errors in the return with respect to deductions, exemptions, and the like. These are some of the most common areas in which errors are found:

- You have claimed deductions for medical expenses without taking into account the stated limitations in the law.
- You have claimed a partial exemption.
- Your reported income does not match the W-2 form your employer has provided, or the 1099 forms that have been provided by various brokers, dealers, and financial institutions. The IRS will cross-check the information it receives on 1099 forms with the information that you report. If you have failed to report any of that income, assume that the IRS knows about it.

If the IRS finds any such errors, you will be notified by mail of the correction. If you disagree with their findings, you can ask for a meeting with an IRS representative, or you can submit whatever information is necessary to support your claim. Matters such as these may be resolved fairly quickly after the filing of your return. But that does not mean you're off the hook with respect to a more detailed audit.

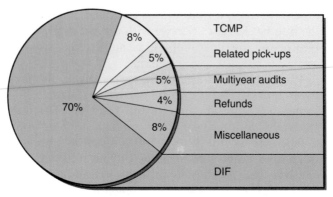

FIGURE 20–1 Reasons for audit selection

Audits

In recent years, the IRS has been auditing about 1 percent of all individual returns filed. Although this may suggest that your chances of being audited in a given year are only 1 in 100, bear in mind that that chance occurs every year, and sooner or later the law of averages might catch up with you.

Out of roughly 100 million returns filed each year, how does the IRS select the 1 million returns for actual auditing? Figure 20–1 illustrates the approximate breakdown of reasons the IRS used to choose returns for auditing.

Exercise 20.4

Discriminate Income Function (DIF)

About 70 percent of the returns chosen for audit are selected by the Discriminate Income Function, or DIF. Computers examine your total income, your adjusted gross income, your deductions, your adjustments and your credits. Based on past statistical evidence, agents can determine which returns have the greatest potential for recovering additional taxes through an audit.

The majority of DIF audits are conducted via correspondence. You may, for example, receive a letter requesting that you send photostats of checks, receipts, or other evidence to support your specific claims. If you can provide such evidence, the audit may be ended quickly. If you are unable to provide the evidence, an additional tax will be payable, or you may be requested to appear at the local IRS office. In some cases, the audit can be at your place of business or home, particularly if the records involved are extensive or if the matter is complex.

Taxpayer Compliance Measurement Program (TCMP)

About 8 percent of all returns chosen for audit are selected via the Taxpayer Compliance Measurement Program (TCMP). This is a random selection by the IRS and is a much more comprehensive and thorough review of your overall situation. A TCMP audit can be very detailed and time-consuming, even if you have nothing at all to hide. The purposes of the TCMP program are to police the voluntary-compliance aspects of the law and to unearth more statistical data to support the DIF program.

Related Pick-ups

About 5 percent of those returns chosen for auditing are based on "related pick-ups." If, for instance, your business partner was chosen for audit, you might also be chosen; the questionable deductions claimed by the one partner might be suspect with regard to the other partner. In addition, if you have not reported all the income that your W-2 and 1099 forms show you actually received, this could be cause for an audit under this category.

Multiyear Audits

About 5 percent of those returns selected for audit are chosen because more than one return is in question. For example, if you had reported deductions from a real estate investment in your 1996 return, you might be audited for your 1995 and 1994 returns as well.

Refunds

About 4 percent of all taxpayers who claim refunds on their returns are audited for no other reason than to verify the facts that would allow a refund.

Miscellaneous

These audits can be searching for verification of capital gains transactions, appraisals of charitable contributions, appraisals of casualty losses, and so forth. The IRS also exchanges tax information with state taxing authorities, and a mismatch of information between your state and federal returns may also prompt an audit in this category.

Audit Red Flags

Aside from the aforementioned ways in which returns are chosen for audit, the following are generally regarded as common *red flags* that will prompt an IRS audit of your return.

- Excessive deductions claimed for travel and entertainment expenses
- Improper deductions claimed for the expense of maintaining an office in your home
- Losses arising out of what the IRS determines to be a "hobby," even though you determine such activity to be an ongoing business

Audit Strategies: Yours

Expenses Income

Subconsciously or otherwise, the government has instilled a fear of the audit procedure in all of us. In so doing, they may hope to encourage taxpayers to be as honest and forthright as possible in preparing their returns, so as to avoid a possible audit. Whatever the reason for our fear of audits, the fact is that most audits really do not have to be feared, particularly if your return is honest and you have the documentation necessary to back up your claims.

Bear in mind that in an office audit you are dealing with another human being. Very likely, you will be treated in much the same way that you treat the auditing agent. If you are surly, don't be surprised if you are met with surliness. If you are pleasant, cooperative, and polite, chances are better that you'll be met with those same traits. If you arrive with your documents in well-organized fashion, you're going to make the agent's job that much easier, which in turn could make your examination that much easier.

If a reasonably small amount of money is involved, you may feel comfortable in handling the audit proceedings on your own. If, however, a substantial amount of money might be involved, consider hiring an accountant or tax attorney to assist you. If you have had a tax preparer do your return initially, that person would be the likely candidate to assist you with the audit.

An audit proceeding is a legal entanglement. Your legal rights and the government's legal rights are in apparent opposition. As in any legal entanglement, you must determine what your likely overall costs will be in terms of money, time, and aggravation. If you feel that your case is weak, it might be better to resolve the matter quickly, pay the tax due (or a lesser negotiated amount if you're able to do so), and save yourself time and aggravation. On the other hand, if you feel that your case is strong and there is enough money involved, you might deem it worthwhile to fight the matter all the way. The IRS looks at the matter in much the same way: the agent's time and energy must be evaluated in line with the hoped-for amount of back taxes that can be recovered. Thus, negotiations are always a possibility.

Audit Strategies: Theirs

An auditing agent of the IRS is expected to produce tax revenues as efficiently as possible. The IRS denies that there is any "quota" as to how much a given agent should produce; but a good agent should justify his or her work by producing as much revenue as possible in the most cost-efficient way. It might be assumed that a good agent, considering a contested amount of, say, $500, might be willing to accept perhaps $350 on the spot rather than to go for the whole $500 over a protracted period of protests and appeals. In short, negotiations are possible, and your success in them will be in direct proportion to the strength of your case.

Be assured that an efficient agent will probe to determine just what your strengths and weaknesses may be. Following, for example, are some of the interrogation guidelines that an agent might use.

- With respect to claims for charitable deductions, the agent will attempt to determine whether the payments were made to properly qualified organizations. If property was contributed, the agent will seek to verify the true fair market value of the property at the time it was given.

- With respect to claimed deductions for interest payments, the agent will ascertain whether the interest payments were made on a valid, existing debt that you, the taxpayer, owed. This may necessitate your providing copies of all the documents relating to the loan agreement.

- With respect to claims for medical deductions, the agent will seek to determine whether any insurance reimbursement has been made to you or is expected by you, and will also probe to be certain that amounts you've claimed as child-care expenses aren't also claimed as medical expenses.

- If a deduction is claimed for a casualty or theft loss, the agent will attempt to determine that a theft or casualty loss has actually occurred and that your loss was the direct result of such an occurrence. The agent will also determine whether insurance proceeds have been received by you or are expected by you.

- If you claim a deduction for educational purposes, it will be the agent's job to determine if your expenses were incurred primarily for the purpose of maintaining or improving skills, or for meeting requirements for retaining your job status. This may necessitate evidence from your employer.

- If you've claimed alimony expenses as an adjustment to your income, the agent may request a copy of the underlying divorce documents for inspection.

These are just a random sampling of the *preliminary* probes you should expect the agent to make. If you are armed with all the necessary documentation at the initial meeting, you might be able to bring the audit to a swift conclusion. If you can't document your claims immediately, the agent will give you a reasonable time to collect the necessary documents and will schedule a future meeting at which the matter should be resolved.

Resolving an Audit: You Agree

If you and the agent agree on the findings at your initial meeting—which could take less than an hour—ask the agent to tell you how much in additional taxes you owe. You will then be asked to sign an agreement, and shortly thereafter you will receive a written report plus a bill for whatever taxes you may owe, plus any interest or penalties that have been agreed on. Note that if you sign the agreement, you waive your rights to appeal in the future. If paying the back taxes in one lump sum will cause a hardship for you, you can ask the agent to put the payments on an installment plan. You have to ask for this, for it's unlikely that they'll volunteer it.

Resolving an Audit: You Disagree

If you are unable to settle the matter in the IRS office audit, you should immediately ask for a written copy of your legal rights under such circumstances. Where disagreement occurs, you can ask for an immediate meeting with a supervisor, with the hope that such a meeting may result in a more favorable compromise.

If you don't reach an agreement with the supervisor, the agent will then send you a report explaining the additional tax liability. You then have the right to request a conference at the district level to see if the matter can be resolved. If a settlement still isn't reached at the conference, you'll then receive a Notice of Deficiency, which is commonly referred to as a "90-day-letter." In this letter, the government notifies you that you will be assessed the additional tax owed ninety days from the date the letter was mailed.

If you still believe that your case is valid, you have ninety days in which to choose one of three courses to further your appeal.

- You can file a petition with the tax court.
- You can pay the tax that the government claims is due and file a refund claim for it. If the refund claim is turned down, you can then sue for your refund in either a federal district court or the court of claims.
- If the amount of the tax is $5,000 or less, you can proceed in the Small Claims Division of the tax court.

The first two choices would be more suitable for claims involving substantial sums of money; and you'd likely need professional representation. In the Small Claims Division procedures are relatively informal and, in many instances, you can plead your own case.

The IRS has been taking a liberal attitude about making compromises with taxpayers who owe overdue amounts. In one recent year the IRS received about 50,000 offers of compromise from delinquent taxpayers. (up from 10,000 two years earlier) and it accepted 18,000 of the 50,000 offers. The total amount the IRS accepted as compromise was $209 million; the original amounts owed totaled $1.38 billion! That's less than 20 cents on the dollar.

As with all tax matters, rules and regulations are subject to change from time to time. If you find yourself involved in a tax dispute, make certain that you know your rights as they currently exist.

STRATEGIES FOR SUCCESS

Bugged by Auditor? Ask for a New One

Most income tax auditing takes place by mail. There's only a remote chance that you will be called upon to deal face to face with an IRS auditor. If you are, and if there is enough money at stake, you might well want to have professional help accompany you. Tension can be high, and personalities can clash when auditor meets taxpayer. Many taxpayers may feel intimidated, "stressed out" by the mere fact of an audit. This can impair your ability to present your own position. If you do feel uncomfortable with the auditor assigned to your case, you *can* ask to have that auditor replaced by another one. Talk to the local IRS supervisor and present your request. There's no guarantee that you'll like the new one either, but at least there is an opportunity to cut the tension. It can work in your favor. But you have to ask for it.

Your Best Protection

There is nothing that can insulate you better from the rigors of a tax audit than an accurate return accompanied by all proper documentation for all claims made. If you have those in hand, an audit should be nothing more than a minor inconvenience. If you lack either a correct return or the proper documentation, an audit can become a major source of stress—not only might you have to pay back taxes, plus possible interest and penalties; the proceedings can also interfere with your day-do-day life. It may seem tempting to put some extra money in your pocket by evading taxes. But the consequences of doing so can ultimately be costly.

PERSONAL ACTION WORKSHEET

Updating Tax Information

You should complete this checklist *before* you read Chapter 20. The information you will gather in completing the checklist will help you to complete the current year's tax returns accurately and quickly.

The information you need to complete this checklist is available in the most recent IRS instructions for the 1040 form as well as in the most recent IRS Publication 17, "Your Federal Income Tax."

Fill in the blanks as they apply to the current tax year:

- **Who Must File a Return?** You must file a return: if you are single, under 65, and had a gross income of $_____ for the year; if you are single, 65 or over, and had a gross income of $_____ for the year; if you are married, both spouses under 65, and had a combined gross income for the year of $_____ ; if you are married, one spouse 65 or older, and had a gross income of $_____ ; if you are self-employed (part-time or full-time); if you had net earnings from self-employment of $_____ or more.

- **Exemptions** The value of each exemption for the current year is $_____ . Generally, if you wish to claim someone as a dependent, that person's gross income for the year may not exceed $_____ . (See exceptions for children and full-time students.)

- **Standard deduction** For married persons filing jointly, and for qualifying widow(er)s: $_____ ; for singles, or heads of household: $_____ ; for married persons filing separately: $_____ .

- **Expenses** Estimate your own actual expenses subject to the tax law limitations in effect for the year: medical and dental expenses that are not reimbursed by insurance, by your employer, or otherwise $_____ ; taxes paid for which deductions are allowable $_____ ; interest paid, including home mortgage, and other debts for which interest is deductible $_____ ; charitable contributions $_____ ; casualty or theft losses not reimbursed by insurance or otherwise $_____ ; other deductions $_____ .

See the text and IRS instructions for specific details. If the total of proper itemized deductions exceeds the standard deduction for your filing status, you should itemize your deductions.

CONSUMER ALERT

Some Tax "Helpers" Can Harm You

Exercise 20.5

Every year without fail—usually between Super Bowl Day and Groundhog Day—the landscape in every town becomes littered with Income Tax preparation signs and newsstands are overloaded with books offering do-it-yourself guidelines for completing your tax returns.

Care should be taken in choosing either a tax preparer or a book. With respect to the preparers, beware of high-sounding promises that they can "guarantee" you lower taxes. The most any preparer can guarantee you is an accurate return, based on the information you provide. Preparers can't create deductions where none legally exist. They must follow the same rules that you must.

Compare prices carefully. Some advertise very low prices, but those might be only for the simplest forms, and extras can add up quickly. Determine, before you commit yourself, what the *total* price will be for the service.

Fly-by-night preparers have been a problem, both for the public and for the IRS. Some have filed false or erroneous returns, leaving the taxpayer to answer to the IRS. Others have pocketed their customer's tax payment or refund checks and disappeared into the night.

Tax preparation services can be helpful, but you must use care in selecting one. How long has it been in business? What personal recommendations can you get from satisfied customers? Don't overlook the regular full-time accountants who don't advertise. They may be no more expensive than the seasonal services, and they're available to assist you all year.

As for the books, some of them are nothing more than reprints of official IRS books that you can obtain at little or no cost from the nearest IRS office. Worthwhile books include J.K. Lasser's *Your Income Tax* and the H. & R. Block annual tax guide. The Lasser book is very comprehensive; the Block book offers an easy step-by-step guide to completing the returns.

Preparers and books aside, though, nobody can help you better than yourself: your ongoing knowledge of and attention to the income tax laws is your best assurance of keeping your taxes as low as possible.

UPS & DOWNS *The Economics of Everyday Life*

Why Income Taxes Go Up and Down

Many, if not most, taxpayers face a rollercoaster of changes every few years. Tax laws change. Your eligibility for deductions changes. (For example, you become a homeowner instead of a renter.) Your number of exemptions changes. (You have a new child.) Your filing status changes. (You get married or divorced.) Your income changes. (You get a raise or your spouse gets fired.) All of these events can mean higher or lower taxes from one year to the next. But there are more substantial aspects of public and governmental policy that strongly influence how we are taxed.

Taxation as a business incentive   Tax breaks given to certain industries can stimulate desired activity. Oil drilling, real estate development, and high-tech research have all benefited from tax breaks when the nation needed the end results: petroleum, housing, space exploration, and so on. When those tax breaks are in place, the companies and their employees benefit, but at the expense of other taxpayers. Sooner or later those favored industries lose their breaks and others get them.

Taxation as a social policy   California passed a steep tax on tobacco products. The revenues were used for nonsmoking advertising. The advertising was so successful that more people quit smoking than had been anticipated. This resulted in such a sharp drop in income from the tobacco tax that the education program had to be curtailed.

Taxation in reaction to international events   How much was defense spending cut as a result of the collapse of the former Soviet Union? How much of those spending cuts were used to reduce the burden on U.S. taxpayers? Or was the money saved from defense cuts (at the expense of defense workers) used to boost some other sector of economic activity (education, health care, welfare, research) to the benefit of those who worked in those fields? In short, some people's taxes can go up and down, while other people's job opportunities ride on the other side of the seesaw.

Taxation in response to special interest groups   It has long been argued whether cutting capital gains tax rates benefits the rich at the expense of the poor. Some argue that lowering capital gains tax rates pushes the tax burden onto those who have no investments. Others say that cutting the tax rates frees investment dollars for economic growth, increasing the wealth of everyone. Both sides lobby Congress ferociously for their respective causes, resulting in changes to the capital gains tax rates over the years.

Taxation as a political football   As with the capital gains issue, the political parties profoundly stress that their tax proposals are better for the public than those of the other party. And taxation can thus go up and down with the fortunes of the respective parties.

Taxation in response to economic trends   When the economy slows down, as in a recession, tax revenues fall—fewer people working means less income taxes being paid. If government spending is not reduced accordingly, then taxes must be increased on the remaining workers to pay the cost of government programs. The alternative is for the government to borrow more, which will put a heavier tax burden on taxpayers years down the road. As the economy grows, so do tax revenues. That increased revenue can be used either to lower taxes or to increase government spending.

? **WHAT IF . . . ?** ————————————————————————————

Test yourself: How would you deal with these real-life possibilities?

1. You add up all your expenses for the past year that are deductible on your tax return. You find that your itemized deductions are $50 more than your standard deduction. To claim the itemized deductions you must file form 1040, instead of one of the simpler forms. Would you itemize? If so, why? If not, why not? What if the itemized deductions were $100 more than the standard deduction? $300?

2. Your spouse, whose earnings are about the same as yours, will not be working for at least one-half of next year. What year-end tax-planning strategies can you utilize this year that would affect your income taxes? Reverse the situation: your spouse has worked only half of this year but next year will work full time. What strategies can benefit you taxwise?

3. Last year the amount that was withheld from your pay for income taxes was $4,200. Your tax bill was actually $3,100, making your refund $1,100. What are the advantages and disadvantages of this situation? What can you do to modify the arrangement?

NUMBER CRUNCHERS

Do the calculations to make decisions in these real-life possibilities.

Exercise 20.6

1. Using the *current-year tax tables,* calculate the taxes due in the following cases: (a) a single person with total income of $24,500, adjustments to income of $1,300, standard deduction, one personal exemption; (b) a married couple filing jointly with total income of $56,700, adjustments to income of $3,300, itemized deductions of $9,350, five personal exemptions; (c) a head of household with total income of $37,900, adjustments to income of $680, standard deduction, two personal exemptions.

2. Based on current law, calculate how much deduction can be taken in the following cases: (a) for medical expenses, when the taxpayer had an adjusted gross income of $32,000 and unreimbursed medical expenses of $4,100; (b) for "miscellaneous deductions," when the taxpayer had an adjusted gross income of $46,500 and had spent $660 on continuing education expenses, $427 on work uniforms and tools, $175 on union dues, and $634 on his homeowner's insurance.

3. With $10,000 to invest you can earn 6 percent on a high-quality tax-exempt bond that has twenty years to run, or 7.5 percent on a federally insured savings plan for three years at your local bank. If your income is taxed at 15 percent, which of these plans will give you a better return? What if your income is taxed at 28 percent? What else should you consider before making your choice?

FOR BETTER OR FOR WORSE

Things beyond our control often impact our personal and financial well-being, for better or for worse. Some are more predictable than others. How could you be affected if the following real-life phenomena happened? Could you have seen it coming? What steps could you have taken to minimize damage or maximize advantage? The better able you are to anticipate and recognize these forces, the better equipped you are to deal with them.

1. You do some freelance work, for which you're paid $1,000. The person who hired you neglects to send you a 1099 form by the required time. So you don't report the income on your return. Months later, the employer tardily sends you the 1099 showing the $1,000 you were paid the previous year.

2. During the year you win $5,000 at the race track. You know that you can offset gambling winnings with gambling losses for tax purposes. So next trip to the track you go about picking up losing tickets after every race to substantiate $5,000 in losses. A stranger in a suit observes you and asks what you're doing. You've heard that the IRS has agents posted at all the tracks, so you don't say a word and walk away with your pocket full of losing tickets.

3. You know that your brother plays fast and loose with his income taxes, evading anything he thinks he can get away with. So far, he's been lucky. You've always been 100 percent honest with all of your tax matters. He invites you to go into a business deal with him. It looks too good to be true, mainly because it involves some tax dodge. But he assures you that if the IRS comes after you for any taxes, he'll pay them on your behalf.

Exercise 20.7

21

Working for Yourself

If you wish in this world to advance, your merits you're bound to enhance. You must stir it and stump it and blow your own trumpet, or trust me, you haven't a chance.

W.S. Gilbert

A man's reach should exceed his grasp, or what's a heaven for?

Robert Browning

Almost everyone has said, at one time or another, "Take this job and shove it! I'd be better off working for myself."

Many people go off on their own and, after hard work and persistence (and often a dose of good fortune), achieve satisfaction in their own business or professional practice. That satisfaction can be a mix of financial success and psychological fulfillment. Many others dive into the deep end, poorly prepared and undercapitalized, and sooner than later face failure. Still others vex and perplex themselves for years, wondering, "Could I? Should I?"—never coming to a conclusion; never scratching the itch to become their own boss.

And then there are those who have already taken the plunge in their own business, but they are unsettled and disturbed that it's not working out the way they had hoped.

This chapter will present:

- The basic considerations that any would-be entrepreneur must take to heart, not just in the planning stages but on an ongoing basis

- The pros and cons of self-employment: the risks that must be faced in order to reap the benefits of independence and financial gain

- Sources of important information on planning and executing a new business venture

This material is only a starting point. The lessons herein may stimulate some to take the chance of a lifetime and embark on the perilous journey of self-employment. And it may prove so precautionary that others will be deterred from doing so, and they might well be grateful for having been forewarned. In any case, you will have at least become familiar with essential elements that make our free-market economy run: entrepreneurism, risk-taking, and the role of capital.

WHEN IS A GOOD TIME TO START A NEW VENTURE?

Many factors will flash "red light" or "green light" with respect to getting started. These same factors may also indicate to a floundering business just why it is floundering.

Personal Factors

Do a lot of self-evaluation and homework before you even think of becoming a successful entrepreneur. Consider the following:

Inflated Expectations

The prospect of being your own boss is exhilarating. Indeed, common sense can fly out the window when one anticipates the joys of self-employment: no more boss to face every day (other than when you look in the mirror); no more timeclock to punch (though you may miss the regular paycheck that is activated by that timeclock); more income than you ever dreamed possible (though those dreams can turn into nightmares); and, above all, freedom! (except when you're beholden to your customers, creditors, landlord, suppliers, and governmental regulators).

In short, when the harsh light of reality shines on your expectations, they may not look as attractive as you had thought. Expectations have a way of getting inflated, sometimes inordinately so, and that can interfere with the process of making sound judgments. Expectations can also be further inflated by well-meaning friends and relatives who, wishing you well, get on the bandwagon without knowing the risks and pitfalls you may be facing. They might tell you what you *want* to hear, not what you *should* hear.

Evaluate your expectations honestly and frankly. You don't get a green light for self-employment until those expectations are reasonable and attainable.

What Do You Really Want to Be When You Grow Up?

Is your ambition based on a solid foundation, or on something that may be frivolous and, therefore, dangerous? Are you aiming for a self-employed career that was born out of an impractical, youthful fantasy? Are you striving to be on your own just to prove a point to someone else, rather than genuinely attempting to reach the greatest potential that your skills and aptitude will allow? Are you honestly seeking a life of self-employment for its own sake, or are you just running away from a bad situation at work, or a troubled home life, hoping that working for yourself will cure those problems? This is the time for serious soul-searching, and the light stays red until you've done it—then let it simmer for a few months and do it again. Vocational aptitude tests might also be in order to help you determine if your ambitions and your capabilities are well-suited to each other.

What Are You Giving Up?

Life is a series of compromises. Leaving a regular job to go on your own entails a lot of trade-offs. You must evaluate giving up a regular paycheck for a questionable inflow of money. You must evaluate giving up the security of fringe benefits—pension, health plan, etc.—for the uncertainty of do-it-yourself protection. You must evaluate giving up a somewhat-predictable ladder of advancement for a totally unpredictable future. This is more than just a whimsical matter. It requires hard and serious number crunching, and the light stays red until you've done it.

Credit

Unless your credit history is squeaky clean you are asking for heartache as an entrepreneur. Landlords, suppliers, lenders, investors, and advertising media will likely shun you unless you have a good track record in the bill-paying department. Until your credit history sparkles: red light.

What's Your Fallback?

It's cruel to make you consider what your situation will be if your business venture fails, but it would be more cruel to let you go off on your own without making sure that you've asked, *and answered,* all the necessary "what-if?" questions. These include:

- "What if I run out of money before I've reached a plateau of success?"
- "What if my venture fails and I find I can't go back to my old job, or get another good job?"
- "What if—despite the money I might be making—I find out that I don't really like working for myself?"

- "What if everything in my new business is going along nicely, but the demands of work are interfering with my family life?"
- "What if my partner, with whom I thought I had an incredible bond, and without whom I thought the business couldn't succeed, turns out to be a totally unreliable and incompetent jerk?"

Energy Sources

The regular job was a nine-to-fiver, plus some overtime now and then. Self-employment must be a labor of love, and there can't be any such thing as "work hours." At least until you're well established and can afford an easier regimen, you might be on call around the clock. Those might not necessarily be hours in the office or shop. They might be hours in the middle of the night when you lie awake worrying whether that big job will come through, or whether the bank will lend you what you need to buy new equipment, or whether the landlord will give you an extra week to pay the rent, or whether you'll get paid by the sharpy you think may have conned you last week.

Working for yourself requires energies that you may never have had to tap before. How deep are your sources? How much energy can you devote to your work without interfering with your other personal interests? It's tough to know the answers to these questions until you're actually in the fray, but no green light until you've pondered this tricky issue.

The Business Plan: Don't Leave Your Regular Job Without It

It is *mandatory* to have a *Business Plan* before you venture out on your own. A Business Plan, most simply stated, is a serious and carefully drawn roadmap of where you want to get to. It is goals, priorities, and hard numbers that will tell you what it will take to get to your destination. Any lender or investor from whom you seek financial support will insist on seeing your Business Plan. (If one doesn't, be suspect. He might not be discerning enough to help you see the possible dangers in your venture, which could just hasten the onset of serious problems.)

Your banker or the Small Business Administration can give you specific material that will help you create your own business plan.

The Small Business Administration (SBA)

Exercise 21.1

The SBA is a federal agency with offices in most cities. It exists to help small businesses get up and running, and stay running. It can help you get loans. It has abundant data on many types of businesses. It provides counseling services. In short, it is invaluable to the would-be entrepreneur, and you can't get a green light until you've visited your nearest office and taken advantage of all it has to offer. Banks, libraries, and bookstores also have information relevant to your particular needs.

To answer the overriding question at the start of this chapter: Once you get green lights flashing simultaneously on all of the preceding items—plus those that follow—*then* is a good time to start a new venture.

Economic Factors

As ready as you may feel—and be—on a personal level, there are forces at work in the economy that may dictate whether it's wise to proceed.

Growth or Recession?

Don't try to swim up a waterfall. If the nation, or your region, is suffering through a recession, that does not bode well for new business ventures. On the other hand, if times are good there is reason to feel encouraged about a new venture. The tides of the economy ebb and flow, so *anticipatory* timing is critical. Base your decisions on what you think the state of the economy will be when you're ready to launch your venture, which may be months, or even a year or two, from today. Yes, accurate crystal balls are hard to come by, but if you're a good student of the economic trends (see chapter 1), you should be able to sense opportunities as they ebb and flow.

Specific Industry Trends

Be aware of any particular trends in the field of your endeavor that could impact on your business venture. While the national or regional economy may be moving in one direction, specific industries may have different forces at work. For example: housing (and all its related components, such as furniture, appliances, lumber, decor, and so on) may be in a boom or bust cycle out of sync with the rest of the economy. The same can hold true in automotive, electronics, leisure and recreation, health care, financial services, aviation, and many other industries. And these trends may vary from locale to locale, which in turn can be of importance to you.

Some business ventures are subject to fads and technological change, and you must take care to avoid traps that can arise as a result. Franchising has its share of fads. At one time it was fast foods, and for every successful McDonald's and KFC there were countless Beauty Burgers and Chicken Pickin's that failed. Then there was the frozen yogurt hoopla and the quick-lube shop phenomena that left the highways littered with more failures.

In the fast-track world of technology, will video rental stores be rendered obsolete if video-on demand through your telephone becomes a reality, as some are predicting? Will the automotive industry be revolutionized by the advent of electric engines? Will books be replaced by digitized readable discs, and bookstores thus merged into electronic/music outlets? The future gets here quicker than we think, and any investments that depend on continuity can be distorted by rapid changes in technology.

To the extent that your venture may be impacted by technological change, you must anticipate how you can avoid being hurt by change, and how you can profitably anticipate change.

Easy Money?

Another trend that can't be avoided is the ever-changing cost of money: interest rates. To the extent that you may be a borrower—either directly from lenders or indirectly, as in having your suppliers extend credit to you—the cost of money can have a major impact on your financial well-being. The easy availability of money—regardless of the cost—can also be a consideration. There are times when lenders tighten their purse strings and make borrowing difficult. Businesses that need to borrow during tight money times can easily find themselves in a most uncomfortable bind. One step to avoid the problem is to arrange for an open line of credit that you can draw against whenever you need to. For small business venturers who own their own homes, a home-equity line of credit can be an ideal way to get protection against tight money times.

Changing Neighborhoods

If your venture requires a specific kind of location, you must evaluate the possibilities of change in the various locations. Timing plays a key role in choosing a location. If you can get into a good location that's on the upswing, and you can lock in a good long-term rental rate, you have the best of both worlds. On the other hand, if a location seems cheap, be wary of the possibility that it may be a decaying area, and moving in might turn out to be a fiasco.

Some other factors to consider:

- If you depend on traffic (foot or vehicular), are any changes in traffic patterns likely to take place in the foreseeable future?
- If you're in a shopping mall and depend on a "magnet" enterprise (such as a major department store or food store), determine if the magnet is likely to remain in place. Your fortunes may be tied to the magnet, and if the magnet shuts down, you may have to do the same. On the other hand, if a weak magnet is about to be replaced by a strong one, that may offer you a very attractive opportunity.
- If your success depends on having clientele with particular demographics (age, income levels, etc.), you want to find a location that will have a stable population representing those demographics.
- You must consider competition as a factor of location. Some kinds of businesses can thrive while in the midst of competitors (a fast-food

stand in the food court of a shopping mall, for example), while others will do better being far away from competitors (a video rental store, for example). It's extremely difficult to control who might move in across the street from you, but in a shopping mall you might be able to get some exclusivity to prevent competitors from being too close.

* Nonretail businesses, such as offices, repair shops, and manufacturing and service facilities, might not be quite as sensitive to changing conditions in a location, but they cannot be overlooked. All businesses must consider the current and future situation regarding parking, loading access, customer access, noise and other pollution, security, and overall appearance of a given area.

While You Wait . . .

As you're carefully watching and waiting for all of these various personal and economic factors to fall into place at approximately the same time, you'll also have to do your homework on the following issues.

TAKING THE LEAP

Choices, choices—and you thought this was going to be easy. As part of your overall planning you must decide on the *legal status* and *start-up form* of your venture. They are two distinctly different matters, and the decisions you make can be critical to your success. Let's examine each.

STRATEGIES FOR SUCCESS

Try It on for Size

Before you embark on any self-employment venture, give it a test run. Do it before you quit your current job, so that you haven't given up anything if the test run tells you that you don't really like the business you thought you'd be so happy with. If you've always wanted to be a travel agent / landscaper / interior decorator / restaurateur / retailer / sales rep / disc jockey / financial planner / whatever. . . . Get a part-time job doing that work for someone else—weekends, perhaps, or evenings. Or do it on your vacation. Or maybe you can get a leave of absence from your current job for a month or so; try on your new career during that time. Get the feel of the rhythms and the stresses of the business. Get a sense of how the work flows, from the initial paperwork down to depositing the payment check when the job is completed. Do it for nothing if you can't get paid for it; the time alone that you invest can bring huge returns in terms of learning experience.

The Legal Status of Your Venture

There are a number of ways you can establish yourself in a business entity. You must discuss the specific legal ramifications of each option with your attorney to determine how the law applies to you, and how it affects your rights. By way of overview, these are the main options, starting with the simplest and working our way up to the most complicated.

Temping

Being a temp, or in a newer format, a leased employee, is perhaps the simplest way to be relatively on your own. A temp may work at a number of different places over the course of time; a leased employee may stay on one job for a lengthy period. In either case you may still be considered an employee in the strict sense of the word. The temp agency or the employee-leasing company pays you and takes the necessary deductions from your check. Temps are less likely to have such benefits as health insurance or a pension plan; leased employees might be better able to negotiate those fringes. Workers' Compensation should be in place to protect you if your are hurt in the line of work. You must also inquire as to what unemployment benefits might exist.

It's essential that you determine the reputation of any placement agency. If the agency fails to pay promptly or to send the payroll deductions to the government, you could be in for some major headaches. Temping might be a good bridge between full employment and full self-employment for many would-be entrepreneurs who want to make their big move one small step at a time.

Independent Contractor

Independent contractors are people who provide services to an individual or business on a direct one-on-one basis. The users pay the contractors directly, and the contractors are responsible for their own payroll taxes, Workers' Compensation, fringe benefits, and public liability insurance.

Many corporations use independent contractors for a wide variety of services: engineering, accounting, sales, marketing consultancy, and so on. For the user corporations there are many advantages, most notably not having to pay for fringe benefits or Social Security taxes, not having to deduct withholding taxes, and not having to provide pensions, Workers' Compensation, or unemployment insurance. Not having to administer all of these matters can save user corporations large sums of money.

For the independent contractors there is a sense of freedom and a chance to move ahead in accordance with one's own potentials, as opposed to being limited by a corporate hierarchy.

It would appear to be a win–win situation, but it's not that simple. The

Exercise 21.2

Internal Revenue Service has something to say about who qualifies as an independent contractor for tax purposes. In the IRS view true independent contractors are those who provide services for a variety of clients, who set their own work schedules, and who use their own tools of trade. The IRS takes a tough position on allowing users to avoid paying withholding taxes by claiming that some workers are independent contractors. If a claimed independent contractor does not meet *all* of the IRS standards, the IRS will disallow the user's claims. That can put the independent contractors back into employee status, whether they like it or not.

It's therefore incumbent on you to determine if your claim to be an independent contractor will jibe with IRS requirements. If not, you're not as free as you'd want to be.

As an independent contractor you'll have to pay your income taxes on a quarterly basis—see IRS form 1040ES and the equivalent state form. You'll report your income from work on Schedule C of the 1040. As a self-employed person, you'll be eligible for the attractive retirement benefits of Keogh, or HR-10, plans.

Sole Proprietorship

For manufacturers and retailers the simplest form of doing business is as a sole proprietor.

You may choose to do business just in your own name or under a business name. The latter will require you to meet local legal requirements for doing business under an assumed name, known more commonly as "getting a D.B.A." (doing business as . . .). This usually requires advertising your assumed name in a local newspaper and paying the proper fees. Get details from your local city clerk's office. Any other local business license fees will also have to be paid.

As a sole proprietor you are personally liable for any harm you cause to anyone in the course of doing business. Depending on the amount of risk you're willing to take, you might want to acquire an insurance policy to protect you. The same conditions hold true for independent contractors.

Sole proprietors are required to pay their income taxes on the quarterly estimated basis (IRS from 1040ES), and they report their income on Schedule C. Many start-up businesses lose money in the first years of operation—indeed, on a broad average it takes about 28 months for new ventures to *break even*. The IRS also keeps an eye on this, and if a business reports losses consistently over a period of a few years, they may take the position that the enterprise is not really a business, but a hobby. And as a hobby, the losses would not be deductible. This could be devastating to the new venture.

Here's an example: You claim to be in the business of buying and selling baseball cards. You claim deductions for expenses incurred in visiting sports shows, entertaining potential "customers" who you take to dinner often, plus telephone, office and equipment costs. These costs are never as much as what you earn from selling cards, so you report a loss year after year on your income tax return. Very likely the I.R.S. will deem your activity to be a hobby, not a business. In addition to disallowing your deductions, you'd have to pay back taxes, interest and possible penalties for previous years in which the same conditions prevailed.

The I.R.S. has used a "3 out of 5" rule to generally distinguish between a business and a hobby. If you can show a profit in three years out of five, you have a better chance of being regarded as a business than as a hobby. In recent years court decisions have begun to nibble away at the "3 out of 5" rule, giving taxpayers a little more room. But there's no assurance how you'll be treated if you're audited on this subject.

The best precautions are to make sure you have all the trappings of a business: a written and updated Business Plan; copies of any advertising, public relations and any other efforts you've undertaken to show that you're an ongoing business; a well-detailed diary showing how much time you've put into the business; copies of all business licenses, DBA certificates and any other legal documents that validate your claim as an ongoing business. And by all means keep a separate bank account, along with copies of all business-related checks you've written (wages, rent, utilities, advertising, etc.).

Exercise 21.3

Self-employed persons are eligible for a particularly attractive type of do-it-yourself pension program called a Keogh, or HR-10, plan. This allows you to put a considerable amount—roughly 25 percent—of your self-employment income into a retirement plan. The amount that you put away each year is tax deductible, and the earnings are tax-deferred. This is similar to IRA plans (see chapter 18), except that a much larger amount can be put into a Keogh plan than an IRA each year.

Sole proprietors and independent contractors should discuss all tax implications with their appropriate advisors.

Partnerships

This is as much a matter of chemistry as it is of law. If you're launching your self-employment with one or more other people, you should have an agreement setting forth all of your rights and obligations, including: Who is contributing what to the venture (labor, ideas, money, property) and what is it to be worth? Who will be entitled to take out how much (money, property) at what times and under what circumstances? Who is to perform what services? Who is entitled to what if the partnership is terminated? Negotiating these issues will tell you a lot about the chemistry between you, for better or for worse. If these matters are not reduced to writing, you are in for painful arguments when questions of money arise. You can buy fill-in-the-blank partnership forms, but the better way to structure your agreement is through a lawyer.

Partnerships are required to file tax returns, but they are for informational purposes only. Partnerships file Form 1065, and individuals report their own partnership income or loss on Schedule K of the 1040. Partners are individually liable for harm to others and are subject to the same tax implications as those for sole proprietors.

Corporations

Forming a corporation can be a complex and costly matter, and the benefits of doing so might not offset the costs until your business is grossing around $200,000 to $300,000 a year.

A corporation is a legal entity in its own right. It can sue and be sued. It pays taxes. It must comply with many difficult laws and regulations. Corporations are creatures of the laws of your state. But in many ways a corporation may also be subject to federal laws; if you have a corporate pension plan, for example, you will have to file voluminous forms with the U.S. Department of Labor, plus additional tax forms with the IRS.

There are two primary reasons why businesses incorporate. The first regards personal liability. If, say, a customer is harmed by some act of the corporation, it is the corporation, and not the individuals behind it, that bears the brunt of liability. In other words, the corporation gets sued and not you. If the corporation does not have any "worth," then a suing party can collect little or nothing.

However, it is well established that individuals can't hide from personal liability behind a corporate veil. A court can "pierce the corporate veil" and hold individuals liable for acts of the corporation. This can also hold true for debts that the corporation owes: individuals will not necessarily escape liability for their corporation's debts if a court finds impropriety in the facts of the case. So, the limitations on liability that are offered by incorporating are certainly not guaranteed.

The other main reason for incorporating is to benefit from the liberal pension programs that a corporation can offer its officers and employees. These benefits can exceed what the generous Keogh plans allow, which in turn exceed what employees can get under their IRA and 401(k) plans. But take fair warning: the paperwork and the legal regulations are a nightmare, and compliance can be costly. You should not entertain forming a corporation for pension purposes unless you're certain that the corporate benefits clearly exceed the Keogh benefits you could otherwise have.

Whether you set up a regular corporation or a Sub-Chapter S Corporation, which is designed for a smaller number of persons, you will need ongoing legal and accounting assistance. Know in advance what these costs will be before you take the plunge.

THE START-UP FORM OF YOUR VENTURE

You can get underway either by starting from scratch or by buying an existing entity. Let's look at some of the complexities you'll have to deal with in evaluating your start-up choices.

Leases

Unless you're going to work at home or float around to various customers' places of business, you're going to need premises—office, store, workshop, whatever. You can rent a place or buy a place. For purposes of this discussion, let's eliminate buying as an option; until your business is on solid footing it can be unwise to tie up capital in premises.

If you're starting from scratch, either on your own or in a franchise, you'll enter into a lease from scratch. If you're taking over an existing entity, you'll take over an existing lease, assuming that the existing lease gives you that right. If it doesn't, you'll have to negotiate that matter with the landlord.

The best lease from the tenant's standpoint is one that gives you short commitments with a lot of renewal options. A one-year lease with four one-year renewal options can be preferable to a five-year lease, even if the rental cost on the options is higher than with the straight five-year plan. Why? Because the options give you *flexibility*. You're just starting out, and flexibility—to be able to move, to close down, to possibly expand—is one of the most valuable assets the budding entrepreneur can have.

Evaluate lease costs from two standpoints: *gross* and *net*. In a gross lease the landlord provides all services: utilities, janitor, maintenance, and repairs. In a net lease, the tenant is responsible for all of those costs. Your base rent will be much higher with a gross lease, but that covers all the services. If you have a choice, and you're confident that you can control your own occupancy costs efficiently, the net lease might be the better choice.

Many commercial leases have percentage clauses. These require the tenant to pay a certain percentage of their income as rent, in addition to the base rent. A percentage clause might say that the tenant is to pay 2 percent of revenues in excess of $100,000 per year. That means that for every dollar of revenue (total income) over $100,000, the tenant will have to pay an extra two cents in rent. So if the business has $150,000 in revenue in a year, the tenant will owe an extra $1,000 in rent ($50,000 is the excess over the base amount, and 2 percent of $50,000 is $1,000).

If a landlord is flexible, any of these terms can be negotiated. And it might pay you to negotiate. Table 21–1 is a comparison of two sample percentage clauses, one calling for 2 percent of revenue in excess of $100,000, and the other calling for 3 percent of revenue in excess of $200,000.

Which is better? In low revenue years, which will presumably be the case at the outset, the 3 percent plan gives you more breathing room. In high revenue years, which will presumably come later, the 3 percent costs more. But for the new entrepreneur, it might be more important to have the extra margin that the 3 percent plan gives early on; if you're that successful later, the 3 percent plan won't hurt you.

If a landlord is willing to build out the premises for you and add the cost thereof to your lease, that can help you conserve capital you may need for other purposes. Indeed, this can be an attractive incentive: in effect, the

TABLE 21–1   **Comparing Percentage Clauses**

Annual Revenue	Extra annual rent based on	
	2% over $100,000	3% over $200,000
$200,000	$ 2,000	–0–
300,000	4,000	$ 3,000
400,000	6,000	6,000
500,000	8,000	9,000
600,000	10,000	12,000
700,000	12,000	15,000

landlord is helping finance the start of your business. And the landlord can get some attractive tax breaks in the process.

When you do negotiate a lease—and remember that all leases are negotiable—get as many options as you can: options to renew, options to enlarge or decrease the size of the premises, and an option to sublease all or part thereof. Options may cost you some extra money, but they provide that all-important flexibility that you need in starting out.

Review the section on income-producing real estate in chapter 16 for more details on seeking a location for your business. As a tenant you'll have many of the same concerns as the landlord regarding building condition, location, lease terms, and so on.

Purchase Contracts

If you are buying an existing business you will enter into a purchase contract with the seller. Before you do, scrutinize all of the seller's income and expense records and be sure that they are all correct. It might be wise to compare those records with the business's tax returns for the past two to three years. A professional audit can also be helpful.

You will need to determine the wisdom of having the seller remain involved with the business after you take over. Will the seller's continuing presence help you or hinder you with respect to retaining the confidence of customers, suppliers, lenders, and regulators? Determine, too, if you want a noncompete clause in your contract. This would prohibit the seller from starting a competing business within an agreed time and place. Any agreements relating to the seller staying on or noncompeting must be in writing.

Terms of payment are critically important. Just as your landlord can help finance your start-up by adding the cost of improvements to your rent, so too can the seller help you by agreeing to a small down payment and stretching out the balance due over a long period of time. Points to negotiate are the rate of interest you pay on the balance due and any share of profits you agree to pay in return for the stretched-out payment schedule.

You should have a lawyer represent you in any such dealings, particularly for a franchise contract.

Franchise Contracts

Exercise 21.4

You must be *extremely* careful to ascertain the difference between the hype that the franchise salesperson presents and the realities that the franchise contract sets forth. See the earlier discussion on "Inflated Expectations": that problem is often caused by the sales pitch for franchises.

Franchise contracts are complex and unyielding. It would be sheer folly to enter into a franchise agreement without having a lawyer assist you. Franchise contracts will dictate exactly how you must run your business and how much you must pay the franchisor. These contracts can run for up to 20 years, and you may not be able to bow out, or move your location, without heavy penalty. Even your right to sell your interest may be restricted by the franchisor's right to approve any successor. There may be little in a franchise contract that your lawyer can actually negotiate for you, but at least your lawyer can make you aware of all the implications more clearly than the small print in the contract will.

While proven franchises can offer good hope for success, you must surrender a lot of freedom to the franchisor, and you may have to work harder than the salesperson indicated to achieve satisfaction.

Keeping these legal issues in the back of your mind, let's now look at the basic start-up forms, beginning with the one with the fewest unknowns and proceeding to the one with the most unknowns. Only you know how much unknown you want to face as you enter self-employment. It will indeed be a time of uncertainties. Everyone must seek his or her own comfort level. I hope this material can guide you accordingly.

Buying an Existing Franchise Operation

You have the track record of the franchise company and the track record of the local operator available to you. If you scrutinize those carefully—preferably with the help of an accountant—you can reduce unknowns to the lowest possible level. This doesn't mean that there aren't risks entailed. There are, but the risks will be more clearly defined. This arrangement might be more costly than the others, but your chances of getting the income you seek and the return on your investment are based more on experience than on guesstimates. Do additional research in trade magazines in the franchise industry and at the Small Business Administration.

Buying an Existing Business (Nonfranchise)

If the business has a long history and well-kept books, this start-up might have very close to the same low number of unknowns as the previous form. The difference would be that the back-up from the franchise company would continue if you were buying into an existing franchise operation, whereas when you buy an independent business there is no such back-up. (The back-up can consist of advertising support, consulting capabilities, and the continuing association with a known "brand name.")

The shorter the history of an existing business, and the less clear its books, the more unknowns you have to conjure with. Given a choice between a long-established and well-documented business and a fairly new entity, those seeking a lesser risk level might prefer the former. In either case you must determine the reason that the business is being sold, and verify that there are no demons hiding in the woodwork who will pop out to harass you.

Buying an existing independent business allows you more freedom and flexibility than you'd have with the franchise. But to many a newcomer, freedom to expand and change means moving into unknown areas. The trade-offs must be carefully evaluated.

Starting from Scratch with a Franchise

You know up front what the franchisor will provide for you, and what the franchisor will expect from you. But there are still a lot of unknowns in the franchise formula. If you're a victim of inflated expectations after hearing the franchise sales pitch, the biggest unknown of all might be, "Why in the devil am I not making the kind of money they said I would make, and why am I having to work so hard to make what I am making?"

Your best protection, *before* you take the plunge, is to interview as many other franchisees of the same company as you can. Don't rely just on the referrals that the franchisor gives you; they're not likely to give you names of any franchisees who will badmouth the company. Seek out all the franchisees within reach, *including* those who have given up the franchise. If possible, examine their books; better still, have your accountant do so. Ask them about their experiences with the franchisor, including the ease or difficulty of communicating with responsible parties; the quickness and fairness with which they deal with problems and disputes; and the promptness with which they respond to calls for assistance. Follow these same steps if you're buying an existing franchise operation.

Before you get in bed with *any* franchisor, whether existing or new, check out their credit standing and overall financial strength. If the company is publicly traded on a stock exchange you can research them through the Standard and Poor's publications at your library. Stockbrokers, bankers, and Better Business Bureaus can also provide information. If a franchisor is not publicly traded, it would be highly advisable to have your accountant and/or banker check them out for you. The franchise industry has had its share of winners, and perhaps more than its share of losers. Buyer beware.

Starting from Scratch Independently

Here almost everything is unknown. And almost everything is possible.

This is the arena for those whose adrenalin pumps fastest at the thought of striving for fullest potential.

It's also the arena wherein one faces the highest risks, and wherein one might find the greatest rewards.

Before you take the plunge, talk to as many people as you can who have done anything remotely like what you're planning on doing. Evaluate their experiences carefully, taking into account their backgrounds, personalities, education, and skills. Reflect discerningly on the failures and successes of others: some might have failed because they went about it all wrong, and others might have succeeded because of a lot of dumb luck.

Take full advantage of what the SBA can do for you. Scour your local library for any books and articles that may be of value: reference librarians can be amazingly helpful. And seek the counsel of your F.A.I.L.-Safe Team of advisors, which will be discussed later.

Some Special Considerations for Professionals

There has been no intention in this chapter to slight the concerns of professionals: lawyers, doctors, dentists, accountants, engineers, architects, financial planners, insurance specialists, therapists, and all others with advanced learning in their chosen careers.

In many respects these professionals have the same interests as the retailers, wholesalers, distributors, manufacturers, artisans, and personal service providers who seek independence. All must look for locations, negotiate leases, prepare Business Plans, develop ways to market their skills, and learn how to work with or manage others.

In other respects the professionals may have certain advantages over the others, arising from the skills and licenses they have obtained as a result of their higher education. Those attributes—the skills and licenses—may be more portable, and thus more valuable, than those of the nonprofessionals. That, in turn, might allow the professional greater liberty in choosing associations. Indeed, they may be wooed by existing groups to join in an already successful practice. The professional might be able to negotiate a considerable amount of independence, while at the same time enjoying the benefits of the practice's clientele and credentials.

Many new professionals are eager to start off on their own. Before they do, they should evaluate the benefits of first associating themselves with a compatible established group. An early association with an existing practice can enable professionals to develop clientele without taking on undue financial risks of overhead. It can help the professional learn the customs, traditions, politics, and taboos of the community and of the local professional society while sheltered under a wing of "the establishment." It can help assure a flow of dependable income during a time when heavy educational debts must be repaid. And it can provide a trial-and-error period during which each individual professional can determine whether a group practice or a solo practice is the better way to go. Perhaps a better time for a professional to go off alone would be after an experiment as just outlined.

WHERE WILL THE MONEY COME FROM?

Probably the most common reason start-up businesses fail—despite all other excuses and rationalizations—is a shortage of capital. This can take a number of forms:

- There wasn't enough there to begin with, either in hand or available from pledged sources. The most visible flaws in planning are that income did not materialize as hoped, or expenses exceeded what was expected.
- There was enough there to begin with, but it was improperly allocated. This involves overspending on some things at the expense of others. For example: too much was spent on rent, and there wasn't enough left to properly advertise. So no customers ever showed up. Or, the restaurateur took out too much in salary, which didn't leave enough to pay the provisioners the cash they wanted, so there was no food to serve to the customers.
- There was enough to begin with, and it was properly spent, but when the business reached a point that it needed a major new capital infusion there was none available at an affordable price because advance plans had not been made for such a contingency.
- The right amount of money was planned, but too much of it was borrowed. When interest rates went up or when lenders declined to renew the loans there was big trouble.

These are not just problems of start-up businesses. They can plague any venture at any time. Planning for capital needs, for the present and for the future, is most important for any entrepreneur. Your Business Plan must deal with this issue. You can get help in projecting your needs from your banker and your accountant. The SBA may have services available to give you further aid. At the outset, this process may seem an overpowering challenge, but as you gain experience it becomes more manageable. You should explore all these possible sources of capital.

Personal Savings

The farther in advance you can plan, the bigger nest egg you can build as the initial stake for your venture. It's best to have a separate fund for your business, rather than tapping into general funds that might otherwise be used for family rainy days, education, or retirement. If you do tap into those other funds, you should make provision to replace them, so that you can be ready to meet those expenses when the time comes.

Family and Friends

They can be of help in a number of ways:

- They might give you money out of the goodness of their hearts.
- They might lend you money, possibly on more favorable terms than you'd get from a bank.
- They might invest in your enterprise, taking their chances that you'll generate profits for them, but willing to risk a failure.
- They might co-sign or provide collateral for you to enable you to borrow more expeditiously from a bank.
- They might network for you, helping you find other possible investors or lenders.

If you do involve friends or family as financial partners in your enterprise, remember these immutable rules:

1. Friends and family who provide financial support usually think that they have the right to give you advice. Take it in the right spirit, being aware of their own agendas in giving you the advice. Be wary that some may be resentful if you don't follow their advice.
2. Nothing can come between friends or relatives more swiftly or more harshly than a dispute over money. Any dealings that you do have with friends or relatives should be handled in the most businesslike way. Put it all into writing so as to minimize misunderstandings.

Lenders

At the earliest possible time start building up a rapport and a line of credit with a local bank. Better still, do it with two local banks in case one changes policy against you. Seek out a lender who will give you guidance on developing a plan for your capital needs. Novice entrepreneurs often find bank borrowing difficult without the help of a co-signer or without some collateral. Don't be offended if you're asked to provide either. In due time, given good payment performance, those supports will no longer be needed. Be most cautious about borrowing from nonbanking sources: interest rates and repayment terms can be harsh. And watch out for the advance fee loan scheme, which often entraps small business operators who are having a hard time finding money. You're promised a loan if you pay a big fee in advance, and then scammers disappear with your money.

"Built In" Credit

As noted earlier, some of your capital needs can be built into other aspects of your venture.

- The landlord can add the cost of certain improvements to your rent, thereby relieving you of the need to finance those items separately.
- Suppliers of equipment and inventory can provide you with payment terms that can reduce your need for some outside capital.
- If you are buying an existing business, favorable terms from the seller can help you conserve your capital.
- Banks, as well as companies known as *factors,* will lend you money with your accounts receivable as collateral. Banks can also finance your inventory acquisitions.

These arrangements will come at a price. But don't turn down any possibility without weighing it seriously.

Governmental Sources

Exercise 21.5

The Small Business Administration can arrange to guarantee loans from banks. An adjunct of the SBA, the Small Business Innovation Research program (SBIR), helps fund technological start-ups, particularly if the product is one in which the government might have an interest.

Many state governments have programs to help new ventures, particularly those that are technologically oriented or minority-owned. Of special interest are ventures that will provide jobs in the community. Your local banker can help you locate these sources.

Other Investors

Aside from friends and family, there may be local individuals who seek business opportunities, and they even advertise the fact in the local want-ads under "Money to Invest" or "Money to Loan." These local versions of "venture capitalists" have big-time counterparts who deal in million-dollar deals. If you're in that class, a local banker or stockbroker can help you find the names of likely prospects.

Many corporations would rather invest in a start-up business that's creating something useful to the corporation than set up a whole new division within their ranks. Whatever product or service you're developing, you might want to explore this route. If you do, though, be alert to the age-old warning against putting all your eggs in one basket.

Tax Breaks

Self-employed persons are entitled to a number of tax breaks (and also subject to one harsh tax cost) that can make a difference to your bottom line. On the good side, self-employed persons can put a lot of their earnings into tax-sheltered retirement plans that are much more generous than IRAs or 401(k)s. Self-employeds can claim a deduction (technically an adjustment) for a major portion of their health insurance costs. This amount is scheduled to increase considerably in the years to come. For the years 1998 through 2002, 45 percent of health insurance premiums can be deducted, for 2003 it is 50 percent, for 2004 it's 60 percent, for 2005 it's 70 percent, and for 2006 and beyond it's 80 percent. If you buy business equipment you can take a deduction for up to $17,000 worth for tax year 1997, and that amount increases to $25,000 by 2003. (The normal situation regarding business equipment is that you must spread the deduction out over a number of years; self-employeds can take it all in one helpful chunk.) You can also take a deduction for that portion of your home you use for business purposes; formerly tight regulations in this area have become more liberal in recent years.

On the bad side, self-employeds must pay self-employment tax in lieu of Social Security taxes, and you must pay an amount that almost equals what you and your employer paid combined when you were an employee. Half of this self-employment tax can be claimed as an adjustment, thus easing the blow.

All of these tax matters should be taken into account in figuring your total income and expenses for your first year of business, and then reviewed each following year.

Debt vs. Equity?

As you raise capital, you will face a question that plagues all businesses: Should you borrow or give up shares of your business in exchange for money? There is no easy answer, but there are some guidelines.

Debt and interest must be paid; that's a cost of doing business. All profits are yours to keep, but if the debt can't be repaid, or if interest costs get too high for you, there could be serious problems. Defaulting on debt can mean the loss of the business: The creditor who has wisely gotten the proper collateral can foreclose and take everything to settle the debt.

Equity—money that's been invested in your business—does *not* have to be repaid. The investors have put their money at risk by investing it with you, and they share your fortunes accordingly. You don't have to pay interest on the equity money, but you would be expected to distribute a fair share of profits to the investors in proportion to their ownership shares, and the investors might require that they have a say in how the business is run. In short, you no longer have total control, and you have to divvy up the profits. A proper investment arrangement requires written agreements, in which you can protect yourself by maintaining ultimate control—a 51 percent ownership interest, whether you're operating as a partnership, a corporation, or any other arrangement by mutual consent. But even if you retain a majority interest, that won't deter the investors from putting demands on you to help protect the money they've entrusted to you.

It's certainly possible to have a blend of debt and equity. And there are some people you might prefer to have as lenders and others as investors; this is a matter of chemistry and personality. You can also shift the balance between debt and equity from time to time. You can have an agreement with lenders in which they might agree to accept a share of ownership in exchange for the debt. You can have an agreement with investors that they will sell their share of ownership back to you on certain terms (and you might have to borrow money to accomplish this). All things are possible, provided you don't get yourself too locked in with too much debt or too much equity. Keep flexible. That's the healthy way.

STRATEGIES FOR SUCCESS

Pay Yourself Last

You're not going into business for yourself just for fun or as an experiment in living. Yes, those might be some of your reasons, but deep down, you can't deny that you want to make money at it. Well and good. You're entitled to. But the rate at which you take money out of your enterprise can bode well or poorly for your long-term success. The temptation is clear to want to pay yourself a regular salary, whether you take it out of earnings or dip into your capital funds. And you want to continue living in the style to which you've been accustomed. But beware: it's likely that something will have to give, at least in the early start-up period. By paying yourself first you may be depriving the enterprise of badly needed capital. Unless you're willing to endure some personal sacrifice, you may starve the enterprise prematurely. Consider paying yourself last—after all other expenses have been met. In doing so you'll see a much more honest picture of the business's potential; and you'll be motivated to work that much harder to meet your own goals.

NIT-PICKED TO DEATH BY REGULATIONS?

Regulations are the bane of many a small business's existence. When you're someone else's employee, some hidden office full of paper-pushers takes care of complying with all the regulations. When you're your own boss, you've got to do it yourself, or else pay for others to do it for you.

The cost of regulatory compliance, and the cost of *failing* to comply, are matters that cannot be overlooked by any entrepreneur. Many of these regulations have been referred to in chapter 2, in the context of your rights as an employee. Review those workplace regulations with the tables turned: you as an employer have to deal with them, like it or not, in correct and timely fashion. It's not a pretty picture, and those are just the *workplace* regulations.

In summary, here are the major areas of regulatory chokehold. When you're an employee you look upon these as rules meant to protect you. As an employer you'll likely look upon them as rules meant to destroy you. It's interesting how the perspective changes.

Employment Regulations

The going gets tough as soon as you have one single employee. If you can hire your needed help as independent contractors or temps (see the discussion earlier in this chapter) you might be able to save yourself a lot of administrative costs. Here's a rundown of the federal, state, and local paperwork you may have to wrestle with regarding employment.

Tax Matters

- W-2 and W-4 forms for employees (and 1099s for independent contractors)
- 1040ES (quarterly estimated returns for yourself)
- Payroll deduction bookkeeping and remittance to proper governmental agencies
- IRS bookkeeping and compliance regarding any pension program you provide for yourself or for your employees

IRS Publication 334, *Tax Guide for Small Business,* can help you deal with these forms and regulations.

Employee Well-being

- Health and safety provisions, including the Occupational Health and Safety Act (OSHA), the Family Leave Act (if you have more than 50 employees), the Americans with Disabilities Act, and workers' compensation

- Unemployment insurance
- Right to work laws: Federal Fair Labor Standards Act, Age Discrimination Act, Fair Employment Practices Law, age and hour laws, plant closing laws, union and labor relations laws
- Health insurance plans, and the cost of providing same, could become a paperwork and financial nightmare

Financial Regulations

Credit Matters

If you don't extend credit to customers, you might sail easily through these waters. But if you do extend credit you may have a raft of concerns. (See the section, "Laws That Govern Financial Institutions and Their Transactions" in chapter 11.) Although the main thrust of these regulations are geared toward banks, they apply to a wide array of small businesses that take customers' IOUs in payment, particularly if the business is charging interest or taking a security interest in the buyer's property. Unless there's some compelling reasons to the contrary, it would seem more efficient for the small business to allow customers to pay by credit card, which can allow a bypass of these regulatory requirements.

Retirement Plans

There is no law that requires an employer to provide pension plans. But if you do offer a pension plan you must comply with governmental regulations, and they can be awesome. Pension plans require compliance with regulations of the Employees Retirement Income Security Act (ERISA) and the Pension Benefit Guarantee Corporation (PBGC). Regular reports have to be made to the IRS and the U.S. Department of Labor.

A much simpler way to proceed, at least until your business is a proven success, is to offer employees a Simplified Employee Pension, or SEP, plan. (See chapter 18 for details.)

Miscellaneous Regulations

On a state and local level, you must comply with regulations regarding:

- Doing business under an assumed name (it's likely that a bank won't open an account for you under your assumed name unless you've complied with local laws on the subject)
- Licensing of your business, if any is required
- Zoning requirements (this might also apply to you if you're doing business in your home)

- Building and safety codes
- Taxes that your business may be subject to
- Sign and advertising restrictions as set by local ordinance
- Pollution controls (federal as well as state and local)

You can't ignore regulations. And they never diminish. Set your mind to those realities at the outset, and you might find them easier to tolerate.

WHERE TO GET HELP: THE F.A.I.L.-SAFE TEAM AND THE M & Ms

Working for yourself is not a day at the beach. But there are people who can help make it more pleasant and productive; indeed, wise use of these helpers can spell the difference between success and failure in your venture.

The F.A.I.L.-Safe Team

This team is composed of professional advisors: Financial, Accounting, Insurance, and Legal. Some may cost a lot of money. Some cost none. But the issue of cost should not deter you from seeking counsel. Without the right counsel the cost consequences could be far worse.

Financial

A cooperative and knowledgeable banker and a friend at the nearest SBA office can be invaluable allies. They can help you determine your credit needs and your credit capacity (see chapter 12). They can help you develop a Business Plan. They can help you project your overall capital needs. And, if all the circumstances are right, they can arrange loans for you. The advice is generally free. The loans cost money.

Accounting

Services can cover bookkeeping, tax preparation, auditing, and documentation (helping you put together your financial statements, profit and loss statements, and Business Plan). An accountant can also evaluate the financial status of anyone with whom you might be doing important business, such as a franchisor, a potential major customer, or a would-be partner.

Insurance

You'll need a knowledgeable agent to help you with a variety of business insurance needs: rental interruption, public liability, casualty coverage for premises and contents, malpractice (if applicable to your work), and appropriate health and disability protection. A good life insurance agent should be consulted with respect to "key person" insurance, which pays off on the death of a person who is essential to the business. It can be wise coverage, particularly if you've invested a lot of your net worth in your business. The insurance proceeds can be used to continue the business or provide for the family of the deceased entrepreneur. As with the banker, the advice is free, the policies cost money.

Legal

Most of the general legal issues you'll encounter have already been discussed: leases, contracts, regulations. You may also benefit from a lawyer's skills in negotiating employment arrangements and contracts for services; for protecting your "intellectual rights" (patents, copyrights, trademarks, etc.); and for being on the alert as to how your rights are being violated so that prompt action can be taken. Not all lawyers are familiar with the business world, however. It's an area of specialized skills, and you'd be wise to seek out one properly equipped to handle your specific needs. Your local Bar Association Referral Service can help you.

The M & Ms

You may be the world's best at what you do, and you have every confidence that working for yourself will be a roaring success. But you may not know enough about marketing and management to fill a thimble, and without those skills you might never find and keep a paying audience.

Marketing and management consultants can play a critical role in your venture. The marketing people can help you design, package, advertise, price, and deliver your goods and services in the most cost-effective way. The management people can help you structure your own operation and can help you best understand the operational structures of the businesses you're trying to sell to.

Seek and You'll Find

In looking for help in these areas, seek referrals from friends and family. Ask past and current customers/clients for reviews of their experiences with any of your prospective helpers. Before you hire any, interview them and get a sense of the chemistry that will be generated between you. And don't be embarrassed to ask any or all of them if they would accept a share of ownership in your venture in lieu of cash payment. Some might, and it might be worthwhile for you to pursue that course.

It's Your Move

No, you're not ready yet to go off on your own. But once you've absorbed all of the information and guidelines in this chapter you're well prepared to start doing the right specific homework that can turn your dream into a reality. Do all that homework as if your life depended on it—in a sense, it does, so take your time. Despite the anxiety to get on with your new career, the worst threat to your success is jumping in before you're *totally prepared*—in terms of capital, skills, energy, and emotions. Be patient. You've waited this long; another few weeks or months for study and preparation can't hurt you. Do it right the first time. If you don't, you may never have the will to try it again.

PERSONAL ACTION WORKSHEET

Set Goals. If You Can't Achieve Them, Let Go.

Do try your best at your new venture. Give it your all. But be ready to let go gracefully if it's not working out. Set realistic goals and strive to achieve them: "Based on my anticipated expenses, I must raise, and/or earn, X dollars within Y months. If I can, I'm on my way. But if I fall short within that time frame, it's time to bow out and say proudly, 'At least I gave it my best shot.'" Don't prolong agony needlessly. The pain of staying in may be worse than the pain of getting out.

Here are some blanks for you to fill in, to help you *start* shaping cashflow goals. One set is for pre-starting expenses; the other is for ongoing expenses. Basic expenses are much more predictable than income. Match the totals with your estimated available capital from all sources, including income. Do best-case and worst-case projections for both income and expenses and design your time frame targets accordingly.

Pre-starting Expenses		Ongoing Expenses	
Legal fees	$ _____	Legal fees	$ _____
Accounting	_____	Accounting	_____
Deposit for rent	_____	Rent	_____
Stationary, supplies	_____	Stationary, supplies	_____
Down payments for equipment	_____	Equipment payments	_____
Licenses	_____	Wages to others	_____
Permits	_____	Payroll taxes	_____
Consultants	_____	Consultants	_____
Advertising	_____	Advertising	_____
Research	_____	Utilities	_____
Initial inventory	_____	Telephone, fax	_____
Fixtures, furniture	_____	Property insurance	_____
Decor	_____	Liability insurance	_____
Other	_____	Personal insurance	_____
Transition costs	_____	Transportation	_____
All personal expenses—food, housing, insurance, etc.—incurred from when you give up your paying job until you can derive a comparable income from your new venture		Postage, delivery	_____
		Payments on debt	_____
		Maintenance, repairs	_____
		Ongoing inventory	_____
		Security	_____
		Other	_____
TOTALS	_____		_____

CONSUMER ALERT ————————————————————————

Snake Oil Sam Strikes Again

Small businesses are terribly susceptible to the wiles of Snake Oil Sam and his army of con artists. That's because of the high level of anxiety that often accompanies self-employment. Here's a brief sampling of some of the more common schemes.

- **Telemarketing**   You receive a call from a so-called office supply distributor offering fantastic deals. You pay, but the goods are never delivered or they are of shoddy quality. And when you try to get restitution, their phone number is no longer in service. Beware, also, of phony investments sold by phone—very slick.

- **Phony invoices**   A favorite is for "renewal" of nonexistent telephone directory advertising. A tight system of cross-checking orders with bills is essential to avoid such scams.

- **Advance fee loan schemes**   See chapter 4.

- **Business investment offerings**   These are rampant in a variety of magazines and tabloid newspapers. If the business ventures being offered were so profitable, why would they be offering you the opportunity? It must be that they will make more money by selling you their "secrets of success" than you will make by trying to put those secrets to work. Simple and compelling logic; be guided accordingly.

- **Bankruptcy scams**   These really hurt. A customer who owes you a lot of money threatens to declare bankruptcy unless you accept, say, 25 cents on the dollar in full payment. Some will actually manipulate the bankruptcy laws to turn a profit and leave you holding the bag. Beware of customers who beg to have a high credit balance and those who show only a post office box for an address and have just an answering machine to take their phone calls.

- **Phony insurance swindles**   Small employers, fearful of the cost of providing health insurance for employees, fall prey to too-good-to-be-true offers of group health plans from con artists. Premiums are paid and the scammers split with the money.

Be extremely cautious when dealing with strangers. Check with the Better Business Bureau for more help on how to protect yourself.

UPS & DOWNS *The Economics of Everyday Life*

Why Do the Fortunes of Small Businesses Go Up and Down?

The fortunes of all small businesses are tied to the ups and downs of many other entities and forces. Aside from the general status of the economy (national and regional), here are some of the specific influences that will increase or decrease your bank account and your peace of mind.

- Your suppliers may raise or lower the prices they charge you. If the former, you can shop for new suppliers. If the latter, be careful that the level of service doesn't drop along with the price.

- Your competition may increase or decrease. If the former, you have to work harder and/or lower your prices to stay afloat. If the latter, don't let yourself get complacent. Don't compromise on your quality or integrity.

- Your capital sources may tighten or expand. If the former, be ready with a fall-back position that will allow you access to funds as you need them. If the latter, determine if now is a good time to acquire more capital, either from lenders or investors, and how can you best put such capital to productive use. It's sometimes wise to get extra capital when the getting is good and invest it safely until you need it for business purposes.

- Your personal energies may ebb and flow, and the dynamics of the business will ebb and flow accordingly. If you're exhausted and in a low funk it may be that you've spread yourself too thin. It may pay to hire someone to help you; the cost of doing so can be justified if it gets your energy back up, which will get your cash flow back up. If you're on a high, on a roll, enjoy it. But be careful of the workaholic syndrome. Make sure you allow yourself enough time to enjoy spending the money you're earning.

?

WHAT IF . . . ?

Test yourself: How would you deal with these real-life possibilities?

1. You are about to embark on your life's dream: opening a shop to make and sell farnolas. You seek advice from various friends. The first is very enthusiastic; he owns a small shopping center with a vacancy in it that you could rent. The second is thrilled for you; she sells the raw materials from which farnolas are made. The third is exuberant; he owns an advertising agency. What are the pluses and minuses of what your friends can offer you?

2. Still another friend knows a famous farnola designer. It's suggested that you and the designer team up and become partners in the venture. The idea has merit, but the designer is a total stranger. What specifically must you learn about the designer in order to make a sound judgment?

3. Your banker agrees to lend you the $25,000 you need to start your venture, but you must provide a satisfactory co-signer or collateral. Who can you call on to help? For real now, not pretend.

NUMBER CRUNCHERS

Do the calculations to make decisions in these real-life possibilities.

1. Your business has earned $70,000 in the year, after all expenses except interest.
   (a) Suppose you had borrowed $100,000 to start the business, paying an interest rate of 8 percent per year. How would this affect your bottom line?
   (b) Suppose that instead of borrowing, friend Pat had invested $100,000, for which you promised to pay 10 percent of your earnings. How would this affect your bottom line?
   (c) Suppose that you had borrowed $50,000 at 8 percent interest, and Pat had invested $50,000, to earn 5 percent of your earnings. How would this affect your bottom line?
   Compare all three scenarios. Calculate others that may be closer to your own real situation.

2. The landlord of the space you want to rent offers you either (a) a 10-year lease at $1,800 a month with no renewals; or (b) a five-year lease at $2,000 a month with an option to renew for five more years at $2,200 a month; or (c) a one-year lease, followed by nine one-year renewal options, the rental to be 20 percent of your gross sales, not to exceed $30,000 in a year. Your business plan estimates that your gross sales will be $125,000 in the first year and $150,000 in the second year. Compare and evaluate the deals.

FOR BETTER OR FOR WORSE

Things beyond our control often impact our personal and financial well-being, for better or for worse. Some are more predictable than others. How would you be affected if the following real-life phenomena happened? Could you have seen it coming? What steps could you have taken to minimize damage or maximize advantage? The better able you are to anticipate and recognize these forces, the better equipped you are to deal with them.

1. To become your own boss you buy Kline's Clothing Store, a small local shop that has had a successful track record for decades. Once you've taken over, the customers stay away in droves. One of them explains to you that customer loyalty was due to Mr. Kline and his sons' delightful personality. And you're not Mr. Kline, nor will you ever be.

2. You do the selling and your partner handles the books. You don't know numbers, and she can't sell worth a darn. It's a good mix, until one day you discover that your partner has embezzled $50,000 from the business.

3. You run a mom-and-pop restaurant in a suburban area outside a big city. The city annexes the suburb, and you must spend an unavailable $25,000 to bring the restaurant up to the city's safety and health code standards.

Glossary

Numbers in parentheses indicate chapter reference. Words are defined in the context in which they are used in the text. Italicized words within the definitions are separately defined within the glossary.

Acquisition fees (7) Expenses that a borrower will have to pay in obtaining a home financing loan. Generally payable to the lender, these expenses can include legal fees, appraisal fees, and *"points."*

Add-on interest (12) One method of calculating *interest* costs in an *installment loan*. Example: If one borrows $1,000 for one year at 10 percent add-on interest, the interest cost—$100—is "added on" to the amount borrowed, making the total debt $1,100. Dividing $1,100 by 12 results in monthly payments of $91.67.

Adjustments (6) In a real-estate transaction, the prorating between buyer and seller of any prepaid expenses (such as property taxes) that the seller has incurred prior to the *closing*.

Adjustments to income (20) In the calculation of one's income taxes, a main category of expenses that can be used to reduce the amount of income subject to taxation.

Administrator (19) A court-appointed person responsible for handling the *estate* of a person who died without a *will*.

Advance fee loan scheme (4) A scam in which a would-be borrower of money is convinced to pay a large fee in advance in order to secure a loan. The loan never materializes and the money paid in advance is lost.

Age Discrimination in Employment Act (2) A federal law that protects workers between the ages of 40 and 65 with respect to hiring and firing problems because of their age.

Amended tax return (20) A tax return that may be filed after the original return was filed to correct errors in the original return.

Annual Percentage Rate (APR) (12) The interest rate that the federal government requires be disclosed to borrowers in most installment loan transactions. The APR is designed to offer an accurate comparison of interest costs on different loan offerings.

Annual Percentage Yield (APY) (11) Determines the amount of money you will earn in one year if you invest your money at the stated percentage. Example: An APY of 6 percent means that an investment of $1,000 will earn $60 in one year. Under the 1993 Truth in Savings law, all banks and other covered institutions must use this standard method of quoting rates they pay.

Annuity (17) A type of investment with an insurance company that guarantees the investor a fixed monthly income for a specific period of time.

Assessment (8) A percentage of the market value of a parcel of real estate, used to establish the property taxes on that parcel.

Assets (2) The total value of everything you own, plus everything owed to you.

Assumable mortgage (7) A *mortgage* that allows future creditworthy buyers of the property to take over responsibility of paying the existing loan.

Attestation clause (19) A clause in a *will* in which the witnesses to the will confirm that they have performed their duties in accordance with the law.

Audit (20) The procedure in which the Internal Revenue Service examines in detail one's income tax return.

Bait and switch (4) An illegal selling scheme in which a seller offers a product at an unreasonably low price (the "bait"). A would-be buyer, lured by the bait, is then "switched" to a higher-priced item.

Balloon clause (7) A provision in a loan agreement (mortgage or installment) that allows the lender to demand full payment of the loan at a set time.

Banker's acceptance (14) A form of investment that arises when a bank holds a foreign company's promissory note (IOU) and sells portions of that note to investors.

Bankruptcy proceedings (12) Federal court proceedings in which the debts of individuals or companies can be wiped out or in which the court may instruct creditors to hold off in their attempts to collect debts due them from the bankrupt person or company.

Beneficiary (17, 19) One designated to receive an inheritance from the *estate* of a *decedent*; also, one who receives the proceeds of a *life insurance* policy on the death of the insured person.

Benefits (17) Money received from an insurance company when the insured party suffers a loss covered by the insurance policy.

Bequest (19) The specific property or money given to a *beneficiary* from the *estate* of a *decedent*.

Blue-chip stock (15) *Stock* of a company considered to have high investment quality: relatively stable prices and strong dividend payment history.

Bond (14) A long-term debt instrument.

Bumping (3) If you are denied a seat on an airplane, and you had had a confirmed reservation, the airline is "bumping" you and must pay you a certain penalty fee.

Buying down (7) A type of "creative" home financing plan whereby the seller pays part of the interest charges for the buyer for a specified period of time.

Cafeteria plans (2, 17) A fringe-benefit program that allows employees to select from a variety of benefits that most closely suits their individual needs.

Call option (15) A contract that gives the owner the right to buy 100 shares of a given common *stock* at a predetermined price (the "strike price") at any time until a fixed future date.

Call privilege (14) The right of a *corporation* or other issuer of debt to pay off the holders of the debt at an agreed-on price prior to the scheduled maturity of the debt.

Cashier's check (11) A check drawn on a bank's own account.

Cash management account (11) A type of account offered by stock brokerage firms that provides a combination of checking, investing, and borrowing capabilities for its customers.

Caveat emptor (4) A Latin phrase that means "let the buyer beware." This is especially important for consumers to remember if they think they're getting something that is too good to be true.

Certificate of deposit (CD) (11, 14) A contractual investment with a financial institution wherein the investor agrees to deposit a fixed sum of money for a fixed amount of time in return for a guaranteed interest rate.

Certified check (11) An individual (or business) check that has been guaranteed by the bank on which it is drawn; that is, the funds are guaranteed to be available when the check is presented for payment.

Churning (15) An improper practice wherein a stockbroker creates excessive trading in a customer's account to generate commissions.

Civil Rights Act (2) See *Fair Employment Practices Law.*

Closed-end lease (5) In car leasing, this arrangement sets a predetermined amount at which you can buy your leased car at the end of the lease, subject to various costs and charges you may have to pay.

Closing (6) In a real estate transaction, the event at which the transfer of *deeds*, money, and promises-to-pay takes place.

Codicil (19) A document that, when properly executed, amends a *will*.

Coinsurance clause (8) A provision in most property insurance policies stating that the insured party will receive full replacement value for losses only if the premises are insured for a stated percentage (usually 80 percent) of full value.

Collision insurance (5) Coverage for the insured's auto for damages resulting from a collision with another vehicle or object.

Commercial paper (14) An instrument of short-term debt issued by a *corporation*.

Commodities (16) A variety of products (such as cattle, wheat, precious metals) whose future values are subject to fluctuation. Commodity markets offer the opportunity to speculate in those future values. (Also known as futures trading.)

Compounding of interest (14) Occurs when the *interest* you earn stays in your account and begins to earn interest itself.

Comprehensive insurance (5) Coverage for the insured's auto for damages resulting from other than collision, such as fire and theft.

Condominium (6) An owned dwelling unit that is part of a multi-unit structure.

Condominium conversion (9) The act of modifying the form of ownership of a multiple-unit building from single ownership of the entire structure to individual ownership of each specific unit within the entire structure.

Contingent beneficiary (17) One who takes the place of an original *beneficiary* (in a *will* or *insurance policy*), should the original beneficiary die before the *testator* or the insured.

Cooperative (6) A type of housing arrangement wherein each resident owns a percentage of the total building and has an agreement with all the owners for the right to use a specific unit in the building for his or her own dwelling.

Corporate bond (14) A long-term debt instrument issued by a *corporation*. Some bonds may contain a *call privilege*. Some bonds are convertible; that is, the owner has the right to convert the bond into *stock* of the same company, upon stated terms and conditions.

Corporation (14) A legal entity created under state law for the purpose of conducting a stated business. A corporation is owned by its stockholders, who in turn elect a board of directors to set the ongoing policies of the corporation. The directors, in turn, select officers to run the day-to-day affairs of the corporation.

Cosigner (12) One who jointly signs a credit agreement with the principal borrower. The cosigner must pay the debt if the borrower fails to do so.

Creative financing (7) A general term describing home financing arrangements that are privately negotiated between seller and buyer, with or without the participation of outside lenders or investors.

Credit bureau (12) A nongovernmental organization that collects and distributes credit information. Merchants and lenders use this information to make decisions on granting credit to those who apply.

Credit capacity (12) The amount of borrowing a consumer can realistically handle, considering his current and future income and expenses.

Credit health insurance (12) A form of health insurance that will pay loan payments if an insured borrower is disabled due to health or accident.

Credit history (12) The record of one's credit activity, as maintained by the local *credit bureau*.

Credit life insurance (12) A form of life insurance that will pay off any balance due on an installment loan should the borrower die before the loan is otherwise paid.

Credit Repair Clinic (4) The term used to describe a shady operation that offers to help debtors get out of trouble. They can create even worse problems by keeping the money the debtor gives them to parcel out to legitimate creditors.

Credit union (11) A type of financial institution that is owned by individuals who have a common bond, such as the employees of a company or governmental agency.

Debt counseling service (12) An agency that assists creditors who are having financial troubles.

Decedent (19) One who has died.

Decreasing term insurance (17) A type of life insurance; the amount of coverage decreases from year to year.

Deductible (5, 8) With respect to insurance, the amount that an insured must first pay out of pocket before the insurance company becomes liable; for example, if one suffers a casualty valued at $200 and has a $50 deductible for such occurrences, the insured will be responsible for the first $50, and the insurance company will then reimburse $150.

Deductions (20) Regarding income taxes, a category of expenses that are subtracted from adjusted gross income to lower the amount of income subject to taxation. Taxpayers may claim *itemized deductions* or *standard deductions*.

Deed (6) A document by which title to real estate passes from the seller to the buyer.

Deficit (1) The status of a budget (one's financial condition) when more money has been spent than has been taken in.

Disability income insurance (17) Insurance that provides some income to a worker who becomes unable to work due to injury or health problems.

Discretionary income (2, 13) Extra money available once one's basic needs have been paid for.

Discriminate income function (DIF) (20) A computerized procedure used by the IRS to select tax returns for *audit*. The computer compares various elements of a given return (income, deductions, etc.) and further compares those ratios to average levels for such claims.

Dividend (15) That portion of a company's profit that the directors vote to pay out to stockholders. Usually paid quarterly.

Double indemnity (17) A life insurance policy provision that will pay *beneficiaries* double the

face value of the policy in the event of the accidental death of the insured.

Dow Jones Industrial Average (15) The most commonly referred to index of stock prices and their movements. It reflects the prices of 30 major industrial stocks.

Down payment (12) That portion of the purchase price (of a house, a car, etc.) paid by the buyer in cash at the time of purchase.

Earnest money (6) A token payment of cash to bind a preliminary agreement between the buyer and seller of a house (or other item).

Easement (6) The right given to someone to use your land for a specific purpose (to cross over the property, to construct utility lines, etc.).

Education IRA (18) A new form of Individual Retirement Account made possible by the Taxpayer Relief Act of 1997. It allows attractive tax breaks for those who are saving money for higher education.

Eminent domain (8) A legal concept that permits a local government to acquire, or condemn, private property when a proven public need for the property exists. For example: to widen a highway, build a school. Owners of the private property must be adequately paid for their property.

Employee Retirement Income Security Act (ERISA) (18) A federal law that protects the right of employees with respect to pension and profit-sharing plans. Also known as the Pension Reform Law of 1974.

Endorsement (11) Writing one's signature on the back of a check (or other negotiable instrument), thereby acknowledging receipt of the cash or credit indicated on the check. Endorsements may be in blank (signature only), restrictive (limiting how the check may be further negotiated), or special (such as when the funds are to be paid or credited to a third party).

Equal Credit Opportunity Law (11) A federal law designed to prevent discrimination regarding sex or marital status of individuals applying for credit.

Equity (9) The difference between what your house (or other property) is currently worth, and what you owe on it.

Escrow (7, 9) (1) A third party who acts as an intermediary in a real estate transaction, seeing to it that the instructions of the parties are complied with. (2) Money paid monthly to a mortgage lender to pay property insurance premiums and property taxes as they fall due. Also referred to as a reserve account.

Estate (19) The legal entity that comes into being upon the death of a person; that is, upon John's death, the estate of John comes into being. Also refers to the net worth of the decedent; that is, John's estate is worth $100,000.

Estate taxes (19) A federal or state tax on the *estate* of a *decedent*.

Exclusion (10) An amount of income that is free of income taxes. For example: if the seller of a home is over the age of 55, he or she may be able to exclude from taxable income up to $125,000 worth of profit on the sale of the home.

Ex-dividend date (15) A date that determines whether a buyer of *stock* is entitled to a recently declared *dividend*. One who buys before the ex-dividend date receives the dividend. One who buys after the ex-dividend date does not receive the dividend.

Executor/Executrix (19) The person or institution designated by a *testator* to carry out the settlement of the testator's *estate*.

Exemptions (20) With regard to income taxes, the number of persons dependent on the taxpayer, including the taxpayer him/herself. For each proper exemption the taxpayer is allowed to reduce his income subject to taxes by a fixed amount.

Face amount (face value) (17) The amount of money that a *life insurance* policy will pay to the beneficiary on the death of the insured person.

Fair Credit Billing Law (11) A federal law that protects the rights of persons who receive erroneous bills from creditors.

Fair Credit Reporting Law (11) A federal law that gives individuals the right to view their *credit history* and the right to take steps to have errors corrected.

Fair Debt Collection Practices Law (11) A federal law that protects debtors from unfair, deceptive, and abusive debt collection practices.

Fair Employment Practices Law (2) A federal law designed to prevent job discrimination because of an individual's race, sex, religion, or national origin. Also known as the Civil Rights Act of 1964.

Federal Deposit Insurance Corporation (FDIC) (11, 14) The federal agency that insures accounts in commercial banks and mutual savings banks against the failure of the institutions.

Federal Fair Labor Standards Law (2) A federal law that protects certain minors with respect to jobs that could be hazardous or detrimental to their well-being.

Federal Occupational Safety and Health Act (OSHA) (2) A federal law that sets health and safety standards for working environments.

Filing extension (20) Available to taxpayers who file the proper form, an added time to file their tax return.

Filing status (20) One of five categories chosen by taxpayers as a part of completing their returns; the choice of category, which is broadly based on taxpayer's marital situation, affects the amount of tax payable.

Fill or kill order (15) An order given to a stockbroker to buy or sell stocks at a specific price, with the understanding that if the order can't be filled immediately at the given price, then the order will terminate.

Financing contingency clause (6) A provision in a contract for the purchase of real estate that allows buyers to be released from their obligations if they are not able to obtain financing at a certain rate of interest by an agreed-on date.

Fiscal policy (1) The policy that determines how a government will raise money, and for what purposes it will spend it.

Flexible spending plans (2, 17) A fringe benefit program that allows employees to set aside part of their earnings on a tax-sheltered basis, provided that the money set aside is used for certain designated purposes, such as dependent care or unreimbursed medical expenses.

Floating rate bond (14) A *bond* in which the interest rate payable to holders fluctuates up and down, usually within set limits and/or in accordance with some outside index.

Foreclosure (7)   The procedure by which a lender can obtain title to property that has been pledged as security for a loan when the borrower has defaulted on that loan.

Foreign exchange (16)   Generally, the currency of other nations. The future values of the currencies of major nations can be bought and sold at commodity exchanges.

Form 1040 (1040A) (20)   The basic forms used to file one's federal income taxes. Taxpayers who wish to claim certain *adjustments, tax credits,* and *itemized deductions* use the 1040 (long form). Taxpayers who do not wish to claim these items use the 1040A (short form).

401(k) plans (2, 18)   A retirement savings plan set up by employers, in which employees can invest a portion of their wages on a tax-sheltered basis. Employers might also contribute to these plans for the benefit of their employees.

Fringe benefit (2)   A form of payment to a worker, other than current money. Examples include insurance protection, pension plans, and profit-sharing plans.

Funding (18)   The placing of money in a pension plan by an employer. Proper funding requires that enough money be placed in the fund to meet future promises to pay benefits to covered employees.

Garnishment (2)   A legal procedure by which a creditor can get access to a debtor's wages to satisfy a debt due the creditor.

General obligation bond (14)   A type of *municipal bond* backed by the taxing authority of the municipality.

Generic products (3)   Grocery, pharmaceutical, and other items with "plain" or nonbrand labels.

Glamour stock (15)   *Stock* of a company that the investment community perceives as "hot," as a "winner." Compared to blue-chip stocks, glamour stocks are relatively less stable in their prices and dividend payment records.

Graduated payment plan (7)   A home financing plan that permits the borrower to make lower than usual payments in the first few years, with payments then increasing in the later years.

Gross lease (16)   A commercial lease that requires the landlord to pay for virtually all expenses relating to the property.

Group insurance (2)   One of many kinds of insurance plans (usually life and health) offered to members of a group, such as company employees or members of a fraternal organization. Because many individuals are covered under a single master policy, the cost to each insured is less than the same insurance would be if purchased individually.

Group venture (16)   The pooling of money among several investors to purchase real estate (or other investments).

Health insurance portability (17)   This federal law gives employees the right to retain health insurance when they change jobs.

Health maintenance organization (HMO) (17)   A prepaid medical care facility.

Hedge value (13)   Generally, the ability of an investment to withstand the effects of inflation.

Heir (19)   One who receives an interest in the *estate* of a *decedent.*

Highball (5)   A selling technique whereby the salesperson attempts to convince you that your property (trade-in car, house) is worth much more than you thought it was, to lure you into doing business with him.

Holographic will (19)   A *will* prepared in the handwriting of the *testator;* not always valid.

Homeowner's insurance (8)   A form of *insurance policy* that will reimburse the owner of a home for losses suffered due to fire, theft, and other causes. Risks covered and cost of policy depend on the type of policy: generally, basic form (the least coverage and cost), broad form (middle range), and comprehensive (highest coverage and cost). (See also *Tenant's insurance.*)

Hospital insurance (17)   A form of *insurance policy* that will reimburse the insured for costs of being hospitalized, including room, board, and other specified services.

Income-producing property (16)   Generally, real estate that is produced as an investment, and from which rental income and depreciation deductions flow to the investor.

Income shifting (20) The procedure whereby a high-bracket taxpayer transfers income-producing assets to low-bracket taxpayers, such as children, so that the income will be taxed at a lower rate.

Income stocks (15) Stocks that are expected to pay a high level of dividend income to holders.

Incontestable clause (17) A provision in an insurance policy that cuts off the rights of the insurance company to challenge statements made in the application after a stated period of time.

Industrial policy (1) Governmental policy that favors certain industries over others, thus shifting economic benefits to one group of companies and their employees and investors and away from other groups.

Individual retirement account (IRA) (18) A do-it-yourself retirement investment plan with attractive tax benefits, available to all workers.

Inflation-proof bonds (14) These are bond investments that pay a lower rate of interest than normal bonds, but their principal value fluctuates in line with inflation, thus assuring that the future spending power of the invested money will not be eroded by inflation.

Inheritance tax (19) A state tax on individuals who receive inheritances.

Installment loan (12) A loan repayable to the lender in equal monthly amounts, customarily over a period of years.

Insurance policy (17) A contract made with an insurance company wherein the company agrees to pay money to the named parties if certain events occur, such as the death, illness, or disability of the insured party; or the destruction of the insured's property (home, car).

Interest (12) The fee paid for the use of another's money.

Intestacy (19) The status of one who dies without a *will*. In such a case, the law of the state in which the decedent resided will determine how the estate is to be distributed.

Itemized deductions (20) A specific listing of all allowable expenses that can be used to reduce the amount of income subject to taxation.

Judgment (6) A binding decision by a court that requires one party to pay money to, or perform services for, another party. Or, contrarily, a decision stating that one party does not have to pay or perform services for the other.

Keogh plan (18) A do-it-yourself retirement investment plan with attractive tax benefits, available to self-employed persons.

Land contract (7) A manner of purchasing real estate wherein the *deed* is not conveyed to the buyer at the *closing,* but rather at some future date, as agreed on by the parties.

Land lease (6) An arrangement for purchasing real estate wherein the buyer buys only the structure and *leases* the land on which the structure stands.

Lease (9) A contract by which the owner of property allows another (the tenant) to use that property for an agreed-on time and price.

Lease with option to buy (9) A lease that also gives the tenant the right to purchase the property at an agreed-on price and within certain time limits.

Lease with right of first refusal (9) A lease during which the tenant is given the right to purchase the property if he or she is willing to match the terms of any bona fide purchase offer the owner receives from outside parties.

Liability (2) A debt; an amount of money owed to someone else.

Lien (6) A legal right obtained by a creditor with respect to property that has been pledged as collateral for a loan made by the creditor to the debtor. Having a lien on the property can allow the creditor to force a sale of the property in order to satisfy the debt.

Life estate (19) A form of bequest wherein the recipient has the use of the subject property only for the remainder of his or her life, after which it passes to someone previously named by the original *testator.*

Life insurance policy (17) An *insurance policy* in which the company promises to pay a fixed sum of money to the *beneficiary* upon the death of the insured (covered) party.

Limit order (15)   An order given to a stockbroker to buy or sell stock within a high and/or low price range.

Limited partnership (16)   A legal arrangement among a number of people, usually entered into for investment purposes. The general partners are those who create the plan; the limited partners are those who put the money in. As a rule, the fate of the limited partners will depend on the contract the general partners have structured.

Liquidity (13)   Generally, how quickly, conveniently, and cheaply you can retrieve your money from a given investment.

Listing contract (10)   A contract between a seller of real estate and a real estate broker, in which the seller gives the broker the exclusive right to try to sell the property, for a specific period of time.

Load charge (14)   The sales commission an investor pays at the time he or she invests in a mutual fund.

Loan consolidation (12)   A procedure whereby one new loan is obtained and the proceeds are used to pay off numerous smaller loans.

Long-Term-Care Insurance (17)   A form of insurance that will pay for nursing home care and in-home care for the elderly and infirm.

Loss leader (4)   A product offered by a merchant at a lower than normal price to lure shoppers to his store.

Major medical insurance (17)   A form of health insurance designed to protect the insured against heavy, even catastrophic, health-care expenses.

Managed care (17)   This is the generic name given to the emerging forms of health-care delivery, such as Health Maintenance Organizations (HMOs), Preferred Provider Organizations (PPOs), and others, wherein a patient's care (diagnosis, treatment, surgery, hospitalization, medication and rehabilitation) are subject to the rules and regulations of the managing institutions (HMO, etc.) and insurance companies, as opposed to being controlled by the patient's own doctors.

Government regulation of managed care institutions is likely to grow.

Margin investing (15)   Buying *stock* partly with your own funds, and partly with funds that you have borrowed from the stockbroker.

Marital deduction (19)   The portion of an estate that is left, in proper legal fashion, to the surviving spouse. The marital deduction amount reduces the taxable portion of the estate.

Market order (15)   An order given to a stockbroker to buy or sell stock at whatever the going price might be.

Medical payments coverage (5)   A part of one's automobile insurance (optional) that reimburses driver and occupants for limited medical expenses arising from an accident. Also available on homeowner's and tenant's insurance.

Medical savings accounts (MSAs) (17)   A savings program that provides tax breaks to those who invest money to be ultimately spent on medical or retirement costs. There are strict limits as to how much can be invested and what kind of medical insurance the investor must otherwise have.

Medicare (17)   A health insurance program administered by the Social Security Administration for the protection of citizens 65 years old and over.

Monetary policy (1)   That part of a government's program that regulates the amount of money flowing throughout the economy.

Money market funds (14)   *Mutual funds* that specialize in acquiring high interest rate *money market instruments*.

Money market instruments (14)   Generally, short-term, high-quality investments, including certificates of deposit, bonds, repurchase agreements, commercial paper, and banker's acceptances.

Mortgage (7)   A debt secured by real estate. When one borrows money to pay for a home purchase, the debt is referred to as a first mortgage, and/or a purchase money mortgage. In some states, that same type of debt is known as a trust deed.

Multiple listing (6)   A service offered by subscribing real estate brokers in a given area, wherein all houses and other properties for sale in that area are listed and described in a frequently published directory.

Multiple-unit housing (6) A structure that contains a number of dwellings. Apartments, condominiums, cooperatives, townhouses, and rowhouses are all considered multiple-unit housing. In most cities there are laws governing health and safety features for residents.

Municipal bond (14) A debt issued by a local governmental agency (state, city, county, or subdivisions thereof). Interest earned by investors in such bonds is exempt from federal income taxes.

Mutual fund (14) A pooling of the money of many investors, which, under professional management, attempts to fulfill stated investment objectives.

National Credit Union Administration (14) The agency that insures accounts in federally covered credit unions.

National Labor Relations Act (2) A federal law that regulates relations between employers and labor unions.

Negotiable Order of Withdrawal (NOW account) (11) A form of checking account that pays interest to the account holder.

Net lease (16) A type of commercial lease in which the tenant is responsible for most, or all, of the operating costs of the property.

Net worth (2) The difference between *assets* and *liabilities;* a measure of one's wealth.

No-fault insurance (5) A type of automobile insurance required in some states, in which an injured party is paid by his own insurance company (up to set limits) regardless of who was at fault in the accident.

Noncupative will (19) A *will* that is spoken by the *testator* to another party; not usually valid.

Nonparticipating (nonpar) policy (17) A *life insurance policy* in which dividends are not paid to policyholders. (See also *Participating policy*.)

Nontaxable income (20) Money received by a taxpayer that is not subject to income taxes, such as inheritances, life insurance proceeds, and Social Security payments.

Nuisances (8) Actions that cause distress to occupants of housing or commercial property. Loud noises, unsightly messes, and unruly behavior are among many types of nuisances. Local laws provide some measure of enforcement against nuisances.

Odd lot (15) A block of less than 100 shares of *stock*.

Open-end clause (7) A clause in a *mortgage* that allows the borrower to borrow back up to the original amount of the loan at the original, or otherwise agreed-on, interest rate.

Open-end mutual fund (14) A *mutual fund* in which the portfolio managers may buy and sell securities as their judgment dictates.

Overdraft (11) The result of writing a check on one's checking account when the amount of the check exceeds the balance in the account.

Participating policy (17) An insurance policy wherein policyholders participate in annual distributions of excess income generated by the company. These distributions are commonly known as dividends. (Also called par policies.)

Pension Benefit Guarantee Corporation (PBGC) (18) A federal insurance program that guarantees retirees a continuation of at least a portion of their promised pension benefits should the company or the *pension plan* fail.

Pension plan (2) A fringe benefit offered by many employers, whereby the employer puts aside a sum of money for the benefit of the employee upon retirement. Some plans also allow voluntary contributions by employees.

Pension Reform Law of 1974 (18) (See *Employee Retirement Income Security Act*.)

Percentage clause (16) A provision in a commercial lease that states, generally, that the tenant must pay the landlord a certain percentage of the tenant's dollar volume of business, under agreed-on conditions.

Permanent insurance (17) Life insurance in which the amount of *premium* paid remains fixed for the life of the policy. Also known as ordinary, straight, or whole life insurance.

Physician insurance (17) A form of health insurance that pays doctors' bills, within stated limits.

Pigeon drop scheme (4) A fraudulent activity wherein the victim is convinced to part with cash in order to share in what appears to be a large sum of money that the perpetrator says he or she has found lying on the street. Many variations.

Pledge value (13) Generally, the ease and cost of borrowing against a particular investment.

Points (7) Added fees that a lender charges a borrower, usually in a home financing transaction. One point equals 1 percent of the amount of the loan.

Ponzi scheme (4) A fraudulent investment activity in which new victims are constantly being lured to participate, and their invested money is used to pay off prior victims. At some point the perpetrator will attempt to disappear with as much money as he or she can elicit from the victims.

Premium (15, 17) In option trading: the cost of purchasing a contract. In insurance: the fee paid for coverage provided.

Prepayment clause (7) A provision in a mortgage that determines to what extent the borrower may make advance payments on a loan, and what penalties, if any, the borrower may also have to pay as a result.

Price-earning ratio (P-E ratio) (15) The price of a given stock, divided by the per share earnings of the company. A low ratio tends to indicate a more conservative investment situation. A high ratio tends to indicate a more speculative situation.

Probate (19) A court proceeding in which the validity of a *will* is proved.

Productivity (1) A measurement of efficiency.

Profit-sharing plan (2) A fringe benefit whereby eligible employees receive a share of the company's profits, either annually or, more usually, on retirement.

Program trading (15) The name given to stock brokerage firms' computer programs that trigger buying or selling of large blocks of stock on the stock market. These triggers are activated by a combination of many complex factors, and they kick in before human beings have a chance to analyze those same factors. Thus, they often cause unexpected sharp up and down movements in stocks.

Prospectus (15) A document that must be published by *corporations* offering securities, in which certain facts regarding the offering must be disclosed.

Proxy (15) A write-in ballot used by stockholders of a *corporation*, which allows them to vote on the election of directors and other pertinent issues; used in lieu of personally attending the stockholders' meetings.

Public liability coverage (5, 8) Insurance that provides legal defense and pays claims if the insured's actions cause bodily harm or property damage to others. Common with automobile, homeowner's, and tenant's insurance policies.

Put option (15) A contract that gives the holder the right to sell 100 shares of a given *stock* at a predetermined price and by a given future date.

Pyramiding (12) A form of credit abuse (largely self-inflicted) that occurs when a loan taken for a recurring purpose (car purchase, vacation) is not fully paid by the time the purpose recurs and a new loan is needed.

Real Estate Investment Trust (REIT) (16) A form of mutual fund for real estate investments.

Reconciliation (11) The process of matching one's checking account balance with the bank's calculations.

Regulatory policy (1) A government's approach to how strictly or loosely it will control how various businesses may operate.

Restrictive covenant (6) A provision in a *deed* that can control certain things that an owner of real estate can or cannot do on the property.

Revenue bond (14) A type of *municipal bond* backed by the revenues produced by the entity borrowing the money (e.g., a toll road).

Reward/risk rule (13) An investment adage that correctly states that the greater reward you expect on an investment, the greater risk you'll be taking.

Right of assignment (6) A contractual clause that permits a party to a contract to transfer his interests in the contract to another party.

Rollover (10,14) Regarding the sale of a home, a technique that allows the postponement of taxes otherwise due on a profit from such sale; also, a form of *IRA plan* that allows postponement of taxes payable on the lump-sum payout of a pension or profit-sharing plan.

Roth IRA (18) A new form of Individual Retirement Account made possible by the Taxpayer Relief Act of 1997. Unlike the standard IRA, which allows tax breaks when money is invested but incurs taxes on later withdrawal, the Roth IRA gives no tax break at the time of investment, but allows the money to be withdrawn free of taxes.

Round lot (15) A block of 100 shares of stock, or a block divisible by 100.

Rule of 78s (12) The most common method of calculating the rebate of prepaid interest charges on an installment loan when the loan is paid off before its scheduled maturity.

Schedules A and B (20) Federal income tax forms, used in conjunction with the *1040 form* for declaring itemized deductions (A) and income from interest and dividends (B).

Securities and Exchange Commission (SEC) (15) A federal regulatory agency that oversees the trading of stocks.

Securities Investors Protection Corporation (SIPC) (15) A federal agency that insures certain aspects of investors' accounts with brokerage firms in the event of the firm's failure.

Security (12) A tangible asset that a borrower pledges to a lender in order to obtain a loan. If the borrower defaults, the security may be sold by the lender to satisfy the debt.

Settlement options (17) Various ways that the proceeds of a life insurance policy can be paid out.

Shared appreciation mortgage (7) A form of mortgage wherein the lender charges the buyer a favorable interest rate in exchange for a share in future profits from the sale of the property.

Shared housing (6) Two or more individuals or families combine their financial resources to purchase a dwelling for themselves.

Short selling (15) A speculative technique that, when successful, allows an investor to profit from the drop in value of shares of stock.

Simple interest (12) One means of calculating loan costs, usually in a loan payable in one lump sum as opposed to installments. The interest cost is expressed as a percentage of the amount borrowed, usually on an annual basis. Example: 10 percent annual simple interest on a $1,000 loan would be $100 for a one-year loan, $50 for a six-month loan, $25 for a three-month loan.

Sinking fund (14) A reserve account set up by a corporation; money is put into the account each year to be used to pay off a debt of the corporation when it falls due.

Sleeping second (7) A creative financing tool involving a second mortgage that will be owed by the buyer to the seller but on which no payments will be required for an agreed-on time.

Standard deduction (20) For taxpayers who choose not to itemize their deductions, this is a fixed amount that can be used to reduce the amount of income subject to taxation. The deduction may be taken whether or not the taxpayer actually incurred such expenses.

Stock (15) Form of ownership of a fractional part of a corporation. One owns "shares of stock." Unless otherwise specified, stock is considered "common." Some corporations also issue another class of stock known as "preferred." Owners of preferred shares have a higher claim to company dividends (and assets in the event of liquidation) than owners of common shares.

Stock investment program (2) A fringe benefit in which employees are offered the opportunity to buy shares of stock in the company at a lower price than they could on the open market.

Stop-payment order (11) Written instructions to a bank, given by the maker of a check, ordering the bank not to pay a specific check that the maker had issued.

Strike price (15) The price at which you can buy the underlying stock in a *call option* contract.

Surgical insurance (17) A form of health insurance that reimburses the insured for surgical and related expenses.

Surplus (1)   The status of a budget (one's financial condition) when more money has been taken in than has been spent. (See also *Deficit*.)

"Take back a mortgage" (16)   Expression that applies to a situation in which the seller of property accepts the buyer's IOU instead of cash. The IOU is secured by a *mortgage* on the property. (Also referred to as "take back paper.")

Takeover operation (5)   A sales technique involving a succession of salespersons, one taking over after the other, at ever increasing pressure; designed to wear down your resistance, especially with automobile sales.

Tax credit (20)   An amount that may be deducted from your computed federal income tax. Every dollar's worth of credit reduces your tax by one dollar. A number of new credits were made possible by the Taxpayer Relief Act of 1997, specifically for families with small children and for certain educational expenses.

Tax-deferred investments (13)   Investments whose earnings are not subject to taxation during the year earned but will be subject to taxation in some later year. (See also *Individual retirement account (IRA)*, *Keough plan*.)

Tax-exempt investments (13)   Investments whose earnings are not subject to taxation at any time. (See also *Municipal bond*.)

Tax rate (8)   With respect to real property taxes, the factor used to determine the amount payable; usually expressed in terms of dollars per $1,000 worth of *assessment* value. For example, a tax rate of $20 per $1,000, applied to property assessed at $40,000, will result in an annual property tax of $800.

Tax tables (20)   With respect to federal income taxes, the format from which most taxpayers can determine their taxes due.

Taxable income (20)   In the calculation of taxes payable, the income on which the tax is figured after having taken into account all proper *deductions, exemptions,* and *adjustments*.

Taxable investments (13)   Investments whose earnings are subject to taxation in the year in which earned.

Taxable transfer (19)   With respect to federal estate and gift taxes, the amount on which the tax is figured after having taken into account all proper deductions.

Taxpayer Compliance Measurement Program (TCMP) (20)   A random selection by the Internal Revenue Service of tax returns to be audited.

Tenant's insurance (8)   A form of property insurance for those who rent their dwellings. (See also *Homeowner's insurance*.)

Term insurance (17)   Also known as temporary insurance; a form of life insurance wherein the premium cost increases as the age of the insured increases. Policies run for a set number of years, and premiums are increased on renewal of policies. (See also *Permanent insurance*.)

Testator/testatrix (19)   A person who makes a *will*.

Testimonium clause (19)   A clause in a *will* in which the *testator* states that he or she is signing the document as his or her true last will and testament.

Time order (15)   An order to a stockbroker to buy or sell stock subject to a time deadline; usually attached to a *limit order*.

Time sharing (3)   An arrangement whereby one buys the right to use a specific dwelling unit (such as at a resort) for one or more specific weeks each year for many years.

Title insurance (6)   Insurance that will reimburse the insured for losses suffered (within stated limits) should a claim be made against the title of property owned by the insured.

Townhouse (6)   (Also known as rowhouse.) A form of dwelling unit adjoined on both sides by similar units.

Trade Policy (1)   Government policy setting forth which nations will be favored or disfavored in international commercial dealings. Trade policy can be used to protect home-based industries from foreign competition, and it can stimulate other forms of competition to benefit home-based companies.

Treasury Bill (14)   A short-term (less than one year) federal government debt instrument, minimum denomination $10,000.

Treasury Bond (14)   A long-term (up to 30 years, or more) federal government debt instrument.

Treasury Note (14)   A medium-term (one to seven years) federal government debt instrument.

Trust (19)   An arrangement, often in complex legal fashion, whereby one person or institution (the trustee) has custody of someone else's (the trustor's) money or property, for ultimate distribution to a named third party (the beneficiary). An *inter vivos* trust is one that comes into being while the trustor is alive. A testamentary trust is one that comes into being upon the death of the trustor.

Truth in Lending law (11)   A federal law which, among other things, requires covered lenders to provide a uniform interest rate quotation to borrowers. (See also *Annual Percentage Rate*.)

"Turnover investing" (16)   With reference to real estate investing: a program of buying property with the intent of reselling it at a profit as soon as possible.

Unemployment insurance (2, 17)   A state-administered insurance program, paid for by employers, that provides financial benefits to employees who are laid off.

Uninsured motorist insurance (5)   A form of coverage in automobile insurance policies that protects the insured if he or she is injured in an accident with an uninsured driver.

Unit pricing (3)   The pricing of food and other grocery products expressed in units of measurement (ounces, pounds, etc.); that is, the price per ounce.

Usury laws (11)   State laws dictating the maximum rate of interest that can be charged for various types of loans.

Vanity rackets (4)   Various schemes, sometimes fraudulent, in which the promoter offers to "publish" your book or song, etc., for a fee, no matter what the quality of the work.

Variable rate mortgage (7)   A home financing arrangement in which the interest rate payable by the borrower may fluctuate up or down.

Vesting (18)   The concept that pertains to one's pension benefits becoming irrevocably due; vesting occurs according to a preset schedule.

Waiver of premium (17)   A clause in an insurance contract (usually life, health, or disability plans) stating that if the insured becomes disabled, the need to pay the premiums on the policy will be waived during the period of disability.

Warrant (15)   Sometimes part of a *stock* offering, it allows the holder to purchase shares of the company's stock at a set price for a limited period of time.

W-4 form (20)   A federal tax form in which a worker claims a number of allowances, which in turn determine the amount of tax withheld from the worker's pay.

Will (19)   A document that, when properly drawn and executed, assures the protection of the state court over the distribution of the individual's (*testator's*) estate, in accordance with his or her wishes as expressed in the document.

Workers' Compensation (2, 17)   A state-administered health and disability program, paid for by employers, which provides certain benefits to workers who suffer job-related injuries or illnesses.

Wraparound mortgage (7)   A creative home financing plan, in which a buyer makes a single monthly payment to the seller and the seller in turn makes two or more payments to actual mortgage holders. The *wraparound*, in effect, is a form of consolidation of two or more mortgage debts.

Yield (13)   Generally expressed as a percentage, the earnings received from an investment; for example, a return of $5 in one year on an investment of $100 equals a yield of 5 percent.

Zone (8)   A specified area within a community that can only be used for specific purposes, such as residential and commercial.

Index